W9-BNY-014

AFRICA AND THE VICTORIANS

The Climax of Imperialism in the Dark Continent

BY

RONALD ROBINSON

FELLOW OF ST JOHN'S COLLEGE, CAMBRIDGE

AND

JOHN GALLAGHER

FELLOW OF TRINITY COLLEGE, CAMBRIDGE

WITH

ALICE DENNY

NEW YORK

ST. MARTINS PRESS

LONDON . MACMILLAN & CO., LTD.

1961

ST MARTIN'S PRESS INC
New York

MACMILLAN AND COMPANY LIMITED
London Bombay Calcutta Madras Melbourne

THE MACMILLAN COMPANY OF CANADA LIMITED
Toronto

PRINTED IN THE UNITED STATES OF AMERICA

FOREWORD

THE ethics of empire have always fascinated the moralist, just as the causes of their rise and fall have perplexed the historian. The prevailing judgements are hostile. 'Imperialism' has become one of the most evocative myths of our time and it colours what Americans and Europeans, Africans and Asiatics think of each others' intentions. Today the motives imputed to national expansion have a world-wide significance. They console those peoples still clinging to memories of imperial glory. They inspire the countries even now extending their influence. They embitter those who, having inherited the achievements of others, may yet plunge into an imperialism of their own. Empires fall; but imperialism is ever resurrected.

This study is an enquiry into the motives behind Victorian expansion. Obliquely, it is therefore a commentary upon the historical truth of modern theories of imperialism, using the classic model of the African partition.

CONTENTS

MAPS

CONTENTS

ABBREVIATIONS OF TITLES OF WORKS AND SOURCES QUOTED IN THIS VOLUME

A.E.	Archives du Ministère des Affaires Etrangères, Paris.
A.E.F.	Archives du Gouvernement-Général, Afrique Equatoriale Française, Brazzaville.
A.E.M.D.	Archives du Ministère des Affaires Etrangères, Mémoires et Documents.
B.D.	*British Documents on the Origins of the War*, 1898–1914.
B.M. Add. MSS.	British Museum, Additional Manuscripts.
C.O.	Colonial Office Records, Public Record Office, London.
D.D.F.	*Documents diplomatiques français*, 1st series.
D.D.I.	*Documenti diplomatici italiani.*
F.O.	Foreign Office Records, Public Record Office, London.
Grosse Politik	*Die Grosse Politik der Europäischen Kabinette*, 1871–1914.
Hansard	*Hansard's Parliamentary Debates.*
M.F.O.M.	Archives du Ministère de la France d'Outre Mer, Paris.
P.P.	Parliamentary Papers.
P.R.O.	Public Record Office, London.
Q.V.L.	*Letters of Queen Victoria*, edited by G. E. Buckle.
S.P.	Private Papers of Robert, Third Marquess of Salisbury, Christ Church, Oxford.

PREFACE

THIS book has been written as a contribution to the general theory of imperialism. We have not tried to write a history of the regions of Africa during the nineteenth century. The morality of the conquest is not here our concern. Its effects in the long run are not our theme. For our purposes, here and now, Africa is the hook on which we hang hypotheses about nationalism and world politics, the framework for discussing the nature of British expansion. The end of the nineteenth century is commonly seen as the great age of imperialism. As the reader will find, we think that theorising of this sort needs to be totally overhauled.

Embedded in the book are fragments of two Fellowship dissertations and a number of ideas beaten into what shape they have by the disputes of the authors. It has been a long time in the writing, and it leaves us beholden to a number of scholars. We are indebted to Professor G. S. Graham, to Mr. Louis Branney and to the late Professor J. Bartlett Brebner for criticising some of our ideas. Dr. G. Kitson Clark of Trinity College and Mr. Edward Miller of Saint John's College goaded us into making a book out of a booklet. One of us owes much to the Colonial Office, especially to Sir Andrew Cohen and Sir John Macpherson, and to the Colonial Social Science Research Council for their generous aid; the other, to the Rockefeller Foundation which enabled him to study the archives in Paris and Brazzaville.

Lord Salisbury kindly allowed us to use his grandfather's papers, and to make extensive quotations from them. We thank him for these most valuable sources. We are also grateful to Dr. J. F. A. Mason of Christ Church, Oxford, to Mr. Timings of the Public Record Office and to Mr. Cheeseman, the Colonial Office Librarian.

For their work in checking references we are grateful to Mr. Clark and Mr. Barnes of the Colonial Office. For their help in cheerfully checking references and typing we thank Mrs. Henry Pommer, Mrs. Jack Davies, Mrs. Olive Burgess, Miss Irmgarde Marschke, and Mr. and Mrs. Roger Childerley.

Lastly, we acknowledge the courtesy of Her Majesty's Stationery

Office in allowing us to use one of Sir Edward Hertslet's maps; and of Messrs. Edward Arnold for permission to reproduce Dr. J. Fage's maps illustrating the progress of the Partition in different parts of Africa. Acknowledgements are also due to the publishers of the following works from which we have quoted extensively: Lady Gwendolen Cecil, *Life of Robert, Marquess of Salisbury*, 4 vols., 1921-32, (Hodder and Stoughton); Sir R. Coupland, *The Exploitation of East Africa 1856-90*, 1939, (Faber and Faber); A. G. Gardiner, *Life of Sir William Harcourt*, 2 vols., 1923, (Constable); S. Gywnn and G. Tuckwell, *Life of Sir Charles Dilke*, 2 vols., 1917, (John Murray); Lord Newton, *Lord Lyons*, 2 vols., 1913, (Edward Arnold).

We should also like to record our best thanks to the Managers of the Smuts Memorial Fund for the Advancement of Commonwealth Studies, who have contributed generously to the costs of publication.

RONALD ROBINSON
Saint John's College

JOHN GALLAGHER
Trinity College, Cambridge

CHAPTER I

The Spirit of Victorian Expansion

The Victorians regarded themselves as the leaders of civilisation, as pioneers of industry and progress.[1] Industry in Britain was stimulating an ever-extending and intensifying development overseas, as her investors and manufacturers, merchants and colonists, railway-builders and officials opened up new continents. Year by year, trade and investment overseas had grown, so that by 1880 almost two thousand million pounds of credit had accumulated abroad.[2] More than twelve million Britons emigrated between Waterloo and the end of the Eighteen eighties, to settle new lands[3] and help supply the growing volumes of food and raw materials consumed in the Mother Country. Business men were gathering the harvests of commercial and naval supremacy from Rio de Janeiro to Hong Kong; and officials, working to improve the Indian peasant or put down the African slave trader, were drawing the Orient and the Dark Continent into the world economy.

The actual powers of industry however were as nothing compared with the expansive spirit which their discovery inspired in the early and mid-Victorians. They were sure that their ability to improve the human condition everywhere was as tremendous as their capacity to produce wealth. And in the exhilaration of their achievements not unnaturally they gave praise for the industrial philosopher's stone to their own domestic arrangements and virtues.[4]

Their secret seemed to lie in releasing private enterprise from the dead hand of the state. Social energy appeared to flow from the happy play of free minds, free markets and Christian morality: from their liberty to think, speak and worship, to inquire and invent, to buy cheap

[1] British National Income: 1851 — £613 millions; 1879–83 — £1109 millions; rise in real income per head, 1851–78 — 27–30%. (J. R. Bellerby, 'National and Agricultural Income, 1851,' *Economic Journal*, LXIX, March 1959, 103, 104.)

[2] A. H. Imlah, *Economic Elements in the Pax Britannica*, (Cambridge, Mass., 1958), 42–81; *idem*, 'British Balance of Payments and Export of Capital, 1816–1913,' *Economic History Review*, 2nd ser., V, (1952), 237, 239.

[3] *Cambridge History of the British Empire*, (1940), II, 443; Brinley Thomas, *Migration and Economic Growth*, (1954), 57.

[4] T. B. Macaulay, *Critical and Historical Essays*, (1854), I, 120–1.

and sell dear, to accumulate and venture capital, to practice thrift and self-help. If a maturing Benthamite bureaucracy in London still disputed with Cobdenite Manchester about the precise degree, all agreed that the state governed best when governing least. Representative institutions as a result worked to pare to the bone the powers of regulating and taxing overseas enterprise. Although doubts grew as the century wore on, most Victorians clung to the gospels of restricted government and free trade. That moral improvement and intellectual enlightenment attended the growth of prosperity, that all three depended upon political and economic freedom, remained their characteristic and passionate beliefs.

This spirit of progress no less than the surpluses and shortages of the industrial community drove Britons outward. Expansion was not simply a necessity without which industrial growth might cease, but a moral duty to the rest of humanity. In the Utilitarian science of political economy, the earlier Victorians beheld the rules for improvement everywhere. They were not the first, nor were they to be the last people, to project their own image as the universal ideal, nor to mistake fortunate trends of national history for natural laws and bend foreigners to obey them. Palmerston stated their earlier faith when in 1842 he asked why the world should be divided between different races living in contrasting climatic zones — and replied:

> 'Why, Sir . . . it is that the exchange of commodities may be accompanied by the . . . diffusion of knowledge — by the interchange of mutual benefits engendering mutual kind feelings. . . . It is, that commerce may go freely forth, leading civilization with one hand, and peace with the other, to render mankind happier, wiser, better.
>
> Sir, this is the dispensation of Providence . . . but in the face of it, with arrogant presumptuous folly, the dealers in restrictive duties fly, fettering the inborn energies of man, and setting up their miserable legislation instead of the great standing laws of nature.'[1]

This was the authentic mid-Victorian outlook on the world. It was suffused with a vivid sense of superiority and self-righteousness, if with every good intention. Upon the ladder of progress, nations and races seemed to stand higher or lower according to the proven capacity of each for freedom and enterprise:[2] the British at the top, followed a few rungs below by the Americans, and other 'striving, go-ahead' Anglo-Saxons. The Latin peoples were thought to come next, though far

[1] *Hansard*, 3rd ser., LX, col. 619, 16 Feb. 1842.

[2] 'Enterprise, the desire to keep moving, to be trying and accomplishing new things for our own benefit or that of others. . . .' (J. S. Mill, *Considerations on Representative Government*, People's ed., 1867, 24.)

behind. Much lower still stood the vast Oriental communities of Asia and north Africa where progress appeared unfortunately to have been crushed for centuries by military despotisms or smothered under passive religions. Lowest of all stood the 'aborigines' whom it was thought had never learned enough social discipline to pass from the family and tribe to the making of a state.[1]

The Victorians aspired to raise them all up the steps of progress which they themselves had climbed. Few doubted that *gesta Dei per Anglos*, however they might disagree about His choice of method. By the end of the Eighteen sixties this optimistic idealism was cooling, as disappointments piled up and the millennium of peace, brotherhood and free trade receded. The national arrogance perhaps grew less candid. Yet experience had only overlaid the earlier dreams, it had not erased them.

Expansion in all its modes seemed not only natural and necessary but inevitable; it was pre-ordained and irreproachably right. It was the spontaneous expression of an inherently dynamic society. But this expansion was not essentially a matter of empire but of private commerce and influence. Exertions of power and colonial rule might be needed in some places to provide opportunity and to protect. But empire tended to be thought of as an auxiliary, in much the same way as the liberal state at Home. The main engine of expansion was enterprise. Its momentum was attributed to the free energies and aspirations of myriads of individual Britons in search of maximum opportunity. In proliferating their private relations with enterprising individuals and classes within foreign and colonial societies, they were meant to act as yeast and leaven the lump.

Such were the instinctive Victorian assumptions about expansion. Ideally, the British merchant and investor would take into partnership the *porteños* of the Argentine, the planters of Alabama, the railway-builders of Belgium, as well as the bankers of Montreal and the shippers of Sydney; together they would develop the local and metropolitan economies. But this collaboration meant much more than profits. A common concern for peace and liberal reform would knit together the enlightened groups of all these communities.[2] At the same time the trader and missionary would liberate the producers of Africa and Asia. The pull of the industrial economy, the prestige of British ideas and

[1] *vide ibid.*, 15 *et seq.*

[2] As Peel put it in 1842: 'trade agreements would offer more reliable guarantees for mutual amity and co-operation than political treaties . . . because the interests of commerce are permanent and must be defended by all administrations.' (V. Puryear *International Economics and Diplomacy in the Near East*, 1935, 184.)

technology would draw them also into the Great Commercial Republic of the world. In time the 'progressive' native groups within the decaying societies of the Orient would burst the feudal shackles and liberalise their political and economic life. Thus the earlier Victorians hoped to help the Oriental, the African and the Aborigine to help themselves. Many would be called and all would be chosen: the reforming Turkish pasha and the enlightened mandarin, babus who had read Mill, samurai who understood Bentham, and the slaving kings of Africa who would respond to the Gospel and turn to legitimate trade.

But however liberal in principle, Victorian statesmen in practice never minimised the role of government in all this. Like Clarendon, they looked '. . . to what may be most for the honour and advantage of England, and to what offers the fairest prospects of extending her commercial relations and the sphere of her influence and power.'[1] If the Cobdenites objected that the exercise of power interfered with the growth of trade,[2] the practical statesmen found that the two worked together. The Palmerstonians insisted that the expanding economy needed the protection of power and that it was also one of the weapons of power. Disraeli was stating their principle when he said in 1863: 'There may be grave questions as to the best mode of obtaining wealth . . . but there can be no question . . . that the best mode of preserving wealth is power.'[3] Power remained an end in itself, although it was now often deployed in ways impossible for such mercantilist statesmen as Cromwell or Chatham. It was still used to give security in Europe and to enforce the *pax Britannica.* But now liberation, not acquisition, was more often the aim of power; and free trade, not monopoly, was its device.[4] All over the world the Canningites and Palmerstonians exerted their strength to bring about political conditions favouring commercial advance and liberal awakening. During the first half of the century they were generally ready to confront despotism and Holy Alliances, and to give aid and comfort to rebels in South America, Greece, Belgium or Hungary, and to Texans rightfully struggling to be free. Even after 1850 they still sympathised with Garibaldi's Redshirts and the insurgents of the Argentine.

Trade and hegemony were manipulated deliberately as reciprocating

[1] Clarendon Memo., in Clarendon to Palmerston, 14 Mar. 1840, Sir H. Maxwell, *Life and Letters of . . . the Fourth Earl of Clarendon,* (1913), I, 188.

[2] *vide* the debate on intervention in China in 1839, *Hansard,* 3rd ser., LIII, cols. 669–836, 845–955. For Cobdenite opposition to intervention in Turkey *vide* Puryear, *op. cit.,* 27.

[3] W. F. Monypenny and G. E. Buckle, *Life of Benjamin Disraeli,* (1910–20), IV, 335.

[4] J. Gallagher and R. E. Robinson, 'The Imperialism of Free Trade,' *Economic History Review,* 2nd ser., VI, no. 1, (1953).

elements. Political influence was used so as to extend and secure free exchange; commerce and anglicisation, to spread political influence and weld alliance. 'It is the business of Government', Palmerston had said, 'to open and secure the roads for the merchant,'[1] Before the technique of collaborating classes would work, power must break open the world to free trade. It would not work either where antiquated *régimes* could not keep order or receive and respond to European influences.[2] All this in official thinking was necessary work for diplomats with gunboats in the offing. From the beginning of the century onward they were spreading the rule of free trade from Buenos Ayres to Constantinople, from the Niger and the Oxus to the Yangtse-kiang. Annexations were to be avoided if possible. Power was extended in its subtler forms — prestige, cajolery, threat, the dangled loan reinforced occasionally with blockade, bombardment or expedition. By such means foreign tariffs and monopolies were broken down, the gouty empires of China and Turkey opened to British influence, and innumerable lesser sheikdoms, sultanates and chieftaincies were drawn into the invisible empire of informal sway.

But the results of this imperialism of free trade among non-European peoples were disappointing, even disquieting. By the Eighteen sixties and seventies the Victorians were less sure of their panacea for the East and Africa. Neither the Son of Heaven[3] nor the Commander of the Faithful[4] had been attracted along the narrow ways of liberal reform. Among the invincibly conservative Confucian and Islamic rulers, no effective westernising collaborators had been found. Their responses had not been what the political economists had foretold. It appeared from the Tai'ping rebellion[5] in China and growing chaos in the Muslim states[6] that European agencies could destroy as well as re-create. No waves of

[1] Palmerston to Auckland, 22 Jan. 1841, C. K. Webster, *The Foreign Policy of Lord Palmerston*, (1951), II, 751.

[2] e.g. the reforms in the Ottoman Empire which *The Times* of 12 Feb. 1856 suggested were prerequisite to regeneration: 'The removal of all obstacles to the purchase of land by foreigners, the establishment of a sound financial system and of the guarantees for the security of the capital invested in roads or harbours, must be the diplomatic labours most immediately productive of large results. A rich and unworked land is before us, and the industry of the West may go in and possess it.' (D. C. Blaisdell, *European Financial Control in the Ottoman Empire*, (New York, 1929), 47, fn. 1.)

[3] *vide* N. A. Pelcovits, *Old China Hands and the Foreign Office*, (New York, 1948).

[4] *vide* D. E. Lee, *Great Britain and the Cyprus Convention Policy of 1878*, (Cambridge, Mass., 1934); F. E. Bailey, *British Policy and the Turkish Reform Movement, 1826–1853*, (Cambridge, Mass., 1942); D. C. Blaisdell, *op. cit.*

[5] J. Chesnaux, 'La Révolution Taiping d'après quelques Travaux récents,' *Revue Historique*, CCIX, (1953), 39–40.

[6] F. R. Flournoy, *British Policy towards Morocco in the Age of Palmerston*, (Baltimore, 1935); M. Emérit, 'La Crise syrienne et l'Expansion economique française en 1860,' *Revue Historique*, CCVII, 217–21; Bailey, *op. cit.*

regeneration such as Palmerston and T. F. Buxton[1] had dreamed of had rolled along the trade routes across tropical Africa nor into the central Asian steppe.[2] In China after 1860 Victorian governments relaxed their pressure for reform lest they should become involved in governing a tottering empire.[3] In Turkey a decade later, their eagerness to improve had been swallowed up in concern to preserve its integrity.[4] Trade and investment, it is true, had grown in both these regions. But if the 'Old China Hands' had developed the regional trade, few of the expected three hundred million Chinese customers for Lancashire had come forward.[5] The uncongenial spirit and inflexible institutions of the two empires clouded their commercial prospects and raised too high the political risks of realising them. The spectacular successes of collaboration, liberalism and free trade lay elsewhere.

By 1880 British business was concentrating above all in Europe and the Americas, and next in India and Australasia.[6] Except where lesser

[1] T. F. Buxton, *The Remedy . . . to the Slave Trade*, (1840); C. Buxton, *Memoirs of Sir Thomas Fowell Buxton*, (1849).

[2] C. K. Webster, *op. cit.*, II, 540–57. [3] Pelcovits, *op. cit.*, cap. I.

[4] Lee, *op. cit.* [5] Pelcovits, *op. cit.*, caps. III and IV.

[6] *Regional Inclination of British Economic Expansion*

(Trade figures in quinquennial annual averages and millions of pounds sterling; emigrants in thousands; investments as notional in millions of pounds)

	U.S.A.	*Canada*	*S. America*	*Australasia*	*India*	*S. Africa*	*Egypt*	*Trop. Afr.*
1865–9 imports	39	7	12	12	32	3	12	1,3
1865–9 exports	24	6	10	12	20	2	7	1,0
1870 investment	200	20	85	74	160	—	20	—
1870 emigration	153	27	—	17	—	—	—	—
1880–4 imports	97	11	10	27	35	6	9	1,5
1880–4 exports	28	9	13	22	30	6	3	1,3
1885 investment	300	113	150	240	270	34	30	—
1885 emigration	138	20	—	39	—	3	—	—
1890–4 imports	98	13	13	30	30	11	10	2·4
1890–4 exports	26	7	17	20	32	8	4	2·0
investment	525	205	350?	389	305?	200?	30	—
	(1899)	(1902)	(1900)	(1900)	(1900)	(1900)	—	—
1891–5 emigration	66	23	—	21	—	10	—	—
1909–13 imports	131	28	64	56	45	19	13	6
1909–13 exports	63	21	49	40	54	16	6	8
1911 investment	688	373	587	380	351	351	44	—
1911 emigration	122	185	—	81	—	31	—	—

Sources: P.P. (1870), LXIII, 2–3, 284; P.P. (1886), LXIV, 2–3; P.P. (1890–1), LXXXIX, 50–1; P.P. (1901), LXXXVI, 56–7, 130–1; P.P. (1914), LXXXIII; W. Schlote, *British Overseas Trade from 1700 to the 1930's*, (Oxford, 1952), 108–9; A. K. Cairncross, *Home and Foreign Investment*, (1953), 183, 185; Brinley Thomas, *Migration and Economic Growth*, (1954), 60, 266, 304.

trades brushed its northern shores and its southern tip, the entire African continent remained almost untouched between the strenuous activity of the Atlantic on the one hand, and the Orient on the other.

By far the largest sphere of enterprise was in the United States. The Victorians bought and sold more there than in any other single country.[1] Most of their emigrants and most of their foreign lending went there.[2] In the Americas also were smaller but still promising partners — Canada, the Argentine, Chile and Brazil.[3] In 1880 as in 1914 about half of Britain's commercial exchanges and investment outside Europe were with northern and southern Americans. The remainder was mostly with Australians and Indians, and to a much lesser extent with white south Africans, Levantines, Chinese and Japanese.

Their commercial experience impressed a single portentous fact upon the Victorians. All their most successful trading associations, with the exception of the Indian empire, were with Europeans transplanted abroad; so much so that by 1914 Britain had lent them about seven-tenths of her investment overseas.[4] It is easy to see why. The white communities of the temperate zones had the outlook and institutions favourable to progress which Asiatics and Africans seemed to lack. They offered customers with European tastes and money to spend. Here there were comparatively stable governments and superior guarantees for life, capital and property. Affinities of kinship, sentiment, and religion made the paths of intercourse and political connection comparatively straight. By the Eighteen seventies few tiresome exertions of power or Downing Street rule were usually needed in these lands. Where mutual self-interest and understanding were joined, the private business of Great Britain commingled freely with that of Greater Britain and the once-colonial societies of the New World. Hence independent American republicans and self-governing British 'colonials' seemed to be the best collaborators in the Victorian world mission.

The success of these partnerships gave force to the Victorian statesman's deepest convictions about the role of empire in the expansion of the economy. They vindicated brilliantly the superiority of informal ties

[1] N. S. Buck, *The Development of the Organisation of Anglo-American Trade*, 1800–1850, (New Haven, 1925); F. Thistlethwaite, *The Great Experiment*, (1955), 64–90; W. Schlote, *op. cit.*, 79–88.

[2] R. W. Hidy, *The House of Baring in American Trade and Finance: English Merchant Bankers at Work*, 1763–1861, (Harvard, 1949); Brinley Thomas, *op. cit.*, 56–71; A. K. Cairncross, *op. cit.*, 185, 189.

[3] J. B. Brebner, *Atlantic Triangle*, (New Haven, 1945), 148–97; A. C. Wilgus (ed.), *Argentina, Chile and Brazil since Independence*, (Washington, D.C., 1935); H. S. Ferns, 'Investment and Trade between Britain and Argentina in the Nineteenth Century', *Economic History Review*, (1950).

[4] H. Feis, *Europe, the World's Banker, 1870–1914*, (New Haven, 1930), 23.

of trade and influence over those of imperial control. And so British leaders strongly preferred influence to political possession as a means to national prosperity and world power. For one thing, the merchant and manufacturer could usually overcome all competitors, given an open market; for another, the Treasury normally had little money to spare for more colonial activities. Above all, connections with self-governing white communities seemed everywhere the most profitable and least troublesome. Over half of Britain's investment overseas and two-thirds of her exports and imports went outside the regions coloured red on the map. And so for this reason nearly all Victorians stood firmly for free trade and held protective tariffs and imperial preference to be commercial suicide. The formal empire of rule was but a part of the informal empire of trade and influence. Commercially speaking, colonies were the lesser part of the iceberg visible above the water-line.

The white colonies had always been the exception to this preference for informal influence over imperial rule. In both official and unofficial thinking, the natural, as well as the most rewarding mode of imperial expansion was the spread of British settlers. To the Victorians the formal empire was 'Greater Britain'. Seeley described it in 1880: 'four great groups of territory [Canada, Australasia, South Africa and the West Indian Islands], inhabited either chiefly or to a large extent by Englishmen . . . and a fifth great territory India . . . inhabited by a completely foreign race. [When we inquire into the Greater Britain of the future], we ought to think much more of our Colonial than of our Indian Empire.'[1] Ideally, empire meant the extended family of mother country and colonial sons. By comparison the Indian empire seemed unnatural, almost improper, like some extra-marital responsibility incurred in youth. There was a strong prejudice against allowing it to happen again.

Hence ministers were usually willing to annex more provinces only when their colonists required them. Where the settler was expropriating the lands of the Aborigine, the Maori and the Kaffir, there was no alternative government at first to 'Mr. Mother Country'. But by the mid-century the Victorians were tiring of guarding their extending frontiers, of trying to enforce justice between black and white.[2] The colonists, equally, were becoming bitter against Downing Street control. Granting self government solved the immediate problem, but few intended there-

[1] Sir J. R. Seeley, *The Expansion of England*, (1880), 11–12.

[2] *vide* the instructive episode of the Fugitive Slave Circular, 1875. The Admiralty was willing to surrender fugitive slaves in certain circumstances. At the last moment the Disraeli government decided that humanitarian opinion was still too strong for this to be sanctioned, (G. E. Buckle, *The Life of Benjamin Disraeli*, (1920), V, 296–8.)

by to separate from the colonies.[1] The aim rather was to avert the loss of colonies and more American wars of independence. Responsible government was meant to conciliate Canadian, Australian and Boer sensibilities; to bind them perpetually to Britain and to relieve the imperial military and financial strain. Devolution was carefully measured out so as to keep British influence over the colonies and to strengthen the imperial links. Hence responsible government was normally withheld until a colony was mature enough to keep order and defend itself locally. Even then, the imperial authority went on with its duties of external protection against hostile tribes and rival European powers. It still reserved space for the colonists to advance up to the uttermost natural frontiers of white settlement, and acquired and pacified more territory as the colonists came forward to occupy it.

By the Eighteen seventies, confederated Canada, responsibly governed Australasia and the Cape were regarded as constitutional embodiments of collaboration between British and colonial interests working at its best.[2] The further slackening of formal bonds by colonial governments, it is true, raised qualms about the future of imperial unity. Yet the policy-makers felt sure that their self-governing colonials, bound with the silken cords of kindred, tradition and self-interest, would continue to be their most loyal and energetic partners in spreading British influence and multiplying British commerce. Unlike the financial and trading enterprises which were thrusting into Oriental empires, those of the white colonist were proving commercially and politically creative. They had the supreme virtue of being self-propelling. The impetus to expansion was soon coming, not so much from the Metropolis as from the colonial communities themselves.

Yet no one system could co-ordinate or comprehend this world-wide profusion of expansive activities. Although governments often used or regulated its processes, they were usually unplanned and beyond official control. Contradictions abounded amid the variety of options and regional circumstances. Furthermore the achievements of the mercantilist era of expansion were left curiously embedded in the more modern mosaic.

The Indian empire to all Victorians was the exception to every rule. Begun before the loss of the American colonies, formal dominion there was spreading to its natural mountain frontiers long after policy toward other Oriental countries had become grounded on mere influence. India

[1] *The Elgin-Grey Papers 1846–52*, (ed. A. G. Doughty, 4 vols., Ottawa, 1937); W. P. Morrell, *British Colonial Policy in the Age of Peel and Russell*, (1930).

[2] As had been foreseen by Sir. J. Stephen, 'On Colonization as a Branch of Social Economy,' *Trans. Nat. Soc. Promotion Social Sciences*, 1858.

again was no field for the colonist. Yet it was irretrievably under imperial rule. There was another paradox as well. In the so-called era of *laissez faire* the country was being turned into a satellite of the industrial economy chiefly by state enterprise.[1] But such inconsistency rarely worried the pragmatic British. Plainly, India was not a country where commerce could dispense with dominion. As Dilke put it in 1862:

> 'Were we to leave Australia or the Cape, we should continue to be the chief customers of those countries: were we to leave India or Ceylon, they would have no customers at all; for, falling into anarchy, they would cease at once to export their goods to us and to consume our manufactures.'[2]

One principle at least held good in India as in white colonies. The British would expand by trade and influence if they could; but by imperial rule if they must. Conversely, as soon as their subjects provided reliable collaborators with British purposes and could keep order themselves, London gladly relaxed imperial control. But India by the mid-century no longer seemed likely to offer loyal partners on whom authority might safely be devolved. The Victorians accepted the fact, and comforted their liberal consciences with the duty of an indefinite but benevolent trusteeship which pushed beyond the mental horizon teasing questions about nationalities struggling to be free.

Yet the experience of governing Hindus and Muslims strongly prejudiced the later Victorians against acquiring more Oriental possessions. The grand schemes of the early Utilitarian administrators for anglicising India had gone down in the Residency at Cawnpore. Other optimistic designs for endowing the Chinese and Ottoman empires with progressive rulers had blunted against the crassness of mandarins and pashas. The Indian Mutiny and the social upheavals which followed hard on the heels of European penetration throughout the Near and Far East left a lasting disenchantment in London and Calcutta about the possibility of westernising the Oriental.

The Victorians had learned that westernisation was a dangerous and explosive business. Perhaps non-Europeans after all were not potential English gentlemen who had been unluckily retarded, but races inherently different and apart. Victorian rulers had learned much more about the depths of reactions and racial fanaticisms which too much meddling could stir up in Oriental societies. They were becoming aware for the

[1] J. B. Brebner, 'Laissez Faire and State Intervention in Nineteenth-Century Britain,' *Journal of Economic History*, Supplement, VIII, (1948); D. Thorner, *Investment in Empire*, (Philadelphia, 1950), 168–82; W. J. Macpherson, 'Investment in Indian Railways, 1845–1875,' *Economic History Review*, (1955), 177–86.

[2] Sir C. W. Dilke, *Greater Britain*, (1868), II, 394–5.

first time of the disturbing effects of one culture upon another. In India, the more cautious 'Guardians'[1] prevailed over the apostles of anglicisation, as the administration became more institutional and formalised. Perhaps it was safer to take native society for what it was, and concentrate on honest government and raising living standards. The white rulers became increasingly absorbed with the mechanics of administration and sought to solve their problems less in social and more in narrow administrative terms. Even before the Mutiny, ministers were growing acutely aware of the high risks of rebellion and racial feeling, the enormous military burdens, the huge liabilities which had been undertaken so lightly in subjecting India to British rule. Their uneasiness about India, coupled with the success of their white colonies and wider commercial empire confirmed the preference for the modes of free trade and settlement and the prejudice against adding to the number of non-European jewels in the Crown. As late as 1883 the axiom was that 'the policy of England discourages any increase of territory in tropical countries already occupied by native races'.[2]

Still, the Indian empire seemed essential, so that whatever its enigmas and risks it had to be held. Since the middle of the eighteenth century the eastern arc of expansion had become an ever more important component of British world power.[3] By the Eighteen eighties, India at its centre had become of the first importance to the economy. The British had invested some £270 millions there, not much less than one-fifth of their entire investment overseas.[4] India had become a valuable exporter and importer, taking about 19 per cent of British exports.[5] In addition much of the regional trade with other parts of Asia fell into British hands because India was a key to the regional system of exchange.

But more than that, India was the grand base of power in the East. Throughout the nineteenth century the central feature of Britain's expansion there was the symbiosis between her trade with Asia and her power in India. The growth of India's trade, and so of its revenue, nourished the military forces of the Indian government; and this force in turn secured and promoted trade and investment throughout India,

[1] E. Stokes, *The English Utilitarians and India*, (1959), 47–81, 140–233.

[2] J. S. Cotton and E. J. Payne, *Colonies and Dependencies*, Part II, 114.

[3] For the genesis and objectives of the 'swing to the east' *vide* V. T. Harlow, *The Founding of the Second British Empire, 1763–1793*, (1952), 62–145; for the strategic value of India as a base, C. N. Parkinson, *War in the Eastern Seas, 1793–1815*, (1954), 47; for French appreciation of this, J. F. Cady, *The Roots of French Imperialism in Eastern Asia*, (Ithaca, N.Y., 1954), 138–9.

[4] A. K. Cairncross, *Home and Foreign Investment, 1870–1913*, (1953), 185; A. H. Imlah, 'British Balance of Payments and Export of Capital, 1816–1913,' *Economic History Review*, 1952, 237–8.

[5] P.P. (1890–1) XC, 686–7; P.P. (1901) LXXXVI, 49.

south-east Asia, and the Far East.[1] This reciprocal action of power and trade depended on dominion in India.

The *ultima ratio* of that rule was the army of India. But it also had another function. The Indian army provided the means of over-awing and, in the last resort, of crushing the resistance of Asiatic rulers who obstructed British influence and trade. The ambit of Indian power is described by the movement of her troops: to China in 1839, 1856 and 1859; to Persia in 1856, to Ethiopia and Singapore in 1867, to Hong Kong in 1868, to Afghanistan in 1878, to Egypt in 1882, to Burma in 1885, to Nyasa in 1893, and to the Sudan and Uganda in 1896.[2]

This vital instrument of security had been re-organised after the Mutiny, so that the proportion of non-European troops to Europeans 'should never greatly exceed two to one'. The regular army settled down at some quarter of a million men; and in addition there was a vast reserve of Indian manpower which could be drawn on at need. Control of India meant the control of an army and of an almost inexhaustible reserve.[3]

Although some protested against the usage, India was indeed 'an English barrack in the Oriental seas'.[4] It had the added advantage of being a barrack over which Parliament could exercise little control. The freedom of action which this gave to ministers was well summed up by Hartington in 1878:

> 'The Indian Army is not limited in numbers by an annual Vote of Parliament. It is not voted by Parliament at all; its numbers are not enumerated in the Mutiny Act; and the native portion of the Indian Army is not even subject to the Mutiny Act. In fact, it may be described as a

[1] M. M. Greenberg, *British Trade and the Opening of China, 1800–42*, (1951), 9–14; H. T. Lambrick, *Sir Charles Napier and Sind*, (1952), 205. For the fluctuations of this trade *vide* G. C. Allen and A. G. Donnithorne, *Western Enterprise in Indonesia and Malaya*, (1957), 38–9; for instances of the importance of Singapore within it, F. E. Hyde, 'The Expansion of Liverpool's Carrying Trade with the Far East and Australia, 1860–1914,' *Transactions of the Royal Historical Society*, (1956), 145–6, 149–50.

[2] These examples are only the most conspicuous cases of the use of the army of India. Its use was often advocated elsewhere. In 1863 there was a proposal to send it to New Zealand, (*Hansard*, 3rd ser., CLXXII, col. 1291); in 1878 Disraeli wanted to send it to Cyprus and Alexandretta, (G. E. Buckle, *Life of Benjamin Disraeli*, (1920), VI, 273); in 1884 it was planned to send it to Hong Kong, (E. V. G. Kiernan, *British Diplomacy in China, 1880–1885*, (1938), 146); in 1899 Curzon wanted to send it to the Persian Gulf, (the Earl of Ronaldshay, *Life of Lord Curzon*, (1928), II, 100).

[3] In 1880 there were 66,000 British and 130,000 Indian troops in the Indian Army. (R. Temple, *India in 1880*, (3rd edition, 1881), 392.) The numbers in the armies of the princely states in the Eighteen eighties were estimated at 350,000. (Sir Charles Dilke, *Problems of Greater Britain*, (1890), II, 66.) Writing of the regular army in the Eighties, Sir John Strachey remarked that 'In case of necessity there would be no difficulty in making at short notice a large addition to their numbers.' (*India, Its Administration and Progress*, (4th ed., 1911), 482.)

[4] *Hansard*, 3rd ser., CXC, col. 406, 28 Nov. 1867.

non-Parliamentary Army, as compared with the Army which is maintained at home and in the other Dependencies of the Crown.'[1]

That was the state of affairs throughout the remainder of the century, as it had been since 1829.[2] Not only did the Indian taxpayer bear the cost of his own occupation, but something like half the British Army was billetted upon him. The Indian empire thus provided a uniquely self-financing army, which allowed Victorian governments to exert power in the Far and Near East without always having to foot the whole bill.

And so the Raj, with its relative freedom from Parliamentary scrutiny and Treasury control, provided a formidable expansive power, which was all the more so for being unfettered. Admittedly, the defence of India was itself a heavy strategic burden upon the British Empire, but to Victorian statesmen it seemed the essential supplement to British sea-power. The power derived from India saved them from some of the restrictions of anti-imperialist and democratic influences in British politics; and it helped them to shrug off the objections usually raised against the spreading of trade by the use of power.

Hence the Indian empire was of great political and economic value. Its revenue and manpower provided the rod of order, the shield of defence and the sword for further advance from Zanzibar and Basra eastwards to the Yellow Sea. This was partly the case in the southern seas as well, for the Indian bastion helped to protect Australia and New Zealand. Between them, the sepoys and the Royal Navy guarded the commercial empire throughout the eastern seas and the Pacific.

To all Victorian statesmen, India and the British Isles were the twin centres of their wealth and strength in the world as a whole. Their main commerce with the Americas had little need of the aid of power. But the Orient and Australasia, the other major arc of the expanding economy, depended heavily upon the naval and political arms. It seemed essential to build up positions of strength against Russia as she sprawled out westwards and eastwards from the Asiatic heartland. At the same time, the flow of forces and trade eastward through the Mediterranean was vulnerable to the Powers of Europe. So throughout the century it seemed imperative to make sure of the communications between the British Isles and India, if the spine of prosperity and security was not to be snapped. British positions and interests in half the world stood or fell upon the safety of the routes eastward.

Up to the Eighteen eighties Africa appeared in these world-wide

[1] *Hansard*, 3rd ser., CCXL, col. 272, 20 May 1878; cf. C. Ilbert, *The Government of India: Being a Digest of the Statute Law Relating Thereto*, (2nd ed., 1907), 90, fn. 1.
[2] C. H. Philips, *The East India Company, 1784–1834*, (1940), 11.

considerations as but the huge, unopened land mass interposed between Britain and the East. In the main her merchants and colonists had been concerned with the sea-ways around the continent; and her statesmen, with keeping them open and clear of rival Powers. Africa's only major significance so far lay in the transitory importance of its shores to the enterprises flowing past them. Where Africa stood in the government's world picture is illustrated by the headings used by the clerks to file correspondence about it. Egyptian affairs were approached through 'Turkey' — the major concern in the Mediterranean, and indeed in the European balance. Much of the correspondence about the east coast went to Bombay, since Zanzibar was regarded merely as an outpost of India. The rest ended up in London with the more important missives from the west coast under the general title of 'Slave Trade'. Only the despatches from the Cape and Natal colonies were invariably grouped under their specifically African titles.

For the most part ministers did not contemplate Africa in itself. This was because it had not yet been caught up in any of the grand processes of British expansion, except one — the crusade to expiate past sin and cut off the supply of African slaves to the trans-Atlantic economy. But that mission had been fulfilled on the west coast by the Eighteen sixties. For the sake of humanity, a once-prosperous arm of European trade had been lopped off. What was left seemed unpromising enough. There were three tiny, poverty-stricken colonies; a few useful but difficult fields of private enterprise, notably on the Niger; hundreds of anti-slave trade treaties with minor chiefs, and paramount influence along a vast stretch of coast. London was dead against extending territorial responsibilities and warned its local agents to keep to coastal and riverine influence. War was endemic among the congeries of tribal kingdoms; and trade and revenues during the Sixties and Seventies stagnated. With its lethal climate, its barbaric tribes, its disorders and difficult communications, its single small staple, its lack of disciplined labour and purchasing power, west Africa seemed no place for colonial expansion.

A similarly negative policy of coastal influence applied to the east coast. What trade there was consisted of slaves, slave-grown cloves, and slave-portered ivory, organised by Arabs and Banyans. The British government was putting it down with the help of naval blockade and of its puppet, the Sultan of Zanzibar. The slave economy had to be destroyed; but what could replace it had not appeared. For the rest, Bombay was content to keep the Sultan in his vague possessions as a sentinel against the intrusion of European rivals upon the African flank of the short route to India. Ministers put imperial rule in east Africa out of the question. According to the official canons, there seemed no reason for empire anywhere in tropical Africa. British enterprise did not look like providing the necessary capital or colonists; and certainly African societies could not provide the trade, the revenue or the collaborators.[1]

It was somewhat different in the temperate southern sub-continent. Here there were colonists, but few were British. The Boer farmers were spreading northward across the Orange and the Vaal, subjugating the Bantu as they went. Yet the Victorians, in spite of their liking for white colonisation, were hardly pleased with this movement. The Cape Colony had been annexed to secure 'the master link of connection between the western and eastern world'[2], not as a base for colonising the sub-continent. During the first decades the imperial authorities had sympathised more with the Bantu than with the Boer. They had tried to restrict settlement, partly to save the Kaffir, partly to avoid frontier wars, and partly because they were seriously concerned only to command Simon's Bay and the coast-line, which had a bearing on the

[1] It is, of course, the central argument of the various theories of economic imperialism that Africa could provide these essentials. *vide* J. A. Hobson, *Imperialism, a Study*, (1902, 3rd ed., 1938); R. Hilferding, *Das Finanz Kapital: eine Studie über die jüngste Entwicklung des Kapitalismus*, (Vienna, 1910); V. I. Lenin, *Imperialism, the Highest Stage of Capitalism*, (1916); *New Data for Lenin's Imperialism, the Highest Stage of Capitalism*, (ed. E. Varga and L. Mendelsohn, 1939); R. Luxemburg, *Die Akkumulation des Kapitals, ein Beitrag zur ökonomischen . . . Erklärung des Imperialismus*, (Berlin, 1921, English translation, 1951); F. Sternberg, *Der Imperialismus*, (Berlin, 1926); *idem, Die Kritiker vor der Imperialismus*, (Berlin, 1929); *idem, Capitalism and Socialism on Trial*, (1951); G. Hallgarten, *Imperialismus vor 1914*, (Munich, 1951). None of these discussions seems to pay much attention to the concrete facts of the African economy or the evaluations of it by Europeans. True, the imperial federation movement in politics had its counterpart in business opinion, but it was no more than the opinion of a small minority. The prevailing view among businessmen was that in the circumstances of the 'depression', the need was to consolidate the existing empire of trade rather than to extend the empire of rule. By contrast, business opinion scouted the prospects of northern and tropical Africa. The commercial geographer, Yeats voiced the prevailing doubt whether west Africa would ever repay railway investment or the most rudimentary form of administration. (J. Yeats, *Recent and Existing Commerce*, (3rd ed., 1887), 70.) The *Economist* said of the Congo Basin that '. . . the rudiments of civilisation do not exist' (8 Mar. 1884, p. 627); and of east Africa: 'It is probably an unprofitable possession' (8 Oct. 1892, 1262). The trade with Egypt could be described in 1887 as 'fluctuating, but most of it is a transit trade and is of little significance'. (Yeats, *op. cit.*, 126.) In the middle of the territorial partition The *Economist* summed up the prevailing view of Africa's trading future: 'The trade of South Africa is in our hands and is considerable. The trade of the Lower Niger is also in our hands. But, apart from these, Algeria, Tunis and Egypt, are alone the countries of which the trade and finance are not really infinitesimal. There may be mining surprises in store. But the lands of tropical Africa are not usually suitable for a European population, and the present inhabitants are races which it must take a far longer time to civilise than those who look for immediate big results appear to think of. We do not, apart from surprises, look for any rapid development of either trade or financial success from these territories . . .' (30 Aug. 1890, 1109).

[2] Macartney to Dundas, 10 Jul. 1797, *C.H.B.E.*, VIII, 181.

defence of the long route to the East. The subsistence farmers colonising the northern hinterlands, although they impinged upon this purpose, were extremely inconvenient to it. Their land-hunger brought no benefit to the British economy. Yet they were lengthening and disturbing frontiers which placed an increasing strain upon the imperial Exchequer, the War Office and the tempers of Cabinet and Parliament. The south African colonies for these reasons were by far the most unpopular of all the white dominions up to the Eighteen seventies. They had colonists, but produced little trade or revenue, attracted no capital and few immigrants. Since the commercial ties were slender, the colonists alien and the Africans hostile, the methods of devolution and collaboration suitable in Canadian and Australasian circumstance, proved hard to work. But the Victorians were all the more in haste to apply them. There was little incentive to penetrate north of the Orange River beyond Kimberley; and much to shuffle off existing commitments. Imperial expansion in southern Africa had been extremely weak.

British commercial enterprise was seeking far brighter horizons than any to be found in Africa; and except in the south, it went on doing so until the century's end. James Stephen of the Colonial Office put the official view which held good until the Eighties:

> 'I cannot but think that even if our National resources were far more potent than they at present are, it would be very bad policy to employ in Africa that part of them which is available for Colonisation. In North America and in Australia we have vacant continents to occupy, and every shilling well expended there may be made to yield a large and secure return. But in Africa we cannot colonise at all without coming into contact with numerous warlike tribes, and involving ourselves in their disputes, wars and relations with each other. If we could acquire the Dominion of the whole of that Continent it would be but a worthless possession.'[1]

This precept also inspired the outlook on the Muslim states of north Africa. After Palmerston had broken them open for free trade, they had become useful fields of British business. But by the Eighteen seventies financial chaos had halted their commercial growth. And as in China and the rest of the Ottoman empire, the British became mainly concerned lest they should be sucked into the vortex and involved in responsibility for their government. Egypt, where the Suez Canal had been opened in 1869, concerned ministers above all. But their highest ambition was to guard the second lifeline to India, not by taking possession of Egypt, but by paramount influence over its rulers.

[1] Minute, 21 Dec. 1840, on Governor of Sierra Leone to Russell, 29 Jul. 1840, no. 34, C.O. 267/159.

Thus stood Africa in Victorian estimation in the Eighteen seventies. All the powerful processes of social expansion, except that of philanthropy, were passing that continent by. The local enterprises nibbling at its fringes — palm oil traders on the west coast, missionaries and explorers on the east, republican Boers in the south, investors in Egyptian bonds — had been making weak efforts at imperial expansion locally for half a century. But only the white pastoralists had been able to make headway, without the imperial arm to break the paths. The Home government had consistently refused to extend colonial rule. Africa remained peripheral to the Mediterranean, the Indian empire and the routes to the East. And therefore paramount influence over coasts and the Canal had sufficed. A far-reaching experience of colonisation, commerce, influence and dominion confirmed the conclusion: it was just feasible that the south might one day turn into another Canada or Australia; but no more Indias were wanted in northern or tropical Africa.

Nevertheless the Victorians after 1882 saw an almost unbelievable revolution in their political relations with Africa, as if their former calm and rational courses had run into some freakish whirlwind in the dark. As Lord Salisbury observed: 'I do not exactly know the cause of this sudden revolution. But there it is.'[1] Against all precept and prejudice, against the experience and trends of previous expansion, the British occupied Egypt and staked out a huge tropical African empire. What was more, they were ready by the end of the century to fight major wars for Sudanese deserts and south African *Kopjes*. Why, after centuries of neglect, the British and other European governments should have scrambled to appropriate nine-tenths of the African continent within sixteen years, is an old problem, still awaiting an answer.

At the centre of late-Victorian imperialism in Africa lies an apparent paradox. The main streams of British trade, investment and migration continued to leave tropical Africa practically untouched; and yet it was tropical Africa that was now bundled into the empire. There is a striking discrepancy of direction here between the economic and imperial arms. The flag was not following trade and capital; nor were trade and capital as yet following the flag. The late-Victorians seemed to be concentrating their imperial effort in the continent of least importance to their prosperity.

What were the causes and incentives? Which of them were merely

[1] Speech at Glasgow, May 1891, G. Cecil, *Life of Salisbury*, (1922–32), IV, 310.

[2] W. L. Langer, *American Historical Review*, LV, 568; L. Ragatz, 'Must We Rewrite the History of Imperialism?', *Historical Studies* (Australia and New Zealand), VI, Nov. 1953–May 1955, 90–8.

contributory and which decisive? The question of the motives for African empire may be opened afresh. There are several well-known elements in the problem. Perhaps the late-Victorians were more enthusiastic imperialists than their fathers. Possibly business men were driven to bring the unopened continent into production and so relieve surfeit and depression. The custom was once to account for the partition in such terms. Or it may be that heightened rivalries between the Powers in Europe made them seek relief in Africa from their tensions nearer home. For any or all of these reasons, the forces of imperialism in Britain and in Europe may have intensified dramatically in the last quarter of the century and caught up all Africa as they did so.

But in the British case at least, there are other possible elements which have sometimes been neglected. It cannot be taken for granted that positive impulses from European society or the European economy were alone in starting up imperial rivalries. The collapse of African governments under the strain of previous Western influences may have played a part, even a predominant part in the process. The British advances may have been the culmination of the destructive workings of earlier exercises of informal empire over the coastal *régimes*. Hence crises in Africa, no less than imperial ambitions and international rivalries in Europe, have to be taken into account. Allowance has also to be made for the diversity of interest and circumstance in the different regions of Africa. It seems unlikely that the motives in regions as dissimilar as Egypt, the Niger and south Africa can be fitted easily into a single, simple formula of 'imperialism'.

Another factor must be included. Victorian expansion by the Eighteen eighties had long historical roots and world-wide ramifications. Its manifold workings tended sometimes to build up, and sometimes to break down the societies drawn under its influence. While in some countries, British agencies helped to create vortices of disorder and nationalist reaction, in others they helped local communities to grow until they became expansive in their own right. In these ways the processes of expansion were soon receding out of metropolitan control. Some satellites tended to break up; others were beginning to throw off galaxies of their own. It is not unlikely that both these tendencies helped to drag British ministries into African empire. Lastly, it is quite possible that they did not acquire a new empire for its intrinsic value, but because Africa's relationship to their total strategy in Europe, the Mediterranean, or the East had altered.

The elements in the problem might seem so numerous and disparate as to make it insoluble. Some unified field of study has to be found where all possible incentives to African empire may be assembled without becoming indistinguishable in their several effects. Historically, only the government in London registered and balanced all the contingencies making for British expansion in Africa. In following the occasions and motives, all roads lead ineluctably to Downing Street. The files and red boxes which passed between ministers and officials at the time contain the problem in its contemporary proportions.

The collective mind of government assembled and weighed all the factors making for and against advances. Party leaders and Whips anxiously consulted the tone of the Commons and the trend of the by-elections. Secretaries for India, the Colonies and Foreign Affairs, along with the Chancellor of the Exchequer and the Service ministers, gauged the pressures: the condition of domestic and European politics, the state of the economy, the expansive demands from India and the white colonies, the risks and crises in Africa and in the whole world. Furnished with intelligences from distant ambassadors, governors and consuls, they took the rival theses of their departments to the Cabinet; and there, the Prime Minister and his colleagues argued out the differences and balanced the considerations of profit and power.

A first task in analysing the late-Victorians' share in the partition is to understand the motives of the ministers who directed it, and the study of official thinking is indispensable to this. Policy-making was a flow of deliberation and argument, of calculation and mediation between differing impulses. Secondly, it was a reading of the long-run national interest which stayed much the same from ministry to ministry, regardless of the ideological stock in trade of the Party in power. Ministers in their private calculations used a complex political arithmetic to decide whether to advance or not. Their thinking included analogues for the expansive pressures coming from business enterprise and Home politics, from foreign rivals and British agents on the spot.

By trying to reconstruct the calculations behind the higher decisions, the interplay of these elements as they worked at different levels may begin to emerge. The study of government's own reasoning is the obvious yardstick for measuring the urgency of incentives and contingencies at the point of action. Policy-making, in other words, is the unified historical field in which all the conditions for expansion were brought together.

This is not to say that ministers and their advisers were fully aware of the forces at work, or that they knew to a nicety where they were going. Neither is it to say that they were in control of the process of expansion and could start and stop it at will. Again, their recorded arguments for this course or for that did not always bring out fully their unconscious assumptions. What is more, there are many things too well understood between colleagues to be written down. There is no denying these limitations to the study of policy. But for all its shortcomings, official calculations throw most light on the deeper reasons for imperial expansion into Africa. They offer the unique method for making a first approximation to the relative strength of the different drives.

But the study of policy-making may not only advance the subject of motives, it may in addition help toward a break-through into the crucial problem — the objective causes of the partition of Africa. Once the weights in the balance of decision have been recorded, it may still be necessary to check the scales themselves. The official mind has to be taken along with the other elements in the problem as a possible cause in its own right.

Statesmen did more than respond to pressures and calculate interests; their decisions were not mere mechanical choices of expedients. Judgements and actions in fact were heavily prejudiced by their beliefs about morals and politics, about the duties of government, the ordering of society and international relations. And their attitudes to such questions tended to be specialised and idiosyncratic because they felt that their unique function and responsibility set them apart. If official thinking was in one sense a microcosm of past and present experience of expansion, in another sense, it was consciously above and outside those processes. The aristocrat by right, the official by *expertise*, both felt socially superior and functionally detached from those who pushed trade and built empires.[1] It was their high calling to mediate between jarring and selfish interests and to keep the state from being used as the tool of any of them. As governors, their profession was to take the long and the broad, not the short and narrow view, to reconcile one principle with another in action — and, in a hard-headed way, even to do right and eschew wrong. Whether a man entered the ruling circle through patronage, which was still usual, or through examination, which was becoming less rare,[2] aristocratic traditions of duty to the whole nation and disdain for its parts persisted, as did the legalism with which they approached their problems. Those who governed still thought of themselves as arbiters above the tumult, slightly contemptuous of the short-

[1] e.g. Stephen's castigations of the London merchants who governed the Gold Coast forts: '. . . nothing is less wonderful than the affected ignorance of commercial men of any rule of Law which interferes with their gains. . . . It is almost too great a temptation to throw in the way of commercial men.' (Minute by Stephen, 2 Apr. 1840, on Maclean to Russell, 27 Jan. 1840, C.O. 267/162.)

[2] S. E. Finer, 'Patronage and the Public Service,' *Public Administration.*

sighted business man, the impractical philanthropist and the ignorant populace alike.

But the London policy-makers' detachment from their problems overseas was physical as well as professional. In Africa they were usually dealing with countries which they had never seen, with questions apprehended intellectually from reports and recommendations on paper. Their solutions and purposes on the other hand, were charged with the experience and beliefs of the society in which they lived and worked. Inevitably, the official idea and the African reality, the analysis of Whitehall and the local significance of Arabi or Kruger, of Goldie or Rhodes, were worlds apart. Yet in the end it was the idea and the analysis of African situations in Whitehall, and not the realities in Africa as such which moved Victorian statesmen to act or not to act. The working of their minds is therefore of the utmost importance in establishing the motives of imperialism. Because those who finally decided the issue of African empire were partly insulated from pressures at Home, and remote from reality in Africa, their historical notions, their ideas of international legality and the codes of honour shared by the aristocratic castes of Europe had unusually wide scope in their decisions.

The possibility that official thinking in itself was a cause of late-Victorian imperialism, although once brilliantly suggested by an economist,[1] has usually been neglected by historians. England's rulers had inherited not only a world empire but the experience gained in bringing it together, and the assumptions and prejudices accumulated from past successes and failures inevitably influenced their behaviour in the partition. In the course of events, the great Departments of State and the Indian Service had compiled special historiographies of their own.[2] Time and practice had ingrained upon the minds of the oligarchy who still controlled policy abroad special notions of the national interest, and of supremacy and security in the world. England's rulers shared an esoteric view of desirable and undesirable trends stretching from the past and present to the future. And they had evolved well-tried techniques for dealing with certain situations and swinging the issue in Britain's favour.

[1] J. Schumpeter, 'Zur Soziologie der Imperialismen,' *Archiv für Sozialwissenschaft und Sozialpolitik*, XLVI, Dec. 1918, 1–39, June 1919, 275–310, translated into English in F. M. Sweezy (ed.), *Imperialism and Social Class*, (1951).

[2] 'There is a certain Pharisaism of intellect which is created or fostered by the habits of official, and especially of departmental life. It is a dangerous thing for a man to live with all the official data he can want for any decision always within his reach, docketed in pigeon-holes, with intellectual labourers always at his command to search, investigate, and condense for him. . . . They hold themselves . . . culpably deficient in self respect if they listen at all to the lessons of popular conviction. . . .' (The *Economist*, 5 Feb., 1859.)

The tradition of policy had come down unbroken from Pitt and Canning to Palmerston and Clarendon. And in the great country houses of the land, their apothegms had been passed on to the descendants of the favoured few. The continuity of Victorian leadership was remarkable. New faces were few and far between. Almost all of Gladstone's colleagues of 1868–74 served with him again between 1880 and 1885; while most of Disraeli's second ministry returned to office under Salisbury in 1886. The homogeneity of leadership was equally striking, for all its hardy individualism. Most ministers had been born in the Eighteen twenties and thirties, read classics or mathematics at Oxford or Cambridge and served their political apprenticeships in junior posts under Palmerston or Disraeli in the late Fifties and Sixties. Their cast of mind had been fixed by the personalities and experiences of their mid-Victorian prime. As Colonial Secretary under Peel, the young Mr. Gladstone's mind had been formed upon the confident assumptions of early Victorian expansiveness, and they still inspired the ageing Prime Minister of the Eighteen eighties. As Secretary for India in the Sixties, the youthful Lord Cranborne had formed that high view of its worth which resolved the later Lord Salisbury to protect it at any cost. And the lesser officials in Whitehall, Calcutta, Cape Town and Cairo shared the tradition. It was a tradition in which the Indian, the Colonial, the Palmerstonian and the Cobdenite views of expansion commingled. Hence situations were reported from abroad and judged at Home through the distorting glass of inherited prejudice and preconception. The policy-makers' choices may have been fuddled by the distortions of this special historiography, or indeed by sheer ignorance of Africa; but their peculiar angle of vision made them take decisions which might not have been made for any other reasons in any other circumstances.

How far this official mind in all its different facets was itself a cause of partition partly depends on the relation of government to society at the time. It was a relation in which a mature élite of birth and talent continued to lead, provided that it respected popular sentiments and to some extent responded when they could no longer be denied. The coming of the mass-vote, the redistribution of seats, and the rise of the modern party all set narrowing limits to the independent action of the Whig and Tory dynasts. But if the control was tightening in some fields, it remained slack in others. Ministers of both parties were careful to court the new voter in domestic affairs. They entreated his opinion about the schooling of children or the limiting of drink. But the higher statecraft of empire and world security they usually managed to seal off from his ignorant enthusiasms. Throughout the partition of Africa, the Foreign Secretaries were all peers and great landowners. Foreign policy, of which African policy was part, was still made at house parties, not by the man in the street or the man in the Stock Exchange. But this freedom abroad had its conditions, and the party leaders were careful to observe them. They had to respect the public's thirst for peace, economy and prestige, its traditional shibboleths of trusteeship and anti-slavery. No powerful business interests must be offended or jettisoned. Disasters in Britain's foreign ventures had to be avoided.

The mass voter was still an enigma to England's governors. Fearing that *demos* was a Radical, they presumed that he was also an anti-imperialist. Gladstone, it seemed, had roused him for peace and against extensions of empire, and had thereby won an overwhelming victory in the 'Midlothian Election' of 1880.[1] The risks of another Midlothian haunted ministers throughout the partition. They feared that the country was turning against imperial expansion, and they knew that it was set against expense. Since such imperial enthusiasm as there was in the Eighties was directed to consolidating the white empire and not to extending tropical dependencies, leaders of the day might well wonder with the fifteenth Earl of Derby whether the democracy would tolerate for long the burdens of defence and empire;[2] several of them prophesied that to annex more provinces would over-tax the nation's financial strength and open the way to bankruptcy and class war.[3]

Altogether the Eighties were years of harrowing uncertainty rather than ebullient confidence in British politics. It was the Irish, not the African question which held the stage, and old party loyalties, shaken already by the reforms of Gladstonian Liberalism, were being dislodged by the struggle over Irish Home Rule. Amid this confusion no ministry commanded more than a composite and conditional majority between 1881 and 1895. As to affairs abroad, Salisbury could complain in 1888 that:

> 'The misfortune — the root difficulty — we have in dealing with [such] questions . . . is that public opinion in its largest sense takes no note of them. . . . The Members of the House of Commons are each like a ship without an anchor.'[4]

[1] This is not to say that in historical fact the election of 1880 was won for these reasons. *vide* H. J. Hanham: *Elections and Party Management*, (1959), 227–32.

[2] C. A. Bodelsen, *Studies in Mid-Victorian Imperialism*, (Copenhagen, 1924), 201–2; cf. J. E. Tyler, *The Struggle for Imperial Unity, 1868–1895*, (1938).

[3] For Salisbury's views *vide* his anonymous article 'Disintegration,' *Quarterly Review*, Oct. 1883, vol. CLVI, 559–95; Cecil, *op. cit*, III, 65–6, 69–77; G. E. Buckle, (ed.), *Letters of Queen Victoria*, (henceforward *Q.V.L.*), 3rd ser., II, 172 *et seq.*; A. G. Gardiner, *Life of Sir William Harcourt*, (1923), II, 196.

[4] Salisbury to Baring, 22 Dec. 1888, Earl of Cromer, *Modern Egypt*, (1908 ed.), 397, fn. 1; Cecil, *op. cit.*, IV ,136–7.

To ministers pondering the dangers of democracy, the Irish rifts, the ingrained dislike of expenditure and tropical dependencies, there seemed to be no clear call in British politics for imperial expansion in Africa. When it came to acting there they did so more in fear of the nation's criticism than in hope of its approval.

Although there was little instructed public interest in Africa during the Eighteen eighties, some of the vague benevolence released by Wilberforce and Livingstone still persisted. Most Britons still agreed on the need for preaching the Gospel of Christ in the Dark Continent, if few regarded it as a duty of the state. That is why the lonely end of Livingstone and Gordon's martyrdom on the steps of the palace at Khartum haunted the imaginations of their fellow-countrymen. But these archetypal figures were but the heroes of an hour. Popular attention was never directed toward Africa for long. Ministers too approached their African problems with minds deeply influenced by feelings of ethical and religious obligation. All this was common doctrine, whether in Downing Street or in Exeter Hall. The official mind took pleasure in supposing that in the pursuit of the national interest it was also putting down the slave trade and spreading sweetness and light. Hence it was natural rather than hypocritical for government to clothe its African actions in the public garb of philanthropy. But since public interest in Africa was vague and intermittent, ministers feared to rely on it for support of vigorous intervention.

In business no more than in political opinion did party leaders perceive any strong incentives to African empire. Industrial growth might be slowing down after the Eighteen seventies; but as the official inquiry into the so-called depression found, it was to the established markets of America, Australasia, India and China that nearly all chambers of commerce were looking for relief.[1] The hazardous speculations of northern and tropical Africa did not attract them.[2] Throughout the partition, only the southern sub-continent, its prospects newly gilded with gold, was to draw British commercial enterprise powerfully into Africa.

[1] It is true that in the Midlands the 'Fair Traders' were spreading their influence. (A. Briggs, *History of Birmingham*, (1952), II, 179.) But the evidence submitted to the Royal Commission on the Depression of Trade and Industry shows that business opinion as a whole was not interested in fair trade or imperial solutions for its troubles. It looked for relief to the great regions of white settlement, outside as well as inside the empire, and next to railway-building in the Far East. (P.P. (1886) XXI, 75–117, (App. Pt. I), 614–62.) Of all the Chambers of Commerce which made a case before the Royal Commission only two mentioned the possibility of developing tropical Africa. (*ibid*, 97, (App. Pt. I), 639.) cf. Goschen's remark in 1885: 'Our chief hope [lies] in the prospect that the teeming millions of the old country [may] find customers in the teeming and increasing millions of Greater Britain.' (*Essays and Addresses on Economic Questions, 1865–1893*, 1905, 214.)

[2] S. H. Frankel, *Capital Investment in Africa*, (1938), cap. V.

All these considerations stress once again the paradoxical nature of late-Victorian imperial expansion in Africa. Not only was it unaccompanied by any corresponding thrust of the expanding economy, except in the south, but in the Eighteen eighties at least, strong social impulses toward a new African empire do not appear on the surface of British opinion or politics.[1] Yet it was in this decade that the ground plan of African dominion was truly laid. If the impulses from the British Isles were as weak and sporadic as they seem at first sight, then the contribution of the official mind is even more in need of investigation. For its role must have been correspondingly greater.

Naturally, government's ability to intervene would have been stronger if it had been backed by a deep social impetus. But as things stood, its powers of action were restricted. On the other hand, if ministers could evade the electorate's indifference and zeal for retrenchment, they would be that much freer to follow their traditional canons of policy. Whether confronted with European rivals or African crises, they would be guided by their own esoteric concepts. But they would have to find African governments or private agents to act on their behalf; or — and this they much preferred — they would have to ward off foreign action with diplomatic bargains. All this strengthens the possibility that the inherited notions and biases of official thinking may have been a significant cause of this imperialism without impetus.

It would seem then that we must turn from the sophistications of social analysis to the humbler tasks of chronology. We must learn the grammar of the policy-makers and construe their texts. We must go deeper than the symbolism of their conscious calculations, down to the objective causes of which these are in some sense the image. The aim is to try and disentangle the continuities of purpose from the play of circumstances and personalities. Evidently these continuities are sometimes broken. Policy is fragile to the touch of individuality, and the peculiar influence of each new-comer has to be reckoned. But decision by decision it may be possible to make out something of the broad notions, the illusions and apprehensions, the tone and spirit of the collective mind which more or less directed, and perhaps partly impelled the imperial movement into Africa.

The task of this book is to re-open by the use of such methods the historical question of the partition. This is not simply a history of African policy; it is rather, a history of the processes of Victorian expansion and of African reaction to them, as seen through the policy-

[1] *vide* R. Koebner, 'The Concept of Economic Imperialism', *Econ. Hist. Rev.*, 2nd ser., II, no. 1, 1–29, for an earlier analysis on these lines.

makers' own eyes and thoughts. The enquiry will analyse each of the larger British decisions to advance in Africa, so as to bring into the open the conceptions, prejudices and interests which lay behind it. After examining these decisions, the highest common factors in the total calculations of ministers may begin to emerge, and the constant elements in the African situations with which they were dealing may slowly be discerned. The chief issue is to settle why ministers decided to advance where they did and when they did. Finding the answers to these questions of timing and selection is the essential step towards understanding the motives of the partitioners. Beyond this lies the concluding task. If the workings of the mind of government can be deciphered, it may then be possible to translate back from the symbols of policy-making into the terms of why the partition really took place.

CHAPTER II

Moral Suasion in Guinea and Zanzibar 1815–1880

Since the Evangelical revival and the rise of secular liberalism, the issues presented by tropical Africa to the British nation had been derived from the ethical constructs of these movements. The duty to free the slaves and to convert the heathen had been thrown into high relief by the statute of 1807 which declared the Slave Trade illegal, and throughout the century the Churches and anti-slavery societies were to keep up the call of duty. Concern for Africa flowed from some of the most vivid experiences of Victorian religious and political life. And for this reason the chief African questions for the Victorians were ones of atonement and duty. The chains had to be struck from the African's neck. He must be converted. He would be civilized. He should be traded with. But for all their enthusiasm, the earlier Victorians refused to rule him.

This popular outlook derived more from virtue and imagination than from knowledge or selfish hopes. All that was generally known about Africans consisted of horrible tales of the 'Middle Passage', fables about noble savages degraded by muskets and gin, and infant races awaiting the Gospel's dawn. Ignorant of realities and intoxicated with the exuberance of their own generosity, the British conceived tropical African issues as problems of ethical behaviour — a habit which has endured.

Official attitudes at first were no more sophisticated, but as the ambitious schemes of the humanitarians broke one by one against the facts of Africa, statesmen became more and more hard-headed. They saw clearly that no concrete national interest would be served by serious state intervention in tropical Africa. Yet in a region where they had little other concern, they carried on the routines of the anti-slavery campaign, long after the fires of Wilberforce had sunk low in Downing Street.

On the tropical coasts until the Eighteen eighties the result had been generally one of success against the slave trade and of disappointment with conversions and commerce. The British connection with the west coast had stemmed from the Atlantic slave trade. Beginning in the sixteenth century, European merchants shipped millions of west Africans to work the growing plantations of the Americas. Yet the connection with west Africa during the eighteenth century remained as superficial as it was destructive. Invariably the slaving captains bought their cargoes at the water's edge. It was the African middlemen who went up-country to the slave markets and drove the slaves down to the waiting ships. Only a tiny handful of whites ever pushed inland, and they were speculators such as André Brüe and Bartholomew Stibbs, or explorers such as Mungo Park.[1] The relations of black men with white were still confined to the sea coast.

The stopping of the slave traffic involved the British in the affairs of the Coast far more than the trade itself had done. Although the Act of 1807[2] closed the business to British nationals, foreign slaving during the Eighteen thirties was to rise to a greater volume than ever.[3] In response British humanitarians were powerful enough to conscript their government into the anti-slaving crusade, and the politicians built a network of colonial footholds along the coast, Sierra Leone in 1808, the Gambia in 1816, the Gold Coast in 1821. They were intended as bases from which legitimate commerce and civilisation would drive out the slave traffic. But the trade they did was trifling, the political conundrums they presented were irritating. In Sierra Leone several thousand former slaves were left to squat on infertile soil and some of them enslaved each other.[4] The settlement at the Gambia was for ever at odds with its African neighbours and in the pocket of its French customers. The forts on the Gold Coast fell foul of the Ashanti confederacy which dominated the hinterland; serious fighting broke out and the Ashanti closed the trade paths. This was too much for the British government, which thankfully handed over the forts to a group of merchants in 1827. Captain George Maclean, the political agent of the Company, smoothed down the Ashanti and re-opened the routes into the interior. From 1830 until 1843 he extended British influence over the Fanti tribes inland in the form of an unofficial and illegal

[1] For documents concerning the aims of Brüe *vide* Bibliothèque Nationale, MSS. FR. NOUV. ACQ. ff. 41–3, 49–50, MSS. FR. 24222, ff. 306–64. For the journal of Stibbs' voyage up the Gambia in 1723, *vide* F. Moore, *Travels into the Interior Parts of Africa . . .*, (1738); Park's account is in his *Travels in the Interior Districts of Africa*, (1799).

[2] 46 Geo. III, cap. 36.

[3] J. Gallagher, 'Fowell Buxton and the New African Policy, 1838–1842,' *Cambridge Historical Journal*, X, 1950.

[4] Govr. of Sierra Leone to Goderich, no. 17, 29 Jun. 1831, C.O. 267/109; same to Glenelg, no. 85, 21 Dec. 1838, C.O. 267/148.

jurisdiction. In trying to trade, the merchants were being drawn into affairs inland. But to keep peace along the trade paths, Maclean had to pay the Ashanti their price. The European merchants on the coast were forbidden to trade directly in the interior.[1] Maclean had made straight the paths of trade, but at the cost of warning the white man off them. He had brightened the prospects of the settlements, so that the British government in another impulse of anti-slave trade feeling annexed them all over again; but British merchants were still unable to deal directly with the native producers at source, and the external trade of the Gold Coast remained a stagnant business and the expansive tendencies very weak.

The record and potentialities of the formal colonies were miserable enough. But the British government had to go on dragging these burdens because public opinion would not give up these symbols of the fight against the slave trade. Ministers generally consoled themselves by forbidding their extension.

There was a time at mid-century when it was hoped that these responsibilities might be devolved. As Colonial Secretary between 1846 and 1852, the third Earl Grey, who had extended large measures of self-government to the white colonies, hoped to carry out the same process of disengagement in west Africa. The aim of policy on the Gold Coast was to be '. . . the formation of a government upon the European model'.[2] Grey assumed that taxes would be collected by the local chiefs, but neither their prestige nor their pockets stood to benefit by their acting as the agents of Downing Street. It was the same with the Colonial Office plans for Sierra Leone. In 1851 a tax on lands and houses was introduced. The response was only moderate. Disengagement failed for lack of revenue. The inhabitants of Freetown and Cape Coast simply refused to behave like the citizens of Montreal or Sydney.

Self-financing self-government would not work on the west coast; and so the colonies remained as irritating violations of the canons of mid-Victorian expansion. To make matters worse, the customs dues they imposed stimulated ships to steer away towards those parts of the coast which did not enjoy such resources of civilisation. Hence the trade returns of the colonies remained abysmally low and gave strong arguments to their critics. Another Ashanti war in 1863 and 1864 was the last straw. With the inland paths blocked, the foreign commerce of the Gold Coast came practically to a standstill. In 1865 a Select Com-

[1] Committee of Gold Coast Merchants to Grey, 28 Nov. 1837, C.O. 267/144.

[2] Earl Grey, *The Colonial Policy of Lord John Russell's Administration*, (1853), II, 286.

mittee of the House of Commons recommended a change of policy towards all the settlements, 'with a view to an ultimate withdrawal from all, except, probably, Sierra Leone'.[1]

The report of 1865 has often been criticised as shortsighted, but on the assumptions of the mid-Victorians it was perfectly sound. Its authors did not advocate a withdrawal from west Africa as such, but merely from those irritating hostages to fortune, the colonies of west Africa. At the same time the Committee genuflected towards the humanitarians by consenting to stay in Freetown. All that was proposed was that Britain should cut her colonial losses and concentrate on the more profitable regions where the gains of trade were not cancelled by the liabilities of rule.

But it was not to be as easy as that. When it came to the point, any proposal to discard a colony brought humanitarian and commercial pressure groups into action. 'In the present tone and temper of the public mind,' noted a junior minister in 1873, 'no abandonment of territory would . . . be permitted by Parliament, or sanctioned by public opinion.'[2] Not even a colony as futile and minute as the Gambia could be jettisoned, as the Colonial Office discovered when they tried to fob it off on the French, although as Carnarvon plaintively pointed out, there were scarcely twenty whites in the territory.[3]

Downing Street still carried its mill-stones with a bad grace. Spasmodically attempts were made to apply the old plans that had failed already. If only the boundaries of Sierra Leone could be delimited, then smuggling would drop and the revenue might rise. If only the Dutch could be shifted from their forts on the Gold Coast, then it too might achieve solvency. If only the Fanti confederation could be turned into a political reality, then ministers might thankfully devolve responsibility.[4] When none of these schemes worked, it was hoped at least to avoid further commitments. But the processes of expansion working among the tribes of the west coast made this difficult to achieve. Disorder was endemic in these communities, and trade and alien influence sharpened their rivalries and disturbed their customs. On the Gold Coast a long series of wars between the coastal Fanti and the Ashanti of the interior had punctuated the history of the colony; but the British government had refused to pacify the hinterland. It looked as though this policy could go on no longer, when in 1873 the Ashanti

[1] *Report from Sel. Comm. on West African Settlements*, PP. (1865) V.
[2] Minute by Knatchbull-Hugessen, 18 Feb. 1873, C.O. 96/104.
[3] A. Hardinge, *Life of . . . Carnarvon*, (1925), II, 143–4.
[4] *vide* C. Gertzel, 'Imperial Policy towards the British Settlements in West Africa, 1860–1875,' (unpublished Oxford thesis, 1953), esp. 84, 99–100, 163.

invaded the Fanti territory and threatened to wipe out the British stations. At last London was provoked into a sharp exercise of supremacy, and General Sir Garnet Wolseley was sent out to deal with another small colonial war. But even in this extremity, it was not in the minds of Gladstone's Cabinet to subjugate or rule Ashanti. Wolseley was warned not to take measures which might bring on 'a complete break up of the King's Government and power'.[1] He was instructed to smite them a Palmerstonian blow which would chasten the unruly, but leave their political organisation independent and intact. After this lesson, they were expected to keep to their own territory, allow trade to flow freely, and to collaborate respectfully with British purposes. It was the policy of 1831 all over again, helped this time by Sir Garnet and the big battalions, but still it was a policy of influence and minimum intervention.

Wolseley duly punished the Ashanti and then withdrew, leaving them to stew, it was hoped co-operatively, in their own juice. But on the coast itself, some change was unavoidable. The sole guarantee against further Ashanti attack lay in a strong defensive grouping of the Fanti under British protection. It was a reluctant decision,[2] but in July 1874 the Gold Coast Colony came formally into being. So much for the pipe-dreams of 1865, but the Colonial Secretary consoled the Lords by remarking that the Fanti might now be made to pay for their own defence.[3] In the decent obscurity of official files another minister tartly observed: '. . . I suppose something of the kind will have to be attempted until the vulgar prejudice which is nowadays dignified by the name of "Public Opinion" veers round to a common sense and unsentimental view of this question.'[4]

It turned out on the Gold Coast as elsewhere that government had enlarged its commitment without curing disorder or improving trade. Once the colony had been set up, the Aborigines Protection Society pressed government to end domestic slavery within its jurisdiction. Against his better judgement Carnarvon did so,[5] and in imposing European standards, he destroyed a tribal institution vital to the Fanti economy. For lack of slave porters, the caravans from the interior

[1] Kimberley to Wolseley, 24 Nov. 1873, P.P. (1874) XLVI, 239–41.

[2] '. . . I do not . . . think that we could make any good use of such an organization as the erstwhile proposed Fantee Confederation. . . . I am not at all sure that the annexation of the whole Protectorate (which I look upon with horror), is not the only cheap and safe alternative to retirement. . . .' (Minute by Herbert, 17 Apr. 1874, C.O. 96/114.)

[3] *Hansard*, 3rd ser., CCXIX, col. 162.

[4] Minute by Lowther (Under-Secretary for the Colonies), 20 Apr. 1874, C.O. 96/114.

[5] Gertzel, *op. cit.*, 205.

switched their business to other parts of the coast where ethics were less stringent. Their revenues and authority diminished, the Fanti chiefs became increasingly dependent on British power for protection and peace. To make matters worse, the Ashanti confederacy threatened to fall to pieces. The Palmerstonian blow had succeeded all too well, for defeat destroyed its cohesion, and the anarchy within spread across the frontiers into the colony. For twenty years to come, the tumult in the hinterland throttled trade; in the colony on the coast the economy could not grow, and the administration was hard pressed to make ends meet.

This was the state of the British west African colonies on the eve of the scramble for Africa. Their strategic importance was trifling.[1] The value of their trade was miserably low.[2] The politicians longed to be rid of the Gambia, they vetoed the expansion of Sierra Leone. They annexed the Gold Coast to cut its costs, they kept out of Ashanti to cut their losses. In a region lacking in strong incentives, their only shred of policy was to continue the routine of moral influence. Yet this technique was becoming ineffective. European contiguity helped to sap the vigour of tribal societies drawn into the orbit of superior power and competence. So far was this erosion from inspiring dreams of conquest, that Downing Street found the situation positively embarrassing. As the tensions within African communities grew, the coastal middlemen and the inland producers competed more fiercely for the white man's favours. Their brawling and warring dammed the trickle of trade, and the old-fashioned coastal influence no longer sufficed to keep the peace. All this makes it understandable that the settlements should have seemed worthless to most politicians, and that in 1882 one of their advisers should have written: 'Personally, I wish the policy recommended by the House of Commons' Committee in 1865 could be carried out, and that we could

[1] Freetown, however, was recognised to be of secondary importance as a coaling station and a naval base.

[2] *British Trade with British West African Colonies* (*in £000's*)

	BRITISH EXPORTS TO				BRITISH IMPORTS FROM			
	Gold Coast	*Sierra Leone*	*Lagos*	*Gambia*	*Gold Coast*	*Sierra Leone*	*Lagos*	*Gambia*
1870	156	212	273	45	191	81	299	22
1875	270	253	331	64	241	113	271	17
1880	284	322	244	103	352	104	256	8
1881	302	261	160	57	275	125	160	12
1882	306	272	280	98	260	189	267	36
1883	295	302	314	90	251	169	259	46
1884	404	330	338	87	331	157	250	19
1885	345	229	293	35	342	122	195	10
1886	262	187	223	30	334	111	309	19

Sources: P.P. (1881) XCIV, 22–3, 28–9; P.P. (1890–1) XC, 686–7, 692–3).

retire from the West African Colonies.'[1] The mission against the slave trade had been accomplished. The humanitarians could no longer persuade government to enlarge its duties in west Africa. On the other hand, it dared not offend the sense of moral obligation which the anti-slavery campaigns had instilled and give up the colonial responsibilities already undertaken.

The Old Coast System: the Niger, the Congo and Lagos

There were, however, parts of the coast less unrewarding than the colonies. Farther to the south lay the mouths of the great rivers, and the deltas of the Niger and the Congo seemed to offer the easiest access to inland trade. The ending of the slave trade had destroyed the commerce on the Congo, but in the second half of the century legitimate trade began slowly to revive. In 1866 the Liverpool firm of Hatton and Cookson found a river route into the rubber-bearing region of the Ogowe;[2] and step by step the white men built a trade in ivory and rubber, palm oil and gum. They were not all subjects of Queen Victoria; the region was no-man's-land, and the Dutch, the Belgians, the Portuguese and the Spaniards had a firm apiece working there, while the French had two. But the British had six, and by 1882 they were selling goods worth half a million sterling there.[3] British commercial pre-eminence was such that even in the French colony of Gabon the gallon, the yard and the pound were the normal trading units.[4] It was small business of course, and trifling in the eyes of the strategists of mid-Victorian expansion; but at least it was on the increase, at least it could be carried on without the irritating overhead charges of formal empire.

In the Niger Delta the case was even clearer. Here, where they were unprotected by the formal authority of Britain, the trading interests were at their strongest. Debarred from slaving by the sensibilities of Westminster, the Liverpool merchants had cast around for a substitute trade, in which their African connections and know-how could be turned to new advantage. They had improvised a trade in palm oil, and by the middle of the century it had become a minor success story.

[1] Minute by A. W. L. Hemming, 19 Mar. 1882, C.O. 806/203, Appendix 1, 7.

[2] E. D. Morel, *The British Case in French Congo*, (1903), 29.

[3] Foreign Ministry Memo., 'La Question du Congo,' n.d. [1884], Archives du Ministère des Affaires Etrangères, Mémoires et Documents, (henceforth A.E.M.D.), Afrique, 89.

[4] Commandant of Gabon to Ministry of Marine, 10 Dec. 1883, Archives du Gouvernement-Général de l'Afrique Equatoriale Française, (henceforth A.E.F.), 2, B 25.

Prices were buoyant, shipments rose, and since the bulk of the trade was done in the Niger Delta, this sharply cut back the volume of slaving there.[1] Here then was a striking proof of the virtues accruing from private enterprise. Human wants were satisfied. New customers were created. Problems of sovereignty did not arise. Slavery and other barbarities were being edged out of existence.

Admirable; but was this enough? The embattled humanitarians of England did not think so, and they pressed government to take more forceful measures of moral regeneration. Ministers themselves were not unwilling, for they had not abolished their own slave trade to make life easier for the slavers of other nations. From 1819 a squadron of cruisers took up station along the coast; by 1850 there were two dozen of them.[2] It is far from clear that these vessels were a successful deterrent against the bootleg trade in slaves, but certainly their presence created an undeclared British paramountcy along the shores of Sierra Leone, Liberia, the Ivory and Gold Coasts, Dahomey, the Niger Delta and as far south as the mouths of the Congo. They forced anti-slavery treaties upon the coastal chiefs; they hunted for Portuguese, American and Cuban slavers; and they were on hand to advise, to encourage or to warn the British supercargoes plying their trade in the rivers. After 1844 the squadron had a new function, for there was now an unofficial representative of the Foreign office to be carried to the rivers, charged with the tasks of fighting the slavers and controlling the bad tempers of the old west coast hands.[3] In 1849 Captain John Beecroft was formally appointed as British consul to supervise the trade of the Niger Delta; three years later a consulate was established at Lagos. Legally, the authority of the British government might be restricted to the formal colonies, but in fact its power was supreme along vast stretches of the coast whenever it suited British interests. In the eyes of early Victorian lawyers, most of the coast of west Africa might be *res nullius*, but it is manifest nevertheless that this region was being brought under informal British control.

This official activity was important. The palm oil ruffians disliked state intervention on the coast; but in fact their trade often relied on official support. The influence of cruisers and the consuls helped to spread free trade and quell strife. British governments usually worked

[1] P.P. (1850) IX, Q. 3745; *Journal of the Royal Statistical Society*, XXX, 47.
[2] C. Lloyd, *The Navy and the Slave Trade*, (1949), Appendix C.
[3] Beecroft to Palmerston, 16 Jul. 1849, F.O. 84/775. This describes thirteen occasions in which he had been taken by the Squadron since 1844 to help in the making of treaties and the settling of disputes. The Foreign Office had wanted to appoint him as consul as early as 1844.

on Palmerston's theses for African policy: 'to encourage and extend British commerce and thereby to displace the Slave Trade.'[1] To his way of thinking, these two objectives were ultimately identical. Self-interest and the general good were interchangeable categories — a sure index of expansionist thinking. He had no more desire than the other architects of mid-Victorian empire to scramble for colonies in Africa. Trade and influence were the sole requirements, and the more of Africa opened up by any nation the better, since Britain's industrial pre-eminence would quickly win her the lion's share.

> '[The Palmerstonians] . . . wishing most earnestly that civilization may be extended in Africa, being convinced that commerce is the best pioneer for civilization, and being satisfied that there is room enough in . . . Africa for the commerce of all the civilized nations of the rest of the world, would see with pleasure every advance of commerce in Africa, provided that such commerce was not founded on monopoly and was not conducted upon an exclusive system.'[2]

Free trade was the necessary condition for improving Africa. To apply this policy properly, Palmerston saw the need to set up bases from which order, trade and the useful arts could radiate through Africa. It was hardly necessary that these bases should be annexed, merely that they should be areas where British influence could bear rather heavily upon native authorities and turn them into tools working for British purposes. What the Palmerstonians had done in China, in Turkey, in Morocco they also attempted on a tiny scale on the west coast. In 1852 Palmerston imposed an anti-slave trade treaty on Lagos.[3] Similarly he was resolved to defend the missionary settlement of Abeokuta, fifty miles inland from Lagos against the powerful kingdom of Dahomey,[4] and on several occasions in the Eighteen fifties he proposed to turn Whydah, Dahomey's chief port, into another Lagos.[5] With its slave trade gone and its rulers over-awed by Palmerston's gunboats, the independence of Lagos existed on paper only; and when in 1861 it was decided to annex the port, the Foreign Office correctly judged that the change would be slight since 'the Consul has in fact for some years been the *de facto* ruler of the place'.[6] Britain had yet another possession

[1] Palmerston to Beecroft, no. 1, 30 Jun. 1849 (cancelled passage), F.O. 84/775.

[2] Minute by Palmerston, 20 Dec. 1850, on C.O. to F.O., 15 Nov. 1850, F.O. 2/4.

[3] Minute by Palmerston, 2 Feb. 1851, F.O. 84/816; Minute by Palmerston, Palmerston to Beecroft, no. 4, 21 Feb. 1851, F.O. 84/858.

[4] Minute by Palmerston, 14 Dec. 1851, on Beecroft to Palmerston, no. 64, 4 Oct. 1851, F.O. 84/858.

[5] e.g. Minutes by Palmerston, 7 Jun. 1857, on Consul at Lagos to Clarendon, no. 9, 4 Apr. 1857; 6 Oct. 1857, on same to same, no. 24, 1 Aug. 1857, F.O. 84/1031.

[6] Minute by Wylde, 11 Jul. 1861, on Acting Consul at Lagos to Russell, no. 2, 7 Jun. 1861, F.O. 84/1141.

on the west coast. The Colonial Office was disgusted — 'Lagos is a deadly gift from the Foreign Office,' wrote one of its advisers.[1] They could foresee all too clearly that it would join the queue of west African pauper possessions lining up for a Parliamentary grant-in-aid.[2] All the same, on Palmerstonian principles the move was right. The new colony would be confined to the coast.[3] It would lend support to Abeokuta. It would canalise the oil trade from the palm belt west of the Niger. It would check the French at Porto Novo.

The British government intervened in the affairs of the Niger in another way which was to prove momentous. In the Eighteen twenties ministers were already dreaming of opening trade with the great Moslem emirates around the middle reaches of the Niger.[4] The difficulty, of course, was to find a way to them; but in 1830 Richard Lander proved that Mungo Park's Niger was the same river which flowed into the huge Delta in the Bight of Biafra.[5] Two years later Macgregor Laird and Lander, using the new technical resources of the age, managed to take an iron steamship some four hundred miles up the Niger. They had demonstrated not only that the hinterland could be reached, but that oil could be bought there much more cheaply than on the coast.[6] In 1841 government itself took a hand, and sent an elaborate expedition upriver, only to find that if the ascent of the Niger was technically feasible, it was fatal to health.[7] The white traders stayed where they were on the coast, deterred from adventuring upcountry by malaria, the middlemen, and the conservatism of the Liverpool oligarchs. But they were not left in peace for long. In 1854 Her Majesty's Government encouraged Laird to launch another luckier expedition. This time Dr. Baikie steamed up the Niger and the Benue and returned to the coast without the loss of a single life. Science had struck another blow at the old trade, this time in the form of quinine.[8] From now on

[1] Minute by Barrow, 22 Apr. 1864, on Govr. of Lagos to Newcastle, no. 13, 9 Mar. 1864, C.O. 147/6.

[2] e.g. 'In Lagos we have assumed a government without as yet a revenue . . . there is not yet one self-supporting settlement on the West Coast of Africa.' (Minute by Elliott, 30 Nov. 1861, on F.O. to C.O., 28 Nov. 1861, C.O. 147/2.)

[3] 'It is the policy of the Gov[ernmen]t to confine our acquisition in the neighbourhood of Lagos to the smallest limits. . . .' (Minute by Rogers, 20 Nov. 1862 on Govr. of Lagos to Newcastle, no. 56, 9 Oct. 1862, C.O. 147/1.)

[4] Bathurst to ruler of Bornu, n.d. 1825 (to be delivered by the Clapperton mission), C.O. 392/3.

[5] R. and L. Lander, *Journal of an Expedition to Explore the Course and Termination of the Niger*, (1832).

[6] M. Laird and R.A.K. Oldfield, *Narrative of an Expedition into the Interior of Africa by the River Niger*, (1837), I, 103–4; II, 401–9.

[7] C.O. 2/23 and 2/24, *passim*.

[8] H. W. B. Baikie, *Narrative of an exploring Voyage up the Rivers Kwora and Binue*, (1856), 5, 453.

the picture was changed. The Niger could be ascended, malaria could be mastered. The Foreign Office revived the old dream of developing a connection with the Moslem states of the north. In 1857 they agreed to subsidise Laird to send five annual expeditions up the river[1] and instructed Baikie to make for the great emirate of Sokoto.[2]

In opening up the Niger, the Foreign Office was attacking the vested interests of the oil traders on the coast. In the Delta, oil might cost up to £24 per ton;[3] further up the river it could be had for £13.[4] By backing the trial voyages to the confluence and beyond, government threatened to bring white traders into the heart of the palm belt, and so to leave both the African middlemen chiefs and the white supercargoes high and dry. Moreover, official support of another of Laird's ventures, the African Steamship Company, plying between Liverpool and the Delta, weakened the old system still further. The steamers gave new men the chance to ship independently by using their regular freight services and to break the monopoly of the oligarchs. Already by 1861 more than 10 per cent of the palm oil coming to Liverpool was carried by Laird's line.[5] Technical innovation represented by the coming of the steamer was working to transform the British connection with the Niger. In the interior the steamer could outflank the coastal monopolists. On the coast it could undercut them.

Throughout the middle decades of the century the Foreign Office deliberately encouraged free trade and expansion against monopoly and restriction in the Delta and upriver. The Foreign Secretary, Lord Clarendon, wrote that the interlopers '. . . *must* be upheld against the supercargoes'.[6] The permanent head wrote that the Niger must be kept open for trade 'on every ground'.[7] Four years later the aims of this policy were summed up by one of his assistants:

> 'The profits of the Oil Trade have hitherto been so great, that the few great merchants engaged in the traffic have been quite content to let matters remain *in statu quo*, and have not troubled themselves to push up the rivers, the trade of which they monopolised at the mouth. . . . We have laboured hard for some years past and successfully to break up this monopoly, and if we can open out the Niger to the trade of this country, it will be another and a considerable step in the right direction.'[8]

[1] Admiralty to F.O., 21 Apr. 1857, F.O. 2/23. [2] F.O. to Baikie, 1 May 1857, *ibid.*

[3] Baikie to Clarendon, 11 Oct. 1856, F.O. 2/23.

[4] Glover to Russell, 28 Feb. 1860, enclosure, F.O. 2/34.

[5] Oil shipped to Liverpool, 1861: by sail 17,277 tons; by steamer 2,008 tons. Figures calculated from Liverpool Customs *Bills of Entry* (Picton Library, Liverpool).

[6] Minute by Clarendon, 17 Dec. 1856, on Governor of Sierra Leone to Clarendon, no. 12, 27 Oct. 1856, F.O. 84/1003.

[7] Minute by Hammond, 1 Mar. 1860, on Glover to Russell, 28 Feb. 1860, F.O. 2/34.

[8] Memo. by Wylde, 28 Apr. 1864, F.O. 97/434.

Here are the Palmerstonian principles in action. Naval power was being used to break up the barriers of artificial monopoly and restriction whether European or African, so that trade could expand through the cracks, carrying with it the essentials of liberal civilisation and British paramountcy. To put trade into the hinterland of the Niger would increase British commerce. It would open the way to the emirates. It would extend the region of informal influence. Moreover, by damaging the sources of slaving, it would serve as well the true interests of Africa. Commerce and philanthropy would advance hand in hand.

By the middle of the Eighteen sixties it seemed to the Foreign Office that this happy ending was in sight. The inland trade was growing, so that the subsidy could be withdrawn in 1865 on the sound Victorian argument that the trader must now learn to stand on his own feet.[1] It seemed that he might manage to do so. From now on British firms became active upcountry. By 1871 there were five steamers on the river, doing a trade worth some £55,000 a year, and edging further along the Niger, until voyages as far as Egga became matters of routine.[2] By the end of the Seventies the trade had come to be worth annually some £300,000.[3] It was small change to the counting houses of England, but it did stand for economic growth, for a local expansive impulse, for private enterprise seizing its opportunities.

But after the Eighteen sixties the outlook began to change for the worse along the whole line of coast. In the colonies of the Crown commercial stagnation continued to be the rule, while political disturbances with the surrounding tribes became more baneful than ever. In the regions under the private influence of the merchants, the period of growth was at an end. Palm oil prices had risen to their peak during the Crimean War; thereafter they fell steadily until the end of the century.[4] Moreover the chaos and disruption of the inland market grew wilder.

[1] Minutes by Layard, 15 Dec. and Clarendon, 17 Dec. 1865, on Memo. by Wylde, 13 Dec. 1865, F.O. 97/435.

[2] W. N. M. Geary, *Nigeria under British Rule*, (1927), 170; J. Whitford, *Trading Life in Western and Central Africa*, (1877), caps. VI and VII.

[3] Consul Hopkins to F.O., no. 40, 18 Nov. 1878, F.O. 84/1508.

[4] *Palm Oil Prices, 1866–87 (£ per ton) and Imports from 'West Coast':*

	£	£		£	£
1866	40·21	1,422,937	1883	35·11	1,738,367
1870	36·48	1,721,632	1884	33·50	1,477,659
1875	33·35	1,727,765	1885	26·90	1,232,649
1880	29·45	1,890,599	1886	20·92	1.063.626
1881	29·09	1,585,373	1887	19·48	1,098,712
1882	30·49	1,725,375			

Sources: P.P. (1881) XCIII, 104–5, 32–3; P.P. (1890–1) LXXXIX, 134–5, 50–1. Note 'West Coast of Africa' excludes any British, French or Spanish possessions.

As trade slumped and turmoil spread in the hinterlands, the old coast system was becoming slowly unworkable. Nevertheless, Her Majesty's Government would not be driven into replacing the old system by a new *régime* of imperial administration and order. What had taken place in Sierra Leone and on the Gold Coast was repeated in the palm belt between Lagos and the Niger country. The time-honoured bases of exchange, of inter-tribal politics, of the relations between producers and middlemen were upset by the presence of the European, by his innovations and by the play of the world market. Instead of spreading peace, commerce seemed to have encouraged unrest and corroded tribal authority in ways which upset all the Palmerstonian calculations.

The gulf between intention and effect is illustrated by the events around Lagos. Britain had annexed it, ended its slave trade and worked to make it the outlet for the western side of the palm belt. But in overthrowing the hidebound slave economy of the country, Britain had turned the relations between the coastal and the inland peoples topsy-turvy. The forcible conversion of Lagos to legitimate trade had put it on the worst of terms with the great slaving power of Dahomey. Secondly, the annexation of 1861 completely upset the old power balance, and set Lagos at odds with the littoral tribes of the Egba, who were themselves thrown into enmity with the inland peoples. The Ibadans, who produced the palm oil, wanted a route to the sea; the Egba stood in the way — to this extent it was the familiar west coast conflict between the ambitious producer and the unreconstructed middleman. The result was a chronic state of chaos, incurable in terms of the old techniques of mere influence. Glover, the administrator of Lagos, tried to settle it with a high hand; his immediate successors switched to a policy of appeasement and then of hopeless quiescence. The local field of trade had been shaken out of its old pattern of mutual advantage, and jerked into a condition of tumult. It was to persist for three decades and it crippled the trade of Lagos.[1] The colony remained a failure, another skeleton in the imperial cupboard. Only determined British intervention in the politics of the hinterland could have turned it into a success; but no British government was willing to contemplate such a step. In 1881 the Colonial Secretary could write:

> 'Her Majesty's Government, whilst ready to promote by any friendly means the settlement of these long-standing dissensions which . . . seriously affect the prosperity of Lagos, could not approve any measures involving direct interference with the inland tribes. Such a course would not fail to

[1] For the relations of Lagos with its hinterland, *vide* S. O. Biobaku, *The Egba and their Neighbours, 1842–1872*, (1957), 64–95.

involve the Colonial Government in dangerous complications, and would entail on this country an extension of responsibilities which Her Majesty's Government are not prepared to undertake.'[1]

On the eve of the Scramble Lagos was still regarded as a liability.

In the Niger Delta itself the disturbances worked among tribal communities by European penetration put Palmerstonian calculations even more out of true. By 1864 there were twenty-one British firms operating in the Delta and in points south,[2] all ferociously competing against each other, bolstering the buying price of palm oil in Africa, even as its selling price was falling in Europe. The rugged individualism of Liverpool could never reconcile itself to a common buying policy. In mid-century, when oil prices were still buoyant, this did not much matter; but as they started to sag, so cutthroat a business came to look absurd. As Richard Burton in the Sixties wrote of the river where the trade was greatest: 'The commerce of the Bonny River is a subject for the antiquary.'[3] Liverpool firms of the Delta and the African middlemen who supplied them, stirred up tribal resistance against the British firms who were tapping the trade at source upriver.[4] The drive into the hinterland threatened to destroy the prosperity and the prestige of the Delta chiefs. Upstream as a result the steamers ran into violence and gunplay. It had happened to Lander in the Thirties. It had happened to Laird's captains in the Fifties. It was still going on in the next decade.[5] By this time it was only part of the general unrest which forced the British in 1869 to remove their new consulate from Lokoja, at the confluence of the Niger and the Benue, and which led them after 1871 to send gunboats on annual punitive sweeps up the river. The Foreign Office in 1878 still believed in the prospects of the upriver traffic, despite its difficulties. By that date four British firms were trading up the Niger, more than six hundred miles inland.[6] To the officials in London this seemed to justify some self-congratulations:

> 'The trade in this River increases annually. . . . I have no hesitation in stating that this River never would have been thrown open to British Trade if it had not been for the Expeditions we have from time to time sent up the Niger. . . .'[7]

[1] Kimberley to Govr. of Gold Coast and Lagos, 26 Aug. 1881, C. 4957, 9.

[2] Total calculated from Consul Burton to Russell, 15 Apr. 1864, F.O. 84/1221, (also as a Confidential Print in F.O. 2/45).

[3] *idem.*

[4] e.g. Baikie to Russell, no. 6., 13 Jan. 1861, F.O. 97/433; Company of African Merchants to Palmerston, 11 Mar. 1864, F.O. 97/434.

[5] Minute by Wylde, on Glover to Russell, no. 26, 6 Nov. 1863, F.O. 84/1201.

[6] Consul Hopkins to Sec. of State, no. 40, 18 Nov. 1878, F.O. 84/1508.

[7] Minute by Wylde, 21 Jan. 1879, on above, *ibid.*

But the reactions of the tribes were deeper than Downing Street allowed for. The following year the consul had a different story to tell; this time he was reporting 'the lawlessness, the murders, and the slave buying and selling' taking place at the inland markets.[1] Here was a mounting social crisis. Ought Britain to be dragged into the interior to deal with it by assuming some outright control? The Foreign Office was clear that she should not: 'It would be impossible for Her M[ajesty]'s Gov[ernmen]t to undertake to protect Merchants in every quarter of the globe.'[2]

In any case the trade itself did not seem worth the exertions of empire. The firms trading upriver were undercapitalised[3] and overstrained. They had set up some fifty-eight stations and were not doing enough business to justify such overhead costs. The slump in palm oil prices was turning these speculative ventures into doubtful propositions, since trade was too expensive on a falling market. They responded to this situation by undercutting each other. The result was that the inland region remained 'a no man's land traded in to a trifling extent by three or four petty companies quarrelling like kites and crows.'[4] The country was turbulent, the merchants were weak, the trade was small, the prospects were poor.

The mid-Victorians had attempted to bring about favourable conditions for a system of informal commercial influence, but African reactions were making progress on these lines difficult. Their traders had set the Delta to work for the market; their consuls and gunboats had rigged up a flimsy structure of order. Stage by stage the region had been linked to the British economy without the expense of linking it with the British Crown. Here the initiative of the trader had set up local British interests with only a bare minimum of intervention by the British government.

The Old East Coast System

On the east coast of Africa the position was somewhat different from that on the west. There, it was the government which had set up the British interests, with only a bare minimum of action by the trader. On

[1] Consul Hopkins to Salisbury, no. 19, 19 Jul. 1879, F.O. 84/1541.
[2] Minute by Wylde, n.d. [7–14 Sept. 1879] on above, *ibid.*
[3] This may be deduced from these facts. In 1885 the subscribed capital of the National African Company was 'about' £1,000,000. Of this less than one-third had come from the 'survivors of the smaller companies which had created the Niger-Benue trade.' (Goldie Taubman to Salisbury, 28 Dec. 1885, F.O. 84/1879.)
[4] Goldie Taubman to Anderson, Private, 6 Nov. 1885, *ibid.*

the east coasts as on the west, the long war on the slave trade and the arduous search for legitimate commerce had left a vague paramountcy of influence to the late-Victorians. The slave trade was continuing on the east coast, but on the west by the Eighteen sixties it had been put down. The east coast had not yet attracted the British merchant, whereas on the west, the palm oil traders of Liverpool and London were plying a small but regular commerce. On the west the web of paramountcy was spun intricately of relations with myriads of African chieftaincies scattered among the towns and rivers of the steaming coasts. But on the east, there was a Sultan of Zanzibar through whom British influence could be generally exerted. The connection with the east was much more recent. Trade and influence had not penetrated into the hinterlands. Yet the record of failure and disenchantment, the resolve of British governments against undertaking colonial responsibilities was the same.

Along the east coasts, Britain had enjoyed an unchallenged supremacy since the Napoleonic wars. Its ultimate sanction was naval power in the Indian Ocean. From Mozambique in the south to Somaliland in the north, the island Sultanate was the chosen instrument of British sway over the coast-towns of the mainland and their hinterlands. The inconveniences of rule were thus avoided. This east African paramountcy was but part of a wider web of influence over the shores of the Indian Ocean, the Persian Gulf and the Red Sea. It linked with others based upon Muscat, Aden and Cape Town covering the approaches to the Indian Empire from the west. All along the Arabian and African coast, except at one or two key points, British influence was of this informal type. Forceful agents or residents scattered here and there, an occasional visiting gunboat showing the flag, and Arab or African allies kept loyal by treaty, subsidy or threat, were its tools.

British aims were better served by Arab allies than by an army of British administrators; and Seyyid Said,[1] Imam of Muscat and Sultan of Zanzibar, (1806–56), had been one of the most valuable. As early as the Eighteen twenties the policy of mere influence and no commitments was enforced. The government of that day sent Captain Owen to survey the east African coast-line. Personages in the East India Company thought that east Africa's trade with India could be increased. There were suspicions of French designs on the east coast which might turn out to be strategically awkward. And the humanitarians in England were as anxious to strike a blow against the slave trade in east as in west

[1] For the career of Seyyid Said *vide* R. Coupland, *East Africa and Its Invaders*, (1938).

Africa. Owen decided that the best way to serve these purposes was to proclaim a protectorate over Mombasa, but the government would have none of it. To have done so would have alienated the Sultan of Zanzibar in whose dominions Mombasa theoretically lay, and British interest in the country was dubious and trivial. Informal influence through the Sultan was quite enough.[1]

During the Eighteen forties the British began to develop this policy more fully. They encouraged Said to move his capital from Muscat to Zanzibar, and posted a consul to guide him. They helped him win back his authority, from Warsheikh in the north to Cape Delgado in the south. They implicitly protected his possessions against foreign encroachment and prompted his policy behind the scenes. As Cogan, one of Palmerston's agents had suggested, the Sultan of Zanzibar was being used '. . . not only as a powerful political engine as regards our Eastern Possession [sc. India] but [one] through whose means education and morality might be introduced to an unlimited extent in . . . Africa.'[2]

There were good reasons why the Foreign Office made fuller use of Said. His enlightened policy was turning Zanzibar into a promising *entrepôt*. He did his best to encourage the merchants of British India and provided ready-made the political order which their enterprises required. In partnership with the Swahili traders who were pushing inland, the Banyans promised to open up the regions westward as far as Lake Nyasa, Tanganyika and Victoria.

But however bright the possibilities, the actual trade of Zanzibar remained of slight value to Britain or to India, and the mid-Victorians valued the Sultan most as an instrument of strategy. During the Eighteen forties and Eighteen fifties French expansion towards the east revived. Their occupation of the islands of Nosse-bé and Mayotta between 1840 and 1843 suggested that they aspired to footholds on the mainland at Mombasa and even further north. This danger was averted by British aid to its Arabic overlord.

Already sentinel of the African coast opposite India and protector of its traders, the Sultan had now to serve a third purpose. Although it was foreign to his authority and would weaken him in his other capacities, the Foreign Office expected him to be the Wilberforce of east Africa and lead the fight against the slave trade. An anti-slave-trade treaty had been forced on him at Muscat in 1822. Not content with treaties, the humanitarians advocated establishing settlements at

[1] M. V. Jackson, *European Powers and South East Africa*, (1942), 107–8.

[2] For knowledge of Palmerston's policy toward Zanzibar we are indebted to the work of Mr. Robert Gavin on Palmerston's African policy.

selected points along the coast of Africa. In 1838 Buxton had urged Palmerston to begin such a settlement at Mombasa.[1] He refused: 'In order to extirpate Slave Trade by commercial settlements you must begird with them the whole circumference of Africa.'[2] The Foreign Office persevered with its system of influence and treaties. In 1839 the earlier agreement was more stringently defined, and six years later Said was induced to put an absolute ban on the export of slaves from his African dominions.[3]

Palmerston himself saw something of the contradictions inherent in such a policy. The Sultan was the patriarch of a chain of self-governing Arab trading communities, not a despot at the head of a centralised administration and a powerful army. His vassals drew much of their prosperity and prestige from slaves and slave-trading. The trade provided him with much of his revenue, and it was sanctioned by the Muslim religion of which he was a leader. To use Said in this way was likely to provoke revolt, to break up his empire and to encourage French influence.[4] The more he was forced to act as an agent of humanitarianism, the less effective as a tool of trade and strategy did he become. But the fervour of British philanthropy brushed aside this consideration and forced him to carry out the anti-slave-trade treaty of 1845. 'You have put on me', he complained to the British agent, 'a heavier load than I can bear.'[5] Said was right. After his death in 1856, there was a revolt, and the British had to step in to save the *régime*. The crisis came in 1859. Said had divided his realm between his heirs, and Zanzibar was now separated from Oman. A succession dispute followed at Zanzibar, in which the British backed one candidate, the French another, while the Omanis tried to reunite Zanzibar to Oman.[6] Bombay and Whitehall saw the struggle as one between British and French influence, as a contest between progress and reaction in Arab society. Quasi-feudal Oman could not be allowed to throttle the commercial expansion of Zanzibar. A British sloop and a few marines imposed a settlement, and Mejid was put into power. In 1861 the Viceroy of India finally decreed the separation of Zanzibar and Muscat. Consul Rigby's argument in favour of this course sums up British policy towards east Africa during the age of Palmerston:

[1] Glenelg to Palmerston, 10 Sept. 1838; Palmerston to Glenelg, 14 Oct. 1838; F.O. 54/2.

[2] Palmerston to Glenelg, 24 Sept. 1838, F.O. 54/2.

[3] Coupland, *op. cit.*, 502–3, 514–6; *British and Foreign State Papers*, XXXV, (1846–7), 632–3.

[4] Palmerston to Cogan, 28 Sept. 1838, Jackson, *op. cit.*, 167–8.

[5] Sir R. Coupland, *The Exploitation of East Africa*, (1939), 12.

[6] For the details of the crises, *ibid.* cap. II.

'From Port Natal to Cape Guardafui the only state from which any progress or stability can be hoped is Zanzibar . . . it bids fair to become the chief emporium of trade on the east coast. Its population possesses valuable elements for commerce in the wealthy and numerous settlers from India, and the enterprising Arabs and Swahili who travel over Central Africa, distributing foreign goods in exchange for the products of the country. . . . If Zanzibar should be an independent state, the dominion of its ruler would probably soon extend into the interior . . . and . . . might form a considerable African kingdom.' Nothing of the kind, Rigby declared, could be expected if it remained a dependency of Muscat. In that case, Zanzibar would '. . . gradually . . . lose its power over the territories of the mainland, the petty chiefs and sultans would soon become independent; the treaties for the suppression of the Slave Trade would be disregarded; foreign settlements would be established; and all hope of progress would be destroyed.'[1]

Here Rigby put in a nutshell the Palmerstonian technique for suppressing the slave trade and developing and civilising the interior of tropical Africa by means of legitimate commerce. Although the idea of acquiring territory was rejected out of hand, the method was essentially political. The Foreign Office sent its agents into Africa to seek out the native centres of order and stability and to bring them under British influence. The states that were the quickest to adopt British notions of lawful trade and moral behaviour were to be made the agents of peace and progress in Africa. The search had been continuous. In their quest for pliant native powers the British ranged from Sokoto and Dahomey to Abyssinia and Zanzibar; but by the late Eighteen sixties this policy had met with one failure after another. The Foreign Office was discouraged to find that receptive African rulers were not strong, and that strong African rulers were not receptive; and although they could make headway with the puny rulers of Abeokuta, they could do little in the strong warrior kingdoms. Consequently the interior stayed virtually closed to their enterprise. London took Rigby's rosy forecasts about east Africa with a grain of salt. The Cabinet sanctioned the intervention at Zanzibar in 1859, but hardly because they believed in a bright future for its mainland trade. They were chiefly concerned with safeguarding Indian life and property, and excluding French influence. In 1862 the dispute with France was settled, and the two governments agreed to respect the independence of Zanzibar and Muscat. As was normally the case on either coast before the occupation of Egypt, the two Powers composed their African conflicts without forcing each other to make unwanted protectorates or annexations.

[1] Rigby to Coghlan, *Disputes Commission Report*, 72–3, quoted in Coupland, *Exploitation of East Africa*, 29–30.

After the intervention of 1859–61, the influence of the British at Zanzibar was stronger than ever; yet during the Eighteen sixties and seventies they went on using it in the way which would cut the ground from under their own feet. When Majid died in 1870, the British agent made Barghash Sultan, on one condition, that he should intensify his effort against the slave trade.

> 'The decided attitude of this Agency,' the Consul reported, 'with regard to the succession of Seyyid Barghash has closed the mouths of many who were inclined to reject his candidature . . . while the Prince was made to understand that he himself had no chance if Her Majesty's Government were against him. . . . the new Sultan has pledged himself to do everything in his power to be agreeable to the British Government.'[1]

Instead, the new Sultan rebelled against his masters and attacked their interests in the name of conservative Islamic tradition. He interfered with British Indian property rights and free trade. Worst of all he refused to end the slave export from his mainland territories. To do so, he protested, would deprive the clove culture of Zanzibar of labour, ruin the Sultanate, and provoke revolt among his subjects. Humanity's business none the less could not wait. Something more than iron-fisted diplomacy was needed to exterminate the traffic. The 'Sentimental squadrons' blockading the coasts had merely diverted it into other channels. Indeed, the trade seemed to grow and prosper more than ever as the slavers resorted to smuggling and opened new overland routes. The British therefore were determined to use the Sultan and his governors on the mainland as the only administrative means of suppressing the trade on land. It was for this purpose that they imposed the Treaty of 1873 and the Procalmations of 1876.

To dragoon the *sheikhs* and *walis* into what was for them a disastrous task, the British had to prop up the *régime* and change its character. The outlawing of the slave trade, so Dr. John Kirk, the Consul General, reported was 'the most unpopular step' a Sultan had ever taken. 'His people to a man [were] against him,' for there was '. . . not a house that [was] not more or less affected.' The Sultan and his officials would do nothing unless compelled; and resistance was certain. In using the Sultanate to outlaw the traffic, to exact obedience to a Christian ethic, its Muslim authority was being destroyed.

> 'If we make it seen that the Sultan's authority will be maintained while he acts with us,' wrote Kirk, 'the new concession will be a reality. Otherwise, his authority being set aside, the law will be broken, and in the end we shall

[1] Churchill to Bombay, 8 Oct. 1870, *ibid.*, 88.

be forced to take [those measures of] direct and independent interference which I hoped to have spared the Government . . . .'[1]

There were indeed humanitarians in Parliament pressing government to take direct possession of Mombasa and the main of Zanzibar; but as usual, the Cabinet ignored them and stuck to its habitual method of influence. The British lent alien sinews to the tottering Sultanate when the Navy put down the slavers' rebellions at Mombasa and Kilwa in 1875 and 1876, and forced Barghash's authority upon the rest of his ports before revolt could begin. At Kirk's suggestion, the Sultan was strengthened further by a small army, trained and commanded by a British officer.[2]

In order to strike down the slave traffic, the British had perforce improvised what was in effect a 'new Sultanate'.[3] Behind the forms of the old institution, their influence was hardening into something very like control. The real, if not the nominal Sultan from now on, was the British agent, Dr. Kirk; and with the change, the former suzerainty over the Arab communities of the coast was being turned into centralised direction with real authority behind it. External paramountcy was passing into a barely disguised informal control, as it was doing in so many Muslim countries in the nineteenth century. The Sultanate of Zanzibar was going the same way as the *régimes* in Turkey, Egypt, Tunis and Java; but whereas it was foreign economic penetration which sapped their power, in Zanzibar the Sultan's authority was destroyed by the struggle over the slave trade. Its fate was strikingly similar to that which overtook the Khedivate of Egypt, although the causes of decline were not the same. The Khedivate was broken more by the expansion of the European economy, by the extent of its debts and the suspicions of its creditors; the Sultanate by the extension of European morality, by the attack on the slave trade and the zeal of the humanitarians. In the one case Ismail's creditors put in the bailiffs, who turned the Khedivate into an agency for collecting taxes; in the other, Barghash's protectors turned the Sultanate into an instrument for enforcing an alien ethic. But in both cases the result was a native revolt against a *régime* which had been converted into the medium by which foreigners gave orders. The retort to the bondholders was to be the revolt of Arabi; the response to the humanitarians was the revolt of the slavers; and the effect of these rebellions in Zanzibar as in

[1] Kirk to Derby, 20 Apr. 1876, *ibid.*, 227.
[2] For the officer in command of this force and the work it carried out *vide* R. N. Lyne, *An Apostle of Empire . . . The Life of Sir Lloyd William Mathews*, (1936).
[3] Coupland's phrase; *Exploitation of East Africa*, cap. XII.

Egypt was to weaken the *régime* still more and to deliver it further into European control.

In 1875 there was a sharp clash between the interests of Egypt and Zanzibar. The Khedive Ismail, deep in projects of southern expansion, sent an expedition under Gordon up the Nile towards Lake Victoria, while an Egyptian naval force was sent to seize the port of Kismayu and open an overland supply route for Gordon's column from the east coast. The following year Gordon annexed the Upper Nile for the Khedive. Egyptian ambition was encroaching on the northern mainland territories of Zanzibar, and the British stepped in to protect their client's interests. To Barghash and to Kirk the prospect of an Egyptian occupation around the Lakes seemed intolerable. In the face of this Egyptian threat they considered in 1877 a plan for handing over to the rule and safe-keeping of a British company all the Sultan's mainland possessions from the coast up to the Lakes.

Since the Eighteen thirties British agents at Zanzibar had aspired to use the Sultanate to pacify and develop the interior, but it had never been strong enough for the purpose. British humanitarians in their turn had tried to persuade government itself to undertake the work directly; but they had always been rebuffed. In 1877 Kirk and the philanthropists hoped to enlist business enterprise in the cause so long frustrated by the Sultanate's impotence and the Home government's inertia.

There were indications that Mackinnon,[1] a businessman with shipping interests in the Indian Ocean might raise the money, while his reputation as a philanthropist was a guarantee of respectability. He wanted the mainland, and Barghash was willing to let it go. Kirk for his part tried hard to engineer the concession. But it came to nothing.

Precisely why it failed remains something of a puzzle, but the more general reasons are plain enough. A handful of enthusiasts for imperial expansion in tropical Africa by themselves could no more make an imperialist summer in the late Eighteen seventies than they could in the Eighteen forties and Eighteen fifties. Their fabricated appeals to high national and commercial interests in the east African interior met with little response, for there existed in Britain no deep urges to expand there. The government respected the overwhelming weight of prejudice and tradition against official or even semi-official ventures in central

[1] William Mackinnon (1823–93); founded British and India Steam Navigation Company, 1862; established steamship service between Aden and Zanzibar, 1872; one of the original subscribers to the *Comité d'études du Haut Congo*, and continued to work with Leopold II during the Eighteen eighties, founded East Africa Association, 1887, and the Imperial British East Africa Company, 1888.

Africa because it saw no large purpose in them. Lord Derby at the Foreign Office would not budge from the long-standing policy of refusing any commitment in east Africa;[1] and Salisbury, then Secretary for India, probably objected even more strongly.[2] Mackinnon was told that his enterprise did not require official sanction and in any event, this could not be given. He would receive 'such support as [government] . . . can properly afford to such an undertaking'; but the Foreign Office was careful to point out that this did not include guaranteeing the projected Company's territory against invasion by foreign Powers.[3] What it amounted to was this: if private enterprise could go it alone, well and good; but government would have no hand in the affair, at least in the pioneering stage. Mackinnon for his part found that money was not forthcoming on these terms. Without public risk there would be no private enterprise, and Mackinnon's plans fell through. In commercial as in political terms, there was still no impulse towards expansion in east Africa.

The Liberals were as determined as the Conservatives to keep out of east Africa and Gladstone's ministry showed this on several occasions before 1884. Early in 1881, Granville rejected Kirk's suggestion that the extent of the Sultan's dominions inland should be defined. Like Derby before him, the Foreign Secretary feared that delimitation might commit Britain to defend the territory later on, and such a commitment was still anathema in London. Later in the same year, Barghash, fearing that there would be faction fights after his death, asked the British government to settle the succession and take powers of regency. It amounted practically to a request for a protectorate.[4] Kirk advised that it should be accepted. Dilke, the Under-Secretary of the Foreign Office, also favoured it. 'Are you going to let Zanzibar die without a kick?' he asked Northbrook.[5] Dilke's question and Barghash's request showed how utterly the new Sultanate depended on British influence to keep it together. But in Zanzibar, if not in Egypt, the British could take big risks with anarchy since no vital interest was involved. Ripon, the Viceroy of India threw cold water on the scheme. We should

> '. . . avoid implicating ourselves,' he wrote, 'in matters over which we could exercise no real influence without an expenditure of money and a display of strength out of all proportion to the advantages to be gained.'

[1] cf. Coupland, *ibid.*, 312–3.
[2] de Kiewiet, *History of the Imperial British East Africa Company*, (London University Doctoral Thesis, 1955), cap. I.
[3] Pauncefote to Mackinnon, 19 Dec. 1877, Coupland, *Exploitation of East Africa*, 312.
[4] A translation of the Arabic text of Barghash's deed is given in *ibid.*, 377.
[5] Dilke to Northbrook, 16 Nov. 1882, S. Gwynn and G. M. Tuckwell, *Life of Sir Charles Dilke*, (1917), I. 535.

Stability at Zanzibar *was* an advantage to British India, he admitted, but it was not in the least crucial.[1] Gladstone and most of the Cabinet frowned on the offer. The French might regard an acceptance as a breach of the joint Declaration of 1862; the Liberal Alliance was far more valuable than the trivial and inconvenient interest in Zanzibar.[2] As late as 1883, the traditional policy was as decided as ever. Paramountcy was still enough for British purposes in Zanzibar.

Such was the system of influence on the east African coast before the coming of the Scramble. To British public opinion by far the strongest reason for keeping it up was to put down the slave traffic, and to substitute a mellower trade and civilisation. But although public opinion might be stirred by a Buxton or a Livingstone, with their pleas for spreading Christianity and commerce, no serious national interest in the east African interior existed. Decades of failure had dimmed Buxtonian hopes. The country lacked anything which the world wanted to buy (except slaves), and so the lawful trade never became more than an appendage to philanthropy. The humanitarians put forward plan after plan for the development of the interior; but humanitarianism was not enough.

Strategically too, Zanzibar and the coast were of secondary importance. From the viewpoint of Bombay it was perhaps as well to deny bases on that coast to other Powers; but so long as Britain kept her supremacy at sea, this was not vital. Enemy harbours were bound to fall into the hands of whichever navy controlled the Indian Ocean, and there was little doubt which navy that would be.[3]

Although east Africa was not a region of high importance to British policy, out of the anti-slavery campaigns had grown an informal paramountcy along the coast, the work of ambitious consuls and naval officers. In the absence of foreign competition they found this easy to build; and government acquiesced, more because influence fell into its lap than because it was seriously desired. But London steadily refused to let influence grow into territorial commitment. It would guard the coastal possessions of Zanzibar, since there was an anti-slave-trade squadron in those waters which could do so at no extra cost; but it would not push the Sultan's influence into the interior, since this was more than the navy could do. Hence the opening of the hinterland was left to private action, and by the Eighteen eighties missionaries, explorers and concession hunters of several nations had done something to penetrate

[1] Coupland, *Exploitation of East Africa*, 380.
[2] Gwynn and Tuckwell, *op. cit.*, I, 535; Coupland, *op. cit.*, 380, 82.
[3] Third Report of Royal Commission on Imperial Defence, 22 Jul. 1882, C.O. 812/38, para. 27.

along the trade routes up to the Lakes. Private treaties of trade and friendship were being made. Mission stations were being set up. Travellers were reporting the wonders of the interior. But the governments of Europe refused to pacify or administer the mainland, and for all the humanitarians' appeals for protection, the Powers remained cold and indifferent.

From this experience of enterprise on the east and west coasts since 1815, it is perhaps easier to understand why by 1880 the idea of taking more tropical African colonies had become officially unthinkable. A noble atonement for the eighteenth-century slave trade was being made on the east coasts and had been accomplished on the west. Yet the eager projects for commerce to carry Christianity and material improvement far inland had blunted against realities.[1] What trade there could be on the east had not yet appeared. What trade there was on the west was useful but stagnating. The merchants had prospered most where the authority of the Colonial Office did not run, and they did not want colonial rule which would have to be paid for out of their profits. Nor did ministers believe that the trade would yield customs revenue enough to bear any extension of rule. They therefore left the trader to make his own way privately with the help of such official influence as was customary and easily exerted.

Under official aegis nevertheless small enterprises had been launched. And if government refused them the support of the flag, it was unable and unwilling to inhibit them. However limited in extent, without the imperial power behind them, tendencies to expansion had been set off locally. Their workings among the different African authorities and communities did not stop. The business of imposing European ethics and pushing European trade disturbed native authorities more often than it regenerated them. Thus on the east, the result of putting the Sultan to work against the slave trade had been to undermine his authority over his subjects. British power, although informal, tended to be drawn in to fill the vacuum which it had helped to create. In this negative way, expansion was at work through erosion of the Sultanate

[1] *British Trade with Tropical Africa Before and After the Partition:*

(In thousands of pounds sterling)

	Total Exports	*Exports to Trop. Africa*	% 2 : 1	*Total Imports*	*Imports from Trop. Africa*	% 5 : 4
annual	1	2	3	4	5	6
1877–79 average	194,427	1,249	·64	375,394	1,805	·48
1898–1901	267,266	3,062	1·19	500,161	2,572	·51

Sources: W. Schlote, *British Overseas Trade from 1700 to the 1930s*, (1952), 122, 125, 168–9.

on the east coast. The workings of commercial influence on the west were more positive, and there was no large-scale African polity to disrupt. Nevertheless, trade at the ports depended upon peace along the rivers and trade paths into the producing hinterlands; and hence British influence tended to be drawn inland to supply the lack of strong native authority, to put down tribal wars and keep the way open.

There were therefore local tendencies toward extension on both the tropical coasts; and they were provoking deepening African resistance. But the propensities were too weak, the interests too negative or unpromising to draw forth the arm of empire. The imperial government here could afford to let British enterprise in tropical Africa grow or die according to its private energy; to ignore turmoil or quell it with mere influence.

Meanwhile, far greater and more catastrophic crises were coming to a head elsewhere in Africa. It was along the shores of the eastern Mediterranean, in the Turkish empire and in Egypt where vital strategic interests were involved, that European influence by the Eighteen seventies had eroded once powerful states and provoked dangerous nationalist reactions against foreign sway. In south Africa at the same time, British efforts to incorporate the republican Boers in an imperial confederation aroused another dangerous disturbance in a region vital to imperial security. But whereas the Turkish and Egyptian crises stemmed from the decay of Muslim empires under European influence, the Transvaal crisis arose from the processes of colonial growth. Yet a third crisis nearer Home, brought on by a nationalist uprising against British domination, accompanied the two in Africa. It was wrought by a movement of British expansion centuries older than either of them. By 1880 the Irish tenant was in revolt against the alien landlord, and the Parnellites were beginning their struggle for Home Rule. This concatenation of crises in the unwinding processes of expansion in places far apart was the setting for the partition of Africa.

CHAPTER III

The Revolt of the Afrikaner 1877–1881

The south African crisis which led to the first Boer War of 1880–1, occurred because the British government claimed to be the paramount authority and trustee of south Africa, and the trek Boers rejected the claim. This clash between a liberal, multi-racial imperialism and a racialist republicanism had a long history.[1] For thirty years after the British had taken the Cape Colony in order to secure the route to the East, their rule had been more often pro-Bantu than pro-Boer. The Colonial Office under James Stephen earnestly carried out its duty of protecting the Bantu tribes against 'the cupidity . . . and crimes of that adventurous class of Europeans who lead the way in penetrating the territory of uncivilized man'.[2] Imperial officials had attempted to impose liberal, Christian standards upon the Boer colonists in their relations with the coloured and Bantu population. The slaves were freed. Masters were restrained. Servants were given liberty of contract and equality in the courts, the tribes protected in possession of their lands, and the principle of political equality was laid down.[3] It was not a purely humanitarian policy, for the Colonial Office was convinced that without justice there could be no peace on colonial frontiers, no security within them, no economy in defence or growth of trade. Partly to protect the Bantu and partly to avoid expense, the British tried to stop the spread of colonisation. The Cape route could be secured without meddling in the interior. The colony was to be restricted to the purpose of guarding the naval base at Simon's Town. But trusteeship and restriction broke against the local environment. The Boer frontiersmen, hungry for land and determined to preserve

[1] Much of the argument in this chapter is based on the research of Professor C. W. de Kiewiet into British colonial policy in South Africa, especially his *British Colonial Policy and the South African Republics, 1848–1872*, (1929), and *The Imperial Factor in South Africa*, (1937); and Professor E. A. Walker's work, especially *A History of South Africa*, (2nd ed., 1941), and *Lord de Villiers and His Times*, (1925).

[2] Report: Aborigines (British Settlements), H. of C. 425), P.P. (1837) VII, 75.

[3] *vide* The Cape of Good Hope Constitution Ordinance, Order in Council, 11 Mar. 1853.

white supremacy and black inferiority, streamed out of the Cape Colony northward and eastward across the Orange and Vaal Rivers in the Great Trek of 1837–44.

Henceforward, the imperial strategic interest became entangled with the wanderings of the trekkers and their colonisation of the interior. Their independence and animosity, the Colonial Office feared, might one day endanger control of the coast-line. In pursuit of order and security, the empire gradually extended paramountcy in one form or other over the entire region occupied by the trekkers. The tiny Boer republic on the coast at Port Natal first seemed to endanger the India route. Its people were suspected of inviting French or Dutch protection. The British annexed Natal in 1844[1] 'to prevent the Emigrants from ever acquiring a dangerous importance as an independent community . . . and to finally exclude the idea of foreign interference'.[2] Lord Stanley, the Colonial Secretary, assured Parliament that 'Her Majesty's Government would not recognise, would not acknowledge, and would effectually resist any attempt on the part of the Boers to place themselves under foreign protection'.[3]

Imperial paramountcy for the next thirty years was based on these principles: to exclude foreign Powers from the coast-line: to deny the trekkers independent access to the sea: to ensure that the colonies dominated the trekker republics; and so to smother the potential dangers of Boer independence to imperial security.

Since the Boers in trans-Orangia and the trans-Vaal did not at first endanger imperial control of the coast-line, the Colonial Office gave them their independence in the Bloemfontein Convention of 1852 and the Sand River Convention of 1854. Henceforward, these poor and ramshackle republics were to be dominated rather than ruled. As long as they were kept shut in the interior and dependent on colonial ports, the weight of British influence seemed enough to prevent them from threatening imperial control of south Africa. Wherever the expansion of the republicans touched upon imperial supremacy, the Colonial Office intervened. They were thwarted for example in their attempts to reach a free port at Delagoa Bay in 1860 and 1868, and at St. Lucia Bay in 1861 and 1866. At other times, paramountcy was exerted to tilt the balance of development against the republics in favour of the colonies. Lest the republics should become too strong, the Governor of the Cape

[1] Sir E. Hertslet, *Map of Africa by Treaty*, (3rd ed., 1909), I, 199–200.

[2] Colonial Land Board to C.O., 11 Feb. 1841, C. J. Uys, *In the Era of Shepstone*, (Lovedale, 1933), 10.

[3] *Hansard*, 3rd ser., LXII, cols. 1169–70.

forbade their union under Pretorius in 1860. Ten years later they were denied their claims to Basutoland and Griqualand West; and these regions were annexed to strengthen the imperial position in south Africa. The mid-Victorians gave the inland Boers independence with one hand and kept hold of their destiny with the other. The British would not rule directly north of the Orange River and they had little interest in colonising the territory. It was being colonised against their will. But because the trekkers' activity endangered Colonial frontiers and might eventually threaten imperial control of the coast-line, the mid-Victorians extended informal influence over the interior. Their main strategic purpose had become caught up in a local movement of Republican *Voortrekkers*. As the Governor of the Cape Colony put it in 1868: 'The British possessions . . . as commanding the whole accessible seaboard, must inevitably take part in and control . . . the relations of the interior.'[1]

Security through Imperial Confederation, 1868–1877

The south African possessions still seemed the most troublesome, expensive and unprofitable of all the white colonies in the Eighteen sixties. They gave little trade. They attracted few British settlers or investors. For half a century the British government, it seemed, had been spending men and money in defence of colonists mostly of Dutch origin, who were occupying tribal lands which the empire did not want. Their advance was marked by native wars. No sooner was peace imposed upon one frontier, than strife broke out on another, spreading tumult into the settled lands. British administrators of the Eighteen sixties despaired of peace on the colonial frontiers unless south Africa could be brought under one government. Politicians in London resigned themselves to the fact that nothing but natural boundaries would halt the colonists' advance. Facing this prospect of endless troubles, the imperial authorities turned to plans for confederation.

By this time responsible government was the conventional device for achieving financial economy at Home without inhibiting commercial expansion, and for reconciling imperial unity with colonial aspirations for independence. The Canadian, and to a great extent the Australasian,

[1] Wodehouse to Buckingham, 18 Jul. 1868, C.O. 48/441 D. 62, quoted in de Kiewiet, *Colonial Policy*, 261.

colonists had already been made responsible for the expense and administration of their own internal affairs. By devolving authority, the British persuaded the colonists to share the burdens of colonial expansion without sacrificing imperial supremacy. Imperial expenditure and garrisons were thus reduced at the same time as the colonists' resentment of Colonial Office rule was smoothed. But the responsible colonial governments, bound to the empire by kinship, culture and interest, were expected to remain loyal agents of British colonisation, trade and power in their various parts of the world. So far from being anti-imperialist, this policy of devolution and retrenchment was only intended to make expansion cheaper and more efficient. The mid-Victorians were re-shaping the old colonial rule to conform with the prejudices and nature of a liberal state. The statesman who granted responsible government to the colonies intended to admit the colonists into a junior partnership in empire-building. But before doing so, the Colonial Office tried to ensure that devolution did not endanger ultimate imperial control.

In south Africa as elsewhere, the Colonial Office took care to tighten British supremacy over the entire region on a lasting basis before it proceeded to relax its authority. Immediately the Canadian concepts of responsible government and confederation began to be applied to south Africa, the independence of the Boer republics with their alien culture and nationalism ceased to be convenient and became an obstacle to the imperial design.[1] There could be no withdrawal unless this potential danger to imperial paramountcy and the route to the Far East was first removed. The republics sooner or later would have to be absorbed into the empire; otherwise, the eagerly-desired withdrawal from direct responsibility could not take place without risk to the strategic interest. Sir Philip Wodehouse, the Governor of the Cape, pointed out as early as 1867 that this was best done while the republics were still weak.[2] Twenty years before the gold of the Rand turned the Transvaal Republic into a formidable opponent of empire, its eventual absorption had become necessary to British plans. The ambition was not born of a new economic imperialism in the Eighteen nineties; it was inspired by thoroughly mid-Victorian schemes for reducing expenditure and devolving authority without sacrificing supremacy.

The British aim from the Eighteen sixties onwards was to cajole the republics into a federation with the Cape and Natal Colonies. The advantages would be very great; for the federal government would take over the expensive business of keeping order and carry out a com-

[1] de Kiewiet, *British Colonial Policy*, 120–1, 139 *et seq.* [2] *ibid.*, 269.

prehensive native and frontier policy; and the far more populous, wealthy and loyal Cape Colony,[1] would dominate the trekker elements and watch over imperial interests. But first the Cape colonists had to be brought to accept the duties of responsible government. Until they mustered enough local revenues and forces to defend their own frontiers, the imperial authorities could not safely shift the burden on to them and withdraw the British garrisons. Gladstone's first ministry annexed Basutoland in 1868, in order to make the Colony's north-eastern frontier more easily defensible. Three years later the Liberals over-rode the republics' claims to the ownership of the newly-opened Kimberley diamond fields and annexed Griqualand West on behalf of the Cape Colony. The British motives were plain. As Kimberley, the Colonial Secretary argued, to yield the diamond fields to either of the republics would be to raise their revenues and strengthen their resistance to imperial supremacy and confederation. Griqualand West was taken for the Colony in order to make responsible government feasible financially and to preserve its preponderance over the republics.[2] With these extensions of territory, a constitution of responsible government was accepted by the Cape colonists in 1872.

Gladstone's government thought they had taken the first step toward a south African federation, but in fact they had done so at the cost of arousing strong resistance in south Africa. The republics, further embittered by the loss of Basutoland and Griqualand West, were in no mood to give up independence for the flag of their 'oppressors'. Ironically, the Cape colonists used their self-governing powers to obstruct the making of a federation in which they would have to help carry the financial and defence burdens of the poorer states. The *Voortrekkers*' national feeling against the empire, together with the particularism of the Cape Dutch, had been aroused against the British plan; but the changing circumstances of south Africa during the Eighteen seventies made the Colonial Office all the more determined to carry it out.

[1] *European Population* (*000's*) / *Govt. Revenues Annual Average* (*£000's*)

	Cape	*Natal*	*O.F.S.*	*Transvaal*		*Cape*	*Natal*	*O.F.S.*	*Transvaal*
1854	112	7·6	15	25	1850–2	289	27·3	—	—
1873	236	18·6	27	40	1854–7	407	28·6	11·6	—
1892	377	47	78	119	1855–9	416·5			
					1866–9	537	95·8	64	31·5
					1871–5	668	127	127	54·9
					1875–9	1,648	272		64

Source: C. G. W. Schumann, *Structural Changes and Business Cycles in South Africa, 1806–1936*, (1938), 38, 50–52. Frankel, *op. cit.*, 56–7; M. H. de Koch: *Economic History of South Africa* (Cape Town, 1934), 388, 395, 398, 40.

[2] For details of this policy see de Kiewiet, *British Policy*, caps. XIV and XVII.

'All the conditions of South African politics', wrote a British official, looking back over the Eighteen seventies, 'have been altered by the recent discovery of diamonds.'[1] The diggings at Kimberley brought a surge of development to the stagnant south African economy. Diamonds attracted capital investment, which in turn stimulated trade. Eight million pounds had been sunk in Kimberley by 1881, largely from colonial sources;[2] and the Cape government had been able to borrow ten millions mostly for railway building from London on the strength of its improved revenues.[3] Diamonds almost trebled the value of south African foreign trade within the decade.[4] But Disraeli's Conservative administration which came to office in 1874 was more concerned with the political problems which the beginnings of economic growth brought in its train. The investment of the Eighteen seventies gave a fillip to colonisation inland. The inflow of immigrants and speculation in rising land values gave fresh impetus to the colonists' expropriation of tribal lands; and the unconquered Chwana of the north-west, the formidable Zulu in the east and the Ba-pedi in the north were hard-pressed by the colonists. The old competition for land between black and white, colonies and republics sharpened; and their frontiers were ringed with explosive land disputes and potential native wars.

Confronted with this sea of troubles, Carnarvon, the Colonial Secretary, and his colleagues were convinced by 1875 that the 'balkanisation' of south Africa was becoming an anachronism. They decided to press forward with confederation as the only hope of peace and order. 'The most immediately urgent reason for general union', the Cabinet was told, 'is the formidable character of the native question, and the importance of a uniform, wise and strong policy in dealing with it. . . .'[5] This was an old argument for bringing the Boer Republics under direct imperial control at once; but Carnarvon and his advisers had other reasons for thinking that the time had come to consolidate the British hold over the regions between the Orange and the Limpopo Rivers, and to convert hegemony into a more permanent control. The Transvaalers after 1870 renewed their efforts to escape from commercial dependence upon colonial ports and to break away from imperial domination. Already their attempts to expand eastward and reach Delagoa Bay had prompted the British government to claim possession of that port against the Portuguese, but without success. Burgers, the Transvaal President,

[1] E. Fairfield, Colonial Office Memo. on the Zulu Question, 19 Mar. 1879, C.O. 806/119.

[2] Frankel, *op. cit.*, 61.

[3] *ibid.*, 56, table VI.

[4] Schumann, *op. cit.*, 44.

[5] de Kiewiet, *Imperial Factor*, 69.

toured Europe in 1875 in search of German and Dutch aid to build a railway joining Pretoria to Delagoa Bay. The Boers' ambition to establish their commercial independence and to draw other European Powers into south African affairs seemed proof enough for the Conservatives of a threat to imperial supremacy. Delagoa Bay in Carnarvon's mind was the 'key position on the eastern coast'.[1] It seemed essential to prevent the Transvaalers from winning free access to the sea; otherwise the colonial merchants would lose their monopoly of interior trade; and the British grip on the republic would be loosened. With the beginnings of economic growth therefore, the threat of the independent Transvaal to British control seemed increasingly serious. Carnarvon and the Conservatives concluded that since the Transvaal had some day to be absorbed into the empire, it had better be done before the Boers grew stronger.

Supremacy in southern Africa seemed indispensable to British statesmen of the Eighteen seventies and eighties for much the same reason as it had to Pitt. The Cape route eastward, despite the opening of the Suez Canal in 1869, had lost little of its commercial and none of its strategic importance. In 1871 a Colonial Office official wrote of '. . . the importance of Cape Town as . . . the true centre of the Empire . . . clear of the Suez complications, almost equally distant from Australia, China, India, Gibraltar, the West Indies and the Falklands. . . .'[2] This traditional strategic doctrine was re-stated by the all-party Commission on Colonial Defence (1879–81), presided over by Carnarvon himself. It continued to inspire the pursuit of south African supremacy for the remainder of the century. The Commission reported that commercially, the defence of Cape Town remained enormously important. Ninety-one million pounds' worth of British trade passed to or round the Cape in 1878, compared with sixty-five millions going through the Suez Canal.[3] But in wartime, the Commission feared, the entire Suez trade

[1] Carnarvon to Queen Victoria, *C.H.B.E.*, VIII, 453; Uys, *op. cit.*, cap. VI; de Kiewiet, *Imperial Factor*, 66, 105 *et seq.*

[2] R. Herbert, Minute on Barkly to Kimberley, 31 May 1871, C.O. 48/455.

[3] *Value of British Trade via the Cape of Good Hope and the Suez Canal in 1878 in Pounds Sterling.*

To or from	*via Cape of Good Hope*	*via Suez Canal*
India, China and the East -	59,033,000	54,416,000
Australasia - - - - -	21,525,000	11,244,000
South Africa - - - - -	10,794,000	
Totals - - - - - -	91,352,000	65,660,000

Source: 1st Report of the Royal Commission on Colonial Defence, 3 Sept. 1881, in Papers laid before the Colonial Conference of 1887, C.O. 812/38, 411. This Commission also included Sir H. Holland, later Lord Knutsford, Colonial Secretary, 1887–92.

might have to be diverted to the Cape route to escape enemy cruisers in the Mediterranean:

> 'The general result of these inquiries . . . is that the security of the route by the Suez Canal might, under certain contingencies, become very precarious, and the risk attendant on sending commercial ships through it so great as practically to preclude its use; in which case the long sea route would be the only one available. . . .'

If the Commission regarded the Cape route as commercially invaluable, they placed its strategic value even higher:

> 'The Cape route . . . assumes a far higher degree of importance to the Empire at large, as being essential to the retention by Great Britain of her possessions in India, Mauritius, Ceylon, Singapore, China, and even Australasia. It is by this route alone that reinforcements of troops . . . could, under the contingencies alluded to, be sent from the United Kingdom with any degree of certainty or security . . . the uninterrupted supply of men and material to meet the ordinary demands of our Eastern garrisons and squadrons is of such importance that the integrity of this route must be maintained at all hazards, and irrespective of cost.'[1]

This conception of the central importance of the Cape in imperial strategy was generally accepted among British leaders. The safety of the whole empire, it seemed, might hang one day upon control of the naval base at Simon's Bay and the south African shores; and this in turn, required the exclusion of other European Powers and control of the potentially hostile republics inland.[2] These were chief among the arguments which moved Carnarvon and his colleagues to confederate south Africa. It is significant, as Professor de Kiewiet wrote, that 'the earliest document contained in Carnarvon's Memoranda on South African Affairs is a discussion . . . in which a consideration of the value of Simonstown led directly to . . . [the] conclusion that in South Africa "strength is therefore to be sought in federation".'[3]

But Molteno, the Cape Prime Minister, and President Brand of the Orange Free State both raised difficulties, and the London Conference of August 1876 proved a fiasco. A month later however, Carnarvon was presented with what seemed a golden chance of obtaining the cession of the Transvaal and of federating the republics with the colony of

[1] *ibid.*, 412.

[2] Frere re-iterated these arguments, which Wodehouse had used in the 1860s: 'Your object is not conquest, but simply supremacy up to Delagoa Bay. This will have to be asserted some day and the assertion will not become easier by delay.' (Frere to Carnarvon, 19 Dec. 1877, J. Martineau, *Life and Correspondence of Sir Bartle Frere*, (1895), II, 259); Frere to Hicks Beach, 17 Jan. 1880, *ibid.*, II, 371.

[3] De Kiewiet, *Imperial Factor*, 66; *vide et* Frere to Carnarvon, 16 Feb. 1880, Martineau, *op. cit.*, II, 370.

Natal, when Sekukuni and the Ba-pedi heavily defeated the Transvaalers. The republican government was on the verge of bankruptcy and its weakness invited the long-feared onslaught of Cetewayo's Zulu armies. There appeared a good chance under these circumstances that the Transvaalers might be only too glad to accept imperial rule and protection. The cession would also eliminate the complications to be feared from a Delagoa Bay railway. Carnarvon pressed upon Disraeli the immediate annexation of the Transvaal 'to prevent a great S. African war' and bring 'the *consequent* confederation . . . in sight'.[1] He and his advisers hoped in this way to avert the Zulu danger.[2] Such were Carnarvon's motives for ordering Shepstone's annexation of the Transvaal in 1877.[3] He wrote:

> 'I attach to a cession [of the Transvaal] the greatest importance. It solves a legion of difficult questions; it relieves us from many real and pressing dangers and it puts us as regards [South] African politics in a position more favourable than any which we have as yet occupied.'[4]

Having been told that a majority of the burghers would acquiesce, the British government annexed the Republic of the Transvaal in April 1877.

Although Carnarvon and Disraeli might delight in the name of 'imperialist' and call their Liberal predecessors 'Little Englanders', their aims in south Africa were essentially those of Newcastle and Kimberley before them. The self-styled new imperialists differed only in their bold attempt to achieve federation at once. There seems to have been no purely commercial necessity for the extensions of rule in the Eighteen sixties and seventies, such as the theory of economic imperialism would suggest. British enterprise had ample opportunity to exploit the diamond fields of Griqualand West, whether imperial rule was extended there or not; the empire took them for their weight in the local balance of power. Nor was the Transvaal acquired because of its commerce. When it was first annexed, British trade and investment were concentrated in the Cape Colony, leaving the republic practically untouched. The continuity between mid and late-Victorian policy is impressive. The annexations of the Eighteen seventies were made to uphold a traditional paramountcy for the old strategic reasons, and to perpetuate it in an orderly confederation in which the colonists would take over the military and financial burdens of empire.

[1] Carnarvon to Disraeli, 20 Sept. and 15 Oct. 1876, G. E. Buckle, *The Life of Benjamin Disraeli*, (1920), VI, 414–15.

[2] E. Fairfield, Memorandum on the Zulu Question, 19 Mar. 1879, C.O. 806/119.

[3] Hertslet, *op. cit.*, I, 223.

[4] Carnarvon to Barkly, 20 Sept. 1876, G.D. 6/32, de Kiewiet, *Imperial Factor*, 110.

Disraeli's ministry now tried to drive federation home. The burghers of the Transvaal, it was hoped, would accept incorporation in an imperial dominion in return for a restoration of self-government.[1] At the Cape, the Governor, Sir Bartle Frere, managed to get rid of the unco-operative Molteno, and the succeeding Sprigg ministry was willing to take a lead and call a conference to consider federation. Frere removed another obstacle in the middle of 1879, when he crushed the Zulu military power which menaced the Transvaal, Natal and ultimately the Cape.[2] The Colonial Secretary in 1879 informed the Cabinet:

> '. . . There is no question as to the increased necessity of uniting . . . South Africa under a confederation or union charged with the full responsibility of defence against the Natives. . . . Unless and until this is done there is clearly no prospect of avoiding the periodical recurrence of wars carried on at great cost to this country and to the Colonies. Confederation therefore is to be kept in view as the one object to be attained as speedily and as completely as possible.'[3]

With the Cape ministry willing, and the Transvaal and Natal under Colonial Office control, the moment for federation seemed at hand. The need had been apparent since the days of Sir George Grey; and Carnarvon was bold enough to take grave risks to bring it about. But courage and conviction could not save the maturing policy from the kicks of British party politics, nor from public hostility to its expense. In south Africa the bitter reaction of Boer and Bantu against the empire which was rough-hewing them to its design, thwarted the plan and ended by threatening British supremacy itself.

Success with closer union in south Africa, as its administrators well knew, required four conditions — peaceful frontiers, contented Bantu, full colonial treasuries and Boer consent. It was the misfortune of Carnarvon and Frere that these could not be brought about artificially or simultaneously. Before handing over the responsibilities of internal defence to the colonial governments, the imperial authorities attempted to pacify the frontier regions and settle the struggles between white and black for possession of the new lands. But the imposition of peace and the division of land meant war. The Gaika, the Ba-pedi, the Griqua, Batlapin and Baralong, the Zulu and Basuto rose up between 1877 and

[1] Frere to Hicks Beach, 3 Dec. 1879, C.O. 806/149, 639; Hicks Beach to Wolseley, 20 Nov. 1879, C.O. 806/155, 3–4.

[2] For Frere's correspondence on the Zulu problem *vide* Martineau, *op. cit.*, II, cap. XIX.

[3] Sir Robert Herbert, Cabinet Paper, 'Future Policy in Zululand and South Africa Generally,' 10 Mar. 1879, C.O. 806/123, 1.

1880 to defend what was left of their patrimony. All these wars appeared to Frere and Shepstone to be portents of a great connected Bantu uprising led by the Zulu against white civilisation.[1] Prospects of federation were damaged, as the bloody business of suppression drained money out of colonial and imperial treasuries.[2] As had happened often before, a forward policy aroused strong criticism in Britain, both on grounds of humanity and expense. The Aborigines Protection Society branded the Zulu War as 'morally indefensible'[3]; and humanitarians attacked the injustice of handing the Bantu over to Boer rule.[4] Gladstone in Opposition called for the dismissal of Frere and included the Zulu War and the annexation of the Transvaal in his general indictment of Beaconsfield's extravagant policy abroad. The tribal uprisings were at last put down, only to give place to bitter conflicts between the settlers and the Colonial Office over the allocation of the conquered areas. Native policy had always been a main source of Boer antagonism to British rule; and in insisting upon large land-reserves and labour rights for the defeated Zulu and Basuto, the imperial authorities strained their relations with the colonial leaders, who were mainly interested in land and labour for Europeans. In the circumstances of 1877–80, the conditions for successful confederation were turning out to be mutually incompatible: peace on the frontiers could not be obtained without emptying treasuries; and measures which might have made the Bantu content antagonised the settlers. Worse still, when Gladstone's second ministry came into office in May 1880, it found that Carnarvon's attempt to lever the burghers of the Transvaal into federation had provoked Afrikaner dissent.

The South African Crisis of 1877–1881

By 1880 the annexation of the Transvaal was stirring Boer feeling throughout south Africa against British imperialism; out of this revulsion came the modern Afrikaner political movement.[5] Once they had been rescued from the Ba-pedi and the Zulu, the Transvaalers

[1] Frere to Herbert, 18 Mar. 1878, Martineau, *op. cit.*, II, 223 *et seq.*

[2] Imperial expenditure was very heavy. Up to 30 Sept. 1879, the amounts were: £5,137,878 for the Zulu War; £543,465 on the Transkei War; £222,000 on the Rising in Griqualand West, and £380,000 on the Sekukuni War. (Grant Duff, *Hansard*, 3rd ser., CCLVI, col. 870.)

[3] *vide*, J. A. Froude, 'Africa Once More', *Fortnightly Review*, Oct. 1879.

[4] Sir G. Campbell, *Hansard*, 3rd ser., CCLVI, cols. 880–4.

[5] Sheila Patterson, *The Last Trek, A Study of the Boer People and the Afrikaner Nation*, (1957).

threw over Burghers who had consented to annexation, and followed Kruger and Joubert in reclaiming their independence. Their hatred of imperial rule broke out once more, with all the weight of trekker tradition behind it. Of all the Boers those across the Vaal River were the most anti-British. They had dedicated their republic to the conservation of white supremacy in Church and State and of 'true burgher-like freedom, equality and fraternity'. Their church likewise clung to the harsh Calvinist orthodoxy of the seventeenth century, unmellowed by the liberal theology of later times. They had trekked out of the colonies to defend these things against anglicisation, only to find themselves snatched under British rule once more. To Transvaalers the empire represented alien officialdom over burgher freedom, racial equality in place of white supremacy, and laxity and latitudinarianism instead of Calvinist discipline. At the extreme, the conflict between the *Voortrekkers* and the British was one of seventeenth-century Calvinist frontiersmen against the official representatives of a nineteenth-century liberal and humanistic metropolis. Between the two stood the far less exclusive and fanatical burghers of the Orange Free State and the wealthier and more sophisticated Cape Dutch. These Boers of the south were torn between their community of culture and kinship with the Transvaalers and their commercial and cultural ties with the British; and they normally favoured conciliation and compromise. Nevertheless, by 1880 the annexation of Griqualand West and, even more, of the Transvaal swung the sympathies of the Orange Free State behind the Transvaalers' struggle for independence. In Cape politics, the Dutch and Afrikaans language movements and the rise of Jan Hofmeyr's Farmers' Protection Association marked the growth of Afrikaner group consciousness in reaction to the stronger anglicising influences brought by the diamond boom. The spread of the Afrikaner Bond in the Cape Colony, Transvaal and Orange Free State showed Boer nationalism organising against assimilation in defence of its own identity. Both Hofmeyr and President Brand of the Orange Free State, who had acquiesced at first in the annexation of the Transvaal, were by 1880 supporting Kruger's claims to independence. Hofmeyr wrote: 'The annexation of the Transvaal has taught the people of South Africa that blood is thicker than water. It has filled the (Cape) Africanders, otherwise grovelling in the mud of materialism, with a national glow of sympathy for the[ir] brothers across the Vaal. . . .'[1] Carnarvon's attempt to consolidate British supremacy had provoked a dangerous Afrikaner national challenge.

[1] *ibid.*, 26.

While out of office, Gladstone and the Radicals had criticised 'the injustice' done to the Transvaalers and the Zulu. At Midlothian in the election campaign Gladstone had spoken of:

> 'The Transvaal, a country where we have chosen most unwisely — I am tempted to say insanely — to place ourselves in the strange predicament of the free subjects of a Monarchy going to coerce the free subjects of a Republic, and to compel them to accept a citizenship which they decline and refuse. . . . There is no strength to be added to your country by governing the Transvaal.'[1]

While their leader had expressed British liberal sympathy with Kruger's aspiration for self-determination, Chamberlain and Bright had voiced the protests of the humanitarian conscience of Britain against Frere's suppression of the Bantu. But the Liberals once in power turned from principle to pragmatism and tried to complete Carnarvon's work. Out of the Afrikaner nettle they would yet pluck the flower, confederation. Determined to retrench the appalling expenditure in south Africa, Kimberley, once again Colonial Secretary, ordered his officials to avoid any more native wars and extensions of jurisdiction.[2] He kept the much-criticised Frere as Governor of the Cape in order to consummate federation, and assured him that the Liberal government, like its predecessor, would refuse the Transvaalers' demand for self-government until they had agreed to join a British dominion.[3] Gladstone explained to the Commons: 'Confederation is so important . . . it eclipses and absorbs every other consideration,'[4] including apparently the Transvaalers' right to independence which he had handsomely acknowledged in Midlothian. Closer union now seemed to him the only hope of bringing about healthy relations between Boer and Briton, colonist and native, and of achieving economy without risk to supremacy. Opposed though it was by Chamberlain and Bright, the decision had been taken to go on ruling the Transvaal for the time being. It disappointed the Transvaalers' hopes that Gladstone would restore their republic. English party politics had encouraged the pan-Afrikaner reaction against the annexation and helped to bring on the crisis.

By June 1880 the sympathy of the Cape Dutch with their annexed kinsfolk across the Vaal had destroyed all chance of early unification; and the Colonial Office felt once more the exasperation of having to

[1] Speech at Dalkeith, 26 Nov. 1879, *Hansard*, 3rd ser., CCLVI, col. 860.

[2] Kimberley to Frere, 18 May 1880, C. 2586, P.P. (1880) LI, 239; Kimberley to Colley, 27 May 1880, *ibid.*, 251–4.

[3] Kimberley to Frere, 20 May 1880, *ibid.*, 250.

[4] *Hansard*, 3rd ser., CCLII, cols. 461, 459–64.

rely on an unco-operative colonial ministry as the main agent of imperial interests. At the instance of Kruger and Joubert, Hofmeyr and the Cape Farmers' party, aided by colonial irritation against the imperial land settlement in Basutoland, defeated Sprigg's federation proposals in the Cape Assembly. The colonists' representatives refused to consider any scheme until the Transvaal Republic had been restored.[1] The Transvaalers and the Cape Dutch had turned the tables on the British. The British attempt to lever the Transvaal into a union by withholding self-government was thwarted by the Cape Assembly's rejection of federation until the republic was freed. At the end of 1880 Kruger and his burghers raised an armed rebellion against British rule and proclaimed a republic. Gladstone's ministry feared, not without reason, that the Orange Free State Boers might come to the aid of the rebels. There were rumours of a rising in the Cape Colony itself. The continuation of Carnarvon's attempt to consolidate and withdraw had raised the danger of a general Boer rebellion throughout south Africa in defence of Transvaal independence.[2]

This was the crisis of imperial paramountcy in the south, as it appeared to the government in London early in 1881. If exaggerated, the British fears were none the less real. As men sometimes do who make policy detached by distance and experience from the country where it is applied, Gladstone's government tended to conceive the south African crisis in more familiar terms. To the Cabinet at least it seemed as if south Africa was on the verge of becoming another Ireland, the inveterate hostility of whose people might only be held down at tremendous cost by main force. In the Transvaal as in Ireland by 1881, the question for Gladstone and the Liberals was whether a nationalist reaction should be met with coercion or concession. There were three different opinions among British politicians, and all were represented in the Cabinet. Forster stood for the small minority of humanitarian imperialists. Since the days of Glenelg and the Aborigines Committee of 1837, they had fought a losing battle for Colonial Office rule over the tribal communities, against the prevailing tendency toward handing over powers of native administration to the colonial governments. So now the humanitarians wanted the government to re-impose its authority on the Transvaal and carry out the duty of native trusteeship. For the same reason they wished to retain the Griqua and Basuto and to bring the Zulu under direct British administration. The Whig peers in the Cabinet, particularly Hartington and Kimberley, held another and

[1] Frere to Kimberley, 6 Jul. 1880, C. 2655, P.P. (1880) LI, 353–5.
[2] *vide* Kimberley's account of the situation in *Hansard*, 3rd ser., CCLX, 281–6.

more influential opinion. They maintained that it was in the national interest to suppress the Boer rebellion, not only for the sake of humanity, but of prestige and supremacy. Gladstone, Bright, Chamberlain and Dilke represented a more liberal view, and on grounds of principle sympathised with the Transvaal struggle for self determination. British colonial experience, the Gladstonians held, proved that while genuine national movements could rarely be eradicated by force, they could usually be accommodated with concessions of home rule. Hence they contended that coercion of the Transvaal rebels, as of the Irish malcontents, would only endanger the interests which the Whigs supposed it would preserve; and they proposed to conciliate the nationalists as the only way to lasting security. But in the political circumstances of 1881 the doctrine most likely to triumph was that which would soonest stop the heavy imperial expenditure in south Africa which the futile effort at unification had involved.

In the months following the failure of confederation, retrenchment had been Kimberley's chief aim. He had brushed aside the humanitarians' demand for the annexation of Zululand and the undertaking of native trusteeship there. He had over-ridden their objection to placing the native people of Griqualand West under a colonists' administration when he tried once again to persuade the Cape government to take over the territory from the Colonial Office. Economy rather than trusteeship was also the dominant aim at first in the Transvaal. Only the hope of achieving the ultimate economies of federation had induced the government to defend and administer the poor and fractious republic. By August 1880 it seemed pointless to continue this expensive occupation, and Liberals and Conservatives alike were anxious to get rid of the burden and grant the Transvaalers responsible government under the Crown.[1]

But the burghers' revolt of December 1880 complicated the issues. It meant more imperial troops and money for the Transvaal than had been expected.[2] The repercussion of the rebellion in the Cape Colony and Orange Free State was to show that its suppression might endanger the Imperial government's position throughout south Africa. Yet if the rebellion strengthened the argument for conciliation, on the one hand, it dramatised the question of imperial security throughout south Africa

[1] Sir M. Hicks Beach, *Hansard*, 3rd ser., CCLVI, cols. 857–8; Grant Duff, *ibid.*, col. 879.

[2] Kimberley calculated that, apart from the heavy cost of repressing the rebels, the expense of holding the country thereafter would not fall much below £220,000 per annum. (Kimberley Minute on Lanyon to Sec. of State, 8 Dec. 1880, C.O. 291/7, D. 199.)

on the other. To Whigs and Conservatives who had learned from Palmerston the power of prestige, a revolt in the Queen's dominions had to be put down at any cost. The Transvaalers were confirming British fears of their hostility which had been present since the Great Trek. It seemed that if imperial authority was not vindicated, British security would suffer a heavy blow. Hence the Transvaal crisis brought the interest in retrenchment into collision with the concern with supremacy, and divided British opinion between the two different principles of liberalism and imperialism. The issue however was not to be decided upon its south African merits alone. It became enveloped in the Irish question and the struggle for power in the Liberal Party. As ever, imperial policy was decided as much by domestic beliefs and politics as by specific interests in, and ideas about empire.

The Boer and the Irish crises came upon Gladstone's ministry at the same time, and the coincidence had startling effects upon the making of south African policy. From July 1880 until March 1881, Ireland was the decisive field of a conflict between Radicals and Whigs for predominance in the government. The two wings of the Party were divided on principle and in temperament. Hartington and Kimberley, the Whig leaders joined with Forster in demanding stronger powers of coercion against the Irish malcontents. On the other hand, Chamberlain and Dilke, with whom Gladstone sympathised, opposed the Coercion Bill and stood for land reform and other concessions to placate Irish discontent. The rift in the Party was embittered by tactical manœuvres. The Whigs held most seats in the Cabinet;[1] but the Radicals, when supported by the Irish Nationalists, had greater influence in the House of Commons.[2] Chamberlain and Dilke seized upon the Irish question as a chance of ousting Whigs from the ministry and winning more offices for themselves. In a smaller way the Transvaal question opened the same rift of principle and offered the same tactical opportunity as

[1] Gladstone's Second Cabinet (formed Apr. 1880) — 1st Lord of the Treasury and Chancellor of the Exchequer: W. E. Gladstone; Lord Chancellor: Lord Selborne (cr. Earl 1881); Lord President: Earl Spencer; Lord Privy Seal: Duke of Argyll; Home Secretary: Sir William Harcourt; Foreign Secretary: Earl Granville; Colonial Secretary: Earl of Kimberley; Secretary for War: H. C. E. Childers; Secretary for India: Marquess of Hartington; 1st Lord of the Admiralty: Earl of Northbrook; President of the Board of Trade: Joseph Chamberlain; President of the Local Government Board: J. G. Dodson; Chief Secretary for Ireland: W. E. Forster; Chancellor of the Duchy of Lancaster: John Bright. Important Cabinet changes — July 1882: Bright resigned, and Kimberley combined Bright's office with his own; Dec. 1882: Gladstone resigned the Exchequer to Childers; Hartington succeeded Childers at the War Office; Kimberley to India Office; Lord Derby to Colonial Office; Sir Charles Dilke to Local Government Board; Dodson to Chancellor of Duchy of Lancaster.

[2] The distribution of seats was: Liberals and Radicals — 349; Conservatives — 234; Irish Nationalists — 60.

the Irish issue. Coercion was the Whig policy for the Transvaal as for Ireland; concession and conciliation, the Radical solution for both. The Radicals saw a good chance of 'dishing the Whigs' over the Transvaal, since the Irish Nationalists sympathised with the Boers, and Kimberley, who was Colonial Secretary and responsible for south African policy, was a Whig. Furthermore, Bright was strongly with the Radicals on the Transvaal and only lukewarm in his sympathy with their Irish policy. Hence Chamberlain and Dilke fought hard for the Transvaal's independence, not only on principle, but as a weapon against the Whigs in the Irish question, and as a means of forcing Kimberley's resignation.[1] Out of this curious pattern of circumstances, some of which were irrelevant to the question of south Africa, emerged the British response to *Voortrekker* nationalism.

At first the Whigs carried the Cabinet, and on 6 January 1881 the government announced to the Commons a policy of suppressing the Transvaal rebels. Kimberley, Hartington and Forster, with support from the Queen, the humanitarians and the handful of imperialists, seemed to have got their way. They appealed to the instinctive respect for law and order, the constitutional dislike of rebellions, the pride in British prestige, the concern to protect the tribes — in short, the ingrained prejudices of Victorian society. The Radicals, Irish Nationalists and the Fourth Party replied with a demonstration of strength in the Commons. Rylands, a Radical back-bencher, moved a censure on the government for its coercive policy in the Transvaal; and the five Radical ministers abstained from voting for the ministry of which they were members.[2] As Lord Randolph Churchill had gleefully expected: '. . . the question of reducing the Boers [divided] the Liberal party by a sharper and more insuperable line than any Irish question.'[3] It was this Radical protest combined with warnings from President Brand about the Orange Free State's sympathy with the rebels, that brought the ministry to consider a peaceful settlement at the same time as it was preparing to use force. As early as 10 January Kimberley began to negotiate with Brand to probe out the chances of agreement.[4] In the first week of February, Gladstone and Kimberley seem to have persuaded their colleagues to offer the rebels some form of self-government

[1] Dilke, *Diary*, 2–5, 14, 19 Mar. 1881: B.M. Add. MSS. 43934; Dilke, *Memoir*, in Gwynn and Tuckwell, *op. cit.*, I, 368.

[2] *Hansard*, 3rd ser., CCLVII, col. 1109 *et seq.*; Gwynn and Tuckwell, *op. cit.*, I, 366.

[3] Churchill to Wolff, 27 Dec. 1880; W. S. Churchill, *Life of Randolph Churchill*, (1906), I, 195.

[4] For Kimberley's account of the negotiations with Brand and Kruger, *vide Hansard*, 3rd ser., CCLX, cols. 278–95.

under the Crown. And so direct negotiations began with Kruger.[1] But Kruger made it plain that he would fight on until he had won back republican independence for the Transvaal rejecting the offer of colonial responsible government which was as far as the Whigs would go. Then, on 26 February, news reached London of the humiliating defeat of British forces at Majuba Hill. The Horse Guards and the Court demanded that the government should order the Army to wipe out the affront to British arms. A black mood of vengeance rose up momentarily in the country strengthening Kimberley and the coercionists in the ministry. In Gladstone's absence they won a Cabinet decision to break off negotiations and crush the rebels. On 2 March the Radical ministers told Gladstone that they would resign unless the negotiations were resumed. Dilke wrote in his Diary:

> 'Chamberlain had an hour and a half with Bright and got him to write a strong letter to Gladstone about the Transvaal, which we put forward as our ground for proposed resignation, although of course the strength of the [Irish] coercion measures, the weakness of the [Irish] land measures and the predominance of the Whigs in the Cabinet are the real reasons. . . .'[2]

Gladstone agreed with Bright[3] and asserted his authority with his colleagues. All along he had blamed Carnarvon for the mischief in south Africa, and he regarded his own task as one of avoiding the 'blood-guiltiness' arising from the Conservatives' sins.[4] The policy of conciliation at last prevailed.

Kimberley's new terms[5] were accepted by Kruger, and the Pretoria Convention was signed. The recently annexed colony became a republic once more, although it remained vaguely under British suzerainty. But the empire retained a power of veto over the republic's relations with foreign powers and bordering tribes and took other safeguards for native interests.[6] In Parliament, the Conservatives criticised the government for its vacillation and for its betrayal of the native population to the Boers.[7] The Opposition contended that the rebellion should have been crushed before making a settlement. Yet even they admitted that the terms they would have imposed would have been somewhat similar. The main body of Parliament seemed prepared to agree with Kimberley

[1] Dilke, *Political Diary*, 21 Feb. 1881, B.M. Add. MSS. 43934.
[2] Dilke, *Political Diary*, 2 Mar. 1881, B.M. Add MSS. 43934.
[3] *ibid.*, 3 Mar. 1881.
[4] Gladstone to Granville, 7 May 1881, P.R.O. 30/29/124.
[5] Kimberley to Royal Commissioners for the settlement of the Transvaal, 31 Mar. 1881, C.O. 806/181, 1–4.
[6] Hertslet, *op. cit.*, I, 223–7.
[7] *Hansard*, 3rd ser., CCLX, cols. 249–319; CCLXIII, cols. 1756–1876.

when he declared: '. . . We cannot hold [the Transvaal] . . . with any proper regard for the interests of our Colonies in South Africa or of the whole Empire', and we have secured 'all that is valuable to retain'.[1]

The retrocession of the Transvaal was the triumph of British Liberals and Irish and Transvaal nationalists over Whigs and humanitarian imperialists. It was a victory of moderation, all the more remarkable for being won on the threshold of the so-called age of imperialism. If there was one thing more likely to anger the Victorian public than heavy expenditure on empire, it was the cession of any of the Queen's possessions, however undesirable. Yet Gladstone's government had not only hauled down the flag in the Transvaal, they had left a rebellion unpunished and a humiliating defeat unavenged. The compromise with *Voortrekker* nationalism embodied in the Pretoria Convention could hardly have been made if the jingo-spirit had been uppermost. Those who made it were prompted above all by anxiety to avert a 'race war' between British and Dutch — a civil war in south Africa.

It had become plain by June 1880 that the annexation of the Transvaal had defeated its own objects. It had diverted Boer attention from the need for unity to the defence of a romantic particularism, from the creation of a nation to suspicion of an empire. Hence the attempt to unite ended in deeper division; the effort to consolidate supremacy only endangered it; and what was intended to bring on colonial self-government provoked an Afrikaner reaction in defence of republican independence. Kimberley explained to Gladstone:

> '. . . Bitter experience has proved that the g[rea]t majority of the Boers will resist our rule to the uttermost. We know that if we conquer the country we can only hold it by the sword, and we have every reason to believe that the continuance of the war w[oul]d have involved us in a contest with the Free State as well as the Transvaal Boers, if it did not cause a rebellion in the Cape Colony itself.'[2]

This belief in associating peoples with Britain in free partnerships, this refusal to rule by the sword alone, was the hallmark of the Cobdenite Gladstonians. On the same principle, they were soon to advocate Home Rule as the only solution to the problems of Egyptian and Irish nationalism. The Boer reaction, it seemed, was beginning to undermine the imperial position throughout south Africa and heavy expenditure would be required to suppress it.

[1] *Hansard*, 3rd ser., CCLX, col. 292.
[2] Kimberley, Memo., 29 Apr. 1881, *Gladstone Papers*, B.M. Add. MSS. 44627, 1–12. (We thank Mr. David Hoskin for this quotation.)

Gladstone's ministry was forced on to a different tack from Disraeli's. They met the crisis by compromising with the Transvaalers and reverting to the old system of external paramountcy over the republic which had been founded upon the Conventions of 1852 and 1854. The Liberals were no less determined to preserve supremacy in south Africa than the Conservatives; and they took care to strengthen the old system against the danger of another pan-Afrikaner challenge such as that which had frightened them in the first Transvaal War. If the empire was once more to dominate the republic from outside, British suzerainty had to be much tighter and more explicit than before. In taking control of the republic's foreign relations, the Liberals tried to reinforce the mid-Victorian informal supremacy with formal sanctions. Gladstone explained to the House of Commons that the Convention '. . . gives us a great deal more power [over the Transvaal] than we should have had if we could have established . . . Colonial Parliamentary government with responsible Ministers'.[1] However wildly imperial policy vacillated with changes in British and south African politics, the pursuit of a permanent supremacy remained constant.

The Imperial position in south Africa had been shored up for the time being; but the experience of the crisis of 1880–1 left deep marks upon the future. Apparent victory in the war gave the exclusive and particularist burghers of the Transvaal a new faith in themselves. With fresh vigour they set about breaking the remaining fetters of imperial domination. Moreover, Boer solidarity and suspicion of the British had been heightened throughout south Africa. A growing Afrikaner national feeling was to put the compromise of 1881 under increasing strain. The British on the other hand did not forget the shocks of the crisis. Majuba rankled long with the jingoes. More important, British statesmen had been confirmed in the opinion which they had held ever since the Great Trek, that Boer independence represented a real threat to the empire; and they were more resolved than ever to thwart it. The Colonial Office furthermore had had a startling insight into the difficulty of maintaining supremacy through the medium of colonial politics. Its normal influence, except in Natal, now depended once more upon the co-operation of Afrikaner-dominated ministries in the Cape Colony and Orange Free State and upon its suzerainty over the South African Republic. The first Transvaal war had shown how easily these sources of British influence might be swept away in a general Afrikaner reaction against the empire. It became a great point with every Colonial Secretary from 1881 until 1895 to avoid provoking another Boer challenge and

[1] *Hansard*, 3rd ser., CCLXIII, cols. 1859–60.

another Boer war. Direct imperial intervention as a result diminished henceforward, the British thinking it safer to work through influence and the agency of the Cape government wherever possible. Whitehall concluded that any further attempt to force south Africa into confederation would be folly; and any further designs on the republics seemed out of the question. The British sat back to wait for the colonial leaders to unite south Africa spontaneously from within, at the same time hoping to bind the future dominion to Britain.

In south African policy, all the elements of the Victorian imperial tradition were at odds. Not only did the duty of native trusteeship there conflict with the liberal principle of colonial self-government; but in south Africa, as nowhere else in the British settlements overseas, the policy of retrenchment and devolution had to be carried out without endangering a vital strategic interest. Apparently the upkeep of imperial influence was the constant imperative behind the extensions and withdrawals of British rule in south Africa from the beginning. Cabinets of both parties obeyed it. The pursuit of paramountcy was almost instinctive. It was a tradition so deeply ingrained in the close-knit generations of imperial ministers and officials that they rarely defined it explicitly as a concept of policy.

Supremacy originally had entailed no more than excluding foreign Powers from the coasts. From the Great Trek it had also meant shutting the republicans inland and dominating the interior by controlling their access to the sea. With the growth of south Africa from the Eighteen sixties onward, supremacy came to mean nothing less than the power to shape a loyal British self-governing dominion. And in this form, the doctrine was fully acceptable to mid and late-Victorians alike. As the Defence Commission of 1879–81[1] showed, paramountcy in southern Africa still seemed necessary to imperial security in the world at large — because of Indian, Australasian and Far Eastern reasons. This is not to deny that commercial and humanitarian interests in south Africa itself also played their part. But the British investor, merchant and immigrant were not to become deeply involved in developing the sub-continent until after 1885; and so security and sentiment, rather than economic expansion, prompted London to turn south Africa into another imperial dominion.

The more the reasons for the imperial government's acts in south Africa are studied, the more it appears that they were inspired by concepts peculiar to the official mind, rather than by the pressure of

[1] 1st Report of the Commission on Colonial Defence, C.O. 812/38, 411–14; *vide* Tyler, *op. cit.*, 24.

commercial or philanthropic lobbies in Parliament. After the mid-century, these imperialist 'interests' were rarely strong enough to rally British opinion behind the cause of imperial control in south Africa. Their influence seems usually to have been dwarfed by the massive canons of Gladstonian economy; and Cabinets usually ignored their cries for imperial rule. The humanitarians in London agitated for British rule wherever the south African colonists advanced, wherever the trekkers warred with the Bantu, wherever there was hope of trade — in Trans-Orangia, the Transkei, Basutoland, Zululand, Bechuanaland and Swaziland. They objected to the Conventions of 1852 and 1854, when the Colonial Office placed Bantu peoples under Boer rule, they opposed the grant of responsible government to the Cape, the retrocession of the Transvaal and the London Convention. But the government, while doing its best to safeguard native interests, continued to transfer the responsibilities of trusteeship. Nor did the timing and incidence of annexations correspond closely to that of humanitarian and commercial agitation. Upholding the imperial connection appears to have been the deciding reason for the action of the Cabinet in most cases. Natal was annexed chiefly to protect the India route; Basutoland and Griqualand West, in order to ease the Cape Colony's progress toward self-government; the Transvaal, to consolidate supremacy in an imperial federation. But as Dilke, an acute student of imperial affairs, wrote: '. . . the greatest of our dangers in South Africa is . . . the difficulty of inducing Parliament to sanction a continuous expenditure without direct return.'[1]

If strategic security and imperial sentiment prompted the search for supremacy in south Africa, it was the financial constraint of Parliament and Boer dislike of British rule which dictated its characteristically indirect and tentative forms. The impulses which drove colonisation forward were local rather than metropolitan; nevertheless the British government was drawn ever deeper into the problems of order and justice on the inland frontiers of settlement. Yet Colonial Secretaries had great difficulty in persuading the British public to accept the responsibility of administering the interior, as the frequent retrocessions and transfers of annexed territory to local control showed. A Colonial Office official explained this recurrent dilemma:

> 'When we lean to the policy of controlling all sections of the population, and regulating their mutual relations, we find that a huge bill has been run up. Then the advocates of retirement and retrenchment have their day,

[1] Sir Charles Dilke, *Problems of Greater Britain*, (1890), I, 575–6.

until it is perceived that retirement and retrenchment have involved the abandonment of some weak and friendly tribe to the mercy of the Africander, or the triumph of anarchy among the natives themselves. Then there is a cry for a resumption of responsibility.'[1]

Every Colonial Secretary had the problem of maintaining supremacy; but at the same time he had to devolve his authority. As a result, paramountcy by 1881 was once more embodied in an indirect system which rested upon the Cape ministry and external controls of the Transvaal Republic. It had to be worked through the medium of south African politics. Only thus could supremacy be reconciled with Westminster's demand for retrenchment and the Boer demand for freedom. But this compromise had not been achieved without interventions and collisions in the internal movement of colonisation which stimulated the beginnings of an Afrikaner reaction against British domination. The extrusion of imperial influence was becoming the aim of Cape colonists and Transvaal republicans alike by 1885. But within the next decade economic growth in south Africa and the political changes and rivalries which it touched off were to undermine British paramountcy and to solidify the Afrikaner national movement still further.

[1] E. Fairfield, Memo. 'Vacillation in Policy in South Africa,' 4 Aug. 1885, C.O. 806/250, 1–2.

CHAPTER IV

The Suez Crisis, 1882

No sooner had Gladstone's ministry patched up the Transvaal crisis and applied reform and coercion to Ireland than the Egyptian revolt broke upon them. But whereas the Afrikaners and the Land League were struggling against settlement and foreign rule, what drove the *fellahin* into revolt was the damage done by informal influence and foreign creditors. Moreover, the Victorians approached the crisis on the Nile with different political models in mind and different historical analogies in memory from those which informed their Irish and south African policies. In south Africa, they had tried to confederate and make another Canada; and they had desisted to avoid turning it into another Ireland. In Egypt on the other hand, the Liberals tried to deal with Arabi as Palmerston had dealt with Mehemet Ali; but they ended by turning the country into another Indian princely state, and the repercussions were felt throughout tropical Africa.

Mid-Victorian Strategy in the Eastern Mediterranean

At first sight it seems remarkable that the Egypt of the Khedive had escaped occupation until 1882. Since Napoleon's strike at India through the Nile Delta, Britain and France had been rivals there. Egypt was important to the security of both in the Mediterranean and as the key to the best short cut to India and the Orient. These national interests were not the invention of the so-called age of imperialism. More than forty years before the occupation of Egypt, Palmerston had sent the Royal Navy, as he said characteristically, to 'chuck' its Pasha, Mehemet Ali into the Nile so as to prevent a French *protégé* from controlling the short routes to India.[1] The French during the Eighteen forties had opposed the British building of the Cairo-Suez railway, fearing that it would increase their rival's influence in Egypt; and the British for the

[1] H. C. Bell, *Lord Palmerston*, (1936), I, 304.

same reason had obstructed the French project of the Suez Canal in the Fifties and Sixties.[1] Each Power felt bound to deny the other supremacy in Cairo. The Palmerstonians were on guard against the French raising up an empire in north Africa which might one day counter-weigh their empire in India, while they were even more determined to stop the French from establishing themselves across the Suez route to India and the East. Yet although the fate of the Orient might depend upon the turn of fortune on the Nile, both nations until 1882 had been able to find security in Egypt by means of influence over its rulers. Neither had found it necessary to occupy the country. In Egypt, as in Tunis and Morocco, the game of power for decades past had been played with gun-boat diplomacy, commercial concessions, loans, railways and canals.

There were excellent reasons why the two Powers hitherto had gone no further. Divided though they were in Cairo, they were more or less united in defence of a greater interest at Constantinople. They feared Russia far more than they feared each other. The Palmerstonians' nightmare was the Russian advance towards the Dardanelles, Persia, India and China. The French were no less worried by the Russian advance towards the Mediterranean. To protect and strengthen the Turkish empire as a shield against Russia therefore, was the first priority in the Mediterranean; and compared with this interest, the advantage to be gained by lopping off the Sultan's Egyptian provinces was negligible. The logic of British strategy in the eastern Mediterranean from 1838 onwards ran dead against occupying Egypt. Naval supremacy gave Britain the power to seize Egypt and hold the Suez route to India against the French, in case of war. A British garrison in Egypt could add little to that security. The Navy alone, on the other hand, could not prevent a Russian army striking at Suez through Asia Minor. But Asia Minor, not Egypt was the obvious line of defence against this danger on land. The British therefore relied upon a combination of the Navy with allied Turkish armies in the near East to protect the India routes against Russia. Hence they preferred to watch over Egypt from Constantinople rather than from Cairo; and they subjected their local rivalry with France in north Africa to the broader community of interest in the rest of the Ottoman empire. The English method was to turn the Sultan and the Khedive into reliable allies rather than to seize their territories.

The outlook of the mid-Victorians on the rest of the world did as much as calculation and interest to give their expansion this particular

[1] H. L. Hoskins, *British Routes to India*, (1928), 302, caps. 12 and 14; C. W. Hallberg, *The Suez Canal: Its History and Diplomatic Importance*, (New York, 1931), 101–215.

shape. If the Palmerstonians sought no exclusive territorial advantage, it was largely because they were sublimely confident of dominating the Near East without it.

Palmerston, the greatest exponent of the imperialism of free trade, perfected the policy of protecting strategic interests in the Near East by trade and influence. Between 1838 and 1841 he forced the Sultan and the Pasha of Egypt to give up their monopolies and to throw open their dominions to free trade, believing that British merchants, given this opportunity, could not fail to capture and multiply Turkish commerce. A thriving trade, Palmerston expected, would fill the Sultan's treasury and pay for stronger armies, to be trained by British officers. British advisers would guide Ottoman policy and bring the Sultan to introduce liberal reforms which would give the subject peoples representation in government and property rights in the Courts. The productive classes were to be freed from the exactions of their quasi-feudal Moslem overlords whose rule, the British believed, had kept the country backward and poor for centuries. Once liberated, the peasant would produce more for the market, the Oriental merchant would accumulate capital and his enterprise would develop the economy in partnership with the British merchant. The inflowing trade would spread liberal notions of justice and freedom. In the end, rulers and ruled, grateful both for prosperity and enlightenment, would look to Britain as their mentor. Those classes of Turkish society whose interests and outlook were identified with the British, would come to power and perpetuate the partnership with Britain.[1] With such a theory, it is no wonder that the Palmerstonians preferred influence as a far more potent mode of expansion than rule, or that they put commerce to work to secure their strategic interests in the Near East.

During the next thirty years their conception was partially realised, but in the end it defeated its own object. British merchants captured most of the growing Turkish and Egyptian trade. British, and even more French investors began to build railways and to lend large sums to the Sultan and the Khedive. But Moslem conservatism and Russian intrigue blocked every attempt at liberal reform; and as a result the technique of the collaborating class did not work. Yet commerce and naval power gave Britain the leading influence at Constantinople; while loans from Paris usually gave France a similar position in Cairo. The two Powers, allied with the Turk, fought the Crimean War to halt the Russian advance towards Constantinople and the Straits. The

[1] *vide* Sir Charles Webster, *op. cit.*, II, cap. II; Bell, *op. cit.*, I, cap. XIV; V. Puryear, *International Economics and Diplomacy in the Near East*, (Standford, 1935), *passim.*

Sultan, although he had to be shored up more and more, served well for a time to secure the short routes to India against Russia.

In the course of their rivalry for trade and influence, the two Powers by the Eighteen seventies had reached something like a working compromise in a shared hegemony at Cairo and Constantinople. They had learned from experience that their influence over the Sultan and Khedive was far more effective when they co-operated than when they competed for supremacy. Rivalry and changes of balance continued within the system, but the two Powers had managed so far to settle their different strategic interests within the framework of influence and the *status quo*. Prospects of continuing this collaboration seemed even brighter during the Eighteen seventies. The long struggle over the Suez Canal had ended with the opening of the waterway in 1869. After the defeat by Germany and the advent of the Republic, France drew closer to Britain in a liberal *entente*;[1] and the old conflicts in the Mediterranean merged into the broader partnership. In Egypt by the end of the decade, they were sharing the dominant influence over the Khedive on a basis of parity. Nothing could have been fairer or more settled from the British and French points of view than to go on protecting their interests in north Africa and the Near East by means of commerce, capital and influence. But by this time the Turkish governments on which Britain and France had built their security in the Mediterranean were breaking down. All the European schemes for regenerating a rotten empire with trade, loans and reforms proved only to have helped on its disruption.

The Breakdown of Dual Paramountcy in Egypt, 1876–1881

From the Crimean War onwards the Turkish empire showed increasingly the strains imposed upon its antiquated structure by war and free trade. With his currency in disorder, his foreign trade unbalanced and his revenues falling short of expenditure, the Sultan borrowed heavily from London and even more from Paris, mortgaging his land revenue to get the loans. His decrepit administration however only squandered the capital. As his debts mounted, his attempts to force up land taxes strained his authority and helped to provoke the Christian and national revolts in Bosnia and Herzogovina. At last the Sultan could no longer find new money to repay old loans.

[1] *vide* A. J. P. Taylor, *The Struggle for Mastery in Europe, 1848–1918*, (1954), 285.

In 1876 his credit collapsed and his regime went bankrupt.[1] Anglo-French trade and investment, and the use of the Sultan as a shield against the Russians had proved too much for an antique administration and an inflexibly conservative society.

Financial crisis and rebellion led on to the shackling of Turkish political independence and to the Eastern crisis of 1878 in European politics. There was grave danger that the Turk empire might be entirely divided among the Powers under the aegis of the Russians who intervened on behalf of the Balkan rebels. This was not so much because the Powers now had higher ambitions, or fiercer rivalries in the region than they had had before; but because the Turkish power seemed to be crumbling away.

Intensifying Anglo-French influence by the end of the Eighteen seventies, was working similar effects in the rickety Turkish states of north Africa.[2] In Egypt the Khedivate, like the Sultanate, was cracking. Twenty years after Palmerston had opened Egypt to free trade, the Khedive Ismail[3] had begun his ambitious attempt to develop his country with the aid of foreign loans. He did much in the Eighteen sixties to improve irrigation and agriculture. Thousands of labourers were digging the Canal and building a railway. Foreign trade grew. Ismail, it seemed, was exactly the kind of enlightened Oriental collaborator that Palmerston had dreamed of; and yet every step forward took the Khedive further into the thicket of debt and difficulty. Egyptian imports soared high above the exports, and expenditure above revenues. The capital invested was not producing enough new wealth to cover its cost.[4] European bankers who charged the Khedive high rates of interest were partly to blame; but the vices of Oriental administration played their part in bringing on the eventual disaster. 'Immense sums', it seems, were 'expended on unproductive works after the manner of

[1] *vide* D. C. Blaisdell, *European Financial Control in the Ottoman Empire,* (New York, 1929), caps. I–V.

[2] *vide* F. R. Flournoy, *British Policy toward Morocco in the Age of Palmerston,* (Baltimore, 1935); A. Raymond, 'Les Tentatives anglaises de pénétration économique en Tunisie,' *Revue Historique,* CCXIV, 48–67.

[3] *vide* G. Douin, *Histoire du Règne du Khedive Ismail,* (Cairo, 1937).

[4] *Table: Growth of the Egyptian Economy, 1860–75.*
(Values in Egyptian pounds)

	Exports	*Imports*	*Revenue*	*Expenditure*	*Public Debt*	*Private Debt*
1860	2,535,651	2,604,933	2,154,000	2,984,000		
1865	13,045,661	5,753,184	5,356,000	10,785,000		
1870	8,680,702	4,502,969	5,389,000	12,309,000		
1875	13,333,334	5,619,467	10,542,468	10,026,476	76,000,000	15,000,000

Source: A. E. Crouchley, *The Economic Development of Modern Egypt,* (1938), 137, 275.

the East, and on productive works carried out in the wrong way, or too soon'.[1] Ismail, for all his economic liberalism, shrank from political and administrative reform; and he worked to develop the country through an administration whose outlook and method was alien to nineteenth century enterprise. As his expenditure far outran his income, the Khedive came to live from loan to loan. As his credit in London and Paris dwindled, the interest rates became more and more exorbitant. He managed to squeeze more out of the Egyptian taxpayer, but at a heavy cost in political discontent among peasants[2] and pashas alike. In 1876 when the European money market shut its doors upon the Sultan, they closed also for the Khedive. His government owed foreign creditors over ninety million pounds and the debt charges absorbed almost two-thirds of his annual revenue.[3] The Sultan was as badly off. He owed some two hundred million Turkish pounds and had pledged over half his income. The foreign bailiffs were knocking at both their gates; their discontented subjects were heaving under their thrones; while they, without money, had lost their power to resist or command.[4]

French and British economic enterprise in the Near East and north Africa, had helped to undermine the two *régimes* on which British and French statesmen had built their systems of Mediterranean security.[5] As long as the Sultan and his nominal vassal, the Khedive kept their dominions together in peace, the Powers had been able to guard their rival interests by mere influence. But now the Turkish instruments of influence were breaking in the Europeans' hands. There could be no safety in influence, no security for the different European interests except by partition and occupation, unless the power of the Sultanate and Khedivate could be revived. The very danger of their fall sharpened

[1] Stephen Cave (Paymaster General) Report, (C. 1425), P.P. (1876) LXXXIII, 101.

[2] M. Sabry, *La Genèse de l'Esprit National Egyptien, 1863–1882*, (Paris, 1924).

[3] Feis, *op. cit.*, 386.

[4] Disraeli wrote: '. . . This dreadful Herzogovina affair, wh[ich] had there been common energy, or perhaps pocket-money even, among the Turks, might have been settled in a week.' (Disraeli to Lady Chesterfield, 21 Aug. 1875, Buckle, *op. cit.*, VI, 13.)

[5] *Foreign Investment in Egypt, 1876–1914**

(Millions £ Egyptian)

	Public Debt	*Joint Stock Coys.*	*Total*
1876	85	negligible	85
1884	90	6	96
1892	101	6	107
1897	98	11	109
1902	92	22	114
1914	86	71	157

(estimated British: 44.†)

Sources: * A. Crouchley, *Economic Development of Modern Egypt*, (1938), 273.
† H. Feis, *Europe the World's Banker 1870–1914*, (New Haven, 1930), 23.

international rivalry, as each Power cast about for alternative safeguards in case of need. After groping for more than a decade, the British eventually stumbled into a different strategy based upon north-east Africa instead of Asia Minor, upon the Nile, not the Straits. More than any other cause, the danger of a general Ottoman collapse set off the partition of Africa and brought on the rise of new European empires in north and tropical Africa.

Disraeli's and Salisbury's handling of the Eastern crisis between 1876 and 1880 shows that they had no more territorial ambition than the Palmerstonians on the shores of the eastern Mediterranean, and certainly not in Egypt. The Conservatives, faced with the prospect of a partition of the Turk empire, tried to stop it. Turkish weakness and Russian aggression endangered the traditional arrangements for securing the short routes to the East. Gladstone's campaigns against Turkish atrocities whipped up British sympathy for the Christian rebels against the Sultan and made the old pro-Turk policy unpopular. Disraeli found it harder to keep up the old British supremacy of influence at Constantinople, because of the decline of French, and the rise of German prestige. Despite all the difficulties, the Conservative ministers strove throughout to prop up the Turk and preserve the mid-Victorian system.

For the British, the line of defence against Russia was still the Turkish empire in Asia. Its pivot rested upon Constantinople, not upon Cairo. Disraeli's reasons were thoroughly Palmerstonian:

> 'Many in England say, Why not? England might take Egypt, and so secure our highway to India. But the answer is obvious. . . . If the Russians had Constantinople, they could at any time march their Army through Syria to the mouth of the Nile, and then what would be the use of our holding Egypt? Not even the command of the sea could help us under such circumstances. . . . Constantinople is the key of India, and not Egypt and the Suez Canal.'[1]

Leading British statesmen rejected the very idea of occupying Egypt as 'moonshine'.[2] Divided though they were as to the morality of defending the oppressor of Christians against a Christian Power, they risked war with Russia in 1877–8 to defend the Turkish empire in Asia.[3] To achieve this object, the British at the Congress of Berlin made large concessions to Russia in the Balkans. They rejected Bismarck's barbed invitation to take Egypt as compensation, because they regarded occupation as a useless encumbrance which would mean breaking with their

[1] Barrington, Memo., 23 Oct. 1876, Buckle, *op. cit.*, VI, 84.
[2] Disraeli to Derby, 21 Oct. 1876, *ibid.*, 100.
[3] Cabinet Note, and Derby's Diary, 27 Mar. 1878, *ibid.*, 264–6.

French ally.[1] Instead, the Conservatives strove to put new teeth into the old system for securing the road to India, in case the Turkish collapse should go further. Cyprus was occupied as 'the key of Western Asia'.[2] Britain guaranteed Asiatic Turkey against Russian invasion. Although Palmerston's hopes of reforming and reviving the Ottoman empire had faded, Beaconfield and Salisbury had only modified the mid-Victorian arrangements in the light of Turkish weakness.[3] They had rejected out of hand the idea of occupying Egypt. They continued to rely upon influence, naval power at Constantinople, reinforced by a *place d'armes* in Cyprus and military consuls in Armenia, and the Anglo-French *entente*. The conservatism of these plans suggests that the occupation of Egypt four years later was an involuntary response to the continuing collapse of the Khedivial *régime*, not the outcome of a new Mediterranean strategy or of a purposeful new imperialism.

Since Egypt remained of lesser importance than Asia Minor, the British had no higher ambition in the crisis of the Khedivate than to restore its finances and to keep the old parity of influence with France. Disraeli's purchase of the bankrupt Khedive's shares in the Suez Canal Company in November 1875 was not a bid for exclusive supremacy in Cairo. It was intended only to give the British a voice in the management of the waterway and to keep the balance of influence even with France. 'The question for us', Derby, the Foreign Secretary, explained, 'is not one of establishing an exclusive interest, but of preventing an exclusive interest from being established as against us.'[4] Two years later he wrote privately: 'We want nothing and will take nothing from Egypt. . . . We shall continue to work in harmony with the French, and hope and expect the same from them.'[5] Salisbury, at the Foreign Office from 1878 until 1880, also wanted to interfere in Egypt as little as possible, and to go on protecting the British interest by mere influence. He had three good reasons: it would be dangerous politically for the government to appear before the public as debt-collector for the Egyptian bondholders; it would be equally unpopular to involve the taxpayer in responsibility for the Khedive's debts; and thirdly, Salisbury was determined to avoid a joint occupation of Egypt with France, because if things could be kept fluid on the old basis, he 'had faith in

[1] Disraeli to Salisbury, 29 Nov. 1876, *ibid.*, 104, 353; Salisbury to Waddington, 7 Jul. 1878, P.P. LXIX, 1347.

[2] Disraeli to Queen Victoria, 5 May 1878, Buckle, *op. cit.*, VI, 291.

[3] For this modified Conservative policy in the Near East, *vide* D. Lee, *Great Britain and the Cyprus Convention Policy of 1878*, (Cambridge, Mass., 1934), *passim.*

[4] Derby to Lyons, 27 Nov. 1875, Lord Newton, *Lord Lyons*, (1913), II, 92; Disraeli to Lady Bradford, 25 Nov. 1875, Buckle, *op. cit.*, V, 449.

[5] Derby to Lyons, 21 Dec. 1877, Newton, *op. cit.*, II, 122.

the English influence in Egypt drawing ahead'.[1] Sobered though it was by experience and disappointment, the mid-Victorian confidence in informal expansion still remained.

In Cairo as at Constantinople nevertheless, bankruptcy was to lead to foreign financial control. The British, in keeping in step with France, were dragged into interfering politically in Egypt. In May 1876 the Khedive Ismail had been forced to hand his pledged revenues over to an international *Caisse de la Dette Publique*. An English and a French controller were set over the Egyptian finance departments to supervise the Khedive's remaining resources on behalf of the foreign bondholders. Unlike the French, the British government at first officially disassociated itself from these arrangements. It looked upon them as private matters between the bondholders and the Khedive.[2] Ministers felt an aristocratic distaste for mixing politics with business, except in the service of strategy; and generations of free trading faith had raised strong prejudices against government pulling private enterprises out of foreign fires. It was fear of the French, not tenderness for the bondholders, which drove the British to share in setting up the joint financial control of the Khedive's government. As Salisbury wrote:

> 'It may be quite tolerable . . . to the French Government to go into partnership with the bondholders; or rather to act as sheriffs' officer for them. But to us it is a new and very embarrassing sensation. . . . We have no wish to part company with France: still less do we mean that France should acquire in Egypt any special ascendency [*sic*]; but subject to these two considerations I should be glad to be free of the companionship of the bondholders.'[3]

But Disraeli's ministers had to swallow their qualms. When the financial arrangements of 1876 failed two years later, the French insisted on a thorough-going reform of the Egyptian fiscal system to secure payment of Ismail's debts. The British felt compelled to go on with them. The two Powers forced the Khedive in return for a new loan, to surrender his autocratic powers and his personal revenues and estates to a responsible ministry, headed by Nubar Pasha and including a British and a French minister. These enforced reforms were meant to turn the absolutist Khedivate into a liberal constitutional monarchy, and to promote fiscal reform and solvency.[4] But the European attempts to

[1] Salisbury to Lyons, 10 Aug. 1878, Cecil, *op. cit.*, II, 335.
[2] A. D. Elliott, *Life of . . . Goschen*, (1911), I, 170.
[3] Salisbury to Lyons, 10 Apr. 1879, Newton, *op. cit.*, II, 175.
[4] The British Minister in Cairo, Rivers-Wilson, noted that Ismail's authority in the country was badly shaken by the reforms, (C. R. Wilson, *Chapters of My Official Life*, (1916), letter of 29 Jun. 1878.)

introduce equitable and efficient taxation and to cut expenditure alarmed the privileged classes of the old *régime*, and united the Army, the landlords and the *Ulema* against foreign control.[1] Ismail astutely placed himself at the head of the opposition. In April 1879 he defied the British and French governments, dismissed his European ministers and overthrew the alien controls. In retaliation, the Powers brought the Sultan to depose Ismail and to set up Tewfik as Khedive. Anglo-French financial control was restored, but in more covert form.

All along the British had felt that the French were going too far. They were squeezing the lifeblood out of the Egyptian peasantry in order to meet the coupon. Salisbury complained: 'Egypt can never prosper so long as some 25 per cent of her revenue goes in paying interest on her debt.'[2] He detested the Bourse policy of France, and he wanted to go back to the old informal methods of domination by influence:

> 'Actual authority we cannot exercise. We tried to do it through the European Ministers, but . . . the disbanded officers proved to us that two pairs of arms are not much use against two thousand. The only form of control we have is that which is called moral influence, which in practice is a combination of nonsense, objurgation and worry. In this we are still supreme. . . . We must devote ourselves to the perfecting of this weapon.'[3]

The high priests of Disraeli's so-called new imperialism, no less than Gladstone and the Liberals, were strongly against bringing more Oriental peoples into the empire. The mid-Victorian preference for 'moral influence' was as strong as ever in the Eighteen seventies and Eighteen eighties. Neither the Indian, nor the Colonial school of imperialists wanted another empire in the Near East or north Africa. The Indian Mutiny perhaps had been warning enough of the dangers and difficulties of ruling coloured subjects. Disraeli and Salisbury, who had made the Queen Empress of India in an attempt to meet some of these difficulties, had not the least ambition to turn Egypt into another India.

The Foreign Secretary nevertheless admitted that 'after having a Khedive deposed the character of non-intervention is not easy to retain'.[4] Once again the British felt bound to go along with the French in reasserting financial control and imposing reform and a settlement upon Egypt. After the deposition of Ismail in 1879, a British and a French Controller-General were given broad powers of inspection.

[1] *vide* Cromer, *op. cit.*, (1908), I, caps. V–VII.
[2] Salisbury to Lyons, 10 Apr. 1879, Newton, *op. cit.*, II, 175.
[3] Salisbury to Lyons, 15 Jul. 1879, *ibid.*, II, 355.
[4] Salisbury to Lyons, 17 Jul. 1879, *ibid.*, 357.

Unlike the former European ministers they had no formal administrative authority. Ostensibly the Khedive and a responsible Egyptian ministry continued to govern. But the foreign controllers, in conjunction with the Debt Commissioners, were practically dictators in finance. As Baring put it: 'The Controllers would have to pull the strings behind the scenes, but appear on the stage as little as possible.'[1] Six Powers signed the complicated Law of Liquidation of July 1880, which completed the settlement of Egypt's debt and finances. Under these arrangements sixty-six per cent of the revenue was assigned to the budget for the Debt. This income was put in the hands of a Debt Commission representing Britain, France, Austria, Italy and Germany; but Britain and France together had a majority of votes. The remainder of the revenue was set aside for administrative expenditure and left nominally in the hands of the Egyptian government. Indirectly however, the Debt Commissioners had wide powers over the administrative budget also, for they could veto changes in taxation and fiscal legislation and prevent the raising of new loans. More important, the Commissioners were empowered to draw upon the administrative revenues to make up deficits in the Debt budget; whereas the Egyptian government could not touch surpluses in the Debt revenues without the consent of the Commission. Lastly, a maximum was laid down for administrative expenses which could not be exceeded without permission. As Alfred Milner put it, Egypt under this *régime*, was financially '. . . tied hand and foot, unable to move, almost unable to breathe, without the consent of Europe'.[2]

Egyptian insolvency and opposition to foreign interference were driving Britain and France from informal sway into a veiled direction of Egypt's internal affairs. Beaconsfield's ministry had tried to keep to the Palmerstonian policy of 'moral influence'. If they had been driven further into intervention than they wanted, it was not by imperialist enthusiasm, but by the internal crisis in Egypt and their French ally's determination to settle it. Salisbury's own explanation of the British motives rings true:

> 'When you have got a . . . faithful ally who is bent on meddling in a country in which you are deeply interested — you have three courses open to you. You may renounce — or monopolise — or share. Renouncing would have been to place the French across our road to India. Monopolising would have been very near the risk of war. So we resolved to share.'[3]

[1] Cromer, *op. cit.*, (new ed., 1911), 130.
[2] A. Milner, *England in Egypt*, (1904 ed.), 52.
[3] Salisbury to Northcote, 16 Sept. 1881, Cecil, *op. cit.*, II, 331–2.

The Anglo-French Control was meant to make Egypt solvent again and to strengthen the Khedivate. Yet the governing institution had been badly damaged in the attempt at restoration. The Khedive's power had always been poised upon the narrow base of a personal autocracy, a Turkish official and landowning class, and in the last resort, upon the army. As the Sultan's viceroy, he had been the defender of Islam, entitled to command the faithful; and as the Khedive of Egypt he represented Egyptian aspirations to be free from the Turkish yoke. But by 1880 he had lost most of these claims to his subjects' allegiance. In using his government for their own purposes, the Powers were separating him from the native sources of authority. They had taken away his wealth and made him into a constitutional monarch. In setting Tewfik in Ismail's place, they had shown the Khedive to his people as a Christian puppet. They had turned him into a debt-collector for the *effendi*. In using his authority to re-assess and raise the land tax and to abolish tax-exemptions,[1] they had deprived him of his natural allies, the landlords. The severe retrenchment of military expenditure loosened his hold on the army and made it rebellious. The Anglo-French financial arrangements were provoking a national revolt against Turkish oppression and foreign control.

There were four disparate elements in the movement: the liberal reformers, led by Cherif Pasha and inspired by nationalist resentment against Turkish overlordship and a belief in a western constitution; the Moslem conservatives, who denounced the spread of Christian influence; the great landowners, fighting to preserve their fiscal privileges under the guise of ridding the country of the foreigners; and Arabi and the colonels, who challenged the Dual Control so as to re-instate their brother officers[2] and enlarge the Army. Beneath the ruffled political surface, the peasantry who had been squeezed to pay for Ismail's industrial schemes and squeezed again to pay his debts were near to revolt.[3] By 1881 the Khedivate was going the way of many Oriental *régimes* eroded by penetration of European influences. The country was on the verge of anarchy. The symptoms were unmistakable: the restless peasantry, the discontented landlords, the immature liberal opposition, the broad movement against the foreigner, the collapse of traditional authority leading to a military *Putsch*.

After the mutiny of the regiments in February 1879, Arabi Pasha and the Army became the spearhead of the nationalist reaction. The

[1] For the fiscal reforms, *vide* Cromer, *op. cit.*, (1908), I, caps. VII, X.

[2] Sir A. Colvin, Memo., Cromer, *op. cit.*, (1911), 170–1. For one view of the army's discontent *vide* E. Malet: *Egypt, 1879–83* (1909, for private circulation), 97–103.

[3] French Consul-General in Egypt to Gambetta, 17 Jan. 1882, *D.D.F.*, IV, no. 237.

malcontent colonels mustered their forces a second time on 1 February, 1881, in protest against the economies imposed on the Army, and compelled Tewfik to dismiss the Minister for War. On 9 September the crisis was reached. Arabi and his officers surrounded the Khedive's palace and demanded the dismissal of his ministry, the restoring of the Army to its former strength and the calling of the Chamber of Notables. The Khedive had no choice but to yield. On the advice of the Anglo-French Controllers, he accepted the liberal Cherif Pasha as his first minister, hoping to divide the civilian from the military elements in the national opposition. The new ministers hoped to win the support of the Chamber of Notables and fend off Arabi's challenge to the Dual Financial Control. Cherif promised to co-operate with the Controllers, and so won Anglo-French approval. But for all that, power, if not authority, continued to pass from the Khedive and his ministers to Arabi and the colonels. The French Consul-General reported that Tewfik had lost all prestige.[1] Malet, the British representative, found at the end of November that 'the Khedive . . . considers the country to be in the hands of Arabi Bey and has little confidence in the Chamber of Notables showing either wisdom or moderation.'[2] The British Controller-General, Sir Auckland Colvin, observed that Arabi was being swept to power by an 'Egyptian national movement' which was partly the result of 'the growing emancipation of the Egyptian mind owing to its close contact with Europeans', and partly a reaction against the oppression of Turkish Pashas and European dictation.[3] The Khedivate was being crushed under the weight of the Anglo-French hegemony on its back.

By the end of 1881 Egypt was in deep crisis. But about this crisis one fact is clear. Its origins were not to be found in any new imperialism arising in Europe after 1870; they lay in the corrosive effect locally in Egypt of half a century of informal expansion by Britain and France. The two governments remained satisfied in principle to protect their strategic interest in Egypt by influence alone. When the Turkish *régimes* through which they had exerted their influence broke down financially and politically after 1876, they strove to repair them in order to restore the old system of security. But in Egypt by 1881, Anglo-French attempts to shore up the Khedivate with a liberal constitution and fiscal reform had further undermined its authority. Their efforts to restore solvency by means of financial control had

[1] French Consul-General in Cairo to Saint-Hilaire, 11 Sept. 1881, *D.D.F.*, IV, no. 122.

[2] Malet to Granville, 28 Nov. 1881, F.O. 141/151.

[3] Colvin, Memo., Cromer, *op. cit.*, (1911), 170–1.

led on to an increasing degree of European direction within the Egyptian government. This tightening control had provoked a national opposition which threatened to sweep away the Dual Control along with the discredited Khedivate.

The Gladstonian Approach

Gladstone and the Liberal ministers who came to power in 1880 had to choose between going forward or drawing back. All their sentiments, principles and conceptions of the national will and interest determined them to draw back; but in the end, ironically, it was they who occupied Egypt, with Gladstone in the unexpected role of invader.

Of all British statesmen it is Gladstone whose character is the most convoluted. Others abide our question; but with him the snap judgement and the glib formula will not fit. The ambiguities which bedeck his speeches and letters, the prolixity, the lurches into the conditional mood and the qualifying clause — these marked the intricacy of his nature. He could chop logic with the most sparkling of the High Churchmen, yet frame budgets with the grimmest of the utilitarians. He had learning without taste, eloquence without style, sweetness without light; he could toss moral judgements into the affairs of state, and yet conduct politics as one of the fine arts. Hence at all stages of his career friends and enemies were starkly divided about the roots of his nature. To Palmerston he seemed an opinionated prig, to Cobden the only politician with principles; Disraeli thought him a bore, Northcote found him an inspiration; for Morley, the Irish adventurer revealed the ancient hero on his last crusade, for the Queen it showed the old spellbinder up to his tricks once more.

Perhaps there was truth in all these judgements. The vehemence, the scalding, volcanic objurgations which poured up from the craters of his personality were calculated to attract some temperaments and repel others. Not everyone liked their politics couched in terms of the categorical moral imperative. But more than that, it was Gladstone's peculiar fortune that the casings and centre of his nature became of greater political value as he grew older. Just as his character was larger than life, so his career was longer than time out of mind. He was everything by turns. He had met Canning. He was to lead Lloyd George. From decade to decade his career was to broaden down from mutation to mutation. The sententious young graduate of the Eighteen thirties who had seen himself as the hammer of Benthamism modulated into the earnest economist working fourteen hours a day to dismantle the tariffs and cut government's costs. After 1867 he was the first politician to exploit the mass vote, because he, and only he, could supply the *persona* which symbolised the issues of the day to the new electorate. It might seem a long step from the conventional member for Oxford University at mid-century to the People's William of later years, but Gladstone's own temperament assisted the change. The moral ardour and theological zeal which once attracted only intellectuals such as Frederic Rogers and Newcastle, now appealed to the popular taste for ethical simplicities and hectic religiosity, and rallied the farm labourer and artisan to the Liberal polls.

At the head of his great administration of 1868–74, Gladstone had defined a new kind of politics for a new period. Reform of the Civil Service, the Army and the Irish Church had established the Liberals as the enemies of the privileged, the nepotist and the effete. Then their demand for greater efficiency at lower cost had looked like a policy of iconoclasm on the instalment plan. But by 1880, what did Gladstone stand for? At the opening of his second ministry he prophesied:

> 'The new parliament . . . will not draw its inspiration from me. . . . I expect it to act in the main on well-tried and established lines. . . .'[1]

After its fall in 1885, he told Argyll:

> 'I deeply deplore the oblivion into which public economy has fallen; the prevailing disposition to make a luxury of panics . . . and the leaning of both parties to socialism, which I radically disapprove.'[2]

The electorate had struck its tents and was on the march towards collectivism, but Gladstone was no longer marching at their head.

Just as his domestic policy had been evolved in reaction against those who favoured too little liberty, so his approach to problems overseas came from reaction against those who pressed for too much intervention. It was in contradistinction to Palmerstonian policies of unlimited intervention that he placed so much reliance on the Concert of Europe, and from this he went on to erect a schematic version of the rules of foreign policy:

> 'The first thing is to foster the strength of the Empire by just legislation and economy at home, thereby producing two of the great elements of national power — namely wealth . . . and union and contentment. . . . My second principle . . . is . . . that its aim ought to be to preserve . . . the blessings of peace. . . . My third principle . . . to strive to cultivate and maintain, ay,

[1] Gladstone to Doyle, 10 May 1880, John Morley, *The Life of William Ewart Gladstone*, (1903), II, 631.

[2] Gladstone to Duke of Argyll, 30 Sept. 1885, *ibid.*, III, 221.

> to the very uttermost, what is called the Concert of Europe. . . . My fourth principle is that you should avoid needless and entangling engagements — My fifth principle is to acknowledge the equal rights of all nations.'[1]

There was a good deal of the Manchester School about Gladstone's views of the world at large. But no man would have achieved high office as a full blown member of that sect, and Gladstone was always careful to distinguish himself from Cobden's pacifism. Yet the overtones — peace, good neighbourliness and good trade — are unmistakably those of Cobden. Gladstone took for granted the pre-eminence of England through the expansion of England's trade; he went on to postulate that since the country was playing from strength in economics and politics, it should give a lead to the world in ethics. Secure in her wealth, her power and her morality, England did not need to carry a big stick, since the pulling power of the English *ethos* would win the goodwill of others. But his anger against the interventionists in the late Eighteen seventies sprang more from his dislike of Disraeli's swagger and bluster than any fundamental disagreement over the objectives of policy. The one kept his politics in his bosom, the other wore his morals on his coat sleeve.

The Liberals had been at cross purposes from the onset of the troubles in the Turkish empire and its Egyptian provinces. While in opposition, Hartington and the Whigs in the Party had tacitly approved the Conservatives' measures in the eastern Mediterranean. Like Disraeli and Salisbury, they were pragmatists and Palmerstonians. They had no more sympathy with national movements in the Orient than in Ireland or the Transvaal; and they rejected as an illusion dangerous to imperial security the idea that liberal principles could be applied in the East as in the West. They accepted as right whatever was necessary to protect the national interests of wealth and power. Gladstone and the liberal-radical wing on the other hand, had publicly denounced the Conservatives' intervention in the Near East as barefaced 'jingoism'. High Anglican though he was, Gladstone spoke for the liberal and nonconformist conscience in foreign affairs, for the Cobdenite opposition to Palmerstonian belligerence and interference in other peoples' politics. The Gladstonians believed that foreign as well as domestic policy should be conducted on moral principle. Unlike the Whigs, they believed within limits in the right of oppressed nationalities to be free, and in encouraging their progress toward representative government. They stood against the amoral pursuit of national interests.

[1] Gladstone, *Political Speeches in Scotland*, (1880), I, 115–7.

They preached instead the settling of international disputes by arbitration. Gladstone in Midlothian had called upon every nation to respect the equal rights of its neighbours, whether strong or weak, and to submit their selfish aims to the collective will of a Concert of Europe.[1]

These were the principles which Gladstone in opposition had hurled at Disraeli. The Liberal leader had laid most of the trouble in the Near East at the door of his rival's 'forward policy'. In 1875, he had criticised the purchase of the Suez Canal shares because he expected that they would turn out to be 'the almost certain egg of a North African Empire'.[2] He had come out of retirement and resumed the Liberal leadership from Hartington to thunder against Disraeli's pro-Turk policy, and to appeal on behalf of the Bulgarian Christians and peace with Russia. Gladstone in his Midlothian campaigns had denounced the Conservatives' interference at the Straits, in Cyprus, Egypt, the Transvaal and Afghanistan as 'gratuitous, dangerous, ambiguous, impracticable and impossible'.[3] The appeal of peace, Christianity and conscience appeared to have won the Liberals an overwhelming victory at the Elections of April 1880.[4] They congratulated themselves that they had deposed 'King Jingo' and exorcised his 'baleful spirit of domination'.[5]

The Egyptian question in 1882, like the Boer question a year earlier, turned the Cabinet into a veritable battlefield between Whig and Liberal-Radical principle and prejudice. Yet both issues, although important, were only secondary fields of the conflict. The decisive ground throughout for both sides continued to be Ireland, with the Gladstonians and Radicals contending for concession and conciliation toward the Irish Nationalists, and the Whigs for coercion and autocracy. A struggle for control of the party turned upon this issue. Henceforward the Egyptian question became entangled with the Irish, and the ministry's policy on the Nile tended to become an accident of domestic politics.

Once in office, Gladstone, with Granville as his technician, set out to reform British policy according to their pledges of economy at Home and non-intervention abroad. There were protests from the Whigs, but the electorate seemed to have given a plain mandate, and the Gladstonians directed foreign policy. During 1880 and 1881 the Prime Minister

[1] For this analysis of Gladstone's attitude, *vide* A. V. Medlicott, *Bismarck, Gladstone and the Concert of Europe*, (1956).

[2] W. E. Gladstone, 'Aggression on Egypt and Freedom in the East', *Nineteenth Century*, II, (Aug. 1877), 149–66.

[3] A. T. Bassett (ed.), *Gladstone's Speeches*, (1916), 570–1.

[4] The new Parliament was made up of 349 Liberals, 234 Conservatives and about 60 Irish Nationalists.

[5] Bassett, *op. cit.*, 562.

worked intermittently but passionately to assemble a Concert of Europe which he hoped would 'neutralise and fetter and bind up the selfish aims'[1] of the Powers and make a stable peace. The Liberals tried to set the example. They withdrew from the Transvaal and partly from Afghanistan. British meddling in the affairs of Tunis and Morocco noticeably abated, and they gravely considered giving Cyprus back to its Turkish owner. They tried to lead the collective action of Europe in coercing the Sultan to settle outstanding questions in the Balkans. It was through the same Concert of Europe that the Liberals expected to settle the Egyptian crisis.

Drawn by the noble vision of European comity and a passionate hatred of Turkish oppression, Gladstone and Granville by the end of 1881 had weakened at Constantinople the traditional safeguards for the Suez route. They had dropped the Conservatives' scheme for defending the Turkish empire in Asia from Cyprus and Armenia. By asserting the rights of the Christian nationalities against the Porte, they had lost the influence over the Sultan which Disraeli had tried to preserve. It was just as important to the Liberals as to the Conservatives to secure the routes to India and maintain the *status quo* in the Mediterranean. But Gladstone and Granville felt morally bound to dispense with the 'unspeakable Turk' as an ally, because they also thought that they could do so with safety. For security they relied entirely upon naval power, the Anglo-French *entente*, the European Concert and parity in an independent Egypt.

It was the old Palmerstonian chair, but with only three legs; the fourth — the Turkish — was missing. By the end of 1881 the Concert of Europe was missing too; for Bismarck's secret alliances with Russia, Austria, and shortly afterwards with Italy, now divided Europe and he did not always choose to make a Concert to help Britain in the Mediterranean. It was Bismarck also who now occupied the seat left vacant at Constantinople. British security for the moment thus depended more than ever before upon Egypt and the liberal *entente* with France. At the same time the Liberals wanted to draw back from further intervention there. So it was that the Egyptian national revolt against financial control hit Gladstone's half-formed system unawares at its vulnerable point.

The Liberals' problem was to carry out their promises of peace and non-interference without giving up the French alliance or losing equality of influence in Cairo. They could only reconcile conscience with security if they could settle the Egyptian crisis from outside and per-

[1] Medlicott, *op. cit.*, 30.

suade the French to do the same. In this they were attempting the almost impossible. From September 1881 until June 1882 Gladstone and Granville tried one compromise after another, only to drive the nationalists to extremes and to strain the *entente* with France. At last they were overtaken by events in Egypt and by a Whig revolt against conscience on behalf of security; and direct intervention became the one course which could not be avoided. It is important to trace in detail the Liberals' wrestling with Egypt, because, without their realising it, this turned out to be the deciding struggle between British imperialism and anti-imperialism in Africa.

Motives of Intervention

Non-intervention remained the ministry's principle in north Africa throughout 1881. When the French took Tunis under their protection early in the year, Granville wrote: 'I own to jealousy of France getting an overwhelming proponderance in the Mediterranean'.[1] His colleagues agreed.[2] But they felt bound by Salisbury's agreement with Waddington to give the French a free hand there in exchange for a free hand in Cyprus. Certainly the main consideration was that the French in Tunis did not seem to present any new threat to the vital interest 'of maintaining British influence in Egypt'.[3] The Prime Minister and his colleagues wished 'to do nothing to irritate the French unnecessarily',[4] and so they decided not to oppose French expansion in Tunis. It was not Tunis then which set off Anglo-French rivalry in Africa.[5]

But it was more difficult to avoid intervening in Egypt, where the internal revolution was by now endangering the international Financial Control. After Arabi's military *Putsch* of September 1881, Gladstone's ministry realised that however strongly they preferred inaction, they could not afford to hang back and let the French go in alone and restore the Control. To allow France to steal a march on them in Cairo would give her command of the Suez route. The government's chief concern

[1] Granville to Gladstone, 23 Apr. 1881, P.R.O. 30/29/124.

[2] Gladstone to Granville, 22 Apr. 1881, *ibid.*; Kimberley to Granville, 14 Jul. 1881, P.R.O. 30/29/143.

[3] Northbrook, Cabinet Note, 15 Jul. 1881, *ibid.*; Gladstone to Granville, 28 Apr. 1881, P.R.O. 30/29/124; and Dilke Cabinet Note, 14 Jul. 1881, P.R.O. 30/29/143.

[4] Gladstone to Granville, 28 Apr. 1881, P.R.O. 30/29/124; Gladstone Cabinet Note, 13 Jul. 1881, P.R.O. 30/29/143.

[5] The evidence for these dogmatic statements is contained in A. E., Angleterre, 789, 790, 791. For general accounts *vide* H. Cambon, *Histoire de la Régence de Tunis*, (Paris, 1948), 103–65; M. Reclus, *Jules Ferry*, (Paris, 1947), 247–72; J. Bardoux, *La Défaite de Bismarck*, (Paris, 1953), 7–62; T. F. Power, *Jules Ferry and the Renaissance of French Imperialism*, (New York 1944), 32–72; Medlicott, *op. cit.*, 113–22, 306–11.

was to avert this danger, rather than to seize any positive advantage. On 12 September the Prime Minister was relieved that the French seemed to want British help in handling the crisis.[1] He sketched an Egyptian policy for Granville next day: 'I sum up thus: 1. Steady concert with France 2. Turkish General to go if need be 3. Turkish troops in preference to any others 4. No British or French force, unless ships be needful for *bona fide* protection of subjects 5. Apart from all this, I long for information on the merits of the quarrel.'[2] A month later the Prime Minister and Granville softened their resistance to French ambitions in Morocco '. . . as a help to thorough understanding and co-operation in Egypt'.[3] Fearing that Bismarck was exploiting the Egyptian crisis to split the Liberal Alliance, the government was anxious to demonstrate its unity with France. 'I shall be also glad', Gladstone instructed Granville, 'if you can arrange for some joint act with France which may have the effect of discouraging Bismarck's intrigues.'[4] Accordingly, Malet, the British Agent in Cairo, was told to explore the possibilities.

Gladstone and Granville believed that Anglo-French diplomatic pressure would be enough to check the Arabists and restore the Khedive and the Control. The British wanted above all to stop interference short at diplomacy, and to halt the French at that point. On 15 October Granville made this clear to Dufferin, the ambassador at the Porte: 'We wish to act cordially with France without allowing her any predominance. . . . The *status quo* can be maintained if Turkey, England, and France do nothing to disturb it.'[5] When the French began to talk of an expedition for the purpose, the British had second thoughts about the joint policy. Gladstone still wanted 'to act in accord with France'; but even more he wanted 'to arrive at a *minimum* of interference'.[6] Granville reminded Dufferin that Gladstone had pledged himself to the country against aggression on Egypt.[7] If an expedition should become necessary in the last resort, the British wanted the Turks to make it, not Britain and France. While continuing joint diplomatic action with France, Granville wrote: '. . . There is much to be said against England and France mixing so much in the affairs of Egypt, and I doubt whether

[1] Gladstone to Granville, 12 Sept. 1881, P.R.O. 30/29/124.
[2] Gladstone to Granville, 13 Sept. 1881, *ibid.*
[3] Gladstone to Granville, 5 Oct. 1881, *ibid.*
[4] Gladstone to Granville, 21 Oct. 1881, *ibid.*
[5] Granville to Dufferin, 15 Oct. 1881, Lord Edmond Fitzmaurice, *Life of the Second Earl Granville*, (2nd ed., 1905), II, 252–3.
[6] Gladstone to Granville, 5 Oct. 1881, P.R.O. 30/29/124.
[7] Granville to Dufferin, 10 Oct. 1881, *ibid.*; see Gladstone's article 'Aggression on Egypt and Freedom in the East', *Nineteenth Century*, Aug. 1877.

we ought to extend this interference.'[1] A joint expedition would lead to a joint occupation and '[I] am not sure that baleful as it is the plan of a Turkish occupation would not be preferable.'[2] Gladstone agreed.[3] So to the plan for Anglo-French diplomatic action the British government came to attach a proposal for a Turkish expedition. They were to prove incompatible.

Paris, however, meant to deny the Turk the slightest chance of improving his position in Egypt. The French feared that Arabi's rising was part of a general pan-Islamic movement directed by the Sultan, which was at the same time stirring Moslem revolt against French control in Tunis and Algeria.[4] From the beginning therefore, Paris objected strongly to Turkish intervention and insisted upon Anglo-French action to halt the nationalist movement.

In Britain Gladstone and the humanitarians during the Eastern Crisis had made the cause of the oppressed nationalities against 'the unspeakable Turk' something of a popular passion. They were now, therefore, bound to have serious qualms about interfering with the Egyptian revolution. At the end of 1881 Arabi forced himself into the nationalist ministry, and the Egyptian Chambers of Notables challenged the European Financial Control. Gambetta, the new French Foreign Minister, decided that a strong warning must be sent to the Egyptian nationalists. On 26 December he invited the British to join in a declaration that the two powers were determined to uphold the Khedive and the Financial Control.[5] Although the Cabinet was anxious to co-operate with France, Gambetta's Note went much farther than they wished to go. The projected declaration logically implied a joint expedition, in the last resort, to carry it out. But the British government did not want any kind of expedition. The Prime Minister sympathised with the Arabists and their hatred of the international Control. He wrote on 4 January 1882:

> 'I am not by any means pained, but I am much surprised at the rapid development of a national sentiment and party in Egypt. The very ideas of such a sentiment and the Egyptian people seemed quite incompatible . . . most of all is the case strange if the standing army is the nest that has reared it. . . . [But] it seems to claim the respect due to it as a fact, and due also to the capabilities that may be latent in it for the future. "Egypt

[1] Granville to Gladstone, 4 Oct. 1881, P.R.O. 30/29/124.
[2] Granville to Gladstone, 15 Dec. 1881, *ibid.*
[3] Gladstone to Granville, 16 Dec. 1881, *ibid.*
[4] Lyons to Granville, 30 Sept. 1881, Newton, *op. cit.*, II, 259; Wilfred S. Blunt, *Secret History of the English Occupation of Egypt*, (1907), 182.
[5] Granville to Malet, 6 Jan. 1882, F.O. 141/152; Gambetta to French Consul-General in Cairo, 7 Jan. 1882, *D.D.F.*, IV, no. 226.

for the Egyptians" is the sentiment to which I would wish to give scope: and could it prevail it would I think be the best, the only good solution of the "Egyptian question". . . .'[1]

Gladstone also doubted whether a true nationalist movement could in any case be halted for long. Like Malet, the British Consul-General in Cairo,[2] he regarded '. . . with the utmost apprehension a conflict between the "Control" and any sentiment truly national, with a persuasion that one way or other we should come to grief'.[3] Chamberlain also sympathised with the nationalists[4] and joined Gladstone in opposing the Joint Note, although they were not certain whether the Arabists were responsible nationalist reformers or not.

The opponents of the Note were voicing the earlier Victorian belief that fostering the liberal and 'progressive' groups in other countries must inevitably further British interests, and indeed that flouting such groups would be a futile effort to block the course of destiny. But the world of 1882 had moved on from that which Palmerston knew. It was a world where the upheavals in old non-European societies were growing more violent, where questions about their future increasingly strained relations between the European Powers. To stand aside and allow local revolutions to work themselves out was becoming more difficult.

The majority of the Cabinet decided that it was essential to keep in step with France and preserve the alliance. They accepted the Note as a bluff which they hoped would sober Arabi and the nationalists and bring them to respect the Khedive's authority and Europe's financial rights. It would not come to an expedition, the Liberals assured themselves, and they made it plain that, in joining in the Note, they were not binding themselves to any particular course of action, or indeed to any action whatsoever.[5] The Prime Minister deferred to these opinions, and the Identic Note was presented on 8 January. 'The object,' as Granville explained, '. . . was to strengthen the Govt. of Egypt and maintain the existing order of things.'[6]

Unfortunately the nationalists took the Note as a pretext for making

[1] Gladstone to Granville, 4 Jan. 1882, P.R.O. 30/29/125.

[2] Malet to Granville, 11 Jan. 1882, P.R.O. 30/29/160.

[3] Gladstone to Granville, 4 Jan. 1882, P.R.O. 30/29/125.

[4] '[Their Movement] might be the legitimate expression of discontent and of resistance to oppression. If so, it ought to be guided but not repressed.' (J. Chamberlain, *A Political Memoir, 1880–1892*, (ed. C. D. Howard, (1953), 71.)

[5] 'Her Majesty's Government must not be considered as committing themselves thereby to any particular mode of action.' Lyons reiterated the reservation to the French, *vide* Freycinet to Challemel-Lacour, 3 Feb. 1882, *D.D.F.*, IV, no. 248.

[6] Granville to Gladstone, 12 Jan. 1882, P.R.O. 30/29/125.

another Tunis of their country and reacted as if they had received a declaration of war. Malet reported from Cairo three days later:

> '. . . All seemed to promise to go smoothly until the collective note was presented — Since then, the idea having spread that we intend intervention nothing has been heard of but Araby Bey and his redoubtable Colonels. . . . I confess on the other hand to be so anxious to prevent intervention at all hazards that I would even prefer that the Egyptians should try to manage their own country without the Control.'[1]

In reaction to the Note, the Egyptian Assembly of Notables ousted Cherif's ministry, and demanded a share in making the budget, which was reserved to the Dual Control. The Note, in effect, united Arabi and the colonels with the nationalist politicians in an attempt to remove some of Egypt's foreign fetters.[2] On 5 February an extreme nationalist ministry came into power with Arabi as Minister of War. The Anglo-French bluff had been called.

As the Egyptian situation worsened, the division between the Allies sharpened. Gambetta's determination to put down the Arabists, who had flouted the declared will of Britain and France, now alarmed Gladstone's ministry. They remained '. . . extremely anxious that there should be no apparent difference between the action of the two Governments'. But most ministers wanted above all to avoid direct intervention. '. . . We dislike intervention', Granville wrote privately on 12 January, 'either by ourselves or by others as much as ever.'[3] The French and British also bickered over the terms for a settlement. Gambetta wanted to give more power to the international Control to safeguard the bondholders' rights, but the British Liberals wanted more power for the Egyptian Assembly of Notables and less for the Control. Gambetta, lamented Gladstone, although a Republican, was no true liberal. He showed no respect for 'the popular principle in government'[4] in Egypt.

The failure of the Joint Note now began to strain the alliance. London, not wanting an Anglo-French expedition to enforce the Note, again suggested calling in the Turk and the Powers. Paris would not hear of either. The British in fact did not know what to do, except to do nothing themselves. The Foreign Secretary therefore wrote to Lyons, the ambassador in Paris, that the British saw objections to every kind of intervention. 'M. Gambetta would probably desire joint intervention; the objections to this are immense. . . . Single occupation, by England

[1] Malet to Granville, 11 Jan. 1882, P.R.O. 30/29/160. [2] *idem.*

[3] Granville to Gladstone, 12 Jan. 1883, P.R.O. 30/29/125.

[4] Gladstone to Granville, 31 Jan. 1882, *ibid.*

or by France, still more so. . . . Turkish occupation under . . . control by France and England, although a great evil, would not be less bad than the three alternatives I have mentioned.' Granville asked Lyons how the French would regard the idea of an Anglo-French intervention under a mandate from the Concert of Europe.[1] Malet had suggested this because he thought that 'the [Egyptian] Chamber would . . . listen to the united Great Powers, but would not listen to England and France alone'. Lyons in a forceful reply warned Granville that the French reaction against calling in the other Powers would be so violent that the 'Liberal alliance' would be broken. All Europe, the French would say, would consider this as a sign that the British had given up 'all special intimacy with the French Government':

> 'It would give rise to suspicions that we were trying to use the other Powers for the purpose of ousting France from Egypt. The union of England and France on the Egyptian Question is the principal symbol of there being a good understanding between them. . . .'[2]

Gladstone and Granville saw the force of this argument, but they were still determined to avoid an Anglo-French occupation and to hand the Egyptian problem over to the Powers.[3] Moreover, their fear that Gambetta might steal a march on them in Egypt had faded as the French Premier's government was tottering. 'I doubt his having recourse to the desperate step of anticipating us by a French occupation,' Granville observed, 'and it is very desirable that he should know we object to a joint intervention, and have a slight leaning to Turkish aid.'[4] The British none the less still wanted to save the French alliance and assured Gambetta that they had no ambition to occupy Egypt alone. The cryptic notes which Granville supplied to Lyons for further explanations to the French, showed why:

> 'On the imminence of the crisis: the importance of perfect union between England and France: our strong objection to intervene alone — giving as reasons: — opposition of Egyptians; of Turkey; jealousy of Europe; responsibility of governing a country of Orientals without adequate means and under adverse circumstances; presumption that France would object as much to our sole occupation as we should object to theirs.'[5]

The Liberals had no ambition to take over a bankrupt country in the

[1] Granville to Lyons, 17 Jan. 1882, Newton, *op. cit.*, II, 270–1.
[2] Lyons to Granville, 19 Jan. 1882, and 22 Jan. 1882, *ibid.*, 272–7.
[3] Granville to Gladstone, 21 Jan. 1882, P.R.O. 30/29/125; Gladstone to Granville, 22 Jan. 1882, *ibid.*
[4] Granville to Gladstone, 21 Jan. 1882, *ibid.*
[5] Granville to Lyons, 21 Jan. 1882, Newton, *op. cit.*, II, 274–5.

face of Europe. The Cabinet notes of the end of January show them still wanting to evade the Egyptian dilemma by calling in the Turk and the Powers. In this way they hoped to avert the danger of France intervening, without exerting themselves or sacrificing French friendship. Kimberley, the Colonial Secretary, saw objections to every course.[1] Childers at the War Office, would go along with any policy, except British intervention, but preferred no intervention at all;[2] Selborne and Northbrook, similarly.[3] Hartington and Harcourt alone pressed for further Anglo-French action to restore the Control and the bondholders' rights[4], and to keep up the Liberal alliance. The wretched Granville went on trying to build an Egyptian policy upon the margin of agreement between the British and French views.

In early February there was a change in French policy. Freycinet supplanted Gambetta, and the French attitude to Egypt drew closer to the British. They were agreed that there was no immediate need to act in Egypt. They repudiated the idea of using force, and they did not want the Sultan to send troops.[5] If intervention became absolutely necessary, Granville still wanted it in the form of collective action by the Powers with the Sultan taking part.[6] But the change brought the French little nearer to agreeing to call in the Turk or the Concert of Europe. In England Gladstone's ministry, wracked by a prolonged Irish crisis, was in worse shape for decision than ever. On 30 March, 1882, its majority in the House of Commons shrank to 39. The Parnellites and Radicals were evidently combining with the Conservatives against the Liberals.[7] Whigs and Radicals were at odds in the Cabinet and Party. In Egypt meanwhile, the crisis deepened. In April, Malet reported from Cairo that '. . . the country will soon be governed by nothing but officers'.[8] The Khedive, whom Britain and France had turned into a 'constitutional' monarch, complained bitterly 'of having no party on which he could rely'.[9] His authority had passed to the Army and Notables. Anarchy seemed to be spreading. 'In the Provinces', Malet noted, 'the power of the Governors to keep order is rapidly declining, and business at the Ministries is very nearly at a standstill.'[10] The lives of Europeans might be endangered at any time

[1] Kimberley, Cabinet Note, 30 Jan. 1882, P.R.O. 30/29/143.
[2] Childers, Cabinet Note, 31 Jan. 1882, *ibid.*
[3] Selborne and Northbrook, Cabinet Notes, 28 and 30 Jan. 1882, *ibid.*
[4] Hartington and Harcourt, Cabinet Notes, 31 Jan. and 1 Feb. 1882, *ibid.*
[5] Freycinet to French Ambassador in London, 3 Feb. 1882, *D.D.F.*, IV, no. 248.
[6] Granville to Lyons, 7 Feb. 1882, *ibid.*, p. 240, f.n. 1.
[7] J. L. Hammond, *Gladstone and the Irish Nation*, (1938), 290.
[8] Malet to Granville, 4 Apr. 1882, P.R.O. 30/29/160.
[9] Malet to Granville, 18 Apr. 1882, *ibid.* [10] *idem.*

Malet warned Granville on 25 April that further European action to put down Arabi would only lead to bloodshed and that the only hope of quelling the mutinous Army peaceably would be to call in the Turk.[1] In European diplomacy meanwhile, Bismarck was doing his best to exploit the Egyptian crisis in order to drive Britain and France apart, while Granville clutched at every chance to hold them together.

The Cabinet in March 1882 was still desperately looking for a way of averting forcible intervention by anyone, and Granville, at his wits' end, asked Malet how this could be done. The British Agent suggested that a Turkish Commissioner should be invited to arbitrate between the Arabists and the Khedive. A naval demonstration, he added, would be needed to enforce the Commissioner's decisions.[2] But Freycinet still refused to agree to Turkish intervention. Granville had proposed to send a Turkish general to restore discipline in the Egyptian army by 'moral force'; but the French insisted upon an English and a French general. Granville by this time had as he said, few eggs left in his basket. He compromised on three generals, one Turkish, one French and one British; not that he expected the generals to settle the Egyptian crisis, but he wanted to show that Britain and France were still acting together. 'If the French agree,' he told Gladstone privately, 'it would have a good moral effect to be able to contradict Bismarck and to say that the two Powers are quite agreed.'[3] The Prime Minister however did not want to go as far as generals. '. . . the adoption of any plan of the kind', he objected, 'seems to suppose that there are producible reasons for apprehending a necessity of some kind for doing something precautionary.'[4]

The necessity however was plain to Granville and other ministers; and they were impressed with the possibilities of Malet's plan for a naval demonstration and the preparation of a Turkish land expedition to frighten the Arabists into a settlement. 'A naval demonstration', Malet assured Granville, 'at the same time as the arrival of the Sultan's commissioners would I think make the acceptance of the points demanded certain';[5] and the mere threat of a Turkish expedition should clinch the matter.[6] It seemed then that this more elaborate plan of threat and bluff offered a good chance of overthrowing Arabi's government and preserving the Anglo-French alliance, if the French would agree.

[1] Malet to Granville, 25 Apr. 1882, *ibid.*
[2] Malet to Granville, 21 Mar. 1882, *ibid.*
[3] Granville to Gladstone, 23 Apr. 1882, P.R.O. 30/29/125.
[4] Gladstone to Granville, 24 Apr. 1882, *ibid.*
[5] Malet to Granville, 2 May 1882, P.R.O. 30/29/160.
[6] Malet to Granville, 16 May 1882, *ibid.*

Early in May, the French, moved by the deepening Egyptian crisis and fearing that Bismarck and his allies might push the Turk into Egypt on their own terms, pressed the British to act with them.[1] Freycinet put forward a plan on 12 May which went some way toward agreeing with Granville's and Malet's ideas. He agreed to an Anglo-French show of naval force at Alexandria. He remained strongly against independent Turkish intervention. France even opposed for the moment the Turkish commissioner's going to Egypt, although later she sanctioned this, and with Britain warned the Porte not to send troops independently. But the French now conceded that, if a landing should become necessary, Turkish troops under Anglo-French control and upon Anglo-French terms, should pacify Egypt. They further agreed to exclude any landing of British or French troops.[2] The plan once again went too far for Gladstone or Granville. They tried to turn the proposed naval demonstration into an affair of all the Powers,[3] but the French refused.[4]

To the British nevertheless, the French plan appeared to hold out two great advantages. It would avert either an Anglo-French or a British occupation, and it would avoid a rupture with France and a possible war. The French had now agreed to a Turkish landing in the last resort, although the terms upon which the Turk was to be called in had not yet been worked out. Here at last Granville believed was a compromise on which Britain and France could act together, bring Arabi to heel and remove the danger of any major Power interposing across the Suez route to India.[5] On 15 May the two governments announced to the Powers that their joint fleet was on its way to Alexandria, to strengthen the Khedive and safeguard law and order.[6] Nine days later Granville called upon the French to bring into effect the second part of the plan and invite the Turk to send his land forces to Egypt. But Freycinet wavered and refused,[7] because Turkish intervention was so unpopular in the Chamber. All now hung on the naval demonstration alone, although both the British and French Consuls-General in Cairo had insisted that the Turkish troops must be ready to be called in, if the plan was to succeed. Like many joint plans, it was a

[1] French Ambassador in Berlin to Freycinet, 5 May 1882, *D.D.F.*, IV, no. 309; and French Ambassador in Constantinople to Freycinet, 5 May 1882, *ibid.*, no. 308.
[2] Freycinet to French Ambassador in London, 12 May 1882, *ibid.*, no. 316.
[3] French Ambassador in London to Freycinet, 13 May 1882, *ibid.*, no. 318.
[4] French Ambassador in London to Freycinet, 15 May 1882, *ibid.*, p. 309, f.n. 1.
[5] Granville, Minute, 13 May 1882, P.R.O. 30/29/125.
[6] Freycinet, Circular Telegram, 15 May 1882, *D.D.F.*, IV, no. 320.
[7] Freycinet to French Ambassador in London, 24 May 1882, *D.D.F.*, IV, no. 337, and 27 May 1882, *ibid.*, no. 342.

compromise made up of the acceptable features of several different proposals. Any one of them if applied in entirety, might have had a chance of success; but pieced haphazardly together, they were almost bound to fail.

With the fleets at Alexandria, the Khedive on 25 May was nerved enough to dismiss the Arabist ministers. But Egyptian reaction to this *coup* was so strong that Arabi was able to force his way back into power five days later. Malet reported that the nationalists were circulating petitions for Tewfik's deposition.[1] The naval demonstration, unsupported by the threat of a Turkish landing, failed to overawe the Egyptian nationalists; like the Joint Note it only consolidated Arabi's power, and weakened the Khedive and the moderates still further. The British Agent's reports from Cairo from the last days of May onwards were those of a man sitting on a powder keg. Anti-European feelings flared up at Alexandria on 11 and 12 June, when fifty Europeans were massacred and the British Consul was assaulted. Malet lived in terror of the Khedive being assassinated.[2] His telegrams now warned that 'the fleet is a menace likely to lead to disturbance and not to protection'.[3] In stirring the Egyptian pot, Britain and France had made it boil over.

Muddled as the British government's actions may seem, their intentions were far removed from any imperialist ambition to seize the country. The Liberals' policy was in fact the exact opposite. Their first aim throughout was to prevent any major Power from occupying Egypt, and to avoid doing so themselves. Their second purpose was to avoid breaking the French alliance; but the crisis in Egypt made it difficult to achieve both at once. If the British occupied Egypt on their own, the Anglo-French *entente* would be broken. If on the other hand, Britain and France occupied the country together, the forces of a major foreign Power would be interposed across the Suez route to India. Gladstone's government in fact could only gain both their objects if they could end the Egyptian crisis by means short of occupying the country, either alone or with France. Of necessity, therefore, their plans were all for keeping out rather than for going into Egypt; and for bringing order into its politics while safeguarding the Suez route from outside.

At the same time, Gladstone and Granville accepted the necessity for a settlement of Egypt. Ideally, they would have been happy to leave the Egyptians to settle their own quarrel with the foreign bondholders and to set up a liberal constitution. But they could not afford to gamble

[1] Malet to Granville, 30 May 1882, P.R.O. 30/29/160.
[2] Malet to Granville, 12 Jun. 1882, *ibid.* [3] Malet to Granville, 14 Jun. 1882, *ibid.*

that France and other Powers would do the same. The only real solution, as the Prime Minister had said, was to come to terms with Arabi and the nationalists. Time after time indeed, the Liberal government tried to do so on a basis of concessions to the Chamber of Notables, but the French objected to the slightest delegation of authority to the Egyptians. And the British, in order to keep up the alliance and their parity of influence in Cairo, were dragged in the wake of France, away from the policy of negotiating with the Egyptians, into the French policy of breaking the national movement. Egyptian national aspirations were not to be reconciled with continuing the full international Financial Control which the French demanded. Not that the Liberals felt tenderly for the bondholders; but as long as the threat of anarchy and interference with the Control remained, the way lay open to a foreign occupation. As a result, Gladstone's ideal solution of conciliating the Arabists became impracticable because of the priority given to concord with France and the Concert of Europe.

It was for these reasons that the Liberal government joined with the French in the Joint Note and the naval demonstration to break the Arabists by external pressure; and yet insisted upon a Turkish rather than an Anglo-French expedition as the last resort. From the British point of view, a Turkish landing had fewer disadvantages than any other, if only Paris could be brought to agree to it. It might be difficult to get the Sultan's troops out of Egypt once they had gone in. But acting together, the Powers would be strong enough to compel him to evacuate. Egypt would be settled and the French *entente* preserved. Once the internal crisis in Cairo was resolved, Britain and France could return to their old system of domination through 'moral influence' which had served both their interests so well in the past. With a stable *régime* in an independent Egypt once more, the Royal Navy would secure British control of the Canal and the country, should it be needed in peace or war. A British or an Anglo-French occupation would not serve half as well. The height of British ambition on the Nile in 1882 was to revert to the old system of influence and to avoid occupation. Unfortunately they did not understand the nature of the Egyptian revolution; nor was this altogether surprising since Arabi's movement was one of the first Oriental liberal-national revolutions against European control. It proved indifferent to mid-Victorian techniques of external persuasion. Every turn of the screw by Britain and France since 1879 had only weakened the Khedive, and strengthened the nationalists. By keeping in step with Paris, Gladstone's Cabinet had changed the crisis in Egypt into an emergency.

The failure of the naval demonstration and the massacre at Alexandria began the transition; and London pressed Paris to join in preparing a Turkish intervention with a mandate from the Concert of Europe. Although the French at the end of May called a Conference of the Powers to deal with the Egyptian Question, they refused to join Britain in putting forward a proposal for the sending of Turkish troops to Egypt.[1] Gladstone moreover feared that the Germans would wreck the Conference,[2] which was to meet on 23 June at Constantinople. In their anxiety to keep in step with the French over Egypt, the British had lost influence at Constantinople; it was already damaged by their taking of Cyprus, their ally's taking of Tunis, and the Anglo-French dealings with Egypt without consulting the Porte. Bismarck, who with the Austrians and Russians, had predominant influence at the Porte, now refused to press the Sultan to send a Turkish expedition.[3] On 3 June the Turks refused to attend the Conference at Constantinople at all. It looked as though all Granville's plans for avoiding direct intervention by calling in the Sultan's troops were falling through. His Egyptian policy was now challenged by Hartington. The Secretary for India took the Foreign Minister to task for failing to get the French to agree to Turkish military preparations in support of the joint naval demonstration at Alexandria. Impatient with Granville's bungling, and even more with French bad faith, Hartington ironically congratulated the Foreign Secretary on 27 May on settling the Egyptian problem:

> 'At least I suppose it is settled, as there has been no Cabinet, and you are I hear out of town. But I am rather anxious to know how it has been settled, as by the last telegrams it seems very far from that point. Has Arabi Pasha given in, or has M. de Freycinet been persuaded to get out of bed? I wonder whether any human being, (out of Downing St.) would believe that not a word has been said in the Cabinet about Egypt for a fortnight, and I suppose will not be for another week, — If then.'[4]

Hartington demanded a meeting of the Cabinet. The Foreign Secretary replied that a meeting now would not help. Hartington's answer shows something of the confusion of Egyptian policy-making in a government which was fully absorbed in Irish struggles.

'I dare say that Cabinets would not give you much assistance; but I

[1] Freycinet to French Ambassador in London, 24 and 27 May 1882, *D.D.F.*, IV, nos. 337 and 342.
[2] Gladstone to Granville, 30 May 1882, P.R.O. 30/29/125.
[3] See Busch's account of his interview with the Chancellor on 8 Jun. 1882, M. Busch, *Bismarck, Some Secret Pages of His History*, (1898), III, 51–3. Also French Ambassador in Berlin to Freycinet, 5 Jun. 1882, *D.D.F.*, IV, no. 369.
[4] Hartington to Granville, 27 May 1882, P.R.O. 30/29/132.

think that it is very much in consequence of the extreme rarity of the occasions on which our opinion is asked, that you find such a want of suggestion when it is asked. We have been supplied lately very liberally with telegrams and correspondence, but unless these are supplemented by some occasional discussion, it is not very easy to understand from them the actual position, or the objections to any alternative course.'[1]

So far indeed the government as a whole had given little study to the fundamentals of the Egyptian crisis. Granville and Gladstone had been content to go from expedient to expedient, intent upon avoiding risks rather than achieving a settlement.

But the Secretary for India's chief complaint was against the French:

'The French seem to be behaving worse than badly. Freycinet's communication . . . appears to be nothing less than a breach of faith. . . . Unless the French keep their word to us and are prepared to go in for Turkish intervention at once, we had much better cut ourselves loose from them. What is the use of such Allies? They have brought us into the frightful mess we are in, and I believe it would be easier to act with the Turks, and with the whole of the remaining European Powers, than with them alone.'[2]

From this time onward the heir to the duchy of Devonshire was to have as much influence upon Egyptian policy as Gladstone and Granville. The leader of the Whig interest, his one object in politics was to uphold the great traditional interests of the nation abroad. He was an avowed disciple of Palmerston, who had been his first political chief.[3] Hartington in fact was one of that select and aristocratic company which included Salisbury and Rosebery, who worked to keep foreign policy above party politics in an increasingly democratic age. He affected to be bored with politics and to have no ambition. But a friend noted that nobody 'ponders longer over State problems; the bent of his mind is slowly critical and very slowly constructive. . . . No personality, even the loftiest, and no sentiment, however pathetic, would prevail with him, against the plain, dry duty . . . of a citizen to the State.'[4] The Secretary for India distrusted Gladstone's sentimental Cobdenite notions of foreign policy as a danger to the national interests abroad; and he disliked almost as much Granville's watered down version of Palmerstonian principle and his appeasement of France. Convinced that British supremacy in India and in the Mediterranean was now at stake in Egypt, Hartington reacted as Palmerston might

[1] Hartington to Granville, 29 May 1882, *ibid.*
[2] Hartington to Granville, 30 May 1882, *ibid.* [3] Holland, *op. cit.*, I, 30, 268–9.
[4] Brett to Stead, 22 Apr. 1886, *Journals and Letters of Viscount Esher*, (ed. M. V. Brett), (1934), I, 125–6.

have done. It seemed intolerable to him that the disorderly and unprogressive Egyptians should be permitted any longer to endanger a vital Imperial interest. He was determined that no longer should Britain's weakness in dealing with the French, the Turk and the Egyptians flaw her strength in the world.

The Alexandria riots swung several other ministers in this direction. They blamed Arabi for the massacre and for unleashing anarchy, although some of them later admitted that they had been misinformed and mistaken in this.[1] However at the time, it seemed to Gladstone[2] and the Radicals, Chamberlain and Dilke, that Arabi had thrown off the mask. He had shown himself to be, not as they had supposed hitherto a national leader struggling to free his country, but 'a military adventurer' whose 'uncontrolled supremacy would very shortly bring about bankruptcy and anarchy'.[3] The two Radicals now insisted upon suppressing the Arabists, upon reparation for the massacre and upon releasing the Chamber of Notables — 'the nucleus of a really national and patriotic party' — from the grip of military dictatorship.[4] Under the shock of anarchy in Egypt, a forward party formed behind Hartington. As well as the Radicals, the Whigs, Northbrook and Kimberley, joined to press for military measures to protect the Canal.[5] They wanted above all some sort of effective action. Their spokesman, Hartington, wrote to Granville on 19 June: 'I am afraid that we are going to give in and submit to a complete defeat in Egypt. I do not think that I can stomach this, whatever may be the risks of any other course.'[6] His faction threatened to resign unless the Prime Minister and Granville got some kind of expedition sent to Egypt.[7] A Turkish expedition would be the lesser evil, Hartington and Northbrook agreed; but they doubted whether it could come quickly enough. The Sultan, they suspected, was making a bargain with the Arabists. If the Turk could not be brought to restore order, then an Anglo-French expedition should be sent. Hartington himself, and Hartington alone, went even further. He was ready, if all else failed, to send a British expedition,[8] and he wanted to prepare the force at once with the fullest possible publicity. 'I believe', he wrote, 'it would now be the best chance of stimulating the Turks, France and the other Powers to some effective action; and if it fails in this, the sooner we are prepared to act the

[1] Dilke *Memoir*, Gwynn and Tuckwell, *op. cit.*, I, 460.
[2] Gladstone to Granville, 2 Jun. 1882 P.R.O. 30/29/125.
[3] Chamberlain *op. cit.*, 71.
[4] Chamberlain, Cabinet Memo., 27 Jun. 1882, P.R.O. 30/29/143.
[5] Hartington to Granville, 16 Jun. 1882, P.R.O. 30/29/132.
[6] Hartington to Granville, 19 Jun. 1882, *ibid.*
[7] Hartington to Granville, 20 Jun. 1882, *ibid.* [8] *idem.*

better.'[1] It was the first time that any of the Cabinet had seriously proposed a single-handed British invasion of Egypt. Even now, none of his colleagues, except Northbrook, was ready to go so far. That Hartington should have proposed a British expedition mainly as a way of compelling the Sultan and France to act, was a recognition of his colleagues' lack of ambition to seize Egypt and monopolise power there.

Hartington felt so urgently the need for action in Egypt and was so disillusioned with the French as partners, that he insisted that Britain prepare for the worst: while on the other hand Gladstone and the rest of the Cabinet were loathe to consider the possibility of a British expedition.[2] Nevertheless in order to mollify Hartington, they agreed to send two battalions of reinforcements[3] to the Mediterranean. As to occupying the Canal, either single-handed or with France 'without reference to the authority of Europe', the Prime Minister and the Foreign Secretary would not hear of it.[4] But yielding a little to Hartington, the Cabinet asked Childers and Northbrook to look into the best means of protecting the Canal with the French,[5] should it become necessary. The French replied that the Suez Canal Company was sure that the Canal was safe, and that the only danger to it would arise from foreign intervention to protect it. This alone, the Company believed, would probably provoke Egyptian attacks on Canal traffic.[6] Gladstone agreed with the French view. It was enough, he thought on 24 June, to get assurances for the Canal's safety from the Khedive.[7] He and Granville wanted to do nothing until the outcome of the Conference at Constantinople was known. Until then, Granville observed, 'the question is hardly ripe for discussion. We do not know the ground we stand upon.'[8] He was still against joint intervention with France; but he agreed to bring more pressure upon the Turk to send an expedition. The Cabinet on 21 June had agreed to ask the Conference to authorise other military intervention than Turkish, in an attempt to scare the Sultan into an expedition.[9] The Foreign Secretary summed up his own view of policy thus:

> 'I am ready to go any lengths for reparation, and I set great store about making the Canal safe. But I own to dreadful alarm at occupying Egypt

[1] Hartington, Cabinet Memo., 18 Jun. 1882, P.R.O. 30/29/132.
[2] Granville to Hartington, 20 Jun. 1882, *ibid.*
[3] Cabinet letter for the Queen, 21 Jun. 1882, *ibid.*
[4] Gladstone to Granville, 21 Jun. 1882, P.R.O. 30/29/125.
[5] Cabinet letter for the Queen, 21 Jun. 1882, P.R.O. 30/29/132.
[6] Freycinet to French Ambassador in London, 24 Jun. 1882, *D.D.F.*, IV, no. 408.
[7] Gladstone to Granville, 24 Jun. 1882, P.R.O. 30/29/125.
[8] Granville to Hartington, 20 Jun. 1882, P.R.O. 30/29/132.
[9] Gladstone, Memo., 'Decisions of Cabinet,' 21 Jun. 1882, P.R.O. 30/29/125.

militarily and politically with the French. I think the majority [of the Cabinet] would rather like to do this. . . . It is a nasty business, and we have been much out of luck.'[1]

But the ministry's fondest hope was still of a Turkish expedition under a mandate from the Powers,[2] and so of avoiding a British landing, either alone or with France. At the end of June, this outcome still seemed feasible. 'There is a streak of daylight in Egyptian matters,' Granville wrote. 'It is quite on the cards that the Sultan will send troops after all.'[3] Hartington himself was more hopeful; but he would not wait much longer for action. 'It would seem to be almost the last chance of making anything out of the Conference,' he noted on 2 July, 'and of avoiding the necessity for separate action.'[4] Even now, the Cabinet as a whole did not want to intervene directly in Egypt, and certainly they did not want to occupy it. Gladstone and Granville indeed rejected out of hand the Sultan's offer on 25 June to hand over the virtual protectorate of Egypt to Britain alone.[5] The Prime Minister and the moderates by July seemed to have fended off Hartington's demand for a British expedition as a last resort. On that day, Gladstone set down the points on which Ministers had agreed. They would demand reparation for the Alexandria massacres; and they would decide upon no definite course in Egypt until the Conference had dealt with, or refused to deal with, the problem.[6]

During the next fortnight however, hopes of Turkish intervention faded. Fears of the French stealing a march got on ministers' nerves. 'It looks', Granville warned, 'as if the French were about to cotton to Arabi.'[7] Anxiety lest the French were settling separately with Arabi and the Khedive, and so heightening their influence in Cairo at Britain's expense,[8] worried even Gladstone. In such a case it would be almost impossible for the British to regain their position without a major war.[9] And Freycinet's original refusal of 24 June to join with Britain in protecting the Canal strengthened this suspicion.[10]

[1] Granville to Spencer, 22 Jun. 1882, Fitzmaurice, *op. cit.*, II, 265.

[2] Granville to Spencer, 26 Jun. 1882, *ibid.*, 266; *vide* Cabinet Minutes on Dufferin to Granville, 30 Jun. 1882, P.R.O. 30/29/143.

[3] Granville to Spencer, 26 Jun. 1882, Fitzmaurice, *op. cit.*, II, 266.

[4] Hartington, Minute, 2 Jul. 1882 on Dufferin's telegram of 30 Jun. 1882, P.R.O. 30/29/143.

[5] Q.V.L., 2nd ser., III, 302–3; Gwynn and Tuckwell, *op. cit.*, I, 463.

[6] Gladstone to Granville, 1 Jul. 1882, P.R.O. 30/29/126.

[7] Granville to Spencer, 26 Jun. 1882, Fitzmaurice, *op. cit.*, II, 266.

[8] French Ambassador in London to Freycinet, 3 and 4 Jul. 1882, *D.D.F.*, IV, no. 422–3.

[9] Gladstone to Granville, 1 Jul. 1882, P.R.O. 30/29/126.

[10] Freycinet to French Ambassador in London, 24 Jun. 1882, *D.D.F.*, IV, no. 408.

At the same time ministers became more anxious about the security of the Canal, and in their uneasiness, a minor question of the safety of the fleet brought them to take what proved to be an irretrievable step into aggression. At Alexandria the Egyptians were raising shore batteries commanding the anchorage. Seymour, the British admiral, wanting to remove the danger to his squadron, asked permission to bombard if the works were not stopped. When the French were asked whether they would join in the proposed ultimatum, they excused themselves because the French Chamber was unlikely to approve,[1] and withdrew their fleet to Port Said. Their action heightened British suspicions of a bargain with Arabi.[2] Should Seymour be allowed his ultimatum?

It was this question which opened the decisive struggle between the moderates and the forward school in the Cabinet. Ministers weighed the possibility that if the fleet bombarded the forts at Alexandria, the Arabists would probably block the Canal; and most of the Cabinet now agreed that any immediate danger to the Canal could hardly be met without landing an expedition.[3] Hartington and four other ministers by 7 July were prepared to accept the risk of Seymour's ultimatum and in the last resort to land British forces and occupy the Canal.[4] Hartington and Northbrook demanded a landing to protect the Canal and restore foreign financial control. On the other hand, Chamberlain and Dilke insisted upon putting down Arabi, not in order to restore the foreign Financial Control and to save the bondholders, but to protect the Canal and exact reparations for the Alexandria outrages. These Radicals wanted intervention on condition that it was directed towards freeing the Egyptians from foreign control. Otherwise, the Radicals feared '. . . liberal opinion in the country will be extremely restive at the idea of armed intervention'.[5] Gladstone, Granville and Bright 'now stood alone against the rest of the Cabinet in supporting a let-alone policy'.[6] Bright's objection was sane and simple. 'Surely,' he minuted, 'if the attack on the port endangers the Canal, the attack should not be made.'[7] The Prime Minister opposed the idea of a British landing on principle and asked characteristically: 'Is there any great necessity for a step at

[1] Freycinet to French Ambassador in London, 5 Jul. 1882, *D.D.F.*, IV, no. 426.

[2] French Ambassador in Constantinople to Freycinet, 9 Jul. 1882, *D.D.F.*, IV, no. 436.

[3] Cabinet Opinions on the protection of the Canal, 1–9 Jul. 1882, P.R.O. 30/29/143 and 30/29/126.

[4] *idem*. The four were Northbrook, Kimberley, Childers and Chamberlain.

[5] Chamberlain Cabinet Minute, 21 Jun. 1882, J. L. Garvin, *Life of Joseph Chamberlain*, (1932), I, 448; and Dilke, *Memoir*, Gwynn and Tuckwell, *op. cit.*, I, 465.

[6] Dilke's *Political Diary*, B.M. Add. MSS. 43935, 5–7 Jul. 1882.

[7] Bright, Cabinet Minute, 7 Jul. 1882, P.R.O. 30/29/143.

present?'[1] But Granville, who hoped that a bombardment of Alexandria might still break Arabi's power and who was doing his best to keep his colleagues together, wavered. When he asked Gladstone to call a Cabinet to give Admiral Seymour fresh orders, the Prime Minister refused. '. . . Hurried and frequent Cabinets create much stir,' he complained. 'I do not understand what fresh order Beauchamp Seymour could have. . . .'[2]

By 9 July the ministry seemed on the point of breaking up, not so much because of its divided opinions about Egypt as because of its Irish quarrels. Gladstone was on the verge of resignation. Bright, Chamberlain and Dilke were prepared to go out with him, although the two latter agreed with Hartington on the need for action in Egypt.[3] Nobody knew whether Hartington would try and go on with a Whig ministry or let the Conservatives into power. In the midst of this confusion, the Cabinet decided the question of Seymour's ultimatum. The Prime Minister gave way to the forward party for the moment. About the ultimatum he wrote: 'I do not feel the necessity but I am willing to defer to your decision and judgements.'[4] The old man, already at full stretch with the Irish Arrears Bill, for the moment had lost his grip on Egyptian policy. Even he had caught the Cabinet's jitters for the safety of the paramount British interest in the security of the Canal. On 8 July Granville wrote: 'Gladstone admitted to me yesterday for the first time that we were bound to protect the Suez Canal.'[5] Now at last the danger to the Indian route had convinced most of the Cabinet that in the last resort they must sanction the British landing which hitherto they had been intent to avoid. Their disillusionment with Arabi's liberalism, despair of Turkish and international action, suspicion of French loyalty, anxiety for the Canal, and their Irish confusions had driven this non-interventionist ministry to the point of action. Seymour was allowed to send his ultimatum at Alexandria; and the war departments were authorised to prepare, but not to send, forces to occupy the Canal if necessary.[6]

It was a compromise between cross purposes, rather than a clear-cut decision. All the ministers who accepted the ultimatum did so with different intentions. They all realised that a bombardment at Alexandria might put the Canal in danger and accepted the calculated risk.

[1] Gladstone to Granville, 7 Jul. 1882, P.R.O. 30/29/132.
[2] Gladstone to Granville, 7 Jul. 1882, P.R.O. 30/29/126.
[3] Dilke, *Memoir*, Gwynn and Tuckwell, *op. cit.*, I, 446–8, 464–8.
[4] Gladstone to Granville, 9 Jul. 1882, P.R.O. 30/29/126.
[5] Granville to Hartington, 8 Jul. 1882, P.R.O. 30/29/132.
[6] Hartington to Granville, 10 Jul. 1882, P.R.O. 30/29/132.

Hartington and the forward party seized upon the pretext of the earthworks at Alexandria to set in train direct British intervention to crush the Arabists in the course of protecting the Canal. They gathered at the Foreign Office, eagerly awaiting news of the bombardment.[1] The rest of the Cabinet, except Bright, acquiesced unwillingly but with their eyes open. Gladstone did so to keep his ministry together, and sacrificed his policy of non-intervention in Egypt to the Irish Arrears Bill. Granville and other moderates went over to Hartington in the end because they hoped that a bombardment, combined with preparations for a landing, would persuade the Egyptians at last that Britain was in earnest and would bring down Arabi without landing an expedition. Single-handed action to protect the Canal remained hedged about with contingencies; whether Arabi would accept the ultimatum and cave in: whether the Conference at Constantinople and the Turk could yet be frightened by the threat of drastic British action into sending an expedition on Anglo-French terms;[2] or whether the French would now join with Britain in protecting the Canal and putting down Arabi. On 6 July the Porte had refused the Conference's invitation to send an expedition to Egypt.[3] The government as a whole had not decided upon the invasion of Egypt, or even upon the measures necessary to protect the Canal. Most ministers had agreed to Seymour's ultimatum and the readying of troops as a Palmerstonian stroke which would avert the need for a military invasion. But, whatever their intention, they had left that question to be decided by the outcome at Alexandria.

The Admiral added to the confusion by exceeding his orders. He demanded the 'surrender' of the Egyptian forts instead of the stoppage of work on them. Gladstone told Granville: 'The Admiral's telegram is bad but I am at a loss to understand the meaning of the word "surrendered". What title can he have to demand the surrender of any forts? And this without instructions.'[4] Nevertheless the rest of the Cabinet did nothing to stop Seymour. The ultimatum expired, and the fleet bombarded the forts on 11 July. On hearing the news, several ministers expected the Arabists to break under the blow. Granville declared: 'It is well for a country whose strength is maritime, that naval demonstrations should not be thought to be absolutely without a sting.'[5] The Foreign Secretary was still living in the age of Palmerston.

[1] Dilke, *Political Diary*, B.M. Add. MSS. 43935.
[2] French Ambassador in Constantinople to Freycinet, 9 Jul. 1882, *D.D.F.*, IV, no. 436, p. 141, f.n. 1.
[3] French Minister to Bucharest to Freycinet, 7 Jul. 1882, *ibid.*, no. 431.
[4] Gladstone to Granville, 9 July. 1882, P.R.O. 30/29/126.
[5] Granville to Ampthill, 12 Jul. 1882, Fitzmaurice, *op. cit.*, II, 267.

He thought that the bombardment had 'greatly simplified the position. . . . It is possible that matters may be settled by the accomplished fact of yesterday'.[1]

But Seymour's cannonade only fanned the Egyptian blaze. It strengthened the Arabists' hold on the country. Anti-European riots spread from Alexandria to the interior, and Arabi proclaimed a holy war on the British.[2] The Khedive himself fled to Alexandria and placed himself under the protection of the fleet. His officials were driven from their posts in the Canal towns and replaced by Arabi's colonels. Bright's worst fears of the effect of the bombardment had been realised. European life and property were in peril everywhere in Egypt; the Canal seemed in immediate danger; and the military revolution was complete. On 20 July ministers heard that 'Arabi had turned the salt water from the Lake into the great fresh-water canal'.[3] de Lesseps himself, who had hitherto trusted the Arabists not to touch the Canal, appealed to his government on 19 July to protect it,[4] for Arabi had warned him that he would destroy the Canal in the defence of Egypt.[5] Neither the British nor the French doubted any longer that the Canal was in real and immediate danger. This danger was to complete the conversion of the Liberal Cabinet from naval and diplomatic bluffing to urgent and direct action, with or without the Powers.

Hartington once again took the lead. He proposed to ask the Powers to authorise sole British intervention, even at the cost of giving up any pretence of special alliance with France.[6] The struggle between Gladstone and the moderates on the one hand, and Hartington and the forward party on the other, went on. But the Prime Minister insisted upon action through the alliance and the Conference, and his view prevailed. He told Granville: 'I think you will probably still wish to work with the French but to avoid the danger of seeming to ask the Conference for a monopoly or privilege.'[7] On 13 July the British once more invited the French to take joint measures to protect the Canal and Freycinet accepted.[8] Granville was relieved at this revival of co-operation, which would he thought prove 'an immense national advantage, and ought to relieve us from many dangers'.[9] On 19 July

[1] Granville to Queen Victoria, 12 Jul. 1882, *Q.V.L.*, 2nd ser., III, 309.
[2] The text is given in C. 3391, P.P. (1882) LXXXIII, 184–5.
[3] Dilke, *Memoir*, Gwynn and Tuckwell, *op. cit.*, I, 472.
[4] French Actg. Consul-General to Freycinet, 19 Jul. 1882, *D.D.F.*, IV, no. 458.
[5] C. Beatty, *Ferdinand de Lesseps*, (1956), 276; Hallberg, *op. cit.*, 266.
[6] Hartington to Granville, 12 Jul. 1882, P.R.O. 30/29/132.
[7] Gladstone to Granville, 14 Jul. 1882, P.R.O. 30/29/126.
[8] For these negotiations see *D.D.F.*, IV, p. 424, f.n. 1 and 2; p. 425, f.n. 1–3; and no. 453.
[9] Granville to Lyons, 19 Jul. 1882, Newton, *op. cit.*, II, 289.

France and Britain formally applied to the Conference for authority to take joint measures for the defence of the Suez Canal.[1] They sent an ultimatum to the Porte, that if it did not send troops on the Powers' conditions within twelve hours, other Powers would be invited to intervene at once.[2] It looked as though events in Egypt had driven the British at last to accept the Anglo-French intervention which they had hitherto tried to avoid.

But at this critical moment the British Cabinet was riven by Irish no less than by Egyptian disputes; and once more its fall seemed imminent. Although all ministers, except Gladstone, now agreed upon the need for acting, they disagreed about how far they should go. Gladstone and Harcourt were 'peace men' as Bright had called them.[3] If they had to act at all, they wanted to go no further than a naval police action with France to protect the Canal zone.[4] Northbrook at the Admiralty also agreed at first that the Navy alone could do all that was needed. Hartington, Chamberlain and Dilke on the other hand, particularly after Arabi's proclamation calling upon Moslems throughout the Orient to rise against the British, insisted upon putting down the Egyptian revolt once and for all, as well as upon safeguarding the Canal. There could be no safe road to the East, the forward party declared, as long as anarchy reigned in Cairo. 'The question', Hartington wrote on 18 July, 'is no longer what form of intervention is on general grounds most unobjectionable, but in what form it can be most promptly applied.' We should act with anyone who will act with us; and if need be, alone.[5] The forward party therefore demanded the despatch of a large British military expedition to go to Cairo, to put down Arabi and restore the Khedive.

The 'row' in the Cabinet, as Dilke called it,[6] came to a head between 18 and 22 July amid the utmost confusion. Bright who had been on the point of resigning ever since the bombardment of Alexandria now left the government. Most of the remaining ministers were raining threats of resignation upon each other, if not over Egypt, then over Ireland. Gladstone and the Radicals were at daggers drawn with Hartington and the Whigs over the Irish Arrears and Crimes Bills. Between 7 and 20 July indeed, the Prime Minister was threatening to retire to the Lords.[7]

[1] French Ambassador at Constantinople to Freycinet, 19 Jul. 1882, *D.D.F.*, IV, no. 460.

[2] British Ambassador in Paris to Freycinet, 19 Jul. 1882, *D.D.F.*, IV, no. 462.

[3] G. M. Trevelyan, *The Life of John Bright*, (1913), 435.

[4] Gladstone to Granville, 16 Jul. 1882, P.R.O. 30/29/126.

[5] Hartington to Granville, 18 Jul. 1882, P.R.O. 30/29/132.

[6] Dilke's *Political Diary*, 22 Jul. 1882, B.M. Add. MSS. 43935.

[7] Dilke, *Memoir*, Gwynn and Tuckwell, *op. cit.*, I, 471–2, 446–7.

Chamberlain and Dilke believed that Hartington might soon be Prime Minister, and after thinking of going out with Gladstone, they actually discussed their terms for serving under Hartington.[1] At the time of decision in Egypt, Gladstone's influence with his colleagues was waning and Hartington's rising, so that the Irish question worked for the moment in favour of the war party. Northbrook now supported Hartington's demand for an expedition to Cairo; and next, Granville himself who had been trimming industriously between the two factions, went over to the forward party.[2] Hitherto, he had dreaded the thought of an Anglo-French expedition to Cairo, because it would mean giving the French a half share in the occupation of the route to India.[3] But by 20 July it seemed unlikely that Freycinet could find enough support in the French Chamber to send a force to Cairo, although he had agreed to share in protecting the Canal. The Cabinet therefore now felt reasonably sure, though by no means certain, of 'a qualified partnership with France',[4] if they decided to go to Cairo on their own. This assurance was important, because it seemed to mean both that the Liberal alliance would survive a British intervention, and that Britain would have the major, and France the minor share in making the Egyptian settlement.

In these circumstances the forward party got their way at the Cabinet on 20 July, with Gladstone protesting impotently. It was decided to send an expeditionary force under Sir Garnet Wolseley to Cyprus and Malta, where it would be ready 'for operations in any part of Egypt'.[5] The size of the force moreover showed that the Government was determined to pacify Egypt, and to do it alone, if need be. Two days later Hartington was asking how long the occupation of Egypt would last, in order to prepare his estimates for Indian troops. Nobody knew the answer.[6] The Cabinet also decided to ask the House of Commons for a vote for these 'large proceedings' in Egypt.[7] But the Prime Minister at least still regarded single-handed British action as a last resort, as he wrote to Granville:

> 'I do not think I can travel quite at the pace you propose. I am far from asking you to exclude sole action, and will say nothing myself in that direction but viewing the probabilities of the case, as well as what one ought to desire, namely the exhaustion of every effort to procure collective or joint action, I think it would be highly proper, even for those who can

[1] *ibid.*, I, 446–7. [2] Trevelyan, *op. cit.*, 435.

[3] Granville to Lyons, 19 Jul. 1882, Newton, *op. cit.*, II, 289.

[4] Gladstone to Granville, 13 and 23 Jul. 1882, P.R.O. 30/29/126.

[5] Childers to the Queen, 20 Jul. 1882, Spencer Childers, *The Life . . . of Hugh C. E. Childers*, (1901), II, 96–7.

[6] Hartington and Duke of Cambridge to Granville, 22 Jul. 1882, P.R.O. 30/29/132.

[7] Hartington to Granville, 22 Jul. 1882, *ibid.*

so distinctly contemplate acting alone in case of need, at this moment to intimate a contingent decision of which the conditions are still remote.

'The nearest point to you which I could reach would be to say that after the exhaustion as above, we should not be deterred by any apprehension as to the magnitude of the enterprise, or the amount of force required, if the way be clear in point of principle.'[1]

At Gladstone's insistence, the British in the weeks before intervening in Egypt tried desperately to associate the Powers with their projected action. It had proved impossible to obtain a formal mandate from the Conference at Constantinople, largely because of the German and Turkish attitudes. Therefore from a diplomatic point of view, partnership with France was all the more important. The two governments informed the Conference at Constantinople that since none of the Powers had dissented, they would protect the Canal by themselves or with any other Power willing to take part.[2] The British government invited France and Italy to join in immediate action to put down the Egyptian revolt, and to decide with Britain the proper division of labour.[3] But Freycinet on 23 July made it clear that while the French would co-operate in protecting the Canal, they would not share an invasion of the interior of Egypt.[4] But 'a qualified partnership with France' still seemed assured.[5] Having obtained Germany's moral support,[6] the two Powers agreed to occupy the Canal zone together, the French to take Port Said and Kantara, and the British, Ismailia and Suez.[7] Both partners '. . . disclaimed any intention of seeking any territorial or other advantages which any other nation should not be able to obtain'.[8] There was a streak of opportunism in the British pressing their invasion forward, when it was known that the French government was tottering and could not share fully in the movement. But they had certainly exhausted 'every effort to procure collective or joint action', and for Gladstone the way had been cleared 'in point of principle.' They had come this far with French diplomatic support; now it remained to be seen whether France would act to preserve her parity in Egypt.

On 24 July, the government asked the Commons for £2,300,000 to

[1] Gladstone to Granville, 22 Jul. 1882, P.R.O. 30/29/126.
[2] Note of the British Ambassador, 22 Jul. 1882, *D.D.F.*, IV, no. 469.
[3] Gladstone, Cabinet Memo., 22 Jul. 1882, P.R.O. 30/29/126.
[4] Freycinet to French *chargé d'affaires* in London, 23 Jul. 1882, *D.D.F.*, IV, no. 470.
[5] Gladstone to Granville, 23 and 25 Jul. 1882, P.R.O. 30/29/126.
[6] Note du Département, 24 Jul. 1882, *D.D.F.*, IV, no. 472.
[7] Freycinet to the French Agent in Egypt, 26 Jul. 1882, *ibid.*, no. 476; Lyons to Freycinet, 26 Jul. 1882, *ibid.*, no. 478.
[8] Draft Protocol, enclosed in *idem*.

pay for the expedition. The Prime Minister proposed to meet the bill by increasing income tax by three-half-pence. It was one of the rare occasions when Gladstone set aside his financial canons in favour of a foreign adventure and shows the supreme importance which a restoration of order in Egypt had now assumed. He had always held that British sea supremacy was enough to secure the Canal,[1] as long as it remained unfortified, so that territorial control of the zone seemed dangerous and unnecessary. But Gladstone now assured the Commons that a British expedition was the last hope of protecting the Suez Canal. There is little doubt that his public explanation reflected the private motives of his colleagues. He explained that '. . . the insecurity of the Canal, it is plain, does not exhibit to us the seat of the disease. The insecurity of the Canal is a symptom only, and the seat of the disease is in the interior of Egypt, in its disturbed and its anarchical condition'. Therefore, the Prime Minister declared, Britain must substitute the rule of law for that of military violence in Egypt, in partnership with other Powers if possible; but alone, if necessary.[2] Another minister, Dilke, stressed the supreme Imperial interest in Egypt. 'As regards the Suez Canal,' he told the House of Commons,

> 'England has a double interest; it has a predominant commercial interest, because 82 per cent of the trade passing through the Canal is British trade, and it has a predominant political interest caused by the fact that the Canal is the principal highway to India, Ceylon, the Straits, and British Burmah, where 250,000,000 people live under our rule; and also to China, where we have vast interests and 84 per cent of the external trade of that still more enormous Empire. It is also one of the roads to our Colonial Empire in Australia and New Zealand.'[3]

Hartington, Chamberlain and the other ministers faithfully repeated these arguments for suppressing Arabi and protecting the Canal. The vote was carried by 275 to 19, and Gladstone reported to the Queen that '. . . the entire House, with infinitesimal exception, recognises the necessity and justice of the steps now about to be taken'.[4]

This widespread support was all the more remarkable in a House which had been elected amid the thunderings against jingoism in Lancashire and Midlothian. But the votes for intervention were cast for many contradictory reasons, and conflicting purposes underlay the apparent unanimity. The British bondholders, as would be expected,

[1] Gladstone to Granville, 13 Nov. 1870, Fitzmaurice, *op. cit.*, II, 252.
[2] *Hansard*, 3rd ser., CCLXXII, cols. 1586–90, 24 Jul. 1882.
[3] *Hansard*, 3rd ser., CCLXXII, col. 1720, 25 Jul. 1882.
[4] Gladstone to Queen Victoria, 27–28 Jul. 1882, *Q.V.L.*, 2nd ser., III, 314.

warmly supported intervention, and Goschen spoke strongly in this sense.[1] But their favour was a liability rather than an asset to the government, since the Radicals and many Liberal supporters suspected their leaders of fighting a 'bondholders' war'.[2] Intervention however now had the support of far more powerful interests than Egypt's creditors. The shipping and the great Eastern trade interests which depended on the Canal called for action. Dilke had already noted on 7 July that the shipping magnates were in the 'Jingo Gang'.[3] Chambers of Commerce and shipping associations throughout Britain were pressing the government to protect the Canal.[4] Yet it was not the pressure of these interested parties which converted the many Cobdenites in the Liberal majority to an invasion of Egypt. It took all the authority of Gladstone and the Radical leaders to set the liberal conscience at ease. The Prime Minister's speech was a masterly appeal to Liberal sentiment, presenting intervention as the only hope for peace and progress in Egypt.

> '... When ... a reign of law is substituted for that of military violence, something may be founded there which may give hope ... for free institutions ... even in a Mohammedan people ... a noble thirst may arise for the attainment of those blessings of civilized life which they see have been achieved in so many countries in Europe.'[5]

Gladstone also expressed the general indignation against the 'atrocities' committed upon European life and property in Egypt, and his attacks on Arabi[6] revived something of the religious fury which he had fanned when the Turks were slaughtering Bulgarian Christians. In this way he swayed the humanitarian and nonconformist conscience of Victorian liberalism into accepting a policy of aggression. As Northcote, the leader of the Opposition, complained, 'the Government are attempting to make war upon peace principles, and such an attempt must always fail.'[7] Such liberal doubts as remained, Gladstone and his ministers quietened with assurances that intervention would promote Egyptian independence. They led the House to believe that intervention would be short; it would result in a quick settlement and an early withdrawal, leaving the Egyptians 'to manage their own affairs' [8] Their case was the more convincing because the Cabinet sincerely believed this forecast.

[1] *Hansard*, 3rd ser., CCLXXII, cols. 1872–89. [2] e.g. *ibid.*, col. 1777.
[3] Dilke Political Diary, 7 Jul. 1882, B.M. Add. MSS. 43935.
[4] French Ambassador to Freycinet, 14 Jul. 1882, *D.D.F.*, IV, no. 449.
[5] *Hansard*, 3rd ser., CCLXXII, col. 1590, 24 Jul. 1882.
[6] Dilke *Memoir*, Gwynn and Tuckwell, *op. cit.*, I, 468–9.
[7] A. Lang, *Life ... of Sir Stafford Northcote*, (1891), 348.
[8] *Hansard*, 3rd ser., CCLXXII, col. 1711–12, *et seq.*

In the end, only the reputations of Gladstone and his Radical colleagues as bitter opponents of jingoism united their Party in favour of the expedition. The Conservatives supported it 'on the ground of national interests',[1] but for many Liberals it took all the prestige of Gladstone himself to bring them to look upon the intervention as an inescapable police action and not another imperialist adventure.[2] The French Chamber's attitude was very different.

On 29 July Freycinet's ministry was overwhelmingly defeated when it asked for a vote of credit for the expedition to the Canal. He had asked for only one-sixth of the sum which Gladstone obtained from the Commons: yet the majority in the French Chamber against intervention was almost as heavy as the majority in favour of it at Westminster. Gladstone's success and Freycinet's failure showed the difference between the British and the French outlook on Egypt and the Canal. Commercially and strategically, the waterway was important to so many British interests that its safety was generally accepted as a vital national concern. For the French, on the other hand, Arabi's revolt did not seem a serious danger to national security. Indeed, a great many deputies voted against an Egyptian expedition because it would deflect attention from the Rhine. Arabi's revolution threatened directly only the French bondholders' interest. As Freycinet admitted afterwards: 'We can admit today that the financial question had too much influence over our diplomatic policy.'[3] Anxious as the French government was to restore financial control and to go hand in hand with Britain in order to prevent her from gaining an exclusive influence in Cairo, the *rentiers* by themselves failed to rally broad and popular support for the policy. Duclerc's 'sea-side ministry' which followed Freycinet's, had to withdraw from the joint plan to protect the Canal and could do nothing further in Egypt. On the same day that Freycinet fell, the Italians refused to join the British in their Egyptian enterprise. At the last minute the Sultan attempted to intervene. The British warned him off. The accidents of French domestic politics and of European diplomacy had thwarted all the British schemes for international action, and for associating France with it. Gladstone's ministry, relieved perhaps that they had at last struggled through to a decision and assuring themselves that they had done everything possible to share the venture with the Powers and with France, felt surprised and even pleased at the outcome.[4] Their consciences were clear.

[1] Lang, *op. cit.*, 348–9.
[2] Chamberlain's Cabinet Minute of 18 Oct. 1882, Chamberlain, *op. cit.*, 74.
[3] C. de Freycinet, *Souvenirs, 1878–1893*, (Paris, 1914), 216.
[4] Gladstone to Granville, 2 Aug. 1882, P.R.O. 30/29/126.

So they were left with the field to themselves: and on 29 July Wolseley was ordered to seize Ismailia, assure the fresh water supply for the Canal towns and then to crush Arabi's army in the interior. The first objective was to safeguard the Canal.[1] The expedition landed on 16 August 1882, and having built up his forces, Wolseley utterly broke the Egyptian army at Tel el Kebir on 13 September. With Arabi a prisoner and British garrisons in Cairo and Alexandria, Gladstone's ministry found itself in control of the country.

This single-handed conquest of Egypt was plainly the outcome which the British Liberals had intended above all to avert, at least until the later days of July. They had not wanted to saddle themselves with a bankrupt country or to strain the French *entente* or to give hostages to Europe. They had no long-term plan to occupy Egypt and saw no strategic need to do so. They had muddled and drifted with events. Each fateful step seemed to be dictated by circumstances rather than will. Each decision snatched out of disagreement between ministers and with the French, was a makeshift on which they could all go on together, rather than a move in a premeditated direction. As Granville recalled later: 'The misfortune . . . had been that we hardly ever had anything but bad alternatives to choose from. The objectors to whatever was decided were pretty sure to have the best of it.'[2] The many-sided Irish tensions in the Cabinet coinciding with the strains of Egypt were partly responsible. But the root of the confusion went deeper; the British fell into Egypt between the two stools of their liberal conscience and their national security. Gladstone had stood upon the one, Hartington in the end, upon the other.

The nationalist revolution in Egypt had indeed taken the Liberals' half-formed system unawares at an unprotected point. The French proved more of a handicap than a help in controlling the crisis and averting intervention; for in keeping up with their ally, the Liberals were dragged a long way towards armed aggression. They had relied upon the *entente* as a source of strength and a sanction of peace. But it turned out to be a dangerous flaw in their security. The Concert of the Powers, manipulated by Bismarck, likewise proved illusory. In their extremity, Gladstone and Granville turned to the Sultan to deliver them from French belligerence and the necessity of direct intervention, only to find Bismarck occupying Britain's old position of influence at Constantinople which they themselves had scorned.

It was Gambetta and the forward party in France who initiated the

[1] Granville to Spencer, 18 Aug. 1882, Fitzmaurice, *op. cit.*, II, 272.
[2] Granville to Baring, 18 Apr. 1884, Cromer, *op. cit.*, (1908), I, 499.

Anglo-French policy of swagger and bluff against the Egyptian national movement. But it was Hartington and the British forward party which insisted at last on implementing the threats. The Egyptian revolution showed that Gladstone's and Granville's system for guarding Egypt was a rope of sand. With the Canal in immediate danger from the anarchy in Egypt, Hartington and the Whig realists were able to take charge of policy. When, as they considered, the vital imperial interest was at stake and British prestige shaken throughout the Orient, they did not hesitate to exert force to recover both. It was not until the last minute that a streak of opportunism entered into the Cabinet's motives. Not until the expedition had become necessary to protect the Canal did most ministers console themselves with the notion that for all their blunders, they had by chance got themselves into a position to steal a march on the French in Cairo. Wolseley's expedition was sent under the necessity imposed by events in Egypt. To seize supremacy does not seem to have been the original or the decisive reason for the invasion. It was something of an after-thought. Ministers, strangely enough, gave no serious thought to what advantages Britain should claim in Egypt, until after Wolseley's force had set out. Their thinking, on paper at least, had got no further than their old aim of restoring the Khedive, withdrawing the troops and getting back to the old system of 'moral influence' without direct responsibility. The final British intervention in Egypt rested upon this same false premise, this same misunderstanding of the Egyptian problem, as her earlier interferences. Gladstone and most of his colleagues did not think of themselves as occupying Egypt when they decided upon the invasion. Their deliberate intention was to intervene and withdraw, and the plans they laid after Wolseley's victory at Tel el Kebir were still all in this sense.

CHAPTER V

Gladstone's Bondage in Egypt

The victory of Tel el Kebir encouraged British opportunism. Ministers still intended to withdraw quickly from Egypt; but they now resolved to make British influence supreme in Cairo before they left.

On 10 August the Prime Minister '. . . adverted to it as a possibility that the time might be close at hand when . . . we might . . . set forth the character, intentions and limits of our action in Egypt'.[1] Two days after Tel el Kebir, he drew a plan which he felt represented the views of the rest of the Cabinet. They would bring the leaders of the military rebellion to trial, restore the Khedive, train and equip him with a loyal army, and, as soon as he was strong enough to keep order and deal with any further Arabis, they would withdraw their troops from the country.[2] None of the government wanted to turn Egypt into a British protectorate.[3] Gladstone wanted instead: 'The withdrawal of the foreign occupation as early as possible. This will be regulated exclusively, and from point to point by the consideration of security for life and property.'[4]

Gladstone's further proposals however qualified this principle of withdrawal. Before coming away, Egypt was to be brought under informal British 'suzerainty', French influence was to be ousted and the old Dual Financial Control abolished. Institutions of Egyptian self-government were to be developed under British auspices. Then the Powers would be asked to guarantee the independence of Egypt for the future and to 'neutralise' the country on Belgian lines.[5] The Prime Minister inquired whether the Canal should also be neutralised. '. . . If and when the military matter is well over, our position in Egypt,' Gladstone expected, 'will "naturally" be something like that which

[1] Gladstone to Granville, 10 Aug. 1882, P.R.O. 30/29/126.
[2] Gladstone to Granville, 15 Sept. 1882, P.R.O. 30/29/126.
[3] Dilke, *Memoir*, Gwynn and Tuckwell, *op. cit.*, I, 544.
[4] Gladstone to Granville, 15 Sept. 1882, P.R.O. 30/29/126.
[5] *idem.*

Russia now has in Bulgaria, not the result of stipulation, but of effort and sacrifice crowned by success.'[1]

The Government framed its policy on these lines. Granville wrote: '. . . The three objects should be not to throw away the advantages we have gained, to avoid any just accusation of having abandoned our pledges, and to enlist the sympathies of the Egyptians with us and not against us. . . .'[2] The Queen herself impressed upon her ministers '. . . the absolute necessity . . . of . . . securing to ourselves such a position in Egypt as to secure our Indian Dominions and to maintain our superiority in the East. . . .'[3]

'The great question of British interest [was]', as Gladstone declared, 'the Canal, and this turns upon neutralization, aye or no.'[4] Anxiety for its safety had moved the British to go into Egypt while the French had hung back. So now to guard the Canal for the Empire more certainly in the future became the over-riding object. Gladstone's ministry therefore decided to demand guarantees for the 'free navigation', not the neutralization, of the Canal from the Powers[5] and a larger share in its management from France.[6] The intention was to make certain that British war ships should be free to use the Canal in peace and war.[7] It was also to make sure of the Canal that the Liberals wanted sway in Cairo over a stable Khedivate. The Anglo-Indian official mind prevailed, and Northbrook stated its view: 'As long as India remains under British rule the interests of England and of India . . . go far beyond the traffic in the Canal, for [they] demand that no other nation should be allowed to dominate Egypt.'[8]

For this purpose, the British decided to seize their chance and scrap the Dual Financial Control. The system whereby a British and a French official jointly supervised the Egyptian finance departments seemed to Gladstone anathema. He wanted to get rid of '. . . the kind of responsibility for advising and therefore supporting the Khedive with which we found ourselves saddled under Salisbury's arrangements'.[9] What was more, the whole Cabinet by this time agreed upon abolishing the Control, whether or not it meant the end of the Anglo-French

[1] *idem*; and Gladstone to Granville, 9 Sept. 1882, *ibid.*
[2] Granville to Harcourt, 18 Sept. 1882, Gardiner, *op. cit.*, I, 460.
[3] Queen Victoria to Harcourt, 22 Sept. 1882, *ibid.*
[4] Gladstone to Harcourt, 17 Sept. 1882, *ibid.*, I, 459.
[5] Cabinet Opinions, Sept.–Dec. 1882, P.R.O. 30/29/143.
[6] Dilke, *Political Diary*, 14 Nov. 1882, B.M. Add MSS. 43935.
[7] Childers to Gladstone, 19 Sept. 1882, Childers, *op. cit.*, II, 132–3.
[8] Northbrook to Baring, 27 Sept. 1882, B. Mallet, *Thomas George, Earl of Northbrook*, (1908), 170.
[9] Gladstone to Granville, 21 Sept. 1882, P.R.O. 30/29/126.

entente.[1] As Malet put it bluntly, to get rid of the old Egyptian dualism was the best way of 'consolidating a permanent influence for Britain' and 'breaking the co-equal power' of France.[2]

The Cabinet resolved lastly to create a stable, self-governing Egypt. An early evacuation of the country would be impossible without it; and concessions to Egyptian aspirations for independence would help to establish a pro-British Khedive and ministry in power and perpetuate British influence after the withdrawal. 'We have now reached a point', Gladstone declared, 'at which . . . the choice lies between *more* intervention and less, and the question is fairly raised whether we are to try and prepare Egypt for a self-governing future. I believe our choice has been made.'[3] The Prime Minister realised that if Egyptian self-government was delayed, Britain would be drawn into administering the country.

There were other reasons why most ministers were anxious to withdraw from Egypt quickly. Their followers were restive at the rising cost of the Egyptian garrison.[4] Radicals and Liberals alike increasingly suspected the motives behind the invasion and pressed the government to fulfil its promise of independence for the Egyptians. Chamberlain and Dilke reported to their colleagues: 'There is great anxiety lest after all the Bondholders should too evidently be the only persons who have profited by the war.'[5] The dissatisfied Radicals, represented by Harcourt, asserted: 'There . . . was a general desire [in the country to] come away as quickly as possible' and doubt 'whether we ought ever to have gone.'[6] Gladstone and Granville also wanted 'to get out of it as soon as we could properly do so'.[7] As Chamberlain recalled later: '. . . In the early stage of our occupation we were all desirous of a speedy evacuation and believed that the conditions which we had laid down would be accomplished in the course of a year or two at the outside.'[8] Already in September 1882, the government was making out a timetable for retiring the British forces from Egypt;[9] and a month later it ordered the withdrawal of the main body to begin, leaving a small garrison to support Tewfik until his own army was trained.[10] As yet the Liberals did not suspect that they had 'occupied' Egypt. They still genuinely believed that they had merely 'intervened'.

[1] Tissot to Duclerc, 4 Nov. 1882, *D.D.F.*, IV, no. 555.
[2] Malet to Granville, (circulated to the Cabinet), 3 Sept. 1882, P.R.O. 30/29/160.
[3] Gladstone to Granville, 16 Sept. 1882, P.R.O. 30/29/126.
[4] Gladstone to Queen Victoria, 30 Sept. 1882, *Q.V.L.*, 2nd ser., III, 345.
[5] Chamberlain, Minute, 18 Oct. 1882, Chamberlain, *op. cit.*, 75.
[6] *ibid.*, 81.
[7] Granville to Gladstone, 29 Nov. 1882, Fitzmaurice, *op. cit.*, II, 303.
[8] Chamberlain, *op. cit.*, 81.
[9] Gladstone to Childers, 22 Sept. 1882, P.R.O. 30/29/126.
[10] Childers to Gladstone, 22 Oct. 1882, *ibid.*

The men of conscience and the exponents of *Realpolitik* in Gladstone's ministry could all agree to these broad Egyptian aims. At first the objects of an independent yet stable Egypt under British supremacy seemed entirely compatible with those of withdrawing quickly, of reconciling France, and of obtaining an international settlement. There appeared to be no invincible difficulty about combining Egyptian self-government with guarantees that Egypt would fulfil her financial obligations. If all these aims could be achieved together within the space of a year or two, the Liberals would have collected the fruits of opportunism without violating their principles. But when they discussed how all these things were to be done in detail, ministers began to discover that their plans for Egypt were riddled with paradoxes. Some of their aims might have to be subordinated to others; and in making the choice, the Liberal sheep parted once more from the Whig goats. They remained agreed on setting up a supremacy of influence at Cairo to guard the Canal; but they were divided about how to do it. They were still determined to get rid of the Dual Financial Control, but could not agree upon what to put in its place. They all wanted to promote Egyptian self-government, yet differed upon the extent to which it was safe. And in the end, those who would have given up some of their opportunities in Egypt to get out of the country were separated from those who would stay and make full use of them.

The Radicals were preaching 'Egypt for the Egyptians'. Dilke favoured Labouchere's idea: '. . . We should warn off other Powers, hand Egypt over to the Egyptians but, establishing our own influence over the Canal, remain masters of the position so far as we needed to do so.'[1] Chamberlain proposed to hand over to the Egyptian Chamber of Representatives the financial powers exercised hitherto by the Foreign Controllers. He would have left the bondholders to fend for themselves, although he admitted, 'the difficulty . . . of conciliating the natural intentions and wishes of English Liberalism with the privileges claimed by the other European Powers and especially by France.' The gratitude of Egypt for this relief from servitude to foreign creditors, Chamberlain argued, would be the best guarantee of a lasting British paramountcy.[2] Gladstone and Granville sympathised with Chamberlain's view, but they felt less optimistic, fearing that the politically immature Egyptians would provoke the Powers again, if their independence was entirely restored.[3]

[1] Dilke, *Memoir*, Gwynn and Tuckwell, *op. cit.* I, 546.

[2] Chamberlain, Cabinet Memo., 18 Oct. 1882, Chamberlain, *op. cit.*, 74–8.

[3] Gladstone to Harcourt, 17 Sept. 1882, Gardiner, *op. cit.*, I, 459; Chamberlain to Dilke, 22 Oct. 1882, Garvin, *op. cit.*, I, 452.

At the other end of the Cabinet, Hartington, Northbrook and other Whigs argued that the powers of financial control should be retained and placed in the hands of a single British controller. Unlike their colleagues, these two ministers from the beginning had made the restoring of the Control a principal aim of intervention. But they had more in mind than simply protecting the bondholders. The Whigs had little faith in experiments with liberal institutions in Oriental societies. They feared that if the Egyptian Chamber was given powers over finance, they would be used to repudiate the foreign debt, once the British had gone.[1] And this would provoke French intervention and revive the recent danger to British influence and the Canal. While the Radicals argued that liberality towards the Egyptians would contribute to the British strategic purpose, the Whigs feared that it would only defeat it. The incompatibility of the several British aims was already beginning to emerge, with the Radicals wishing to hand power over to the Egyptian Chamber, and the Whigs, to a strong Khedive under British financial control. At the Cabinet on 21 October, both sides accepted a compromise from Gladstone and Granville. The dual controllers were to be replaced by a single European Financial Adviser to the Khedive; but unlike the former controllers, the new official was to have no administrative powers over the Egyptian finance departments; nor was he to be an official representative of the British government.[2] But as Dilke observed in his Diary the adviser in effect would be 'a single English (not to be so expressed) controller (not to be so called)'.[3] There was still to be some sort of constitutional advance in Egypt, to satisfy the Radicals. But the Cabinet was content for the moment to put off the more difficult problem of striking a balance between its divergent aims. Lord Dufferin was sent to Egypt to report upon the whole Egyptian question. His instructions showed the delicate shades of opinion within the Cabinet and the paradoxes behind the Liberals' policy:

> 'Her Majesty's Government, while desiring that the British occupation should last for as short a time as possible, feel bound not to withdraw from the task thus imposed on them until the administration of affairs has been reconstructed on a basis which will afford satisfactory guarantees for the maintenance of peace, order, and prosperity in Egypt, for the stability of

[1] Dilke, *Memoir*, Gwynn and Tuckwell, *op. cit.*, I, 547.

[2] Granville to Lyons, 23 Oct. 1882, *D.D.F.*, IV, no. 548. This was not acted upon until 8 Jan. 1884: *vide* Granville to Dufferin, 28 Dec. 1882 and 8 Jan. 1883, C. 3462, P.P. (1883), LXXXIII, 34–6, 40.

[3] Dilke Diary, 21 Oct. 1882, Gwynn and Tuckwell, *op. cit.*, I, 546.

the Khedive's authority, for the judicious development of self-government, and for the fulfilment of obligations towards foreign Powers.'[1]

Granville in negotiations with Paris found at the same time that the abolition of the Dual Control in Cairo meant the end of the French alliance. Duclerc's ministry at first had taken the British conquest quietly. Indeed from some points of view they welcomed it.[2] But they bitterly resented being ousted from the old partnership in the Control;[3] and they scorned Granville's petty consolations as insults added to injury.[4] The *haute* and *petite finance* of Paris regarded the British plans for securing payment of the Egyptian debts as wholly inadequate.[5] In trying to advance Egyptian self-government, the British were pursuing one purpose at the expense of another — the reconciliation of France to their supremacy in Cairo. If France was antagonised, supremacy would in turn work against their hopes of an early withdrawal. As Lyons warned Granville from Paris: 'If we leave [the French] bitterly discontented with arrangements in Egypt, I hardly see when we shall be able to withdraw our troops and still maintain the influence which is a necessity to us.'[6] Supremacy was beginning to become inconsistent with evacuation, Egyptian self-government incompatible with reconciling France and the Powers. But while some ministers wanted to take a high tone with the French, others wanted to try and salvage the connection with Paris by giving compensations elsewhere. In Madagascar, Granville's policy of appeasing France prevailed. The Cabinet decided not to answer the islanders' appeal for help against French subjugation, and British missionary and trading interests there were sacrificed in an attempt to mollify France.

On 4 December, the government took a momentous decision. It had proved impossible to agree with the French upon the Egyptian settlement, Gladstone wrote, and the government therefore decided '. . . to bring about forthwith the execution of the [British] arrangement in Egypt itself, and to make known their proceedings to France and the Powers . . . not inviting an opinion. . . .'[7] Confident of German good will, Britain had determined to settle Egypt alone; and in ejecting the French from the Control, ruptered the *entente*.[8] In the circular note of 3

[1] Granville to Dufferin, 3 Nov. 1882, C. 3462, P.P. (1883) LXXXIII, 15.
[2] French Ambassador to Duclerc, 14 Sept. 1882, *D.D.F.*, IV, no. 525.
[3] Granville to Lyons, 23 Oct. 1882, *ibid.*, no. 548.
[4] Duclerc to French Ambassador in London, 28 Oct. 1882, *ibid.*, no. 551.
[5] Lyons to Granville, 14 Nov. 1882, Newton, *op. cit.*, II, 229.
[6] *idem.*
[7] Gladstone to Queen Victoria, 4 Dec. 1882, *Q.V.L.*, 2nd ser., III, 366–7.
[8] Duclerc to French Ambassador in London, 28 Oct. and 13 Dec. 1882, *D.D.F.*, IV, nos. 551 and 576; Lyons to Granville, 2 Feb. 1883, Newton, *op. cit.*, II, 309–11.

January 1883, Britain stated to the Powers her terms for leaving Egypt. She claimed the paramount position in Egypt and asked Europe to guarantee free navigation in the Canal. The Liberal government served notice in effect that they would retire as soon as this position had been established and recognised by the Powers.[1]

On 6 February, Lord Dufferin, the Whig diplomatist,[2] reported to the ministry upon Egypt. With Granville as his prompter, he dressed up a middle plan between liberal idealism and Whig realism. Echoing the Cabinet's reasons for getting out of Egypt quickly, he wrote:

> 'The Valley of the Nile could not be administered with any . . . success from London. . . . [It] would at once render us objects of hatred and suspicion to its inhabitants. Cairo would become a focus of foreign intrigue . . . against us, and we should soon find ourselves forced either to abandon our pretentions under discreditable conditions, or to embark upon the experiment of a complete acquisition of the country.'[3]

Dufferin's job was to chart a quick way back from occupation to the traditional system of 'moral influence'; and on paper at least he found it.

He proposed to strengthen the Khedivate and gain Egyptian friendship by giving the *fellaheen* their first taste of efficient and honest administration and prosperity. Dufferin's plans for the wholesale reform of land tenure, irrigation, taxation and education, and of all the departments of government, were on the best Indian lines. British officials were to supervise their execution. A beginning was to be made with representative government, which would satisfy liberals at Home, reconcile Egyptian nationalists and bring a class of pro-British pashas to power. But the envoy could not recommend much delegation of authority to an elected Egyptian Assembly. Too many of its members might become French or Turkish tools and work against British influence.[4] Such risks were not taken even in India, where the imperial position was much stronger.[5] Nor could the Assembly be given enough powers to endanger the debt payment, and so provoke another foreign intervention. To begin with, the Legislative Council was to be merely advisory, and the Assembly mainly a consulting body,[6] although many of its members were to be elected, and it was to be given a veto over

[1] Granville, Circular, 3 Jan. 1883, C. 3462, P.P. (1883) LXXXIII, 38–40; *D.D.F.* IV, no. 592.
[2] Sir Alfred Lyall, *Life of . . . Dufferin*, (1905).
[3] Dufferin to Granville, 6 Feb. 1883, C. 3529, P.P. (1883) LXXXIII, 89.
[4] Dilke, *Memoir*, Gwynn and Tuckwell, *op. cit.*, I, 551.
[5] Dufferin to Dilke, Dec. 1882, *ibid.*; Dufferin to Granville, 6 Feb. 1883, C. 3529, P.P. (1883) LXXXIII, 95–6.
[6] *ibid.*

new taxes. The British stake was too high, and international claims upon Egypt too heavy to carry out liberal intentions any further.

Power for the time being was to remain in the hands of the Khedive and his Council of State. He was to be equipped with new forces, trained and commanded mostly by British officers. And so, with British leaders at the head of the administrative and military departments, with the collaboration of the Khedive, the 'liberal' pashas and a peasantry grateful for release from injustice and crushing taxation, Egyptians were expected to co-operate with British purposes without the dictation of direct control. In Dufferin's nice phrase, he was 'enabling [the Egyptians] to govern themselves, under the uncompromising aegis of our friendship.'[1]

There were, he admitted, difficulties. The finances were overburdened. Out of a total revenue of eight and a half million pounds, almost forty-four per cent went to Egypt's creditors.[2] The Egyptians would need another large loan to pay indemnities for the Alexandria massacres and the cost of the British occupation. These contingencies apart, Dufferin expected that '. . . by the close of 1884 the Egyptian finances will have recovered their normal state'.[3] On this slender thread of revenue hung the Liberals' plan for a stable government, a contented pro-British Egypt and a satisfied Europe. Again, Dufferin pointed out the danger of a conservative reaction against the progressive pashas. 'It is absolutely necessary to prevent the fabric we have raised from tumbling to the ground the moment our sustaining hand is withdrawn,' he insisted.[4] There remained the problem of making sure 'that no subversive [foreign] influence will intervene between England and the Egypt she has re-created'.[5]

Dufferin had recommended stability before liberty, administrative reform in preparation for constitutional advance. It was a scheme for implanting British influence more radical than Palmerston's plans for regenerating Turkey. Where he had relied on free trade and private enterprise to reform the 'Orient', it was clear by the Eighteen eighties that commerce and ideas alone were not enough. Success in India had shown what could be done through administration; hence Dufferin's method was administrative rather than commercial. But it was to be an Anglo-Egyptian administration without annexation or military occupation. As soon as the Khedive's new army and police were trained, the British garrison was to leave the country; and although no definite date was set, Duffering implied that the military occupation could be safely

[1] *ibid.*, 89. [2] *ibid.*, 128. [3] *ibid.*, 127. [4] *ibid.*, 129. [5] *ibid.*, 130.

ended within a year or two.[1] Gladstone's ministry were delighted with his proposals and hastened to put them into effect. They were assured that with administrative reform begun, they could safely transfer responsibility to the Khedive. They would soon be able to evacuate Egypt, as they had Afghanistan and the Transvaal.

The government throughout 1883 intended to extricate itself from the Nile. Occupation was so distasteful to liberal opinion in the country that, according to Chamberlain, Bright could have broken the government if he had chosen to attack it. The garrison on the Nile was a heavy drain on the Exchequer and on Egyptian revenues. Liberal consciences in the Commons were troubled so that the government's majority upon the Egyptian question dropped to thirty-five in February, even though ministers promised Parliament a speedy withdrawal.[2] They were pledged to the Powers to do so. Moreover, Cherif Pasha, the Khedive's chief minister, wanted the British troops to retire from Cairo, in order to increase his popularity.[3] On 9 August, 1883, the government announced that after November the garrison would withdraw to Alexandria,[4] and it decided to reduce this force to about 3,000 men.[5] 'The Cabinet', Granville told Sir Evelyn Baring, who was by now in charge at Cairo as Consul-General, 'is anxious that this should be done. . . .'[6]; while Northbrook added that '. . . the main question for us is, how soon our troops can safely leave Cairo'.[7] The projected retirement to Alexandria implied that the Khedive was to rule once more. Thenceforward, Granville instructed Baring: '. . . the main responsibility for preserving order throughout Egypt will . . . devolve upon the Government of the Khedive . . . [although] they may rely upon the full moral support of Her Majesty's Government.'[8]

For Gladstone, Granville and most of the Cabinet, the retirement to Alexandria was the first step toward complete evacuation. They were so anxious to extricate themselves that they would take risks for this purpose. But there were others who refused to gamble on complete evacuation until Britain had made certain of the rewards of intervention. The Queen and Hartington, on advice from Baring in Cairo, approved the retirement to Alexandria, but only as a tactical move. The rest of the

[1] Dufferin to Granville, 1 Jan. 1883, *ibid.*, 51; Granville to Dufferin, 8 and 29 Dec. 1882, C. 3462, *ibid.*, 28, 36–7.
[2] *Hansard*, 3rd ser., CCLXXVI, cols. 7–63, 98–164, 178–250; Dilke *Memoir*, Gwynn and Tuckwell, *op. cit.*, I, 551; and Dilke Diary, 25 Oct. 1883, B.M. Add MSS. 43935.
[3] Cromer, *op. cit.*, (1911), 733.
[4] *Hansard*, 3rd ser., CCLXXXII, col. 2140.
[5] Dilke, *Memoir*, Gwynn and Tuckwell, *op. cit.*, I, 554.
[6] Granville to Baring, 31 Aug. 1883, Zetland, *op. cit.*, 88.
[7] Northbrook Letter, 5 Sept. 1883, *ibid.*
[8] Granville to Baring, 1 Nov. 1883, Cromer, *op. cit.*, (1911), 736.

government deferred so far as to give Parliament no definite day by which the evacuation of Egypt would be completed. But compromise only overlaid the fundamental divergence of aim which dogged the Liberals thenceforward. Some ministers looked for withdrawal in a matter of months; but others, and the Queen, herself, considering the realities in Egypt, resigned themselves to staying for 'many years'.[1]

Baring, with all his Indian experience, was alarmed at the Cabinet's haste to withdraw and gave a version of the realities in Egypt very different from Dufferin's. 'Under present conditions,' he declared, a speedy retirement and constructive reform were 'almost a contradiction in terms'. The road to solvency and stability would be long; and the need to obtain the assent of the Powers at every step would make uphill work of it. If, on the other hand, Baring continued, we leave Egypt to anarchy: '. . . We may again find ourselves . . . obliged to interfere or stand aside whilst others, probably the French, take up the work which we . . . had failed to accomplish.' 'I do not see my way out of this dilemma,' Baring confessed.[2] But the difficulty went much deeper. 'Recent events', he reported, 'have completely shattered the system of government. . . .'[3] In restoring the refugee Tewfik, the British showed that he was no longer an Egyptian ruler but a foreign puppet. His restoration emptied the Khedivate of authority and popularity, as much as the deposition of Ismail had done. What was worse, Baring explained, was that '. . . the whole tendency of the reforms we now have in hand is to weaken it still further'.[4] We were expecting the traditionally autocratic Khedivate to support '. . . a top-heavy and exotic superstructure, such as an enormous external debt, Western law courts,'[5] representative institutions and an efficient and progressive administration, all of which antagonised the Pashas and landowners — the Khedive's natural allies. Baring touched here upon the fundamental fault in the Liberals' policy. All along they had ignored the essential impotence of the Khedive's government, as it became ever more plainly the tool of European purposes. As a result, Gladstone's ministry had intervened to restore the *status quo ante* Arabi — only to find that it no longer existed. They planned to reform and regenerate the country through the Khedive; but too late, they discovered that he retained no authority but that which British power could lend him. They intended a quick withdrawal,

[1] For the Queen's correspondence with the government on this issue in October 1883 *vide Q.V.L.*, 2nd ser., III, 445–51.

[2] Baring to Granville, 28 Oct. 1883, Cromer, *op. cit.*, (1911), 738–9.

[3] Baring to Granville, 9 Oct. 1883, *ibid.*, 743.

[4] Baring to Granville, 9 Oct. 1883, Zetland, *op. cit.*, 90. (Baring himself seems to have excised this phrase in his version printed in Cromer, *op. cit.*, (1911), 743–5).

[5] Baring to Granville, 28 Oct. 1883, Cromer, *op. cit.*, (1911), 739.

leaving British influence supreme in Cairo, and found that they could not risk leaving a vacuum. Baring however failed to convince the Cabinet of all this. It was the events in the Sudan which opened British eyes to the extent of their misunderstanding and miscalculation.

Disaster in the Sudan

As the British forces were about to retire from Cairo and Baring was busy with reconstruction in Egypt proper, the collapse of the Khedive's authority was still going on in the Sudan. Even before the British invasion of Egypt, the Mahdist revolt had been breaking the Egyptian hold there.[1] Wolseley's annihilation of the Egyptian army had enabled the rebels to move northward toward Khartum. As early as October 1882, Malet warned Granville that the way lay open for a Dervish advance into lower Egypt.[2] But three months later the danger seemed to be passing. The Khedive sent ten thousand men under Hicks Pasha into the Sudan. Dufferin took it for granted that with these reinforcements the Egyptians would be able to hold the northern Sudan and keep the Dervishes away from the Egyptian frontier.[3] In this fools' paradise, Gladstone's ministry was blind to the profound implications of the Mahdist movement in the south for their plans in Egypt proper. They imagined that they could reconstruct Egypt while rejecting all responsibility for the defence of upper Egypt. Granville in his anxiety to limit British commitments insisted that the Sudan was the Egyptian government's affair.[4] After Hicks' victory in May 1883, Tewfik and his ministers decided to reconquer Kordofan. The British who wanted to avoid further strain upon the Egyptian revenue and the untried army, discouraged it. As Childers wrote in June 1883: '. . . We had no interest in keeping up the dependency of the Sudan on Egypt.'[5] But they did not prohibit the Kordofan expedition. Since they were about to hand over responsibility to the Khedive for order in Egypt proper, they 'abstain[ed] as much as possible from interference',[6] making it plain that what was done in the Sudan was none of their business.[7] On 8 September, 1883,

[1] For the origins and background of the Mahdist revolt *vide* R. Hill, *Egypt and the Sudan, 1820–1881*, (1959), 143–70; P. M. Holt, *The Mahdist State in the Sudan, 1881–1898*, (1958), 37–57.

[2] Malet to Granville, 2 Oct. 1882, C. 3461, P.P. (1883) LXXXIII, 401.

[3] Dufferin to Granville, 6 Feb. 1883, C. 3529, P.P. (1883) LXXXIII, 92–3; and 2 Apr. 1883, C. 3693, *ibid.*, 350.

[4] Malet to Cherif, 22 May 1883, in Malet to Granville, 22 May 1883, C. 3802, *ibid.*, 594–5.

[5] Childers to Granville, 8 Jun. 1883, Childers, *op. cit.*, II, 175.

[6] Granville to Malet, 8 Aug. 1883, C. 3802, P.P. (1883) LXXXIII, 647.

[7] Granville to Cartwright, 7 May 1883, *ibid.*, 84; Dilke, *Memoir*, Gwynn and Tuckwell, *op. cit.*, I, 552–3.

Hicks Pasha with 10,000 men marched out of Omdurman against the Mahdi. The news reached London on 22 November, 1883, that the entire expedition had been annihilated.

It was this disaster which first awoke the government in London to the interdependence of the Egyptian and Sudanese questions. They could not build up the Khedive's power in Egypt proper, so long as he squandered his last resources in the Sudan. Baring reported that Tewfik could not hold Khartum, or indeed prevent the Mahdi from advancing to the frontiers of Egypt proper. Egypt itself was in danger, and the British position there with it. If the whole of the Nile Valley south of Wadi Halfa was to be abandoned, Baring prophesied, '. . . the political and military situation here [in Cairo] will become one of very great difficulty'.[1]

The enormity of the disaster struck the ministry in London. Hartington at the War Office proposed, on Wolseley's advice, that British officers should help Egypt to hold Khartum and the Sudan east of the White Nile. To insist on abandoning these provinces, he believed, would arouse bitter feeling against Britain. Furthermore, he declared, the Red Sea ports of the Sudan, particularly Suakin, should be defended in order to protect the route to India. In the Sudan, as in Egypt, the first thoughts of Britain's military strategists were of securing communication eastward. The commander of the East India station was ordered immediately to protect the Red Sea Coast. But the provinces west of the Nile, Hartington suggested, should be given up, with the exception of the district between Khartum and Debbeh.[2] Northbrook at the Admiralty also hoped that Egypt might hold Khartum.[3] Granville by 7 December saw that Britain was on a knife's edge in Cairo, as a result of the catastrophe in the Sudan.[4] Five days later, the Cabinet had to bring its policy more closely in touch with realities. In the first place, they decided to order the Egyptians to give up the whole of the Sudan,[5] and withdraw to Wady Halfa and the frontiers of Egypt proper. The government could not '. . . agree to increasing the burden on the Egyptian revenue by expenditure for operations which even if successful and this is not probable, would be of doubtful advantage to Egypt'.[6] In

[1] Baring to Granville, 22 Nov. 1883, P.R.O. 30/29/161.

[2] Hartington to Granville, 23 Nov. 1883, Holland, *op. cit.*, I, 411–2.

[3] Gladstone to Granville, 29 Nov. 1883, B.M. Add. MSS. 44547.

[4] Granville to Baring, 7 Dec. 1883, P.R.O. 30/29/199.

[5] Northbrook's Memo., 11 Dec. 1883, Mallet, *op. cit.*, 174–5; Dilke *Memoir*, Gwynn and Tuckwell, *op. cit.*, I, 555; M. Shibeika, *British Policy in the Sudan, 1882–1902*, (1952), 121–2.

[6] Granville to Baring, 13 Dec. 1883, Temperley and Penson, *op. cit.*, 422; and 16 Dec. 1883, P.R.O. 30/29/127.

the second place, the Cabinet accepted the necessity of defending Egypt proper, together with the Red Sea ports, against Mahdist invasion.[1] Egypt could not defend itself, since the British had destroyed its army. The Dervishes in Egypt would be a greater menace to British interests than the Arabists. 'We have now been forced', Northbrook bitterly complained, 'into the position of being the protectors of Egypt.'[2] Baring was actually asking for British reinforcements to defend the Egyptian frontier and the Prime Minister hoped against hope that he could do without them by negotiating a peace between the Mahdi and the Khedive.[3]

Rarely had a ministry been caught napping as this one now was. Ministers wrote to each other in tones of consternation, for they were catching a glimpse of the Egyptian realities which their own false assumptions had hidden from them. They began to see something of the maze which they had unknowingly entered. How much more immense than they had expected was the task of building a permanent influence in Egypt. The danger from the Sudan was making sport of their plans for an early withdrawal.[4] In dictating the abandonment of the Sudan, the British were dealing another blow to the prestige of the Khedive and their Egyptian collaborators, the reforming Pashas. The chances of creating a popular Egyptian leadership which would serve imperial purposes loyally after the British had gone, were dwindling.

Baring in Cairo was already painfully aware of these reactions in Egyptian politics. On 16 December, 1883, he warned London that the Khedive and his ministers would almost certainly refuse to give up the fight for the Sudan. To do so would anger all politically conscious Egyptians. It would swell the hordes of the Mahdi for an invasion of Egypt proper. If London insisted on yielding those provinces, Cherif would almost certainly resign. Baring doubted whether any other Egyptian leaders would serve the Khedive on such terms. To enforce their command, the British would have to take practical control of the Egyptian government and be responsible for it. At worst, a ministry of British officials would have to be imposed on the Khedive. The policy of giving up the Sudan, Baring concluded, would prolong the British occupation for five or ten years. Nevertheless it seemed to him the only course.[5]

Ministers in London were shocked by this candid analysis. Their

[1] Northbrook, Cabinet Memo., 24 Dec. 1883, P.R.O. 30/29/139.
[2] *idem.* [3] Gladstone to Granville, 18 Dec. 1883, P.R.O. 30/29/127.
[4] Cabinet Opinions, 24–5 Nov. 1883, P.R.O. 30/29/143.
[5] Baring to Granville, 16 Dec. 1883, P.R.O. 30/29/127; Chérif to Baring, 22 Dec. 1883, and Baring to Granville, 22 Dec. 1883, Cromer, *op. cit.*, (1908), I, 380–1.

original notions of what they were doing when they sent the expedition to Egypt, their plans for taking advantages, their ideas of how long it would take to secure them, and of the cost — had all been exploded. The Cabinet was 'greatly troubled'[1], and not least about what would be said when Parliament met.[2] Northbrook feared that 'our Egyptian position . . . seems in danger of becoming universally unpopular'.[3] He even suggested that the government should make much of defending the Red Sea forts of the Sudan as a measure against the slave trade in order to make its Egyptian policy more acceptable.[4] This was a tribute to humanitarian sentiment and to the nation's lack of imperial ambition in Egypt. It was also perhaps the germ of an idea which helped to send Gordon, the anti-slavery champion, to Khartum. The Cabinet had to choose between insisting on the surrender of the Sudan and retaining Egyptian co-operation. The Prime Minister was appalled at the thought of forming an Egyptian ministry of British officials. 'It would be a great mischief at best', he wrote, 'to become provisionally administrators of the country. I suppose bastinadoed fellaheen would be reported to Parliament at the rate of a hundred cases a month.'[5] Gladstone was talking once more of throwing the Egyptian problem back into the lap of the Powers, and Northbrook of inviting the Turk to defend the eastern Sudan. But in the end the Cabinet chose to alienate the Egyptians rather than get involved in fighting the Mahdi, and on 4 January, 1884 stood by their 'advice' to the Khedive's government. Ministers decided that they would still be able to withdraw from Egypt more quickly without the southern provinces than with them. Even Northbrook scorned the possibility of empire in the Sudan:

> '. . . We are satisfied that Egypt should no longer be hampered by the attempt to govern a piece of the world as large as Europe when she cannot find a Corporal's guard fit to fight . . . or . . . a hundred thousand pounds to pay troops without plunging deeper into bankruptcy . . . we are not going to spend the lives of Englishmen or of natives of India in either supporting Egyptian rule in the Soudan or of taking half Africa for ourselves and trying to govern it.'[6]

The Liberals now realised that in any case withdrawal from Egypt proper would have to be deferred until Egypt had recovered from the loss of the Sudan.[7] Northbrook's impression was that '. . . we shall be

[1] Northbrook to Granville, 24 Dec. 1883, P.R.O. 30/29/139.
[2] Northbrook to Granville, 27 Dec. 1882, *ibid.*
[3] Northbrook, Cabinet Memo., 24 Dec. 1883, *ibid.*
[4] *ibid.* [5] Gladstone to Granville, 5 Jan. 1884, P.R.O. 30/29/128.
[6] Northbrook to Ripon, 13 Feb. 1884, Mallet, *op. cit.*, 178.
[7] Granville to Baring, 28 Dec. 1883, Shibeika, *op. cit.*, 130.

forced to assume the direct government of Egypt for a fixed time, and I should like to take the bull by the horns and announce this at once'.[1] This seemed to him preferable to '. . . the practical assumption of the administration, which appears to be inevitable, without a term'; and he feared that Britain would have to make financial sacrifices on behalf of the Egyptian government.[2] But the Prime Minister stamped upon any idea of openly taking the responsibility of Egyptian government for a period of five years. It would be, he objected, a breach of faith with the Powers, a step towards a permanent annexation or Protectorate, and unpopular with the Radicals.[3] The Cabinet nevertheless accepted the fact that for the time being they would have to take practical control of the Khedive's administration. As long as the British occupied Egypt, Granville instructed Baring, the Khedive and his ministers henceforward must carry out British 'advice' in all matters affecting the safety or administration of the country.[4] Cherif's ministry must either evacuate the Sudan or resign. The catastrophe had drawn the Liberals into responsibility for the government and defence of Egypt.

This decision killed all hope of Egyptian co-operation for the time being. Cherif resigned on 7 January 1884, protesting at the loss of Egyptian independence. There were rumours that the Khedive himself might abdicate. He doubted whether any Egyptian could form another ministry on such terms.[5] Riaz and Tigrane refused to serve unless Khartum was saved. Fortunately the Khedive was persuaded to remain. Nubar Pasha agreed to carry out British orders and managed to rig up a ministry of sorts.[6] But, as the Sirdar, Sir Evelyn Wood, remarked, 'Chérif carries more weight than a dozen Nubars, because the latter is *novus homo* and a Christian.'[7] Only the facade of Khedivial rule had been saved.

As the loss of the Sudan forced the Liberals to stay in Cairo, they became more deeply entangled in its financial difficulties. The vain efforts to put down the Mahdists and the cost of the British garrison drained the Egyptian treasury still further. The Powers moreover insisted that Egypt should pay several millions in compensation for the destruction of European life and property at Alexandria in 1882. It was

[1] Northbrook to Ripon, 4 Jan. 1884, Mallet, *op. cit.*, 171.
[2] Northbrook to Granville, 8 Jan. 1884, P.R.O. 30/29/139.
[3] Gladstone to Granville, 11 Jan. 1884, P.R.O. 30/29/128.
[4] Granville to Baring, 4 Jan. 1884, Cromer, *op. cit.*, (1908), I, 382.
[5] For a French view of the crisis see Barrère to Ferry, 7 Jan. 1884, *D.D.F.*, V, no. 185.
[6] Cromer, *op. cit.*, (1908), I, 383–4.
[7] Wood to Ponsonby, 1 Feb. 1884, A. Ponsonby, *Henry Ponsonby . . . his Life from his Letters*, (1942), 229.

largely because Egypt was once more on the verge of bankruptcy that London had dictated the abandonment of the Sudan. At the end of 1883, there was a deficit of nearly a million pounds in Egypt's administrative budget.[1]

Gladstone and his colleagues now faced these financial troubles of staying in Egypt. Early retirement had become incompatible with stability and a supremacy of British influence at Cairo. They also found that reform and development did not go well with bankruptcy. As long as they occupied Egypt, the Powers held them responsible for Egypt's financial liabilities, and so they could not withdraw safely until Egyptian independence had been refounded in solvency. But the more they took charge of Khedivial affairs, the less became the possibility of a return to independence. British dealings with Egyptian finance provide another historical test of the motives behind the occupation of Egypt.

On 16 January, 1884, Childers, now Chancellor of the Exchequer, warned the Prime Minister: 'This is a very serious question, affecting our finance in more than one way. . . . I mean whether anything, and if so what, should be done for the finances of Egypt.'[2] The Alexandria Indemnity could not be met without raising another loan; and a loan could not be raised except with a guarantee by Britain or the Powers. Again, Egypt's administrative deficit could be made up only by reducing the interest rate paid to its creditors and diverting the money saved from the Debt to administrative expenditure. For most of these urgent financial operations the consent of the Powers was required by international treaties. Entangled in Egypt's financial crisis, Gladstone's government during 1884–5 became highly vulnerable both to international pressure and to attack at Westminister. As Baring put it, 'the main question . . . is this — who is to be sacrificed, the bondholders or the English taxpayers? You will either have to reduce the rate of interest on the debt or bear the expense of the army of occupation. The alternatives are exceedingly unpleasant, but they have to be faced.'[3] The one would anger the French, the other, the House of Commons.

Withdrawal had now come to depend mainly upon Egyptian financial recovery and internal politics; and Childers on 17 January saw only three possible ways to solvency, all of them long and hard. The Cabinet might pursue 'the natural development of the last fifteen months' policy', stay in Egypt, and wait for the country to recover financially by its own efforts. But, the Chancellor warned, this would mean pro-

[1] Cromer to Salisbury, 3 Feb. 1896, F.O. 78/4761.
[2] Childers to Gladstone, 16 Jan. 1884, Childers, *op. cit.*, II, 198.
[3] Baring to Childers, 26 Feb. 1884, *ibid.*, 201.

longing the occupation indefinitely. The second possibility was to declare Egypt a protectorate, giving the country 'the benefit of our credit and our autocratic administration'. Britain would thus undertake direct responsibility for the solvency of Egypt; but the Chancellor pointed out that no good ever came of underwriting bankrupt governments. The last possibility was to quicken Egypt's recovery by guaranteeing her a large loan; indeed a loan of some kind was the only chance left of getting out of Egypt quickly and safely. But the Chancellor recalled: this was '. . . what we did for Turkey when we guaranteed her War Loan. We set her on her legs with a vengeance, and she never stopped borrowing and wasting till she blew up'.[1] The ministry was in a cleft stick and could settle nothing at the Cabinet on 22 January.[2] Six weeks later the Egyptian government received a bill of four and a half million pounds for the Alexandria riots. Childers faced 'difficulties — which are enormous — in the way of a satisfactory solution'.[3]

The Liberals and the country knew by the beginning of 1884 how deeply they were sinking into the Egyptian bog. They had fallen into the business of defending Egypt proper and the Red Sea ports against the Mahdists. They had taken over the Khedive's government and were entangled in its financial liabilities. They were open to heavy diplomatic pressure from the Powers and reduced to going cap in hand to the French and Germans who were combining against Britain. The Prime Minister acknowledged the fiasco of his Cabinet's plans for limited intervention and quick withdrawal which alone had persuaded them to go into Egypt, and which had achieved the exact opposite of their intention. At the end of the Cabinet meeting on Egypt of 2 April, Gladstone wearily summed up: 'We have done our Egyptian business, and we are an Egyptian government.'[4]

On every hand the government was now paying for its blunders and under the strain they fell out among themselves. There were bitter recriminations between the Radicals and moderates on the one side, and the forward party on the other. In the Commons the ministry which had pleased nobody by its Egyptian imbroglio, not even its own followers, was by February divided and in trouble. The evacuation of the Sudan, which had mollified the Radicals, had alienated another wing of Liberals, headed by W. E. Forster and the anti-slave trade crusaders. *The Times*[5] and the *Pall Mall Gazette* accused the government of

[1] Childers to Money, 17 Jan. 1884, *ibid.*, II, 198–9.
[2] Dilke, *Memoir*, Gwynn and Tuckwell, *op. cit.*, II, 30.
[3] Childers to Gladstone, 21 Mar. 1884, Childers, *op. cit.*, II, 204.
[4] Dilke, *Memoir*, Gwynn and Tuckwell, *op. cit.*, II, 46.
[5] For this agitation see *History of the Times*, (1947), III, 22, 24, 28, 37.

abandoning the cause of civilisation in the Sudan. The ministers' failure to bring about the conditions for retiring from Egypt, so the extermists argued, showed that the road to India could be safeguarded only by means of prolonged occupation. A few imperialists went so far as to demand a protectorate in Egypt, but they gained little support. The government was not to be driven back into the Sudan; but their humanitarian critics received one slight consolation.[1] On 18 January, 1884, a Cabinet Committee consisting of Hartington, Granville, Northbrook and Dilke sent General Gordon to evacuate the beleaguered Egyptian garrisons from Khartum and to do what he could by personal influence to secure the Egyptian frontiers against the Mahdists.[2] But on 4 February the tide of disaster had engulfed the eastern Sudan. Baker Pasha's raw *gendarmerie* were crushed by Osman Digna and the Dervishes. Tokar and Sinkat fell, and the British force in the Red Sea port of Suakin was besieged.[3] Gordon as a result, was in peril at Khartum.

At this further shock, the Conservatives moved a censure on the government for its failures in the Sudan, hoping to exploit Liberal dissensions and bring down the ministry. The Opposition leaders blamed the government for the loss of Hicks and Baker. Ministers, it was said, had completely misunderstood the Egyptian problem and by their shillyshallying had made it ten times worse. Worse still, extremists on both wings of the Liberal party voted against the ministry. Several Radicals supported the Conservative censure, on the ground that the government should never have invaded Egypt in the first place; it had acted as the lackey of the bondholders and taken away the Egyptians' right to independence. The more vehement of the forward Liberals attacked the ministry from the opposite standpoint. Forster opposed the evacuation of the Sudan; and another Liberal ex-minister, Goschen, supported the censure. Gladstone and his ministers replied with the arguments they had used in 1882 to justify their intervention. In Egypt and the Sudan, the Prime Minister repeated, his policy was one of 'Rescue and retire'; it was impossible to evacuate until a native government had been set firmly in power in Cairo.[4] But the disastrous results had blunted the old argument. The censure passed the Lords by a majority of a hundred votes.[5] After a five-day debate, the government majority in the Commons dropped to only forty-nine votes. The

[1] Northbrook, Cabinet Memo., 24 Dec. 1883, P.R.O. 30/29/139.

[2] Gwynn and Tuckwell, *op. cit.*, II, 29–31; Bernard Allen, *Gordon and the Sudan*, (1931), 227–34; Holland, *op. cit.*, I, 414–24; Childers, *op. cit.*, II, 176–8.

[3] Wolseley to Hartington, 8 Feb. 1884, Holland, *op. cit.*, I, 425–6.

[4] *Hansard*, 3rd ser., CCLXXXIV, cols. 912–3, 14 Feb. 1884.

[5] *Hansard*, 3rd ser., CCLXXXIV, col. 656.

attack continued. On 15 March Radicals, Irish Nationalists and Conservatives combined to challenge the ministry on its decision of 12 February to send a small expedition to relieve Suakin.[1] Labouchere, Morley, and O'Donnell went into the same lobby as Randolph Churchill, Gorst and Hicks Beach. In an ominously small House, the government was defeated by seventeen votes.[2]

The Liberals in the Cabinet as in the Commons were badly shaken. Now that the compromise of 'rescue and retire' on which they had gone into Egypt had broken down, they were all at sixes and sevens about how to get out. Several ministers regretted that they had ever sent an expedition to Cairo. Their smug contemplation in 1882 of what they would make of their Egyptian opportunity had given way to an agitated search for escape routes from a frightening liability. Harcourt and the Radicals wanted to throw up the sponge in Egypt. 'We must get out of Egypt', Harcourt wrote in March, 1884, 'as soon as possible at any price. The idea of our administering . . . [Egypt] or of the Egyptian army defending it is equally out of the question.'[3] The Prime Minister and Childers, still shocked by the financial liabilities of the occupation, sympathised with Harcourt. At the other end of the Cabinet, Hartington and Northbrook resigned themselves to facing facts and shouldering the burdens of a prolonged occupation which could no longer be avoided. Both sides knew that they were sinking deeper into the Egyptian quicksands. But one side felt that if they stayed longer, they would only sink deeper; while the other side accepted the need to stay until withdrawal could be made safe. Granville as usual continued his search for the golden mean between his colleagues. The balance of opinion in the Cabinet was swinging in favour of cutting the ambitious conditions for leaving Egypt laid down at the end of 1882, so as to evacuate within two or three years. But there was violent resistance from Hartington's section before this outcome was reached. From March 1884 onward, the questions of Gordon's safety at Khartum, of the financial crisis in Egypt and of the lowering of Britain's terms of withdrawal were all drawn together into the same underlying struggle between those who would cut their losses and those who would stay until things improved.

At the end of March, 1884, Baring and Wolseley warned the Cabinet

[1] *vide* Cabinet Opinions on this, 7–12 Feb. 1884, P.R.O. 30/29/144.

[2] *Hansard*, CCLXXXV, col. 1725, 15 Mar. 1884. For the debates on Egyptian policy see *Hansard*, CCLXXXIV, cols. 64 sqq., 5 Feb. 1884, cols. 684 sqq., 12 Feb. 1884, col. 582 sqq.; CCLXXXV, col. 1653, 15 Mar. 1884.

[3] Harcourt to Dilke, Mar. 1884, Dilke, *Memoir*, Gwynn and Tuckwell, *op. cit.*, II,

of Gordon's danger in Khartum and pressed for an expedition to relieve him.[1] Hartington wanted to prepare an expedition to Khartum.[2] Selborne threatened to resign if it was not sent, and Harcourt, if it was.[3] Chamberlain suspected that Hartington was using Gordon as a pretext for dragging the government into reconquering the Sudan and for prolonging the Egyptian occupation. 'Once more,' Chamberlain wrote to Dilke, 'Hartington, and you and I, are at opposite poles. For one, I do not mean to be forced any further in the direction of protectorate.'[4] The Prime Minister shared this view. Unless Gordon was in immediate danger, he wrote, 'as far as I can see sending English troops to Khartoum . . . would be the most vital and radical change that could be made in our policy.'[5] A few days later, Chamberlain and Dilke were persuaded of Gordon's danger and joined the advocates of an autumn expedition, while still resolved to prevent it from prolonging the Egyptian occupation or reversing the abandonment of the Sudan. But the Prime Minister still opposed sending an expedition.[6] By 23 April, 1884, there were six ministers for an autumn expedition and five against it.[7] Northbrook's diary breathes the tension in the Cabinet: 'Cabinet 3 till 7. Great difference of opinion. Question of immediate steps for consideration of expenditure to support Gordon deferred. . . . I think Government will probably break up.'[8] Saving Gordon was put off, and his fate became entangled in the Liberals' disagreement about Egypt's future.

But almost everyone in the Cabinet now wished devoutly to be rid of Egypt. The occupation was wrecking party unity. Its diplomatic penalties were mounting as well. Lyons reported from Paris the 'ill will towards England . . . which seem[s] to become more and more prevalent here'.[9] Gladstone and his friends were frightened above all at the horrid prospect of asking the British taxpayer to shoulder financial liabilities in Egypt. By the beginning of April, the government was more than ready to give up many of its Egyptian ambitions to escape from the trap. The Prime Minister wrote of the need to respect the law of Europe, and of his 'indisposition to extend the responsibilities

[1] Baring to Granville, 24 Mar. 1884, Allen, *op. cit.*, 311–2; Wolseley to Hartington, 13 Apr. 1884, Holland, *op. cit.*, I, 441 *et seq.*

[2] Hartington to Gladstone, 11 Apr. 1884, Holland, *op. cit.*, I, 439–40.

[3] Dilke, *Memoir*, Gwynn and Tuckwell, *op. cit.*, II, 45.

[4] Chamberlain to Dilke, 2 Apr. 1884, *ibid.*, 47.

[5] Gladstone to Hartington, 13 Apr. 1884, Holland, *op. cit.*, I, 440.

[6] Gladstone, Cabinet Memo., 23 Apr. 1884, P.R.O. 30/29/128.

[7] The six in favour were: Hartington, Northbrook, Selborne, Derby, Chamberlain, Dilke; the five against were: Gladstone, Granville, Harcourt, Kimberley, and Dodson. (Dilke, *Memoir*, Gwynn and Tuckwell, *op. cit.*, II, 48.)

[8] Mallet, *op. cit.*, 186.

[9] Lyons to Granville, 27 May 1884, Newton, *op. cit.*, II, 328.

of this country'[1] for Egyptian finances. There had been talk of the possibility of pulling the Khedive out of bankruptcy by giving a British guarantee of the Egyptian Debt — a step which would also have given Britain supreme influence. But the majority of the Cabinet bilked at going to Parliament with such a proposal. On 2 April the government decided instead to go to the Powers and offer to withdraw from Egypt as soon as possible, if only they would agree to alter the Law of Liquidation in Egypt's favour and grant her an international loan. There seemed no other way out of the financial difficulty[2] but to take risks with Britain's claim to a 'sole and privileged position' in Cairo.[3] Granville called a European Conference to settle Egyptian finances and worked to come to terms with France before the meeting. When Jules Ferry's ministry offered to agree to 'neutralise' Egypt and not to send in French troops, if the British would evacuate the country within two years,[4] most of the Cabinet were relieved and delighted. The Prime Minister enthused at this new hope '. . . because it is all in the sense of giving back to Europe what had been held exclusively'.[5] Gladstone had had an uneasy conscience about Egypt from the beginning. His colleagues also welcomed the idea of an international agreement which would 'neutralise' Egypt on Belgian lines. Northbrook wanted it because it would revive the Anglo-French Alliance;[6] Chamberlain and Dilke because it would mean early evacuation;[7] and Granville, Derby, Kimberley, Selborne and Harcourt[8] because 'neutralisation — annexation — are the two alternatives. All between the two is a temporary expedient', and they abhorred annexation.[9] They acclaimed the policy of neutralisation as the best means of 'relief from the intolerable burden of a continued occupation'.[10] Hartington alone was sceptical. It was unrealistic, he believed, to think that Britain could set up a stable order in Egypt and withdraw within two years. 'What is it which prevents an immediate evacuation?' he asked. 'I suppose it is the probability of revolution or disturbance in Egypt on our departure. . . . Is there any probability that the force of such reasons as these will be diminished in a period of less than five years?'[11]

[1] Gladstone to Granville, 22 Mar. 1884, P.R.O. 30/29/128.
[2] Gladstone, Report to the Queen of Cabinet Proceedings, 2 Apr. 1884, P.R.O. 30/29/128; Dilke, *Memoir*, Gwynn and Tuckwell, *op. cit.*, II, 46.
[3] Gladstone to Granville, 22 May 1884, P.R.O. 30/29/128.
[4] Waddington to Ferry, 2 May 1884, *D.D.F.*, V, no. 258; 20 May 1884, *ibid.*, no. 274.
[5] Gladstone to Granville, 3 May 1884, P.R.O. 30/29/128.
[6] Northbrook, Cabinet Minute, 22 May 1884, P.R.O. 30/29/143.
[7] Chamberlain, Cabinet Minute, 21 May 1884, *ibid.*
[8] Minutes of 21 May 1884, *ibid.* [9] Derby, Minute, 13 Jun. 1884, *ibid.*
[10] Chamberlain, Minute, 21 May 1884, *ibid.*
[11] Hartington, Minute, 21 May 1884, *ibid.*

He preferred to stay in Egypt with all its financial penalties rather than to leave the security of the route to India once more at the mercy of Egyptian disorder. But his colleagues were so anxious to get out and to agree with France, that they were for withdrawing within three, and, some, even in two years,[1] although the Queen wrote protesting against anything less than four.[2] In the end Granville agreed with the French to evacuate Egypt within three and a half years, if the country was by then sufficiently stable. The French promised not to occupy Egypt after the withdrawal except with British consent, and to join in guaranteeing its neutrality.[3] The agreement nevertheless was conditional upon the Conference accepting the British financial proposals. There seems no reason to doubt that most of the Cabinet were still eager to escape from Egypt if they could get reasonable terms from the Powers. Dilke himself, a cynical enough critic of his Whig colleagues, surmised in his Diary on 12 June: '. . . if Mr. Gladstone [were] to stay in . . . we should come as regards Egypt to evacuation and neutralisation. Under the Tories, or under Hartington, the *status quo* may be tried for a long time.'[4]

In spite of the preliminary Anglo-French agreement, France led the Powers in rejecting all the British proposals for balancing the Egyptian budget at the London Conference which met on 28 June, 1884. She refused to reduce the interest on the Egyptian debt or to transfer any portion of the debt revenues to meet the cost of administration and defence. France denied that Egypt was bankrupt. Ferry's ministry had bowed to the objections of the French bondholders and the opposition in the French Chamber to doing anything which might help the British in Egypt.[5] Gladstone blamed Bismarck and the French Chamber for wrecking the Conference.[6]

The diplomatic situation by June was turning in favour of the French, and Ferry saw prospects of a far better bargain with Britain if he delayed a settlement. Bismarck, using as his pretext Granville's and Derby's obstruction of his colonial claims in south and west Africa[7] and in the western Pacific, was forming an *entente* with France against Britain on the Egyptian and colonial questions. By the beginning of August, Britain in Egypt was faced with the united hostility of the

[1] Cabinet Minutes, 21 May–22 Jun. 1884, *ibid.*
[2] Queen Victoria to Gladstone, 7 Jun. 1884, P.R.O. 30/29/128.
[3] Waddington to Ferry, 17 Jun. 1884, Annexes I and II, *D.D.F.*, V, no. 311.
[4] Dilke, *Diary*, Gwynn and Tuckwell, *op. cit.*, II, 55; 52–5.
[5] Lyons to Granville, 3 Jun. 1884, Newton, *op. cit.*, II, 330–2.
[6] Gladstone to Granville, 28 Aug. 1884, P.R.O. 30/29/128.
[7] *vide infra* 173–5.

Continental Powers. Granville tried to buy the Triple Alliance's help in solving Egypt's financial crisis by accepting German claims in the Cameroons, Angra Pequena and New Guinea, by giving up the Anglo-Portuguese Congo agreement,[1] and by accepting an international conference about west Africa. But it was all in vain. In mid-August, Granville observed, 'I am afraid that we shall find Bismarck a great difficulty in our path.'[2] For the next nine months, the Franco-German *entente* was to harry the British positions throughout the world. The occupation of Egypt had by the middle of 1884 made Britain highly vulnerable to pressure from the Continental Powers; and Africa had become an important pawn in the European balance of power. Germany, in particular, as Gladstone remarked, could '. . . do extraordinary mischief to us at our one really vulnerable point, Egypt'.[3] The occupation moreover gave France and Germany the opportunity and the provocation to invade British spheres of paramountcy elsewhere in Africa and Asia which hitherto had not been seriously challenged.

The Egyptian financial crisis, the Franco-German *entente*, the frustrated hopes of neutralising Egypt and evacuating it, the Radicals' cries for getting out at once and the Whigs' insistence on staying, 'created', according to the Prime Minister, 'a very formidable state of things at a moment when we have already on our hands a domestic crisis of the first class likely to last for months, and a foreign crisis of the first class, hardly certain, however, to be developed in a few days.'[4] The Radicals and the Whigs were at each others' throats over the Franchise and Redistribution Bills. Ministers expected the government to break up altogether.[5] Hartington in particular was expected to go on this issue. On 31 July, he and Selborne also threatened to resign if the Cabinet did not agree to an expedition to rescue Gordon from Khartum.[6] At last the rest of the Cabinet's sense of Gordon's actual danger got the better of their suspicion of Hartington's territorial ambitions in the Sudan. On 1 August the Cabinet agreed at last to go to the House of Commons for a vote of £300,000 for an expedition, should one become necessary, making it plain that its object was solely to rescue Gordon and come away, and not to conquer the Mahdi or to establish stable

[1] Hertslet, *op. cit.*, III, 1004–5.
[2] Granville to Northbrook, 16 Aug. 1884, P.R.O. 30/29/139.
[3] Gladstone to Derby, 24 Dec. 1884, Aydelotte, *op. cit.*, 166.
[4] Gladstone to Granville, 31 Jul. 1884, Holland, *op. cit.*, I, 477.
[5] Dilke, *Memoir*, 10 Jun. 1884, and 31 Jul. 1884, Gwynn and Tuckwell, *op. cit.*, II, 55, 61.
[6] Selborne's Cabinet Memo., 29 Jul. 1884, is given in Roundell, Earl of Selborne: *Memorials Personal and Political, 1865–1895*, (1898), II, 141–4; Hartington to Granville, 26 Jul. 1884, P.R.O. 30/29/134; and 31 Jul. 1884, Holland, *op. cit.*, I, 476–8.

government in the Sudan.[1] The War Minister insisted frankly upon using the expedition to capture and hold Khartum and Berber; in effect to reverse the abandonment of the Sudan. But the rest of the Cabinet wanted to do no more than rescue Gordon, and they watched Hartington's military arrangements with distrust.[2] As was usual when Gladstone was losing an argument, the decision was to get ready to do something rather than to do it.

The struggle within the Cabinet over Egypt's future reached a climax toward the end of 1884; and, after the failure of the London Conference, it was bound to turn upon ways and means to Egyptian solvency. On 2 August ministers agreed to send Northbrook to Cairo to find the shortest financial path back to evacuation. But they could not agree on any but the vaguest of instructions.[3] Northbrook himself thought the Egyptian occupation would have to go on for five more years; Hartington objected to laying down any dead-line; Chamberlain and Dilke pressed for a limit of three and a half; Harcourt, for evacuation as soon as Gordon was safe. Hartington wanted Britain to guarantee the whole Egyptian debt; Northbrook, a guarantee of minimum rates of interest on it; while Chamberlain and Dilke declared in favour of an announcement that Egypt was bankrupt and of a heavy cut in the bondholders' coupon.[4] The Prime Minister himself shared the Radicals' fear that if Britain undertook further responsibility for the Debt, temporary occupation would be drawn out into annexation. He greatly doubted 'whether Parliament would or should assume new responsibilities for Egyptian finance, and take as an equivalent full "financial control" '. He feared that '. . . such control is a certain though circuitous path towards annexation, and has been the root of the present mischief and embarrassment'.[5]

It was not to be expected that Northbrook's reports would unite so divided a Cabinet. Hartington indeed advised him not to try for a compromise, but to propose something definite which would force the Cabinet to a decision, even if this meant the resignation of several ministers. 'It strikes me,' he wrote, 'that what we have always done has been to look at things as we wished them to be, and hoped they would be, and have always declined to look at them as they were.' And there

[1] Dilke, *Memoir*, Gwynn and Tuckwell, *op. cit.*, II, 61. For the debate *vide Hansard*, 5 Aug. 1884, 3rd ser., CCXCI, cols. 1757–95.

[2] Hartington to Granville, 16 Sept. 1884, P.R.O. 30/29/134; Gwynn and Tuckwell, *op. cit.*, II, 61; Gladstone to Hartington, 21 Aug. 1884, and Hartington to Granville, 22 Aug. 1884, Holland, *op. cit.*, I, 481–4.

[3] Dilke, *Memoir*, 5–6 Aug. 1884, Gwynn and Tuckwell, *op. cit.*, II, 57–8.

[4] Dilke, *Memoir*, 18 Jul., 5–6 Aug., 22 Sept. 1884, *ibid.*, 56–9.

[5] Granville to Northbrook, 12 Sept. 1884, P.R.O. 30/29/139.

was some truth in this judgement of the government's Egyptian policy since January 1882. He still held that Khartum and the Eastern Sudan should be saved from the Mahdi. 'Temporary occupation, temporary sacrifices by the bondholders, and temporary sacrifices by the British taxpayer will have to go together. . . . We had much better make up our minds to do what is necessary if we are going to remain [in Egypt] and let those who do not like the policy leave the Government. . . .'[1]

Northbrook's proposals certainly brought matters to a head in the Cabinet. He declared it unsafe to fix a time limit for the evacuation. He advised the Egyptian government to break its international agreements and divert the surplus from the debt revenues to make up its administrative deficit. And he proposed a loan of nine million pounds to be guaranteed by the British Treasury.[2] 'The effect of the proposals', he concluded, '. . . will undoubtedly be to substitute the financial control of England for . . . international control,'[3] but this seemed inevitable in view of the hostility of the Powers. As Hartington had wanted, Northbrook's reports brought to a climax the struggle between the advocates of early evacuation and prolonged occupation. Only it was Hartington and Northbrook, not Gladstone and the Radicals, who were driven nearest to resignation.[4]

From September 1884 until January 1885, the tussle went on over Northbrook's scheme for ruling Egypt until its finances had been set in order. Gladstone disliked the proposals intensely and even more, the idea of defending them in the Commons.[5] Chamberlain asked Dilke how many M.P.s would support Northbrook's plan. Dilke answered, none.[6] The Liberal leaders in the Commons plainly believed that opinion against staying in Egypt and under-writing its finances was far stronger than that in favour of it. The bondholders, humanitarians and imperialists remained in a minority. On 19 November, 1884, something like a vote of the Cabinet was taken on Northbrook's proposals. According to Dilke,

> '. . . The opinions stood: Mr. Gladstone, Childers, Chamberlain, Harcourt, Trevelyan, and Dilke against Northbrook's scheme; for it, Lord Granville, the Chancellor, Hartington, Spencer, Kimberley, Derby, Carlingford, and

[1] Hartington to Northbrook, 11 Sept. 1884, Holland, *op. cit.*, II, 2–4.
[2] Northbrook to Granville, 21, 22, 23, 27 Sept. 1884, P.R.O. 30/29/139.
[3] Northbrook to Granville, 2 Sept. 1884, *ibid.*
[4] Hartington to Gladstone, 20 Jan. 1885, Holland, *op. cit.*, II, 5; Lewis Harcourt's Journal, 21 Jan. 1885, Gardiner, *op. cit.*, I, 514; Northbrook to Hartington, 22 Dec. 1884, Holland, *op. cit.*, II, 4.
[5] Granville to Northbrook, 25 and 26 Sept. 1884, P.R.O. 30/29/139.
[6] Mallet, *op. cit.*, 194–5.

Northbrook himself. All the Lords on one side, curiously enough, and all the Sirs and Mr.'s on the other; eight to six against us. But . . . Mr. Gladstone is so strong that we shall win. As we did.'[1]

None the less the fiasco of its policy in Egypt and the mounting penalties for its failure nearly broke the ministry[2] and almost dissolved its following in the Commons.

Ministers were by now thoroughly demoralised. They were painfully aware that they had blundered into Egypt on false premises. They admitted frankly in private that the plan which had inspired their original intervention had proved wildly impracticable. They had expected to solve in a year or two the financial and political problem of Egypt which had been maturing for several decades. Within a year or two they had imagined that they could build up supremacy of influence at Cairo and evacuate Egypt. But the Liberals knew only too well by the end of 1884 that instead of these easy and inexpensive accomplishments they had become the government of Egypt. They had fooled their followers as well as themselves and united all Europe against Britain.

Dilke was one who expressed the chagrin of the Liberal ministry. Of this time, he wrote:

> 'The Egyptian policy of the Government had now become thoroughly unpopular, and those of us who, although we had favoured intervention as necessary at the time, had deplored alike the engagements of our predecessors which had made it necessary, and the occupation which unnecessarily in my opinion, followed it, were as unpopular as were those like Hartington, and the majority of the peers in the Cabinet, who had insisted not only on going, but on staying — at least in Cairo.'[3]

The peers in the Cabinet however, were as dissatisfied as Dilke. At the end of 1884 Selborne wrote:

> 'I am among those who now look back with sincere regret, after experience of its consequences, to our original interference in Egypt; and I am most anxiously desirous of finding the best possible way out of it. But I think the honour and the interest of this country . . . must forbid our leaving Egypt with ignominy and humiliation, or abandoning . . . the Egyptian people to mere anarchy, until they fall into the hands of France.'[4]

But it was Harcourt who gave the most candid review of past blunders and present difficulties. In a Cabinet memorandum of 16 November,

[1] Dilke to Brett, 19 Nov. 1884, Gwynn and Tuckwell, *op. cit.*, II, 59. f.n. 2.

[2] Granville to Northbrook, 26 Sept. 1884, P.R.O. 30/29/139; Gwynn and Tuckwell, *op. cit.*, II, 94–5, 98, 100; Holland, *op. cit.*, II, 5.

[3] Dilke, *Memoir*, Gwynn and Tuckwell, *op. cit.*, II, 93.

[4] Selborne, Memo., Selborne, *op. cit.*, II, 133.

1884, he wrote: 'The theory on which we originally undertook the management of Egypt was that after the overthrow of Arabi we should be able to set Egypt on its own legs within a comparatively brief period and, having constructed an adequate native Government, leave the country to administer itself.' Harcourt went on to explain why this scheme had turned out to be unrealistic. 'This theory, however plausible it may have been,' he declared, 'has completely broken down.' It had broken down for several reasons: the disaster in the Sudan, the Alexandria indemnities, the financial insolvency and the failure to build, amidst this confusion and continuing disintegration of Khedivial authority, a popular and co-operative ministry to which power could be transferred safely. 'And, what is worst of all,' Harcourt continued, 'it must now be admitted that [Egypt] does not contain the elements out of which Civil Government or Military organisation can be constructed.'

> 'If, then, we are to remain in Egypt we must contribute to her finance, we must find her troops, we must man her Civil Service. In short, the administration of Egypt must be in substance an English Administration, maintained in part at the cost of the English taxpayer. There is no longer any probability that if we enter on this task we can escape from it in any calculable period. Our presence will be as indispensable in the future as today.'

Such were the implications which Gladstone, Harcourt and the Radical ministers saw in Northbrook's proposals for sole British financial control in Egypt and a loan guaranteed by the Treasury. Harcourt went on to state the overwhelming objections to staying in Egypt. First, the occupation would have to be continued '. . . in the teeth of Europe, and that is a terrible risk which we are not justified in incurring. Indeed, there is no possible English interest commensurate with such a risk.' 'But Egypt', Harcourt declared, 'is practically a European province. . . . In Egypt all the great Powers have equal rights with ourselves. . . . Russia, France, Germany would be for ever tripping up our heels.' If Britain attempted to administer Egypt, Harcourt feared, 'we should always be in hot water with the Powers. We should have all the evils of becoming a Continental State.' Prolonged occupation in fact was making England so vulnerable to international pressure that it was being drawn inextricably into the European alliance system on one side or the other. Egypt was not worth such a price.

Secondly, Harcourt was worried by the Parliamentary dangers of prolonging the occupation. '. . . The Administration of Egypt', he judged, 'will always afford to the Opposition in Parliament, as it now does, a constant and convenient weapon with which to harass a Government . . . to carry on the administration of Egypt under such conditions, both of European and parliamentary obstruction, is an impossibility.' If the Cabinet asked Parliament to give the Northbrook guarantees of Egyptian finances, Harcourt foretold, '. . . the Government will be defeated by a combination of the Tories, Irish and Radicals.' He admitted that it might also be defeated upon a policy of evacuation. But he concluded, 'If, as is possible and even probable, we shall be beaten on either alternative, it is far better to be beaten on a policy consonant to our other principles and those of our Party.'

The political and international disadvantages of Britain's position in Egypt had become so grave that all the ministers in the Commons, including the Prime Minister, were prepared to forego the idea of establishing a perpetual supremacy of influence at Cairo, in order to get away quickly. As Harcourt put it, '*Retire from Egypt*, *quam celerrime*'; indeed, within the year. Britain should accept responsibility for Egypt's finances and administration for another twelve months only; but after that, she should hand over the entire task to the Powers of Europe.[1]

Chamberlain agreed in general with Gladstone and Harcourt. The Radicals were for 'immediate bankruptcy, communication to the Powers of our fixed intention to leave, declaration that we would not allow intervention by other Powers in our place, and Conference to settle details of neutralization.'[2] Harcourt however, shrank from the idea of declaring Egypt bankrupt and repudiating the debt, because it would provoke the Powers still further. Chamberlain and Dilke on the other hand, were for defying France and Germany, and making the bondholders suffer.[3] Thus although by January 1885 the Cabinet was divided into two factions for and against exclusive British financial control and responsibility for Egypt, it was split into three on the details. As Chamberlain described it: the Radicals wanted to 'scuttle and repudiate' responsibility for the Egyptian debt; Hartington and Northbrook were determined to 'pay and stay'; while Harcourt wanted to 'pay and scuttle'.[4]

Gladstone and the advocates of early retirement prevailed. At the end of 1884 they rejected Northbrook's and Hartington's proposals for an exclusive British control of Egyptian finances and an indefinite

[1] Harcourt, Cabinet Memo., 16 Nov. 1884, printed in Gardiner, *op. cit.*, I, App. II, 601–6.

[2] Chamberlain to Dilke, 5 Jan. 1885, Gwynn and Tuckwell, *op. cit.*, II, 96.

[3] Dilke to Brett, 19 Nov. 1884, *ibid.*, 59, f.n. 2.

[4] Lewis Harcourt's Journal, 22 Jan. 1885, Gardiner, *op. cit.*, I, 515

occupation,[1] and they refused to pay out the Egyptian bondholders with English money. Northbrook and Hartington threatened to resign,[2] but the ministry decided upon another approach to France, on the basis of continuing the international control of the debt revenues, reforming the Law of Liquidation, neutralising Egypt, and guaranteeing free navigation in the Canal.[3] Supported by all the interested Continental Powers, the French put forward counter-proposals; and a majority of the Cabinet jumped at the chance of compromising with France and Germany, which would relieve them also from going to Parliament for a British guaranteed Egyptian loan. The French insisted on an international Egyptian loan guaranteed by all the Powers. The *Caisse de la Dette* would remain. In return, the French would allow the Egyptian government to tax the coupon for two years, and to use for administrative purposes any surplus in the revenues earmarked for Debt payments.[4] Northbrook and Hartington had proposed to free Egypt from international financial control and substitute exclusive British control. They had intended to cut away the tangle of international powers and so give Britain a free hand in Egypt. The French scheme would do the opposite. It would entrench international control over Egyptian finance; and British control of the Egyptian government as a result would be dependent at every turn upon the consent of the Powers. Baring and his officials in Egypt naturally disliked the French proposals. They complained of being bound hand and foot by the international *régime*. 'We have . . . managed somehow', Baring complained, '. . . to drift into a hybrid form of government, to which no name can be given. . . . It involves almost all the disadvantages of governing the country directly, without any of the advantages.'[5] The French financial proposals meant that the government of Egypt was still to be the football of European diplomacy.

It is hardly surprising therefore that Northbrook and Hartington should have rejected them as utterly impracticable from the point of view of a prolonged British occupation of Egypt; but the Cabinet brushed their protests aside.[6] The French proposals were tolerable enough on the other hand, if it was genuinely intended to withdraw from the responsibility of administering Egypt in the near future. The

[1] Gladstone to Granville, 8 Sept., 17 Oct. 1884, and Gladstone to Northbrook, 19 Dec. 1884, P.R.O. 30/29/128.

[2] Hartington to Granville, 28 Dec. 1884, P.R.O. 30/29/134; Granville to Gladstone, 26 Dec. 1884, P.R.O. 30/29/128.

[3] Gladstone to Granville, 19 and 26 Dec. 1884, *ibid.*

[4] For the working of this arrangement see Milner, *op. cit.*, 188 *et seq.*

[5] Baring to Northbrook, 4 Apr. 1884, Zetland, *op. cit.*, 117–8.

[6] Hartington to Granville, 28 Dec. 1884; Minute, 24 Mar. 1885, P.R.O. 30/29/134.

Cabinet's rejection of Northbrook's scheme and acceptance of the French proposals showed that a majority of ministers were still fixed on carrying out the original intention of extricating themselves from Egypt as soon as possible. Derby stated this implication when he bitterly criticised the opponents of the French plan:

> '. . . Those who object to a proposal of this kind will be compelled to show their hand, and to say " we do not mean to go out of Egypt at all, either now, or hereafter". It will be a happy result if we can bring the matter to that issue. Then we shall know whom we have to fight. . . . I believe we should have the English public with us — and I do not think the House of Commons would go against us.'[1]

Granville, Childers[2] and Gladstone[3] were all anxious to agree with France. And so when the French proposals came before the Cabinet on 20 January, 1885, the two factions in favour of neutralisation and early retirement over-ruled Hartington and Northbrook. Gladstone, Granville, Kimberley, Derby, Harcourt, Dilke and Selborne agreed to accept the 'French Proposals as a basis'.[4] The London Convention which embodied the plan was signed in March 1885. Waddington, the French Ambassador in London stressed the importance of this event:

> '. . . It implies the eventual supervision of Egyptian finances by Europe. It means the start of international control for Egypt. After the negotiations over the freedom of navigation for the Canal, will come the question of neutralising Egypt and consequently the British evacuation of the country.'[5]

The majority in Gladstone's Cabinet was willing to go a long way towards sharing its influence at Cairo with the Powers, in order to get out of Egypt quickly. Only a minority now thought it worth while to accept the heavy disadvantages of staying in Cairo for the sake of making sure of exclusive British supremacy.

At the same time as these international and Cabinet crises over Egyptian finance came to a head, the last and greatest of the string of Sudanese disasters hit the divided Liberals. On 5 February, 1885, news reached London that Khartum had fallen and that Gordon was dead. The public was shocked and there were loud cries for revenge. On 6 February the Cabinet, fearing the danger to lower Egypt and the upsurge of opinion, took up Hartington's policy and ordered Wolseley's Nile expedition to grapple with the Mahdi. Hitherto the expedition's

[1] Derby to Granville, 17 Jan. 1885, Granville Papers, P.R.O. 30/29/120.
[2] Childers to Granville, 10 Jan. 1885, Childers, *op. cit.*, II, 212.
[3] Gladstone to Granville, 26 Dec. 1884, P.R.O. 30/29/128.
[4] Dilke, *Memoir*, Gwynn and Tuckwell, *op. cit.*, II, 100–1.
[5] Waddington to Ferry, 22 Jan. 1885, *D.D.F.*, V, no. 533.

aim had been restricted deliberately to saving Gordon.[1] Gladstone's government now reversed this policy, and told Wolseley to defend the exposed Egyptian frontier either at Berber or if possible, even at Khartum. The details were left to the ill-prepared Commander. Once more the Liberals were advancing in order to mollify the Whigs, on condition that they retired again to please the Radicals. It was another variation of that compromise of 'rescue and retire' which ran throughout their Egyptian policy. But this time compromise was not enough to stop an explosion of Liberal dissension.

The Conservatives on 23 February moved a vote of censure upon the ministry's record in the Sudan and upon the 'betrayers of Gordon'. Northcote in the Commons, and Salisbury in the Lords called upon the government to establish peace in those parts of the Sudan essential to the security of Egypt,[2] before evacuating the Sudan. Several Liberals of the forward party supported the Conservatives against their own colleagues. Northbrook agreed essentially with Salisbury in the Lords debate.[3] In the Commons the right-wing Liberals, Forster and Goschen satirised the futility of 'smashing the Mahdi' only to retire again at once. Goschen accused the Cabinet of having decided 'to go to Khartoum to please the Whigs' and 'to retire from Khartoum to please the Radicals'. They both wanted a prolonged occupation of Egypt which, they held, required the defence of the Upper Nile at least as far south as Berber. If the Cabinet had followed Hartington's policy, Forster and Goschen would have voted for the government; but they felt compelled to vote against it because it was Harcourt's policy of early evacuation that prevailed.[4] Hartington's argument, ostensibly for the government, plainly disclosed that he agreed with the right-wing Liberals. To withdraw from the whole of the Sudan, he declared, without establishing a stable order over at least part of it, would put back the revival of Egypt.[5] Public indignation over Gordon's death gave new heart for the moment to the forward school in both parties.

The extreme anti-imperialists attacked the ministry as bitterly from the opposite standpoint. John Morley, the Radical leader, moved an amendment against continuing the Nile expedition and urging the earliest possible evacuation of Egypt. The Radicals and left-wing Liberals feared that in deciding to 'smash the Mahdi', Gladstone was

[1] Hartington to Wolseley, 6 Feb. 1885 and Wolseley to Hartington, 8 Feb. 1885, Holland, *op. cit.*, II, 13–6.

[2] *Hansard*, 3rd ser., CCXCIV, cols. 1052 *et seq.*

[3] *ibid.*, 26 Feb. 1885, cols. 1343–4.

[4] *ibid.*, Goschen, cols. 1251–63; Forster, cols. 1690–9.

[5] Holland, *op. cit.*, II, 24.

going back on the policy of withdrawal.[1] Sir John Lubbock moved another amendment condemning the Sudan expedition but approving the policy of defending Egypt at Wadi Halfa.[2] Harcourt in the Commons[3] and Derby[4] in the Lords made it plain that they sympathised with the Radical point of view. They hinted that it was a mistake ever to have gone into Egypt, in the first place. Harcourt thought that it would be suicidal to stay much longer. The Prime Minister himself, although he dressed his thoughts in ambiguity appealing to Radical and Whig in turn, admitted that his ministry had blundered into Egypt and the Sudan.

> 'I have often owned in this House that the difficulties of the case have passed entirely beyond the limits of such political and military difficulties as I have known in the course of an experience of half a century. Therefore, I do not ask the House to believe that what we have done is necessarily right, but as to honesty of purpose, painful as the course we have had to pursue has been to me, I felt that we had no alternative. We have been bound from the time that we first covenanted to keep the Khedive upon his Throne, and at no point have we had before us the choice or the possibility of return. . . . There has been no want of honesty, but possibly want of judgment [*sic*] has made me at least, a party to these decisions, which, sad and deplorable as they may have been in themselves, were yet unavoidable under the circumstances and at the moment when we were called upon to take them.'[5]

Gladstone renounced any idea of attempting to govern the Sudan, although a part of it might have to be pacified. But that he was determined on withdrawing from the sad business of Egypt, was plain enough.

Gladstone and Harcourt had done their best to soothe the Radicals. Hartington had tried to placate Forster and Goschen. But the old compromise of 1882–3 was no longer plausible even in debate after the experiences of 1884–5. The slogan of 'Rescue and retire' had been thoroughly discredited. It was now, as Derby and Harcourt had declared, a straight choice between an evacuation within two years and a prolonged protectorate. Both the Radicals and the Liberals of the right, for opposite reasons, were tired of evasion and attacked the ministry because it would not make up its mind. Despite the public outcry against Gordon's betrayal and for revenge upon the Mahdi, Morley's amendment for immediate evacuation obtained over a hundred votes. This two-headed revolt among the Liberals, added to the defection of the Parnellites,

[1] *Hansard*, 3rd ser., CCXCIV, cols. 1075 *et seq.*
[2] *ibid.*, col. 1198.
[3] *ibid.*, col. 1454 *et seq.*
[4] *ibid.*, col. 1389.
[5] *ibid.*, cols. 1093, 1079–1100.

brought the government's majority on its actions in Egypt and the Sudan down to fourteen votes. There were 288 votes against them and only 302 for them.[1] Six Liberals and thirty-one Parnellites voted with the Conservatives; while thirty-six Liberals abstained.

This long debate, which ranged over the government's Egyptian policy since 1880, gives a sense of Parliamentary opinion. For all the emotion stirred by Gordon's death and for all the Opposition's success in making his tragedy the accusing symbol of the ministry's blunders — the Liberal rank and file still stood firm against a forward policy in the Sudan. The Liberal imperialists and advocates of the civilising mission represented by Goschen and Forster, had won at most only forty-two Liberal votes, although the moment seemed so fortunate for their cause. Indeed, the Radicals who called for immediate withdrawal from the Sudan counted far more votes than the forward school and in the end, they voted for the government. The vast majority of Liberals, it is clear, approved the evacuation of the entire Sudan. More remarkable still, the Conservative leaders carefully avoided committing themselves to holding it and concentrated on the muddle and indecision of the Liberals. Nor did the Opposition leaders preach an indefinite occupation of Egypt. One or two Conservative back-benchers alone pressed for a protectorate. Although they called upon the ministry to set up stable government in Egypt and to defend it in the Sudan, the Opposition talked almost exclusively about Gordon — the topic of the moment rather than the issue of the future. There could be no better evidence of the trivial influence in both Parties of the handful of extremists who wanted a permanent protectorate over Egypt and the Sudan. It was the general sense of Parliament that the entanglement in Egypt was a thoroughly bad job; but there was no consensus on how to make the best of it. The dangers of staying seemed as alarming as the risks of evacuating without guarantees. Party leaders were at a loss for an agreeable policy, and the Opposition refrained from proposing one. Altogether, the House of Commons did not express the strong popular demand for a permanent occupation that theories of imperialism have so often taken for granted.

The disunity among the Liberals exposed by the debate almost broke up the government. Its members were at odds with each other over Irish policy and social reform as well: and their morale had cracked. Most of them during the debate on the Sudan censure were only too anxious for defeat or resignation.[2] But they managed to cling together

[1] *ibid.*, cols. 1719–23.
[2] Dilke, *Memoir*, 28 Feb. 1885, Gwynn and Tuckwell, *op. cit.*, II, 111 *et seq.*

for four more months, chiefly in order to see the Distribution of Seats Bill through Parliament.[1] By April 1885 the Cabinet felt safe in going back to their former course of retreating from the Sudan altogether. Wolseley himself reported that little could be done there, except at heavy risk and high expense. It now appeared that the danger of a Mahdist invasion of Egypt had been greatly exaggerated; and the Nile expedition no longer seemed necessary to its defence. The ephemeral enthusiasm for smashing the Mahdi and avenging Gordon moreover had died down.[2] Even Forster and the forward Liberals could now see no object in staying in the Sudan. 'I fear such abandonment', Forster wrote, 'is the only way out of the hopeless mess which the Govt. has made.'[3] In the Russian war scare arising out of the Penjdeh Incident, ministers found the occasion for withdrawing the Nile expedition. The Prime Minister declared: 'I am not prepared to go on [in the Sudan] upon any terms, Russia or no Russia.'[4] On 15 April, the Cabinet reverted to its former policy and ordered the evacuation of the whole of the Sudan. When the Conservatives took office (June 1885–February 1886 and July 1886–August 1892) they did nothing to reconquer it, despite their criticism of the evacuation when in Opposition. The new House of Commons was no more eager to vote money for the purpose than the old one had been; and the new government continued the old policy of Egyptian evacuation inherited from the Liberals.

The Motives of Intervention

After this tragi-comedy of the Liberals and Egypt, it seems incongruous to return to the question which the theories of imperialism would answer. What moved the Liberals to occupy Egypt? Intention was often lost in a maze of compromise and misconception. Ministers' actions sometimes belied their purposes. Parliament approved their plans but not necessarily the results. The unforeseen in European diplomacy as in domestic politics — influences essentially irrelevant to the Egyptian problem — none the less entered unpredictably into its solution. The motives plainly were nothing so simple as a new imperialist urge or a new strategic or economic need to seize the Nile. There was no straight line from cause to effect, from change in British opinion or

[1] *idem.* [2] Hartington to Wolseley, 17 Apr. 1885, Holland, *op. cit.*, II, 33–6.

[3] Forster to Allen, (Secretary of the Aborigines Protection Society), 30 Apr. 1885, A/S Papers, F. 2nd Bundle. (We are grateful to Dr. Roger Anstey for this quotation.)

[4] Dilke, *Memoir*, 11–14 Apr. 1885, Gwynn and Tuckwell, *op. cit.*, II, 117.

European diplomacy leading to a change of policy and a simple executive decision to acquire Egypt.

The seizing of Egypt, on the other hand, was not entirely due to absence of mind. If there were vacillation and half measures in it, there was also purpose. The accidental and the predictable curiously combined to bring the occupation about; and the one may sometimes be distinguished from the other.

It was plainly predictable that Gladstone's ministry, like every government since the end of the eighteenth century, would be vitally interested in the fate of Egypt. Few interests had higher priority than the routes to India and the East. Yet until 1882 they had been protected satisfactorily without occupation. Parity of influence with the French, and informal sway over the Sultanate and the Khedivial governments had proved enough; and at the end of the Eighteen seventies the old methods seemed surer than ever, because of the Liberal alliance. Why then did the long-standing security by influence in Egypt break down? That at least, the Europeans did not desire or design. It broke down because of the financial and political collapse of the Khedivial authority on which it stood.

The Egyptian crisis after 1876 was no accident. Although both the French and British misunderstood its character, it was not unusual for European influence in the end to bring about a nationalist reaction and the fall of a collaborating Oriental *régime*. The internal crisis was worked by the extension of European influence into Egypt since the beginning of the nineteenth century; and when the insidious effects had come to a head, the occasion of direct European intervention had arisen.

It was the Egyptian crisis, rather than a new rivalry with France or a new imperialism in Britain, which decided the time of intervention. Beaconsfield's Cabinet could hardly be suspected of designs to occupy Egypt, for they had laid plans for safeguarding the Canal route by an altogether different method in Cyprus and Armenia, and against a very different danger — Russia. The Liberals, after Midlothian and their denunciations of empire in north Africa, could hardly be mistaken for imperialists with ambitions for occupying Egypt. They faced the crisis with the strongest faith in the sufficiency of moral and commercial influence and a passionate aversion to unnecessary occupations. If they could be called imperialists at all, they were of the mid, not the late-Victorian variety; and their prejudice and principle went no further than the old Palmerstonian methods of external pressure and moral suasion, to restore the Khedive's authority and Anglo-French supremacy at Cairo. Until January 1882, the French took the initiative in this, and the Liberals, like the Conservatives before them, followed, partly to preserve parity, partly to keep up the alliance, and altogether to safeguard the road to India. Each fresh interference however only weakened the Khedive further and strengthened the Arabist reaction; while with each fresh defiance, the two Powers became more and more committed to enforcing their demands.

The British interest in Egypt and the crisis there were predictable. But it was an accident in French domestic politics, and the further progress of the Arabist revolution which brought the British in the last resort to intervene alone. The fall of Gambetta and the weakness of Freycinet could hardly have been foreseen in the beginning. Yet this random element determined that Britain, having been committed so far upon the premise of an Anglo-French restoration of the old dual influence through external pressure, should be left to carry it out single-handed. For Gladstone and several other ministers, the French defection at first seemed to relieve them of the unpleasant duty of interfering further. Inaction would no longer endanger parity nor strain the *entente*; and Egypt, they hoped, would right itself in the end, if only she was left alone. If not, perhaps another turn of the wheel in Paris might revive Anglo-French action; or the Concert of Europe or the Turk might be persuaded to put down the Arabist revolt; or the next naval demonstration might have more effect in over-aweing Arabi than the last one. Until just before the bombardment of Alexandria, Gladstone's ministry as a whole plainly had several plans for avoiding direct and single-handed intervention and none for going in alone. Most, if not all ministers, looked upon the crisis and the impotence of France, not as a unique opportunity to seize Egypt for Britain, but as a dangerous liability to be escaped if at all possible.

Again, the circumstances which persuaded the ministry to take the final and irretrievable step into Egypt with or without France, were partly rational and partly fortuitous. Above all, ministers seem to have been converted to intervention by the growing evidence of anarchy in Egypt which, they believed, endangered the Canal. The Radical ministers were convinced of this by the Alexandria riots; the moderates, by Arabi's declaration of a holy war against Britain throughout her Moslem empire in the East, and the spread of anti-European demonstrations after the bombardment of Alexandria; the Prime Minister, last of all, perhaps by rumours of Arabi's design to block the Canal. The great Eastern trade and shipping interests also became alarmed. When Egyptian anarchy reached the point of endangering the Canal, it was predictable that a British government, whatever its political complexion, would be forced to protect it.

Only this national interest perhaps was big enough to overcome the Liberals' distaste for the task. They claimed to stand for non-intervention and self-determination for oppressed peoples, for peace and the Liberal alliance with France. They would be accused of fighting for the bondholders and striking down freedom. They risked losing their ally. They had just withdrawn from Afghanistan and the Transvaal to make peace. There was an appalling inconsistency in going into Egypt to make war. Hence they had exhausted every other chance of solving the problem.

At the same time the accidents of Party politics and Gladstone's age conspired to persuade ministers to accept the inevitable. The Party and ministry was already racked with dissension over the Irish question. The Prime Minister's threat of retirement weakened the objectors to going into Egypt and strengthened Hartington's insistence on it. At the last minute some ministers reconciled themselves to doing the job, with the idea that it might be turned to advantage. Granville in particular early in July began for the first time to look upon the necessity of restoring the Khedive, if it had to be done, as a possible opportunity to set up British, in place of Anglo-French supremacy. But it is most unlikely that the idea of setting up British supremacy in Cairo decided the greater part of the Cabinet to invade Egypt. This was something they consoled themselves with once they had accepted the necessity of protecting the Canal.

Therefore, the final decision to send an expedition represented a muddled compromise between a few opportunists and many 'innocents'. But without carrying the Radicals and moderates, and Gladstone himself, the forward group could have done nothing. It was the 'innocents' who carried the Commons. The Liberals were all alike however, in conceiving intervention in Palmerstonian terms. What they intended was a quick restoration, not an occupation. Their sole purpose was to restore the conditions for a return to the old system of security through influence; only this time it was British influence which should be supreme. In purpose and in method, it was a thoroughly mid-Victorian policy. A brisk intervention and withdrawal, designed to leave behind a supreme British influence, had impressive sanction in past experience. A similar method had worked well enough in the Turkish empire in 1839–41, and in China in 1842 and 1858–60. These same Liberals had themselves launched similar expeditions in Abyssinia in 1869 and Ashanti in 1874. They had no reason to foresee that they were committing themselves to anything more than this in Egypt in 1882; and this was all that Parliament had approved. Not until a year later did the government discover that they had done something quite different from what they had intended and had plunged into an ever-lengthening occupation and ever-increasing responsibility for administering and defending Egypt. Plainly, this outcome was shaped far more by circumstance than policy. Gladstone and his colleagues had intended a supremacy of influence. They achieved instead a territorial occupation, financially insolvent, vulnerable to European hostility, unpopular among their own followers and in Egypt itself. Conflicts of intentions in London, further disintegration in Egypt and the alienation of France forced the British to stay. With the disasters in the Sudan and the alienation of France, the risks of a quick withdrawal became too great; for it might lead to a revival of the Egyptian revolt and the intervention of another Power.

The security of the routes to the East was the one interest with which British cabinets could not afford to gamble. It was the *sine qua non* of the British movement into Egypt. The downfall of Khedivial authority would not have brought this anti-jingo Government to intervene, except that it involved the Canal. If the Canal had not been the lifeline to the East, it would have been easy enough to take the risks of early evacuation instead of the road to governing the country. After all, there was a decisive motive behind the movement into Egypt, although the form and time of that movement were partly accidental. It was a long delayed corollary of British trade and power in India and the East. But the corollary was only brought into effect by the internal revolution in Egypt, worked by the slow erosion of European influence, and ironically enough, it was left to an anti-imperialist ministry to carry out the logic without being convinced by the argument.

Yet however self-interested or involuntary a nation's expansion may be, its spirit and aims are eventually shaped by its domestic morality and particularly by the terms in which it justifies to itself the control of other peoples. So it was in Egypt. Once in power, the Anglo-Indian officials in Cairo, with the approval of the Home government, set about cleaning up directly the corrupt and oppressive Turkish government which had troubled the Liberal conscience for so long and which Palmerston had failed to remove indirectly through the imperialism of free trade. The mid-Victorians had propped up Turkish despots. The late-Victorians in Egypt found that they could do this no longer and eventually resigned themselves to the task of turning the despot's subjects into an allied people by good government and economic development.

CHAPTER VI

Repercussions south of the Sahara

Although Egypt and the Transvaal had divided Gladstone's second ministry, it was Ireland that was to destroy it. The cleavage which in 1886 resulted in ninety-three Liberals, led by Hartington and Chamberlain, leaving Gladstone over Irish Home Rule had been widening since 1880. The Egyptian and Boer problems had multiplied these dissensions. Indeed, the three crises had much in common. They were all caused by national rebellion against British sway. All three movements came to a head together in crises which were more or less unsolved when the century closed. Each in a different form set the problem of how to deal with nationalist challenges without damaging imperial unity and security; and in all three the choices lay between different degrees of conciliation and coercion, between conceding rights of self-determination and asserting imperial authority.

These questions stirred the liberal and imperial sentiments of the Victorians against each other and set the exponents of different traditions of national expansion at odds. In the Irish, as in the Boer and Egyptian crises, the Gladstonians' approach was cautiously Cobdenite. They sympathised with national sentiment, and if they could not concede all its aspirations, they inclined to accept it as a creative force which could not and should not be suppressed. They continued to rely on influence, trade and liberty to protect British interests and unite the empire and its allies. They preferred to attract peoples, rather than to coerce them or keep them under centralised control. Home rule had reconciled colonial nationalists to Britain in the past. And the Gladstonians saw no other way of binding the Irish, the Boers, and in the end, even the Egyptians for the future.

Whig 'realists', such as Hartington and Northbrook, who were to become Liberal unionists after 1885, disagreed with these Cobdenite views for much the same reasons as Palmerston had done, namely, for not recognising sufficiently that trade, liberty and international peace depended upon power and prestige. They distrusted popular political movements, whether at Home or abroad, and rejected the possibility of liberal constitutions working in Oriental circumstances. Their aristocratic prejudices were confirmed by the apparent soundness of the authoritarian Indian tradition. Temperamentally, they inclined in the last resort to intervene, to vindicate authority and even to impose control. It was by the concentration not the dissipation of power that empires were preserved; and accordingly they insisted on coercion in Ireland, as in an emergency they had done in Egypt and the Transvaal.

It was upon the Irish issue that the crucial choice between the liberal and the unionist solutions to these nationalist challenges was to be made. In stiffening unionist, and weakening liberal feeling in England, the Home Rule struggles of 1885–93 were to work in favour of imperial advances in Africa. Conversely, events in Africa helped to discredit the old Cobdenite and Palmerstonian prescriptions for collaborating classes and informal sway. In south Africa in 1881, the Gladstonians had compromised with the Transvaal nationalists and saved the former indirect hegemony. But the efficacy of generosity seemed more doubtful when four years later, the Liberals had to bring Bechuanaland under the flag to contain the republic which they had just set free. In Egypt on the other hand, the Palmerstonian prescription had turned out to be a spectacular fiasco, with unforseen ramifications in Europe and the rest of Africa. The course of African events seemed less and less predictable according to the old historiography of expansion. It seemed as if the former techniques were ceasing to work well in a world where nationalist protests and irrational colonial rivalries were intensifying; and ministers were driven much against their will to apply Indian solutions to Africa.

These disillusioning experiences in Africa, combined with the Irish disaffections, gradually changed the official mind. The so-called imperialism of the late-Victorians began as little more than a defensive response to the Irish, the Egyptian and the Transvaal rebellions. Their 'imperialism' was not so much the cause as the effect of the African partition. The paradoxical conduct of Gladstone's ministry shows that the taking of a new African empire originated in an almost involuntary reaction to African national movements, and not in a stronger will to empire in Britain. The crucial changes which had upset the Liberals were taking place in Africa rather than in Europe. Eventually, their failure to come to terms with the Egyptian nationalists necessitated the occupation of the Sudan and much of tropical Africa besides. At the southern end of the continent, the Voortrekker challenge to imperial supremacy necessitated the extension of empire over Bechuanaland, Zambesia and the Transvaal itself. The British movement into

Africa stemmed from these two crises of informal empire wrought by nationalists.

Gladstone's second ministry was the true founder of the twentieth-century African empire. In stumbling into Egypt, it set off the international rivalry which led to the partition of the tropical regions.

However fortuitously, its single-handed intervention altered the European balance of power. Baring's rule in Cairo was the worst French humiliation since the defeat of 1871; and it drove Britain and France apart. The French search for adequate compensation led to attacks on exposed British interests in west Africa. Britain in Egypt became highly vulnerable to pressure from the Powers, since she could not set Egypt's finances in order without their consent. In this way, her luxurious isolation from the Continental balance was reduced; while her dependence on Bismarck's goodwill in Egypt strengthened Germany's pivotal position in Europe.

By altering the European balance, the occupation of Egypt inflated the importance of trivial disputes in tropical Africa and set off a scramble. Quickened by the hope of prising the British out of Cairo, the French drove deep into west Africa, while the Germans took their opportunity to irrupt into east and west Africa, in an attempt to extort British support in Europe. Hence the taking of Egypt ended the age when private merchants and consuls, acting through African authorities, could dominate the east and west coasts by influence alone. Once the French and German governments for diplomatic purposes began to back their own traders against British firms, trade turned into a business of territorial claims. As long as the British remained trapped in Cairo, France and Germany had the opportunity and the incentive to challenge Britain in Africa.

In this roundabout way, the occupation of Egypt triggered off at last a secondary rivalry for possession of tropical Africa; and despite its small intrinsic value, began its partition among the Powers at the Berlin Conference of 1884–5. Some diplomatic historians have suggested that the African Scramble was generated by new tensions within the European balance of power. But it was the internal crisis on the Nile, leading to the Egyptian occupation, which both altered that balance and brought its rivalries for the first time into Africa.

West Africa, 1882–1889

Without the occupation of Egypt, there is no reason to suppose that any international scrambles for Africa, either west or east, would have begun when they did. There seem to have been no fresh social or economic impulses for imperial expansion which would explain why the partition of tropical Africa should have begun in the early Eighteen eighties. Gladstone's second administration was totally devoid of imperial ambitions in west Africa. Granville was unimpressed by the dingy annals of the west coast. Kimberley, at the Colonial Office, was eager to give sleeping dogs every chance of lying. The pessimistic Derby, who succeeded him in 1882, was temperamentally opposed to any suggestion, however modest, for expansion on the west coast. Finally there was Gladstone, himself, who knew little and cared little about the problem. In so far as these men possessed any coherent view of the situation in tropical Africa, it was the view sometimes of Cobden, sometimes of Palmerston and the mid-Victorian imperialism of free trade. As in Gladstone's first ministry, they still concurred in looking on tropical Africa as a third-rate adjunct of the British economy, which might be worth the exertion of coastal influence, but did not justify the effort of administration inland. There were none of them likely to plant the flag in the middle of the African bush in a fit of absence of mind.

For decades all the European governments concerned with the coast of Africa both east and west had tacitly agreed not to allow the petty quarrels of their traders and officials to become occasions for empire. The ministries in London and Paris wanted nothing more than to continue their gentleman's agreement, although each faintly suspected the other of wanting to break it. There was little reason for this. Napoleon III had nourished a few sporadic projects for African expansion, but the catastrophe of 1870 had halted them. The Third Republic had pulled out of the Ivory Coast, contemplated renouncing its options in Dahomey, and had hoped to get rid of Gabon and the unpromising claims in the Congo. In Senegal, however, there was a stronger interest. The colonial government there had gradually developed a local expansive power of its own, which derived not so much from its economic potential as from the French army's proprietary feeling and its influence in Paris. In 1879 Brière de l'Isle began the portentous advance from the old colony towards the Upper Niger; two years later the Chambers voted credits for a railway which should link the Senegal to the Niger.

Analysis of this line of policy does not concern us here, but it had implications for Gladstone's Cabinet. The rulers of Senegal were extending not only eastwards but southwards. In 1877 they took a further step towards the encirclement of the Gambia; in 1881 Brière de l'Isle made a treaty with Fouta-Djalon which threatened to cut off the hinterland of Sierra Leone; at the same time private French firms had started to compete for the trade of the Niger Delta.

To Granville and Kimberley in London, these moves were faintly disturbing. Poverty-stricken though they were, it would have been feckless to stand idle while Sierra Leone and the Gambia lost their hinterlands, and with them, all chance of ever becoming solvent. Hence the British Cabinet tried to amplify the traditional understanding by a formal agreement.[1] In 1880 they made two separate suggestions to Paris. They proposed that the frontier between the Gold Coast and the French settlement at Assinie should be delimited; and secondly that there should be a standstill arrangement between the two Powers to the north of Sierra Leone, to be followed by a commission of demarcation.[2] The French government accepted both these suggestions. They had to do with regions which in themselves meant little to the diplomats of the Quai d'Orsay. To their minds it was much more important to keep in alignment with Great Britain because of 'the interests of our policy in general'.[3] The French government wanted to go into Tunisia and keep in line with London over Egyptian policy. Obviously, it would go more than half way to meet the wishes of the Gladstone government in west Africa. The British wishes, for their part, were plain enough. Best of all, they would have liked to continue the standstill arrangement along the whole line of coast, so as to save the hinterlands of Sierra Leone and the Gold Coast for any future development, and to keep the Deltas of the Congo and the Niger free from French interference. Unwilling to advance their own formal authority, their simple ambition was to ward off French tariffs. All the political problems of the west coast would go on being shelved; there would be no bidders for its territory; there would simply be a partition of informal influence. Britain and France could still both consent to a policy of self-denial. Nobody would annex anything, and furthermore France would promise

[1] Throughout the Seventies schemes for a consolidation of the understanding by means of a general partition of influence had been seriously discussed, *vide* Freycinet to French Ambassador in London, 6 Mar. 1880, *D.D.F.*, III, no. 52.

[2] Lyons to Freycinet, 20 Apr. 1880; Minister of Marine and Colonies to Freycinet, 4 Jun. 1880, A.E.M.D., Afrique, 77; Lyons to Saint Hilaire, 14 Feb. 1881; Ministère des Affaires Etrangères, Correspondence Politique, (henceforth A.E.), Angleterre, 789; same to same, 9 Mar. 1881, A.E. Angleterre, 790.

[3] Saint Hilaire to Minister of Marine, 17 Feb. 1881, A.E.M.D., Afrique, 57.

not to raise any discriminatory tariffs against British trade. Such were the maximum demands of the British. In practice they had to settle for less. A commission of demarcation in 1881 agreed that Britain should not interfere on the coast between the northern frontier of Sierra Leone and the Gambia; while France bound herself to non-intervention between the southern frontier of Sierra Leone and Liberia.[1] The expansion of Senegal had been checked. The Quai d'Orsay could console themselves by recalling that '. . . the British Government promised us more co-operation in our other affairs if we regulated the west African question to their satisfaction'.[2]

Granville and Kimberley were able to stick to the old ruts of west African policy. The delimitation talks with France in 1881 were based on the assumption that the north-eastern hinterland of Sierra Leone was expendable. In the same year Kimberley refused to sanction any step intended to pacify the warring tribes behind Lagos.[3] The following January, the Cabinet had to consider a new offer fudged up by the traders of the Cameroons, and he told Gladstone firmly that 'we have already quite enough territory on the West Coast'.[4] The Colonial Secretary took an equally strong line about the Niger Delta. When Consul Hewett urged that a loose protectorate should be formed between Benin and the Cameroons, Kimberley would not hear of it:

> 'Such an extensive protectorate as Mr. Hewett recommends would be a most serious addition to our burdens and responsibilities. The coast is pestilential; the natives numerous and unmanageable. The result of a British occupation would be almost certainly wars with the natives, heavy demands upon the British taxpayer. . . .'[5]

Looked at commercially, the Niger was the best of a poor lot of trading prospects, and it was worth keeping open to British merchants. But it was not worth the expense of administration. If a protectorate was set up, it would certainly not pay for itself. Moreover, there seemed to be no immediate danger that any other Power would rush in where Kimberley feared to enter on tip-toe. True, Galliéni had made a treaty with Segou, and Borgnis-Desbordes was moving on Bamako; but there are more than three thousand kilometres of Niger between Bamako and the Delta. Since 1880 a French firm had been established in the Oil

[1] The proceedings of the commissioners are in A.E.M.D. Afrique, 57.

[2] Minute by Affaires Etrangères on Minister of Marine and Colonies to Saint Hilaire, 8 Aug. 1881, *ibid.*

[3] Kimberley to Governor of Gold Coast and Lagos, 26 Aug. 1881, C. 4957, P.P. (1887) LX, 15.

[4] Kimberley to Gladstone, 2 Jan. 1882, P.R.O. 30/29/135.

[5] Minute by Kimberley, 6 Apr. 1882, C.O. 806/203, Appendix I, 7.

Rivers, but there were plenty of British firms as well. As late as 1882 the British and French governments saw no reason to upset the old coast arrangements for territorial self-denial.

It was the British invasion of Egypt which shattered this system, because it shattered the general Anglo-French collaboration. When France came out in open opposition to the new *régime* in Egypt toward the end of 1882,[1] she began to cast around for ways of putting pressure on London. There was plenty of scope for a policy of pin-pricks in west Africa, and these now began in earnest. Two French firms were on the lower Niger, trading not only at the coast, but pushing into the interior. The alarming feature of this activity was that the French consular agent in the river was now hard at work making treaties as far upstream as the kingdom of Nupe and along the Benue.[2] In Paris they had no illusions about their chances on the lower Niger, for the British position seemed too strong. But the Minister of Marine and Colonies had high hopes of the Benue:

> 'On the Niger, from the Delta up to its confluence with the Benue, our only aim must be to make sure of the freedom of our trade. . . . But on the Benue we can win a more privileged position by signing political or commercial conventions. . . . Such a policy, if it is skilfully pursued, would give our traders a route to Lake Tchad and to the rich markets of Adamawa and Bornu.'[3]

Plans of this sort meant a clash with the British firms upriver. Since 1879 they had been grouped into one concern with a capital of £300,000 and Lord Aberdare as chairman.[4] It was a rather more impressive group than the freebooters who had gone before. It had its merger. It had its peer. Above all, it had its Goldie.[5]

From 1879 until 1898, George Goldie was to dominate the affairs of the Niger. In a sense he was the residuary legatee of the old west coasters, but whereas they had been content to take the cash and let the politics go, he perceived that their methods were out of date. If the inland trade was to be made to pay, there must be a framework of law and order over those lesser breeds without the Foreign Jurisdiction Act; and since consuls and gunboats were few and far between, the merchants

[1] Duclerc to French Ambassador in London, 4 Jan. 1883, *D.D.F.* IV, no. 594.

[2] The records of French activities in the Delta, here very summarily referred to, are in A.E.M.D., Afrique, 78, 80, 85, 86.

[3] Minister of Marine and Colonies to Duclerc (Foreign Minister), 25 Jan. 1883, A.E.M.D., Afrique, 86.

[4] Formerly H. A. Bruce, Home Secretary, 1868–73, President of the Council, 1873–4.

[5] George Goldie Taubman (1846–1925). He later became Sir George Taubman Goldie. We shall refer to him as Goldie.

themselves must supply it. Only the merchant turned administrator could make a success of the hinterland. 'Energetic and unceasing political work' as Goldie put it, 'was at the root of success';[1] and on this principle he made treaties and assumed control on a scale no earlier trader had dreamed of.

From one point of view this showed the man's foresight. From another it suggested recklessness. Indeed he possessed both. The young candidate for the Royal Engineers who had taken his final examinations 'blind drunk', the odd man out who had fled England to escape from the sound of church bells, the company promoter who hopefully amalgamated four broken-down firms — it is all of a piece. Like many another great imperialist, Goldie was a great eccentric, although he differed from many African men of action in having no fear of women. He was an empire builder with a taste for anonymity, an atheist who wrote religious verse, a Rhodes with less money but more oddities.[2] This man, of a character ardent, articulate and acrimonious, was to do much in the making of British Nigeria. In 1881 his newly formed National African Company asked for a charter to administer the countries upriver, an offer which would have given the Queen a territory on the cheap and Goldie a monopoly on the rebound. The Foreign Office turned it down. The fact was that on the eve of the Scramble both the company and the inland trade were interests too small to engage the serious attention of the British government. The Foreign Office had opened the Niger, but beyond that it would not go. The push into the hinterland was a local expansive impulse of a sort, since the breakdown of the old trading methods and the need to dodge the consequences of falling prices had driven some of the merchants to go upstream. But for all the optimistic talk about the prospects of rubber and shea butter, the trade figures made a poor showing; and this was at a time when the old sentimental appeal of anti-slavery was muted. Lacking any larger implications, either economic or humanitarian, this local impulse failed to get forceful backing from Home. Not all the arts and pressures of Goldie could induce government to move. From the standpoint of official thinking at this time, he was no more than a reckless and expendable intruder.

But after the occupation of Egypt, when France was beginning to press on the lower Niger, he emerged as a personage of consequence to the policy-makers. Early in 1883 he and Aberdare were warning

[1] Goldie Taubman to Pauncefote, Private, 9 Dec. 1885, F.O. 84/1879.

[2] For an account of Goldie as the elderly eccentric lion *vide* D. Wellesley, *Sir George Goldie* (1934), 91–162.

ministers about the new threat to British interests. They urged that the gentleman's agreement between the two governments should be patched up. France should undertake not to acquire political influence on the lower Niger or the Benue, and in return she would be allowed to disregard the recent delimitation and to extend her rights between Senegal and the Upper Niger. Since Aberdare was careful to add that the political status of the Delta would remain unchanged and that nothing would be added to the government's burdens,[1] ministers caught eagerly at the suggestion. But the time for gentleman's agreements had passed. They had not worked in Egypt, and so the French did not intend that they should work in west Africa. The British ambassador in Paris reported that the suggested *modus vivendi* with the French was out of the question, since feeling against Britain was so exacerbated by her actions in Egypt.[2]

By March the Foreign Office was resigning itself to taking some sort of action in defence of the region;[3] but in the Colonial Office they were still determined not to take delivery of any more white elephants. The Assistant Under-Secretary minuted that:

> 'The view of the Foreign Office, which was pressed on Lord Kimberley, was that England should annex all unoccupied territory between Lagos and the French settlement of the Gaboon. Now this would be a tremendous undertaking. We could not annex it without making ourselves responsible for peace and order there. This would mean a task as heavy as governing the Gold Coast in a country and climate still severer. We should have to obtain a revenue which could only be obtained by levying customs dues, and I doubt English traders wishing for this.'[4]

Here indeed was the trouble. Nobody in government wanted to see the trade of the Delta and the potential trade of the interior whisked away behind the French tariff. But on the other hand, that trade was so small that the merchants would not help to carry the cost of annexation. So who would pay? Ministers would have to ask for a grant from the restive Radicals in the Commons. And by 1883 the Gladstone administration had enough troubles in the Commons without causing more crises of conscience among its backbenchers.

At the same time, another British sphere looked like slipping away. Trade in the Delta of the Congo was dominated by British firms; in the interior Lieutenant Cameron had made a set of treaties in the Seventies

[1] Aberdare to Granville, 28 Feb. 1883, enclosed in F.O. to C.O., 12 Mar. 1883, C.O. 806/203, Appendix 2, 8–10.

[2] Minute by Hemming, 24 Mar., on F.O. to C.O., 12 Mar. 1883, *ibid.*, Appendix III, 11.

[3] *idem.*

[4] Minute by Meade, 28 Mar. 1883, on above, *ibid.*

which gave the United Kingdom an option on the inner basin of the river.[1] Then Her Majesty's Government had rejected it. Now French and Belgian private enterprises were ready to take the Congo seriously. There was a vast river behind the mouths of the Congo, as Stanley had shown; and it had become possible to break into the hinterland, as Brazza had found. King Leopold II of the Belgians, who had floated an International Association to explore central Africa at the end of the Seventies, launched Stanley on another mission to open communications between the navigable Congo and Stanley Pool in the interior. At the same time Brazza too went back, acting in the name of the French section of the International Association. Here was a scramble, but only at the personal level of two explorers racing each other to the interior, each with the skimpiest of credentials. Stanley was little more than the personal agent of a petty monarch, for the International Association was a piece of mummery, and the Belgian Parliament would have nothing to do with its King's speculations.[2] The status of Brazza was no less peculiar. He too was nominally the agent of the International Association. Although his expedition was given a tiny grant by the French government,[3] the chief inspiration of his mission came from his own pleadings.[4] Paris had little desire to be involved in his adventures. Brazza however had heard that Leopold intended to seize all the interior basin of the Congo,[5] and this would cut off the French colony of Gabon from its hinterland and cast it into bankruptcy. To avoid the ruin of their colony, the French government in 1879 authorised Brazza to make a treaty at Stanley Pool. Just as the Foreign Office in the Eighteen fifties had worked to open the Niger hinterland, so the French government in the Eighteen seventies worked to open the Congo basin. They were far from wanting to extend their political control into the interior; their aim was simply to block the political extensions of others. Brazza's treaty was meant to 'reserve our rights, without engaging the future'.[6]

[1] A. B. Keith, *The Belgian Congo and the Berlin Act*, (1919), 27.

[2] The most complete accounts of the early African ventures of Leopold II are contained in four monographs by A. le R. P. Roeykens, *Les Débuts de l'Oeuvre africaine de Léopold II; Le Dessein africain de Léopold II (1875–76); Léopold II et la Conférence géographique de Bruxelles (1876); La Période initiale de l'Oeuvre africaine de Léopold II (1875–83), Académie, Royale des Sciences Coloniales, Classe des Sciences morales et politiques, Nouvelle série*, t. I, X *ter*.

[3] Between 1877 and 1882 the French Committee of the International Association was given 100,000 francs by the Ministry of Public Instruction and 22,000 francs by the Ministry of Marine and Colonies, President of French Committee to Freycinet, 4 Jul. 1885, A.E.M.D., Afrique, 93.

[4] le Général de Chambrun, *Brazza*, (Paris, 1930), 86.

[5] *idem*.

[6] Brazza to Ministry of Public Instruction, 1879, R. Maran, *Brazza et la Fondation de l'A.E.F.*, (Paris, 1941), 153.

Between 1880 and 1883 Stanley and Brazza played out their game in the Congo. This raised awkward questions for the British government. Leopold was a puny rival, and his Association could be pushed into the wings if the need arose. But after Brazza had made his treaty at Stanley Pool, the Foreign Office had to rely on the French disinclination to move in central Africa. In April 1882 the British ambassador in Paris asked the Quai d'Orsay whether the Congo mission had an official character. The discussion that followed showed that in the opinion of the Ministry of Marine and Colonies Brazza had no right to have made a treaty at all.[1] But on the Congo, as on the Niger, all this was to change. After the Egyptian affair had reached its climax, Paris did not feel the old need to pay deference to British susceptibilities; on 10 October the Foreign Minister over-rode the protests of the Marine, and announced that he intended to ask the Chamber to approve the treaty.[2] Ratification followed on 30 November. On 15 December the Foreign Office countered by recognising Portugal's claims to the Congo and its hinterlands[3]— claims which Britain had steadily rejected for the past forty years. In return Britain was to enjoy most favoured nation treatment in the trade of the Congo, a maximum tariff rate, and the setting up of an Anglo-Portuguese commission to supervise the traffic on the river. The treaty took fifteen months to complete, because the Portuguese went on hoping to get better terms from France than from the United Kingdom; but its purpose was always painfully clear. When it had at last been signed, the French ambassador in London caustically defined it as:

> '. . . A security taken by Britain to prevent either France or an international syndicate directed by France from setting foot in the Congo Delta. . . . The British Government . . . would rather parcel it out with Portugal, whom it can influence at will, than leave France with an open door.'[4]

That was true enough. During 1883 and 1884 the Gladstone Cabinet hoped to use the Portuguese as a sort of holding company which would decently veil the pre-eminence of British interests. Lisbon would do the governing, London would do the trade. In fact, British optimism

[1] Jauréguibéry (Marine) to Freycinet, 7 Jun. 1882, A.E.M.D. Afrique 59.

[2] Duclerc to Jauréguibéry, 10 Oct. 1882, *ibid.*

[3] This was not a new notion. It had been sketched in the Eighteen seventies by Morier, the British minister in Lisbon, who hoped to get counter-concessions from Portugal at Delagoa Bay. But the whole matter had lapsed in 1881, (*vide* S. E. Crowe, *The Berlin West African Conference, 1884–1885*, (1942), 16–22). Portugal asserted that by discovery and prior occupation she had a title to the line of coast between 8° and 5° 12′ South Latitude.

[4] Waddington to Ferry, 4 Mar. 1884, *D.D.F.*, V, no. 214.

went further than that. It was rumoured in the Foreign Office that King Leopold's own organisation might become '. . . as I hear is not unlikely, an English company'.[1] Both these sanguine hopes are very revealing. As a direct result of the Egyptian occupation, British interests in the Congo were now threatened by Leopold and the French. If their sphere was to be saved, then ministers could no longer rely on the old gentleman's agreement; from now on, official acts of policy would be needed. This they understood. Yet they refused to meet the new situation by any territorial extension of their own. Instead, they fell back on a variant of their technique of informal empire. Others could administer on paper, while they enjoyed the trade. With the King of Portugal as their caretaker on the coast and the King of the Belgians as their manager in the hinterland, all might still be saved, thanks to these regal subordinates.

For all the apparent dexterity of this solution, it was full of difficulties. As negotiations for the treaty with Portugal dragged on in 1883, the French hostility to the project became plainer. In London they badly wanted Egyptian concessions from Paris. Was the Congo worth the cost of rendering those concessions harder to get? Already in May the First Lord of the Admiralty was expressing his doubts to Granville: 'I presume we don't want to get into a quarrel with anyone in order to carry out a measure of which the advantage is so doubtful.'[2] The Congo was not much of a prize, that was common ground; and from there it was a short step to draw a new conclusion. Since the British position on the west coast was under pressure, ministers would have to resign themselves to the loss of some sphere or other. If the Congo was expendable, then what could be bought with it? Kimberley by June was arguing that the treaty should be scrapped and moreover that the Gambia should be sacrificed, if in return the government could '. . . above all get control of the Niger so as to prevent the possibility of our trade there being interfered with'.[3] Now at last ministers were compelled to work out their priorities for the west coast.

But precisely how was the Niger Delta to be kept? In November, a Cabinet committee decided 'to establish an efficient Consular Staff in the Niger and Oil Rivers District'. which should make treaties with the chiefs and induce them to accept British protection.[4] Action to forestall official French encroachment had become urgent. This was the largest

[1] Minute by Lister, 28 Feb. 1883, F.O. 84/1803.
[2] Northbrook to Granville, 2 May 1883, P.R.O. 30/29/139.
[3] Kimberley to Granville, 12 Jun. 1883, P.R.O. 30/29/153.
[4] Memo. by H. P. Anderson, 'On Events Connected with the West African Conference,' 21 Oct. 1884, F.O. 84/1813.

possible measure of agreement that could be found in that distracted Cabinet, but it represented the smallest possible measure of official commitment in the threatened region. At most, it meant a wider and a more intensive system of consular rule; but even this was to be whittled down by the caution of ministers. More consuls would mean more salaries; who ought to meet the bill? The traditionally-minded group in the Cabinet were clear that government should not find the money, and the Treasury took the same view. The whole plan was delayed, while efforts were being made to cajole the British firms in the Niger trade to help with the costs. None of them, except Goldie's National African Company, would do so.[1] The outcome of all this shilly-shallying was that not for another six months did the government nerve itself to pay, and Consul Hewett did not sail on his treaty-making mission until 28 May, 1884. He was to go down in the folk-lore of the west coast as 'Too-late Hewett'; but the real procrastination was that of his masters.

In fact, British plans went astray both in the Niger and in the Congo. Ministers had had their doubts already over the Anglo-Portuguese Treaty. They were to end by thoroughly repenting of it. Although the treaty had been designed to guarantee the interests of British traders, they were loud in opposition to it, because of the nominal Portuguese control and the actual Portuguese tariff.[2] Their protests were joined by the ancestral voices of the Anti-Slavery Society and the Baptist Union.[3] Behind all this agitation there may have lain, as Granville suspected, the fine hand of King Leopold.[4] The complaints of these pressure groups however were not enough to stop the treaty. That it failed was another of the consequences of the Egyptian crisis. After the occupation of Cairo, it seemed to French observers that Britain was driving for African empire. French diplomacy attacked the Anglo-Portuguese arrangement, both as a way of keeping the Congo open, and of putting pressure on the British in Egypt. The treaty was signed on 26 February, 1884, and during March the Quai d'Orsay was actively

[1] The negotiation is worked out in H. R. Rudin, *Germans in the Cameroons, 1884–1914*, (1938), 24–7.

[2] Manchester Chamber of Commerce to F.O., 6 Mar. 1884, (C. 4023), P.P. (1884), LVI, 89–93; G. H. Wright, *Chronicles of the Birmingham Chamber of Commerce*, (1913), 305.

[3] British and Foreign Anti-Slavery Society to F.O., 12 Apr. 1884, P.P. (1884) LVI, 112; Baptist Union to Her Majesty's Government, 28 Apr. 1884, *ibid.*, 119.

[4] Granville to Aberdare, 20 Feb. 1884, Fitzmaurice, *op. cit.*, II, 356. It is interesting to note that J. F. Hutton of the Manchester Chamber of Commerce wrote to the French firm of Daumas, Beraud et Cie, asking them to urge the French government to make a protest against the treaty. (Enclosure in Daumas, Beraud et Cie to Ferry, 18 Feb. 1884, A.E.M.D. Afrique, 89.) Hutton was an associate of Leopold's Congo schemes.

inciting opposition in Belgium, Holland and the United States, the Powers with trading interests in the Congo.[1] But in his search for supporters Ferry hooked a bigger fish than these. On 31 March he tried to get the Germans to join the resistance.[2] This overture was to begin the partition of west Africa.

Bismarck too had his grievances against British policy. To his rooted dislike of Gladstone as a man fit only to chop down trees and make up speeches,[3] he could now add a splenetic indignation at Granville's dawdling. In February 1883 he had enquired whether Britain would be ready to protect the German settlement at Angra Pequena; in December he repeated the enquiry. But for a further six and a half months the only reply he could get from London was a series of vague observations about British claims in that region. In part the muddle was caused by the objections of the Cape, in part by the British feeling that the colonial politicians had to be listened to, if south Africa was one day to be united around that province. But it was an important muddle. The occupation of Egypt gave Bismarck the chance to deepen the rift between Britain and France and to enter the African game.[4] In March and April of 1884 the Germans took steps to assert their own protectorate over Angra Pequena, but the ambiguity of their statements and the imperceptiveness of Gladstone's ministers (one of whom as late as June did not know where Angra Pequena was) left the British as naively ignorant as ever about where their attitude was taking them. It was beginning to take them a long way. On 5 May Bismarck hinted at this in two messages to London, in which German colonial claims and the question of the Congo were ominously linked.[5] By another in this chain of muddles the messages were not delivered.[6] Thereafter Bismarck swung the weight of Germany behind the Congo revisionists and then against the whole British position in west Africa. On 7 June he let the Foreign Office know that Germany refused to recognise the Anglo-Portuguese Treaty and wanted a conference to settle the Congo question. Granville was too discouraged to press on with ratification, and that was

[1] Ferry to diplomatic representatives at the Hague, Brussels and Washington, 15 Mar. 1884, *D.D.F.*, V, no. 219.

[2] Ferry to Courcel at Berlin, 31 Mar. 1884, *ibid.*, no. 226.

[3] *The Holstein Diaries*, (ed. N. Rich and M. H. Fisher), (1957), 18 Jan. 1884, 59–60.

[4] This episode has been minutely studied. We follow the general conclusions of W. O. Aydelotte, *Bismarck and British Colonial Policy, the Problem of South-West Africa, 1883–85*, (Philadelphia, 1937), *passim*; S. E. Crowe, *The Berlin West African Conference, 1884–85*, (1942), 34–49; A. J. P. Taylor, *Germany's First Bid for Colonies*, (1933), *passim*.

[5] Bismarck to German ambassador in London, 5 May 1884, *G.P.* IV, no. 738; Crowe, *op. cit.*, 28–9.

[6] *ibid.*, 51–5; Aydelotte, *op. cit.*, 62–3; Taylor, *Germany's First Bid for Colonies*, 33–5.

the end of the Treaty. But the retreat did not stop there. On 4 August the Germans suggested to the French that they should co-operate over west African questions generally at the impending conference,[1] and at the end of the month the French persuaded their new collaborators to join in an onslaught against the least expendable of the British spheres — the Niger.[2]

By now the whole of the British position along the coast seemed to be in danger. The Germans were established at Angra Pequena; on 5 July they had proclaimed a protectorate over Togoland, and on 14 July another over the Cameroons, where Hewett had indeed been too late. In addition, British designs in the Congo had been blocked, and now, as a final twist of the knife, their control of the Lower Niger was being challenged.

What had brought about this rout? Fundamentally, the cause was the British intervention in Egypt and its effects on the European balance. In the aftermath a resentful France had been driven into repudiating the former standstill arrangement throughout west Africa;[3] and now Germany was enabled to press heavily upon the British government. One of the worst penalties of the Egyptian occupation, so ministers found, was the torment of the Egyptian budgets. By 1884 it looked as though they might have to ask the British taxpayer to meet the deficits. Rather than run this political risk, they summoned a conference of the Powers to modify the law of liquidation. This was the moment Bismarck chose to withdraw his grace and favour. The desire to discipline Gladstone, the chance of having a colonial flutter in Africa, the decision to edge closer to France, all these worked to change Bismarck's approach to the Egyptian question. When the Egyptian conference opened on 28 June, the French stated their opposition to the British request. That was predictable; but Lord Granville suddenly woke up to the fact that the Germans were opposing it too, and he hurriedly dissolved the conference on 2 August.

This fiasco made a number of points clear. The Foreign Office had long been uneasily aware of how much they depended on Bismarck to underpin their position in Egypt. Rather than risk a drubbing from his

[1] Hatzfeldt to Bismarck, 11 Aug. 1884, *G.P.*, III, no. 681; Courcel to Ferry, 11 Aug. 1884, *D.D.F.*, V, no. 361; c.f. *Holstein Diaries, op. cit.*, 27 Aug. 1884, 155–6.

[2] Memo. by Ferry, Aug. 1884, *D.D.F.*, V, no. 376; Bismarck to Busch, 30 Aug. 1884, *G.P.*, III, no. 688.

[3] So much so that the Anglo-French delimitation remained unratified by the French throughout the whole west African crisis. Even at the end of 1885 the Marine were still holding back, on the ground that the convention damaged the future expansion of Sénégal. *vide Note pour le Ministre*, 4 July 1885; Freycinet to Minister of Marine, 31 Oct. 1885, A.E.M.D., Afrique, 86.

bâton égyptien, they had gone into retreat in west Africa. They had abandoned Angra Pequena, they had given up the Portuguese treaty, yet Berlin was still not satisfied. Soon it was to be the turn of the Niger.

THE CLAIMING OF THE NIGER

By the end of September 1884, Bismarck and Ferry had reached agreement over the official bases for the west African conference. It was to regulate the division of Africa by defining the concept of effective occupation, and to discuss the measures needed to assure free trade in the Congo and liberty of navigation on that river and on the Niger — issues which brought up the whole question of jurisdiction in those regions. In October, Granville accepted an invitation to the conference, but in doing so he specifically objected to any form of international control over the Lower Niger.[1] Routed elsewhere along the coast, he was at last beginning to defend the British sphere in the Delta.

In July Consul Hewett had reached the Niger at last, and he had started snapping up territory in the Delta by treaties of protectorate with the chiefs. He hurried on to the Cameroons, but arrived five days after the German protectorate had been proclaimed on 14 July. From then until November Hewett carried on in the Delta with his treaty forms, collecting a strong hand for Granville to play at the conference. His case on the coast and in the Oil Rivers, at any rate, would be a good one.

But there were others to the rescue as well. This was to be Goldie's opportunity. If Granville was to claim that British interests were already supreme throughout the Lower Niger, what of the French firms operating there, with their treaties and their ambitions on the Benue? By the autumn of 1884 they were reporting that their stations had been pushed four hundred miles up the Niger, and five hundred miles up the Benue.[2] The French companies posed a problem insoluble at government level. If they could not be driven out, they might be bought out. Goldie had waged a violent price war against the *Compagnie du Sénégal* and the *Société française de l'Afrique Equatoriale* since 1880.[3] The inland trade needed a monopoly to make it solvent. By October 1884, as the diplomats prepared to settle the fate of the Niger, Goldie had bought out the

[1] For the British attitude toward the proposed conference *vide* C. 4205 and C. 4241, P.P. (1884–5) LV.

[2] Mattei (French consular agent in the Niger Delta) to Ferry, 13 Oct. 1884, A.E.M.D., Afrique, 86.

[3] Report of Lieutenant Cavalier, 29 Aug. 1883, encl. in Under-Sec. of Colonies to Ferry, 12 Feb. 1884, *ibid.*

Compagnie du Sénégal and was negotiating for the other company.[1] Shareholders of the *Société française* were tired of trading at a loss,[2] and they sold out shortly afterwards.[3] Goldie was monopolising the river traffic once more, and his agents made a series of treaties with the riverain chiefs. He next turned to monopolising the trade of the Moslem emirates far beyond the confluence. At the end of December he induced Joseph Thomson, the celebrated explorer, to undertake the task. While the conference was sitting at Berlin, Thomson was moving through northern Nigeria, making treaties for the National African Company in Sokoto and Gandu.[4] Goldie had moved quickly and done much. Whether the French threat to the Lower Niger was ever as great as he liked to claim is doubtful;[5] but his enterprise had considerably strengthened the British thesis at Berlin.

With this collection of treaties, purchases and promissory notes, the British government struggled to hold its sphere on the Niger. All this zeal in the manufacturing of evidence was rewarded in Berlin. A timely swing towards the British position by Bismarck, who had little wish to go to extremes with his Francophil policy, and the prudent concession of the Congo, enabled the Foreign Office to make good their claims to the Lower Niger. By 1 December they had managed to lay the bogey of an international status for the river.[6] The conference went on to frame a definition of effective occupation, so admirably vague that it mollified the Gladstonians' dislike of extended claims in west Africa.[7] While the Congo basin was divided between Portugal, France and the International Association, the navigation of the Upper Niger was placed under French, and that of the Lower Niger under British control. It remained for the Foreign Office to decide how its new responsibilities were to be carried out. The critical period was over. At the onset of the scramble, ministers had been almost swept off their feet; under

[1] Captain of the 'Dumont d'Urville' to Marine, 14 Oct. 1884, encl. in Under-Sec. of Colonies to Ferry, 5 Dec. 1884, *ibid.*

[2] Mattei to Ferry, 13 Oct. 1884, *ibid.*

[3] Goldie to Anderson, 1 Nov. 1884, F.O. 84/1814; c.f. *The Royal Niger Company . . . Proceedings at the Tenth Ordinary General Meeting . . . 29 July, 1890.*

[4] J. B. Thomson, *Joseph Thomson, African Explorer*, (1896), 137, 143, 160.

[5] There is a mystery here. Why did the French government make no effort to stop the sale of the two French companies to Goldie? There seems to be nothing in the archives of the Ministère des Affaires Etrangères or of the Ministère de la France d'Outre-Mer to throw light on this. But it is worth noting that Ferry rejected an earlier scheme for buying neutralisation of the Delta by concessions to Britain elsewhere by asking: 'Are our immediate interests in the Lower Niger large enough to justify the sacrifices which we might thus find ourselves driven to?' (Ferry to Minister of Marine, 11 June 1884, A.E.M.D. Afrique, 86.)

[6] Crowe, *op. cit.*, 75–7, 127.

[7] *ibid.*, 176–91.

pressure they had at last been forced to determine their priorities. They had staked their claims, they had underwritten their bids, and at Berlin they had got their way.

MOTIVES FOR CLAIMING THE NIGER

Why, amid their general retreat along the west coast, had ministers decided to hold the Lower Niger? Here was the region with the best trade. Here was the best waterway into the interior. Here lay the best opportunity of breaking the power of the African middlemen. In so far as British policy during the west African 'scramble' was governed by any clear motive, it was to protect trade.

Yet the motives were very different from those postulated in the theory of economic imperialism. It was not the case that the merchants pressed the Crown to pacify and develop the Lower Niger for them. Most of the traders still wanted to operate in a *res nullius*, where there would be a fair field and no tariffs, without an imperial authority to tax them and get in their way. All they asked for was protection against the interference of foreign governments[1] and help in breaking the power of the middlemen. Neither was it the case that industrialists and investors at Home looked on west Africa as the remedy for their difficulties during the Great Depression. Nor had government when it claimed the Niger the slightest intention of employing the power of the state to administer and exploit it. Indeed, the traditionalists of the Cabinet acquiesced in the sphere on the Niger because they thought it the one region where merchants could be made to pay the bill. The official programme fell a long way short of administering the region or turning it into a colonial estate. There is no sign that British public opinion was hungry for west African territory. In 1884 and 1885 opinion was agitated about the Franchise Bill, anxious about the crisis in Ireland and in Afghanistan, agonised about the fate of Gordon.[2] The scramble for the west coast aroused very little interest. At no time before, during or after the Berlin Conference was there a parliamentary debate about its aims or its results.

It seems then that any attempt to analyse British policy in terms of some one decisive factor breaks down before the facts. There is nothing

[1] As late as 1883 west African merchants were still demanding all help short of control. They urged the Earl of Derby to see to it that foreign annexations between the Gold Coast and Lagos should be blocked — but they did not call for British annexation as the way to block them, (Manchester Chamber of Commerce to C.O., 4 Dec. 1883; Merchants of London trading to West Africa to C.O., 7 Dec. 1883, C.O. 806/212, 108–9.

[2] H. M. Lynd, *England in the Eighteen-Eighties . . .*, (New York, 1945), 218–25.

for it but to approach the problem from another direction. Instead of postulating a single, necessary and sufficient cause of these events, it is well to be less pretentious and to define them as the result of an interplay between non-recurrent factors in the early Eighteen eighties. Government policy in west Africa seems to have evolved as a by-product of three major crises, one in Egypt, another in Europe, a third in the domestic politics of Great Britain, and a minor crisis on the west coast itself.

The Egyptian affair had started off the 'scramble'. It had ended the standstill arrangement in Africa. It had run British policy into a noose held by Bismarck. When Germany's policy swung towards France, the two of them squeezed hard on the British position in west Africa. That position was already susceptible to change, as the bases of tribal societies and economies were eroded by the gradual commercial penetration of the interior. So long as other things stayed equal, Gladstone's Cabinet thought it could cope with the results of this erosion by making only small adjustments in its traditional policy. But things did not stay equal, and the Egyptian aftermath shifted the European balance, blowing these calculations sky-high.

This left the Cabinet in a dilemma. On a rational view of priorities, it was sensible to give ground in such places as Angra Pequena, Togoland, New Guinea, Samoa, the Congo and the Cameroons, so as to hold ground in Egypt. But this involved some political friction at Home. During the nineteenth century the political nation was seldom interested in the expansion of British frontiers, but opinion in general, and vested interests in particular, were usually averse to the contraction of their trading empire.[1]

The Liberal administration had come a long way since the glad, confident morning of 1880. By now the Whigs and the Radicals were at each others' throats, and their quarrels had riven the Cabinet apart. The Egyptian misfortunes and Parnellite manoeuvres had brought its prestige so low that in March the government was beaten by seventeen votes.[2] From February until December 1884 the government was pushing its Franchise Bill through the Commons and then wrestling over its consequences with the Lords. Whig ministers were alarmed at the prospect of Irish peasants with votes, their Radical colleagues were alarmed lest there should not be enough of them.[3] On top of all this friction and intrigue were superimposed the Franco-German *entente*

[1] For example, over the Gambia in the 1870s and again in 1881.
[2] *Hansard*, 3rd ser., CCLXXXV, col. 1725.
[3] Chamberlain, *op. cit.*, 137–8; Hammond, *op. cit.*, 345, 351.

and Bismarck's bid for colonies. On this issue the forward party in the Cabinet was able to exploit the Cabinet splits to press their policy on the traditionalists who kept their rooted dislike of African adventures. The Radicals, Chamberlain and Dilke, wanted action. For tactical reasons they were both willing to stomach the German irruption into the Cameroons,[1] but they were determined to make a spirited stand somewhere. They could see the political risks of passivity, and anyhow it did not agree with their temperaments. This was the spirit of Chamberlain when he wrote, 'I don't give a damn about New Guinea and I am not afraid of German colonisation, but I don't like being cheeked by Bismarck or anyone else;'[2] and by Dilke when he blamed ministerial dawdling for letting the Germans into the Cameroons.[3] But it was not only the Radicals who wanted to do something in west Africa. Granville himself came to think that the Lower Niger must be safeguarded, if need be by the extension of official control.[4] Even so orthodox a Whig as the Lord Chancellor, Selborne, wrote:

> 'I must confess to a feeling of humiliation at the passive part which we have played, and are still playing, under the idea that a breach with Germany, at this juncture, would make our chances of honourable extrication from the Egyptian difficulty even less than they are.'[5]

The restiveness in the Cabinet finally overbore the moderates. It was common knowledge that the right-wing ministers, Hartington, Northbrook and Selborne might split off, and that Chamberlain and Dilke might do the same on the left.[6] Gladstone in the middle might dislike the whole quarrel over these west African affairs, but under pressure from both the dissident groups in his government he had no alternative but to let the spirit blow where it listed. The future of the Delta cut only a small figure amid the many racking dissensions of that government; but the dangers contained in those other dissensions helped to decide the fate of the Lower Niger.

It would seem that the claiming of the Niger in 1884 was motivated neither by increased enthusiasm for enlarging the empire nor by more pressing economic need to exploit the region. The incentive to advance

[1] Memo. by Herbert Bismarck, 24 Sept. 1884, *G.P.*, IV, no. 753; Herbert Bismarck to Fürst Bismarck, 7 Mar. 1885, *ibid.*, no. 760.

[2] Chamberlain to Dilke, 29 Dec. 1884, Garvin, *op. cit.*, I, 497.

[3] Dilke's *Diary*, 22 Sept. 1884, B.M. Add. MSS. 43936A.

[4] Fitzmaurice, *op. cit.*, II, 341; Gwynn and Tuckwell, *op. cit.*, I, 431–2.

[5] Selborne to Gordon, 31 Dec. 1884, Earl of Selborne, *Memorials. Part II: Personal and Political, 1865–1895*, (1898), 131.

[6] Morley to Spence Watson, 5 Jan. 1885, F. W. Hirst, *Early Life and Letters of John Morley*, (1927), 208–9.

here was no stronger than of old. It sprang from a passing concatenation of minor trade rivalries in west Africa with major changes of front by the Powers in Europe and the Mediterranean, mainly provoked by British blunders and difficulties in Egypt. The Liberals claimed the Lower Niger merely to prevent an existing field of British trade from disappearing behind French tariff walls; and they limited their new commitment to this negative purpose. They had not decided to found an ambitious west African empire. All they had done in the face of French hostility was to make a technical change in the international status of the Lower Niger. Henceforward the Powers recognised this country as a British sphere, but government still had no serious intention of administering, developing or extending it.

The Charter and Its Enemies

By the terms of the Berlin Act, the Liberals were now committed to a semblance of effective occupation on the Lower Niger. Any direct annexation was out of the question: it would have been against the prejudices of their supporters. Gladstone and Granville had drifted into the Niger like a couple of imperial Micawbers looking for something to turn up. An expanded consulate could be rigged up for the coast itself, and there were good reasons for hoping that Goldie could be saddled with the cost of policing the country upriver.

Goldie's own plans were clearcut. The best guarantee for keeping his monopoly in the hinterland lay in seizing political control of it; and so he wanted a royal charter for his company. He could expect a warmer welcome now than he had received in 1881. By his swift action in the crisis Goldie had deserved well of the Foreign Office, a point he was not slow in making. The public flotation of the company had shown that it was financially reliable, and it had a social *cachet* which the palm oil ruffians had never enjoyed. But what above all endeared it to the Foreign Office was that it offered a way of meeting the requirements of effective occupation for nothing. As an Assistant Under-Secretary wrote enthusiastically:

> '[The Company] . . . is perfectly able and willing to discharge the duties of administration for which H[er] M[ajesty's] G[overnment] have become responsible, and unless it sh[oul]d be considered necessary that this country sh[oul]d go to the great expense of setting up the machinery of gov[ernmen]t upon the two rivers where the Co[mpany] now rules supreme, there seem

to be no other course open, and certainly no better one, than that of legalizing and affirming the position of the Co[mpany] and placing the business of administration into its hands.'[1]

This was a comforting argument for Gladstonians, and it was supplemented by the aristocratic persuasions of Lord Aberdare. The company made formal application for the charter on 12 February, 1885, and in a supporting letter its chairman drew a seductive picture of the inland regions. Prospects were so glittering that it was '. . . not only probable but certain that their existing trade, large as it is, will speedily be developed in proportions and directions hitherto unexpected'.[2] A gorgeous vista indeed.

At first the projected charter attracted most of the Cabinet as a way of avoiding any direct territorial responsibility. Granville wanted to grant the charter as '. . . the cheapest and most effective way of meeting [the obligations imposed by the Niger Act of Navigation]'.[3] Nearly all ministers agreed, believing mistakenly that the charter would involve no new commitment and would merely recognise the private *de facto* jurisdiction of the company.[4] But several ministers were much disturbed when the lawyers told them that they must declare a protectorate before they could give the charter. Selborne, Harcourt, Childers and Derby all had their doubts, and it was only the fear of immediate German inroads into the region which reconciled them to it.[5]

The Foreign Office timetable was drawn up. First, there must be a rough delimitation between the 'Niger Districts' (as the hinterland was to be called) and the German Cameroons; this was done by an exchange of notes in May and June. 'The second step was to be notification of protectorate, the third the charter.'[6] The new status of the Niger Districts was gazetted on 5 June;[7] but the charter had run into trouble. Goldie wanted a charter on the lines of the North Borneo arrangement, which would practically have given him autonomy and a legal monopoly.

[1] Memo. by Villiers Lister, 30 Jan. 1885, F.O. 84/1879.

[2] Aberdare to Granville, 13 Feb. 1885, F.O. 84/1879.

[3] Lister to Herbert (C.O.), 6 Jan. 1885, F.O. C.P. no no., ('Further Correspondence *re* the West African Conference'), Jan. 1885.

[4] Derby to Granville, 20 Oct. 1884, P.R.O. 30/29/120; Memo. by Derby, 19 Feb. 1885, F.O. 84/1879.

[5] Memos. on the proposed charter, written by almost all members of the Cabinet are in F.O. 84/1879.

[6] Anderson to Pauncefote (Permanent Under-Secretary), 12 May 1885, *ibid.*

[7] The Niger Districts were defined as including 'the territories on the line of coast between the British Protectorate of Lagos and the right or western bank of the Rio del Rey', and also the 'territories on both banks of the Niger, from its confluence with the River Benue at Lukoja to the sea, as well as the territories on both banks of the River Benue, from the confluence up to and including Ibi'. (*London Gazette*, 5 Jun. 1885.)

Naturally Granville backed the draft, but the Cabinet as a whole would not pass it. Goldie then tried again, still holding out for large powers. Anderson reported:

> 'The opinion of the Cabinet was decided [*sic*] against such a charter, and I have repeatedly told him that the only one that would have a chance of acceptance would be one in which the Government control would be in some shape definite. . . .
>
> Mr. Goldie Taubman is a most able man, but he is, body and soul, devoted to the interests of the Company and finds it difficult to comprehend the necessity of tending [*sic*] to considerations of policy.'[1]

The matter was still stuck here in May when the Gladstone government fell. Nor did Goldie fare much better with Salisbury. The Law Officers pointed out that the large powers which he wanted suffered from the tiresome drawback of being illegal.[2] There were more delays, and Goldie dropped a hint that '. . . if the charter was not granted it might be necessary in the interests of the shareholders to hand over the Co[mpany]'s rights to the French'.[3] It was no wonder that the Foreign Office began speculating that consular officers might be needed after all for the government of the Niger Districts.[4] The negotiators went on floundering over the degree of official control that Goldie should have to endure. At the end of the year another complication arose. The Berlin Act committed the signatories to free trade on the Niger. Goldie, as everyone knew, wanted a monopoly. In December the Germans protested against his claim to exclusive rights,[5] and Salisbury responded by trying to scale down the Company's pretensions. At this point his administration fell in its turn, to be replaced by another Gladstone ministry. The question of the charter was then considered by a third Cabinet and a third set of Law Officers. This time it was granted. The charter was finally approved by an Order in Council of 25 June, 1886.[6] The Company was empowered to administer justice, to enforce treaty rights, to collect customs duties and to spend the receipts solely on the expenses of rule. The projected monopoly had been scrapped on paper; but in return Goldie was freed from any direct interference by government. From now until the end of the century the Lower Niger was to

[1] Memo. by Anderson, n.d. but *c.* 12–18 May 1885, F.O. 84/1879.

[2] Law Officers to Salisbury, 8 Aug. 1885 and addendum, 20 Aug. 1885, *ibid.*

[3] Warburton (of F.O.) to Pauncefote, 26 Aug. 1885, (record of conversation with Goldie), *ibid.*

[4] Memorandum by Pauncefote, 30 Aug. 1885, *ibid.*

[5] *Note Verbale*, German Embassy to Foreign Office, 2 Dec. 1885, *ibid.* c.f. Goldie Taubman to Salisbury, 28 Dec. 1885, *ibid.*

[6] The charter was published in the *London Gazette*, 13 Jul. 1886.

be ruled by a chartered company, the Royal Niger Company, as it was soon to call itself.

Out of this involved record of haggling there emerge two wider considerations. Nearly a year and a half went by between the signing of the Berlin Act and the granting of the charter. This was caused first and foremost by the awkward fact that the Liberals were chartering a confessedly monopolistic company for the purpose of carrying out their international obligation to maintain freedom of trade in the Lower Niger. This alarmed the German government, who could foresee that the Cameroons might be cut off from its hinterland; they therefore threw obstacles in the way of the charter and helped to delay it — this at a time when Bismarck was disposed to go to any reasonable length to restore good Anglo-German relations,[1] and when the British still badly needed his support in Cairo and Constantinople.

Moreover, the Royal Niger Company, once chartered, was certain to arouse the wrath of Liverpool, as a government-backed device for throttling their trade. Goldie was an expert in the gentle art of making enemies, and the monopoly which he asserted in spite of the charter (and which everyone knew he would assert) teemed with chances of friction and complaint. 'Nothing in this our Charter', so it was recited, 'shall be deemed to authorise the Company to set up or grant any monopoly of trade.' But this disavowal was belied by the other clauses. The granting of political authority meant that government was giving back to Goldie with one hand the monopoly it had taken away with the other. It was too much to expect that once he had been conceded jurisdiction, he would concede competition. The Company absolutely needed the monopoly. The inland trade could not be made to pay without it. Palm oil prices had fallen from more than £35 per ton in 1883 to less than £21 in 1886, and they were still on their way down.[2] The directors of the Company had to admit at the end of 1885 that it had been a bad year, and they predicted that there might be need to make a call on the partly paid-up shares.[3] What was more, the Stock Exchange was taking a bleaker view of the commercial prospects of the western Sudan than Lord Aberdare had done. The £2 shares of the company had now dropped to 10s.[4]

[1] e.g. After the agreement in principle on a delimitation between the Cameroons and the Niger Districts (May–Jun. 1885), the Foreign Office had avoided a detailed delimitation until Goldie's men had penetrated as far as Yola on the upper Benue. Rather than risk a conflict in that region, Bismarck had reined his own men back. (Rudin, *op. cit.*, 66–7.)

[2] P.P. (1890–1) LXXXIX, 134–5.

[3] *Special Report of National African Company*, 8 Dec. 1885.

[4] Unsigned statement on copy of above (in Goldie's writing) encl. in Goldie Taubman to Pauncefote, Private, 8 Dec. 1885, F.O. 84/1879.

The result was that British policy over the charter went round in a vicious circle. To make the new protectorate pay, it was necessary to push inland. To push inland, it was necessary to use the Company. To use the Company, it was necessary to grant it a monopoly. To grant it a monopoly, it was necessary to face the complaints of Germany and Liverpool. Goldie was not a Rhodes. There were no gold and diamonds to bear the cost of his push to the north.

So resolved were the imperial authorities against enlarging their responsibilities in the Niger, that they hoped to get the merchants to take over the Delta as well as the lower river. Liverpool had refused to share the cost of the floating consulate in 1883–4. But Goldie in 1885 was anxious that his charter should be widened to cover the Oil Rivers,[1] and the Foreign Office looked forward to his combining with the Delta merchants for this purpose. But the negotiations turned out to be thorny. When Consul Hewett complained that his powers and his staff were hopelessly inadequate, Anderson in the Foreign Office explained why the Oil Rivers had been kept in this Cinderella status:

> 'We have been waiting in the hope that the Niger Co[mpany] would be able to come to terms with the Oil Rivers traders and bring the district within their system — this hope is not likely to be realized.'[2]

This was understandable. Obviously Liverpool did not find Goldie's scheme congenial, since his charter was upsetting the business of '. . . 10 firms, whose trade is 3, 4 or 5 times as great as that of the Niger Company'.[3] To them Goldie was an *arriviste* whose arrival was not made any the more palatable by his connection with government, an intruder whose intrusion challenged the pre-eminence of the houses which had built up the oil trade. Their operations were mainly confined to the coast,[4] as they always had been, and their prosperity still seemed to depend on the prosperity of the coastal middlemen. When the Royal Niger Company obstructed the African brokers in fetching oil from

[1] This seems a legitimate deduction from a letter from Goldie to Anderson, saying: 'I have been thinking of a remark of yours that we have an urgent "present" question to think of and must not look too far forward. . . . The bird in the hand is worth two in the bush, but in catching the first is there any need to bind oneself not to take the other two afterwards? Ten or twenty years hence Bonny will be an important question for Great Britain.' (Goldie Taubman to Anderson, Private, 6 Nov. 1885, F.O. 84/1879.)

[2] Minute by Anderson, 18 Oct. 1887 on Memorandum by Hewett, 15 Oct. 1887, F.O. 84/1828.

[3] Fergusson (Foreign Under-Secretary) to Salisbury, 18 Apr. 1888, Salisbury Papers, (Fergusson). The Salisbury Papers, Christ Church, Oxford are henceforth referred to as S.P.

[4] But the old-established firm of Hatton and Cookson also traded upriver. They too opposed the claims of the Royal Niger Company. (Hatton and Cookson to Rosebery, 14 Jul. 1886, F.O. 84/1880).

upcountry, then Liverpool had to pay more for it, a bitter thought in the late Eighties, when selling prices were steadily dropping. So towards the end of 1886, the African Association was firing the first shots in what was to be a long war against the charter.[1] The following year they were supporting the middlemen of New Calabar and Brass against the regulations of the Royal Niger Company.[2] But even Liverpool had middleman troubles of its own, and the Association clashed with Ja Ja, the great African trading chief at Opobo. This led to the celebrated breaking of Ja Ja by the cocksure consul, Harry Johnston;[3] but, more important than that, it revealed how far the traditional basis of trading relations in the Delta was being shattered by the penetration of European trade.

The Foreign Office supported the African Association in the Ja Ja affair since it disposed of a restraint of trade.[4] But officials would not listen to its protests against the restraint of trade upriver caused by the charter. In one of the raciest of his memoranda the head of the African Department explained why:

> 'Till recently the trade in this part of Africa was carried on in a loose sort of fashion by houses doing, individually, no large trade. They worked through the coast middlemen who barred them from the interior markets. With them the traders sometimes stood in, sometimes wrangled, settling disputes in a patriarchal fashion through mercantile courts under the fatherly casual superintendence of consular officers. There was no publicity so few questions were asked.
>
> The rush for Africa has broken up the little family party: and the rich and powerful Niger Co[mpany] on the one hand, the Germans on the other, have broken through the middlemen crust and forced their way to the interior markets. The Liverpool men are fighting the battle of the middlemen. . . . Their object is to reform the broken crust. Were they to succeed they might benefit till it was broken again, which would not be long delayed, and would stifle the brilliant prospect, for trade generally, of free access to the comparatively civilized Mahometan tribes of the interior. Their demand is now as complete an anachronism as would be a petition for the restoration of mediaeval guilds.'[5]

So it was a disappointment for Anderson to find that Goldie had not managed to haul the Liverpool interests into his net. That would have

[1] African Association to Iddesleigh, 29 Nov. 1886, F.O. 84/1880.

[2] Macdonald, Documents *re* Niger Delta, 9 Jun. 1890, cap. 5 and 6, F.O. 84/2109.

[3] This episode is discussed in W. Geary, *Nigeria under British Rule*, (1927), App. I; A. N. Cook, *British Enterprise in Nigeria*, (Penn. 1943), 64–5; R. Oliver, *Sir Harry Johnston and the Scramble for Africa*, (1957), 107, 23.

[4] e.g. Minute by Anderson, 24 Oct. 1887 on Johnston to Salisbury, no. 18, 24–28 Sept. 1887, F.O. 84/1828.

[5] Memo. by Anderson, 15 Mar. 1887, F.O. 84/1880.

strengthened the chartered company, and it would have saved government the trouble of supervising the Rivers. Next, Anderson considered whether the Delta should be added to the Lagos protectorate.[1] But within a few weeks government's hope of shuffling out of the Rivers had revived once more. Liverpool might be the middleman's friend, but the pace of change in the Delta was so fast that even the palm oil ruffians were beginning to move with the times. At last the African Association began to glimpse the facts of life. Instead of competing briskly against each other for oil, they formed buying rings (the move which had ended by putting Ja Ja on board ship for the West Indies); instead of sitting on the coast and waiting for supplies, they started to trade inland, to those markets which were still outside the range of Goldie's monopoly. Their 'long dull slumbering apathy', as Consul Hewett remarked, with his love of the redundant adjective, had disappeared; and now they were '. . . really exerting themselves to extend the basis of their trading operations to the inland market'.[2] If they could not beat Goldie, they could join him. An agreement to extend the charter to the Oil Rivers would cut the new Liverpool cartel into a larger sphere of monopoly, which they would enter, not as prisoners, but as allies. So negotiations began once more between Goldie and the African Association.[3] This delighted the Foreign Office. By 1888 Anderson was taking it as a matter of course that 'if the present negotiations succeed the whole coast will go under the Niger co[mpany]'.[4] It looked as though they might. In April Rogerson, the chairman of the African Association, told the government that he was '. . . pretty confident of making a fair arrangement with the Niger Company . . . if it is understood that the Charter is to be extended to the Oil Rivers'.[5] The campaign against Goldie was magically transformed into sympathetic understanding. By two agreements of 12 October and 6 November 1888, the African Association declared its willingness '. . . to fuze with the Royal Niger Company on condition of an extension of the Company's Charter'.[6] At last it looked as though the trials of the Foreign Office were over, and

[1] Minute by Anderson, 24 Oct. 1887, on Johnston to Salisbury, no. 18, 24–8 Sept. 1887, F.O. 84/1828; Minute by Anderson, 29 Nov. 1887, on same to same, no. 22, 21 Oct. 1887, *ibid.*

[2] Hewett to Salisbury, no. 34, 10 Nov. 1888, F.O. 84/1881.

[3] Minute by Anderson, 15 Jan. 1888, on Johnston to Salisbury, no no., 13 Dec. 1887, F.O. 84/1828.

[4] Minute by Anderson, 15 Jan. 1888, on Johnston to Salisbury, no no., 13 Jan. 1887, F.O. 84/1828.

[5] Fergusson to Salisbury, 18 Apr. 1888, S.P. (Fergusson).

[6] Macdonald to Salisbury, no. 11, 12 Jun. 1889, F.O. 84/1940 (also printed as an F.O.C.P. and bound in the same volume).

that they had finally managed to get the Oil Rivers off their hands.[1]

But it was all too good to be true. Three factors worked against the plan. In the first place Liverpool decided to play for higher terms. Within three months of having signed the agreement, members of the Association were hinting that what they really wanted was a charter of their own.[2] Secondly, the plan ran into obstacles in the Delta itself. On 17 January 1889 Major Claude Macdonald was sent to the Niger to enquire into the proposed extension of the charter.[3] He found that local opinion was solidly against it. Naturally, the chiefs and the African traders of the Rivers were opposed to coming into the grip of Goldie. But so too were the local agents of the African Association, who gave the Commissioner views culled 'from their employers at home'. Evidently Liverpool was dreaming of a separate charter. The missionaries and the Africans wanted the region to become a colony. The Liverpool men, who associated colonies with customs, wanted it to remain under consular rule.[4] There were too many difficulties in the way of the plan. Evidently too, the old consular system as operated by a swashbuckler such as Johnston or a general factotum such as Hewett, had proved quite inadequate.[5] For the time being the Foreign Office contented itself with widening and overhauling the consular jurisdiction in the Delta,[6] although it was becoming harder and harder to leave things at that. Then in 1890 a third factor worked to destroy Goldie's hope once and for all. Since the chartering of his company, it had been constantly criticised by the German government as a monopoly exerted in flagrant violation of the Berlin Act, and as a hindrance to free

[1] It is noteworthy how utterly the Foreign Office in the pursuit of its long-standing objectives completely disregarded the advice of its men on the spot. Vice-Consul Johnston wanted the Oil Rivers to be made into a colony. (Memo. on the Oil Rivers, 26 Jul. 1888, F.O. 84/1882.) Consul Hewett began challenging the treaties and the tariffs of the Niger Company at the end of 1888. (Hewett to Salisbury, telegram, no no., 5 Nov. 1888; same to same, telegram, no no. 9 Nov. 1888.) Anderson minuted, 9 Nov. that 'this . . . sudden activity against the Co[mpany] at the present moment is very unfortunate'. And again: 'I suspect Hewett thinks we are going to make the Oil Rivers a Colony and is playing for the Governorship,' (F.O. 84/1881.)

[2] '. . . The Association would rather have a distinct and separate Company, with a separate Charter.' (Rogerson to Hewett, 5 Feb. 1889.) 'The newspapers are pegging away at the Niger Company. At the present moment any connexion with that Company would not enhance the credit of our Association in the eyes of the public.' (Holt to Hewett, 5 Feb. 1889.) Both letters are quoted in Macdonald to Salisbury, no. 11, 12 Jun. 1889, F.O. 84/1940.

[3] Lister to Macdonald, 17 Jan. 1889, F.O. 84/1940.

[4] Macdonald to Salisbury, no. 11, 12 Jun. 1889, (report of his commission of enquiry), *ibid.*

[5] *vide* e.g. minute by Anderson, 1 Aug. 1888 on Hewett to Salisbury, no. 25, 20 Jun. 1888: '. . . the absolute failure of our attempt at consular adminstration. . . . The result is chaos.' (F.O. 84/1881.)

[6] F. E. Hodges, *Consular Jurisdiction in Her Majesty's Protectorate of the Niger Coast*, (1895), 89–179, (text of the Order in Council), 12–24 (analysis).

navigation and fair trade in the interior. Possession of the Cameroons was proving as much of an embarrassment to Berlin as possession of the Oil Rivers to London. London wanted to strengthen the Royal Niger Company, so as to cut its costs in the Rivers; Berlin wanted to weaken it, so as to cut theirs in the Cameroons. During the Anglo-German negotiations of 1890, which were to give Salisbury his all-important concession in the valley of the Nile, the Germans returned to the old grievances against Goldie and demanded '. . . an expression of our intention not to place the Oil Rivers under a Chartered Company'. No objections of substance were raised by the British. They were playing for higher stakes at Berlin than the future system of rule in the Delta, and they promised that 'it is understood that as regards the Niger a fresh start will be made'.[1] The German intervention was decisive. From now on there could be no more hankering after Goldie's solution; and there was nothing for it except to bring the region under a more elaborate consular system than before. In 1891 Macdonald was to become Consul-General with six vice-consuls under him. The new *régime* was simply '. . . to pave the way for placing the Territories over which Her Majesty's protection is and may be extended, directly under British rule'. Here at last was the genesis of a more formal government in the Rivers. It came in 1893, when the region was organised as the Niger Coast Protectorate. But the scale remained petty and the attitude pinchbeck. London remained resolute against incurring expense in the dismal place, and it was laid down that the cost of administration was to be met by customs duties.[2] Government had not got the best of both worlds. It had finally been driven into a larger commitment; but it had taken steps to see that the merchants, not the taxpayers, would meet the cost. Liverpool had got the worst of both worlds. It had failed to win the longed-for charter; and it had been landed with the cost of governing the region.

That the Egyptian crisis was the moving cause behind the flurry of claim-staking in west Africa between 1883 and 1885 is shown by the relative calm there during the following decade. The ending of the short-lived *entente* between Berlin and Paris, itself a consequence of the Egyptian occupation, took much of the sting out of west African rivalries. French expansion went on challenging British interests, because Paris still resented the *fait accompli* in Cairo. But now that this challenge was no longer supported by German diplomacy, the British

[1] Anderson to Malet, no. 14, 21 Jun. 1890, encl. in Malet to Salisbury, no. 77, Africa, 21 Jun. 1890, F.O. 84/2032.

[2] Macdonald to Salisbury, no no., 21 May 1891, F.O. 84/2111.

were not to be stampeded into extending their improvisations of 1884. As a result, British policy now had more liberty to buy and sell in west Africa, and usually the decision was to sell. The west African partition became for Britain merely an expendable item in the greater game for the vital interests in the Mediterranean and the valley of the Nile.

REPERCUSSIONS OF EGYPTIAN OCCUPATION: EAST AFRICA, 1884–1888

On the east coast as on the west, the occupation of Egypt had repercussions which shattered the old coast system. Here also Bismarck was to threaten the British with the '*baton égyptien*', and their troubles in Cairo made them eager to yield his claims. As the Franco-German understanding over Egypt and West Africa was ruining their precautionary arrangement with Portugal for the Congo, Granville at the Foreign Office and Kirk at Zanzibar expected similar trouble in east Africa. The Foreign Office in July 1884 showed unusual interest in the reports on the Kilimanjaro highlands sent in by Harry Johnston — then a young botanist and not yet a vice-consul. He declared that the region would make an excellent colony. It commanded important trade routes, and a settlement there would help cut off the slave traffic. Johnston's argument was but the threadbare stuff of many such schemes turned down by the Foreign Office during the past sixty years. But this time the Foreign Office at least listened — from fear of France and Germany.

> '. . . I am specially to point out,' Granville instructed Kirk, 'that at the present moment the attention of European Powers is directed to an unprecedented extent to the question of the formation of Settlements on the African coast, that action has been in recent cases prompt and secret, and that it is essential that a district situated like that of Kilimanjaro . . . should not be placed under the protection of another flag.'[1]

The Foreign Secretary and other ministers perhaps were inspired not so much by a sudden interest in the east African interior as a jejune notion that Bismarck was getting the better of them. The Angra Pequena affair had caused hard feelings against Germany on the part of M.P.s and the man in the street alike. Not that anybody thought that south-west Africa had any intrinsic value, but Bismarck had affronted national prestige; and sooner than see him do it again in east

[1] Granville to Kirk, 9 Oct. 1884.

Africa, the Foreign Office talked of action. An official suggested three possible methods of forestalling the Germans: annexation — which nobody wanted; a Kilimanjaro railway which would enable the Sultan to occupy the region; but this was financial heresy; or treaties of protection which, although they might cost nothing, would hardly serve to shut out Foreign Powers.[1] But the Cabinet did not aspire to turn east Africa into another India, nor yet a British protectorate. Ministers would have liked nothing better than to 'neutralise' the region by agreement with Germany on the lines of the Anglo-French agreement of 1862.[2] Meanwhile they preferred that the Sultan should make his own territorial claims good. They still held to the old indirect method. On 5 December Granville encouraged a Zanzibari expedition to bring Kilimanjaro within the Sultan's dominion,[3] and his flag was hoisted there in April of the following year. Since the force soon withdrew again, this was but flimsy defence against a German invasion. Granville in fact was far more worried about the coast than the interior:

> 'Its annexation by France or Germany, and the seizure of a port would be ruinous to British . . . influence on the East Coast. The proceedings of the French in Madagascar make it all the more necessary to guard . . . our sea route to India.'[4]

Kimberley at the India Office agreed, 'From an Indian point of view I regard it as of very serious importance that no Foreign Power should oust us from that coast.'[5] The Ministry therefore, took another paper insurance and Kirk got the Sultan on 6 December to promise that he would cede no part of his dominion without British consent.[6]

Perhaps the strategic argument was compelling with regard to the coast line; but it was no reason for holding regions such as Kilimanjaro in the hinterland. Ministers themselves were divided about supporting the Sultan's claims in the interior. The Prime Minister broke out fiercely against any such innovation.

> 'Terribly have I been puzzled,' so runs his celebrated protest to Dilke, '. . . on finding a group of the soberest men among us to have concocted a scheme such as that touching the mountain country behind Zanzibar with

[1] Clement Hill, F.O. Memo., 29 Nov. 1884, P.R.O. 30/29/143.
[2] Cabinet Min. on Hill's Memo., 1–12 Dec. 1884, *ibid.*
[3] Granville to Kirk, 5 Dec. 1884.
[4] Granville, Minute on Kirk to Granville, 23 Nov. 1884, F.O. 84/1679.
[5] Kimberley to Granville, 21 Dec. 1884, Coupland, *Exploitation of East Africa*, 394; Kimberley to Granville, 24 Nov. 1884, A. J. P. Taylor, *Germany's First Bid for Colonies*, (1938), 85.
[6] The text is given in Coupland, *Exploitation of East Africa*, 388.

an unrememberable name. There *must* somewhere or other be reasons for it which have not come before me. I have asked Granville whether it may not stand over for a while.'[1]

The Foreign Office did its best to explain. Dilke prompted Clement Hill, a Foreign Office official, to write another memorandum for the Prime Minister. This may be taken as the forward school's programme for dealing with the sudden rush for tropical Africa, set off by the West African Conference at Berlin. It was a policy of conceding west Africa to other Powers and concentrating British efforts on saving the eastern regions.

'The geographical position of the East Coast lays it more within the general area of our foreign policy than that of the West Coast,' Hill argued. 'Our alternative route by the Cape to India may at any time make it important that we should have possession of or at least free access to good harbours. The importance is not less since the French move to Madagascar. Is it not worth considering whether in view of the European race for territories on the West Coast . . . we might not confine ourselves to securing the utmost possible freedom of trade on that coast, yielding to other Powers the territorial responsibilities . . . and seeking compensation on the East Coast where . . . we are at present, but who can say for how long, without a European rival; where the political future of the country is of real importance to Indian and Imperial interests; where the climate is superior; where commerce is capable of vast extension, and where our influence could be exercised . . . in the extension of civilisation, and the consequent extinction of the Slave Trade for which we have so long laboured?'[2]

The forward school's doctrine plainly implied that east Africa should be brought within the British sphere — a revolutionary change. Five years later, although for different reasons, Salisbury was to carry some of Hill's ideas into effect. But in December 1884 they were far too heretical for most ministers. Kirk still hoped to save east Africa through the Sultan. Gladstone for his part remained entirely unconverted:

'The Kilimanjaro papers . . . leave me . . . wholly mystified. I cannot see . . . an adequate reason for our being "*dans cette galère*". The tone of the Memo prepared by F.O. people disquiets me . . . and in places savours of annexationism, as for instance when it is laid down that we are to seek [exclusive advantages for ourselves on the East Coast while] concurring in measures *equal for all* on the West Coast. [I cannot see] . . . the necessity of doing anything.'[3]

[1] Gladstone to Dilke, 14 Dec. 1884; Gwynn and Tuckwell, *op. cit.*, II, 83–4.
[2] Foreign Office Memorandum, 9 Dec. 1884.
[3] Gladstone to Granville, 12 Dec. 1884, P.R.O. 30/29/143.

The forward party had to give way to him. On 2 December he had threatened to retire if his colleagues accepted Northbrook's proposals for settling Egyptian finances and for increasing the naval estimates. The Prime Minister had his way on these matters as well as on Zanzibar, for no-one but Gladstone could hold together a ministry hopelessly divided over Egypt and Ireland.[1] Again, the Cabinet badly needed German support if the Egyptian finances were to be straightened out, and once in December and again in January, 1885, Bismarck roundly declared that this support would depend upon their acceptance of German claims in Africa and New Guinea.[2] With German agents active in east Africa, the Liberals could see compelling Egyptian reasons for avoiding British protectorates there.

Thus it happened that after 14 December the forward party in the Cabinet dwindled away. Ministers ruled out any idea of committing themselves to a direct hold over any part of east Africa, and least of all, over the interior. If the Sultan could hold Kilimanjaro by his own unaided effort, well and good.[3] But the Liberals who were trying to get out of Egypt, would not get into another colonial quarrel with Germany in order to help him. It is true that on 7 January the Cabinet decided to warn Bismarck that the Sultan's possessions lay within a British sphere of influence,[4] but they did so in Gladstone's absence, and in any case this effort at diplomatic support quickly petered out. The warning left the Germans a free hand on the mainland unless the Sultan's claims there were defined. When Kirk reported German activity at Lamu, a Foreign Office official minuted: 'here are the Germans in Zanzibar territory. Should we not now advise the Sultan to issue a proclamation defining his territory?' 'The Cabinet will not agree to this', Granville replied, '. . . we had better leave it alone.'[5] The fact was that once Gladstone and the moderates defeated Hartington and the forward group over Egypt, the tendency to surrender to Germany in east Africa became irresistible. The forward party which had launched the Kilimanjaro project was resigned by February to selling the hinterlands in return for German support in Egypt and German goodwill during the Penjdeh crisis. Not only did the ministry refuse to support

[1] Dilke, *Political Memoir*, 2 Dec. 1884; Gwynn and Tuckwell, *op. cit.*, II, 86.

[2] Bismarck to Munster, 5 Dec. 1884; same to same, 25 Jan. 1885; *Grosse Politik*, IV, nos. 756, 758. cf. *The Journals and Letters of . . . Viscount Esher* (ed. M. V. Brett, 1934), I, 97–8.

[3] Granville to Kirk, 20 Dec. 1884, Coupland, *Exploitation of East Africa*, 393, 414.

[4] Dilke, *Political Memoir*, 7 Jan. 1885, Gwyn and Tuckwell, *op. cit.*, II, 96.

[5] T. V. Lister, Minutes 27 Jan. 1885, on Kirk to Granville, 31 Dec. 1884; F.O. 84/1679.

the Sultan's claims in the interior,[1] it also refused a charter for Mackinnon's company to do so.[2] Gladstone wrote to Granville on 6 March,

> 'It is really impossible to exaggerate the importance of *getting out of the way the bar to the Egyptian settlement*. . . . if we cannot wind up at once these small colonial controversies, we shall before we are many weeks older find it to our cost.'[3]

Dilke summed up for Bismarck's benefit the British attitude toward Zanzibar:

> '. . . we must maintain an especially preponderant position on that coast' but 'as regards the Hinterland . . . you have a free hand. . . . Public opinion here will . . . accept your establishments in the Cameroons and behind Zanzibar, if you allow the greatest possible freedom of trade.'[4]

The Prime Minister went further, and gave a public welcome to Germany's civilising aspiration in Africa.[5]

The Palmerstonian vision of using the Sultanate one day to open the interior for British trade had faded in Cairo. A hypothetical interest of commerce had been sacrificed to an urgent interest of strategy. Egypt made the east African hinterland expendable and it was expended. On the coast however, the government still hoped to keep its old supremacy for the safety of the India route.

Bismarck was quick to take advantage of British acquiescence. His *Schützbrief* of 3 March, 1885, brought under German jurisdiction the inland regions acquired by Carl Peters on behalf of the Society for German Colonisation. The new protectorate lay some two hundred miles inland, at the back of the ports of Pangani and Dar-es-Salaam, and across some of the main trade routes between Zanzibar and the interior. It was clear that this was only a beginning. German agents were making treaties elsewhere around Witu near the coast, and it was rumoured, as far as Buganda and Lake Victoria.

Once more Mackinnon and Hutton, a Manchester businessman, joined by members of the Foreign Office and the consular service, tried to persuade the government to salvage something out of the wreck. In April 1885, Consul Holmwood stirred up Hutton to revive Mackinnon's concession scheme of 1878. He also proposed the building of a railway from the port of Tanga to Kilimanjaro, which would later be linked

[1] Coupland, *Exploitation of East Africa*, 422.

[2] Lister to Mackinnon, 2 Feb. 1885, P.R.O. 30/29/270, p. 12. For Mackinnon's earlier application, *vide supra*, cap. II.

[3] Gladstone to Granville, 6 Mar. 1885, Fitzmaurice, *op. cit.*, II, 431–2.

[4] Herbert Bismarck to Bismarck, 7 Mar. 1885, *Grosse Politik*, IV, no. 760.

[5] *vide* Aydelotte, *op. cit.*, App. IV.

with Lakes Victoria and Albert and with the Upper Nile.[1] Hutton, Aberdare and Mackinnon pressed for the support of the Foreign Office against the Germans.[2] But the Cabinet was much more interested in getting German friendship than east African trade, and the Foreign Secretary referred the company scheme to Bismarck, saying that Britain would not support it if it meant a clash with German interests.[3] In any case Hutton and his friends showed up the trade at its true value in requiring so much state aid before they would move a step. After an interview with Hutton, Anderson of the Foreign Office reported that the group would do nothing without a large concession from the Sultan.[4] Even then, the concession would be worthless unless government saw to it that the Germans were kept out of the territories in question. But the government refused to resort to a charter, much less a protectorate for this purpose.[5] The notion of a Treasury guarantee for a Tanga-Kilimanjaro railway which Hutton and Mackinnon had demanded, was almost preposterous. Indeed, so little were British businessmen interested in developing east Africa that Anderson[6] and Holmwood spent much time trying to prod them into activity; but with little effect. Whereas in west Africa, the merchants were urging on the government, in east Africa officials were vainly trying to get business to take a hand. Thus in October 1885 Anderson pressed Hutton to take up Johnston's Kilimanjaro concessions in order to establish British claims there.[7] But Hutton and Mackinnon refused to do much without cast-iron assurances from government. 'The truth is', an exasperated Anderson broke out, 'that we [the Foreign Office] not only do not neglect the Manchester interests, but have to stir Manchester up to look after its interests.'[8] Government would give neither charter nor guarantees of territory or of railway capital; the businessmen therefore remained uninterested; and east Africa remained wide open to German treaty-makers.

The conciliators of Germany dominated the forward party. When Barghash protested to Berlin against the *Schützbrief*, a German squadron sailed to Zanzibar to over-awe him, and Kirk was told by the Foreign Office that the Sultan must yield to German demands or risk losing his independence. Britain would defend his claim to the interior no longer.

[1] Holmwood to Hutton, 10 Apr. 1885, Coupland, *Exploitation of East Africa*, 425–6.
[2] Aberdare and others to Granville, 22 Apr. 1885, F.O. 403/93, 33–42.
[3] Coupland, *Exploitation of East Africa*, 427–8.
[4] Anderson Memo., 9 Jun. 1885.
[5] Coupland, *Exploitation of East Africa*, 428.
[6] Anderson, Memo. of Interview with Hutton, 2 Jul. 1885, F.O. 403/94, p. 6.
[7] Anderson, Minute, 30 Oct. 1885, on Johnston to Anderson, 29 Oct. 1885, *ibid.*, 6.
[8] Anderson, Minute, 3 Nov. 1885, *ibid.*

On 3 June, 1885, Granville and Bismarck agreed to a joint delimitation of the Sultan's remaining possessions on the mainland. A day later the Germans declared a protectorate over the Sultanate of Witu near the coast. The coming to power of the Conservatives made no difference, for Salisbury simply continued the policy of giving up the hinterland. It was clear to the Foreign Office that Holmwood's railway, Mackinnon's concession and Johnston's Kilimanjaro colony were all proving broken reeds. Accordingly, Anderson advised the Prime Minister to settle with Germany on the basis of independence for Zanzibar and a friendly delimitation of the mainland. All that Britain really needed, he concluded, was a German guarantee of free trade and access within their sphere.[1] At the end of June Bismarck agreed to a settlement of this kind and promised German adherence to the Anglo-French Declaration of 1862 respecting the Sultan's independence. But his own claims on the other hand, were still being extended. On 8 August, 1885, Kirk reported that German treaties now covered the Kilimanjaro districts, which only a month or two ago the Sultan's agents had been encouraged to occupy. Once more there were appeals from Hutton and Mackinnon that government should protect their claims.

Salisbury was no less in need of German aid in Cairo against France, and in Constantinople against Russia, than his predecessor. He was if possible even more contemptuous of Mackinnon's trade interests and his reliance on government to make money for them. Apart from the need to keep German friendship, the Prime Minister failed to see the importance of reserving the hinterland territories.

> '. . . If we had no motive for standing well with G[erman] G[overnment], I do not quite see our interest in this Zanzibar quarrel. Keeping every other nation out on the bare chance that some day or other our traders will pluck up heart to go in is a poor policy.'[2]

To Salisbury as to Granville, it was much the same thing whether Germany or the Sultan ruled on the east African mainland, so long as free trade and access was everywhere guaranteed.[3] No less than his predecessor, Salisbury would have preferred if possible 'to save [the]

[1] Anderson Memo., 9 Jun. 1885; Anderson Memo., 'Pending Questions in African Dept.,' 23 Jun. 1885.

[2] Salisbury, Minute, *c.* 17 Sept. 1885, Coupland, *Exploitation of East Africa*, 433.

[3] His subordinates in the Foreign Office were not so sure of this. T. C. Lister, one of the Assistant Under-Secretaries, urged on Salisbury that a failure to support the Sultan of Zanzibar would have a bad effect on the Indian Princes; but he admitted that 'from a purely com[mercia]l point of view Brit[ish] trade w[oul]d gain by the substitution of German colonists for Arabs & savages.' (Lister to Salisbury, 19 Sept. 1885; S.P. (Lister).)

whole of [the] coast territory'[1] from the Germans; but when the Germans insisted on a share of the coast-line and the port of Dar-es-Salaam, he saw no reason to demur. The Prime Minister indeed seems to have thought that Zanzibar was less important than before to the India route.[2] Accordingly, he began to work for an understanding with the Germans, and left it to a boundary commission to work out the details. Salisbury felt no pangs about it. 'This matter of equality [of opportunity between British and German traders]', he commented, 'is the only point in which the whole negotiation really touches Englishmen.'[3] The Germans were perfectly willing to concede this. On the whole, he was well satisfied with the outcome at Zanzibar. 'On the Zanzibar question', he wrote in September, 'there does not seem to be any material difference between us. . . .'[4] He was even more pleased with the dividend elsewhere. 'I have been using the credit I have got with Bismarck in Caroline Islands and Zanzibar to get help in Russia and Turkey and Egypt. He is rather a Jew, but on the whole I have as yet got my money's worth.'[5] So had Bismarck. On 20 December, 1885, Barghash signed a treaty with Germany recognising her protectorates.

This was a bad knock to the Sultan's prestige and to British prestige as well. The power which had defended his suzerainty for so long seemed to have been shouldered aside. By the middle of 1886 the commission had cut back the Sultan's claims so savagely that the whole of the hinterland lay exposed to renewed advances by the Germans, and indeed they were still signing treaties. The defences were down, and it was useless to look to private enterprise to prop them up. Bereft of government backing, Hutton and Mackinnon had done no more than send an agent to establish a claim in the Taveta district. The shock to the truncated Sultanate, the establishment of another Power in the region were putting an end to the old system of influence, and British business could not fill the gap. Most of east Africa lay wide open to German expansion. In June 1886 Kirk surveyed the wreckage of the paramountcy which he had helped to build:

> '. . . One cannot assume that the relations of Germany and Zanzibar will long remain what they are or that our position will continue to be what it is . . . [Germany] will be compelled by the inevitable course of events to obtain possession of the coast opposite. Treaties, agreements, or commissions will all be powerless to stop her. . . . Nor will the occasion be difficult

[1] Salisbury to Kirk, (private), 12 Aug. 1885, S.P. 40.
[2] Waddington to Freycinet, 23 Dec. 1885, *D.D.F.*, VI no. 148.
[3] Salisbury to Malet, 24 Aug. 1885, Cecil, *op. cit.*, III, 230.
[4] Salisbury to Drummond Wolff, Private, 8 Sept. 1885, S.P. 36.
[5] Salisbury to Iddesleigh, 24 Aug. 1885, Cecil, *op. cit.*, III, 230.

to find since she has to deal with an Oriental prince to whom are not accorded the usual rights prescribed by international law. The time is . . . not far distant when the Sultan's authority, unable to bear the constant strain to which it is now being exposed . . . will give way. . . .'

The Sultanate would then be of no further use to British policy. Was anything to be substituted for it?

'The question to be decided is practically this,' Kirk concluded; 'Whether we are prepared to see Germany paramount over all the Zanzibar coast . . . or whether some compromise cannot be come to whereby our influence is upheld . . . as legitimately paramount over a certain district, without necessarily affecting the independence of the Sultan of Zanzibar so long as that State hangs together.'[1]

Such a partition of paramountcy turned out to be perfectly feasible. Bismarck was willing to divide East Africa into German and British fields of political activity, provided of course that his claims were liberally conceded. Otherwise, he hinted as usual, Salisbury would lose his aid in Egyptian affairs.[2] The Prime Minister on his side, was well content to get what he could without paying penalties in Cairo or Constantinople. With things as they were, the balance of compromise tilted heavily in favour of Germany. Under the Anglo-German Agreement reached at the end of October 1886, the German African Company[3] gained control of Dar-es-Salaam and Pangani; and Britain implicitly accepted the German claim to a protectorate over Witu and the coast fronting that Sultanate. The two Powers recognised the Sultan's possession of the islands and of the coasts to a depth of ten miles between Minengani at the head of the Tunghi River in the south and Kipini in the north; together with certain ports to the north as far as and including Warsheik; while they divided the hinterland along a line running northwestwards from the mouth of the River Wanga near the coast, to the eastern shore of Lake Victoria Nyanza. The British got the northern zone while the Germans got the southern.[4] Salisbury without enthusiasm had managed to rescue by diplomacy part of what could no longer be saved in full by mere influence. It was easy to get, so he got it.

[1] Kirk to Rosebery, 4 Jun. 1886, Coupland, *Exploitation of East Africa*, 471–2.

[2] Malet to Iddesleigh, 2 Oct. 1886, *ibid.*, 473. On hearing that the British wanted to settle colonial questions with Germany, Bismarck commented that Germany should not demand more than she could digest and that the German Colonial Jingos' eyes were bigger than Germany's stomach for colonial acquisitions. (Bismarck, Minute on Hatzfeldt to Bismarck, 19 Oct. 1886, *Grosse Politik*, XXIII, no. 801.)

[3] This was the *Deutsch-Ostafrikanische Gesellschaft* which had grown out of the *Deutsche Kolonialverein* on whose behalf Peters made his treaties.

[4] Hertslet, *op. cit.*, III, 882–7, 684–7.

He had satisfied a number of minor interests while he had been about his major task of conciliating Bismarck. He had retained Mombasa. Kirk and Rosebery wanted that port to counter a possible German base at Dar-es-Salaam, even though the Admiralty said that it was not worth the expense of fortification.[1] The treaty also preserved free access to the supposed markets around the Lakes — a traditional but always a prospective point of British policy — and to the missions in Buganda. Here at least was something for businessmen and humanitarians alike. But it was not much. Faced with the collapse of the old system of influence, government had rigged up a new 'sphere of interest' over part of the region. But this was the slightest, the most tentative advance towards a more direct commitment, and it was far from denoting any new 'imperialist' urge. The interests to be protected at Zanzibar seem to have been no more important in the Eighteen eighties than they had been before. They now had to be sanctioned by treaty because of the breakdown of influence in east Africa, a fortuitous result of the occupation of Egypt and its effects upon the European balance.

The British East Africa Company's Charter

At the end of 1886 the British government once more showed its indifference to the fate of the hinterland. News reached Zanzibar in the autumn that the Kabaka of Buganda was persecuting the missionaries and their converts, and that he had murdered Bishop Hannington upon his arrival in the kingdom.[2] Shortly afterwards a message came from Emin Pasha, the Khedive's governor of Equatoria in the Sudan. Cut off from Cairo by the Mahdists, Emin was apparently still in control of his province, with a considerable garrison at his back. What was more, he had reportedly offered to hand over his charge to the British, if they would supply him from Mombasa.[3]

Holmwood, who was acting Consul at Zanzibar, saw in the martyrdom of the Bishop and the survival of the Pasha a good opportunity to get control of the headwaters of the Nile. An expedition to save Emin and the missionaries might be dramatic enough to rally philanthropic sentiment at Home behind a policy of occupying Uganda and Equatoria; and he suggested that a military force should be sent to punish Mwanga and

[1] Coupland, *Exploitation of East Africa*, 471.

[2] See R. Oliver, *The Missionary Factor in East Africa*, (1952), 103 ff.

[3] *vide* Iddesleigh to Salisbury, Private, 22 Nov. 1886, S.P. (Northcote); H. M. Stanley, *In Darkest Africa*, (1890), I, 11–48.

relieve Emin.[1] Several missionary and humanitarian societies did indeed press government to answer this appeal. But neither philanthropists nor consuls could move Salisbury and his colleagues. They knew only too well that Parliament and the public strongly disliked adventures in tropical Africa, and so Holmwood's proposal was brushed aside. Far from sending help, Iddesleigh at the Foreign Office advised the missionaries in Uganda to withdraw.[2] Two years later, the Cabinet was to be equally indifferent to the plight of the missions on Lake Nyasa.[3] However much ministers sympathised privately with the Cross in its widening struggle with the Crescent in Africa, officially they still looked upon missions as private rather than national enterprise, in fact much as they regarded the traders.

Nor was the Cabinet greatly interested in Emin's plight or in his offer. 'There was talk of a military expedition to assist him', the Foreign Secretary reported, 'but this would never have done, and we decidedly negatived it.' Mackinnon was already getting up a private relief expedition to be led by Stanley;[4] but the government wanted nothing to do with it, lest Stanley turn out to be another Gordon, and Wadelai another Khartum. Ministers decided to avoid '. . . any action which may by any possibility lead to our being obliged to rescue the rescuing party'.[5] The Prime Minister himself was so indifferent to the fate of Equatoria as to suggest irritably that the Germans should be told about Emin's troubles. 'It is really their business', he minuted, 'if Emin is a German.'[6]

But by 1887 Salisbury no longer objected to the notion of private enterprise occupying the coasts and eventually the whole of the sphere allotted under the Anglo-German Agreement. The sooner this territory was occupied, the better. Along the coast, German rivalry was an accomplished fact. The Sultan was plainly too weak to stop the spread of German influence without help. The occupation could now take place without fear of German reprisal in Cairo or Constantinople. But if it was to be done, it would have to be without public expense.

[1] Holmwood to Baring, 25 Sept. 1886, quoted in A. Low, *The British and Uganda* (Oxford Ph.D. Thesis, 1957), 92.

[2] Iddesleigh to Holmwood, 25 Sept. 1886, F.O. 403/98

[3] *vide infra*, 224.

[4] There is some information on Mackinnon's scheme in F.O. 84/1794 and 1795. Mackinnon was urged on by Kirk at Zanzibar. For an assessment of the role of Leopold II *vide* R. T. Anstey, *British Policy towards West Central Africa, 1816–1887 . . .* (London Ph.D. Thesis, 1957), 189–200, where it is argued that Leopold intended to make Emin's territory a province of the Congo Free State, and so to open a way to the Nile; while Mackinnon was ready to acquiesce in this.

[5] Iddesleigh to Salisbury, Private, 28 Nov. 1886, S.P. (Northcote).

[6] Salisbury, Minute on Holmwood to Iddesleigh, 23 Sept. 1886, F.O. 84/1775.

Mackinnon had founded his British East African Association, and the Foreign Office began to encourage him to establish it on the mainland. It was at least encouragement, compared with the entire lack of sympathy shown hitherto; yet it remained lukewarm and severely restricted. Salisbury smiled upon his efforts to revive the concession scheme of 1878. On 24 May the Foreign Office approved the Sultan's lease to Mackinnon of the coastal strip along the northern mainland.[1] At the same time, the government renewed the small subsidy enjoyed by Mackinnon's British India Steam Navigation Company for its east African sea-mail service.

Anderson explained to the Treasury why his master was giving these few crumbs to Mackinnon and his friends. Although then as now, cases for expenditure put up by Departments were sometimes less than candid, this particular explanation rings true enough. The Foreign Office hoped that the East African Association would strengthen British influence at Zanzibar and along the coast, and in particular would secure the port of Mombasa. This makes it plain that government looked on the Association as no more than a way of strengthening the Sultan and keeping out the Germans, without committing the government to a protectorate.

Salisbury's gaze was still fixed upon the coast rather than the hinterland, for it was there that the immediate German danger lay; but Anderson was already suggesting something more for the Association to do. It might eventually occupy the interior from its base at Mombasa. Indeed, Mackinnon had asked for a royal charter authorising his company to do this. But Salisbury would not yet consider giving Mackinnon that much support. He distrusted the man's capacity. Financially, the Company was much too slight for so great a task. Should it fail after being chartered, the government might find an unwanted territory dumped into its lap.[2] There was no reason to fear that Bismarck would not respect the British sphere for the moment,[3] although German agents in east Africa might not. Therefore Salisbury restrained Anderson's enthusiasm for a charter. He would give the Company no more aid than government usually gave to a private venture. Characteristically enough however, he did not altogether exclude the possibility of a charter, should the German danger become serious. The Foreign Office went so far as to tell the Treasury in May of

[1] Concession, Sultan of Zanzibar to British East African Association, 24 May 1887, Hertslet, *op. cit.*, I, 339–45.

[2] Salisbury's Minute, 18 May 1886, quoted in Low, *op. cit.*, 105.

[3] Salisbury to Malet, 2 Jul. 1887, C. 5315, P.P. (1888), LXXIV, 457; Scott to Salisbury, 28 Jul. 1887, *ibid.*, 463.

1887 that it expected to charter Mackinnon's Company and hoped to see the Company push its influence inland, in much the same way as the Niger Company had done in west Africa. If Mackinnon was one day to undertake all these responsibilities under a charter, so Anderson concluded in his letter to the Treasury, he must have his mail subsidy.[1]

The subsidy was renewed, but Salisbury would not be hurried over the charter. He does not seem to have been greatly interested in the affair. Urged on by his official advisers, he slowly accepted the need of an advance which would cost the country so little. At the end of the year, he was ready to give Mackinnon his charter, if only he would organise a company with capital enough to make it worth chartering.[2] On 18 April, 1888, the East African Association responded by turning itself into the Imperial British East Africa Company, with a quarter of a million pounds capital.[3] This proof of energy seems to have removed Salisbury's last doubts. He remained sceptical of serious German designs upon the British sphere, but Anderson at least foresaw trouble sooner or later over Uganda and the regions to the north of Lake Victoria, none of which had been settled by the agreement of 1886. Preparing for an occupation of the Lakes region had been a frustrated Foreign Office ambition since Palmerston's day; and Anderson wanted a chartered company for the specific purpose of going up and making sure of Uganda. 'When we gave a Charter to the E. Africa Co.,' he recollected in 1890, 'we understood that its main idea was to push up to Uganda,'[4] Two years later he gave a fuller explanation of the original purpose behind the charter. The aim, he wrote, had been to take Uganda, and so prevent the Germans from linking up their west coast sphere across the Upper Nile to their east African possessions.[5] Anderson is surely the best authority on his own motives, but whether Salisbury as yet shared his adviser's fear of the Germans or his enthusiasm for Uganda is much more doubtful. It is more likely that in the middle of 1888 the Prime Minister was still mainly interested in using the Company to strengthen the Sultan at the coast rather than in securing Uganda. For when the Germans and Italians in September of that year seemed likely to overthrow the Sultan and rob him of his remaining possessions, Salisbury determined to defend

[1] F.O. to Treasury, 19 May 1887, F.O. 403/101, 77–8.

[2] Salisbury, Minute, 10 Dec. 1887, quoted in Low, *op. cit.*, p. 116. Here we follow Dr. Low's thesis.

[3] Founders' Agreement, printed in P. L. McDermott, *British East Africa or I.B.E.A.*, (2nd ed., 1895), App. II.

[4] Anderson, Minute on Euan-Smith, 31 Mar. 1890, M. Perham, *Lugard; the Years of Adventure*, (1956), 181.

[5] Anderson, Cabinet Memo., 7 Sept. 1892, F.O. 84/2258.

him. 'The English and Indian interests' in the Sultan's survival, the Prime Minister wrote, 'are both too strong' to give up.[1] A week later, he was 'thinking of making a formal agreement with the Sultan . . . to protect his two islands from attack';[2] and he was by now interested enough in keeping British influence on the coast to brush aside several ministerial objections and to send a squadron to back up the Sultan.[3]

For all these reasons the government chartered the East Africa Company on 3 September, 1888,[4] but strictly at the risk of the promoters: government could not help them, since it was afraid to ask Parliament for money. Mackinnon and Anderson might have large plans to seize the Upper Nile and the territory between Lakes Victoria and Tanganyika in pursuit of their fantasies of Cape to Cairo or Niger to Nile, but as yet the politicians left it to private enterprise to decide the fate of these countries. The issue was not important enough to the nation for government to do more. In granting the charter, Salisbury and his colleagues seem to have been taking a small and inexpensive insurance on their east African options against German and Italian advances.

Repercussions of Egyptian Occupation: South Africa, 1882–1885

While the repercussions of the Egyptian occupation were destroying the old informal systems on the east and west coasts, they were also unsettling the politics of south Africa. Since the mid-century the Convention system, to which the Liberals had reverted in 1881, had seemed to depend upon the exclusion of Foreign Powers, the limitation of republican expansion, the loyal co-operation of the Cape government and the preservation of Cape colonial supremacy in the south African balance of power. But, as a result of the British occupation of Egypt, it was no longer possible to exclude German intervention in southern Africa. The Pretoria Convention did not arrest the spread of Transvaal trekkers over the interior nor appease the republic's territorial ambition. During the next decade Cape colonial enterprise challenged the republicans for possession of the unoccupied interior, in a rivalry big with implications for the future balance of power. But while the British government felt bound to support colonial claims inland for the sake of supremacy, the Cape ministry under the influence of Hofmeyr could

[1] Salisbury to Malet, 18 Sept. 1888, Cecil, *op. cit.*, IV, 234–5.
[2] Same to same (private), 25 Sept. 1888, S.P. 64.
[3] Salisbury to Goschen, 14 Oct. 1888, Cecil, *op. cit.*, IV, 235–7.
[4] *London Gazette*, 7 Sept. 1888; *vide* Hertslet, *op. cit.*, I, 345–59.

by no means always be relied upon to contend against their Transvaal kinsfolk there. In these circumstances, the Liberals by 1884–5 found that they could not be sure of paramountcy over the Transvaal without making further territorial acquisitions.

The dilemmas of the renewed Convention policy began in Bechuanaland. In defiance of the Pretoria agreement, trekboers from the Transvaal by 1883 had set up the miniature settlements of Stellaland and Goshen and made war on the Tswana chiefs, Montsoia and Mankaroane. In March, the Opposition in Parliament called upon the government to enforce the Convention against the Transvaal.[1] John Mackenzie, the humanitarian spokesman, and south African business interests in London pressed for the extension of British protection over Bechuanaland, to save the tribes from Boer oppression.[2] The ministry's respcnse showed both its reluctance to intervene and the impotence of imperialist influences in British politics to dictate its actions. At this time Hartington and Chamberlain supported the demand for a protectorate in Bechuanaland; but the Cabinet as a whole rejected it.[3] They would do nothing to provoke the Transvaalers and to run the risk of another Boer war. Kimberley explained:

> '. . . The difficulty of this country was, that in dealing with South Africa as a Native question, we had not the sympathies of the white population. Either we must hold South Africa strongly by force and maintain our policy, whether the Colonists like it or not; or else, we must acquiesce in a great many things being done in these Colonies which the majority of the people in this country do not approve.'

For his own part he did not favour a thorough-going imperialist policy.[4] Lord Derby, who had succeeded Kimberley at the Colonial Office at the end of 1882, declared:

> 'Bechuanaland is of no value to us . . . for any Imperial purposes . . . it is of no consequence to us whether Boers or Native Chiefs are in possession.'[5]

The territory, he went on, had no attractions either for traders or colonists; and he was sure that the public did not want it for another British province.[6] It would require a costly imperial expedition to quell the disorder on the Transvaal's south-western frontier, and the government refused to undertake it. As late as June 1883, Derby's highest hope

[1] *Hansard*, 3rd ser., CCLXXVII, col. 413, *et seq.*, col. 315 *et seq.*

[2] Humanitarians' Memorial, 20 Nov. 1883, C. 3841, P.P. (1884) LVII, 189–90. John M[a]ckenzie to C.O., 20 Nov. 1883, *ibid.*, 190–5.

[3] Dilke's *Memoir*, Gwynn and Tuckwell, *op. cit.*, I, 530; Garvin, *op. cit.*, I, 489–92.

[4] *Hansard*, 3rd ser., CCLXXVII, cols. 339–40.

[5] *ibid.*, col. 328.

[6] *ibid.*, cols. 327–8.

was that the tribes would defeat the Boer freebooters and so remove any reason for imperial intervention.[1]

It was a forthright rejection of designs on Bechuanaland; but the minister for an empire which relied so heavily for its influence upon the agency of a semi-independent colonial government, could not brush aside the requests of the Cape ministry as easily as he did those of British humanitarians.[2] In the Bechuanaland question, as in many others afterwards, the initiative came from Cape Town, and policy emerged as a compromise between colonial demands for imperial extension and British resistance to it. Gladstone and Derby did not want a clash with the Transvaal in Bechuanaland. They feared that it would re-awaken Boer antagonism throughout south Africa.[3] If they sent a British expedition, there would be strong criticism in Britain of the government's extravagance and inconsistency, not least from its own followers. But in Cape Town towards the end of 1883, Scanlen's ministry joined with the colony's merchants in pressing Derby to check the absorption of Bechuanaland into the Transvaal. They pointed out that the road running northward through the Tswana country, between the Kalahari Desert on the west and the Transvaal border on the east, was the colony's only free access to the unoccupied northern interior. If the 'Missionaries' Road' fell under republican control, the future expansion of the colony might be barred from the north, and the south African balance would turn in favour of the republics. Scanlen made his point so vehemently that Derby and the Cabinet by November had accepted the necessity of saving the North Road for the colony, although they resented it.[4] The methods chosen to check the expansion of the Transvaal into Bechuanaland showed how much more difficult informal control had become since 1881. For it had to be done without provoking the sympathy of the Cape Dutch or the Orange Boers for the Transvaal; and therefore it was best done without open imperial action, and if possible, by agreement with the republic. Scanlen was as anxious for kid gloves as Derby. The Colonial Secretary insisted that if, in the last resort, the Road to the north could be saved only by proclaiming a protectorate, the Cape government should bear the charge of it. But Scanlen's ministry, sensitive to the Cape Assembly's sympathies, gave the pledge only on condition that the South African Republic should first agree to the projected imperial protectorate.[5] It was a strange

[1] Derby to Ponsonby, 29 Jun. 1883, *Q.V.L.*, 2nd ser., III, 431–3.
[2] *cf.* E. Fairfield, Memo., 'Vacillation in S. Africa,' 4 Aug. 1885, C.O. 806/250, 5–6.
[3] *Hansard*, 3rd ser., CCLXXVII, cols. 729–30; CCLXXX, col. 675.
[4] E. Fairfield, Cabinet Memo., 'Bechuanaland', 15 Jul. 1885, C.O. 806/247, 4.
[5] *Hansard*, 3rd ser., CCLXXXIV, cols. 149–50.

rivalry, when a colonial government required a republic's permission before collaborating in an extension of empire in its own interest.

Derby nevertheless felt bound to play the game in this way. In the London Convention of February 1884, he persuaded President Kruger to accept a boundary in Bechuanaland which would keep the frontier of the republic east of the North Road.[1] In return, the imperial powers over the Transvaal's internal native affairs under the Pretoria Convention were given up, and the republic received territorial and other concessions. The Colonial Secretary had got Scanlen his road without arousing Afrikaner opinion, and without an expedition, which most of his colleagues wanted above all to avoid. At the same time he had given some protection to the Tswana chiefs, which pleased humanitarian sentiment in Britain. It seemed as if the local conflict of Cape and Transvaal interests, and white and black land hunger, would be settled. As in Basutoland and Griqualand West, the British government had checked republican expansion in order to preserve colonial supremacy.

An unexpected German irruption in south-west Africa in the middle of 1884 overturned Derby's tactful arrangements, and threatened to shake the hold over the interior. The Convention policy had always assumed the absence of a rival European Power with which the republics could combine. And the Colonial Office had always tried to isolate them and to control their foreign relations. Men who had grown old in this tradition were naturally shocked by the German protectorate of August 1884 over Angra Pequena. The monopoly of the south African coasts had been breached. Through a far-fetched chain of circumstance, linking British dependence upon German support in Cairo with Bismarck's *entente* with France, the occupation of Egypt had made Britain powerless to shut Germany out of south, as well as east and west Africa. The advent of Germany on the coast and her claims in the hinterland seemed likely at first to alter the whole balance of south Africa and to make the Transvaal far more dangerous. Bechuanaland, which Derby had described as worthless a year before, suddenly attained high and urgent importance as the territorial wedge between the German hinterland and the Transvaal Republic.

Within a month, Derby's settlement of the Tswana frontiers was challenged anew by the Transvaalers. War broke out again between tribal allies of the empire and the trekker republics. Kruger extended

[1] Derby to Transvaal Delegation, 29 Nov. 1883, C. 3841, P.P. [1884] LVII, 223; Derby to Robinson, 20 Aug. 1884, C. 4213, P.P. [1884–5] LVII, 13; Hertslet, *op. cit.*, I, 227–36.

a provisional republican protectorate over the Boers of Goshen on the North Road and the chiefs whom the Deputy Commissioner, John Mackenzie, had already brought under British protection. There were other signs that the arrival of Germany had stimulated Transvaal intransigence. Kruger granted a monopoly of railways throughout the republic to a German-Dutch syndicate. His plans for railways to join Pretoria with St. Lucia Bay and Angra Pequena threatened the Cape merchants' monopoly of trade with the interior and agitated investors in Cape bonds in London.[1] The Cape government pressed the Colonial Office to annex the entire region between the German protectorate and the Transvaal border,[2] so as to forestall territorial connection between the German port and the republic. The arrival of the Germans and Kruger's defiance of the London Convention seemed to Sir Hercules Robinson, the British High Commissioner, to be undermining the whole structure of British supremacy. It seemed possible that colonial expansion might be shut out from the north, the encirclement of the Transvaal broken and a foreign rival's influence extended far inland. Robinson telegraphed on 24 September 1884: '. . . in view of German annexation and other threatened encroachments calculated to cripple this Colony, decisive measures should be taken for maintenance of British authority in South Africa.'[3] It was essential, he argued, to enforce the London Convention against the Transvaal, and to throw its frontier back from the North Road. It was equally necessary to annex Bechuanaland at once.

Gladstone's Cabinet received these pleas from Cape Town with mixed feelings. Its members were concerned above all to conciliate Germany, and to yield her colonial claims in New Guinea and Africa, in return for Bismarck's help with their serious financial difficulties in Cairo. The Prime Minister himself welcomed German colonial enterprise. He would not be 'bullied' by alarmist colonial governments into an attempt to exclude Germany from the unoccupied parts of the world.[4] Such an attempt would mean enormous increases in naval and administrative expenditure, and it would endanger peace. On the other hand, the spectacle of Germany and France co-operating in the invasion of British spheres of influence in the western Pacific and on the African coasts had shocked British, but even more, colonial opinion. There was

[1] For the mercantile and humanitarian agitation in London after the German protectorate over Angra Pequena, *vide* C.O. African 299, especially Sir. D. Currie to Gladstone, 21 Nov. 1884.

[2] Cape ministers' Minute, 17 Sept., 1884, C. 4252, P.P. (1884–5) LVII, 172–3.

[3] Robinson to Derby, 24 Sept. 1884, C. 4213, *ibid.*, 92.

[4] *vide* W. O. Aydelotte, *op. cit.* App. IV.

a surge of sentiment in Westminster in favour, as Chamberlain put it, of standing up to Bismarck.[1] Of the public reaction to the Blue Books about the Anglo-German negotiation over Angra Pequena, Granville observed to Gladstone that 'there is a wild and irrational spirit abroad'; 'to which I for one', the Prime Minister replied, 'do not feel at all disposed to give in.'[2]

But a forward party had emerged in the Cabinet during the last three months of 1884. Hartington, Chamberlain[3] and even Derby, while agreeing that present German claims had to be conceded, now supported the colonial government's demands for annexations, as a way of forestalling encroachments in the future. On 21 June, 1884, the Cabinet had decided, according to Dilke: 'Angra Pequena—Bismarck to have all he wants.'[4] The Cabinet ended by accepting German territorial claims in south-west Africa, in return for help in Egypt, and having done so propitiated the Cape colonists and strengthened British supremacy against further German or Transvaal expansion by occupying Bechuanaland. The government by 11 November had refused the Cape ministry's request for the annexation of Damaraland and Namaqualand, and handed them over to German jurisdiction.[5] But the forward party[6] in the ministry overcame Gladstone's resistance[7] and sent an expedition under Sir Charles Warren to occupy Bechuanaland and make sure that the Transvaal Republic withdrew from the North Road. The Cape ministry meanwhile, through Cecil Rhodes, was ensuring that the trekkers in Goshen accepted the British occupation peacefully, in order to avert a clash with the imperial troops which would have revived Anglo-Dutch strife. At the end of January 1885, Berlin was informed that Bechuanaland had been brought under British protection.[8] As a Cabinet memorandum recorded later: 'that action was taken

[1] Chamberlain to Dilke, 29 Dec. 1884, Garvin, *op. cit.*, I, 538.

[2] Gladstone Minute, 26 Dec. 1884, P.R.O. 30/29/128. Gladstone defended Derby's lukewarm attitude to the Queen: 'If . . . the real ground of animadversion is . . . to be found in Lord Derby's . . . positive reluctance, to meet the demands now rife in some of the Colonies for a system of annexations intended to forestall the colonising efforts of other countries, Mr. Gladstone . . . himself, for one, is firmly opposed on principle to such a system. . . .' (Gladstone to Queen Victoria, 23 Jan. 1885, *Q.V.L.*, 2nd ser., III, 593–4.)

[3] Dilke, *Memoir*, 4 Jan. 1885, B.M. Add. MSS. 43931, p. 18.

[4] Dilke, *Diary*, 21 Jun. 1884, B.M. Add MSS. 43936 A.

[5] Derby to Robinson, 28 Aug. 1884, C. 4213, P.P. (1884–5) LVII, 40; Derby to Robinson, 11 Nov. 1884, C. 4252, *ibid.*, 203.

[6] Chamberlain, Cabinet Minute, Garvin, *op. cit.* I 492–4; Dilke's *Memoir* Gwynn and Tuckwell, *op. cit.*, II, 81–2, 87.

[7] Dilke, *Memoir*, 10 Nov. 1884, B.M. Add. MSS. 43930, p. 299.

[8] The western boundary of the protectorate was to be the 20th meridian of east longitude; the northern limit was the 22nd parallel of south latitude.

primarily as a precautionary measure, against the fear, now dissipated, of German encroachment.'[1]

It was this same fear of a German-Transvaal junction which decided Gladstone's Cabinet early in 1885 to annex St. Lucia Bay and the still unoccupied coastal region between the Cape and Natal frontiers. The Prime Minister was still dragging his feet. He complained to Granville:

> 'Derby has taken much offence at [Bismarck's] annexations . . . I do not know whether we have reason to complain? I think Derby is quite right in wishing to have a continuous line of coast in South Africa: but as to extending the business northwards . . . I see great objection to it.'[2]

But the majority of the Cabinet by this time was not prepared to let their new neighbour Bismarck beat them out of doors again in Africa; and they reluctantly accepted the Colonial Secretary's case, as he put it to Granville:

> 'I agree with you that there is something absurd in the scramble for colonies, and I am as little disposed to join in it as you can be; but there is a difference between wanting new acquisitions and keeping what we have: both Natal and the Cape Colony would be endangered . . . if any foreign Power chose to claim possession of the coast lying between the two . . . I want to secure the coast-line all round South Africa from the mouth of the Orange River on the west, to the Portuguese possessions on the east.'[3]

The Prime Minister and the Foreign and Colonial Secretaries were all mid-Victorians enough to be astonished at the scramble for colonial trifles in Africa. They were opposed in principle to all extension of British rule. But they were also mid-Victorians enough to carry on the traditional strategy of supremacy in south Africa; and they annexed large territories to secure the North Road for the Cape Colony, to keep the Transvaal Republic encircled and to seal off the imagined German challenge. For the time being, the old indirect control of the republics, with these added safeguards, would be sufficient. Gladstone's estimate of the German danger in south Africa turned out to be nearer the truth than that of the forward party. The Prime Minister had foretold that Germany's presence would strengthen rather than weaken Britain's grip on her colonies in south Africa; and Bismarck's pressure upon imperial interests in the south ceased with the European diplomatic manoeuvre which had chiefly inspired its beginning.[4] The German

[1] Cabinet Memo., Bechuanaland, 15 Jul. 1885, C.O. 806/247, 13.
[2] Gladstone to Granville, 28 Dec. 1884, P.R.O. 30/29/128.
[3] Derby to Granville, 28 Dec. 1884, P.R.O. 30/29/120.
[4] *vide* Taylor, *Germany's First Bid for Colonies*; Aydelotte, *op. cit., passim.*

foothold in south Africa remained inconvenient, and her diplomatic intervention continued to be a potential danger. But as long as Germany lacked a strong navy, she could not seriously threaten the British hold upon south Africa. German rivalry henceforward played only a minor part in the subsequent weakening of imperial supremacy over the republics.

CHAPTER VII

Rhodes' Counterpoise, 1887–1891

After 1887, the disturbance in imperial relations with south Africa, which had begun with the Transvaal rebellion and the German intrusion, continued for new reasons. An inrush of mining and railway enterprise changed the shape of local politics. The commercial drawing together of the region sharpened the rivalry between the divided states to control its resources and decide its future. Within a decade, the shifting balance of wealth and power in south Africa appeared to have overturned the paramountcy which Gladstone had tried to restore between 1881 and 1885. Unwittingly, British capitalists freed the Transvaal nationalists from the colonial yoke and made the republic the leading state in south Africa.

The transformation began in 1886, when the Witwatersrand gold reef was found in the heart of the Transvaal. In London a speculative boom in 'Kaffirs' on the London money market followed in 1888–9,[1] and by 1894 the gold of Johannesburg was believed to be practically inexhaustible. By the end of the second gold boom of 1895–6, £57 millions had been invested in the Rand alone.[2] Five years later, the Rand was producing a quarter of the world's gold supply.[3] South Africa for the first time became big business to the British and European merchant and investor, and the energy of the British expansive economy developed it on a scale comparable to that in Australia, South America and India.[4] Borrowing money in London, the colonies pushed their railways northward in frantic competition for the rich trade of the Rand. Between 1885 and 1895 the railway mileage was almost doubled, and the colonies' public debt rose by about eleven millions. At the same time south Africa's overseas trade almost doubled in value. Prosperity attracted the first substantial immigration. The white population doubled

[1] Frankel, *op. cit.*, 81. [2] *ibid.*, 95.

[3] R. I. Lovell, *The Struggle for South Africa, 1875–1899*, (New York, 1934), 285, f.n. 1.

[4] For the details see Frankel, *op. cit.*, Schumann, *op. cit.*, J. Van der Poel, *Railway and Customs Policies in South Africa, 1885–1910*, (1933).

between 1880 and 1890. South Africa was taking its place among the brightest satellites in the constellation of British world trade.[1]

Politically, the golden Rand after 1887 weighed increasingly against the colonies and the Empire in favour of the South African Republic. The key to the prosperity of southern Africa was falling into the hands of its most anti-imperialist *régime*. As the Transvaal rose out of bankruptcy to solvency,[2] its power to resist imperial confederation increased. President Kruger was winning the means to develop a separatist republican federation in the broad hinterlands of Delagoa Bay between the Vaal and Zambesi Rivers. To the British, his repeated refusals to join a railway and tariff union on imperial terms seemed proof of an

[1] *Trade with south African colonies* 1875–1899[1] (000's of £s)

	Total British Imports	*Imports from S. Africa*	*Total British Exports*	*Exports to S. Africa*
1875	373,939	4,639	223,465	5,800
1880	411,229	8,133	223,060	8,163
1885	370,967	6,559	271,403	5,109
1890	420,691	15,032	263,530	12,043
1895	416,689	11,180	226,128	11,463
1899	485,035	10,191	264,492	12,209

Sources: P.P. [1881] XCIV, 22–3, 28–9; P.P. [1890–1] XC, 686–7, 692–3; P.P. [1901] LXXXVI, 56–7, 130–1; P.P. [1884–5] LXXXII, 35; P.P. [1886] LXVIII, 41.

Notional Figures of Investment in Southern Africa (including Rhodesia) 1880–1913

(millions sterling)

	Public Debt	*Diamond Mining*	*Gold Mines (wits)*	*Total British listed capital*
1875	3,9			
1880	12,5	2,5		
1881		10,5		34
1885	25,3			
1887		23,4		
1890	30,8		22,6	
1895	34,5		41,9	
1900			77,4	230
1905	100,0		104,3	
1913				370,2

Source: Frankel, *op. cit.*, 56–7, 61–4, 95.

[2] The South African Republic's revenue rose from an average of £188,000 in 1883–90 to £4,266,000 in 1895–7. (Schumann, *op. cit.*, 52.) Its white population doubled within a decade and reached 119,128 in 1890. (*ibid.*, 38.)

ambition to build a rival republican axis. The colonies' prosperity and revenues were coming to depend upon traffic with the Transvaal. Their investment in railways linking colonial ports to the Rand seemed to be threatened by the Delagoa Bay line; and Kruger's government obstructed the continuation of the colonial lines across republican territory to Johannesburg. By 1895 the Rand was giving Kruger's government the power to divert economic development in south Africa as a whole. From a dependent of the colonies, the republic was rising to be arbiter over them.

After 1886 therefore, the old imperial interest in federation and strategic security became caught up in the local struggle for supremacy between the Cape Colony and the South African Republic. The considerations of imperial policy in south Africa henceforward become more complicated. Supremacy was now needed to secure a valuable commercial asset, as well as the long route to the East. As a result considerations of wealth and power become more difficult to distinguish; and trading and financial interests both at the Cape and in London played a more obvious part than hitherto. But for all the alteration in south Africa and the rising stakes in its future, British policy became less rather than more imperialistic.

If by imperialism is meant the growth of metropolitan control, imperialism in south Africa between 1881 and 1895 declined. London's aim was still to perpetuate British influence and to shape an imperial dominion. But the terms of the problem were becoming harder. British economic enterprise was expanding and dominant in the sub-continent. Commerce appeared to be coming strongly to the aid of policy for the first time. On the other hand, the state of Home politics forced Cabinets to avoid direct responsibility in south Africa. Although there were imperial federationists in Salisbury's Conservative Ministry of 1886 to 1892 — including the Colonial Secretary, Sir Henry Holland[1]—they were as restrained as the Liberals had been. In the splinter politics of Irish Home Rule crises, imperial ventures were hazardous indeed; the calls for retrenchment and the enigmatic mass electorate worried ministers more and more. So much did the Prime Minister despair of his countrymen's will to keep up the imperial factor in south Africa that he complained: 'In their heart of hearts Members of Parliament have made up their minds to abandon South Africa if it ever threatens to cost them any considerable expense again.'[2]

[1] Holland, who became Lord Knutsford in 1888, is henceforth referred to as 'Knutsford'.

[2] Salisbury to Arnold White, 15 Feb. 1887, S.P. (Secretary's note book).

The danger of provoking Afrikaner nationalism, as much as the indifference of the British electorate, inhibited the Colonial Office from interfering directly. Like other departments of government, it tended to handle existing problems with the idea very much in mind of avoiding past catastrophes. Ministers in these years were especially intent upon averting a repetition of the crisis of 1881, when the separatists of the Transvaal, the Orange Boers and the Cape Dutch had seemed to be uniting against the empire. Henceforth the Colonial Office had an exaggerated fear of arousing pan-Afrikaner sentiment and a hostile alliance between the republicans and the Cape Bond. The shocks of the first Boer war had altered the approach to south African politics. Since conflicts with the Transvaalers tended to stimulate Boer hostility throughout south Africa, British policy became more diffident and conciliatory than in the Seventies.[1] To overcome the republic's separatism by force seemed out of the question. Another Boer war was to be avoided at all cost. Lest the Cape Dutch should be driven into the arms of the Transvaalers, the imperial authorities did their best to avoid open clashes with the republic and to placate Cape opinion. They tended to see Afrikaner anti-imperialism round every corner; and in the attempt to guard against it, they withdrew more and more from control and direct intervention south of the Zambesi. Imperial action in these circumstances became more constricted than it had ever been before.

From the imperial point of view, the south African problem was more political than economic. It was not so much a question of promoting trade and investment, as of manipulating them to strengthen British political influence. The difficulty was to keep preponderance in the face of an expanding and more formidable Transvaal, and a growing national consciousness in both colonies and republics.

Of necessity Colonial Secretaries after 1881 relied chiefly upon informal influence and colonial agency to baffle the rising republican influence without inflaming Afrikaner sentiment. The imperial position had to be built upon the external paramountcy over the Transvaal retained in the retrocession of 1881 and upon the hegemony of the Cape Colony. The challenge from Pretoria was to be met by promoting Cape territorial and commercial expansion to counter that of its republican rival. As Sir Hercules Robinson put it, the only possible policy was 'Colonial expansion with Imperial aid', for there seemed to be 'no permanent place in the future of South Africa for direct Imperial rule on

[1] Both Knutsford and Ripon were only too anxious '. . . to maintain and strengthen friendly relations with the South African Republic and the Orange Free State' (Knutsford to Loch, 4 Nov. 1889, C.O. 806/321.)

any large scale'.[1] It was hoped that commercial partnership would do the rest. Republican government in the Transvaal did not stand in the way of mining development. Railways, immigration and trade connections would inevitably erode Transvaal separatism and unite the colonies and republics.[2] Economic growth would surely strengthen political loyalty and make south Africa part of 'Greater Britain'.

Since the empire relied so heavily upon colonial energies and leadership to redress the shifting balance of south Africa, policy tended to be made in Cape Town and merely approved or amended in London. It was shaped more by Cape politicians than by imperialist and commercial influences in Britain. Colonial Secretaries felt bound to pay 'due regard to the views of the Colonial governments of the Cape and Natal in respect of external affairs affecting the Colony'.[3]

If politicians in London could take a detached and forward-looking view of changing south Africa, the local leaders could not. They were servants of merchants and farmers whose bread and butter and votes bound them to protect and promote local interests against neighbouring competition. Historic antagonisms and sentiments aggravated the economic particularism of the different states. After 1886 a civil war of railways and tariffs spread between the different sections of the country. Each south African government strove against the rest to bring more territory into its own commercial system in an attempt to preserve its political identity and assure future prosperity. As long as the Transvaal stood outside a commercial union, territorial rivalry spread.

The major collisions of 1886–94 took place between the colonists' movement into their northern hinterlands and the Transvaalers' counter-trekking east and west across their path towards the Indian and Atlantic Oceans. With the development of the interior, the republic redoubled its attempts to establish its own communications with the sea, and the colonists did their utmost to prevent it before commercial union took place. This deadlock over a railway and customs union brought on a scramble for territory from the Transvaal, northward as far as Lake Tanganyika, and eastward to Swaziland, Kosi Bay and Delagoa Bay. About these central issues turned lesser struggles: the contest for the favours of the Orange Free State and the commercial competition between the sister colonies themselves. Rivals for the trade of the Rand and contending for different hinterlands, each colony conducted its separate campaign.

[1] Sir Hercules Robinson, Speech at Cape Town, 27 Apr. 1889, C.O. 806/319, 4.
[2] e.g. Ripon to Rosebery, 4 Sept. 1894, L. Wolf, *Life of ... Ripon*, (1921), II, 225–6.
[3] Knutsford to Loch, 4 Nov. 1889, C.O. 806/321, 2.

The Cape colonists concentrated on expansion northward through Bechuanaland to the Zambesi and beyond. Their republican rivals had already been hemmed in on the west by the Bechuanaland protectorate. It remained to draw the circle round the Transvaal to the north. Beyond the Limpopo the Cape drive encountered a second rival in Portugal, who like the Transvaal threatened to bar its northward path. This vast extension of the Cape's hinterland was projected and carried out by the chiefs of its mining and railway industry, with the acquiescence of the farmers and politicians. In power and political importance it entirely overshadowed the Natalians' drive for their north, which encountered the Transvaalers' expansion to the south-east.

Encirclement and Conciliation in Zululand and Tongaland

The situation in Zululand in 1886 was not unlike that in Bechuanaland in 1884. The Natalians looked to Zululand, Tongaland and Swaziland as their natural hinterland, much as the Cape merchants did to Bechuanaland and Matabeleland. In the one region as in the other, invading Europeans were stirring up tribal strife in their rivalry for trade, land and mineral concessions; and the Transvaalers, outdoing the colonists in occupying the territory, had set up an extensive New Republic in Zululand, and were making treaties in Swaziland and Tongaland. Colonists and republicans called upon their respective governments for support against each other. But Natal, too weak for responsible government, was no more able to sustain a protectorate in Zululand than the Cape ministry in Bechuanaland. Although to forestall German intervention in 1885, the imperial authorities had annexed St. Lucia Bay and part of the Zulu coast, they had refused to take the country inland.

At the beginning of 1886, the Natalians and their governor, Sir Henry Bulwer, urged the Colonial Office to check the republicans and reserve the colony's hinterland. Natal needed Zululand as a native reserve for its large African population. It was in the interest of the colony's merchants and railway that the republic should be hemmed in from the sea, especially from Kosi Bay. Lastly, the governor argued, the Transvaalers' advance should be halted to keep the way clear for the extension of the colony's trade and railway through Zululand northward into Swaziland. With these interests in mind, the Natalians pressed the Colonial Office to bring the rest of Zululand under British jurisdiction, and to save Swaziland and Tongaland from the Boers and from the Portuguese.[1]

[1] Sir H. Bulwer, Memo., 6 and 14 Jan. 1886, C. 4913, P.P. (1887) LXI, 409–26.

If the colonists wanted imperial protection for their hinterland, humanitarians and imperialists in Britain wanted it for the Bantu. Forty-two Members of Parliament signed a memorial in favour of snatching the Zulu from Boer hands.[1] The British government's response was discriminating. It followed the old rule for supremacy over the republic and kept the Transvaalers in Zululand from reaching the sea.[2] As a further precaution against Portuguese encroachment[3] and republican access to Kosi Bay, Tongaland was declared a British sphere of influence in February 1888. The Colonial Office's first interest plainly was to retain its indirect hold upon the Transvaal by keeping it dependent upon colonial ports. But at the same time the British government was anxious to conciliate the Transvaalers and their sympathisers in the Cape Colony and Orange Free State. About a quarter of Zululand was yielded to the New Republic in 1886 and later on the Transvaal annexed it. What was more, it was north-west Zululand that was conceded, which meant that the republic had been allowed to cut off the Natal Colony from territorial access to Swaziland. Natal's northern ambitions had been sacrificed[4] to placate Boer opinion, except for eastern Zululand which was annexed to Natal in 1887. There, the British government, fearing to hand over the tribes to the struggling Natal government, kept the administration in its own hands for the time being[5]— a success of sorts for the humanitarian advocates of Colonial Office rule.

In Swaziland however, Salisbury's Cabinet refused to exclude Transvaal expansion or to assume a protectorate. The Colonial Secretary, on Hercules Robinson's advice, wanted to conciliate the Transvaalers there, and to make it plain that he was doing so. Salisbury was wary of doing anything which might offend Portugal, for he was uncertain whether Bismarck might not intervene on her behalf. Other ministers objected to the expense and responsibility of any action in Swaziland. Although Knutsford wanted to send an Imperial Commissioner to settle Swaziland's future,[6] Salisbury forbade it. For all its ineffectiveness, the Colonial Secretary's protest, shows the British attitude toward the Transvaal:

> 'In accordance with your views I have telegraphed to Sir H. Robinson that it is not proposed to send a British Commissioner to assist in settling

[1] Memorial, 26 Mar. 1886, C. 4913, *ibid.*, 449–50.

[2] Stanhope to Havelock, 9 Sept. 1886, C. 4980, *ibid.*, 548; Havelock to Stanhope, 24 Oct. 1886, *ibid.*, 589–96.

[3] Holland to Salisbury, 11 Aug. 1887, S.P. (Holland).

[4] For the colonists' protests *vide* Havelock to Stanhope, 24 Oct. and 19 Nov. 1886 C. 4980, P.P. (1887) LXI, 652, *et seq.*

[5] Holland to Havelock, 9 and 11 May 1887, C. 5143, *ibid.*, 782.

[6] Holland to Salisbury, 21 Mar. 1887, S.P. (Holland).

the Swazi-Portuguese Boundary: I understand that your decision is arrived at on account of political reasons and our relations with Portugal. . . .

We are bound by the Convention of London . . . to secure the independence of the Swazis, and to do this effectually we must (1) take care to keep up our influence with the Swazi King, and not let him think that we take no interest in him, while the Transvaal Govt. are ready to support him; and (2) we must show a willingness to act with the Transvaal Govt. upon any Swazi question, as the peace of S. Africa largely depends upon our working cordially with that Govt.

We should be very much blamed if we let the Boer influence prevail in Swaziland by inaction on our part. . . . But I venture to think that friendly cooperation with the Transvaal Govt. in matters relating to Swaziland would tend to lessen our difficulties not only in Swaziland, but Amatongaland, Zululand and elsewhere where we come into contact with the Boers; and would induce them to put a check upon the marauding Boers who give us so much trouble — This is clearly the opinion of Sir Hercules Robinson, who is a good authority on S. African matters.'[1]

Knutsford's ambivalent attitude to the Transvaal was typical of British policy from 1880 to 1895. He feared, on the one hand, to strain relations with the republic too far, lest he provoke Boer anti-imperialism and Anglo-Dutch strife throughout south Africa. On the other hand, he felt bound to limit the republic's occupation of the interior, in order to protect colonial interests and uphold imperial influence. Yet his power of checking the Transvaal, short of threat and ultimatum, was slight. It was the republic, not the colonies, which was the expanding power in the interior in 1887. Imperial action was shackled by domestic crisis, diplomatic risk and fear of a united Afrikanerdom. It took Knutsford two years to persuade his colleagues to send a British Commissioner to Swaziland. His defence of Natal's hinterland against the Transvaal on the south-east was necessarily modest, compared with the strenuous assertion of the Cape's hinterland rights on the west and later, in the north. His aims were to keep the Transvaal from obtaining a port of its own, until it joined the colonies in a commercial union, and to conciliate the republic with territorial concessions inland.

Salisbury and the Delagoa Bay Gap, 1887–1892

Whatever Knutsford might do about Kosi Bay and Swaziland, it became plain after 1886 that Kruger would eventually release his republic from the colonial commercial monopoly and open his own railway to

[1] Holland to Salisbury, 21 Dec. 1887, S.P. (Holland).

Delagoa Bay in Portuguese territory. The new wealth and traffic of the Rand made it inevitable; and the developing mining industry demanded it. In January 1887, McMurdo's Anglo-American syndicate began work on the Portuguese end of the line. It became equally plain after the abortive railway and customs conferences of 1886 and 1887 that Kruger meant to stop colonial railways from entering the Transvaal and if possible, the Orange Free State also, until his Delagoa line was finished.[1] The President declared: 'Every railway that approaches me I look upon as an enemy on whatever side it comes. I must have my Delagoa Bay line first, and then the other lines may come.' If he seemed ready to join the colonies at times, his burghers insisted on using their new whip hand in trade to drive their republicanism home.

Colonial leaders became alarmed at the economic prospects opened by Kruger's intransigence and Rand gold. Rhodes and Hofmeyr voiced the grave fears of the Cape colonists for the future. The Kimberley diamond magnate prophesied in 1886:

> If the Delagoa Bay Railway is carried out, the real union of South Africa will be indefinitely deferred.
>
> . . . [Unless the Cape railway was soon pushed up to the Rand] we shall be cut off from the Transvaal as far as our trade is concerned.
>
> . . . That trade is bound to go either from Delagoa Bay or from Natal. . . . Before we know what we are about we shall hear of a Customs union between Natal, the Orange Free State, Delagoa Bay, and Bechuanaland [and the Cape may be shut out]. . . . When that comes to pass, I ask what will be the use of our railways?'[2]

Railway connection with the gold fields was no less necessary for the Cape Dutch farmers than for the Cape financial and mining interests. After 1886 Hofmeyr joined Rhodes in preaching an energetic railway policy to join Table Bay with Johannesburg and Delagoa Bay.[3] But Kruger seemed intent on taking the Rand out of the Cape trading system. It was this emerging danger which brought the Dutch agrarian and the English financial interests into political alliance at Cape Town, under the joint leadership of Rhodes and Hofmeyr.

In these circumstances, Cape and Natal leaders saw a chance of keeping their share of the Rand's prosperity by buying control of the Delagoa Bay railway and persuading the imperial government to

[1] *vide* Van der Poel, *Railway and Customs Policies*, cap. II; Walker, *History of South Africa*, 411–5; *C.H.B.E. VIII*, 539–41.

[2] Speech, Cape House, 20 May 1886, Vindex: *Cecil Rhodes, His Political Life and Speeches, 1881–1900*, (1900), 133, 135.

[3] J. H. Hofmeyr and F. W. Reitz, *Life of Jan Hendrik Hofmeyr*, (Cape Town, 1913), 28–32.

protect them against Portuguese and Transvaal confiscation. The colonists hoped in this way to bring the republic to commercial reason. At the end of 1887 they began bidding for McMurdo's company which owned the Portuguese end of the line, and the two colonial governments asked Knutsford for Britain's moral and diplomatic support. He replied that his Department would 'be glad to see the railway in colonial hands', for otherwise it was 'likely to divert traffic which would otherwise have gone through the Colonies'. But as to imperial support, the Prime Minister would not interfere in their negotiations.[1]

Salisbury was old-fashioned enough to think it improper in principle to use British power for the buying and keeping of railways on foreign soil.[2] The government would not guarantee the Delagoa line against interference from the governments through whose territories it ran, even if it could be bought, for that might entail going to war some day with the Transvaal or Portugal in defence of the line.[3] Rosebery in the Lords[4] and Castletown in private warned that British trade and influence would be endangered by the Boer-Portuguese junction, which in turn would open the way to German penetration. Yet Salisbury did nothing. Publicly, his ministry replied that Rosebery had exaggerated the imperial interest in the Delagoa line. Let the Cape and Natal buy it if they could.[5] But the British government would not do it for them. Privately, the Prime Minister admitted that the independence of the Transvaal made the Portuguese presence and German intrigue embarrassing and potentially dangerous. He complained:

> 'There is no part of the world in which Mr. Gladstone's policy has left more fruitful seeds of difficulty. But for him, neither Portuguese, Germans, nor Boers would be in a position to cause us any embarrassment.'[6]

But his first priority was a *rapprochement* with Germany,[7] to safeguard the position in Egypt and the Mediterranean. He did not care to risk this larger object for the sake of wresting the Delagoa Bay railway from Portugal. His ministry felt confident of overcoming the Transvaal difficulty by less desperate means. The growing *uitlander* population in

[1] Holland to Barrington, 3 Dec. 1887, S.P. (Holland).

[2] Salisbury to Castletown, 16 Jul. 1888, S.P. (Secretary's note book). Castletown had asked him '. . . to guarantee from illegal action or attack on the part of either the Boers or Portugal, capitalists who may be disposed to buy the line of railway from Delagoa Bay to the Transvaal'.

[3] *idem.* [4] *Hansard,* 3rd ser., CCCXXII, col. 1466.

[5] *ibid.,* cols. 1467–8. Natal in fact had deserted the Cape in bidding for the line after the break down of the negotiations for a customs union between the two colonies early in 1888.

[6] Salisbury to Baden-Powell, 13 Oct. 1888, S.P. (Secretary's note book).

[7] Goschen to Salisbury, 10 Oct. 1888, S.P. (Goschen).

the republic and the commercial development of south Africa as a whole seemed certain to break down sectional barriers and bring about a general railway and customs union. Salisbury refused to believe that the Transvaal and Portugal would be strong enough to subvert British supremacy, although he admitted that they would try. They might become formidable with serious aid from Germany, but Salisbury felt fairly sure that they would not get it. He wrote in August 1888 to the British capitalists who were still clamouring for his help in buying the Delagoa line:

> 'All that you tell me about the Portuguese is confirmed by my own information, and I can quite believe in the probability of united efforts on the part of the Transvaal Republic and the Portuguese to diminish our influence in South Africa. Their power, however, to do so will not be very great. The more information reaches me, the more sceptical am I as to any real German action in the same direction. There may be here and there a German adventurer, but I think they have no encouragement from their Government.'[1]

The perils to empire in south Africa seemed to Salisbury to be internal rather than external. He weighed the risk of reviving Anglo-Boer strife far more than that of a German challenge. The rise of the Transvaal seemed to him inconvenient; yet not one that the energy of British colonisation could not eventually overcome. Bottling up the republic at Delagoa Bay seemed likely to do more harm than good.

Without imperial support, the offers of the Cape and private syndicates for the railway were rejected in Lisbon. In June 1889, the Portuguese government, in agreement with the republic, confiscated the line and carried it on to the Transvaal border. But the Prime Minister found no legal ground for protesting.[2] Rhodes tried to buy the Transvaal section of the railway from the German-Dutch company which owned the republic's concessions, and was no more successful, because Kruger used state funds to bolster its shaky finances.

Rhodes tried again, this time to buy the whole of the province of Mozambique south of the Zambesi. He failed. These efforts to buy the line or the province went on into the Eighteen nineties. But Salisbury still refused to support them. That Lisbon would part with either was inconceivable to him. He informed the persistent Castletown in 1890 that if the latter could prise them out of Lisbon, he should have a royal charter for the region. At the same time Castletown was not to expect the British government to make Portugal abide by any con-

[1] Salisbury to Castletown, 16 Aug. 1888, S.P. (Secretary's note book).
[2] Salisbury to Castletown, 18 Jun. 1889, S.P. (Secretary's note book).

tracts with his syndicate. Salisbury's government kept to the mid-Victorian view of right relations between diplomacy and private commercial enterprise. As he put it:

> '... On general principles H.M.G. always decline to place the power of the country at the disposal of individual investors to secure the investments which they may think fit to make in the territory of another power.'[1]

Nevertheless, his ministry was to help Rhodes extend his mining kingdom into Zambesia in order to tighten the imperial grip on south Africa. First southern and then northern Zambesia were to be drawn into the strategy of imperial supremacy.[2]

A Counterpoise in Matabeleland, 1886–1888

After 1886 vast new regions were drawn into the struggle for hegemony over the sub-continent. Because the Matabele and Mashona country in the north was reputed as rich in gold as the Rand itself, it suddenly became a cockpit for rival groups. Speculators from the main gold rush in the Transvaal began to push into this region. Germans, Portuguese, Transvaalers and Cape colonists[3] appeared at Lobengula's kraal to barter gin and rifles for the land and mineral rights of his kingdom. Portugal pressed its ancient claims to the possession of the whole of central Zambesia. In 1885 when Warren and Mackenzie had urged the extension of the Bechuanaland protectorate northward to the River Zambesi in order to protect the tribes from the expected white advance,[4] Robinson and the Cape colonists had opposed the idea. But now, anxious to reserve the supposed new Rand for colonial enterprise, they pressed for an imperial protectorate over southern Zambesia. Sir Hercules Robinson's argument for the extension was laid before the Cabinet in 1886. If Matabeleland and Mashonaland were rich in gold, the country would soon be filled with white settlers. The High Commissioner believed it to be vital to imperial supremacy in south Africa that the colonists should be loyalists from the Cape, and not Transvaalers or Portuguese; for whoever developed and controlled this region would be adding weight either to the republican or to the colonial side of the south African balance. To Robinson and some Cape

[1] Salisbury to Castletown, 11 Oct. 1890, S.P. (Secretary's note book).

[2] 'Zambesia' in this book denotes the territories of the central basins of the Zambesi and Limpopo Rivers, lying to the north of the River Limpopo, to the west of Lake Nyasa, and to the south and east of the Congo Free State. The River Zambesi divides northern from southern Zambesia.

[3] Moffat to Shippard, 12 Dec. 1887, C.O. 806/302, 1–3.

[4] *vide* J. Mackenzie, *Austral Africa*; W. D. Mackenzie, *op. cit.*, 387.

leaders at least, southern Zambesia seemed the best place in which to strengthen the pro-British elements in the future south African federation.[1]

Knutsford was sufficiently impressed by the Cape point of view to urge the Foreign Office to resist Portuguese and Transvaal pretensions, and to reserve southern Zambesia for the Cape Colony. He pointed out in December 1887 that 'expansion of trade and settlement from the southward [toward Zambesia] is continuous and is accompanied by the . . . regular occupation of territory'.[2] Since Matabeleland and Mashonaland were certain to be opened up, they had better be reserved for the empire. Salisbury accordingly rejected Portugal's claims to the south of the Zambesi and offered compensation further north. At the same time, Robinson countered a Transvaal treaty with Lobengula by making one of his own; and on the strength of this the Colonial Office notified Kruger that the whole of southern Zambesia was 'exclusively within the British sphere of influence'.[3] Salisbury's government had warned off Portugal and the Transvaal Republic. But he would go no further than diplomacy to secure southern Zambesia for the Cape Colony, fearing lest Parliament should jib at an outright protectorate.[4] Knutsford wrote to the High Commissioner, 'I doubt whether it may be expedient to accept responsibility with regard to Lobengula and his country,'[5] and the Colonial Secretary ruled out any possibility of advancing British protection over chiefs north of the Zambesi River.[6]

SALISBURY'S DIPLOMATIC DEFENCE OF MATABELELAND AND THE SHIRÉ, 1887–1889

It was one thing to claim a sphere of influence; making it good was quite another. Portugal as well as the Transvaal immediately rejected the British pretension; and Bismarck unexpectedly contested the western boundary of Salisbury's claim in the Lake Ngami region.[7] There was a chance that Portugal might be strongly supported. Both

[1] Sir H. Robinson, Cabinet Memo., 'Proposed Extension of Bechuanaland Protectorate to the Northwards as far as the Zambesi River,' 23 May 1886, C.O. 806/268, 1–4.

[2] C.O. to F.O., 2 Dec. 1887, F.O. 403/108, 12.

[3] This declaration covered 'the territory north of the South African Republic and the Bechuanaland Protectorate, south of the Zambesi, east of the 20th degree of east longitude and west of the Portuguese province of Sofala'. (Robinson to Kruger, 25 Jul. 1888, encl. in Bok to Robinson, 30 Nov. 1888, C. 5918, P.P. (1890) LI, 552.)

[4] C.O. to Mackenzie, 13 Aug. 1889, C.O. African (S) 372, 115.

[5] Knutsford to Robinson, 29 Mar. 1888, C.O. 806/302, 15.

[6] C.O. to F.O., 24 Sept. 1888, *ibid.*, 65.

[7] Knutsford to Salisbury, 14 and 15 Oct. 1888, and Sir D. Currie, 'Memo. on Lake Ngami Negotiations' in Knutsford to Salisbury, 7 Jul. 1890, S.P. (Holland).

France and Germany in 1887 had accepted her claims to the whole of Zambesia between Mozambique on the east and Angola on the west coast. At first the British had been contemptuous of Portugal's aspirations. When asked by the Foreign Office toward the end of 1887 whether British and Portuguese claims in Zambesia should be delimited by agreement, Knutsford advised against it. Confident that moribund Portugal had no energy for occupying her paper empire, he felt that to yield anything would be needlessly to fetter the vigorous colonial expansion from the south which must soon effectively occupy the entire region.[1] But from the beginning of 1888 Lisbon showed unexpected activity in sending expeditions along the Zambesi and into the hinterland of Sofala. Ironically, her pioneer companies although headed by scions of the Portuguese nobility were often financed by British capitalists.[2] This expansion forced Salisbury to negotiate with Portugal. He offered to admit her claims north of the Zambesi, if she would admit his to the south. As a result, the question of Matabeleland and Mashonaland in 1888 became bound up in Salisbury's diplomacy with northern Zambesia and the Nyasa question. Colonial expansion from the south became entangled with the fate of British missionaries on the Shiré; and the major plans for planting a colony in Matabeleland to make south Africa more British became linked in Salisbury's mind with a minor project for salvaging humanitarian endeavour from the Portuguese advance.

A legacy from Livingstone, the interests in the Nyasa region were humanitarian, religious and unofficial. Scottish philanthropists and missionaries had been working to cut the slave routes from the interior to the coast, and to destroy the slave trade by legitimate commerce. Missionary traders had formed the African Lakes Company,[3] for this purpose, but their resources were slender, and they had made little headway. Apart from this benevolent enterprise in the Shiré districts, there was no British interest north of the Zambesi until concessionaires looking for minerals crossed the river toward the end of 1889.

Salisbury in 1888 was at one with his predecessors in thinking that these missionary concerns were no good reason to extend British rule

[1] C.O. to F.O., 2 Dec. 1887, F.O. 403/108, 12.

[2] The Zambesi Company and the Companhia de Moçambique, *The Times*, 3 Feb. 1891, 11. For Portuguese policy *vide* J. Duffy: *Portuguese Africa* (Cambridge, Mass. 1959), 213–21.

[3] This Company originated in the Livingstonia Central Africa Company, founded by James Stevenson in 1878, with a nominal capital of £20,000, to supply the mission and foster legitimate trade. All profits after payment of a dividend of 5 per cent were to be re-invested in missionary work. The Lakes Company's capital was exhausted by 1888 by its war with the Arabs. In fact it had paid no dividends up to 1889.

over Nyasa. Granville had refused to do so in 1885, when the African Lakes Company had applied for an imperial protectorate. A year later Rosebery was inclined to accept Portugal's claims to the whole of northern Zambesia in exchange for guarantees of free trade and access in the territory.[1] Once again in 1888, the Lakes Company and the missions, threatened by Portuguese expeditions from the east and fighting a desperate war with the Arab slave traders on the Lake, asked the Foreign Office for protection. They were appealing to a stone. Salisbury and his advisers would not hear of a protectorate or official intervention. All that the Prime Minister would do was to ask the British consul[2] in the region to use his influence on the missions' behalf. As he wrote in May 1888:

> 'I feel that [a consul] represents a compromise between the desire of the missionaries to obtain Protection and the desire of the Home Government not to be involved in expensive operations. To please the missionaries we send a representative of the Govt.: to spare the taxpayers we make him understand that he will in no case be supported by an armed force. The only weapon left to him is bluster.'[3]

Gladstone could not have insisted more emphatically that African missions went at their own risk. Salisbury, speaking in the Lords a month later, was as hard in public as he had been in private. His government would not send military aid to the missions; nor would it extend a protectorate: 'It is not our duty to do it. We should be risking tremendous sacrifices for a very doubtful gain. . . . We must leave the dispersal of this terrible army of wickedness to the gradual advancement of civilisation and Christianity.'[4]

For a man in favour of civilising Africa, Salisbury's indifference to the Nyasa missionaries' plight seems almost cynical. But the humanitarians could raise little enthusiasm in Parliament for official aid to their cause. Several of the Liberal Unionists, upon whom the Conservatives' majority in the Commons depended, especially Goschen at the Treasury, would not hear of more 'white elephant' protectorates in tropical Africa. Their resistance was all the more formidable, since the Gladstonians at this time were trying to tempt the Liberal Unionists back into the Home Rule fold. The position of foreign as of domestic politics dictated indifference. There were German claims to the north-west of

[1] For the official attitude during the Eighteen eighties, *vide* A. J. Hanna, *The Beginnings of Nyasaland and North-Eastern Rhodesia, 1859–1895*, (1956), 123–7.

[2] A vice-consul had been posted in the Shiré district since 1883.

[3] Salisbury, Minute, 15 May 1888, F.O. 84/1922.

[4] *Hansard*, 3rd ser., CCCXXVIII, col. 550.

Lake Nyasa where the Lakes Company's Arab war was taking place. Salisbury had no wish to ruffle Bismarck by sending a force there, when he needed German support against France to protect vital interests in the Mediterranean and on the Nile. For the same reason, the Prime Minister preferred to negotiate rather than to bully Portugal, since Germany and France had already countenanced her Zambesian claims.

His first concern in the negotiations in any case was not with Nyasa but with Matabeleland and Mashonaland. Salisbury had accepted Robinson's case for reserving these regions for Cape colonial enterprise, as a means of strengthening British influence in south Africa. His overriding aim in attempting to settle the whole question of Zambesia with Lisbon was to obtain Portuguese recognition of the British sphere in southern Zambesia. But his religious sentiment and his sense of diplomatic finesse made him try and stretch the bargain, to save the Protestant missions in the Shiré highlands from falling under Catholic rule.[1]

These were the priorities behind the proposals to Lisbon which Salisbury and Knutsford worked out in the first half of 1888. In May the Colonial Secretary suggested that the Zambesi should be accepted as the '. . . southern boundary of Portuguese exclusive influence, provided that free trading along that River [was] secured to Great Britain'.[2] Anderson in the Foreign Office welcomed the idea. Northern Zambesia, he observed, was pestilential and useless to the empire, and it would be enough that Portugal should concede southern Zambesia, while promising to keep out of the British mission field in the Nyasa region. The Foreign Office hoped to kill two birds with one stone. In this way, Anderson concluded, '. . . [We should] get rid of the impracticable idea of a British Protectorate [over Nyasa].'[3] Salisbury on 10 June, 1888 agreed to this neat solution of the whole Zambesi question, with one significant proviso — that the south African colonial governments did not object to the surrender of northern Zambesia.[4]

[1] This may be inferred from Salisbury's minute on Petre's despatch of 24 Dec. 1888 which conveyed the Portuguese government's own admission that Cardozo's expedition was intended to assert Portuguese claims to the Shiré districts. Salisbury instructed: 'Privately inform African Lakes Company and the [missionary] deputation to Sir J. Fergusson.' Barrington, the Prime Minister's private secretary minuted: 'Do you wish the African Lakes Co. to be told even privately that the object of the Portuguese expedition is declared by the govt. themselves to be to affirm Portuguese influence in the Nyassa region. It may do good by raising a storm but I do not like to do it without putting the matter again before you,' (E.B., 26 Dec. 1888, S.P. (Private Miscellaneous), Vol. I.)

[2] C.O. to F.O., 23 May 1888, F.O. 403/108, 39. *vide* Salisbury to Petre, 2 Aug. 1887, C. 5904, P.P. (1890) LI, 71–2; Petre to Salisbury, 30 Oct. 1888, *ibid.*, 151.

[3] Anderson, Minute on C.O. to F.O., 23 May 1888, *ibid.*, 41.

[4] Salisbury, Minute, 10 Jun. 1888, *ibid.*, 41.

Apparently, Salisbury's attitude toward Zambesia was attuned to his delicate relations with Bismarck, the impracticability of setting up more protectorates, and more positively, to Cape opinion and the south African balance. Clearly, his prime purpose was to reserve Matabeleland and Mashonaland for the Cape Colony; this the Prime Minister showed when he disregarded Portugal's claim and declared an exclusive sphere of influence there in July 1888. But whereas he wanted southern Zambesia for a British colony, all he wanted in Nyasaland was neutralisation, stopping well short of a protectorate. For the rest of northern Zambesia Salisbury seems to have had little use. He played down the value of free navigation on the largely unnavigable Zambesi, and decried its trade.[1] Whitehall assumed that climatically the River Zambesi marked the northern limit of white settlement. Since the northern territories, unlike the southern, seemed to be too tropical for European colonists, they had as yet no place in the strategy of imperial supremacy in south Africa.

At the end of October 1888 the British ambassador in Lisbon submitted Salisbury's proposals. Petre insisted that Matabeleland and Mashonaland must be British. North of the Zambesi, on the other hand, he asked for no more than 'a mutual engagement between the two countries that neither of them should attempt to establish exclusive jurisdiction over the Nyasa basin'. With this exception 'Her Majesty's Government would not object to recognise the territory north of the Zambesi as falling exclusively within the Portuguese sphere of influence'.[2] Salisbury apparently had no ambitions for colonial estates north of the River. What is more remarkable, his proposals did not provide for any corridor to connect the British sphere in the south with the Nyasa mission field.[3] The chief architect of the British African empire was not working to a 'Cape to Cairo' design in October 1888. But there were one or two of his subordinates who were.

The project for settling Zambesia proved abortive. Lisbon, with d'Andrade's expedition advancing toward Mashonaland[4] and Cardozo

[1] Salisbury to Knutsford, 12 Oct. 1888, Cecil, *op. cit.*, IV, 241; Knutsford however replied: 'Whether the Zambesi is shallow or not, and whether there is much or little trade going up or down it, I think we ought to secure that that trade should go free.' (Knutsford to Salisbury, 15 Oct. 1888, S.P. (Holland).)

[2] The ambassador's account of his proposals to Gomes is given in Petre to Salisbury, 30 and 31 Oct. 1888, C. 5904, P.P. (1890) LI, 150–2.

[3] Salisbury proposed a line running from the north-eastern corner of the Matabele kingdom to Zumbo as the north-eastern limit of his claims in the south. And in proposing to concede all northern Zambesia except the Nyasa basin north of the confluence of the Shiré and the Ruo, a Portuguese salient would have been left between Matabeleland and Nyasa.

[4] O'Neill to Salisbury, 20 Aug. 1888, C. 5904, P.P. (1890) LI, 76–7.

on the way to the Shiré,[1] did not mean to negotiate for territory which she hoped soon to occupy.[2] For the time being, Salisbury could do nothing to stop these missions. He was probably wary of coercing Lisbon, for fear of Bismarck coming to her aid. But in January 1889 Bismarck relieved Salisbury of some anxiety by offering to accommodate Britain on colonial questions in return for an Anglo-German *entente* in Europe.[3] Two months later, Salisbury, seeing a more favourable chance of settling Zambesia with Lisbon, sent the pushful Harry Johnston to renew the negotiations for 'an understanding about frontiers which would keep the Portuguese out of the Shiré Highlands and Central Zambesia'.[4] Probably Salisbury's purpose still went no further than inducing the Portuguese to yield Mashonaland and to neutralise the Nyasa region. Johnston in fact brought back the basis for a treaty which would have secured Mashonaland, but would have given up the Nyasa mission field and obtained territory which he himself thought far more valuable — the country connecting Matabeleland through Barotseland to the southern end of Lake Tanganyika. The consul justified his choice of northern Zambesia rather than the Shiré district on the ground that it 'may some day serve as a link between Egypt and the Cape'. But it would seem from his protestations that his chief had given him no such instructions. 'I do earnestly hope', Johnston pleaded apprehensively, 'that Lord Salisbury will approve of what I have done and back me up.'[5]

The idea of an all-red connection between Cape Town and Cairo had taken hold of the consul's imagination in the previous summer.[6] But to judge from the proposals he made to the Portuguese at that time, the notion had not appealed to the phlegmatic Salisbury, although Johnston claimed later that it did so.[7] Neither the Prime Minister nor the missionaries were pleased with Johnston's plan for sacrificing Nyasa to the Cape to Cairo chimera. The all-red route indeed, was the aspiration, not of Whitehall, but of the Cape railway and mineral interests. But when the Cape ministers pressed London about the plan, and financial interests offered the means to further it, Salisbury might have to heed their desires. Prodded by Cape Town, Knutsford at least now

[1] Petre to Salisbury, 24 Dec. 1888, S.P. (Miscellaneous, Vol. I., Private).
[2] Petre to Salisbury, 31 Oct. 1888, C. 5904, P.P. (1890) LI, 152.
[3] Bismarck to Hatzfeldt, 11 Jan. 1889, *Grosse Politik* IV no. 943.
[4] Sir H. H. Johnston, *The Story of My Life*, (1923), 231.
[5] Johnston to Lister, 5 Apr. 1889, and Johnston to Salisbury, 22 Apr. 1889, F.O. 84/1969.
[6] 'British Policy in Africa' by 'An African Explorer', *The Times*, 22 Aug. 1888.
[7] Johnston, *op. cit.*, 221–2. cf. R. Oliver, *Sir Harry Johnston and the Scramble for Africa*, (1957), 141, 143.

wanted to secure northern, as well as southern Zambesia for the colony, and welcomed Johnston's scheme.[1]

By 1 May, 1889 however, the imperial outlook in Zambesia had changed abruptly. Salisbury no longer had to try and rescue his Zambesian claims by diplomacy alone. The negotiations with Lisbon could hang fire, for now he had better means. Cecil Rhodes arrived in London at the end of March, to form a British South Africa Company and conclude negotiations which had begun in January for a royal charter.

Knutsford sent Rhodes' offer to Salisbury on 1 May. 'You will see', the Colonial Secretary pointed out, 'he [Rhodes] proposes to help you North of the Zambesi.'[2] Now that Rhodes offered a means of occupying southern Zambesia and countering d'Andrade's and Cardozo's expeditions, there was no need for Salisbury to buy off Portuguese claims with concessions further north. The Prime Minister's intention of yielding northern Zambesia had always been subject to the Cape government's agreement. By the end of 1888 the colonists were protesting strongly. The powerful Rhodesian interests were pressing the Colonial Office hard to reserve northern as well as southern Zambesia.

No sooner did Rhodes arrive in London, than British newspapers took up the Cape to Cairo slogan. From Cape Town the High Commissioner urged Knutsford to claim all of Zambesia for the Colony; and the Colonial Office in turn urged the Foreign Office to extend the projected South Africa Company's field of operations north of the Zambesi.[3] Rhodes offered to bear all the charges of administration in northern as well as southern Zambesia. Sensing Salisbury's predicament in the Nyasa region, Rhodes' opportunism went further. In May he promised to pay the cost of pacifying and administering the Nyasa basin[4] and began his attempt to buy the impoverished Lakes Company. At first the Prime Minister met the great amalgamator's colonial enthusiasm north of the Zambesi with seasoned irresolution. Still intent above all upon drawing support from Berlin to secure the position in the Mediterranean and on the Nile, he wrote:

> 'I am afraid that the new Company . . . will startle people a little in Berlin. I have . . . strongly recommended them in the first instance to confine their proposed region of operations to the south of the Zambesi.'[5]

[1] Knutsford to Salibsury, 27 Apr. 1889, S.P. (Holland).
[2] Knutsford to Salisbury, 1 May 1889, S.P. (Holland).
[3] C.O. to F.O., 16 May 1889, C.O. Africa (S.). 372, 71.
[4] His formal proposal was made in Cawston to Herbert, 1 Jul. 1889, F.O. 403/111, 128–9.
[5] Salisbury to Malet, 12 Jun. 1889, Cecil, *op. cit.*, IV, 244.

What Salisbury would do with Rhodes' cheque book depended partly upon how Bismarck felt about German claims on Lake Ngami and north-eastern Zambesia. For the rest, whether Rhodes should be given his charter was to be decided by broad south African considerations. In that question, as in the negotiations with Portugal, the British government's interest was focused, not upon joining the Cape to Cairo, nor upon commercial prospects in Zambesia as such, but upon the future balance between Boer and Briton in south Africa. For Salisbury as for Knutsford, the crux lay in Matabeleland and in Cape Town. Northern Zambesia was significant only in so far as it might affect colonial politics in the south. The Prime Minister's judgement of Rhodes' projects therefore leaned much upon his Colonial Secretary's advice.[1] It is Knutsford's and Robinson's appraisal of the south African situation which reveals the compelling reasons why Rhodes was to get his charter.

A Stronger Colonial Axis: The Bechuanaland Railway

Ever since the shocks of the first Tranvaal war, Colonial Secretaries had tended to approach south Africa as they might a political volcano. But in Knutsford caution became timidity. He was no politician and he knew it. From an under-secretaryship in the Colonial Office, he had been enticed into Parliament by a family connection.[2] But he was a fish out of water. As described by his son, 'he was a singularly modest man with too little trust in himself and that is why he made no great impression in his political life.'[3] But he was a competent administrator. And Salisbury probably gave him the Colonial Office for his utter loyalty, his *expertise* and his connection with the Imperial Federation League. His own sense of inadequacy as a minister made him a victim of all the south African neuroses which a decade of rising Afrikaner nationalism and Parliamentary criticism had instilled in the British official mind. To Knutsford, the cut and thrust of debate in the Commons was torture.[4] He went in dread of asking Parliament to raise

[1] Salisbury asked Holland: 'Do you mind our driving a hole into your room? It would expedite consultation and the present distance between the Foreign Office and Colonial Office, reckoned by time, is about as long as the distance between London and Berlin,' (Salisbury to Holland, 25 May 1887, S.P. (Holland).)

[2] Sydney Holland, Viscount Knutsford, *In Black and White*, (1926), 71.

[3] *ibid.*, 211.

[4] Salisbury seems to have been kindness itself in bolstering Knutsford's *morale*. After a debate on West African difficulties, Salisbury wrote: 'I am very sorry to hear you are so knocked up. Pray do nothing rash in the way of resigning. I have the strongest hope we shall be able to put a stop to this abominable system of torturing Cabinet Ministers next year, or at least lighten it very much.' (Salisbury to Knutsford, 12 Oct., 1887, *ibid.* 218.)

imperial expenditure and so, of extending protectorates in south Africa. Diffident of his own judgement, he relied heavily on Robinson's.[1]

The High Commissioner was almost as intimidated by south African opinion as Knutsford was by Westminster. Afrikanerdom uniting one day to take south Africa out of the empire, this was his private spectre, as it was the Colonial Office's; and its head and front was the Transvaal. All too often, as it seemed to Robinson, the Cape responsible government appeared ready to furnish the legs. The danger from the Bond at the Cape, and from the South African Republic in the interior, these were the twin themes of his reports. Of all the south African states, the Transvaal alone showed energy in occupying the interior. Unless colonial expansion could be hastened northward to check the territorial extension of republicanism, imperial supremacy seemed unlikely to last. Worse still in Robinson's eyes, the Cape Dutch did not realise this danger. Many colonial leaders did not regard the republicans as potential enemies of the empire. On the contrary, colonists and republicans alike resented imperial interference. 'Africa for the Afrikaner' seemed almost as popular a slogan in Cape Town as in Pretoria. The High Commissioner, in this atmosphere of hostility, concluded that the extension of empire should be left to the Cape government even though, in his experience it had proved a brittle tool. Whatever the Colonial ministry's composition, it could do little without a wink from Hofmeyr and the Afrikaner Bond; but when Transvaal interests were concerned, Hofmeyer rarely winked without a nod from Kruger. Robinson suspected the Bondsmen of being more interested in getting rid of the Colonial Office than in opposing republican expansion and saving the colony's future.

The suspicion might be prejudiced, but it was not altogether unjustified. Kruger and Hofmeyer, the Bond's ministry-maker at the Cape, had spiked too many imperial guns for Robinson to believe in the friendship of the one or the loyalty of the other. The Bondsmen had helped the Transvaal rebels to wreck imperial federation and to bring about the retrocession of 1881. In 1884 and 1885 they had stopped the Cape ministry from fully co-operating with London over Bechuanaland. As a result an expensive protectorate had been left on Colonial Office hands.

Hence in Robinson's mind the first essential of imperial supremacy

[1] Knutsford told Salisbury that Robinson was 'a good authority on S. African matters'. (Holland to Salisbury, 21 Dec. 1887, S.P. (Holland).) Three years later the Colonial Secretary described Robinson as 'the most conspicuous governor of recent years' and proposed him for a baronetcy. (Knutsford to Salisbury, 12 Sept. 1890, S.P. (Holland).)

in south Africa was to make sure of the Cape. Hofmeyr and the moderate Bondsmen had to be detached once and for all from the extremists and from Pretoria. It could not be done as long as the Colonial Office opposed colonial native policy. It could not be done if the British confirmed colonial suspicions of imperialism by refusing to hand over protectorates to colonial rule. That way, Robinson argued, the Cape Dutch would be driven into the arms of the Transvaal. The empire must defer to colonial opinion, if it was to make sure of colonial loyalty. Imperial policy should be aligned on that of the Cape government. It is no wonder that Robinson gained a reputation in London for being more colonial than the colonials. Yet it seemed plain to him that the republicans might win control of the colony and the north unless the loyalists and moderate Afrikaners of the Cape were given their head. In south Africa as in Australasia, the rise of colonial national feeling, as Rosebery observed, meant that imperial policy tended to be dictated more and more from the periphery to the centre.

In the autumn of 1888 the imperial future in south Africa, as it seemed to Robinson, trembled in the balance. The gold of Johannesburg was already beginning to alter the political and commercial configuration of south Africa in favour of the Transvaal. Robinson and Knutsford had hoped that the Cape government would extend its railway[1] northward through Bechuanaland toward the Zambesi. They needed the line to help develop Bechuanaland, to secure Matabeleland and to establish communications between the Cape and the interior, free from republican control. But the Cape leaders wanted to develop the shortest route to Johannesburg through the republics in order to tap the prosperity of the Rand. Colonial merchants and farmers demanded it. Kruger and his allies in the Cape Bond were doing their utmost to block the Bechuanaland extension. But in refusing earlier in 1888 to admit the Cape line into his republic, Kruger seemed to have played into Robinson's hands. The anger of the Cape Dutch against Pretoria gave the High Commissioner and the Sprigg ministry an opportunity to split the Bondsmen, and to carry a Bechuanaland extension Bill, although Hofmeyr and Rhodes with two-thirds of the Bond opposed it.

But by October Robinson was back where he started. Kruger had offered to consider admitting the Cape line if the colonial government would drop the Bechuanaland extension. Hofmeyr and the Bond wanted to accept these terms. Cape opinion, irritated by the Mother

[1] For details of the Bechuanaland railway scheme as remembered by its pioneers, *vide* L. Weinthal (ed.), *The Story of the Cape to Cairo Railway and River Route, 1877–1922*, (4 vols.), (1922–3).

Country's intimations that the Cape Colony was not fit to govern Bechuanaland, swung against a Bechuanaland railway.[1] The High Commissioner foresaw a revival of republicanism among the colonists. Angrily he reported to London that the Bechuanaland extension 'is now not likely to be carried out'.[2] His forecast of the consequences was alarmist. Yet to Knutsford he gave a sense of the south African balance turning in favour of republicanism which was real enough. If there was no Bechuanaland line, then the drawing of the colonial railways into the Transvaal would mean republican control of the empire's communications with Zambesia; and it might mean dooming Bechuanaland to stagnation. Railways and the Rand it seemed, were shifting paramountcy over the interior to the South African Republic. Robinson warned:

> 'The extension from the Cape northwards will now be through one or both of the Republics. The importance of Bechuanaland as a road to the interior will cease. The Cape Colony will then no longer care to be burdened with that territory; and the result will be an expensive, valueless, inaccessible inland Crown Colony will be left indefinitely on the hands of the Imperial Government.'[3]

Without the Bechuanaland extension moreover, it would be hard to save Matabeleland and Mashonaland from republican occupation. In September Robinson had reported a Transvaal trek preparing to enter Matabeleland.[4] Kruger's government rejected Moffat's treaty with Lobengula and the declaration of an imperial sphere of influence. Pretoria claimed that the right to expand northward was implied in the London Convention.[5] What was more, Kruger had just invited France and Germany to arbitrate upon the murder of his agent on the border of Matabeleland. This seemed like inviting foreign intervention. To Robinson the urgent rival in the north was not Portugal but the South African Republic.

According to the abstractions in which the distant imperial government dealt with south Africa, the railway question was crucial — for the future of southern Zambesia, Bechuanaland, perhaps for the turn of

[1] Knutsford wanted to keep direct control of Bechuanaland for the time being to strengthen Imperial influence in the south African interior, although he intended eventually to hand it over to the Cape Colony. (*vide* Knutsford to Salisbury, 4 Oct. 1888, S.P. (Holland).)

[2] For these events see Robinson to Knutsford, 17 Oct. 1888 C. 5918, P.P. (1890) LI, 428–31. For the railway negotiations between Hofmeyr and Kruger, Hofmeyr and Reitz, *op. cit.*, 337–57.

[3] P.P. (1890) LI, 430.

[4] Robinson to Knutsford, 12 Sept. 1888, C.O., 806/310, 22.

[5] Bok to Robinson, 30 Nov. 1888, C. 5918, P.P. (1890) LI, 552–3.

south African politics towards Pretoria or London. British influence seemed to be entering a major crisis — at least to Salisbury's and Knutsford's minds. It hung in the balance whether the Cape Bond and the Orange Free State would swing commercially and politically onto the side of the Transvaal or not. Natal was already defecting to the republic economically. Knutsford's plea for a speedy sanction to the Bill setting up the Cape–Orange Free State Customs Union gives the sense of crisis:

> '[The Cape ministers] are right in saying that it is of the "gravest importance" that the Bill should be at once assented to as to refuse, perhaps even to delay, sanction . . . would tend to throw the Orange Free State into the hands of the Transvaal Republic and to greatly strengthen the Afrikander party.'[1]

Even the 'loyalist' Sprigg ministry in Cape Town was threatening to severe connection with the empire unless the imperial government passed the customs union with the Free State, since the colony's trade and railways depended upon it.[2]

The colony was scrambling to bring the rest of south Africa into its commercial system before the Transvaalers put their fences round it. It was no wonder that Salisbury and Knutsford wished to defer to the Cape's demands and keep the Transvaal out of Zambesia. Nor could Bechuanaland and the north be tied securely to the colony without a Bechuanaland railway. But Knutsford was unable to find money either for a Matabele protectorate or a Bechuanaland extension. No more could the Cape government, with its loyalist members fettered by the Bond. Goschen at the Treasury had banned all increases of expenditure and staff.[3] Hicks Beach at the Board of Trade would have given the Transvaal a free hand in Matabeleland.[4]

The Colonial Secretary had a policy but no means of carrying it out. He was also anxious to avoid conflict with the Transvaal over Matabeleland, which might alienate Afrikaner sentiment in the Cape Colony and the Free State. The only way which he could see out of his difficulties in January 1889 was to bribe the Transvaalers with Swaziland to leave southern Zambesia alone. As he put it to Salisbury:

> 'I apprehend that we intend to prevent the *annexation* of Matabeleland by Boers or any Foreign Power. We should be much abused in this country if we let the Boers annex Matabeleland and Mashonaland, as they are rich

[1] Knutsford to Salisbury, 6 Dec. 1888, S.P. (Holland).
[2] Knutsford to Salisbury, 9 Feb. 1889, S.P. (Holland).
[3] Goschen to Salisbury, 25 Jan. 1889, S.P. (Goschen).
[4] Knutsford to Salisbury, 28 Jan. 1889, S.P. (Holland).

territories, and concessions by Lo Bengula are held by some influential people; but we shall have to face considerable danger of conflict with the Boers; if we bar them from extension to the North, I should be inclined to compromise with them by letting it be known that . . . we shall not prevent them from protecting and annexing [Swaziland]. This will bring them to the sea, which is their chief desire.'[1]

Shut in between Parliament's objection to spending money and the risk of provoking the Afrikaners, Salisbury's ministry could do little. It was left to Rhodes' private enterprise to release the captive government.

Rhodes and the British South Africa Company Charter, 1889–1891

Among the rival speculators in northern mining futures, one company had already offered to begin the Bechuanaland railway, in return for a Colonial Office grant of land and mineral monopolies in Bechuanaland. Lord Gifford's Bechuanaland Exploring syndicate applied for a royal charter for this purpose in July 1888.[2] Knutsford and Robinson had encouraged them to do so.[3] But as yet Gifford's capital was slight. What was more, Hofmeyr and the Bond opposed the English capitalists as catspaws of imperialism.[4] Without the co-operation of the Cape ministry, the Bechuanaland railway extension could not be built. The Colonial Secretary made it plain that he favoured British control and settlement in the north, and he hinted at a better chance of official support if Gifford amalgamated with other concerns.[5] On 30 October Rhodes' agent, C. E. Rudd, persuaded Lobengula to grant a monopoly of all minerals in his kingdom. By the end of 1888 Rhodes had absorbed Gifford's enterprise into his own Central Search Association and was busily buying out other rivals. Financially, Rhodes was irresistible, with the wealth of De Beers diamond monopoly and the Consolidated Gold Fields of the Rand behind him.[6] Investors throughout Europe were rushing into south African gold shares of all kinds; so that he could be confident of raising money for new 'Ophirs' in Bechuanaland and Matabeleland. Whatever Rhodes' personal motives, economic necessity

[1] *idem.*

[2] Robinson to Knutsford, 21 Jul. 1888, C.O. African (S), 372, 1. Gifford offered in the first instance to extend the line from Kimberley to Mafeking; Herbert to British South Africa Company, 24 Jan. 1890, C. 5918, P.P. (1890) LI, 652–3.

[3] Robinson to Knutsford, 17 Oct. 1888, *ibid.*, 429.

[4] Hofmeyr to Kruger, Hofmeyr and Reitz, *op. cit.* 356.

[5] Knutsford to Robinson 20 Aug. 1888, C.O. African (S), 372, 2.

[6] The market value of these concerns at this time Frankel estimates at something near twenty millions, *op. cit.* 63.

plainly forced him to obtain imperial protection for his mineral speculations. Without it, the Rudd concession was vulnerable to Transvaal and Portuguese encroachment and to Lobengula's repudiation. An extension of empire was needed to secure and capitalise these claims, and to confirm the monopoly.

By the beginning of 1889, financial necessity was matched by political opportunity. The event had belied Robinson's Job-like prophecy that the Cape Bond would rage against London's refusal to hand over Bechuanaland. This irritated them less than Kruger's opposition against pushing the Cape line to Johannesburg; and Hofmeyr and the Bondsmen were swinging behind Rhodes' scheme for northward expansion, if it was done by colonial and not imperial agency. The High Commissioner's chance to separate the Bond from Pretoria seemed to have come at last, provided that the imperial government chartered Rhodes' enterprise. On 3 January, 1889, Gifford formally re-opened negotions with Knutsford for a royal charter; and the High Commissioner in support bombarded Knutsford at his weakest points. The choice in Matabeleland, Robinson urged was between

> '. . . letting the country fall into the hands of the South African Republic or of annexing it to the Empire. The latter course would assuredly entail on British taxpayers for some time, at all events, an annual expenditure of not less than a quarter of a million sterling.'

Robinson's propaganda was shrewd if blatant. A chartered company he pointed out would be much cheaper and altogether '. . . the best and most effectual mode of widening the base of British prosperity in that part of South Africa.'[1]

The government in London at this moment suspected Robinson and knew almost nothing of Rhodes. Two months earlier, Rhodes had dared to urge the Colonial Secretary that Robinson should be renewed as High Commissioner. Knutsford commented to Salisbury in a letter which is a curious example of absent-mindedness in empire-making:

> 'I do not think it would be at all desirable to extend Sir H. Robinson's term of office. . . . Any suggestion from Mr. Rhodes (who I may advise in passing is the gentleman who presented Mr. Parnell with £1000 . . .) must be treated with some suspicion.
>
> It is supposed and with good ground, that Mr. Rhodes is working with Mr. Rudd to get very large mining concessions from Lo Bengula, and that Sir H. Robinson favours Mr. Rudd as against others who are trying to get concessions in Matabeleland. Only this morning I have received a protest

[1] Robinson to Knutsford, 18 Mar. 1889, C. 5918, P.P. (1890) LI, 578.

against the conduct of Sir H. Robinson from one of these gentlemen — Mr. Rhodes is not liked by the Cape ministers and he would not improbably lose his place of Secretary to the High Commissioner, if a new High Cr. were appointed.

Both Smith and Goschen are inclined to suspect Sir H. Robinson of being influenced too much by Rhodes and Rudd, and I am disposed to agree with them.'[1]

Rudd in fact had obtained Lobengula's concession two months earlier, although Knutsford did not know it. On the same day, the Colonial Secretary corrected another error: 'I find since I wrote that Rhodes does not hold any office. I was confounding him with a W. Bower — But all the rest of the letter about Rhodes and Sir H. Robinson holds good.'[2] Salisbury's ministry at the end of January 1889 took Rhodes for an enemy of empire. Not only was he an Afrikaner politician associated with the Cape Bond and the Irish Home Rulers, he was competing with influential Unionist supporters for Lobengula's minerals. His appeal on Robinson's behalf made him all the more suspect. The imperialists and humanitarians in the South Africa Committee, headed by Chamberlain and John Mackenzie, were pressing the ministry to drop the pro-colonial Commissioner, to take Matabeleland, and to keep Bechuanaland under United Kingdom instead of Cape control. The Conservatives did not wish to alienate Chamberlain, one of their essential Liberal Unionist allies. Unanimously the Cabinet decided on 31 January against prolonging Robinson's commission at the Cape.[3]

Rhodes however defied the auguries and came to London in March. On the last day of April, after interviews with Knutsford, the emperor of the south African mineral kingdom, the political lieutenant of Hofmeyr sent his formal proposal to the mere ministers of the empire.[4] The commercial advantages required from the charter were put frankly enough. Rhodes' association asked the Colonial Office:

'. . . for an assurance that such rights and interests as have been legally acquired in these territories by . . . this association shall be recognised by and receive the sanction and moral support of Her Majesty's Government.'[5]

[1] Knutsford to Salisbury, 12 Jan. 1889, S.P. (Holland). Rhodes is commonly supposed to have subscribed £10,000 to the parliamentary fund of the Irish Nationalist Party in 1888. It is not clear when this money was paid over, but the balance sheets of the fund in 1890 show a donation of £5,000 from an unknown source. *vide* C. C. O'Brien: *Parnell and his Party, 1880–90*, (1957), 266, n. 4.

[2] *ibid.* [3] Knutsford to Salisbury, 31 Jan. 1889, S.P. (Holland).

[4] Gifford and Consolidated Gold Fields to C.O., 30 Apr. 1889, C.O. African (S), 372, 65. [5] *ibid.*

In return he offered to finance, administer and colonise Matabeleland[1] on behalf of the Cape Colony, to take over the Bechuanaland Protectorate from the Colonial Office and to extend the Bechuanaland railway[2] and telegraph to the Zambesi River. But he would go further. He wanted northern Zambesia and Nyasaland as well. By so much did millionaires exceed Downing Street at empire building.

No African scheme was ever so well conceived for the government to which it was put. Financially it seemed impeccable. Schooled no doubt by Robinson, Rhodes had met all the stock objections to extension of rule. The Cabinet could get no money for the acquisition of Matabeleland and Mashonaland; the Company would provide millions. Where the British government could only make paper claims to exclude Portugal and the Transvaal, the Company would plant a colony to occupy the country. Goschen wished to stop the drain of Bechuanaland on the Exchequer; the Company would do it. The politicians were frightened of taking the responsibility for expansion; the Company would take it for them. Knutsford feared the effect on south African opinion of a clash with the Transvaal in the north; the risk would be lessened if the work was left to a company headed by Cape colonists and approved by Cape Bondsmen. What was more, Rhodes had by now won over many of those British financiers and politicians who had prejudiced the government against him in January. Knutsford now found Rhodes' proposals irresistibly attractive, and on 1 May he commended them to the Prime Minister:

> 'You may like to see the enclosed from Mr. Rhodes, who with Mr. Rudd got the large concession from Lo Bengula, and has now disarmed opposition to that concession by giving his opponents a share in it. I believe he has managed to win over Mr. Chamberlain and Mr. Labouchere.
>
> His plan is now to form a large Company with a Charter if possible like the Niger Company and thus to work the concession south of the Zambesi. . . . You will see he proposes to help you North of the Zambesi.
>
> He and his colleagues are well backed up in the City, and he himself is the richest man by far in S. Africa: This Company will construct the railway through B. Bechuanaland, and hint, if they can get a Charter, of extending it to Shoshong.'[3]

Later, the Colonial Secretary elaborated his argument officially. Of the projected British South African Company, he wrote:

> '. . . Such a body may to some considerable extent relieve Her Majesty's Government from diplomatic difficulties and heavy expenditure. . . . At

[1] Rhodes to C.O., 1 Jun. 1889. *ibid.*, 80. [2] Gifford to C.O., 30 Apr. 1889, *ibid.*, 65.
[3] Knutsford to Salisbury, 1 May 1889, S.P. (Holland).

present nothing could be more unsatisfactory than the condition existing in [Bechuanaland]. Every year large grants have to be obtained from Parliament . . . almost altogether swallowed up in the maintenance of a semi-military police force.'[1]

Robinson's warning that a Matabeleland protectorate would cost a quarter of a million pounds a year had gone home with Knutsford. So had his foreboding of Bechuanaland without a railway left derelict on imperial hands. Knutsford and his colleagues were certain of one thing. Parliament would not provide the 'very large sums' required for an imperial protectorate in Zambesia,[2] nor would it go on much longer with the burden of Bechuanaland. Their fear of the Treasury and the Commons might seem alarmist; but it was not unjustified. So experienced a politician and student of imperial affairs as Dilke saw 'no probability of Parliament consenting to bear the cost which would be involved'.[3] Yet Rhodes and his syndicate could not be prevented from opening up Matabeleland. The white invasion seemed inevitable, with or without a charter. A prospect of endless trouble in the north opened before Knutsford's eyes. All the strife which had plagued British officials and taxpayers for half a century on the Cape and Natal frontiers seemed about to erupt once more in southern Zambesia. White settlement under the shadow of Lobengula and his impis would mean the Zulu problem all over again. Knutsford resigned himself to supervising the movement in theory, but he was determined to avoid direct responsibility for this latest south African frontier. The chartered company would enable him to do both. Without the charter, the Foreign Office was told:

'. . . Her Majesty's Government would not be able effectually to prevent the company from taking its own line of policy, which might possibly result in complications with Native Chiefs and others, necessitating military expenditure and perhaps even military operations.'[4]

To avoid being dragged into administrative commitments in southern Zambesia was one of Knutsford's chief considerations. As he put it, the 'cardinal principle' which induced the Cabinet to accept the charter was that the Company which 'is to enjoy the profits . . . shall also discharge and bear all the responsibilities of government'.[5] In 1889 Conservative

[1] C.O. to F.O., 16 May 1889, C.O. African (S) 372, 71.
[2] C.O. to Mackenzie, 13 Aug. 1889, C.O. African (S) 372, 115.
[3] C. W. Dilke, *Problems of Greater Britain*, I, 572.
[4] C.O. to F.O., 16 May 1889, C.O. Africa (S) 372, 71.
[5] Knutsford to Loch, 26 Jun. 1891, C.O. 806/349, 43.

ministers were more reluctant to push British rule further into south Africa than they had been in 1877. Here is a striking fact. It accords ill with the view that by this time imperialism was on the march.

But to more wholehearted imperialists, Rhodes' ambition for his company seemed pernicious. The resistance to the charter was voiced by the South Africa Committee led by Chamberlain and John Mackenzie, the missionary and former Imperial Deputy Commissioner in Bechuanaland.[1] They spoke for these earnest humanitarians, empire-minded politicians, retired imperial officials and business men, for whom this was the vital phase of their fight to get the government to do its duty in Bechuanaland and Matabeleland. The Committee preached that Britain as the paramount power should protect the tribes against the colonists and administer the territories directly through the Colonial Office. Distrusting the Afrikaners' native policy, the Committee also suspected their loyalty to the empire. Its members tended to think of the Cape Afrikaners no less than those of the republics as enemies of Britain and all it stood for. Hence they added to native trusteeship the policy of developing a specifically British Bechuanaland and Matabeleland under the Colonial Office, to anchor south Africa to the empire against the anti-imperial and illiberal winds blowing from the surrounding colonies and republics. It was for these aims that Forster, Mackenzie, Chamberlain and Warren had contended against the Transvaalers and Cape colonists in Bechuanaland since 1882. The Warren Expedition of 1885 and the proclamation of the Bechuanaland Crown Colony and Protectorate had been the South Africa Committee's triumph. Since that time the Committee had agitated against the transfer of Bechuanaland to the Cape Colony, and worked for the extension of imperial control up to the Zambesi. It had helped to frustrate Robinson's attempt to extract Bechuanaland from Colonial Office control in 1888. And now Rhodes with his chartered company threatened to sweep the board. A radical cleavage of interest and principle heated the Committee's drawn out struggle with Robinson and Rhodes. Imperial trusteeship and central control was set against colonial autonomy and white nationalism; imperial expansion against the extension of colonial rule. Hence the outcome of the battle for the charter may be taken as a test of the new imperialists' strength in British politics.

Throughout 1889 humanitarian societies agitated against giving administrative authority to a commercial company which might use it

[1] The largest monument to the South Africa Committee's work in Bechuanaland, or rather of John Mackenzie's is his *Austral Africa, Losing It or Ruling It*, (1887); for a moving tribute to the great missionary imperialist, *vide* W. D. Mackenzie, *John Mackenzie, South African Missionary and Statesman*, (1902).

to exploit the tribal population.[1] A charter policy, John Mackenzie warned '. . . would have all the disadvantages and unpopularity of shirking responsibilities'.[2] Experienced officials in the imperial service foretold that a chartered company would lead to a Matabele war.[3] Philanthropists were sure that Rhodes' company would expropriate native land and labour. Rhodes was suspected of being a colonial nationalist, with a policy of Africa for the Afrikaner and the extrusion of United Kingdom influence from south Africa. The South Africa Committee attacked the proposal for a chartered company as a betrayal of British trusteeship and commerce.[4] To many British merchants and investors, Rhodes stood for the exclusive and monopolistic Cape mining interest which would close rather than open Zambesia to British enterprise as a whole. His charter was particularly unpopular in the London chamber of commerce. *The Economist* noted that it would confer a practical monopoly of Zambesia's resources upon a handful of Cape Town and London capitalists.[5] On the other hand, *The Times* supported the company which 'ought to be able to draw into [its] nets most of what is worth having in Central Africa'.[6] British business at large was still too loyal to free trade to favour Rhodes' type of enterprise in Zambesia. British commercial interests, in Matabeleland as on the Niger, were sharply divided between rival groups, and the sum of their pressure upon the government for and against the charter as a result was probably ambiguous.

But the opponents of the charter could not stir popular indifference or overcome the aversion to a protectorate. At the end of February, Chamberlain and Mackenzie, having interviewed Knutsford, knew that the government would probably accept the Rudd concession[7]— the basis of Rhodes' entire project. Although ministers afterwards publicly justified the charter as a means of civilising Africa and opening new markets,[8] Britain's philanthropic duties and economic interests were not uppermost in their private minds. What public opinion there was on the matter seems to have pressed a negative policy on them — not to put the flag into Zambesia. The government's compelling reasons for

[1] Aborigines Protection Society to C.O., 5 Feb. 1889, C.O. 806/310, 265.
[2] Mackenzie to C.O., 10 Apr. 1889, C.O. African (South) 372, 40.
[3] C.O. 'Memo. on the Origin and Operation of the British South Africa Charter Company,' 13 Oct. 1892, C.O. African (South) 439, 26.
[4] Garvin, *op. cit.*, II, 465–7.
[5] *The Economist*, 9 May 1891, XLIX, 591–2.
[6] *The Times*, editorial, 15 Oct. 1889.
[7] Mackenzie to Mrs. Mackenzie, 4 Mar. 1889, W. D. Mackenzie, *op. cit.*, 432; Grey to Mackenzie, Jul. 1889, *ibid.*, 435.
[8] Salisbury, Guildhall Speech, 9 Nov. 1889.

granting the charter lay less in the rise of imperial enthusiasm at Home than in their fear of nationalism and republicanism in south Africa.

Salisbury and Knutsford chartered the enterprise first and foremost to tighten the colonial grip on south Africa. From this point of view, Rhodes' scheme offered immense advantages. It promised to perpetuate the rift between the Cape Bond leaders and Pretoria, and to make them more dependent upon London. The Company would engage the colonists wholeheartedly for the first time in the struggle with Kruger for the interior. At last, Robinson's tactic was becoming practicable. Exactly how far these considerations weighed with the Cabinet is unknown. That they weighed heavily may be guessed from the extraordinary deference which ministers henceforward paid to Rhodes' wishes and his company's interests, despite its *peccadillos*. Salisbury and Knutsford acted as men who could not afford to antagonise Rhodes or to lose the opportunities which he alone could give. Because of his connection with Hofmeyr, he appeared to hold the key to Cape politics and might make or mar colonial loyalty. Many imperial federationists and some of the South Africa Committee itself seem to have been converted by this argument, notably Albert, later Lord, Grey. It is not unlikely that Alfred Milner, then private secretary to Goschen, the Chancellor of the Exchequer, echoed the Cabinet's own view when he wrote:

> 'The Cape might be separatist, and South Africa by itself might be separatist, but a South Africa reaching up to the Zambesi, marching into foreign spheres of influence, and needing the protecting arm of Great Britain against Portuguese or German interference with its own development, will lean more and more on us. I think I see the development in Rhodes himself. As a purely Cape politician he was (is perhaps) Africander. As the author of enterprises which look far beyond the Cape and the Transvaal and reach to the Zambesi, and beyond the Zambesi, he must know (he is much too shrewd not to know) that, without Imperial backing, he is lost.'[1]

Some imperialists saw in the charter a magnet to attract south Africa away from republicanism, and Salisbury's ministry certainly granted it to make the eventual federation of south Africa more British. As

[1] Milner to Mackenzie, (1889), W. C. Mackenzie, *op. cit.*, 433–4. *vide* Grey to Mackenzie, Jul. 1889, on joining the Board of the British South Africa Company: 'I should have preferred, with you a bolder Imperial policy, but as this is evidently beyond the thoughts and intentions of the present government, and as they have made up their minds to grant Rhodes a charter, it is, I think, desirable that one like myself who is in close sympathy with you and the South African Committee, should be upon the Board. I am very hopeful that the action of this Company may prove instrumental in developing and stimulating in a very great degree Imperial interests in South Africa,' *ibid.*, 435.

Knutsford explained to the new High Commissioner, Sir Henry Loch, the government's purpose in granting the charter was '. . . to encourage the opening up of [the native territories not now under any form of civilised government] . . . by the gradual introduction of capital and labour *under British control*'.[1] The British South Africa Company was meant to bring southern Zambesia into the imperial scale to counterbalance the rise of the South African Republic. More than that, the enterprise was 'to increase the facilities of communication' with Zambesia.[2] According to Rhodes, the government made him promise to build the Bechuanaland railway before it would give him his charter. 'It was upon the strength of this pledge that my application was favourably regarded by Her Majesty's Government, and that the British South Africa Company has been granted a Charter.'[3] Certainly, he and his associates signed the contract for the extension just before the charter was sealed. The line was crucial in Salisbury's and Knutsford's eyes. It was required to develop British Bechuanaland commercially. The extension would strengthen the Cape Colony's hand in bargaining with Kruger for a railway and customs union. It was needed to bind together the Cape, Bechuanaland and the supposedly rich north. The line was to be the main girder of an extended colonial system of trade and political control, to contain and eventually break down the rival republican axis resting on the Johannesburg Rand and Delagoa Bay. Six years later Salisbury was to disclose this purpose in public, saying: 'See the splendid work Mr. Rhodes has done in the southern end of Africa. . . . The Government of the Transvaal . . . is finding the pressure of English activity all around them so strong that they are slowly giving way . . . they will be compelled to fall into line and to join the great unconscious confederation that is growing up.'[4] Here was the mainspring of official hopes. Austral Africa, developed by Rhodes, would make the loyal colonial elements predominate over the republican constituents in the future dominion.

Rhodes and Robinson were the authors of this grand design. The energies behind its execution were colonial rather than metropolitan. Imperial aid was forthcoming, because Salisbury and Knutsford wanted to further the traditional strategy of British supremacy south of the

[1] Knutsford to Loch, 14 Nov. 1889, C.O. African (South) 439. (The italics are ours.)

[2] *ibid.*

[3] Rhodes to Sprigg, 24 Oct. 1889, Weinthal, *op. cit.*, I, 649. Rhodes at this time seems to have been more concerned to build the Beira railway which would give the shortest access to the sea from Matabeleland, rather than the Bechuanaland-Zambesia extension, *vide* Sir Charles Metcalfe, 'My Story of the Scheme,' and Robert Williams, 'My Story of the Scheme,' *ibid.*, I, 101–11.

[4] *Hansard*, 4th ser., XXX, col. 701.

Zambesi. The British South Africa Company, charter issued on 29 October, showed how heavily they were betting on Rhodes. Full financial and administrative responsibility for the countries '. . . lying immediately to the north of British Bechuanaland . . . to the north and west of the South African Republic and to the west of Portuguese Dominions'[1] was conferred on the Company. It was also authorised to acquire administrative powers in Bechuanaland;[2] but the government later deferred to British humanitarians and imperialists and excluded the protectorate from Company control. Rhodes' syndicates obtained legal recognition for all their treaties and concessions.[3] And the Company was authorised to grant lands and minerals, and to settle Europeans within its territories.[4]

The terms of the charter left little room for effective imperial control. Although the Board in London was adorned with royal dukes, Rhodes had obtained a free hand in south Africa. The company in operation was a colonial enterprise effectively under colonial, not imperial, control. Safeguards for native interests were written into the charter in deference to British opinion. But at first there were no imperial officials in the company's territory to enforce them. Not only did Rhodes demand freedom to colonise without Colonial Office interference; but Knutsford and his successors dreaded the risks of responsibility involved in official intervention. Time and again in 1890 and 1891, Knutsford forbade the High Commissioner, Loch, to interfere in the company's sphere. The Colonial Office ordered: 'No step should be taken practically superseding the Company's Charter and relieving it of its principal obligations. That might make this country liable to have to take over at any time the government of country up to the Zambesi River.'[5] British governments refused to be drawn into the administration of territories almost all of whose taxable resources had passed into the company's private possession. Nor would Salisbury and Knutsford, considering what was at stake in south African politics, risk antagonising Rhodes and Cape opinion. It seemed best from all points of view to leave Rhodes as free as possible of Downing Street for the rough work of planting a white colony on the Zambesi. The imperial authorities intended from the beginning to let the charter run its full term of a quarter of a century, 'the shortest period within which the Company

[1] The British South Africa Company Royal Charter, cap. I (the Tati Concession was excluded), Hertslet, *op. cit.*, I, 271–7.
[2] Knutsford to Loch, 14 Nov. 1889, C.O. African (South) 439, 40.
[3] B.S.A. Co. Charter, cap. II.
[4] *ibid.*, cap. XXIV.
[5] Knutsford to Loch, 28 Jun. 1891, C.O. 806/352, 10.

can be expected to develop and perfect the public part of its enterprise.'[1] No short-term expedient, the chartered company was meant to go on until its colonists were ready to govern themselves and join a south African federation. Whatever Rhodes and the company did, it would be difficult indeed for the imperial government to affront south African opinion and take away his charter — and he knew it. Henceforward he was able to act almost as if he were an independent power in south Africa. In the attempt to retain the Cape colonists' loyalty, the British government gave up freedom of action in Zambesia.

Intrinsically, northern, unlike southern Zambesia was no part of this strategy of supremacy in south Africa; yet after March 1889 Rhodes' habit of thinking big and his Cape to Cairo dream were to make it so. In northern even more than in southern Zambesia, the initiative, the energy and the design for imperial expansion came from Cape Town with Rhodes. Until he arrived in March, Salisbury had been trying to buy Matabeleland and the Shiré region from Portugal by selling her northern Zambesia. There seemed no large imperial or commercial interest in the northern region. The only objection foreseen by Salisbury to its renunciation was a protest from the Cape colonists.

It was Rhodes, backed by Cape opinion, who brought about 'an entirely new scheme of policy' for northern Zambesia[2] and persuaded the British ministry to claim the country instead of conceding it. Exactly how he did it is still obscure. Salisbury and Knutsford may have felt that Rhodes was covering so many of their bids south of the Zambesi that they could not deny him northern Zambesia in the general bargain. Perhaps Salisbury also deferred to Rhodes in this because communication northward from Matabeleland through Barotseland might well be needed if the South Africa Company was to take over the Lakes Company and help secure the Nyasa mission field from the Portuguese. The question of placing Northern Zambesia under the company certainly figured in the final negotiations for the charter to cover Southern Zambesia. Knutsford, prodded by Robinson from Cape Town,[3] suggested the idea to the Foreign Office privately on 1, and officially on 16 May.[4] Rhodes had offered to pay for the police and administration of Nyasa,[5] for the time being through the African Lakes Company, and to take northern Zambesia under the South Africa

[1] Knutsford to Loch, 14 Nov. 1889, C.O. African (South) 439, Appendix, 42.
[2] Johnston to Rhodes, 8 Oct. 1893, F.O. 2/55.
[3] Robinson to Knutsford, 28 Mar. 1889.
[4] Knutsford to Salisbury, 1 May 1889, S.P. (Holland); C.O. to F.O., 16 May 1889; C.O. African (S). 372, 71.
[5] His official proposal is in Causton to Herbert, 1 Jul. 1889, F.O. 403/111, 128–9.

Company. In June however, Salisbury was still dubious about the German attitude in the Nyasa-Tanganyika region, and he had to settle Portugal's claims on the Zambesi. The first draft of the charter therefore restricted the company's field to the south of the river. But Rhodes' demands and assurances were enough for Salisbury to send Johnston off to obtain treaties covering the region south and west of Lake Nyasa. The change of policy toward northern Zambesia and the Nyasa country had been decided in principle. Johnston's well-known account of how it took place is somewhere near the mark:

> 'At [this] juncture . . . when the Government, though wishing to save this country from the Portuguese and the Germans and secure it for England, yet had not a penny to spend on it, you [Rhodes] stepped forward and said: "Make this extension of British supremacy, and I will find the money to administer the new territories" . . . this offer on your part changed the situation at once . . . and within a week of its being made new instructions were drawn up for me at the Foreign Office.'[1]

Rhodes certainly freed the government from its Treasury prison. But Salisbury and Knutsford had not changed their minds about northern Zambesia because they thought highly of its commercial prospects, as Johnston went on to suggest. Of the country's trading future they had always been pessimistic. But it was enough that Rhodes wanted it; and that his power might be used to save the Nyasa mission field from the Portuguese advance. For these combined purposes, Salisbury now turned his diplomacy to claim the territories which would connect Matabeleland, Nyasa and the southern end of Lake Tanganyika.

A provisional understanding with Germany in the summer of 1889 made him much less anxious about Bismarck's opposition in northern Zambesia.[2] When Salisbury realised during the opening of his east African negotiation in December that Berlin needed a general African settlement,[3] he felt better able to deal strongly with isolated Portugal. With its diplomatic anxieties lightening, the Foreign Office in August altered the draft of the South Africa Company's charter to leave the northern boundary of its field open and indefinite.[4] Although the Scottish missions had baffled Rhodes' attempt to absorb the African Lakes Company, he had promised nine thousands pounds a year toward the expenses of taking Nyasa 'pending the settlement of the

[1] Johnston to Rhodes, 8 Oct. 1893, F.O., 2/55.

[2] In the disputed Nyasa-Tanganyika plateau region, the Germans agreed not to press their claims south of the 11th parallel of south latitude. (Hanna, *op. cit.*, 164.)

[3] *vide infra* 290–1.

[4] F.O. to C.O., 16 Aug. 1889, F.O. 403/111, 153.

boundary with Portugal, and ultimate extension of the Charter'.[1] Both Johnston and Rhodes understood that as well as north Zambesia, the Nyasa region including the Shiré highlands, was to be administered by the South Africa Company through its prospective subsidiary, the Lakes Company.[2] Indeed in August the consul recommended Salisbury to charter the latter concern for this purpose.[3] With Johnston, paid by Rhodes, extending his treaty-making tours northward as far as the southern end of Lake Tanganyika and westward to the Barotse country, Salisbury was ready to re-open negotiations with Lisbon and to carry on those with Berlin. What was more he was now ready to repel Portugal from the Shiré mission field. In September he permitted Johnston to bring the Shiré hills under British protection so as to ward off Serpa Pinto's expedition. The following January, a British ultimatum to Lisbon forced the Portuguese to withdraw from the region.

Throughout 1890 Salisbury was doing all he could by diplomacy to satisfy Rhodes' insistent claims in northern Zambesia. Rhodes with Hofmeyr's support had become Prime Minister in Cape Town, and the Rhodesian interest dominated the Colony politically as well as commercially. His wealth, his charter and his premiership enabled Rhodes to exhort, cajole and browbeat Salisbury and Knutsford to meet his territorial requirements. So much did the imperial future south of the Zambesi seem to depend upon the colonial leader that Salisbury did his cautious best to realise Rhodes' Cape to Cairo dream. The Prime Minister himself does not seem to have taken this scheme seriously. It was not related to any of the traditional concepts of standing imperial interests on which his mind always ran. 'Cape to Cairo' represented the aspirations of Rhodes and the Cape expansionists to draw all central Africa into the colony's ambit. Yet sooner than antagonise Rhodes, Salisbury took up the Cape to Cairo project as a secondary objective of his negotiations.

In April 1890 Rhodes and his associates pressed Salisbury to bring into the British sphere of influence the entire Barotse country, together with the regions covered by Johnston's treaties. The High Commissioner, Loch, supported this demand and urged 'that continuous connection to Nyasa and Tanganyika be secured';[4] and Knutsford advised Salisbury to take Barotseland, so as to ensure an alternative British route to Lake Tanganyika, in case the Portuguese claims to the

[1] Cawston to Herbert, 1 Jul. 1889, *ibid.*, 129.
[2] Johnston to Rhodes, 8 Oct. 1893, F.O. 2/55.
[3] Johnston to Salisbury, 9 Aug. 1889, Hanna, *op. cit.*, 143.
[4] Loch to Knutsford, 7 Apr. 1890, F.O. 403/143.

territory between the Lower Zambesi and Lake Nyasa had to be conceded.[1] The Queen herself and the German Foreign Minister asked the Prime Minister not to extort too much from Lisbon lest he bring about the fall of the Braganza dynasty. Salisbury however, managed in the Anglo-Portuguese Convention of 20 August, 1890,[2] to obtain recognition of a British sphere which included much of northern Zambesia west of Lake Nyasa, as far as the Congo Free State and Angola borders, together with the Shiré Highlands. South of the Zambesi, Matabeleland and Mashonaland were also secured, although Manicaland was conceded to Portugal. Even so, Rhodes and his ministry were dissatisfied, especially over the loss of part of the Lochner concession area in Barotseland and of Manicaland through which he planned to run his Beira railway. 'We lose by Treaty', Rhodes telegraphed, 'large portion of our territories. The whole agreement is disapproved in the Colony.' If Salisbury's 'yielding' to Lisbon continued, Rhodes threatened to resign.[3] The Duke of Abercorn, the South Africa Company's chairman, pointed out to Salisbury that Rhodes had to be listened to, for he was powerful at the Cape and the Company's mainspring.[4] Rhodes was indispensable to the empire, and he was taking advantage of it. Understandably, Salisbury was supposed to have had enough of him.[5] The Prime Minister had hoped by his Portuguese agreement to '. . . reasonably suit the British South African without upsetting the Braganza dynasty. But', he added, 'people are not reasonable, either at Lisbon or at Cape Town.'[6] But the Cortes refused to ratify the Convention; and in the final agreement with Portugal signed on 11 June, 1891, Salisbury once more yielded to Rhodes and obtained all Barotseland and the Manica plateau for the South Africa Company, in exchange for a Portuguese salient north of the Zambesi and west of the Shiré highlands.[7]

His own private opinion about all this was:

> 'These Portuguese are the most unsatisfactory people to negotiate with I have ever had any experience of. . . . The difficult point to bring home to them is that it is of no use for them to claim rule over African territory unless they can colonise it. If they cannot provide settlers of their own blood, we can of ours; and we shall do so, whether we — that is Great

[1] C.O. to F.O., 12 Apr. 1890; *ibid.*, Knutsford to Salisbury, 4 Jul. 1890, S.P. (Holland).
[2] Hertslet, *op. cit.*, III, 1006–13.
[3] cf. Salisbury to Sir R. Morier, 11 Feb. 1891, S.P. (Russia, Vol. 74), no. 91.
[4] Abercorn to Salisbury, 22 Sept. 1890, S.P. (Abercorn).
[5] Hanna, *op. cit.*, 168.
[6] Cecil, *op. cit.*, IV, 275.
[7] Hertslet, *op. cit.*, III, 1016–26.

Britain — desire it or not, and a country once inhabited by men of English or Dutch race, the Portuguese had better allow us to govern it; for it is quite certain that *they* will not be able to do so.'[1]

Here the Prime Minister expressed the first principle of his empire-making in southern Africa. It was still the earlier Victorian canon. Wherever private enterprise showed the energy to occupy a region, the empire would help. He would not and could not help those who did not help themselves. It was on this principle that he supported Rhodes, although he still had doubts about the Cape premier's 'loyalty' to the empire and his chances of remaining in power at the Cape. Knutsford and Abercorn[2] however reassured their chief. The Colonial Secretary wrote early in 1891:

> 'I think Rhodes may be trusted, but it is as yet difficult to say whether his position as Premier is safe. His opponents will always be able to criticise that all he does is done in the interest of the B. South Africa Company, but so long as Hofmeyr, who represents the Afrikander party, supports him, he is probably stronger than his opponents.'[3]

Keeping Rhodes in power and in harmony with Hofmeyr was becoming a leading aim of British policy.

Meanwhile, under the Zanzibar-Heligoland Treaty of July 1890 Salisbury managed to add much of the Nyasa-Tanganyika plateau to the British trans-Zambesian sphere, to secure the Stevenson Road and to gain territorial access to Lake Tanganyika.[4] He had thus done as much as he could to satisfy Rhodes and the Cape Colony in this direction; but he had been unable to realise the Cape to Cairo plan. Nor had he tried very hard to obtain the strip of territory between German East Africa and the Congo border which would have linked the British sphere of influence in northern Zambesia with that in Uganda and the Nile Valley. Although Salisbury felt bound to further Rhodes' colonial interests for the sake of imperial influence in south Africa, he gave priority to the imperial interest in excluding Germany from Uganda and the Nile Valley, and so in securing the British position in Egypt. The Anglo German treaty of 1890 sacrificed the Rhodesian Cape to Cairo vision to this paramount British world interest.[5] Salisbury,

[1] Salisbury to Sir R. Morier, 11 Feb. 1891, S.P. (Russia), Vol. 74, no. 91.

[2] Abercorn referred Salisbury to a speech of Rhodes: 'I think when you have read it you will find that Mr. Rhodes is a loyal man.' (Abercorn to Salisbury, 28 Oct. 1890, S.P. (Hamilton).)

[3] Knutsford to Salisbury, 2 Mar. 1891, S.P. (Holland).

[4] Hertslet, *op. cit.*, III, 899–900.

[5] *Grosse Politik*, VIII, nos. 1676–8. *vide* Salisbury to Queen, 10 Jun. 1890, Cecil, *op. cit.*, IV, 298.

defending his arrangement with Germany in the Lords, spoke scornfully of the Cape to Cairo scheme as 'a curious idea which had lately become prevalent'. Of the strip of territory between the Congo and German East Africa which would have made it practicable, he observed, 'I can imagine no more uncomfortable . . . possession.'[1] He wrote to Malet: '. . . to some minds . . . the interior of Africa in the line of the great lakes . . . offered the attractions of the El Dorado of the 16th century. I did not think such anticipations were grounded upon fact.'[2] In this case he had thought it better to anger Rhodes and the Cape colonists rather than the Germans.

The British sphere of influence in northern Zambesia was now handed over, as had always been intended, to the British South Africa Company. In 1891 a supplementary charter extended its administration to include this region. Salisbury's Cabinet however made its one concession to specifically British and humanitarian interests, as opposed to Rhodesian and Cape colonial demands, in exempting the Nyasa mission field and the African Lakes Company region from the South African Company's control. The directors of the Lakes Company had managed to resist Rhodes' attempts to absorb their concern into his own company; while the Scottish missions who had pioneered the Nyasa regions strongly resisted the rule of a commercial company.[3] The government therefore decided to administer Nyasaland for the time being as an imperial protectorate. This was proclaimed in May 1891. But it was a curious protectorate, because Goschen at the Treasury refused to pay its expenses.[4] Its revenue was provided by subsidies from the British South Africa Company, under agreement with the Foreign Office. Rhodes, himself, according to Anderson, believed that the imperial government was 'nursing the Protectorate for the South Africa Company, which will at its convenience add it to the chartered territory'. Johnston, who was appointed Commissioner of the British Central African Protectorate, apparently, 'lean[ed] principally on Mr. Rhodes,' and 'only loosely on Her Majesty's Government'.[5] The Chancellor of the Exchequer complained that he could not distinguish between what Johnston was doing for Rhodes and what he was doing

[1] *Hansard*, 3rd ser., CCCXLVI, col. 1268.

[2] Salisbury to Malet, 21 May 1890, no. 186, Africa, F.O. 84/2030.

[3] Johnston to Rhodes, 8 Oct. 1893, F.O. 2/55.

[4] Salisbury to Johnston, 21 Mar. 1891, S.P. (Secretary's note book). Goschen grumbled: '. . . if we are not extremely careful . . . three administrations in the interior of Africa may be forced upon us — Uganda, Johnston's empire and Mashonaland.' (Goschen to Salisbury, 19 Sept. 1891, *ibid.*)

[5] Memo. by Sir P. Anderson on Interview with Rhodes, 12 Jan. 1894; Anderson Memo., 'Considerations respecting Nyasaland,' 26 Feb. 1894, F.O. 403/184, 5–6, 50–2.

for the Foreign Office.[1] Not until July 1894 did the Foreign Office pluck up courage to substitute a Treasury grant-in-aid for the South Africa Company's subsidies, so little imperial enthusiasm did Parliament show for this new acquisition.

Imperial Purpose of the Charter

When all was done, the Salisbury government's use of the South Africa Company to strengthen the imperial position in south Africa had carried with it, as a strangely adventitious extra, the promotion of Rhodesian colonial enterprise north of the Zambesi; and, an even more curious pendant, the protection of the Nyasa missions from the Arab slave traders and the advance of Catholic Portugal. 'Economic imperialism' would seem to be too simple a description of the mixed intentions and interests behind the chartering of the British South Africa Company. Its shareholders were doubtless '. . . intent more upon a praiseworthy desire to secure . . . a dividend-earning investment, than actuated by any high political or philanthropic motives'.[2] The charter cast the mantle of empire over a gigantic speculation in mineral futures. It gave to extensive and sometimes dubious stock-exchange operations[3] a gilt of patriotism which lured the British investor. Yet Rhodes and the government put the commercial company to some strangely unbusinesslike uses. The incentive to rescue the Nyasa missions seems to have been more a matter of religion and sentiment than profit. But the company was chartered above all as a political instrument in south African politics. British opinion at large probably acquiesced from indifference or vague notions of civilising Africa and opening new markets. Yet imperial enthusiasm in Britain was too faint to support a protectorate. Company rule admittedly was not the best method of carrying out native trusteeship. Nor was monopoly the best way of opening a new country to free enterprise. But as a lever to turn Cape politics in the empire's favour, to off-set the rise of the Transvaal and to anglicise the future dominion, the chartered company alone was apt. These were the Salisbury government's over-riding aims. Although the means were partly commercial, economic ends were incidental to the aim of supremacy in south Africa. Whether the Transvaal or Portugal ruled Zambesia, the government expected that British investors

[1] Goschen to Salisbury, 20 Jan. 1892, S.P. (Goschen).

[2] Duke of Abercorn, *Opening Address, Proceedings of the First Annual General Meeting of the British South Africa Company*, 22 Dec. 1891.

[3] 'Financial Aspects of the Chartered Company,' *The Economist*, 3 Dec. 1892, L, 1510–11

and merchants would take the lion's share, as they were already doing in the republics. But Salisbury and Knutsford chose to promote and secure Rhodes' economic interests, partly because they believed in the man, but more because they expected high political dividends. They extended the empire through the chartered company, not primarily to increase British trade, but to shape the intrinsically neutral movement of commercial development and colonisation to their own political design.

It was characteristic of the Victorians' outlook on the relationship of national wealth and power. If their free trade faith was waning, they still believed in the inevitability of commercial expansion continuing without the aid of extensions of rule. And thinking so, they rarely set out to promote economic expansion as such. They tended to promote British economic interests only so far as they might seem to affect the great enduring political interests of strategy, security and world power. In the calculations behind imperial expansion, economic interests appeared distorted and transformed by the concepts of policy through which they were seen. When British trade and investment were already growing freely in the south African gold boom, there could hardly have been a need for a chartered company to promote economic expansion. But there was an urgent need for the chartered Company to divert south Africa's commercial development towards political unity and an imperial dominion. The political future would partly depend upon the terms of economic unification already taking shape in the railway-building and commercial negotiations between the south African states. Matabeleland and the Bechuanaland railway were needed to strengthen the Cape Colony's hand in these negotiations, and to bring the Transvaal into a railway and customs union. And of all the glittering captains of south African mining finance, Rhodes alone had the will and power to turn its cosmopolitan profit-seeking energy into the manufacture of imperial political influence. The ministry, beggared by Parliament, had no recourse but the king of diamonds.

More than that, the empire needed the aid of Rhodes, the politician and ally of the Afrikaner Bondsmen. The price of a charter seemed little enough to pay for Cape loyalty, and to stem the anti-imperial trends in south African politics. In effect the charter was an admission that the British government was losing its power to shape south Africa's destiny directly. Henceforward until the Jameson Raid, the imperial government clung to Rhodes' coat-tails in south Africa. And the charter committed the empire almost unconditionally to support the Colossus whose shoulders bore the weight of British supremacy.

These impressions of British aims are confirmed by the working of the charter policy between 1890 and 1895. Downing Street deferred continually to south African opinion, in order to keep Rhodes in power and foster his alliance with Hofmeyr. Since head-on clashes with the South African Republic would strain Rhodes' alliance with the Bond, they were to be avoided. Everything possible was to be done to obtain access to Johannesburg for the Cape railway, to inveigle Kruger into a commercial union with the Cape Colony. Nothing was allowed to hinder the making of the imperial counterpoise in the new Rand of the north.

In the chartered company's affairs, Colonial Secretaries all unwillingly danced to the Rhodes' tune. The old-fashioned officials of the Colonial Office were shocked to find in 1891 that the charter had been given under an illusion. So had the million pounds investors had put into the company. They had supposed that the South Africa Company's chief asset was the Rudd concession. But Rhodes and Rudd, in offering the concession to the South Africa Company in exchange for what amounted to half its net profit, disclosed that they had kept the concession in their private hands. Knutsford's civil servants advised him to consider revoking the charter. But by now there was no stopping Rhodes. For the empire to take over the company's field seemed out of the question. The Colonial Secretary resigned himself to making the best of a bad job.

Here were the realities of power. They were shown again when Loch asked for authority to control the company's relations with Lobengula, in order to prevent a Matabele war. Knutsford refused. Ripon, the Liberal Colonial Secretary, had no more control than Knutsford had had. When the war broke out in 1893, the company was suspected of provoking it deliberately, as a means of seizing Matabeleland and boosting British South Africa Company stock. Loch felt that company rule ought to be ended.[1] Distastefully Ripon wrote to Gladstone: 'These companies are really speculative, got up mainly for stock exchange purposes and a good deal blown up in that aspect of their existence . . . they are not pleasant instruments of administration.'[2] If Rhodes was too powerful for the charter to be revoked altogether, the Colonial Secretary at first resolved to have Loch and not the company make the land settlement after the war. But once again, the indispensable Rhodes bludgeoned the Colonial Office with threats of a colonial nationalist reaction against imperial interference. If Ripon intervened in Matabeleland, Rhodes warned, colonial opinion would

[1] C.O. to B.S.A. Company, 24 Oct. 1893, C.O. Afr. (S) 459, p. 1.
[2] Ripon to Gladstone, 4 Nov. 1893, Gladstone Papers, B.M. Add. MSS. 44287.

be antagonised throughout south Africa.[1] It was enough. Rhodes had a free hand in making the Matabele peace settlement, and the government explained to the House of Commons the folly of interfering with the company's charter against the wishes of the south African public.[2] Two years later, Rhodes again showed his power in nominating his own High Commissioner, Robinson, against the wishes of the Queen and several of her Cabinet. As Ripon explained: '. . . More especially Mr. Rhodes has very much to be taken into account. The position between him and Sir H. Loch is now greatly strained. . . . Sir H. Robinson would be acceptable to Mr. Rhodes, in fact, the latter asked for him. . . .'[3] And the Colonial Secretary complied. Fearing that the imperial spirit in Britain was far weaker than national sentiment in south Africa, relying mainly on Rhodes to redress the south African balance in favour of the empire, British ministers gave him almost as much freedom in southern Zambesia as he had in Cape Town.

[1] Cape Ministers' Minute, in Loch to Ripon, 2 Nov. 1893; Rhodes to Loch, 3 Nov. 1893, C.O. Afr. (S) 459, pp. 29–30.
[2] *Hansard*, 4th ser. XVIII, col. 586.
[3] Bigge to Queen Victoria, 26 Feb. 1895, *Q.V.L.*, 3rd ser., II, 483–4.

CHAPTER VIII

Cairo or Constantinople? 1885–1890

While white nationalists were hastening imperial disengagement in south Africa, Egyptian nationalists and a hostile France were forcing Britain to clamp imperial control upon the Nile. The lack of loyal collaborators made for increasing distrust and contempt for Egyptians in particular, and for pessimism about Orientals in general. Salisbury and Baring personified this falling away from the earlier faith in free partnerships for progress. The restored Khedivate showed no sign of turning into a reliable and independent ally. Frustrated but determined, the British stayed on in Cairo. But the repercussions in east and west Africa were as nothing compared with the impact upon the European states-system. What most concerned Salisbury about Africa between 1885 and 1889 was the effect of the Egyptian occupation upon the Mediterranean balance.

The longer the British troops stayed in Cairo, the more marked that effect became; and as long as it went on, French hostility and the Russian threat at Constantinople increased the danger in the Mediterranean. British statesmen were thus placed in a quandary. If they could evacuate Egypt, the rewards would be great. They would reconcile the French, improve their standing in Constantinople and so strengthen the security of the Mediterranean routes to the East. On the other hand, they dared not risk giving up Egypt until they could be certain that the Turk with naval and diplomatic support could hold Constantinople and the Straits against the land power of Russia. For if they withdrew from Egypt and the Ottoman Empire was further divided, the Canal might fall into the hands of another Power. What Salisbury would do about Egypt, and so about tropical Africa, depended above all upon his appraisal of the defences of Constantinople and the stability of Egypt.

It was still the case that the British hoped to preserve the Turk as the guardian of the Straits against the Russians. But the chances of doing so seemed to diminish in the later Eighteen eighties. They were the more reduced because the French, angered by the occupation of Egypt, might not remain neutral should the British fleet have to act against the Russians at the Straits. By the end of 1889, the occupation of Egypt, at first no more than an improvisation, was coming to be a necessary re-insurance against the decline of British strength and influence at the Porte. Ministers came to rely more and more on Cairo rather than Constantinople as the pivot of security in the Mediterranean.

This shift of grand strategy was to decide Britain's future course in tropical Africa. In making sure of Egypt, she was to be dragged further and further into east Africa and the Valley of the Nile. Incongruous as it might seem, the founding of empire in Kenya, Uganda and the Sudan was an incidental result of the major shift in British interest from the European and Asiatic to the African shores of the Mediterranean. It was these large issues which were Salisbury's chief concern.

From 1885 until 1900 the foreign policy of Britain was built on the concepts and designs of Lord Salisbury. Indeed, for most of this time he was himself at the Foreign Office. In his first ministry from July 1885 until February 1886 he was his own Foreign Secretary; when he formed his second government in July 1886 Lord Iddesleigh was for a short time at the Foreign Office, but he was dismissed after six months and Salisbury himself took over. This state of things lasted until the fall of the ministry in August 1892, when Gladstone came back to power and Rosebery became Foreign Secretary. But Rosebery was no more than an unsuccessful Salisbury, and Kimberley, who followed him, an inarticulate Rosebery. From the fall of the Liberals in June 1895 until the Khaki election of October 1900, Salisbury was both Prime Minister and Foreign Secretary once more.

Under Salisbury's direction British policy gained enormously in clarity and in a Machiavellian *virtù*. It acquired, that is to say, a certain brilliance of formulation; but its concepts remained essentially the same as of old. It operated in a world where the old assumptions were becoming more and more doubtful, but although it faced the new facts, it did not positively chart a new course, simply adjusting itself to new dangers in a cautious, empirical and uncommitted way. In these respects it carried the stamp of Salisbury's character and outlook.

As the youthful Lord Cranborne, he had proclaimed that aristocracy was a sham unless it governed, and it was fitting that he should have devoted his gifts to diplomacy, the last refuge of the *grand seigneur* after the widening of the franchise. But it was in any case the abstractions of diplomacy which best set off the pitiless clarity and the strict limitations of his mind. The flouts and jeers which had so annoyed Disraeli, the dislike of cant and the fear of sentiment flowed from the disenchantment and pessimism at the root of his nature. The mockery which runs through the minutes of the Secretary of State, as it had run through the articles of the young writer for the *Saturday Review*, betokened his settled and sardonic belief that things are as they are in the most ironic of possible worlds.

This fundamental defeatism left him with a static view of politics. He saw his time as an increasingly dangerous age which was harshly refuting the mid-Victorian dream of perpetual peace. As he told Baring: '... I do not wish our administration in Egypt to be the cause to which the long European war is to be ascribed by the future historian.'[1] Moreover, these foreign perils were matched by the danger from within. It seemed to Salisbury that the question of Irish Home Rule was driving his country into 'a state of bloodless civil war',[2] 'a controversy which almost threatens her existence,'[3] and he saw himself as one of an unlucky generation charged with conserving intact the abiding national interests during this time of troubles. This was a difficult aim, and it was made harder by the coming of the mass franchise. It was not that the new electorate precluded aristocratic rule, for 'in democracies the capitalist seems to have a crushing power so long as he is content to leave political distinction to other people'.[4] The danger, as he saw it, was that the shifts of ignorant and feckless opinion would more and more hamper the work of diplomacy in the task of safeguarding the national interest. Hence he complained repeatedly that negotiations with the French were ruined by their 'boulevard press',[5] he argued that American chauvinism was a consequence of democracy[6] and lamented that British policy was jeopardised by the whims of faddists and fanatics. It is this queasy view of public opinion which sharply distinguishes Salisbury from Gladstone or from Chamberlain. Where they saw the opportunities offered by the mass electorate, he could see only the risks. To them public feeling could throw an irresistible momentum behind a policy, but to him it threw nothing but confusion. Gladstone and Chamberlain were ready to tell the voters what they ought to believe; Salisbury could only hope that they would not jump to the wrong conclusions.

Although Salisbury's handling of the partition of Africa is his chief diplomatic monument, he began by being little more interested in

[1] Salisbury to Baring, Private, 17 Feb. 1888, S.P., Vol. 55; printed in Cecil, *op. cit.*, IV, 95.

[2] Salisbury to Smith, 5 Feb. 1889, H. Maxwell, *Life . . . of . . . William Henry Smith*, (1893), II, 240.

[3] Salisbury to Queen Victoria, 24 Jan. 1886 (?1887), *Q.V.L.*, 3rd ser., I, 263.

[4] Salisbury to Lytton, 21 Jan. 1888, S.P. 59.

[5] French Ambassador in London to Hanotaux, 7 May 1896, *D.D.F.*, XII, no. 383.

[6] Memo. by Hanotaux, 26 Mar. 1897, *D.D.F.*, XIII, no. 166.

African problems than was Bismarck himself. Indeed, to Salisbury the issues of partition were always to remain curiously abstract, and even academic. They were complicated, they gave great opportunities for the use of *expertise*, and for the exercise of solitary long term planning. Africa for him remained above all an intellectual problem, an elaborate game of bids and counter-bids, of delimitations and compensations. With the consequences for Africa, the development of the new territories and the impact of conquest, he was not greatly concerned: for him the Partition began and ended on the maps of the Foreign Office. He looked on the process with a detached and empty view, in which chances were weighed and puzzles were solved. British policy during the Scramble for Africa was directed with dispassionate precision by the former Fellow of All Souls at the head of the Foreign Office.

When on 11 June, 1885, Salisbury put an end to the sufferings of the second Gladstone cabinet, it was avowedly a stop-gap government that he formed. But this did not prevent him from conducting an active foreign policy. Under the Liberals, Britain had been penned in a dangerous isolation; there was an urgent need to break out of it. By July Salisbury had mended the wire to Berlin[1] with a set of judicious surrenders of expendable areas in east Africa and the Pacific.[2] He went on to win German support where it mattered. He had support at Constantinople, he had the German vote at Cairo, he had elbow-room to salvage British foreign policy.

Egypt was where elbow-room was vital. The garrison in Cairo was a political liability, so long as Egypt remained a European question. Having appeased Bismarck, Salisbury strove to whittle it down to an Anglo-Turkish one. Accordingly Sir Henry Drummond Wolff was sent to Constantinople in August, to make the Turk a small offer. As suzerain of the country, the Sultan was to send troops to the Red Sea ports, where they would offend nobody except the Dervishes. But this was more than window-dressing; to Salisbury's mind it hid an important political purpose, because '. . . until we have the Turkish soldiers in Egypt . . . Europe will be perpetually worrying for a date of evacuation, and . . . with a fixed date before us, there is no hope of doing much good in internal reform'.[3] No evacuation without reform, then? Not quite; it would be more exact to say that in 1885 Salisbury had no specifically

[1] Salisbury to Bismarck, 2 Jul. 1885; Bismarck to Salisbury, 8 Jul. 1885, *Grosse Politik*, IV, nos. 782, 783.

[2] He was ready to see the Germans installed in the Philippines, '. . . which will . . . be much more profitable than any part of Africa,' Salisbury to Malet (ambassador in Berlin), Private, 8 Sept. 1885, S.P. 36.

[3] Salisbury to Malet, Private, 11 Jul. 1885, S.P. 36.

Egyptian policy at all. Profoundly affected by the balance of power and yet profoundly affecting it, dependent on events and the fall of the cards, the future of the British occupation was hemmed around with contingencies. One thing alone was certain: whether the troops stayed or whether they went, Salisbury meant to hold on to supremacy at Cairo. But beyond that, everything was fluid and conditional:

> 'My great objection to fixing a date for our evacuation of Egypt is, that relief from our hated presence is the one bribe we have to offer, the price we have to pay for any little advantages we may desire to secure. If we once part with that, we practically go into the market empty-handed, a practice of which the late Government were fond, but which I never knew come to any good.'[1]

There is a good deal of Salisbury in this remark, the shrewdness, the sarcasm, the scepticism. British policy had finished with the facile optimism of Dufferin. Even if the troops were to sail off some fine day, there must be a right of re-entry built into the arrangement about evacuation.[2] The rewards of Tel el Kebir were not for sale.

Drummond Wolff did not get much for his pains. By the Anglo-Turkish Convention of 24 October, 1885, the Sultan agreed to send a commissioner to study the Egyptian question. It had plenty of students already, but the agreement left Britain with the hope of securing her ends in Cairo by single-handed negotiations with the Turk. Here was a first dividend for Salisbury's new policy of *rapprochement* with Germany.

The coming of the third Gladstone ministry in February 1886 did not upset this equilibrium. It brought Lord Rosebery to the Foreign Office, an appointment which satisfied both the Queen and the Conservative leader. 'Lord Rosebery', reported Salisbury, 'is really sincerely desirous of continuing the policy hitherto pursued . . . but . . . he is rather nervous of Mr. Gladstone's interference.'[3] In fact there was no cause for alarm. Ireland was the be-all, as it was soon to turn out the end-all of the Liberal ministry, and Rosebery was left undisturbed. He gave heed to Baring's warning that 'Berlin, and not Cairo, is the real centre of gravity of Egyptian affairs',[4] and in the event he took a pro-German line in Europe as well as in Africa.[5]

[1] Salisbury to Drummond Wolff, Private, 18 Aug. 1885, S.P. 36.

[2] 'The end to which I would work is evacuation, but with certain privileges reserved for England. I should like a Treaty right to occupy Alexandria when we pleased. . . .' Salisbury to Drummond Wolff, 13 Aug. 1885, Cecil, *op. cit.*, III, 235.

[3] Salisbury to Queen Victoria, 8 Feb. 1886, *Q.V.L.*, 3rd ser., I, 50.

[4] Baring to Rosebery, 9 Feb. 1886, Zetland, *op. cit.* 128.

[5] e.g. Queen Victoria to Rosebery, 16 Mar. 1886, *Q.V.L.*, 3rd ser., I, 82; German ambassador in London to Bismarck, 22 Apr. 1886, *Grosse Politik*, IV, no. 793.

After the defeat of the Home Rule Bill in June 1886, Salisbury returned to power as the head of another weak government. The Conservatives had a majority of forty over Gladstone and Parnell, but there were some seventy-eight Liberal Unionists. It was clear that their leaders, Hartington and Chamberlain, held the Government in the hollow of their hands.[1] 'Our position as a Ministry is very peculiar,' noted the new Premier. 'We have not a majority except on certain vital questions.'[2] Of these Ireland was much the most important; indeed the Irish question which had done so much to split apart Gladstone's Cabinets was the force which bound Salisbury's second ministry together. Here his own position was plain beyond a doubt. 'Ireland', he had written in the more irresponsible and less majestic days before he became a statesman, 'must be kept, like India, at all hazards: by persuasion if possible; if not, by force.'[3] On this position he took his stand. He looked on the call for Irish self-government as the symbol of the pernicious forces which were bent on tearing asunder a unity painfully won by the makers of Great Britain. When he called for a halt to the process of disintegration towards which Gladstone seemed to be speeding, Salisbury had behind him not only the forces of inveterate Toryism but also the men of light and leading in the England of his time.[4]

But what was politically more important than the attitudes of intellectuals, was that the mood of the country was not in favour of Home Rule. Colonial nationalism began outside the United Kingdom; and it was meant to end outside the United Kingdom. Salisbury's political strength derived from the fact that he embodied this determination. The Radical wing of Liberal Unionism might look askance at a government controlled by the head of the House of Cecil, just as the Carlton Club might grumble at the introduction of County Councils; but they had to tolerate the lesser evils to avoid the greater. The crux of politics was the future of the Union, and it was Salisbury who divided its defenders least. Resistance to Home Rule was the making of his political career, as it was to be of Balfour's. So long as Gladstone and Parnell

[1] Lord George Hamilton, *Parliamentary Reminiscences and Reflections, 1886–1906*, (1922), 32–3.

[2] Salisbury to Churchill, 20 Aug. 1886, Churchill, *op. cit.*, 535; during the debate on the Address Salisbury's Lord President noted that the Prime Minister moved as if on ice or among eggs. A. E. Gathorne-Hardy, *Gathorne Hardy . . . Earl of Cranbrook*, (1910), II, 260.)

[3] 'The Position of Parties', unsigned, attributed to Salisbury, *Quarterly Review*, Oct. 1872, vol. 133, 572; *vide* 'Disintegration,' (attributed to Salisbury by Lady Gwendolen Cecil), *Quarterly Review*, Oct. 1883, vol. 156, 559–95.

[4] J. Roach, 'Liberalism and the Victorian Intelligentsia,' *Cambridge Historical Journal*, XIII, 79–80; J. R. M. Butler, *Henry Montagu Butler . . .*, (1925), 97–8.

kept up their attack on the unity of the empire, he was safe from any revolt by the rank and file.

Inside the Cabinet too he gained in stature by his insistence on resolute government. Together with his obvious mastery of foreign affairs, it assured him the support of the Queen, who was as mistrustful of Gladstone's Radicalism as she was tired of Granville's reverses. Withal he was indubitably the leader of his Cabinet and not a mere *primus inter pares*; and this spared his government the faction fights and the backbiting which had been such a feature of the second Gladstone ministry.

In any case, the men inside his Cabinet were not of the calibre to challenge his authority. Cranbrook, Iddesleigh, Cross, Manners — these were the elder statesmen of the party, who had been ministers in Disraeli's day, and who were content to jog along towards retirement under Salisbury. Of the new men Hamilton and Stanhope had fire without ability, and Smith had ability without fire; Lord Randolph Churchill had both, but in December 1886 Salisbury bundled him out of the ministry. 'Did you ever know a man who, having a boil on his neck, wanted another?' So runs his celebrated and ruthless question. He was to take good care that there were no more. The fall of Churchill was the end of faction. The entry into the Cabinet of Balfour and Goschen brought an undeviating toryism into the administration and gave Salisbury a much more reliable Cabinet. From 1887 until the end of the ministry in August 1892, the foreign policy of the country was conducted by Lord Salisbury, without hindrance from his Cabinet, without serious criticism from the Opposition, and without much reference to the advice of the Foreign Office.

But in the six months that Churchill was at the Exchequer he was constantly at odds with the Prime Minister, both over domestic policy and the conduct of foreign affairs. In this sphere it was once again about the Eastern Question that the difficulties arose.

On 20 August 1886, the Bulgarian army staged a *Putsch* against Prince Alexander, and he was removed to Russian territory. The result was another Balkan crisis, and once more the contestants took up their places. To Salisbury it was clear that '. . . the Turkish Empire will be exposed to great danger', and he hoped to bring the Powers of the Triple Alliance to the support of Alexander.[1] They were reluctant to do this, and so it turned out were some members of the Cabinet. Salisbury and Iddesleigh still hoped to block Russian expansion in the

[1] Salisbury to Queen Victoria, 23 Aug. 1886; Iddesleigh to Queen Victoria, 2 Sept. 1886, *Q.V.L.* 3rd ser., I, 182, 197.

Balkans,[1] but the newer blood in the Cabinet thought this policy out of date. The Prime Minister had to tell the Queen:

> 'A section of the Cabinet showed a strong inclination to depart from the traditional policy of this country of resisting the designs of Russia upon the Balkan Peninsula. Lord R. Churchill Lord G. Hamilton, and Mr. Smith were the three who took this view . . . that the real battle with Russia is in Afghanistan, that, having Egypt and Cyprus, the south-east of Europe no longer interests us, and that . . . any further attempt to bar the way to Russia is hopeless.'[2]

For his part, Lord Randolph was prepared to go farther than that. As he saw it, the real need was for an understanding with the Russians which would leave them a free hand in the Balkans in return for steering clear of Afghanistan and for lending 'real support in Egypt'.[3] On such a view, clearly Britain was in Egypt to stay. Towards the end of 1886 Churchill tried to conduct this foreign policy on his own, and Salisbury tolerated him for the moment as he was to tolerate Chamberlain's trespasses in foreign affairs ten years later. Churchill told the German ambassador that Britain would not budge from Egypt, and that as Chancellor of the Exchequer he intended to straighten out the Egyptian financial problem. 'We shall never give up India and we shall stay in Egypt for a long time to come.'[4]

But while the revisionists in the Cabinet were urging that Egypt must be held at all costs, ministers of the old school were pressing that it should be abandoned at the first opportunity. The Foreign Secretary himself, Lord Iddesleigh, wanted Britain to cut her diplomatic losses in this way, as Gladstone and Granville had desired before him. The Conservatives had their Gladstonians as well as the Liberals, just as the Liberals had had their Randolph Churchill in Joseph Chamberlain. Most ministers took the old view that Britain must take her stand at Constantinople and the Straits, and that Egypt alone was not enough.

Exhorted to face both ways at once, Salisbury for the time being chose to face neither. He was unwilling to write off Turkey and rely entirely upon Egypt; neither, on the other hand, would he be rushed into talks about evacuation. To his way of thinking, both these approaches were too clear cut. No less than his Chancellor of the Exchequer, he saw the primacy of India in British policy, but he still

[1] e.g. German ambassador in London to Bismarck, 13 Aug. 1886; same to same, 6 Dec. 1886, *Grosse Politik*, IV, nos. 863, 875.

[2] Salisbury to Queen Victoria, 7 Sept. 1886, *Q.V.L.*, 3rd ser., I, 201–2.

[3] Churchill to Salisbury, 15 Sept. 1886, Churchill, *op. cit.* 553.

[4] German ambassador in London to Bismarck, 20 Sept., 1886; no. 866, same to Herbert Bismarck, 24 Sept., 1886, *Grosse Politik*, IV, nos. 865, 866.

believed that the Indian empire needed defence at the Dardanelles as well as in Egypt. It is true that the difficulties of doing this were growing. British influence at Constantinople was in decline. The Ottoman empire in Europe was visibly breaking up. Nevertheless, the Prime Minister still argued that Constantinople and the Straits must be preserved from the Russians. Since Turkey could not do this alone, she must be protected, and he still hoped that the new Balkan states would obstruct the Russian advance.[1] As he put it to Churchill: 'If Russia attacked Constantinople, and all the other Powers refused to intervene, I am rather disposed to the idea that we should have to act in the Dardanelles. . . .'[2] On the other hand, he was not converted to Iddesleigh's view. No less than his Foreign Secretary, he saw the diplomatic liabilities of remaining in Egypt. But he thought it was far too valuable a safeguard to give up. Both the divisions among his ministers and his own judgement of the Mediterranean situation prompted him to keep all possible courses open.

As he strove to do so, his instinct for ambiguity led him into manoeuvres that were both intricate and opportunist. For the next three years he was to make a flurry of feints and passes, sometimes defending Constantinople while exposing Cairo, sometimes defending Cairo while exposing Constantinople. At the back of this swordplay lay the hope that he would not be driven into sacrificing either of them. It was a simple aim, so simple that his opponents could see it as well. Could he go on getting the best of both worlds, or would he be forced to opt for the better of the two cities?

The pressure to make him choose was unremitting. At the end of 1886 there was much to be said for patching up matters with France. A reconciliation would align Paris with London over the Bulgarian affair, and it would cut down Salisbury's dependence on Bismarck. So between September and November, the Foreign Secretary encouraged Freycinet with fair words about quitting Egypt and regulating the status of the Canal. But there were limits to this kind of manoeuvre. When it came to Egypt, Salisbury was not his own master in the Cabinet, and the opposition group was able to get the whole negotiation quashed.[3]

[1] *vide* L. M. Penson, 'The Principles and Methods of Lord Salisbury's Foreign Policy,' *Cambridge Historical Journal*, V, 94–100.

[2] Salisbury to Churchill, Sept. 1886, Churchill, *op. cit.*, 555.

[3] For the progress of the negotiations *vide* French *chargé* in London to Freycinet, 1 Oct. 1886, *D.D.F.*, VI, no. 324, note; French ambassador in London to Freycinet, 3 Nov. 1886, *ibid.*, no. 342; Freycinet to ambassador, 4 Nov. 1886, *ibid.*, no. 347, note; Iddesleigh to Salisbury, Private, 13 Nov. 1886, S.P. (Northcote); French ambassador to Freycinet, 14 Nov. 1886, *D.D.F.*, VI, no. 351; same to same, 23 Nov. 1886, *ibid.*, 358; Lyons to Iddesleigh, 23 Nov. 1886, Newton, *op. cit.*, II, 377–8. cf. Salisbury to Cranbrook, 26 Nov. 1886: '. . . the machine is moving along with the utmost friction both in home and foreign affairs,' Gathorne-Hardy, *op. cit.* II, 265.

There were too many risks in negotiating with Paris. The alternative was to negotiate with Constantinople, by taking up the thread of the Drummond Wolff talks. At this point Salisbury's trials were lessened by an error on the part of Lord Randolph Churchill. In December, he seriously miscalculated his strength, and the Prime Minister broke him.[1] The fall of this gimcrack Lucifer did not weaken the Egyptian school in the Cabinet, for in the reshuffle Salisbury dropped Iddesleigh, his stern, unbending Gladstonian, and took the Foreign Office himself. With Churchill gone, there was room to manoeuvre, and it was high time. At the beginning of 1887 the new tension between Paris and Berlin was interlocking the two great power struggles, the Franco-German rivalry and the Near Eastern conflict. A war in the west might mean the downfall of the Sultan in the east, and now that it had come to the point, Salisbury was still determined not to let Constantinople go.[2] This is why he brought Britain into the Mediterranean Agreements with Italy and Austria in February and March.[3] But it is characteristic of this hedging and double-thinking that before he would put pen to paper over the agreement with Italy, Salisbury should have screwed out of the Germans an assurance of their 'continued support in respect of Egypt' and their recognition of Britain's right of re-entry.[4]

Once he had the Italian Agreement in hand, Salisbury could be reasonably sure that German support in Cairo would not be cut off, and that the German weight at Constantinople would not swing against British interests.[5] But this was to put him in Bismarck's pocket, and all the more so against the background of the growing troubles between Berlin and Paris. To Salisbury, as to most of his predecessors during the nineteenth century, it was an obvious British interest not to tilt one side of the European balance too hard against the other. There was a lot to be said for not staying in Bismarck's pocket; all the more so, because the Chancellor's vague blessing at Constantinople was not

[1] For the circumstances and the calculations behind his fall, *vide* R. Rhodes James, *Lord Randolph Churchill* (1959), cap. X.

[2] For the formulation of his policy, *vide* Salisbury to Queen Victoria, 24 Jan. 1886 [?1887], *Q.V.L.*, 3rd ser., I, 263. Malet, his most trusted ambassador, told the Germans that his chief believed that 'if the Russians hold Constantinople, we shall be quite unable to keep Egypt and as I think, India also.' (Memo. by Herbert Bismarck, 28 Sept. 1886, *Grosse Politik*, IV, no. 868.)

[3] Texts in A. F. Pribam, *The Secret Treaties of Austria-Hungary*, (Cambridge, Mass., 1920), I, 94–7, 98–100, 102–3; cf. Memo. by Sanderson, 1 Jul. 1902, *British Documents on the Origins of the War* (henceforth *B.D.*), VIII, no. 1.

[4] German ambassador in London to German Foreign Office, 5 Feb. 1887, *Grosse Politik*, IV, no. 884.

[5] Besides hinting at German help over Egypt, Berlin offered 'impartial reserve by our representative in Constantinople in all other questions, without actual opposition to Russia' (*ohne jeden Gegensatz desselben zu Russland*), German ambassador in London to Bismarck, 15 Feb. 1887, *ibid.*, no. 892.

worth many divisions, and a hostile French fleet at Toulon might catch the British ships between wind and water, if they were deployed in defence of the Golden Horn. So the French were worth conciliating too; and with this aim in mind Salisbury launched another negotiation about the evacuation of Egypt.[1]

Egypt was a liability to British policy, that could not be denied. It imposed a dangerous rigidity upon that policy. It left Britain suppliant for the good graces of the Triple Alliance in Cairo, and by extension in Constantinople. The more she became committed to the Triplice, the greater grew the chances of an understanding between France and Russia, which would make nonsense of her plans in the Mediterranean. So there was nothing for it for Salisbury but to run with the hare and to hunt with the hounds. Without Bismarck there was no safety in Cairo against the French; but without French neutrality there was no safety at the Straits against the Tsar. So Salisbury had to hire credit in Paris by paying for it in Cairo. But he could not pay much. He could not risk withdrawing from Egypt, so long as Constantinople stayed insecure, for the break-up of Turkey would leave an undefended Egypt fair game for the first comer. Unless security could be rebuilt at the Straits, it would be impossible to dismantle the occupation of Egypt. But it would be possible to talk about it.

Such was the unpromising background of the second Drummond Wolff negotiation.[2] Salisbury was groping in a situation of the greatest complexity, and so hedged around with ifs and buts was his world view that to ask what precisely was his Egyptian policy at the beginning of 1887 would be to put a question without a meaning. Obviously, an agreement with the Sultan about evacuation would be worthless, unless it was accepted by the Powers, but it was no less apparent that acceptance would not be forthcoming from the Triple Alliance and from France at one and the same time. It was doubtful whether any agreement would mean much unless it won French good will, but it was also doubtful whether any French government could offer good will without being knocked over by Boulanger. All in all, there was nothing Salisbury could do about Egypt except to wait and see, to be patient and to shuffle the cards.

Evacuation was the crux of the second Drummond Wolff negotiation,

[1] For this interpretation of the policy behind the second Drummond Wolff negotiation *vide* F. H. Hinsley, 'Bismarck, Salisbury and the Mediterranean Agreements of 1887,' *Historical Journal*, I, no. 1, 79.

[2] For general accounts of the negotiation *vide* M. P. Hornik, 'The Mission of Sir Henry Drummond Wolff to Constantinople, 1885–87,' *English Historical Review*, LV; C. L. Smith, *The Embassy of Sir William White at Constantinople, 1886–1891*, (1957), 73–86.

which was launched in January 1887. The Prime Minister was adamant for a right of re-entry, for as he told Baring: '. . . it needs no proof that renewal of anarchy if not stopped by us, would be stopped either by French or Turkish troops. I wish to obtain if it is possible some treaty right of re-occupation, under proper conditions and limitations, which would enable us to watch over Egypt from Cyprus or Malta. . . .'[1] Here was the policy aim; the gloss on it was written three weeks later:

> 'Whether we shall get as much as this out of France may very well be doubted: and the negotiations may take a long time. If the present strained condition of affairs in Europe should end in any result to the detriment of France, she might become more open to persuasion than she is now. With a future so uncertain we are not anxious for an immediate close of the negotiations.'[2]

Accordingly, he made a defensive bid — evacuation after five years, with a right of re-entry. Whether he would find a taker was quite uncertain, he told Baring: '. . . under any circumstances I do not see any probability of our leaving Egypt under six years from this date: and our day may be much longer.'[3] In fact he was to lower his terms. The Turks hung out for evacuation after three years, the Germans supported them,[4] and early in May Salisbury 'with very great reluctance'[5] agreed. This clinched the bargain. On the 22nd Drummond Wolff at last got the Turks to sign the convention.[6]

It was to be a dead letter. France and Russia both came out in opposition,[7] and there followed the great diplomatic battle in Constantinople, with Britain and the Triplice urging the Sultan to ratify, and the Russians and the French threatening him with retribution if he dared to do so. He did not. On 15 July Drummond Wolff broke off the talks. Salisbury's proposals for withdrawal had failed. He was not to try again.

Had he ever seriously intended them? The question has been much

[1] Salisbury to Baring, Private, 21 Jan. 1887, S.P. 55.
[2] Same to same, Private, 11 Feb. 1887, *ibid.*
[3] Same to same, Private, 25 Feb. 1887, *ibid.*
[4] H. Drummond Wolff, *Rambling Recollections*, (1908), II, 319.
[5] Salisbury to Drummond Wolff, Telegram, Secret, 3 May, 1887, S.P. 51.
[6] Text in C. 5050, *P.P.* (1887), XCII, 538–45.
[7] It is clear from the archives of the Quai d'Orsay that France came out against the convention with some doubts. In February the Foreign Minister was prepared to accept a right of re-entry, provided that it did not last indefinitely. (Flourens to *chargé* at Constantinople, Telegram, Confidential, 12 Feb. 1887, A. E. Turquie, 473.) In May he wrote that his sole objection now was to this clause (Flourens to ambassador at Constantinople, Telegram, Confidential, 16 May 1887, A. E. Turquie, 475.) The matter was complicated by a ministerial crisis in May, and by the allegations that the London embassy favoured ratifying the convention (Directeur Politique to ambassador at Constantinople, Telegram, Personal, 22 May 1887, *ibid.*)

discussed, but in fact it does not matter. Obviously Salisbury could see all the disadvantages of the occupation, the friction with France, the reliance on Germany, the risks in Turkey. Other things being equal, he might have ended the occupation. But he would not have ended the supremacy. After all, with an indefinite right of re-entry when he should think fit, with a built-in guarantee that no other Power should enter, and with another that evacuation should not start until all the Powers had so promised[1]— with all these safeguards, attached to the convention, Salisbury was not giving much away. Britain would go on ruling Egypt, whether her troops were in Cairo or poised in Cyprus.

The second Drummond Wolff negotiation shows British policy still in a state of balance between the theses that it was at Constantinople or at Cairo that the national interest could best be defended. To hold the position of strength in Turkey, Salisbury was ready to concede a little in Egypt; but he was not willing to endanger the position of strength in Egypt, even if it meant losing ground in Turkey. He had not yet been driven to choose decisively between them; but it had now become clear that no considerations of the balance of power in Europe would drive him into surrendering the substance of British supremacy at Cairo.

Beginnings of the Shift from the Straits to the Nile, 1887–1889

The failure of the 1887 negotiations had effects of the highest importance, both on the balance of power in Europe and on the partition of Africa. The combined onslaught of France and Russia against the convention was a striking act of co-operation, and as Salisbury after his rebuff turned more closely to the central Powers, so the French had no alternative except to turn more closely to the Tsar. The failure of Drummond Wolff's Convention ended the old Franco-British understanding once and for all, and so it paved the way for the new Franco-Russian alliance. But it was above all the question of Egypt which had made the French ready for this switch. By breaking with the policy of his predecessors and demanding that British supremacy there must be guaranteed by a right of re-entry, Salisbury had asked a price that no French government was able to pay. And yet he could not do otherwise. It was too risky to revert to the old external supremacy without a right of return, and Salisbury could not leave. After the diplomatic defeat at Constantinople his first reaction was to say: 'I see nothing for it but to

[1] Salisbury to Drummond Wolff, Secret, 27 Apr. 1887; same to same, Secret, 3 May 1887, both printed in H. Temperley and L. M. Penson, *Foundations of British Foreign Policy*, (1938), 453.

sit still and drift awhile: a little further on in the history of Europe the conditions may be changed. . . . Till then we must simply refuse to evacuate.'[1] Consequently, the balance of power in Europe continued to be deeply influenced by the local situation of collapse in Egypt.

The outcome had important implications for British policy in Constantinople as well. The issue of the Convention had grown into a battle of prestige between the two groups of Powers and an index of their relative influence over the Ottoman Empire. The result showed Salisbury how much French and Russian power had risen, and how much British power had declined at Constantinople. But how then could it be defended? On 2 August Salisbury revived the old thesis of Randolph Churchill, and gave the German ambassador the impression that in certain circumstances he might leave the Turks to their fate.[2] A few days later he was writing to his ambassador in Turkey: 'It would be a terrible blow to lose Constantinople. But have we not lost it already?'[3] This was a dark saying. But it shows something of the heart searching that was now going on in London.

Increasingly Salisbury was to play the old game of defending Constantinople as if he knew the day must come when he would have to give it up. But his preoccupation with the Straits was still serious; and he still meant to stave off a partition of Turkey as long as he could. At the end of 1887 he signed a second Mediterranean Agreement with Austria and Italy. This was designed to protect Asia Minor, the Straits and Bulgaria against Russia,[4] and it held out hopes of stronger German support in doing so.[5] The Prime Minister now felt more confident that there was 'an effective barrier against any possible aggression of Russia'.[6] His concern for the defence of Turkey was still real; but evidently it was not as compelling as of old. Writing to his ambassador in Constantinople, he explained:

> '. . . [I wish] to discourage the idea that our interest in the Turkish domination of their present Empire, and of the Straits, is on the same level

[1] Salisbury to Lyons, 20 Jul. 1887, Newton, *op. cit.* II, 409.

[2] German ambassador in London to Bismarck, 3 Aug. 1887, *Grosse Politik*, IV, no. 907.

[3] Salisbury to British ambassador in Constantinople, 10 Aug. 1887, Cecil, *op. cit.*, IV, 51.

[4] Text in Pribram, *op. cit.*, I, 124–33.

[5] Bismarck to Salisbury, 22 Nov. 1887 (French in original), *Grosse Politik*, IV, no. 930. For an interpretation of this *vide* H. Rothfels, *Bismarcks englische Bundnispolitik*, (Stuttgart, 1924), 112, where it is concluded that 'Gerade die Vermeidung der unmittelbaren deutsch-englischen Bundnisbeziehung und demgemass die Vermeidung der Bindung gegenüber Russland war das entscheidende Widerlager der ganzen diplomatischen Kombination'.

[6] Salisbury to Bismarck, 30 Nov., 1887, (English in original), *Grosse Politik*, IV, no. 936.

as that of Austria and Italy. Though I fully admit the existence of our interest, it is not so imperative and vital as theirs. . . . Of course, it may be said that this plan sacrifices the ideal we have pursued ever since Lord Stratford's days of a leading influence at Constantinople. But is not that idea a chimera? Can any one have that leading influence for more than a month together?'[1]

His mistrust of Turkey is also clear from his refusal to allow the Sultan into the Mediterranean Alliance, although Bismarck had hoped this would be done.[2]

The hope of containing Russia at the Straits through the Mediterranean Agreement, as Salisbury well knew, would also be an illusion in the event of serious French hostility. The failure of the Egyptian negotiation had made this more likely. After 1887, the danger from the French began to emerge ever more plainly so that the British position at Constantinople and in the Mediterranean became increasingly exposed. And, as a result, it became ever more important to hold on to Egypt.

The alarm began in January and February of 1888 when French dispositions turned the naval balance in the Mediterranean against Britain. The Commander-in-Chief, Mediterranean, reported:

'. . . The normal strength of the Squadron in the Mediterranean is insufficient in case of a sudden attack or outbreak of war. . . . [This] is still further accentuated . . . by the fact that France, the principal Naval Power with which we could be brought into conflict, has recently concentrated almost the whole of her ironclad fleet in the Mediterranean.'[3]

The government quickly discovered that the reinforcements available were far too small to make up the deficiency. Politically, no less than technically, the fleet was out of date. The Admiralty reported in May that naval preparations must have both France and Russia in mind. And in the summer and autumn, a Cabinet Committee on National Defence concluded that naval strength must be based on the hypothesis of a Franco-Russian combination, and that with things as they were, the Mediterranean Fleet could not deal with the French ships at Toulon, let alone with the additional commitment of an operation at the Straits.[4] This naval weakness dominated the battle plans of the

[1] Salisbury to ambassador in Constantinople, 14 Dec. 1887, Cecil, *op. cit.*, IV, 78–9. (Lord Stratford was the celebrated ambassador who built up British pre-eminence at Constantinople in the middle of the century.)

[2] Bismarck to German ambassador in Rome, 7 Nov., 1887, L. Israel, *England und der Orientalische Dreibund*, (Stuttgart, 1937), 16.

[3] Duke of Edinburgh to Ponsonby, 21 Apr. 1888, *Q.V.L.*, 3rd ser., I, 399.

[4] Cecil, *op. cit.*, IV, 186–7.

Admiralty during 1888. In the event of war with France, they proposed to use all their iron-clads against the French fleets at Toulon, Cherbourg and Brest.[1] It is plain that this meant stripping the eastern Mediterranean of naval protection.

The naval 'scare' led to political uncertainty and by August, Salisbury's concern about the Straits was mounting, despite the Mediterranean Agreement. It was '. . . the only weak point in the English position. No foreign Power (setting aside France for the moment) is in a condition to threaten England's interests, except Russia by striking at Constantinople.' But France could not be set aside. 'France is, and must always remain, England's greatest danger.'[2] There were sinister signs by the end of 1888 that the two dangers might come together. In December the Russians floated their first loan in Paris. At the same time, the agitation for a Russian alliance reached its height in France.[3] If France should break out of her isolation, the chances of protecting Constantinople would be small indeed. Hence Salisbury was understandably nervous, and he did what he could to mollify the French over Egypt.

Earlier, in the autumn of 1887 he had let them know that an agreement over the Suez Canal would not be impossible.[4] In fact it proved easy. On 24 October a treaty was drawn up and this was the basis of the Suez Canal Convention signed at Constantinople on 29 October, 1888.[5] The treaty laid down a right of free passage through the canal, to be enforced by the government of Egypt, but the British government entered a general reserve against its application during the period of the occupation.[6] The German ambassador in Constantinople caustically remarked that since no one could suppose that Britain was going to leave Egypt of her own free will, the convention represented a kind of decent burial for the French hopes.[7] There was something to be said for this point of view.

[1] A. J. Marder, *The Anatomy of British Sea Power*, (New York, 1940), 130.

[2] Salisbury to Queen Victoria, 25 Aug. 1888, *Q.V.L.*, 3rd ser., I, 437–8.

[3] E. M. Carroll, *French Public Opinion and Foreign Affairs, 1870–1914*, (New York, 1931), 140–2.

[4] French ambassador in London to Flourens, 15 Aug., 1887, *D.D.F.*, VI, *bis.* no. 53; Cecil, *op. cit.*, IV, 51–2.

[5] Text in C. 5623, *P.P.*, [1889], LXXXVII, 791–9.

[6] This reserve had been put forward at the conference of 1885; *vide* C. 4339, P.P. (1884–85) LXXXVIII. It was tacitly accepted in 1888. (R. B. Mowat, *The Life of Lord Pauncefote*, (1929), 97.) For a general discussion of the rights of the territorial sovereign and of the reservation *vide* T. T. F. Huang, 'Some International and Legal Aspects of the Suez Canal Question,' *The American Journal of International Law*, LI, 277–307.

[7] *Aufzeichnungen und Erinnerungen aus dem Leben des Botschafters Joseph Maria von Radowitz*, (Stuttgart, 1925), II, 289.

Salisbury was not so innocent as to think that the French could be fobbed off with a mere formula about the Canal. Fearing Boulanger and his rabble-rousers, he enjoined tactfulness on Baring at Cairo: 'If you were to have a row in Egypt, the excited opinion of the French might turn that way. . . . I should dread any very glaring exhibition of our sovereignty in Egypt at this moment. . . .'[1]

As it turned out, 1888 was an easy year for the Egyptian question, and demands for evacuation were few and feeble. In April the Sultan raised the issue without success; the French too made three routine enquiries,[2] but for the moment, the pressure was reduced; and Salisbury did his best to keep it low. Speaking of Egypt at the Mansion House, he repeated the old thesis that Britain would stay in Egypt until there existed a strong and self-sustaining *régime*; and he went on to give an assurance that '. . . the moment we *are* satisfied that it does exist, we shall gladly relieve ourselves of an unnecessary burden'.[3] This was the same *cliché* as of Granville's day; but Granville's day was done, and the odds against evacuation had become very heavy since then.

French impatience was growing. Such dispassionate diplomats as Waddington and Paul Cambon wanted an *entente* with Britain and were prepared to accept the facts in Egypt in order to get it.[4] But this proved politically impossible for two reasons. At the end of the Eighteen eighties, the Third Republic was plunged into discredit and danger by the Wilson scandals, the resignation of President Grévy and the growing power of *Boulangisme*. As they laboured to keep their leaking ship afloat, the politicians were in no position to concede much over Egypt and to let by-gones be by-gones. The instability of the *régime* put ministries at the mercy of sectional interests. A vociferous anti-British group had sprung up after the occupation of Egypt; but it remained a minority until the prospect of a Russian alliance made better sense of the idea that the Englishman was the implacable enemy.[5] And the power of agitation was enhanced by the ferocity of the French press. As the Republic tottered the journalists flourished.[6]

[1] Salisbury to Baring, 17 Feb. 1888, Cecil, *op. cit.*, IV, 95.

[2] French ambassador in Constantinople to Goblet, 7 Apr. 1888; French *chargé* at London to Goblet, 11 Apr. 1888; French ambassador in London to Goblet, 25 Apr. 1888; same to same, 25 May 1888, *D.D.F.* VII, nos. 93, 98, 108, 122.

[3] Speech of 6 Aug. 1888, Cecil, *op. cit.*, IV, 134–5.

[4] Cambon to Spuller, 11 Mar. 1889, P. Cambon, *Correspondance, 1870–1924*, (Paris, 1940), I, 333.

[5] Carroll, *op. cit.*, 142.

[6] *vide* the tirade of Spuller to the Italian ambassador on 10 Oct. 1889: 'I, who am every day obliged to see many of these men, can assure you that their ignorance, their absurd prejudices and the fierceness of their passions are beyond belief. . . . we may not be held responsible for excesses we deplore. . . .' (*The Memoirs of Francesco Crispi*, (1912), II, 421.)

Therefore every French ministry anxiously sought for some success abroad which would sustain it at home. It was much less dangerous to keep *Boulangisme* in check by acting over Egypt than by agitating over Alsace-Lorraine. And the chances of success would be enormously increased if it was sought in the eastern Mediterranean where Russian co-operation was likely. So, if Freycinet in 1887 looked upon success in Egypt as 'a personal necessity'[1], two years later the necessity was becoming national. In 1889, the French were once more pressing Salisbury hard to evacuate Egypt. Waddington impressed upon him the vital importance '. . . for the Government of the Republic of settling this question before the general elections'.[2]

It was not that the wild chauvinism in France at the end of the Eighteen eighties was clamouring for colonial adventures. Boulanger himself was more concerned to recover Alsace and Lorraine and to denounce internal scandals than to champion imperialism.[3] No more in France, than in Britain, does there seem to have been a strong mass movement for overseas expansion during this time,[4] although it suited the politicians of each country to detect such a movement in the other.

French anger about Egypt did not spring from the hope of annexing it. Their aim was rather to release it from unfriendly hands in order to improve their security in the Mediterranean. The occupation of 1882 had upset the balance in that region. From the British point of view, it might seem a valuable counterpoise to their declining influence at Constantinople, but to the French it represented a blow at their hopes of dominating the southern shores of the Mediterranean. The strategic aim of French policy was to end the situation in which Egypt was held by 'troops of a power already established in Gibraltar, Malta and Cyprus'.[5]

French policy then, both for reasons of internal politics and through anxiety for the Mediterranean balance became committed to the design of forcing the British out of Egypt. It was upon this rock that the Liberal alliance had split. For all the efforts of a Waddington or a Cambon to keep on good terms with London, the French were driven more and more into an anti-British and a pro-Russian attitude.

[1] Lyons to Salisbury, 8 Mar. 1887, Newton, *op. cit.*, II, 392–3.

[2] French ambassador in London to Spuller, 12 Jun. 1889, *D.D.F.*, VII, no. 400.

[3] A. Dansette, *Le Boulangisme*, (Paris, 1946), 148; W. Frank, *Nationalismus und Demokratie im Frankreich der dritten Republik, 1871 bis 1918*, (Hamburg, 1933), 137–252.

[4] c.f. the arguments of T. F. Power, *Jules Ferry and the Renaissance of French Imperialism*, (New York, 1944), *passim*, that Ferry's economic arguments for expansion were an attempt to rationalise unpopular imperialist views.

[5] Ribot to French ambassador in Constantinople, 30 Jan. 1892, *D.D.F.* IX, no. 180.

British anxieties in the Mediterranean by 1889 were piling up. In Egypt the French were pressing for evacuation. In Constantinople, the Russians threatened an exposed position. In the Mediterranean, Britain was too weak in ships to be sure of coping with France alone when she might at any time have to face Russia as well. The Naval Defence Act introduced in March of 1889 was the government's reaction to all these dangers. The principle behind it was the so-called 'Two-Power standard' and Salisbury speaking in the Lords left little doubt which two Powers he had in mind.[1] But even with the Act, this standard could not be achieved until 1894. In the meantime, it was very hard to meet the dangers of 1889. Throughout that year Salisbury's Mediterranean system seemed to be threatened by French warlike moves against Italy. In November 1889 this danger was sufficiently grave for the Cabinet to reinforce the fleet in the Mediterranean; and in December the Admiralty decided that the Channel squadron was to be considered as 'an adjunct to the Mediterranean fleet in case of threatened war with France'.[2] The year 1890 brought further alarms. The British feared that the Tsar intended to rush Constantinople and the Straits. The French too became more active, as they tried to annex Tunis and partition Tripoli while attempting once more to dislodge the British from Egypt.[3] Brought face to face with the likelihood that both Russia and France might act against them, the Admiralty grudgingly concluded that for the time being the Navy could not defend the Straits without endangering the British Isles. On 10 June, 1890, the First Lord of the Admiralty wrote of

> '. . . the extreme danger of the movement not only in itself but in the consequences that must follow. . . . If the attempt by Russia on Constantinople was part of a series of movements to be made in combination with France . . . the position of the British Fleet in the Mediterranean would be, assuming it was wholly absorbed in frustrating the Russian attempt, one of great strategical disadvantage. . . . The naval supremacy of England in the Channel might be endangered. . . . Moreover the presence of a great French fleet at Toulon with nothing between it and the squadrons at Brest and Cherbourg would give to France a strategical position of overwhelming importance.
>
> These and other considerations have been pressed upon and are known to the Government . . . .'[4]

[1] *Hansard*, 3rd ser., CCCXXXVI, col. 1062. [2] Marder, *op. cit.*, 146.

[3] German ambassador in London to German Foreign Office, 1 Aug. 1890, *Grosse Politik*, VIII, no. 1887; Crispi to Italian ambassador in London, 2 Aug. 1890, Crispi, *op. cit.*, III, 45; Ribot to French ambassador in Constantinople, 26 Aug. 1890, *D.D.F.*, VIII, no. 163. The Mediterranean negotiations of 1890 are analysed in W. L. Langer, *The Franco-Russian Alliance, 1890–1894*, (Cambridge, Mass., 1929).

[4] First Lord of the Admiralty to C-in-C., Mediterranean, 10 Jun. 1890, Marder, *op. cit.*, 155.

Accordingly in 1889 and 1890 Salisbury was forced to re-appraise British policy in the eastern Mediterranean. For some years to come, the fleet would be too weak to defend Constantinople against the Russians if the French were to remain hostile. The decay of the Sultanate and the decline of the Fleet were making it impossible to hold the first line of defence in Turkey. Strategically, it would have been folly to give up the second line in Egypt; and Salisbury frankly recognised this by the end of 1889. Furthermore the threat of anarchy in Egypt also made it impossible to leave. As Britain could not be certain of protecting the overlord in Constantinople, she found it essential to be certain of protecting the vassal in Cairo.

CHAPTER IX

New Frontiers of Insecurity

If the strategic reasons for staying in Cairo were strong, the internal Egyptian reasons against withdrawal were overwhelming. By 1889 Baring had convinced the Prime Minister that there could be no stability or security in Cairo without occupation. As the British Agent saw it, the internal crisis which had come to a head in 1882, was still unsolved. Revolution still simmered beneath the surface tranquillity of the occupation. The chances of setting up a reliable Egyptian *régime* and so returning to a supremacy wielded from outside, were smaller than ever.

Baring's judgement bore the stamp of his personality. The proconsul was too much of an Indian administrator to make a success of Egyptian politics. It was in India that he had gained his early experience, first as private secretary to his cousin, Northbrook, the Viceroy, and later as Financial member of the Council. From India also he had drawn most of the British officials who filled key posts in the government of Egypt. In this way something of the administrative tradition of Calcutta was transplanted to the Nile.

It was a tradition with great virtues; and Baring had his full share of them. Like the 'Guardians' of India, he felt too much personal responsibility for the subject peoples' welfare to hand them over to a corrupt and incompetent class of native leaders. For him British rule and influence were ordained by Providence for the progress of the Orient. This faith made him detest nationalists in Egypt as in India. He judged backward Egypt by the standards of a progressive Europe and found it stunted and degenerate. Both on moral and on practical grounds, the old *régime* seemed past praying for. As he declared later,

> 'The country over which the breath of the West . . . has once passed . . . can never be the same as it was before. The new foundations must be of the Western, not the Eastern type.'[1]

With this outlook, it is not surprising that Baring could find no hope of a stable government in Egypt, short of reforming on western lines the whole structure and spirit of the society.

[1] The Earl of Cromer, *Ancient and Modern Imperialism*, (1910), 120.

It was equally characteristic of this matter-of-fact man that he should know of no way of doing this, except by honest administration over many generations. And here again he was echoing the formula of official India. The faith of many early Victorians, that the spread of Christianity and Western education and the growth of free trade would be enough to regenerate the East, had long since been shattered by experience. Baring, like his contemporaries, despaired of assimilating the Oriental to European religion and culture. The one hope he could see for progress in the East lay in gradually reforming its government and improving its material condition. Only when all this had been done, would the Orient adopt that liberal and humanist code of ethics which the Victorians still held must triumph eventually throughout the world.

There was something of Bentham and much of the younger Mill in Baring's certainty that scientific administration was the key to progress. His ideas of government were inspired by Indian experience interpreted in the light of the laws of Utilitarian political economy.[1] To him political order was obviously the first requirement for the improvement of character. He was fond of comparing the role of the *Pax Britannica* in the modern world to that of the *Pax Romana* in the ancient.[2] Political stability to his mind, depended above all upon the contentment and prosperity of the productive classes, especially the mass of the peasantry. For him as for Mill, the backwardness and 'inhumanity' of Oriental society were to be blamed on its quasi-feudal, parasitic rulers who throttled freedom and killed enterprise. The task of administration in Baring's eyes was to break this vicious circle; to release the peasantry from injustice and extortion, to cleanse government of corruption, and to achieve a surplus of revenue. The surplus in turn would permit him to lighten taxes, develop agriculture and public works, and so to improve the lot of the peasant and the prospects of order. Baring was a man of precept and prejudice, rather than philosophy; but he put the essence of his outlook in one commonplace saying. '. . . The inauguration of a sound financial policy', he declared, 'is the necessary and indispensable precursor of all moral and material progress in backward Oriental states.'[3] In the eyes of this financier and administrator mere politics seemed ineffectual and dishonest. From the beginning he looked upon Egypt with a high sense of duty toward the *Fellah*, contempt for the *Pasha* and detestation for the politician.

His outlook indeed had many virtues; but it was hardly congenial to

[1] *vide*, J. S. Mill, *Considerations on Representative Government* (1861).
[2] Cromer, *Imperialism, passim.* [3] *ibid*, 51, fn. 2.

the business of nursing the country quickly back to independence. Moreover he was too much of an autocrat for so delicate a task. As a French diplomat saw him, he was brusque and outspoken, altogether 'the stolid, uncompromising Briton'.[1] Colleagues in Delhi had nick-named him the 'Vice-Viceroy', and in Cairo, 'Over-Baring'. To his superiors as well as to his subordinates, he seemed a man of iron who could be relied upon to surmount any crisis. This strength and self-reliance quickly won for him a remarkable personal authority. Whether under Salisbury or Rosebery, the Foreign Office deferred to his advice and left him a freedom of action given to no other official. Rosebery, on leaving the Foreign Office in 1894, wrote to the Agent in Cairo: 'we have gone through stormy times together, and I have long come to the conclusion that you are a good man to go tiger-hunting with.' Neither the Khedive nor his ministers could escape Baring's control. Quietly yet effectively, he became the puppet-master of Egyptian politics, making all dance to his strings. That he should have ruled Egypt himself, instead of fostering Egyptian rule, was inevitable; for he set out from the beginning to make a new and better Egypt. The old one could not and should not be restored.

It is not surprising that such a man after five years in Cairo should feel that he was only beginning his work. His judgement of the Egyptian situation was as gloomy as his standards were high. At the end of the Eighteen eighties the Khedivial treasury had at last been brought within sight of solvency of a sort. Henceforward, the administration was to find its way out of the red.[2]

As the Egyptian budget began to balance, the occupation looked less

[1] Esher, *Journals*, *op. cit.*, I, 96.

[2] The achievement is shown best in Baring's own figures:

Egyptian Finances since the Occupation

£E

	Surplus	*Deficit*
1883	—	920,000
1884	—	460,000
1885	—	697,000
1886	—	684,000
1887	111,000	—
1888	—	1,000
1889	160,000	—
1890	591,000	—
1891	951,000	—
1892	769,000	—
1893	720,000	—
1894	785,000	—
1895	1,015,000	—

Source: F.O. 78/4761, Cromer to Salisbury, no. 15, 3 Feb. 1896.

like the hostage to fortune it had hitherto seemed to British Cabinets. International controls of course, remained; but with solvency, the Anglo-Egyptian *régime* became far less vulnerable to financial pressure from the Powers. The diplomatic penalties to be paid for occupation were by so much reduced.

The prospect of a surplus at last promised Baring the means to carry on his plans for social reform. In 1889 he proposed to convert part of the Debt to lower rates of interest, and to use the money thus saved to pay wages for keeping the irrigation canals clear. This would do away with the need for the forced labour employed hitherto. The agreement of the *Caisse* was needed for the conversion, and once again the French withheld their consent in the hope of extorting a promise of evacuation. But this was to cast themselves in the sorry role of upholders of the unpopular *corvée*, which the Egyptian National Assembly had unanimously moved to abolish. The British government refused to talk of withdrawal, the French manoeuvre failed, and Baring got his way.[1]

For all that, the British Agent at the end of the Eighteen eighties was reporting to Salisbury that his reforms had utterly failed to set up a basis of self-government. In spite of better justice, land reform, and attempts to improve irrigation and equalise the burden of taxation, the Egyptian peasant seemed to be no better off than before. There were still few signs of that contented and prosperous *fellahin* which Baring believed to be the foundation of order. The peasantry were still ripe for revolt. Early in 1888, his Irrigation officers, whose work brought them closest to the *fellah*, reported that '. . . the spirit of resistance against oppression set alive by Arabi [was] stronger now than ever'.[2] The national feeling against Turk and European which had exploded in 1882 still burned so fiercely that '. . . the Pasha rule would never last, supposing England were to withdraw from Egypt'.[3] This intelligence was of course in line with Baring's opinion. He told Salisbury:

> 'In my belief the chances are that an upset would take place, but it is impossible to foresee whether it would take the form of a palace intrigue, a military mutiny, a popular revolution, *et cetera*.'[4]

This was Baring's theme throughout 1889 and 1890. There could be

[1] *vide*, A. Milner, *England in Egypt*, (1892), 236–42; Cromer, *Modern Egypt*, 786–7; Zetland, *op. cit.*, 154–5, 187; Spuller to French ambassador in London, 7 Jun. 1889, *D.D.F.*, VII, no. 395; Waddington to Spuller, 21 Jun. 1889, *ibid.*, no. 405.

[2] Report by C. W. Forster of the Irrigation Service, 21 Mar. 1888, encl. in Baring to Salisbury, Secret, 24 Apr. 1888, F.O. 78/4145.

[3] *idem.*

[4] Baring to Salisbury, 24 Mar. 1888; F.O. 78/4145.

no stability in Egypt without British troops; and no progress without the supervision of British officials.[1] The heavy fall in prices had swallowed up all the social and political benefits expected from reform, and it had been impossible to cut taxes and lighten the depression, because foreign creditors were the first charge on the revenue. Reforms, Baring declared, had not improved the state of Egypt, they had merely stopped it from getting worse. 'Had the old regime continued', he reported, 'the low prices of the last few years would have brought . . . a hopeless state of bankruptcy.' As it was the improvements

> '. . . have enabled Egypt to meet all its financial obligations in spite of the fall in prices. But they have not done much more than this. From a purely pecuniary point this position of the agricultural tax-payers of Egypt has, by reason of low prices, not been very materially improved.'[2]

So the danger of revolution was still there. Economic grievances kept the peasants as stubble ready for the agitators' fire. Baring again warned Salisbury early in 1890 that 'simmering below the surface is a mass of ignorant fanaticism . . . which is . . . one of the most important elements in Egyptian affairs'.[3] Once more it was the fear of agrarian risings and national revolution that Baring stressed.[4] Without the British, the Pashas now had no hold on the country; and with the British, they had become identified with the foreigner. No doubt, he reported, '. . . the effect of the British occupation has been to make the Pasha class unpopular.'[5] Its rule was upheld only by British bayonets.

Liberal reform had so far failed to produce a more contented peasantry; it had also failed to foster a new leadership. The aim from the beginning had been to set firmly in power a class of Egyptians who would co-operate loyally with British purposes. Until this had been done, there could be no safe return to a system of 'moral' supremacy over the country, exerted from outside. At the end of the Eighteen eighties, Baring was still reporting that this collaborating class could nowhere be found.

Nothing of the kind was to be expected of the Khedive and his Turco-Circassian Pashas. The *fellah* had long hated them as aliens, tax-gatherers and landlords. Pashadom had been on the verge of collapse on the eve of Tel-el-Kebir, and since then it had bowed to the foreigner, carried out his reforms, collected his debts and lost the Sudan. Baring and his officials with their Indian principles, looked on

[1] Baring to Salisbury, 13 Dec. 1889, F.O. 78/4243.
[2] Baring to Salisbury, 20 Feb. 1890; F.O. 78/4308.
[3] Baring to Salisbury, 25 Apr. 1890, Secret, F.O. 78/4309.
[4] Same to same, 24 May 1890; F.O. 78/4310.
[5] *idem.*; and Baring to Salisbury, 24 Mar. 1888; F.O. 78/4145.

the Pashas as both vicious and impotent. They appeared to have no political sense, and what was worse, no idea that they were sitting upon a volcano of discontent. Baring was impressed more and more '. . . by the incapacity of most Egyptians to realise . . . the springs of action which move society whether in Egypt or elsewhere.'[1] In other words, unlike Baring, Egypt's rulers were ignorant of the laws of political economy. 'Until a race of Egyptians has arisen far more competent than any which now exist', Baring told Salisbury, 'the evacuation of the country by the British Army would be attended with very grave risks.'[2]

But it was left to Alfred Milner, one of Baring's staff, to say what the English really thought of the Egyptian ruling caste. It was made up of a small *clique* of Turkish families who were entirely out of sympathy with the mass of the population. The Pasha class, he wrote,

> '. . . is singularly deficient in the industry, the education and the principle which, under the new conditions, are requisite. . . . The great body of this class are, therefore, unserviceable for the work of government. And while they are unserviceable today, with European influence in the saddle, they might become dangerous tomorrow, if that influence were withdrawn.'[3]

The Pashas had proved themselves helpless and hopeless for the British purpose. Beneath them, the sheikhs, village elders and minor officials seemed to be even worse.[4] Milner here faithfully echoed Baring's earlier conclusion.

Egypt seemed by British standards to be a country without suitable political *cadres*. Those that it had were decadent, unpopular or dangerous. This had been the dilemma of the occupation from the start. The British had gone into Egypt because the native government through which they had long secured their interest had broken down under European pressure and national revolt. They had intended to restore the Khedivial *régime* and withdraw within a short time, leaving behind a supremacy of influence. But having come to grips with the Egyptian problem, it was found that the orthodox technique of informal influence beloved of the mid-Victorians,[5] would not work. The Liberals' original scheme remained locked within the covers of Dufferin's facile Report, so little did it correspond with Egyptian realities. The bankers of Montreal, the merchants of Sydney might be trusted to collaborate without compulsion in the process of British expansion, since they were more or less bound up with Britain in interest and outlook. The device

[1] Baring to Salisbury, 24 May 1890 Secret, F.O. 78/4310.
[2] Same to same, 25 Apr. 1890; F.O. 78/4309.
[3] A. Milner, *England in Egypt*, (1892), 404. [4] *ibid.*, 396–7, 398–405.
[5] J. Gallagher and R. Robinson, 'The Imperialism of Free Trade,' *Economic History Review*, 1953, 1–15.

of self-government had proved the safest as well as the most elegant way of preserving the connection. Even the vast and exclusive Oriental empires of the Manchus and the Meijids, after the first troubles, still had enough authority left to meet Western demands without a Western occupation.

But none of this would work in Egypt, as the British belatedly discovered. It was not simply that the strategic importance of the country forbade the British to take the risk of losing it; but rather that the politics of the country offered no basis for collaboration after withdrawal. Britain's intervention as it were, had halted the changes taking place inside the polity at the worst possible moment for her own plan. The alien Pasha aristocracy which might otherwise have served the purpose, would surely have fallen but for the British. On the other hand, the incipient national movement, which would have overthrown the Pashas and might have given Egypt a popular leadership, was still too immature to do so. And Baring was too much of an 'Indian' to do anything but suppress it. It was in this sense that he found Egypt without effective political *cadres*. The occupation had frozen its politics in a state of perpetual 'betwixt and between'. The native authority could hardly revive while Baring ruled. Yet Baring had to rule until the native authority revived. As long as Egypt hung in suspended animation, the British could not withdraw without sacrificing their supremacy and risking a return to anarchy which might draw another Power across the route to India.

The British Agent came up against the same dilemma in the day to day work of administering the country. He had to do this nominally through the Khedive, but a reliable ministry was very hard to find. There were non-Egyptians well suited for the work of reform and westernisation; but they had no support in the country. On the other hand those Egyptian leaders who could command support from the people were hostile to reform and British influence alike. Baring set up ministries of both kinds and was satisfied with neither. After 1884, he had ruled through Nubar Pasha, an Armenian Christian who spoke no Arabic, but had 'no difficulty in grasping a European principle'.[1] By June 1888, the Agent had decided that a Christian first minister in an Islamic country was tempting the Providence of both religions. Moslems had to be brought more into government, even at the cost of slowing down reform. Accordingly, Riaz Pasha, a stern, unbending Moslem replaced Nubar; but Baring in surmounting one difficulty had only set

[1] Cromer, *Modern Egypt*, (1911), 722.

up another. The new first minister was an autocrat and a torturer of the old Turkish school with no sympathy whatever for liberal or creative administration. Although Riaz appealed to the faithful and the conservative, Baring was soon complaining of his ruthless methods and of 'a recrudescence of Mohammedan fanaticism'.[1] Later, he reported that 'Riaz is becoming quite ungovernable',[2] and shortly afterwards, got rid of him.[3] Having failed to find effective collaborators, Baring had no choice but to carry on as Mayor of the Palace.[4] It was a part he was not unwilling to play.

Years later, Salisbury explained why the British stayed in Egypt by saying sardonically that '*l'appétit vient en mangeant*';[5] but the truth went deeper than that. The occupation had to go on because it was the only way of retaining supremacy and keeping the lid on the unsolved internal crisis. In a country where authority had been crushed by European pressure and the national reaction against the foreigner, no way back to an independent order and the old supremacy by influence could be found. The path back to the more fortunate Palmerstonian system had seemed plain and straightforward enough in 1882. Five years later it still seemed feasible, if much longer and more difficult. But by 1889 it had come to look impossible. So withdrawal was out of the question. The 'veiled protectorate' would have to go on. The Khedive was weak and discredited; the Pashas were threatened with agrarian revolt; the nationalist leaders were not to be trusted. None of this offered a basis of trustworthy independence.

By June 1889, Salisbury had come round entirely to Baring's point of view. The British Agent had stated his case in these words:

> '. . . the real reason why the evacuation policy is well nigh impossible of execution . . . is based on the utter incapacity of the ruling classes in this country. . . . [They] are almost exclusively foreigners. . . . Now, all this class are detested by the people, and they are more disliked now than they ever were before . . . if he [Riaz Pasha] were left to himself he would go far to produce a revolution in six months. . . . Really, the more I look at it, the more does the evacuation policy appear to me to be impossible under any conditions.'[6]

Baring warned the Prime Minister that even if the French agreed to give the British a right of re-entry, a withdrawal now would lead to anarchy and disaster for British influence.[7] Moreover he could see

[1] Baring to Salisbury, spring 1890, Zetland, *op. cit.*, 199.
[2] Baring to Salisbury, Jan. 1891, *ibid.* [3] *ibid.*, 200.
[4] Salisbury to Baring, 23 Jan. 1891, *ibid.*, 199.
[5] French ambassador in London to Hanotaux, 3 Oct. 1896; *D.D.F.*, XII, no. 468.
[6] Baring to Salisbury, 15 Jun. 1889, Cecil, *op. cit.*, IV, 138–9.
[7] *idem.*; and same to same, 24 May, 1890, F.O. 78/4310.

another and even worse danger in evacuation. Re-opening the entire Egyptian question would shatter any chance of reconciliation between Britain and France and might well lead to war.[1]

These were no longer simply the opinions of the importunate proconsul on the spot. By the middle of 1889 they had become the matured policy of the Prime Minister. In June Spuller, the French Foreign Minister, tried once more to bring Salisbury to agree upon terms for a withdrawal. The French offered a large concession. In effect they would now accept the terms which Drummond Wolff had asked and they had refused in 1887. The French ambassador told Salisbury that if there was trouble in Egypt after evacuation, 'we should not raise any insuperable objection to the re-entry of British troops.'[2] But Salisbury had by now accepted Baring's view that a right of re-entry was no longer sufficient security for British supremacy. He could see objections everywhere. If Turkey should go to pieces after the British had left Cairo, then what was going to happen to Egypt?[3] He countered the French offer by raising his terms still higher. If there was to be a right of re-entry, then its duration must be indefinite.[4] At last on 21 June he told the French ambassador of the ultimate reason why there could be no more talk of withdrawal on the old terms; and his words came freshly out of Baring's despatches: 'Once our troops go, the Khedive will not last for six months.'[5] Three days later, the Prime Minister again declared that internal dangers in Egypt prevented him from fixing any date for withdrawal;[6] and he broke off the negotiation, saying, 'I cannot see that there is anything more to be done for the present.'[7] It was definitive. Although the French now talked of a right of re-entry, Salisbury would not talk of evacuation. Even in public, he now took a much higher line about Egypt. At the Guildhall on 9 November he declared the government's determination, 'whether it were assisted or obstructed by other Powers', to pursue to the end the task which it had undertaken.[8] He would no longer take the risk of an independent Egypt. Possession seemed to him the only way to security.

If the policy was a new one, the idea behind it was old enough to have been advocated by Clarendon and Ellenborough in the Eighteen forties.

[1] *idem.*
[2] Spuller to French ambassador in London, 7 Jun. 1889, *D.D.F.*, VII, no. 395.
[3] French ambassador in London to Spuller, 12 Jun. 1889, *ibid.*, no. 400.
[4] Same to same, 21 Jun. 1889, *ibid.*, no. 405.
[5] French ambassador in London to Spuller, 21 Jun. 1889; *ibid.*, no. 405.
[6] Same to same, 24 Jun. 1889, *ibid.*, p. 437, note.
[7] Same to same, 1 Jul. 1889, *ibid.*, no. 409.
[8] Cecil, *op. cit.*, IV, 137–8.

It had been pressed from the beginning of the occupation by some at Court and many at the Horse Guards, and even by a few ministers. Hartington and Northbrook had insisted in 1884 that there was no foreseeable escape from the trap. Randolph Churchill had said the same in 1886. But they had been the minority and had been over-ruled. Most ministers would have liked to retire from the heavy liability of occupation, if the vital interest could otherwise be secured. But what if it could not? By the end of the decade the alignment of Europe and the ferment in Egypt had converted most leading politicians to the new view. It was notable that Chamberlain for example, who had demanded early evacuation in 1884, had turned by this time into a fierce retentionist. Rosebery also was firmly for staying. Indeed among the party leaders, only Gladstone and his old guard went on preaching the pure doctrine of withdrawal, and some of them had their doubts. In 1890 the French ambassador spoke of it to the redoubtable Harcourt, hitherto always staunch for withdrawal. He replied, 'the question is very difficult; if we retire, we leave chaos behind us; it is very difficult to take such a responsibility.'[1] It was Baring's thesis once more. And so the policy of the 'veiled protectorate' which hitherto had been one of two alternatives, had now come to be adopted by government as the only course.

Having reached this conclusion by the middle of 1889, Salisbury soon drew others, more momentous still for the future of Africa. Within the next six months he decided at Baring's prompting that if they were to hold Egypt, they could not afford to let any other European Power obtain a hold over any part of the Nile Valley. In so doing, he took what was perhaps the critical decision of the Partition. Henceforward almost everything in Africa north of the Zambesi River was to hinge upon it.

The idea that the security of Egypt depended upon the defence of the Upper Nile was as old as the pyramids; and the government had been reminded of it often enough. Sir Samuel Baker, the well-known explorer and once the Khedive's governor in the Sudan, wrote about it in 1884 and 1888. He pointed at the danger that a hostile Power could readily dam the Upper Nile, starve Egypt of water, and so destroy the country.[2] This had been one of the objections of the forward party to abandoning the Sudan, and for the same reason Riaz Pasha had pressed upon Baring the need to win it back.

'. . . The Nile is the life of Egypt. . . . The Nile means the Soudan. . . . If [any European Power] . . . took possession of the banks of the Nile it

[1] French ambassador to Ribot, 20 Jun. 1890; *D.D.F.* VIII, no. 89; same to same, 9 Sept. 1891, *ibid.*, IX, no. 7. [2] Langer, *Diplomacy*, 105–6.

> would be all over with Egypt. . . . The Government of His Highness the Khedive will never willingly consent, not without compulsion, to such an attack on its existence.'[1]

But the British Agent was not at this time persuaded. He had strongly advised Salisbury against reconquering the Sudan for the time being; and the Prime Minister had agreed.

> 'If an unlucky combination of circumstances had not reduced the finances of Egypt very low,' he told the Queen, 'it might be possible to take this opportunity of restoring the power of the Khedive over the valley of the Nile. But Egypt could not afford an expedition; and the House of Commons would certainly decline to bear the cost.'[2]

To their minds, an advance was out of the question until Egypt could afford it; but already they foresaw that one day circumstance might force them to secure Egypt by regaining the Sudan.

So far they had had good reason to be complacent about the Upper Nile and its headwaters in Uganda and Ethiopia. As long as no other Power was in sight of seizing these regions, they could have little bearing on Egyptian security. The Dervishes who held the Sudan could not cut off the flow of the river on which the life and stability of Egypt depended, for they were no engineers. No European Power had yet reached the point of sending menacing expeditions towards the Upper Nile, and it was still possible that Britain would leave Egypt soon.

But things were very different by 1889. The British were certainly intending to stay. Cairo was becoming more and more the pivot of their Mediterranean strategy. A foreign Power astride the Upper Nile would be in a position either to levy blackmail or to lever them out of Egypt. It was the Italians, advancing from the Red Sea towards the eastern Sudan, who presented the first threat of this kind.

In May 1889, the Italian minister, Crispi made the Treaty of Ucciali with Ethiopia — an agreement designed to give Rome great influence in the country of the Blue Nile.[3] He also laid claim to Kassala which commanded the Atbara tributary of the Nile. With this town as a base the Italians might edge their way towards Khartoum at the confluence of the White and the Blue Nile. Crispi's vaulting African ambition and the challenge at Kassala goaded Salisbury to make up his mind about the Nile Valley as a whole.

[1] Riaz Memo., 9 Dec. 1888; encl. Baring to F.O., 15 Jan. 1889, C. 5668, P.P. [1889] LXXXVII, 769–70.

[2] Salisbury to Queen Victoria, 25 Dec. 1888; *Q.V.L.*, 3rd ser., I, 459.

[3] For a summary of the terms of this Treaty of 2 May 1889, *vide* Hertslet, *op. cit.*, II, 454–9.

How long he had meditated it before putting on paper the policy of closing the Valley of the Nile, who can say? But by August 1889, the Prime Minister was anxious enough about Kassala to ask Baring what he thought about it.[1] The reply must have been emphatically against letting foreign Powers into the Nile Valley, because on 15 November, '[the Prime Minister] concurred fully as to the inviolability of the valley of the Nile even in its affluents. . . .'[2] The doctrine was already fully formed.

The reasons for adopting this policy are plainly disclosed in Baring's correspondence with Salisbury. If the Italians took Kassala, he wrote,

> '. . . They would soon strike the valley of the Nile . . . at Khartoum . . . the establishment of a civilised Power in the Nile Valley would be a calamity to Egypt.'

When Baker and others had put forward similar views in 1888, Baring went on, he had thought them 'unnecessarily alarmist':

> 'The savage tribes who now rule in the Soudan do not possess the resources or the engineering skill to do any real harm to Egypt.'

But the Italian threat had now converted Baring,

> '. . . The case would be very different were a civilised European Power established in the Nile Valley. . . . They could so reduce the water-supply as to ruin the country. . . . Whatever Power holds the Upper Nile Valley must, by the mere force of its geographical situation, dominate Egypt.'[3]

There was already enough discontent inside the country without inviting Foreign Powers to manufacture subversion by drought. But Baring the administrator still guided Baring the strategist. He did not want Salisbury to stop the Italian advance at the expense of a premature reconquest of the Sudan, for this would disorganise the Egyptian finances which the British Agent had been at such pains to set in order. He urged the Prime Minister to keep 'a strictly defensive policy' for the time being;[4] and to keep the Italians out of the Nile Valley by diplomacy.

Just as the Prime Minister in June had concurred in Baring's counsel

[1] Baring to Salisbury, Secret, 15 Dec. 1889, F.O. 78/4243, which mentions that on 25 Aug. 1889 Baring wrote a memo. which Salisbury had requested on Italian activities. This document is not to be found in F.O. 78/4242 which contains the Egyptian correspondence between Aug. and Nov. 1889.

[2] His biographer's paraphrase of Salisbury to Baring, 15 Nov. 1889; Cecil, *op. cit.*, IV, 326.

[3] Baring to Salisbury, Secret, 15 Dec. 1889, F.O. 78/4243.

[4] Same to same, 11 Dec. 1889, Confidential, *ibid.*

to stay in Egypt, so after November he took up Baring's policy of defending the occupation of the Upper Nile.

> 'In respect to Kassala,' Salisbury wrote in March 1890, 'it gives the Power occupying it command over one of the main affluents of the Nile, and therefore a power of diverting a portion of the supply which is vital to Egypt.' And he agreed to '. . . such measures as may be necessary for the purpose of protecting your Nile Valley against the dominion of any outside Power.'

It was, he declared, '. . . essential to the safety of Egypt' that this should be done.[1] The policy was comprehensive. At first it applied specifically to the Italians and Kassala. But Salisbury and Baring had plainly adopted it from November 1889 as a general principle; and the principle held good for all Powers and for all parts of the Nile Valley, indeed as far south as the headwaters of the river in the Uganda country.

Thus the safety of the Nile had now become a supreme consideration, and the policy was quickly put into effect. On 7 March, 1890, Salisbury warned the Italians off the Nile,[2] and later Baring was sent to Rome to try and set safe limits to their advance.[3] The new strategy also forced Salisbury and Baring to reconsider the defensive policy of the past six years in the Sudan. Baring gave three reasons for doing so; in the first place, Egypt's finances had now turned the corner; secondly, 'the dervish movement has been going rapidly downhill'; and thirdly, diplomacy could not be relied upon for ever to ward off other Powers. In the end, occupation alone could make certain of the Upper Nile.[4] The Prime Minister agreed that sooner or later the Sudan would have to be reconquered. But like Baring, he preferred to wait — so long as diplomacy would suffice to keep foreign rivals away. Salisbury as usual was against giving the imperialists at the Horse Guards a free hand. More important, he took it for granted that an 'imperialist' advance would jar upon the prejudices of the electorate at Home.

> 'They were so deeply impressed with the disasters of six years ago,' Salisbury explained, 'and the apparently inexorable necessity which had driven them into situations where those disasters were inevitable, that they shrink instinctively from any proposal to advance into the Egyptian desert. I do not say that this is a sufficient argument to prevent such an advance, if there is a clear balance of undoubted advantage in its favour; but in the

[1] Salisbury to Baring, 28 Mar. 1890, Cecil, *op. cit.*, IV, 328; same to same, 31 Aug. 1890, *ibid.*, 330–1; Shibeika, *op. cit.*, 321–6.

[2] Italian ambassador in London to Crispi, 7 Mar. 1890, F. Crispi, *La Prima Guerra d'Africa*, (ed. Palamenghi-Crispi), (2nd ed., Milan, 1939), 229.

[3] *vide infra*, 303–4.

[4] Baring to Salisbury, 15 Mar. 1890, F.O. 78/4308.

absence of any such evidence, it must be accepted as a strong presumption. As far as I can see matters, I should say that until you have money enough to justify you in advancing to Berber, you had better remain quiet.'[1]

For the time being, diplomacy must remain the chief defence of the security of Egypt in the Nile Basin. If he was not yet ready to re-occupy the region, he made it plain that he would oppose its occupation by any other Power. Having already warned off the Italians, he quickly gave the French and the German ambassadors a similar message. The new strategy was now operating.

For all the worldly wisdom which prompted this strategy, it flowed less from hard-headed reckoning than from a change of heart. Behind it lay a sea-change in the Victorian spirit and the official mind. A new age was struggling to be born. To the old men who sat at the head of affairs — as old men usually do — it seemed that imperialism was entering on its greatest epoch. But European expansion was already at odds with the new forces of colonial nationalism which it had goaded into life. The dynasts were beginning to lose their way in history. The shadows were falling over the times and themes they knew best. The end of the European age was in sight. Beset with problems for which their historiography offered no solutions, the old men in the chancelleries came more and more to combat their manifestations rather than to grapple with their causes.

Salisbury had said that Ireland must be held, by persuasion if possible, by Indian methods if need be. Persuasion had failed. Baring had said that collaboration would not work freely in Egypt. Collaboration had been too risky to try. Both in Ireland and on the Nile, the Unionists had turned to Indian solutions. Before long, Milner was to apply them to the Transvaal. What was more, the gradual merging of the Unionist and the Anglo-Indian creeds was helped by new trends of religious and political belief. Changing ideas about the role of the state, the right relationship between races, the likelihood of a new age of violence — all these contributed profoundly to the emergence of the new spirit.

In the event ministers began to fear that Providence and the laws of progress were no longer working on their side. Shocked by nationalist intransigence and Oriental fanaticisms, jostled by new rivals in Africa and new enemies in the Mediterranean, they were losing their nerve. Self-confidence had carried the English to the ends of the earth. Drop by drop it was dribbling out of them.

[1] Salisbury to Baring, 28 Mar. 1890, Private, S.P. 55. (The last sentence is printed in Cecil, *op. cit.*, IV, 327.)

For the Victorians at mid-century the excellence of moral suasion and free partnership had seemed self-evident. But now this belief was being shrunk by fears of subversion and disloyalty. Too often the old aspirations to liberate and improve the world had been ungratefully accepted or surlily refused. Orientals and Africans had been shown the way. They had not followed it. Boers and Irishmen had been given equal rights with Englishmen. They had misused them. Step by step, the easy British optimism modulated into an injured resentment and a harsher outlook. Since the Irish bit the hand that fed them, they should undergo twenty years of resolute government. Since the Indians could not be assimilated, the Ilbert Bill and the Indian Councils Bill were Radical treachery to the *Raj*. Since the King of Burma was a bad risk, he should be deposed. Having failed to find willing partners by policy, the Victorians condemned them to be involuntary subjects.

Hence they were driven into abandoning creative policy and replacing it by cold administration and control. Prestige became all important to them. So too did insurance. Policy grew more and more committed to the warding off of hypothetical dangers by the advancing of frontiers. When Salisbury put his Nile strategy into practice, the defensive psychology which kept watch over northern India had been transplanted into Africa. The frontiers of fear were on the move.

And so the Prime Minister at the end of the Eighteen eighties had decided upon an enlarged Egyptian policy. Not that there was any popular demand for it. It had emerged from the subjective calculations of national interest made by the small group which still decided such matters. To them supremacy in Egypt was becoming crucial, as the balance in Europe and the Mediterranean shifted. In Salisbury's mind, the pivot of the British position in the Mediterranean, and therefore in the world, was moving from Constantinople and the Straits to Cairo and the Canal, from south-eastern Europe and Asia Minor to the Nile Valley and north-east Africa. The Nile Valley strategy was something of an anomaly among the traditional concepts of the national interest handed down from Pitt, Canning, and Palmerston to Salisbury. He became the first Victorian statesman to discover a vital interest in the middle of tropical Africa, but if he was the first, he was not the last, to do so. The decisions of the winter of 1889 to 1890 set the priorities of British policy for the remainder of the Partition, and the Nile Valley headed the list. Salisbury stamped his new design upon tropical Africa, but it was a new design for an old purpose. Hitherto Britain had given way to her rivals in both east and west Africa, in order to protect Egypt. Henceforward, she could yield only on the west, for the Nile Valley and its approaches from the east coast were now considered vital to Egypt. The Mediterranean and Indian interest, like a driving wheel in some vast machine, was now engaging the lesser wheels of eastern-central Africa and connecting them one by one to its own workings. At the turn of Salisbury's strategy, these once remote and petty interests in the Sudan, Uganda and the northern hinterlands of Zanzibar were changing into safeguards of Britain's world power.

CHAPTER X

Salisbury's Watch on the Nile, 1890

Once he had revised his attitude to the Egyptian problem, Salisbury was driven to revise his assessment of east African questions also. In 1885 he had made no bones about yielding German claims in east Africa to win Bismarck's support in Turkey and Egypt. But by the end of the decade, with the Mahdi in possession of the Sudan, the easiest approach to Uganda and the headwaters of the Nile was from the east coast; and German agents seemed likely to get to Lake Victoria Nyanza first. In carrying out his Egyptian strategy therefore, Salisbury's first priority became to block the Germans in east Africa, so as to exclude them from Uganda and the Upper Nile. Not that the Prime Minister had been converted to the traditional Foreign Office view. The trading prospects of the east African hinterlands and the Lakes left him cold. Neither did his new concern with the region derive from the heady talk of Cape to Cairo or of Niger to Nile. The third Marquess of Salisbury was not an enthusiast. But the country was falling into place inside his Egyptian strategy.

By 1889 the Germans were making better speed inland than Mackinnon's ramshackle East Africa Company, while Carl Peters had pushed inland from Witu with a pocket full of treaty forms.[1] As early as April the Foreign Office was perturbed by the German interest in the interior.[2] But the Foreign Secretary was not. Times had changed, and now when the Russians had floated a loan in Paris, Bismarck needed his good will as much as Britain needed that of Germany. Both Powers had much to gain by collaboration. In January 1889 the Chancellor had offered the British an alliance, and although Salisbury would not push the connection as far as a formal tie, it suited both parties to draw it closer by outward and visible acts of solidarity.[3] In Bismarck's eyes, east

[1] For the development of the Scramble locally in east Africa *vide* Perham, *op. cit.*, cap. X; for the aims of Peters, *vide* C. Peters, *New Light on Dark Africa* (English translation, 1891), 399.

[2] M. P. Hornik, *Der Kampf der Grossmächte um den Oberlauf des Nil*, (Vienna, 1951), 85.

[3] German ambassador in London to Herbert Bismarck, 12 Dec. 1888, L. Israel, *England und der Orientalische Dreibund* (Stuttgart, 1937), 25; same to Prince Bismarck, 16 Jan. 1889, *Grosse Politik*, IV, no. 944.

Africa was admirably suited to become the sacrificial ram on the altar of friendship, and in March his son was dropping heavy hints about a settlement there.[1] In July came a reminder, when Herbert Bismarck told a British emissary that he

> '. . . was very sick and tired of Zanzibar complications. He believed that the commercial value of East African enterprise was altogether fictitious....' Salisbury's agent gathered that '. . . he would be ready to go very far to meet any propositions . . . that would result in a final solution of East African difficulties.'[2]

So it would have been easy enough for Salisbury to go to market. Yet he did not stir. News came that the Baganda Christians were eager for European help,[3] rumour said that Peters would certainly be the first to reach them and to win the obvious reward of a treaty. Moreover, Bismarck in October set up a protectorate over the line of coast north of the British sphere — an ominous move, if the hinterland doctrine should ever be applied to it.[4] Salisbury responded to none of these challenges. And then suddenly on 22 December he suggested to the Germans that some of their colonial differences 'especially Zanzibar', should be taken to arbitration.[5] No response could have been more pedestrian; yet it was the genesis of the great treaties of 1890 which were to shape the political map of eastern, western and central Africa. Again, no response could have been more cautious. By the end of 1889 Salisbury was clear that the whole of the Nile Valley must be reserved, yet December's proposals breathed no word about Uganda. But by raising the Zanzibar issue, the Prime Minister had found a way of probing German intentions and measuring the scope of German concessions in east Africa. What he was after was a large-scale African agreement, which would launch the new strategy of defending the Valley of the Nile.[6]

There were other matters to be cleared up as well. On the west coast

[1] Memo. by Currie, 27 Mar. 1889 on a conversation with Herbert Bismarck, S.P. (Currie).

[2] Euan Smith to Salisbury, 19 July, 1889 (S.P. 79).

[3] Mackay to Mackinnon, 2 Sept. 1889, encl. in Mackinnon to Salisbury, 23 Nov. 1889, S.P. (Mackinnon). For the situation in Buganda *vide* J. M. Gray, *Uganda Journal*, Mar. 1950, 23–49; *A. M. Mackay by his Sister* (1892), 341–442.

[4] But on the same day the German Company at Witu hinted to IBEAC that it was willing to be bought out, (P. L. McDermott, *British East Africa or IBEA*, (2nd ed., 1895), 46).

[5] German ambassador in London to Bismarck, 22 Dec. 1889, *Grosse Politik*, VIII, no. 1674.

[6] This is shown by a note of Anderson's. Referring to a German protest against British claims to the northern mainland possessions of Zanzibar, he wrote that '. . . if a general settlement were arrived at on the basis discussed with Count Hatzfeldt this question would be included in it'. (Memo. by Anderson, 15 Jan. 1890, F.O. 84/2030.)

the boundary between the Gold Coast and Togoland needed adjustment and the German complaints against Goldie's monopoly needed attention. These were trivial affairs, but further to the south a larger issue was looming up. Throughout 1889 Salisbury had been striving to clear a path for a new wave of British colonisation from southern Africa, where private enterprise was showing a creative energy and initiative entirely lacking in its east African counterpart.[1] Rhodes' ambitions in Zambesia collided repeatedly with those of the Portuguese, and if the latter were to be shouldered aside in the interest of the British South Africa Company, Salisbury had to make sure of German acquiescence.

But throughout it was the question of Uganda which dominated the negotiations. With Bismarck tottering towards his fall on 20 March, 1890, Berlin had more urgent things to think about than the partition of Africa, and Salisbury now had strong reasons for believing that the new government would give him what he wanted.[2] So at last he could come into the open. On 29 April, when the discussions were resumed, he served formal notice on the Germans and the French that he intended to reserve Egypt's claims to the Upper Nile,[3] while Anderson declared that the German protectorate over the Zanzibar territories on the northern mainland was 'the chief stumbling block'.[4] Early in May Salisbury made his position still clearer. The German ambassador asked for a standstill agreement, but Salisbury told him that:

> 'Africa was a very large place; we had interests in every part of it; the negociations [*sic*] at Berlin might take a long time; and that we could not undertake to maintain the *status quo* throughout the continent until those negociations were concluded. . . . as far as I could see upon the map, Uganda was within the English and not the German hinterland. . . .'[5]

In the event he won his point with surprising ease. After three days of talks between the experts, the Germans agreed in principle to renounce Uganda,[6] and Salisbury now took personal charge of the negotiations and added to the agenda the question of the disputed

[1] *vide supra*, 225–9.

[2] 'I suspect that the German Government are even more anxious than we are to get all the African questions in dispute between us definitely settled. It would be a feather in the cap of the new Government, while failure would be ascribed to the absence of the master directing mind of Prince Bismarck.' (Malet to Salisbury, Private, 19 Apr. 1890, S.P. 63.)

[3] French ambassador in London to Ribot, 29 Apr. 1890, *D.D.F.*, VIII, no. 49; German ambassador in London to Caprivi, 29 Apr. 1890, *Grosse Politik*, VIII, no. 1779. Salisbury added to the Germans that he wanted to 'recover the lost Egyptian provinces', but that Parliament would not pay.

[4] German ambassador in London to Caprivi, 30 Apr. 1890, *ibid*, no. 1675.

[5] Salisbury to Malet, no. 140, Africa, 5 May 1890, F.O. 84/2030.

[6] Anderson to Malet, no. 4, 9 May 1890, encl. in Malet to Salisbury, no. 53, Africa, 9 May 1890, F.O. 84/2031.

boundaries in central Africa. On 13 May in the abrupt and unofficial way so characteristic of his diplomacy, the Prime Minister flung at the German ambassador what amounted to a matured plan for a complete settlement. Germany was to give up her protectorate over the east African coast between Witu and Kismayu; Britain was to get enough territory west of Lake Victoria Nyanza and north-west of Lake Nyasa to connect up the all red route which Rhodes desired so much; she was in addition to get Zanzibar itself; and the island of Heligoland was to go to Germany.[1] Here was partition with a vengeance.

From the British side it was all take and no give. Heligoland was worth a good deal to the Germans, but not as much as this. Marschall, the new Foreign Minister, was adamant against the all red route, and threatened to hang on to the northern protectorate, unless the project was dropped.[2] Salisbury had to choose, and the choice he made shows clearly where his priorities lay. Security in Uganda called for turning the Germans out of their northern protectorate; they would go, only if he gave ground around Lake Victoria or Lake Nyasa, which would shatter Rhodes' Cape to Cairo dream. Salisbury did not hesitate. The Nile Valley was a tangible interest; the Cape to Cairo route was not. Salisbury did not mix sentiment with diplomacy.

He resolved to give up the route. Either Rhodes or Mackinnon must make the sacrifice, and once more Salisbury was not slow to decide whom it should be. The Germans were willing to leave Britain with the Stevenson Road between Nyasaland and Lake Tanganyika, if Mackinnon could be halted as far to the north as 1° S. This was good enough for the Prime Minister. He told the Cabinet that:

> 'The British *South* Africa Company is a much more reasonable body than their Eastern colleague, and as far as we have had communication with them, they are quite willing to accept this solution of the dispute. . . . That the Germans will give way . . . and allow themselves to be shut out almost entirely from the Congo State is, I think, most improbable. The only alternative, if Sir William Mackinnon's objections are upheld, is that no arrangement at all will be arrived at. . . . To throw up these negotiations now, and come to no result, is a step into the unknown.'[3]

The German Government approved the agreement on 6 June,[4] and four days later the Cabinet did the same.[5] All that remained was for

[1] German ambassador in London to Marschall, 14 May 1890, *Grosse Politik*, VIII, no. 1676.

[2] Marschall to German ambassador in London, 17 May 1890; *ibid.*, no. 1677.

[3] Cabinet Memo. by Salisbury, 2 Jun. 1890, S.P. (Miscellaneous).

[4] Marschall to German ambassador in London, 6 Jun. 1890, *Grosse Politik*, VIII, no. 1687.

[5] Salisbury to Queen Victoria, 10 Jun. 1890, *Q.V.L.*, 3rd ser., I, 613.

the experts to agree on the details, and on 1 July the Anglo-German Agreement was formally concluded.

SALISBURY'S PRIORITIES IN TROPICAL AFRICA

The Agreement was a milestone towards the coming of the British Empire in east Africa, for Salisbury had successfully reserved the territories which were one day to be known as Uganda and Kenya, as well as gaining a protectorate over Zanzibar.[1] So it had in it the makings of an imperialist advance. But Salisbury had not won the option to all these vast regions because he was suddenly enamoured with Africa for its own sake. The Agreement meant to him no more than a holding operation, planned to keep other Powers out of an area which had become relevant to the new British policy of defending Egypt in depth. The Prime Minister's interest in this region began and ended with its bearing on this problem. Private enterprise had failed to reserve the territory for him; popular dislike of African entanglements blocked any official intervention;[2] so diplomacy had to be brought in to do what Mackinnon could not accomplish and Parliament would not sanction.

It is a tribute to the timing of this diplomacy that Salisbury should have bought out so many of the German claims when they were at the bottom of the market. The Kaiser had just become an Admiral of the Fleet, he was beginning his ruinous interest in *Flottenpolitik*, and the

[1] The text of the Agreement, together with a few dispatches, is in C. 6046, *P.P.* (1890), LI, 15–31. In addition, a northern frontier running between Lakes Nyasa and Tanganyika was acquired for the British South Africa Company; Mackinnon's southern frontier west of Lake Victoria Nyanza was put at 1° S.; and Heligoland was ceded to Germany. There were also a number of agreements about lesser matters. They may be summarised as follows:

(*a*) By Article II the German and British spheres in south-west Africa were delimited. The German frontier went up to the 20th parallel, but a narrow strip (the 'Caprivi Zipfel') was extended to bring German territory up to the Zambesi. Britain kept Walfisch Bay.

(*b*) By Article III the frontiers between Togoland and the Gold Coast were delimited. German territory reached the River Volta, and a neutral zone was set up between 8° and 10° N.

Furthermore, the Germans demanded that the Oil Rivers should not come under the control of the Royal Niger Company. It was unofficially agreed that '. . . as regards the Niger a fresh start will be made'. (Anderson to Malet, no. 14, 21 Jun. 1890, encl. in Malet to Salisbury, no. 77, Africa, 21 Jun. 1890, F.O. 84/2032.) For the significance of this *vide supra*, 186–8.

[2] In April 1890, when the Germans were supposed to be far ahead in the race for Uganda, the leader of the House of Commons had commented: 'I am afraid that this is a bad business, and that Mackinnon is allowing everything to slip away from us, but I do not see that we can do anything. You cannot ask Parliament for money and send a Major Wissman out . . . with troops . . . to hold the country'. (W. H. Smith, minute, 2 Apr. 1890 on Euan Smith to Salisbury, Telegram, 1 Apr. 1890, S.P. 80.)

offer of Heligoland was irresistible to him.[1] It was at his insistence that Marschall and Caprivi closed so quickly with the suggestion, and there was some surprise in Germany at the Kaiser's abrupt betrayal of the colonial enthusiasts.[2] Salisbury had baited his trap, and the trap was sprung.

But while the Germans were thinking of Europe, the British were thinking about the larger world. The safety of the Nile was the crucial interest which Salisbury pursued throughout the negotiation. As he put it himself to the Cabinet:

> 'The effect of this arrangement will be that, except as far as the Congo State is concerned, there will be no European competitor to British influence between the 1st degree of S latitude [running through the middle of Lake Victoria] and the borders of Egypt, along the whole of the country which lies to the south and west of the Italian Protectorate in Abyssinia and Gallaland.'[3]

The Germans had already agreed to this in principle, but Salisbury took the greatest pains to see that there should be no loopholes in the formal definition of the sphere. When Anderson started to draft the agreement formally with Krauel, he insisted that the British sphere must extend from Lake Victoria northwards as far as the 'confines of Egypt', and westwards as far as the 'basin of the Nile'. The Germans objected, but had to give way.[4] But even this was not enough for Salisbury. When the draft came back to London, he personally altered the definition of the western boundary from the 'basin of the Nile' to the 'western watershed of the Nile'.[5] The point was gained, and now Salisbury had sealed off the Nile from the Germans, not only at its headwaters in Uganda, but also throughout its upper courses. Neither from the west through the Bahr el Ghazal, nor from the east through Ethiopia and Zanzibar, could the Germans now threaten the valley.

In return, he let the all-red route go. In any case, to so sceptical and

[1] The idea of ceding Heligoland was not new in May 1890. It had been mooted in 1889, but Salisbury put off any discussion until another time. (Herbert Bismarck to Prince Bismarck, 27 Mar. 1889; same to same, 13 Apr. 1889, *Grosse Politik*, IV, nos. 946, 949.) For the Kaiser's interference *vide* Baron von Eckardstein, *Lebenserinnerungen und Politische Denkwürdigkeiten*, (Leipzig, 1919), I, 309–10; for the Kaiser's own recollections about it, *vide* his *Ereignisse und Gestalten*, (Leipzig, 1922), 46–8.

[2] For example the surprise expressed by Waldersee, the Army Chief of Staff. (*Denkwürdigkeiten des General-Feld-Marschalls Alfred Grafen von Waldersee*, (Stuttgart, 1925), II, 131–2.) The treaty had a more formidable critic as well — *vide* O. von Bismarck, *Gedanken und Erinnerungen*, (Stuttgart, 1922), III, 147–52, but of course this criticism was not published until the end of the First World War.

[3] Draft Dispatch, Salisbury to Malet, no. 223, 14 Jun. 1890, (printed for the use of the Cabinet), F.O. 84/2030.

[4] Anderson to Malet, no. 14, 21 Jun. 1890, encl. in Malet to Salisbury, no. 77, Africa, 21 Jun. 1890, F.O. 84/2032.

[5] Emendations in Salisbury's writing to draft treaty, encl. in above, *ibid.*

precise a mind, it seemed no more than a pipe-dream that came from too much map-reading. Both in public and in private, the Prime Minister's irony flickered over the Cape to Cairo idea. In July 1890, he told the House of Lords that there was:

> '... a very curious idea ... that there is some special advantage in having a stretch of territory extending all the way from Cape Town to the sources of the Nile. Now, this stretch of territory North of Lake Tanganyika could only have been a very narrow one. ... I cannot imagine any trade going in that direction. ... But if you look beyond the merely commercial considerations to those which are of a strategic character, I can imagine no more uncomfortable position than the possession of a narrow strip of territory in the very heart of Africa three months' distance from the coast, which should be separating the forces of a powerful empire like Germany and ... another European Power. Without any advantages of position we should have had all the dangers inseparable from its defence.'[1]

The Cape to Cairo dream had the support of flag-waggers, south African millionaires and their courtiers, together with persons who wrote to the newspapers, but towards such groups Lord Salisbury's sympathies were imperfect.[2] It had the support of Foreign Office experts, but Salisbury had a short way with experts. It was to be supported by his successor, but Salisbury was to Rosebery as London was to Paddington.

Apart from the weakness of Mackinnon's Company, Salisbury had other reasons for making the surrender in the north rather than in the south. The Germans set more store by the northern end of the gap; it was, so Marschall put it, 'the most important part of the boundary of our sphere of influence,'[3] and so it would have taken harder bargaining to satisfy Mackinnon than it took to placate Rhodes. It is true that by holding out, Salisbury might have won both the northern and the southern ends of the gap;[4] but his refusal to do so was as much a tribute

[1] *Hansard*, 3rd series, CCCXLVI, col. 1268.

[2] e.g. his comment on the protest of the Rhodesians against yielding the Caprivi strip in central Africa: 'It is ... over an impracticable country, and leading only into the Portuguese possessions, into which, as far as I know, during the last 300 years there has been no very eager or impetuous torrent of trade. I think that the constant study of maps is apt to disturb men's reasoning powers.' (*ibid.*, col. 1269.)

[3] Marschall to German ambassador in London, 25 May 1890; *Grosse Politik*, VIII, no. 1680.

[4] That the German negotiators would have conceded more than Salisbury in the event saw fit to demand, is suggested by Marschall to German ambassador in London, 31 May 1890, *Grosse Politik*, VIII, no. 1683. But there is other evidence of his moderate approach to the question of the northern end of the gap. When Leopold of the Belgians came to London on 24 May 1890, he signed with I.B.E.A.C. the so-called Mackinnon Treaty. By this arrangement Leopold was to extend his territories towards Lado in the Bahr el Ghazal; and in return he was to give I.B.E.A.C. the sovereign rights over a strip of land some ten miles wide between Lake Albert Edward (within his sphere)

to his sense of proportion as the offer of Heligoland was to his sense of timing. For the Agreement was meant to show that Britain and Germany were on the best of terms, and he valued German friendship at Cairo and Constantinople far too highly to risk it for a trivial advantage in tropical Africa.

Another purpose behind the Agreement was to prevent the squabbles of British and German empire-builders in Africa from prejudicing friendly relations between their two governments. This could never be done so long as Zanzibar in particular remained in dispute and the rivalries of consuls and squadrons led to brawling and back-biting. For six years Zanzibar had lain to Bismarck's hand as a stick to beat the Foreign Office; its *dossier* of recriminations and bad feelings was as formidable as that of Samoa; its Sultan, cowed by ultimatum and blockade, was not even a political expression. When Salisbury and Marschall gave their Solomon's judgement on his mainland possessions, there was much to be said for including his island in the verdict. Friendship would not be complete without it.

But this was not the only consideration which led Salisbury to put Zanzibar into the treaty. The inexperienced Germans did not suffer Sultans gladly; and there was always a danger that in their impatience they would one day sweep up the wreckage of the Sultan's empire and bring the Zanzibar islands under their rule.[1] Salisbury wanted to avoid this if possible. Zanzibar had been under British influence for decades, and the announcement of a foreign protectorate would be badly received at Home. Further, some imperial, and more especially Indian, interests were bound up in it. As a strategic base of second-class importance, and as an Indian trading centre, it served useful purposes. By helping to

as far as the northern head of Lake Tanganyika. (*The Autobiograpgy of Sir Henry Morton Stanley*, (1909), 412, 417–8; MacDermott, *op. cit.*, 316–7.) But when Salisbury allowed German territory to close up with that of Leopold north of Lake Tanganyika, the effect of this concession was cancelled; and in any case it had never received the recognition of the British government. For different interpretations *vide* W. L. Langer, *The Diplomacy of Imperialism*, (2nd ed., New York, 1951), 119; Raphael, *op. cit.*, 301.

[1] Anderson in May 1890 reported from Berlin that Krauel, his German opposite number, was clear that the Sultan must be driven off the mainland. ' "Is it not premature", I observed, "to talk of breaking up the Sultan's dominions?" "So Lord Salisbury said", he replied, "when Count Hatzfeldt mentioned it to him last year; but we think the time has come." He proceeded to say that the vexatious sovereign rights of the Sultan must be swept away from all the German concessions. . . . "And the Sultan will then have to content himself with the island of Zanzibar?" I enquired. . . . "Yes", he said "he will have his island to live in," "And on what terms is he to go?" "Bought out," he answered.' Anderson commented that 'I cannot say that the revelation advances the prospect of a settlement, but it at least forewarns us of the direction which German action may take if the present negotiations should be unsuccessful.' (Anderson to Malet, no. 7, 14 May 1890, encl. in Malet to Salisbury, no. 61, Africa, 15 May 1890, F.O. 84/2031.)

arrange the cession of the coastal strip which had been leased to the Germans,[1] Salisbury was doing little more than acquiescing in the inevitable. But he salvaged Zanzibar itself. It was not the case that by the Anglo-German Agreement he was exchanging Heligoland for Zanzibar, but rather for security in Egypt. In that feast Zanzibar was no more than a *bonne bouche*.

Once the treaty had been made, Salisbury was plagued by his familiar fears that in a wave of faction and irresponsibility the House of Commons might upset the fruits of his diplomacy. The difficulty was Heligoland. There had already been trouble enough with the Queen over the cession of this not very large possession[2], and Salisbury seems to have felt uneasy about its reception in the country. 'Of course', he minuted, 'it is in the present state of Parliament very important that the smallest possible surface shall be offered for obstructive comment';[3] and it seems that the Opposition were approached to make sure that the treaty should not be roughly handled. This was not unduly hard to arrange. Throughout Salisbury's conduct of the Foreign Office from 1887 until 1892, the Liberal leaders were inclined to approve his policy (or at least what they knew of it). There were indictments and awkward questions from Labouchere and the Radicals, but so far as the front benches were concerned, both sides were ready to hang together in the defence of national interests. Gladstone himself was still urging that Egypt should be given up, but many Liberal leaders by this time suspected that such a policy was out of date.[4] Evidently, they approved of the arrangement with Germany, and evidently too, they let this be known before it was debated. Rosebery was reported to be anxious not to press the ministry too hard;[5] and on 4 July the Foreign Under-Secretary could inform his chief that 'the attacks on the Agreement will

[1] In August the Germans paid the Sultan some 4 million marks (£200,000) for the coastal strip between the rivers Umba and Rovuma. In June Anderson reported the difficulties of Marschall about this: 'He will not, or cannot put down a mark of ready money' (S.P. 63, Anderson (through Malet) to Salisbury, Telegram, Private, 24 Jun. 1890). It is interesting to see that other governments besides the British found trouble in raising money for African expansion during the period which is supposed to have been so enthusiastic for empire.

[2] Salisbury to Queen Victoria, 8, 10, 12 Jun. 1890; Queen Victoria to Salisbury, 9, 11, 12 Jun. 1890, *Q.V.L.*, 3rd series, I, 610–15.

[3] Minute by Salisbury, n.d. *circa* 4 Jul. 1890 on the constitutional issues arising from the cession of Heligoland, F.O. 84/2032.

[4] French ambassador in London to Ribot, 20 Jun. 1890, *D.D.F.*, VIII, no. 89.

[5] Same to same, 25 Jun. 1890, *ibid.*, no. 96. The German ambassador in Paris reported that he had recently seen Gladstone, 'who seems to have been informed by Lord Salisbury of his intentions,' and who had declared that he would 'raise no difficulties' about the negotiations. (German ambassador in Paris to Caprivi, 19 Jun. 1890, *Grosse Politik*, VIII, no. 1690.)

be of the guerilla order'.[1] And indeed this was all that happened. Salisbury in the Lords on 10 July expounded his settlement candidly enough, arguing that it would help to guard the Nile Valley.[2] Rosebery then followed with a singularly accommodating speech, announcing that he would put up no open opposition: '. . . For my part, I shall offer no such opposition. . . . I, for one, will never be party to dragging the foreign policy of this country into the arena of Party warfare.'[3] The Bill passed its third reading in the Lords without a division, but in the Commons it was too much to hope for the same unanimity. On 24 and 25 July there was a most confused debate. Members got little help from the Foreign Under-Secretary who tried to placate the critics with hoary generalities about the slave trade.[4] Gladstone followed with a long denunciation of the government for bringing the cession of Heligoland before Parliament at all, since it ought to be a matter for the prerogative; but while regretting the precedent, he would not vote against the bill.[5] This high-flying constitutionalism helped to sidetrack the debate. Goschen held forth on the treaty-making power, Harcourt lectured the House on the historical precedents, Balfour drew a distinction between making treaties and ceding territories.[6] It was left to a few interested back-benchers to bring the debate down to earth, and question the substance of the Agreement. Spokesmen for the south African interest criticised it for extending the frontiers of German South-West Africa. One or two East Africa Company men thanked Salisbury for saving them some of their hinterland.[7] But the grounds of opposition to the Bill were trivial: the South Africans' objection to

[1] Fergusson to Salisbury, 4 Jul. 1890 (wrongly dated 4 June), S.P. (Fergusson).

[2] 'As long as the Sultanate of Witu was in the hands of another Power, there was a possibility of annexations and expeditions to the north of us, which would have cut off British influence and British dominion from the sources of the Nile. . . . I do not, by any means, say that is an advantage of which all the results will appear immediately, for, as we know, the valley of the Nile is occupied by another Power which is not European and which just at present is not very much inclined to make room for us. But the advantage of limiting our rivalry to an Asiatic or African tribe is one which those who are engaged in these enterprises appreciate very highly'. (*Hansard*, 3rd series, CCCXLVI, cols. 1263–4.)

[3] *ibid.*, cols. 1283–4. For the attitude of the Liberal Opposition towards Salisbury's foreign policy, cf. the revealing remark of Acton: 'Rosebery would say: "I come in to pursue the continuity of foreign policy. I did it before with the approval of my colleagues and with some success. The principle has been reaffirmed inasmuch as we have abstained from attack, and the front bench always repressed Bryce; and in some cases we have distinctly declared our acceptance of Salisbury's policy," ' (Acton to West, 29 Jul. 1892, *Private Diaries of . . . Sir Algernon West*, (ed. W. G. Hutchinson), (1922), 41.

[4] *Hansard*, 3rd ser., CCCXLVII, cols. 744–52.

[5] *ibid.*, cols. 753–69. [6] *ibid.*, cols. 769–89.

[7] Supporters of South African interests: Baden-Powell (*ibid.*, cols. 792–3), Baumann (cols. 798–800), Philipps (cols. 802–5), Clark (cols. 807–9), Beckett (cols. 813–4), Spokesmen for I.B.E.A.C.: Kennaway (col. 806), Pelly (cols. 816–7).

giving up anything, the sentimental protests against yielding Heligoland, the constitutional qualms of a few lawyers at whittling down the power of the crown, and the Little Englanders' anger over extensions in Africa.[1] Finally, only 61 members voted against the Agreement. Leaderless, abandoned by the Liberal front bench, united by no common principle, the resistance had been no more than the *guerilla* that Fergusson had expected.

It had been a singular debate[2] in many ways. The leaders on both sides had resolutely kept off the point; and of the back-benchers who had spoken, only one had glimpsed the meaning behind the Agreement.[3] Salisbury in the Lords had frankly suggested its bearing on the defence of the Nile, but this found little echo in the Commons. Perhaps the party leaders had agreed beforehand not to relate the Agreement to the crucial issue of Egypt, lest this should lead to awkward publicity in France and awkward criticism from the rank and file of the Liberal Party.

Salisbury had laid claim to the entire valley of the Nile, yet this was hardly mentioned. He had broken the Cape to Cairo dream, but there was hardly a protest; and he had handed over British mission stations north of Lake Nyasa to Germany, yet the humanitarians[4] made but a feeble outcry in the Commons. There were many reasons for the general acquiescence. The Agreement by and large satisfied all the more powerful African interests. Public opinion in the broadest sense was still indifferent to the issues of tropical Africa. Above all the passing of the Agreement showed the way in which Britain's aristocratic leaders could still shape foreign policy according to their own notions of the national interest and sidestep the restrictions of popular control.

THE ANGLO-FRENCH WEST AFRICAN AGREEMENT OF 1890–1891

The Anglo-German Agreement of 1890 was a long step forward in the British strategy for the Nile Valley; and Salisbury now turned to the French. In 1884, Dilke and the Foreign Office had urged that Britain should pursue her interests in east Africa at the expense of

[1] Radical Little Englanders: Labouchere, *ibid.*, (cols. 933–42), Storey (cols. 955–61).

[2] The Bill was also considered in committee and on third reading, but it was mainly its implications for Heligoland that were considered; *ibid.*, cols. 1078–1108.

[3] Sir Richard Temple, the former Indian administrator, defended the Agreement on the ground that it would serve British interests in the Valley of the Nile, *ibid.*, cols. 930–1.

[4] Hanna, *op. cit.*, 165; W. P. Livingstone, *Laws of Livingstonia*, (1921), 252.

those in the west coast, since east Africa was of more value to India.[1] Salisbury from 1889 onward put this principle into effect.

A second occasion for doing so arose from his own inadvertence. It was he who in consultation with the German ambassador had taken all the critical steps in the negotiation, leaving to his advisors only the task of drawing the exact lines on the maps. This was his habit in matters of importance; and it gave to that secretive and brooding mind full control over the main lines of British policy in Africa. But the method had its drawbacks. Salisbury could be careless over details, and his dislike for protocol extended into a disregard for procedure.[2] In 1890 he seems to have forgotten that France had been party to the 1862 treaty regulating the status of Zanzibar, and so she had a right to be consulted about the changes agreed upon by Britain and Germany. The Anglo-German arrangement was badly received in Paris, where the deduction was drawn that it symbolised a further understanding over Egypt.[3] The French raised the issue with Salisbury on 21 June; he explained it by saying that for the last three years the British and the Germans had fallen into the habit of squeezing the ruler of Zanzibar as though he were a rubber doll, but this blunt admission did not turn away wrath, and the French government demanded compensation.[4]

And so another negotiation now followed the Anglo German Agreement. Behind this too loomed the Egyptian question and the struggle for safety in the Mediterranean. In April the Sultan of Turkey had approached the British with yet another project for evacuation, and in this he had French and Russian support. As usual it was cut off sharply by Salisbury, but at the beginning of June the Turks tried again.[5] To add to Salisbury's difficulties that summer, there were rumours that the Russians were planning to rush the Straits.[6] Consequently, both Salisbury and Ribot, the French Foreign Minister, approached their Zanzibar negotiations with Egypt uppermost in mind. To Ribot the main point of the Anglo-German understanding seemed to lie in the renewed support that Salisbury could now expect from Berlin in things Egyptian; and the compensation he wanted was in Tunis, where the

[1] *vide supra*, 190, 202.

[2] French ambassador in London to Ribot, 26 Jul. 1890, *D.D.F.*, VIII, no. 132.

[3] German ambassador in Paris to Caprivi, 19 Jun. 1890; *Grosse Politik*, VIII, no. 1690; French ambassador in London to Ribot, 20 Jun. 1890; *D.D.F.*, VIII, no. 88.

[4] French ambassador in London to Ribot, 21 Jun. 1890; Ribot to French ambassador in London, 24 Jun. 1890; *D.D.F.*, VIII, nos. 91, 93.

[5] Ribot to French ambassador in Constantinople, 1 Apr. 1890; French ambassador in London to Ribot, 9 May 1890; Ribot to French ambassador in Saint Petersburg, 31 May 1890; no. 75, French ambassador in Constantinople to Ribot, 4 Jun. 1890; *ibid.*, nos. 20, 58, 72, 75.

[6] Marder, *op. cit.*, 152–6.

consolidation of French power would do something to restore the Mediterranean balance.[1] To Salisbury, on the other hand, it was imperative that the French should be conciliated as far as possible, if the combined Franco-Russian pressure over Egypt was to be slackened. But the price they were asking was exactly the price he could not pay. The Italian government refused to countenance any French gains in Tunisia, and in this Crispi had the backing of the Germans.[2] Salisbury was in a dilemma. He needed to placate France so as to ease the Franco-Russian pressure against Egypt, but he could not do so at the expense of straining his anti-Russian arrangement in the Mediterranean. There was only one way of breaking the deadlock. France would have to be compensated elsewhere, and so he turned to west Africa. Salisbury decided to offer up some more of this region in the hope of improving the position in the Mediterranean.

The French demands were made known on 1 July. They wanted recognition of their special position in Tunisia,[3] of their protectorate over Madagascar, and a delimitation of their spheres along the Niger and in west Africa generally.[4] It was reasonably clear already that they would not get what they wanted in Tunisia, and their diplomats were not inclined to insist. But the pressures of French domestic politics forced them to do so. Both Right and Left in the Chamber demanded that Tunis should be annexed, and so this remained as a stumbling block.[5] Salisbury might have given way; but he would probably have called for French concessions in Egypt, and these terms were too high for the French government.[6] Nothing could be done here, that was evident; and so Salisbury and the French ambassador could hope to agree about west Africa alone. It had already been settled that France should have the hinterland behind Algeria as far as the northern boundary of the sphere ruled by the Royal Niger Company and extending to the western side of Lake Chad.[7] Once the chance of settling the Tunisian dispute had vanished, Salisbury had to make generous

[1] Ribot to French ambassador in London, 25 Jun. 1890; *D.D.F.*, VIII, no. 95.

[2] *Grosse Politik*, VIII, p. 27, note; *Memoirs of Francesco Crispi*, (English translation), 1914, III, 20; Palamenghi-Crispi, *L'Italia Coloniale e Francesco Crispi*, (Milan, 1928), 30.

[3] More precisely, their demand was that the perpetual treaty between Britain and the Bey of Tunis signed in 1875 should now be brought to an end in 1896 (when the Italo-Tunisian treaty was to end); or earlier, if France reached agreement with the Italians in the meantime.

[4] French ambassador in London to Ribot, 1 Jul. 1890; *D.D.F.*, VIII, no. 101.

[5] German ambassador in Paris to Caprivi, 12 Jul. 1890; *Grosse Politik*, VIII, no. 1691; *D.D.F.*, VIII, p. 154 note.

[6] French ambassador in London to Ribot, 22 Jul. 1890; *ibid.*, no. 127.

[7] *idem.*

additions to this hinterland. At first the British had contemplated a French sphere that would come as far south as Timbuktu; they ended by conceding a French boundary as far as Say.[1] The result was that the French obtained the whole of the Upper Niger, while Goldie's frontier was pinned back to Sokoto.

The Declarations were signed on 5 August, 1890. France acquiesced in the British Protectorate over Zanzibar and Pemba; in return she was given a free hand in Madagascar and the huge territories of the central and western Sudan.[2] Yet it is plain that this gigantic concession did not worry Salisbury in the least. Expounding the agreement in the Lords on 11 August, he mocked at the scramblers for Africa of whom he was not one:

> 'I will not dwell upon the respective advantages of places which are utterly unknown not only to your Lordships, but to the rest of the white human race. . . . Anyone who looks at the map and merely measures the degrees will perhaps be of opinion that France has laid claim to a very considerable stretch of country. But it is necessary to judge land not merely by its extent but also by its value. This land is what agriculturists would call "very light land"; that is to say, it is the desert of Sahara.'[3]

To Salisbury a lessening of Anglo-French tension in the Mediterranean was cheap at such a price.

After France, Italy. Salisbury could write at the end of August that 'we are negociating [*sic*] on these African matters with somewhat greater ease now that we have agreed with France & Germany'.[4] The next step was to dispose of the Italian threat to the Nile. It was decided that Baring should meet Crispi in Naples at the end of September, so as to fix the limits of the spheres of influence around the Red Sea and inwards towards the Sudan. Freed from his other diplomatic struggles, Salisbury could now take a high line in these talks, and this was shown in his instructions to Baring.

> 'I am now writing to say one word about the negotiations. That we should insist on the command of all affluents of the Nile, so far as Egypt formerly possessed them, is agreed. . . . we have no such well defined and imperative interests to safeguard on the Red Sea slope. . . . There is only one point that interests me in that direction — namely that you should not sanction the tribal theory of dominion. . . . we shall have to oppose it vigorously to

[1] French ambassador in London to Ribot, 26 Jul. 1890; same to same, 1 Aug. 1890; *D.D.F.*, VIII, nos. 132, 136.

[2] C. 6130 *P.P.*, 1890, LXXXI; Hertslet, *op. cit.*, II, 738–9.

[3] *Hansard*, 3rd series, CCCXLVIII, cols. 458–9.

[4] Salisbury to Baring, Private, 31 Aug. 1890; S.P. 55.

the South West of Abyssinia. . . . It is possible that you may not persuade the Italians to accept this principle; or to keep their hands off the affluents of the Nile. In that case, we must be content to let the negotiations be adjourned. . . . I do not think England will lose by delay.'[1]

The talks were a failure. Crispi refused 'to give up *a priori* possession of Kassala'; and although the other matters were agreed, Baring would not give way on this.[2] Indeed Salisbury explicitly ordered him not to do so,[3] and the negotiations were broken off on 10 October. For the time being, the Italian threat remained, and Salisbury had to reconcile himself to waiting until the intransigent Crispi should fall. There was not long to wait. In February 1891 Crispi was out of office, and in March and April his successor made two agreements with the British which gave Salisbury the much desired surrender of Italian claims to the valley of the Nile.[4]

The Purposes of Salisbury's Diplomacy

The diplomacy of Salisbury in 1890 finally determined the pattern of British policy towards the division of Africa. In the Anglo-German agreement he edged his most immediate rival out of the Nile Valley. In the Anglo-French agreement he set the seal on the strategy of buying off French threats to Egypt and the Mediterranean by agreeing to a huge French empire in the western Sudan. In his negotiations with the Italians he showed once more that Britain was determined to keep all comers out of the eastern Sudan and the Nile Valley. Baring had pressed hard for this, urging that the British position in Egypt was perilous without it. The work of 1890 was to keep other Powers off the Nile. Until Egypt was ready to re-occupy the Valley, the present rulers of the Sudan had their uses. '. . . The Dervishes are rendering us a service in keeping Italy out', as Salisbury put it. He went on:

'If the Dervishes have occupied the valley of the Nile, they do not pledge the future in any way. Whenever you have money enough to go to Khartoum, the resources of civilisation will be adequate to the subjugation of

[1] Salisbury to Baring, Private, 31 Aug. 1890, S.P. 55; partly printed in Cecil, *op. cit.*, IV, 330–31.

[2] F. Crispi, *La Prima Guerra d'Africa*, (ed. T. Palamenghi-Crispi), (Milan, 1939), 233, 235. [3] *ibid.*, 237–8.

[4] By the agreements of 24 Mar. and 15 Apr. 1891, the Italian sphere of influence was at last defined. Salisbury went to great lengths to conciliate the Italians, agreeing to a western frontier that ran as far west as 35° E. longitude. They were empowered to occupy Kassala, if the military situation demanded it, but the Egyptian government reserved the right to take it over when they were ready to do so. The Italians undertook not to construct any irrigation works near-by, which might interfere with the flow of the Nile. (Hertslet, *op. cit.*, III, 948–50.)

the country. If you leave them for the present where they are they can destroy nothing, for there is nothing to destroy: they cannot erect any domination which shall make the conquest of them a formidable task, for they have, practically speaking, neither cannon nor machine-guns, nor even the ammunition for ordinary rifles. Surely, if you are *not* ready to go to Khartoum, this people were created for the purpose of keeping the bed warm for you till you can occupy it.'[1]

The strategy is summed up by the homely image. Baring would take over the Sudan when he was ready; until that time came, it was the task of diplomacy to keep it clear of rivals. In a similar way, the role of the Foreign Office in central Africa was to peg out the claims and stand watch until the Chartered Company was ready to consolidate the ground. In both these cases, Salisbury's diplomacy achieved its objectives, and in so doing set the course for the remainder of the partition.

But although the results of the diplomatic bargaining of 1890 were crucial for the future of British Africa, this was not because the balance of power determined the course of events. Of course it is true that the Anglo-German *rapprochement* of 1889 helped in the making of the African agreement of 1890; it is true again that Salisbury wanted to avoid the consequences in Europe and in Egypt of a series of diputes up and down east Africa;[2] and it is likely that fear of a joint Franco-Russian policy towards the problems of the Mediterranean made him anxious to give the French their head in west Africa. In a formal sense these were the limiting conditions of the problem. But they were not the reasons why the problem arose. It grew out of the local situations in Africa itself.

The focal points of British interest in Africa lay in Egypt and at the Cape. They were both essential points on Britain's routes to the eastern half of her empire. Long before the scramble for Africa it had been a cardinal element in policy that both these points must be under British influence, no matter what form that might take. But hegemony and the process of economic growth had sharply altered the political structure of both Egypt and Southern Africa; both had been driven into conditions of crisis, which in their different ways imperilled the British position. In Egypt the danger that the compliant native authority would collapse once more, in South Africa the fear that the irreconcilables of the Transvaal would come to dominate the British colonies — these were risks too great to run, and in each case British policy had

[1] Salisbury to Baring, Private, 21 Nov. 1890, S.P. 55.

[2] O. Becker, *Das französisch-russische Bündnis*, Berlin, 1925, 197–8; Salisbury to Queen Victoria, 10 Jun. 1890; *Q.V.L.*, 3rd ser., I, 613–4.

striven to restore their position. In Egypt this meant invasion and a 'temporary' military occupation. But by the end of the Eighteen eighties, it seemed certain that Egypt would have to be occupied for a long time to come. This new axiom of policy led Baring in Cairo to urge that Foreign Powers should be excluded from the whole of the Nile Valley. In 1890 British diplomacy used the balance in Europe so as to make it possible; but it was the development of the crisis in Egypt which made it necessary. In similar fashion the winning of Rhodesia had become one of the aims of diplomacy, because of its effect on the maturing crisis in south Africa, for it was at once a method of encircling the Republic and of righting the balance in the imperial favour.

Salisbury's African diplomacy in 1890 contended with crises in both these regions of supreme British interest. In the one case the valley of the Nile, in the other the lands of Zambesia had to be safeguarded, if the British control over Egypt and South Africa was to stay steady. If the Nile was lost, then the British might be turned out of Egypt, the native authority would collapse, and the Suez Canal would be in danger; if Rhodes' drive to the north failed, then the Transvaal might eventually break the imperial connection with south Africa, and the long route to the East would be in jeopardy. It was Salisbury's diplomatic task to ward off these dangers. His part in the great game was to control the timing of the measures of precaution. It was for him to watch the tremblings of the balance in Europe, and to seize the right moment for winning consent to his advances in Africa. To this extent, then, the balance of power in Europe affected British African policy in 1890, the year of decision; no less but no more.

CHAPTER XI

Uganda, the Rout of Liberalism

The Failure of the East Africa Company

Diplomats might make their elegant dispositions to reserve the headwaters of the Nile; but working politicians had rougher work to hold them when there was little popular interest in doing so. Salisbury had known from the beginning that there was no commercial drive behind the Chartered Company. Apart from Mackinnon himself, its directors were for the most part either humanitarians or Old African Hands, and although such men usually adorned imperial enterprises, there was too much adornment and too little business about the Imperial British East Africa Company. The race for Uganda had begun by breaking Mackinnon's nerve; the effort to hold it broke his company's credit.

Already in 1890 he was despondent; 'I feel so disheartened by the apparent lukewarmness of the support we receive from H[er] M[ajesty]'s Government . . . that I feel great difficulty as to our plans for the future', he wrote to the Prime Minister when asking for an interview. It was refused.[1] The Anglo-German agreement did not mend matters, for the investor was not impressed by the prospects of East Africa or the company. 'I am afraid', so Salisbury observed later in the year, 'they have not capital for their actual work.'[2]

They looked to government for help, only to find that the voter cared no more about their fate than the businessman, and that Salisbury feared Parliament even more than he wanted Uganda. The company still paid rent to the Sultan of Zanzibar for the mainland concession he had leased to them, and one way to lighten Mackinnon's burdens would have been to lower the Sultan's rent. But the landlord thought poorly of this plan. '. . . The Sultan will never commute', reported the Consul-General at Zanzibar, 'unless Her Majesty's Government makes

[1] Mackinnon to Salisbury, 8 Apr. 1890, and endorsement, S.P. (Mackinnon).
[2] Salisbury to Euan Smith, Private, 7 Nov. 1890, S.P. 80.

him, and if he did the Sultanate would collapse. . . .'[1] Salisbury did not make him. There was no point in saving one bankrupt at the expense of another.

The Prime Minister turned instead to another forlorn hope — the project of a Uganda railway. It was not practical politics to make the company a direct grant-in-aid, for as he well knew, 'The H[ouse] of C[ommons] would scoff at a subsidy.'[2] But there was a faint chance that Parliament might sanction a railway guarantee, and in any case he had need of the line. If Britain was to tighten her hold on Uganda and the headwaters of the Nile, there would have to be a railway between Mombasa and Lake Victoria.[3] This railway was not only a strategic necessity. It would also help Mackinnon financially, for a guarantee would improve his company's credit and would be a subsidy in disguise.[4] The Foreign Office admitted that the line could not pay its way for some years;[5] but none the less Salisbury hoped that it would appeal to Parliament and the investor as a philanthropic measure against the slave trade.[6] It mattered little that informed men knew that slave-trading in these regions was on the wane. The Foreign Office habitually explained its African moves to the ordinary voter as measures against the slave trade, for this was all he knew or cared about tropical Africa. Philanthropy was the first resort of diplomacy during the Scramble. And so the Foreign Office proposed a guarantee for a Uganda railway.

The Treasury agreed, provided that Parliament should approve, but their Lordships' comments were very dry. They noted that the railway would save them £100,000 a year, by doing away with the need for the five cruisers used to blockade the Arab slavers of the east coast. 'The public end of suppressing the Slave Trade,' it was observed severely, '. . . alone justifies Her Majesty's Government in taking a direct part in the enterprise.'[7]

In May 1891, the Prime Minister publicly declared his deep interest in this railway 'from a purely Foreign Office point of view', and he stressed the part it would play in civilising Africa.[8] But the project ran into difficulties in the Commons and in the Cabinet. Goschen, the Chancellor of the Exchequer, protested against burdening the taxpayer

[1] Euan Smith to Salisbury, Private, 2 Feb. 1891, S.P. 80.
[2] Salisbury, Minute, 1 Dec. 1890, quoted in Low, *op. cit.*, 258.
[3] Salisbury, *Hansard*, 4th ser., V, cols. 828–9.
[4] Mackinnon himself had asked for a railway subsidy. (Mackinnon to Salisbury, 17 Dec. 1890, quoted in Low, *op. cit.*, 258.)
[5] Foreign Office to Treasury, 20 Dec. 1890, *C.* 6560, P.P. [1892] LVI, 587–8.
[6] Same to same, 9 Feb. 1891, F.O. Print 6124, p. 94.
[7] Treasury to Foreign Office, 10 Feb. 1891, F.O. Print 6124, 99.
[8] Cecil, *op. cit.*, IV, 311.

with the cost of a railway through so unproductive a region.[1] 'There is not much to be done in the way of trade,' the Prime Minister admitted, 'though there is a great work of civilisation. . . . If I had my way and could command the assent of the House of Commons. . . .'[2]—but he could not. The idea of developing tropical Africa by state enterprise was altogether too heretical and unpopular until the beginning of the new century. The danger that the Germans might take Uganda had been removed. The French danger was still to come, and a general election was near. All that the Prime Minister could do was to get Cabinet agreement to a vote of £20,000 for a preliminary survey of the Uganda line. 'All decision upon its results' was put off 'to a future time'.[3]

It was now plain that the Uganda Railway Bill — if there ever was one — would be too late to save the Chartered Company.[4] The directors, unable to raise more money, decided on 16 July, 1891, to withdraw their agents from Buganda. The Church Missionary Society and the Anti-Slavery Society tried to agitate public opinion in favour of a railway subsidy and other aid for the company.[5] They protested that its withdrawal would destroy their religious work in Buganda, it would be a step backwards for Africa. Bishop Tucker refused to leave Buganda, and fatuously talked of inviting German protection.[6] But the government could not afford to be moved. In March 1892 it managed to get the tiny railway survey vote through the Commons; but Liberal opposition was so strong that there was clearly no hope of getting the subsidy itself.[7]

By the end of 1891 the missionaries and their friends had managed to scrape together some £40,000 to stave off the evacuation, but this merely enabled Mackinnon to postpone the inevitable for a few months more.[8] The company was plainly on the rocks. By 1892 its servants were spending at the rate of £80,000 a year, while their income was no more than £35,000.[9] They had laid out almost half a million pounds —

[1] Goschen refused to guarantee capital for a bankrupt company's railway. He warned: '. . . If we are not extremely careful . . . three administrations . . . may be forced upon us, Uganda, Johnston's empire [in Nyasa] and Mashonaland.' (Goschen to Salisbury, 19 Sept. 1891, S.P. (Goschen).)

[2] Salisbury to Goschen, 20 Sept. 1891, Cecil, *op. cit.*, 314.

[3] Salisbury to Goschen, 29 Sept. 1891, *ibid.*, 314.

[4] Mackinnon to Salisbury, Private, 3 Jul. 1891, S.P. (Mackinnon).

[5] C.M.S. to Salisbury, 14 Oct. 1891, and Anti-Slavery Society to Salisbury, 2 Oct. 1891, F.O. Print, 6338, pp. 31–2. cf. Low, *op. cit.*, 260–8.

[6] Portal to Salisbury, 18 Jun. 1892, *ibid.*, 165.

[7] The Survey Vote was passed by 211–23, *Hansard*, 4th ser., I, col. 1836 *et seq.*

[8] IBEAC to Foreign Office, 11 Nov. 1891, F.O. Print, 6338, p. 122.

[9] Portal to Salisbury, 3 Feb. 1892, S.P. 80.

their entire capital;[1] they had failed with the east African trade, and it remained stagnant and small.[2] The chartered company was clearly finished as an instrument of the Nile Valley doctrine, and the Foreign Office was forced to look for other methods of holding Uganda. There seemed to be only two possibilities: either to pay the Kabaka Mwanga a subsidy in the hope of binding him to the British interest; or to install the Sultan of Zanzibar as a caretaker. Salisbury and his officials were once again clutching at straws, and when his Ministry resigned on 10 August, 1892, it left the future of Uganda unsettled. 'The financial views of the next House of Commons will largely affect the course of Her Majesty's Govt., and as it is not yet elected', Salisbury told Portal at Zanzibar, 'we cannot predict its action.'[3] Fear of Parliament and public opinion had strangled all his schemes for occupying the Nile headwaters; and he implied as much when he gave Mackinnon the hint in July 1892 to whip up a public campaign for staying in Uganda.[4]

Salisbury's government plainly perceived no strong urge in Britain to extend the empire in East Africa. Business men were unmoved by tall stories of its bright commercial prospects. Investors refused to sustain the Chartered Company or to build a Uganda railway without a Treasury guarantee which Parliament would not give. Salisbury himself admitted that East Africa had no export staple to develop and that the railway would not pay for many years. Reality in this case hardly fits into the theory of economic imperialism, nor into the hypothesis of a strong imperialist impulse arising in British public opinion. In Salisbury's judgement at least, opinion was more adverse than favourable. The Cabinet had wanted a Uganda railway; yet the political risks of building it were too high to take. Salisbury throughout had the air of a man called to administer the sacred mysteries of African strategy in the face of unreasonable popular objections. He felt safe enough in drawing lines on maps; this was as far as he could go. Deliberately, the government

[1] A. W. Clarke, Cabinet Memo., 1 Nov. 1892, F.O. 84/2263.

[2] *Trade of IBEAC Territories*, 1891–3.

	£ *Imports*	*Exports*
1891	96,000	65,000
1892	130,000	64,000
1893	113,000	80,000

Source: P.P. 1901, LXXXVI, 975.

The parliamentary return issues these figures in rupees of standard Indian value. In 1892 the rupee was worth 1/3d. (Sir J. Strachey, *India, its Administration and Progress*, 4th ed., 1911, 215) and the above table has been calculated on the rate of £1 = 16 rupees.

[3] Salisbury to Portal, 18 Jun. 1892, F.O. Print, 6338, p. 165.

[4] Kemball to Mackinnon, 26 Jul. 1892, Low, *op. cit.*, 269–70.

had left its relation to the Company unofficial and ambiguous,[1] so as to avert charges of jingoism and extravagance and to avoid commitment. Salisbury was quite clear that to bring Uganda into the empire would not be a popular course, and so he preferred to quit office with the issue undecided, rather than risk it in the hurly-burly of an election. He had done as much as he dared to defend the headwaters of the Nile. He had diverted the Germans, blocked the Italians, and tried to buy off the French. What diplomacy could do, he had done. So long as Uganda could be kept as a private intrigue, to be pondered at Hatfield and the Foreign Office, he had fought hard for it; but once the questions of guarantees and subsidies inevitably turned it into a public issue, his defeatism and distrust of the electorate stopped him from pressing the case further. The real nature of the British interest in Uganda was known to none but the happy few. He would not risk its ruin by tossing it to the arbitrament of the many. If Uganda was to be gathered into the empire, it would have to be by a minister with a popular touch surer than Salisbury's. Such a one was about to take office.

Rosebery and Uganda

When Gladstone's fourth ministry took office in August 1892 Lord Rosebery went to the Foreign Office, much to the Queen's relief. A courtier and a wit, a stylist with all the polish of the amateur historian, a grandee of the Turf, a millionaire who appealed to the masses, this Scottish peer who had married into the Rothschild dynasty, was the prince charming[2] of younger Liberal politics. He was the type of colourful grandee in whom the Victorian grocer, baker and candlestick-maker delighted. His private personality was somewhat different. As a friend observed, 'he [was] an extraordinary mixture',[3] a man whose charm and modesty covered an excruciating self-pity and sensitivity which pitched him often into fits of loneliness and depression, as when he was seen by Brett doing his Foreign Office boxes in his billiard room and humming 'Rule, Britannia' to keep his spirits up.[4] In this mood he seemed to personify the 'spoiled child of fortune'.[5] Always craving for sympathy

[1] See for example the plaint of the Consul-General at Zanzibar: 'It would greatly aid me in my relations with the British Company if your Lordship would see fit kindly to inform me how far and in what measure, if any, Her Majesty's Government regard themselves as directly interested or concerned in the success or otherwise of the Company.' (Euan-Smith to Salisbury, Private, 2 Dec. 1890, S.P. 80.)

[2] The phrase is A. G. Gardiner's.

[3] Edward Hamilton to Ponsonby, 1883, Ponsonby, *op. cit.*, 275.

[4] *Journals and Letters of . . . Viscount Esher*, (ed. M. V. Brett), (1934), I, 70–1.

[5] *ibid.*, 186–7.

which he never knew how to get,[1] Rosebery was morose amid his Derby winners or the splendours of Dalmeny. Every man has his own gin shop, as Salisbury used to say, and the consolation which Gladstone found in Homer, and Salisbury in his chemical experiments, Rosebery sought in the eighteenth century. But for him there was no peace of the Augustans, and what is striking about his biographical studies — Chatham, the younger Pitt, Napoleon in exile, Randolph Churchill — is that they all have to do with lonely and star-crossed men.

But in Rosebery the politician, this diffident introvert gave way to a harsher figure. He came to politics as a Whig in a world that was growing unsafe for Whiggery, but he had the popular touch, the ear for a phrase, the sense of the times, which made him, together with Chamberlain and Churchill, the new type of politician in the age of the mass vote. He had little of the moral fervour of Gladstone and the nonconformist wing of the Liberal Party, but much of the realism and cynicism of Salisbury, his mentor, and Churchill, his friend. Again, he was unusual among Liberals in his enthusiasm for imperial federation, his fellow feeling for Cecil Rhodes, and his desire to 'peg out claims for posterity'.[2] For him foreign policy was no place for sentiment, although it had to be presented sentimentally to the voters. He was a *Realpolitiker* in a party which specialised in matters of faith and morals, and his diplomacy was the fixed pursuit of strategy and national interest. In fact the new Foreign Secretary had no new ideas about either, but simply followed the lines laid down by Salisbury. 'For seven years', he could write, 'I have worked hard to make the foreign policy of this country continuous, whether I was in or out of office . . .';[3] and he had succeeded so well in this that Salisbury's diplomacy during his second ministry had been treated with singular respect by the Opposition. For the next three years Rosebery was to continue the policy of his predecessor as closely as he could. But the bow of Ulysses was hard to bend, as he was soon to find out.

From the beginning he was anxious to follow the same policy in Egypt and the Nile Valley, and indeed circumstances made this more essential than ever. Paris and Saint Petersburg were drawing together, and the *Franco-Russe* was on the way. British interests looked like becoming the first casualty of such a pact — indeed this was one of its

[1] A description by his friend, Lord Welby, *Private Diaries of . . . Sir Algernon West . . .* (ed. H. G. Hutchinson), (1922), 35.

[2] On the other hand he was too much of a free trader to expound the new imperialism of developing tropical estates. This was left to Chamberlain, who believed in federation, but also believed in tariffs.

[3] Rosebery to Ponsonby, 21 Aug. 1892, Ponsonby, *op. cit.*, 276.

chief attractions in the eyes of the Russians.[1] Already in 1890 the Admiralty had judged that they could not keep the Russians out of Constantinople, unless the French stayed neutral. Two years later, the theorem could be put more sharply:

> '... unless we are acting in concert with France, the road to Constantinople for a British force bent on a belligerent operation, lies across the ruins of the French fleet.'[2]

It had been left to Salisbury to draw the political conclusion:

> 'If the opinion of the Directors of naval and military intelligence held good, the protection of Constantinople from Russian conquest must cease to be regarded as a great aim of British policy, for we cannot defend it, and our policy is a policy of false pretences.'[3]

Salisbury was notoriously reluctant to take experts at their face value, but this conclusion was hard to gainsay. The Gervais programme had committed France to a vast scheme of shipbuilding, the Russian fleet was expanding, and indeed by 1893 their combined naval estimates were to be larger than the British.[4] Ominous trends such as these made the Naval Defence Act of 1889 look archaic, and the return to power of the Gladstonians in August 1892 meant that the harsh demands of Mediterranean security were unlikely to be met.

The naval situation weakened the hand that Rosebery had to play in foreign affairs. In any case it was weak enough. The closer the collaboration between France and Russia, the greater grew the pressure on Britain, and the more Rosebery was left to look for help to the Triple Alliance. But the Germans simply took advantage of this to charge more for their aid, and the consequent coldness between London and Berlin took much of the force out of the Mediterranean agreements.

These changes in the Mediterranean governed the strange pattern of events which was to unfold over the following six years. A British Cabinet at sixes and sevens over the future of a country in the heart of Africa, a French mission launched from the Atlantic to the Nile, rival diplomats in Ethiopia struggling to tame the Lion of Judah, the stark confrontation at Fashoda, the spectacle of France and Britain almost lurching into war for the Nile — all were consequences at one level or

[1] Memo. by Nelidoff, Apr. 1891, B. Nolde, *L'Alliance Franco-Russe*, (Paris, 1936), 613–4.

[2] Report by Director of Military Intelligence and Director of Naval Intelligence, 18 Mar. 1892, Marder, *op. cit.*, 160.

[3] Minute, 4 Jun. 1892, quoted by L. M. Penson, 'The New Course in British Foreign Policy, 1892–1902,' *T.R.H.S.*, 4th ser., XXV, 134.

[4] Marder, *op. cit.* 162–3.

another of the tilting balance in the Mediterranean Sea, and the repercussions that followed. To be sure, British policy had not yet nerved itself to write off Turkey for good, but with every year that the defence of Constantinople appeared to involve bigger strategic risks and political liabilities, the greater grew the conviction in London that Egypt must be made the basis of Mediterranean defence. The stronger too became the resolution in Paris that the Egyptian question must be solved by some means more heroic than negotiation.

At the end of 1892 their new certainty of Russian support was nerving the French to bring this question back to the boil by working on the Khedive in Cairo and by advancing towards the Upper Nile. This was the background against which Rosebery had to grapple with the problem of Uganda. To evacuate the country would open a gap in the Nile defences; but the collapse of Mackinnon's company made such a withdrawal seem imminent. All this forced Rosebery to look on the safety of Uganda as an even more vital issue than it had appeared to Salisbury.[1]

In the autumn of 1892 Egyptian considerations were uppermost in the minds of British officials as they grappled with the question of Uganda. Wingate, the Director of Military Intelligence in Cairo, supported by his Chief at the War Office, warned that if the chartered company gave up Uganda, then the French might move in. If they did so and then advanced through Equatoria into the Sudan, they would soon be in a position to revive the whole Egyptian question in an acute form.[2] On the other hand, Kitchener, the Sirdar of the Egyptian army, thought that a withdrawal from Uganda would probably lead to its falling into the hands of the Dervishes; but this would be equally undesirable.[3]

The Foreign Office experts agreed with Wingate rather than Kitchener. Anderson observed that 'there is a difficulty which may become serious, *viz.* the non-recognition by France of our sphere and her advance from the Oubanghi to the Upper Nile'.[4] The Permanent Under-Secretary, Sir Philip Currie also stressed the reality of the French danger from the west. He noted: 'France is already claiming a division of territory with the Congo State, which would bring her within measurable distance of Uganda.'[5] Rosebery himself did 'not

[1] German ambassador in Paris to Caprivi, 12 Oct. 1892, *Grosse Politik*, VIII, no. 1743; German ambassador in London to Caprivi, 5 Feb. 1893, *ibid.*, no. 1829; the Marquess of Crewe, *Lord Rosebery*, (1931), II, 400–1.

[2] Memo. by Wingate, encl. in D.M.I. to F.O., 23 Aug. 1892, F.O. 84/2257.

[3] Memo. by Kitchener, 18 Sept. 1892, F.O. 84/2258.

[4] Memo. by Anderson, 27 Aug. 1892, F.O. 84/2257.

[5] Currie, Marginal Note on Wingate's Memo., *ibid.*

think very highly of [Wingate's] memorandum',[1] but this enigmatic comment probably referred to its suitability for circulation in the Cabinet. There is no doubt that both he and his experts concurred with Wingate in the belief that Uganda was vital to Egypt. Early in September the Foreign Secretary presented his case to the Cabinet for taking over Uganda from the company. It had been drawn up by Anderson, who argued that a withdrawal would open the Upper Nile to a French or Belgian advance,[2] which would be against British interests.

Egyptian reasons were the worst possible argument to put to Gladstone's Cabinet, for some ministers rejected its first premise. At the elections a few months earlier, the Prime Minister and Morley had preached an early evacuation of Egypt. Most of Rosebery's colleagues still wanted an agreement with France, and since they hoped to go from the Delta, they saw no need to stay on the Upper Nile. The Foreign Office memorandum re-opened those old Liberal dissensions over Egypt, which had so plagued the second Gladstone Administration. Harcourt, the Chancellor of the Exchequer — no friend to Rosebery in any case — was outraged by the Foreign Office's case. Anderson's Memorandum was pitched '. . . in the highest Jingo tune', he complained to Gladstone, 'advocating the annexation of the whole country up to the Albert Lakes with a view to the "reconquest" of the Sudan via the Upper Nile.'[3] Once again it was the old struggle about reducing or enlarging the Egyptian commitment. Essentially the division was between a pro-French, and a pro-German school of foreign policy; between those who would withdraw from Egypt to conciliate France, and those who would stay in Egypt and rely on Germany. Rosebery long since had joined Salisbury's faction on this; while most of his colleagues still hankered after the Liberal Alliance.

The bitterness of the majority against Rosebery's foreign policy in general was vented upon his Uganda proposals in particular. What possible reason could be found for holding Uganda, Harcourt asked?

> '*Cui bono?* Is it *trade*? There is no traffic. Is it *religion*? The Catholics and Protestants . . . are occupied in nothing but cutting each others' throats. . . . Is it *slavery*? There is no evidence that there is any slave trade question in this region. . . . I see nothing but endless expense, trouble and disaster in prospect if we allow ourselves to *drift* into any sort of responsibility for this business. . . .'[4]

[1] Rosebery, Minute on Wingate's Memo., *ibid.*
[2] Anderson, Cabinet Memo., 7 Sept. 1892, F.O. 84/2258.
[3] Harcourt to Gladstone, 20 Sept. 1892, Gardiner, *op. cit.*, II, 192. [4] *idem.*

The Prime Minister was as horrified as Harcourt at the Foreign Secretary's 'jingoism'.[1] He insisted that there was no Uganda question, and averred tendentiously that Salisbury's government and the Company had decided to withdraw. The great point was to leave it at that.[2] Morley, Asquith and Shaw-Lefevre agreed.

Most of the Cabinet rejected Rosebery's reasons for remaining in Uganda, largely because they did not share his views on Egypt. They were determined that neither the missions nor the Company, should drag them into an expedition or a protectorate. 'These missionaries', Gladstone cried to the French ambassador, 'are always causing trouble.'[3] Neither would the Cabinet hear of a Uganda railway subsidy. All that Rosebery could obtain was one apparently small concession.

Portal had sent the Foreign Office a warning from Zanzibar that an evacuation would lead to a massacre of the Christians in Buganda.[4] The danger was real enough. Here, as in Egypt and at Zanzibar itself, European influence had wrought a crisis in the native polity;[5] but this time it was largely the work of a few missionaries. In the struggle for religious influence at the *Kabaka's* court, political factions, British Protestant and French Catholic, Arab and pagan, had swiftly grown up. Their rivalries were sundering the kingdom and inviting the intervention of its enemies among the neighbouring states. And so after 1886, persecution replaced polemic, as revolution followed revolution, *Kabaka* succeeded *Kabaka*, and Arabs, Catholics and Protestants enjoyed in turn a brief span of bloody supremacy. Whether as victors or victims, the European missionaries were implicated willy-nilly in the civil strife. At last in 1892, Lugard, at the head of the East Africa Company's caravan, had managed to defeat the Muslims, over-awe the Catholics enough to get them to work with the Protestants, and patch up a settlement. But shortly afterwards, the Company ordered him back to the coast. Uganda was to be evacuated by the end of the year. It seemed impossible that Lugard's settlement could survive the counter-attacks from the Arabs and pagans and the strife between the two Christian factions, without the support of his maxim gun. That civil war would break out afresh was certain. The missionaries would be once more in peril. Another local crisis in Africa brought on this time by disruptive religious influence from Europe, was bedevilling the hapless Liberals.

It was this danger which enabled Rosebery to extract his crumb of

[1] Perham, *op. cit.*, 406.
[2] Gladstone to Morley, 26 Sept. 1892, Gladstone Papers, B.M. Add MSS. 44257.
[3] Waddington to Ribot, 2 Nov. 1892; *D.D.F.*, X, no. 38; cf. Perham, *op. cit.*, 406–7.
[4] Portal to Rosebery, 13 Sept. 1892, *ibid.*, 405.
[5] For a full account of this, *vide ibid.*, caps. XII–XV.

comfort from his unsympathetic colleagues. The Cabinet agreed to subsidise the Company, if it would stay on for another three months in order to cover the missionaries' withdrawal. But it was decided that the general evacuation must go on. Rosebery wrote apologetically to the Queen, who was strong for retention, that the decision was 'not what he would wish, but it is more than this morning seemed attainable'.[1] That was something; but plainly the Cabinet as a whole had no intention of being dragged into responsibility for the Buganda crisis. The spectre of Gordon still haunted Downing Street.

Rosebery had won a stay of execution for Uganda. Saving it, and the Egyptian stakes encapsulated in it, was a harder matter. He could try to make his colleagues see reason by threatening to resign; but first of all he needed to strengthen his own position by calling up sentiment to the support of *Realpolitik*. In September several newspapers started a campaign in favour of a Uganda railway and protectorate (the Liberal press as a whole was still strongly against them both), while Stanley and later Lugard stumped the country in the cause. On 20 October Rosebery encouraged a deputation from the Anti-Slavery Society to agitate for retention, admitting at the same time that he himself could not say what the government would choose to do about Uganda.[2] Local churches and missionary societies, stimulated by the Church Missionary Society, joined with a few chambers of commerce, local political associations and town councils in begging the government to keep Uganda and to build the railway.[3] Salisbury and Balfour added their voices to the agitation.

This was by no means a spontaneous outburst of imperialist enthusiasm. The campaign was sedulously manufactured with the scarcely veiled encouragement of Rosebery; and for this reason perhaps, its success was greatest in organising the converted. A humanitarian appeal produced a humanitarian response, but it did not gain much purely political support.[4] In fact, the campaign fell flat just where success was most needed — in the Liberal ranks. It could be said that 'not a single Liberal or Radical Society in the country had passed a

[1] Rosebery to Queen Victoria, 29 Sept. 1892, *Q.V.L.*, 3rd ser., II, 159–60.

[2] Crewe, *op. cit.*, II, 405–6.

[3] For this campaign see: Perham, *op. cit.*, cap. XX; D. A. Low, 'British Public Opinion and the Uganda Question,' *Uganda Journal*, 1954. The resolutions are collected in F.O. 84/2192. It should be noted that the campaign's effect upon the governmental decision to keep Uganda was far smaller than would appear from the viewpoint of the biographer of Lugard.

[4] Of 174 resolutions sent to the Foreign Office, 101 were sent by religious bodies, 24 by chambers of commerce, 13 from Town councils and 34 from public meetings: Perham, *op. cit.*, 425–6.

resolution in favour of the retention of Uganda'.[1] The agitation, of course, succeeded in strengthening Rosebery's hand with his colleagues; but its effect was far from decisive. For all the effort they made, the forward party was simply not strong enough to force the government's hand, and Rosebery made this clear to Mackinnon in mid-November. Of the railway subsidy, he said, '. . . I would not hold out any prospect of the Government proposing that railroad.' Mackinnon replied 'that grave public feeling in the country would be excited on behalf of a railroad'; and the Foreign Secretary answered: 'I should have no objection to being forced by the country in that direction, but . . . nothing would be done spontaneously by Her Majesty's Govt, and [you] must remember that several of my colleagues hold the strongest opinions and were publicly pledged against it, but I could not, indeed, propose the railway to them' or the resultant commitment to stay in Uganda.[2] Rosebery himself at the peak of the campaign, was surely admitting here that its effect in the Cabinet was something less than compelling.

On the other hand, the humanitarian campaign served to point his threat of resignation. Although the Liberals distrusted Rosebery's 'jingoism' and Francophobia, they had great need of him as a leader. Therefore it was a serious matter for the ministry when, at the end of September, he threatened to resign over Uganda. Several Liberal leaders pointed out to Gladstone through his secretary, Sir Algernon West, what a heavy blow this would be to the Party[3] and the cause of Irish Home Rule. The old man replied darkly that it would be worse for Rosebery than for the ministry. The Prime Minister nevertheless became most anxious not to 'drive our friend [Rosebery] to despair'.[4] The Foreign Secretary's position was a strong one; and his intimate, Reginald Brett, described and accounted for it when he wrote: 'He is absolute at the F.O. He informs his colleagues of very little, and does as he pleases. If it offends them, he retires. We shall remain in Egypt, and the continuity of Lord S's policy will not be disturbed.'[5]

His offer to resign forced ministers by the beginning of November to compromise with him over Uganda, rather than risk a break in the ministry.[6] Gladstone and Harcourt had softened so far as to consider handing over the territory to the Sultan of Zanzibar;[7] while the Foreign

[1] A. C. Morton in the House of Commons, 6 Feb. 1893: *Hansard*, 4th ser., VIII, 571.

[2] Rosebery, Memo. of interview with Mackinnon, 17 Nov. 1892. F.O. 403/168, 241.

[3] West, *op. cit.*, 60–2. West was Gladstone's Private Secretary and *alter ego*.

[4] Gladstone to Harcourt, 28 Sept. 1892: Gardiner, *op. cit.*, II, 196.

[5] Esher, *op. cit.*, I, 162.

[6] West, *op. cit.*, 62, 72, 75; Crewe, *op. cit.*, II, 406.

[7] Rosebery to Gladstone, 20 Oct. 1892, Gladstone Papers, B.M. Add MSS., 44290; Harcourt to Gladstone, 20 Oct. 1892, Gardiner, *op. cit.*, II, 198.

Secretary had given up for the time being his demand for a protectorate and a railway.[1] The government could not agree on how to deal with the problem; but it could agree to postpone it.

On 3 November Rosebery put up his notion of a suitable compromise. Uganda, he took it for granted, was not to be given up. He proposed to send an Imperial Commissioner to take over from the Chartered Company and to set up a token administration.[2] At the same time, the Foreign Secretary mentioned Rhodes's offer to take Uganda under the British South Africa Company in return for a subsidy;[3] but, although this notion appealed to Harcourt, Rosebery himself disliked it, preferring to work towards committing the government directly to take over the country. But his bland proposal was still too much for other ministers. Gladstone, Harcourt and Morley insisted that Rosebery's Commissioner should not go out to administer, but merely to inquire and report.[4] And in the end this was the compromise which Harcourt and Rosebery jointly brought to the Cabinet for approval on 23 November.[5] It was ambiguous enough to save both their faces. Gladstone and Harcourt expected the Commissioner to keep an open mind on this question of withdrawal and of handing Uganda over to Zanzibar,[6] even though Rosebery had told them that this solution was financially impracticable.[7] Rosebery, on the other hand, still expected the Commissioner to take over the administration of Uganda, making his report merely as a formal justification of the act. The Prime Minister took care to strike out of the Commissioner's draft instructions the references to 'administering' Uganda, which the Foreign Office had inserted;[8] but the Foreign Secretary was able to over-ride the Cabinet and press forward his own policy. The officer chosen for the commission was Sir Gerald Portal. Everyone knew that this well-connected *protégé* of Salisbury's was a strong advocate of keeping Uganda; yet none of the Cabinet questioned the choice. What was more, Rosebery gave Portal private instructions. The Commissioner was not for a moment to consider withdrawing from Uganda, except as a matter of form.[9] He was to assume that the government would take over by some means or

[1] Rosebery, Memo., 3 Nov. 1892, F.O. 403/168, 202. [2] *ibid.*, 202–4.
[3] *ibid.*; see also, Gardiner, *op. cit.*, II, 199; Rhodes to Rosebery, 29 Oct. 1892, F.O. 84/2262.
[4] Perham, *op. cit.*, 427–8.
[5] Rosebery Memo., 22 Nov. 1892, F.O. 403/168, 255.
[6] Gladstone to Rosebery, 9 Dec. 1892, Gladstone Papers, B.M. Add MSS. 44290.
[7] Rosebery to Gladstone, 28 Oct. 1892, *ibid.*
[8] Gladstone to Morley, 13 Dec. 1892, *ibid*: see also Perham, *op. cit.*, 429–31; West, *op. cit.*, 91–2.
[9] Rosebery to Portal, 1 Dec. 1892, Perham, *op. cit.*, 431.

other, short of a protectorate. Rosebery was confident that time was on his side. Public sentiment, he believed was swinging in favour of staying.[1] Portal was to report upon the best means of doing so. His official orders stuck to the compromise reached on 23 November; but his secret orders were more in the sense of Rosebery's proposal which the Cabinet had turned down three weeks earlier. If Rosebery had agreed to postpone a decision until Portal had reported, he had gone far to make sure that the decision would be in his favour. 'The mission of Gerry Portal to Uganda', wrote Brett in his journal, 'will be much canvassed, but it is good. Rosebery's colleagues commit themselves thereby to his views.'[2]

Whether the Cabinet had any unwritten understanding of this kind with Rosebery, or whether his colleagues accepted it implicitly as the price for keeping him in the government, one thing is certain; Rosebery henceforward was strong enough to over-ride the Prime Minister and the rest of the Cabinet and to carry on Salisbury's foreign policy. For Rosebery much more than Uganda was at stake. The Cabinet quarrels over Uganda were really quarrels over Egypt; and having got his way on the local issue, Rosebery had gone far to win freedom of action for his broad strategy in Egypt and the Nile Valley.

How was it that Rosebery by the end of 1892 could dictate foreign policy to a majority of angry colleagues? His authority did not derive from the missionaries' agitation over Uganda; for nothing would have been less likely to make his colleagues regard him as indispensable. Rosebery's pre-eminence in foreign affairs decided the fate of Uganda; but it was not Uganda that gave him his power. It was rather the peculiar balance of domestic politics which he exploited to win a free hand in foreign affairs. Even when the ministry was being formed, it had been clear that the Liberals could not do without him, and they showed it by the way they pleaded with him to join. Morley had told him: 'If you do not join the Government it is hamstrung; it cannot last three weeks after Parliament begins.'[3] Both wings of the party needed him as leader of the Liberal minority in the Lords;[4] and the Whigs moreover were looking to the future. Gladstone was obviously failing; and in Rosebery they saw their best hope of edging out of the succession the radical and vitriolic Harcourt. Spencer also begged Rosebery to join, hoping to serve under him in the Lords and 'later on . . . in the Cabinet'.[5]

[1] Rosebery to Portal, 9 Dec. 1892, *ibid.*, 431.
[2] Brett's Journal, 6 Dec. 1892, Esher, *op. cit.*, I, 166.
[3] Rosebery's diary, 3 Jul. 1892, Crewe, *op. cit.*, II, 391.
[4] Gladstone to Rosebery, 4 Aug. 1892, *ibid.*, 398.
[5] Spencer to Rosebery, 4 Aug. 1892, *ibid.*, II, 395.

Gladstone himself hinted that Harcourt could never lead the Party and that the leadership in the Lords would carry the '*jus successionis*';[1] and Morley, who carried the hint to Dalmeny, agreed.[2] But there was a third, and still more compelling reason why the Liberals had to woo the temperamental peer out of his tent. The Queen wanted him for Foreign Minister; and she would have no other.[3]

With all these advantages, Rosebery had been able to join the ministry on something like his own terms. The Queen's Secretary, Sir Henry Ponsonby wrote that Rosebery's 'conditions . . . are believed to be that he shall not be interfered with especially on the question of Egypt, or briefly that he will not abandon Egypt as many insist upon'.[4] Lord Acton, the intimate of both Rosebery and Gladstone, went to and fro during the negotiations. 'If Rosebery accepts [office]', Acton told Gladstone's secretary, 'it is hardly likely that . . . he will accept *sans phrase*. The minimum I take to be that he would say: "I come in to pursue the continuity of foreign policy". . . . In fact, the innocent device I imagine R[osebery] to propose would imply the abdication of the Premier. . . . I would venture to hope that Mr. G. would not yield more than this: that he undoubtedly intended to give a general approval of Salisbury's Continental [and Mediterranean] policy, so far as it was manifest, patent, and documentary, and as it aimed at the maintenance of peace.'[5] It is highly probable that Rosebery and Gladstone agreed upon some such arrangement; and this would explain why the Cabinet dissensions over Uganda were so much concerned with what Salisbury had or had not decided to do about Uganda before he left office. Such an arrangement left many loop-holes for disagreement about the scope of Rosebery's freedom. But however ambiguously defined, it was obviously large, and Rosebery was able to make it larger. His correspondence with the Prince of Wales shows how this could be done.

> 'There are many grave questions . . . affecting our interests in India, Egypt and Morocco,' wrote the Prince, 'and it requires a very watchful eye — to prevent Russia and France from harming us — and a thorough knowledge of the subject which nobody possesses more than you do. Let me therefore implore you to accept office — (if Mr. Gladstone will give you a free hand in Foreign Affairs . . .) for the Queen's sake and for that of our great Empire!'[6]

Rosebery's answer implied that Mr. Gladstone had done what was

[1] Rosebery's Diary, 5 Aug. 1892, *ibid.*, 397. [2] West, *op. cit.*, 70.
[3] Queen Victoria to Ponsonby, 10 Aug. 1892, Ponsonby, *op. cit.*, 217.
[4] Crewe, *op. cit.*, II, 400. [5] Acton to West, 29 Jul. 1892, West, *op. cit.*, 41.
[6] Prince of Wales to Rosebery, 14 Aug. 1892, Crewe, *op. cit.*, II, 401.

asked of him: '. . . The matter has now been . . . settled in the way that Your Royal Highness wishes.'[1]

However vague the original contract under which Rosebery agreed to take the Foreign Office, he was now in a strong position to enforce his own interpretation of it. The circumstances of the Party and government eventually forced the Liberal leaders to follow him. In the House of Commons, they had a shaky majority of forty over the Conservatives and Liberal Unionists, and they were utterly dependent for this advantage on the votes of the Irish Nationalists.[2] This meant that they were obliged to make Irish Home Rule their first concern. With this Irish burden on their backs, they could not afford to challenge Rosebery's control of foreign affairs. As he had shrewdly remarked to the Liberal chiefs in December 1891, 'the Government which *simultaneously* gave Home Rule to Ireland and evacuated Egypt would be a bold one. . . .'[3] Indeed, this saying was truer of the Liberals' Parliamentary position in 1892–5 than Rosebery could have foreseen. They held office on two conditions: that they fought for Irish Home Rule; and that they accepted the foreign policy of Salisbury and Rosebery. For if they followed this policy and their Radical wing voted against it in the Commons, they could rely on Conservative votes to sustain them. If, on the other hand, they chose to throw over Rosebery's policy, the defection of his followers to the Opposition might bring down the ministry and ruin the Irish Cause. They chose to swallow their distaste of jingoism in foreign policy for the sake of survival. Having lost the Liberal Unionists over Ireland, the Liberals could ill afford to lose Rosebery and the Liberal imperialists over Egypt and Uganda. It would have ended the ministry and finished the Party. And so in the end, Rosebery was indispensable to the Liberals. However much they protested against it, Gladstone and his colleagues could go on in office only by going on with Home Rule; and they could go on with both only by going on with Rosebery in Egypt and the Nile Valley.

Perforce, they went. The humanitarian agitation may have contributed a little strength to Rosebery's position and to the sending of Portal to Uganda. But Rosebery's authority in the matter was not essentially the product of democratic pressure or a rising imperialism. His was a more personal triumph made possible by some curious freaks of parliamentary representation joined with some powerful survivals from a more aristocratic age. The electorate in 1892 had chosen the

[1] Rosebery to Prince of Wales, 15 Aug. 1892, *ibid.*, II, 402.
[2] Lyons, F.S.L.: *The Irish Parliamentary Party 1890–1910* (1951), 225.
[3] Rosebery's Diary, Crewe, *op. cit.*, II, 376.

Liberals so tentatively, and they were themselves so divided and confused, that the Court and the Opposition through Rosebery still controlled the nation's foreign policy. And so it came about that Portal's mission was a small part of a far greater price which Rosebery's colleagues paid for the survival of the Party and the ministry.

The government went on in this way throughout the year 1893, while Portal was in Uganda, carrying out Rosebery's private orders. The East Africa Company's agents there handed over to him in April, and on 29 May he made a provisional treaty with the *Kabaka* of Buganda,[1] by which the government could take over the Company's protectorate if it wished to do so. The Commissioner was in no hurry to make his report to the Foreign Office. He knew that the delay in producing it would serve Rosebery's purposes far better than his recommendations could do. At Home meanwhile, the ministry turned all its energies upon the struggle for the Home Rule Bill and for the time being the public had eyes for nothing else. Abroad, Rosebery continued to play his free hand amidst the impotent protests of his 'friends'. During the first months of the year the war in the Cabinet flared up once more over the Egyptian question. The outcome was that Rosebery became more determined than ever to make sure of Uganda, as part of his struggle to defend Egypt against France.

In January, Abbas II, the new Khedive, carried out a *coup d'état* against British control. Prompted (so Cromer suspected) by the French and Russian Consuls-General, Abbas dismissed his ministers and replaced them with men whom Cromer thought dangerous. These events, he feared, might bring on another nationalist revolution against British control and European privilege which might sweep away the Khedivate and Pasha rule altogether. He asked London to send him more troops and to authorise him to seize the public offices and reinstate the fallen ministers. At once his telegrams revived the bitter dissension in the Cabinet over policy towards Egypt and France.

Gladstone, Harcourt and Morley again formed a triumvirate for early evacuation, and they were backed by most of the Cabinet against Salisbury's apostle, Rosebery, and his agent, Cromer. 'Mr. Gladstone said to Harcourt that they might as well ask him to put a torch to Westminster Abbey as to send more troops to Egypt.'[2] Along with Harcourt, Morley and Ripon, he was furious with Cromer for insisting on putting down the Khedive 'at any cost'. '. . . We are now able to understand what Lord Cromer means by "at any cost",' Harcourt

[1] Hertslet, *op. cit.*, I, 393–5. [2] West's Diary, 20 Jan. 1893, *op. cit.*, 123.

fumed, '*viz.*, a conflict with France. The means that he proposes is a military *coup d'état* by England . . . this amounts to the annexation of Egypt . . . and is an entire breach of the European understanding on which our occupation rests. . . .'[1] Against his angry colleagues Rosebery coolly backed Cromer and stood his ground. 'There is a Cabinet on Monday', the Foreign Secretary wrote to Cairo, 'and if you do not receive the powers you ask on Monday evening, the Foreign Office will have passed into other hands.'[2] Once more Rosebery's offer to resign brought the Cabinet to heel. His opponents had to admit that his going would bring down the government.[3] West went the round of ministers telling them that the danger in Egypt was real, that their opposition to Rosebery would end any chance of Irish Home Rule, and that they would have to acquiesce. He was right — and for the right reasons. Rosebery got his way, Cromer got his powers and his troops. The Foreign Secretary still held his colleagues in a vice.

However much they wished it, they could not return to the old Liberal policy of conciliating France. The French had protested strongly against Cromer's high-handed measures. On 30 January, Gladstone spoke to Waddington, the French ambassador, about the need for an Anglo-French agreement and a withdrawal from Egypt on the lines of the Drummond Wolff proposals of 1887. Two days later in the House of Commons the Prime Minister offered what Waddington took to be a public invitation to France to resume negotiation,[4] and the ambassador found that Gladstone,[5] Harcourt and Morley wanted a conference of the Powers to settle the Egyptian Question. For a time things looked promising. In May, Dilke and the Francophil Radicals in the Commons pressed for agreement with France and evacuation from Egypt;[6] while later that summer, Gladstone and Harcourt were still hoping for a French agreement.[7] But Waddington by this time had found that these were fancies. Gladstone's words, he reported, counted for nothing. Rosebery was the master;[8] and Rosebery followed Salisbury's policy of possession. The Opposition leader had warned the Lords that the risks of withdrawal from Egypt had become greater than ever with the making of the Franco-Russian alliance; and that the danger of an Egyptian revolution remained.[9] Rosebery refused to re-

[1] Gardiner, *op. cit.*, II, 226.
[2] Zetland, *op. cit.*, 203. *c.f.* Earl of Cromer: *Abbas II*, (1915) *passim.*
[3] West's Diary, 21 Jan. 1893, *op. cit.*, 124–5.
[4] Waddington to Develle, 1 Feb. 1893, *D.D.F.*, X, no. 155.
[5] Waddington to Develle, 5 May, 1893, *ibid.*, no. 224.
[6] *Hansard*, 4th ser., XI, cols. 1634–81. [7] Gardiner, *op. cit.*, II, 240.
[8] Waddington to Develle, 1 Feb. 1893, *D.D.F.*, X, no. 156.
[9] *Hansard*, 4th ser., VIII, cols. 18–19.

open talks with France. He preferred the *status quo*[1] in Egypt to the hazards of evacuation. Fear of France and Russia kept the Liberals trapped in Egypt, just as it had trapped the Conservatives.

Snubbed in London and checked in Cairo, the French now began the study of a great coup on the Upper Nile which would drive the British willy-nilly into negotiation. On 3 May President Carnot launched a plan for putting a French force near the confluence of the White Nile and the River Sobat, in the region beyond the effective power of the Dervishes. Fashoda was the point he chose, since it was also near the confluence of the Bahr el Ghazal with the Nile, and the natural terminus for travellers from the stations of the Congo[2]. Here then would be the attack from the west. The French were already considering a supporting move from the east through Ethiopia to the Nile. The two forces were to unite at Fashoda.[3] So even the remote and shadowy land of Prester John was to be dragged into the struggle for security in the Mediterranean. By the treaty of Ucciali the Italians had already thrown a noose around the Emperor Menelek; but he was clearly eager to break free, and for aid he looked to France. In September 1893 Carnot sent him a letter, vague but unmistakably friendly, and Menelek caught the drift so well that he asked for rifles and ammunition.[4]

Like many another French project during the partition, this had a certain heroic sweep. The French thought big in Africa, the British thought big elsewhere. But for all the cartographical elegance of the scheme, it involved high risks. To take position astride the water supplies of Egypt might well jerk the British into appeasement; but might it not equally well mean a head on collision with London that would ricochet back against France's position in Europe? Rather than run these risks, the directors of French policy preferred to negotiate for the time being, and to keep the *coup de main* in reserve. As for Menelek, he had troubles of his own with the Italians; and if his new French rifles irritated Rome, so much the better.

[1] Waddington to Develle, 1 Feb. 1893, *D.D.F.*, X, same to same, 5 May 1893, *ibid.*, no. 224.

[2] On the origins of the Fashoda mission, *vide* Monteil to Under-Secretary for Colonies, 7 Mar. 1894, Archives du Ministère de la France d'Outre Mer (henceforward M.F.O.M.), Afrique, III, 16–19, dossier, 19A; partly printed in *D.D.F.* XI, 65; P. L. Monteil, *Quelques Feuillets de l'Histoire Coloniale*, (Paris, 1924), 65–72; H. Labouret, *Monteil, Explorateur et Soldat*, (Paris, 1937), 157–60. The French Government had been pondering the plan since March, according to Monteil.

[3] C. Maistre, 'La Mission Congo-Niger,' *Communications et Procès-Verbaux de l'Académie des Sciences Coloniales*, séance du 21 juin, 1933, pp. 17–18; *L'Afrique française*, Mar. 1932, 156–7.

[4] Develle to French ambassador in Rome, 19 Jun. 1893, *D.D.F.*, X, no. 269; Menelek to President Carnot, 5 Jan. 1894, *D.D.F.*, XI, no. 5; same to same, 10 Jan. 1894, *ibid.*, p. 6, fn. 2; Governor of Obok to Carnot, 9 Dec. 1893, *ibid.*, p. 85, fn. 1.

Moves of this sort had become classified as threats to British interests since Salisbury had worked out the Nile Valley strategy. The French might hesitate to thrust at the Upper Nile, but there were others who did not. By April 1893 it was from Leopold of the Belgians that the threat was coming. 'The sovereign of the Congo', so Rosebery told the Queen, 'has sent a large filibustering force into the British sphere of influence, and it has occupied Lado, an important post on the Nile.'[1] As the heir of Salisbury's strategy, he found himself urgently compelled to take action.

Uganda remained the pivot of his strategy. Without consulting any of the Cabinet,[2] he ordered Portal 'to protect the important interests of this country on the Upper Nile'.[3] He was to 'negotiate any treaties [with the indigenous rulers] that may be necessary for its protection',[4] especially at Wadelai and in the Nile basin, and to build a chain of forts commanding the region between Buganda and Lake Albert. Although Portal had yet to report to the Cabinet, Rosebery was already extending British claims over further regions of Uganda so as to ward off the Belgians. At the same time he tried diplomatic methods of shutting out the French. In November 1893 he agreed that the frontier of the German Cameroons should be pushed as far eastwards as the Nile watershed, so as to set up a barrier against a French advance.[5] It was even clearer by 1893 than it had been in 1890 that the over-riding purpose of British policy in Uganda and the Nile Basin was neither to protect missions nor to peg out claims for posterity, but to defend the British occupation of Egypt.

By this time Rosebery's independence in foreign affairs was well-nigh invincible. In March 1893 he had easily brushed aside a revolt of Labouchere and forty-six Radical dissidents against his Uganda policy, since the Conservatives had voted with the government, and turned

[1] Crewe, *op. cit.*, II, 423–4. The best account of Leopold's ambitions on the Nile is in J. Stengers, 'La Première Tentative de Reprise du Congo par la Belgique,' *Bulletin de la Société royale belge de Géographie*, LXIII, 1–80. The French in the Congo were in no condition at this time to mount a threat against the Nile without substantial reinforcement from Paris; *vide* the letters of Captain Decazes (second in command of the proposed mission from Congo to Nile), 25 Jun. 1893–30, Jan. 1895 (28 letters in A.E.F. (Decazes).

[2] Harcourt to Kimberley, 14 May 1894, Gardiner, *op. cit.*, II, 315.

[3] Rosebery to Portal, 10 Aug. 1893, Low, *op. cit.*, 364–5.

[4] Gardiner, *op. cit.*, II, 315.

[5] By Article IV it was agreed that 'the influence of Germany, in respect to her relations with Great Britain shall not extend eastwards beyond the basin of the River Shari, and that Darfur, Kordofan, and Bahr-el-Ghazal . . . shall be excluded from her influence. . . .' (C. 7230, P.P. (1893–94) CIX, 125–31.) cf. A. J. P. Taylor, 'Prelude to Fashoda: The Question of the Upper Nile, 1894–95,' *English Historical Review*, 1950, 53.

an otherwise certain defeat into an overwhelming victory.[1] Thanks again to Conservative favour, Rosebery had over-ridden the Radicals' demands for an early withdrawal from Egypt. The Liberals were finding that there was no holding their Foreign Secretary. The Radicals were trying, but failing to do so; and the moderates had given up trying.

There were good political reasons why the party should come to heel. As early as October 1893 the Foreign Secretary stood out as a likely successor to Gladstone.[2] His jingoism was still anathema to his colleagues, but it was becoming clear that he was the only man who could keep the ministry together, once Gladstone went.[3] At the beginning of the New Year, Lewis Harcourt, who had been lobbying for his father, reported that Rosebery had probably won the succession.[4] He had not won because he was a jingo, but in spite of that notorious fact. His victory followed from the poverty of the Liberal leadership, gone to seed under Gladstone's awful shadow, from the feuds and backbiting that had become a feature of Liberal Cabinets, and from the support of the Crown. The Queen may have wanted an imperialist Prime Minister; the Party did not. That she got her way was not a sign of the strength of imperialism but of the weakness of the Party.

Hence when Rosebery at last brought Portal's report to the Cabinet on 20 December 1893[5] it was, as he had always intended, a mere formality. Nobody could stop Rosebery from keeping Uganda. He was being tapped for the leadership, and in any case events were strengthening his hand. Franco-Russian hostility was written plainly round the world from Afghanistan and Siam to Egypt and the Nile Basin. The French fleet had been to Kronstadt, the Russian fleet had been to Toulon, and the great naval scare had begun. Most of the Cabinet wanted to enlarge the fleet and repair the naval weakness in the Mediterranean.[6] The question of withdrawing from Egypt was practically dead; that of giving up Uganda had died with it.

Consequently, the fate of Uganda was decided by considerations of grand policy which had little to do with the country itself. The interest of Portal's report lies not so much in what he said about Uganda as in its relation to these larger issues. There were good reasons for holding it, as Portal could see, but they were not commercial. On the contrary,

[1] Labouchere's motion to reduce the vote for Portal's Uganda mission was lost by 368 votes to 46. (*Hansard*, 4th ser., X, cols. 539, ff., 20 Mar. 1893.)

[2] West's Diary, 6 Oct. 1893, *op. cit.*, 204.

[3] *idem*; Crewe, *op. cit.*, II, 395.

[4] Lewis Harcourt's Journal, Gardiner, *op. cit.*, II, 263.

[5] For the incubation of this Report, see Perham, *op. cit.*, 448–51: also Rosebery, Minute, 10 Sept. 1893, on Portal's Report, F.O. 83/1242.

[6] Queen Victoria to Ponsonby, 16 Dec., 1893, *Q.V.L.*, 3rd ser., II, 332.

he wrote, 'those of a purely economic character would appear to weigh on the side of evacuation, since no hope need be entertained of Uganda being able, at all events for some years to come, to defray the cost of its occupation.' The country therefore was not worth bringing under close British administration. Nevertheless, Portal came out strongly 'in favour of the maintenance of some form of British preponderance.' There were philanthropic arguments for this, since an evacuation would be a blow to the progress of civilisation and it would invite Arab expansion; but Portal tacked even this point to his over-ruling strategic thesis. 'Any other European power would be justified', he observed, 'in taking the British place in Uganda if there is an evacuation, because of the Arab aspect of the problem.' On these grounds too he rejected the idea of handing over Uganda to the rule of the Sultan of Zanzibar. The Sultan was not strong enough. Moreover, he was a Muslim. It would hardly do to hand over Christian missions to his rule.

Implicitly Portal's whole case rested upon the importance of Uganda in Egyptian and Nile Valley strategy. He argued that the only way of keeping other Powers out was to occupy Uganda. '. . . It is hardly possible that Uganda, the natural key to the whole of the Nile Valley,' he wrote, '. . . should be left unprotected and unnoticed by other Powers because an English Company has been unable to hold it and because Her Majesty's Government has been unwilling to interfere.' Clearly then, there were limits to philanthropy. If the chief aim had been to 'civilise' Uganda, Portal would hardly have been so anxious to prevent other Powers from sharing the task. The preoccupations of Portal and his masters were much more those of the strategist than the evangelist. 'All question of a complete evacuation of Uganda', the Commissioner concluded, 'at all events for the present, should be set aside.' One or two British officials should hold the country by their influence over the rulers. It was a makeshift solution, he admitted; but a tighter grip on Uganda would have to wait until the Uganda railway could be built.[1]

The Foreign Office had got the report which it expected. Anderson thought it 'admirable' and could find no word of criticism.[2] Rosebery's colleagues raised no difficulties about it, and even Gladstone agreed that the only trouble would be over the East Africa Company's demands for compensation.[3] The truth was that the year-old purpose of the report had long been overtaken by events.

Very soon news of French and Belgian plans forced Rosebery to go

[1] Portal's Report is contained in F.O. 83/1242.
[2] Anderson to Currie, 30 Aug. 1893, F.O. 83/1242.
[3] West's Diary, 21 Dec. 1893, *op. cit.*, 230.

far beyond Portal's recommendations, if the Upper Nile was to be saved. The Foreign Office knew by 11 February, 1894 that the device of letting in the Germans up to the western watershed would fail to keep the French out of the Nile Valley, for Germany had now agreed to let the French in.[1] And so on the next day Rosebery declared that the Uganda question must be decided at once. Portal had only gone as far as suggesting a 'sphere of influence'. This was not enough for Rosebery. In view of the British interests at stake, he wrote, withdrawal was impossible. There was now only one way of securing them, and that was a formal protectorate.[2]

The next day Anderson set down some of the reasons why the Foreign Office wanted a tighter grip on Uganda. 'It is certainly probable', he observed, 'that when the [French] negotiations with Germany are concluded Captain Monteil will push towards the Nile.'[3] A protectorate was now needed to forestall the long-range threat of a French advance. It was more immediately required to halt the Belgian drive toward Uganda from Wadelai. By 4 March, Rosebery was Prime Minister; a day later, the Foreign Office offered to lease the Bahr-el-Ghazal to Leopold II, in order to stall the Belgian thrust and shut the French out of the Nile Basin on the west. Lugard, sent at the same time to Paris to divine more of the French intentions, returned with the news that a French expedition was to march on Lado or Fashoda.[4] The way was opened for them by the Franco-German agreement, reached on 4 February and confirmed on 15 March;[5] a week later, Rosebery and Kimberley, his successor as Foreign Secretary, brought the Cabinet to agree to a protectorate over Uganda,[6] although they refrained as yet from asking for the railway as well. Harcourt, Morley and the Radicals fought in the last ditch against the protectorate, but they fought in vain.[7] In the ensuing debate in the Commons, Grey, the Foreign Under-Secretary, defended the protectorate with all Portal's arguments, embellished with high hopes of commercial gains, which Portal's report had flatly denied.[8] Once again the Radical revolt would have been large enough to bring down the government, if the Conservatives had not come to the rescue. With their aid the Uganda vote was carried

[1] A. J. P. Taylor, 'Prelude to Fashoda: The Question of the Upper Nile, 1894–95,' *English Historical Review*, Vol. LXV, no. 254, Jan. 1950, 53–4.

[2] Rosebery, Memo., 12 Feb. 1894, F.O. 403/180, 130–4.

[3] Anderson, Minute, 13 Feb. 1894, on Plunkett to Rosebery, 11 Feb. 1894, quoted in Taylor, *loc. cit.*, 54, fn. 2.

[4] Lugard, Memo., 10 Mar. 1894, *ibid.*, 54.

[5] Hertslet, *op. cit.*, II, 657–60.

[6] Rosebery to Queen Victoria, 22 Mar. 1894, *Q.V.L.*, 3rd ser., II, 385.

[7] Rosebery to Queen Victoria, 7 Apr. 1894, *ibid.*, 389; Dilke's Amendment, 30 May 1895; *Hansard*, 4th ser., XXXIV, 736 *et seq.*

[8] *ibid.*, 4th ser., XXV, 181 *et seq.*

by 218–52.[1] Rosebery had his protectorate at last,[2] and that would keep the French away from the Lakes. He had also secured in Uganda a base for protecting the rest of the Upper Nile basin.

THE ANGLO-CONGOLESE TREATY OF 1894

But to the north and west of Uganda, the Prime Minister still had to rely on diplomacy to exclude the French. When the Prime Minister brought his colleagues to agree to the new protectorate, he had practically completed an arrangement for leasing to Leopold of the Belgians the former Egyptian provinces of Equatoria and the Bahr-el-Ghazal; indeed, the two moves were complementary parts of the one strategy. Rosebery distinctly stated the paramount aim that 'the Nile is Egypt and Egypt is the Nile, and . . . as the occupying Power our first interest was to obtain a recognition of this principle by the Great Powers'.[3] Here he was faithfully following the conception of Salisbury and Cromer. And Kimberley, faithfully following Rosebery, made the over-riding aim even clearer to the choleric Harcourt, who had been told nothing of the negotiations:

> 'The object is to prevent the French, who are about to send an expedition . . . to [the Bahr-el-Ghazal] from establishing themselves there, and to settle with the Belgians, who are there already. . . .
>
> The arrangement . . . present[s] many advantages. We shall have a friendly neighbour; we shall not be under pressure to extend our operations in that district; we shall prevent the French from interfering. The presence of the French there would be a serious danger to Egypt. . . .'[4]

It was a new version of an old policy. From 1889 Britain had worked to build up the defences of Egypt in east and central Africa. Salisbury had kept watch and ward against Germany and Italy; Rosebery was fending off the challenges from Belgium and from France. The methods altered; but the aim did not change.

The Anglo-Congolese agreement was published on 12 May, 1894.[5]

[1] *ibid.*, 270. For an account of this debate, *vide* Perham, *op. cit.*, 459–62.
[2] Uganda British Protectorate Treaty, 27 Aug. 1894, Hertslet, *op. cit.*, I, 396.
[3] Crewe, *op. cit.*, II, 448.
[4] Kimberley to Harcourt, 28 Mar. 1894, Gardiner, *op. cit.*, II, 313.
[5] Text of the agreement in *P.P.* 1894, XCVI, 25–9; comment in German minister in Brussels to Caprivi, 1 May 1894, *Grosse Politik*, VIII, no. 2030; Marschall to German ambassador in London, 10 May 1894, *ibid.*, no. 2031; Casimir-Périer to French minister in Brussels 26 May 1894, *D.D.F.*, XI, no. 109. For interpretations of the agreement *vide* M. P. Hornik, 'The Anglo-Belgian Agreement of 12 May, 1894,' *English Historical Review*, 1942; A. J. P. Taylor, 'Prelude to Fashoda: The Question of the Upper Nile, 1894–5,' *ibid.*, 1950, 52–80; M. P. Hornik, *Der Kampf der Grossmächte um den Oberlauf des Nil*, Vienna, 1951, 104–22; W. L. Langer, *The Diplomacy of Imperialism*, 128–41.

Rosebery's aims are shown in its terms. Indeed the arrangement would have given him all he wanted, if it had ever gone into force. Leopold recognised the British sphere on the Upper Nile which had been laid down in the Anglo-German arrangement of 1890. In return the British leased to him those regions which corresponded with the former Egyptian provinces of Equatoria and Bahr-el-Ghazal, on the understanding that he would claim no rights of sovereignty there. Thirdly — and this was no more than an afterthought — Leopold leased to the British a corridor running along the eastern border of the Congo State and adjoining the western frontier of German East Africa. The corridor was meant to re-open a way for Rhodes' Cape to Cairo extension. Since the winter of 1893 the French had been trying to persuade Leopold to leave open their way to the Nile from Lake Chad and Ubangi. Once they had got there, the Egyptian question was to have been re-opened; Rosebery had bought off Leopold, so as to keep it closed.

Rosebery seemed to have scotched both the Congolese and the French thrusts from the west, by bribing the one to block the other. At the same time he was hastening to seal off the Nile Valley from the east. If Ethiopia collaborated with French designs, this could throw all the defences into disarray. Menelek claimed all the territory up to the right bank of the Nile, and he aspired to push the limits of his empire as far as Khartoum and Victoria Nyanza. These were no more than empty words, as long as the Italians were trying to bundle him into the decent obscurity of a protectorate; but they could become fighting words, should the French help him to shake off Italian domination.

All this gave Rosebery two reasons for encouraging the Italians in Ethiopia. One was that he did not want to frustrate a Power on whose support he was counting in the Mediterranean; the other was that if the Italians mastered Menelek, this would dispose of the chance that he might appear in the Nile Valley as a French ally. The Anglo-Italian agreement of 5 May, 1894, was satisfactory in both respects. The published part merely delimited the British and Italian claims along the Somali coast, but the kernel of the bargain lay in the secret annexes. Here, Britain recognised Italian sway in Ogaden and Harrar — and so over Menelek; what was more, she was empowered to treat Harrar as part of her own sphere until Italy was ready to take it over.[1] Once under

[1] For the published part of the Agreement *vide* Herslet, *op. cit.*, III, 948–50. The suppression of the annexes is examined in L. Woolf, *Empire and Commerce in Africa*, (1920) 170–1, 221–7. Mr. Woolf denied the existence of the *Déclaration Secrète* which turned Harrar over to Britain, but it was admitted at the time; cf. Hanotaux to Dufferin, 26 Jun. 1894, *D.D.F.*, XI, p. 174, fn. 4; *Grosse Politik*, VIII, p. 362, fn. 2.

British sway, the province would bar the way between Ethiopia and French Somaliland.

Rosebery's diplomacy had built barriers against any incursion into the Nile Valley, whether from east or west, but in the event these paper defences did not last the summer. The Germans feigned resentment against a corridor at the backdoor of their east African sphere and threatened to retaliate against Britain in Egypt.[1] Marschall wished to show that he could flourish Bismarck's *bâton égyptien*, and he attacked the Anglo-Congolese agreement as a useful way of forcing Britain closer to the Triple Alliance.[2] Britain was no longer so frightened of the big stick in Cairo as she had been in the Eighteen eighties, but it was still a formidable weapon. Moreover, the French were violently opposed to the agreement,[3] and the double onslaught forced Rosebery to give ground. On 22 June the Foreign Office thought it better to give up its afterthought — the Cape to Cairo corridor.[4]

French threats in Brussels quickly compelled Leopold to withdraw from the remainder of the treaty. The King of the Belgians asked whether Britain was ready to go to war with France in order to sustain him in the Nile Valley agreement.[5] And the rising wrath of Europe delivered Rosebery into his colleagues' hands. Harcourt and Morley in particular had protested that the Treaty would mean a war with France. Events seemed to have proved them right and the Cabinet insisted that Leopold should get no support of any kind.[6] Without it the King quickly caved in to the French. By August the agreement had been shattered, leaving the Upper Nile once more exposed to a French advance. Kimberley could talk sadly of foreign jingoes,[7] Rosebery could write fiercely of giving the Germans a lesson,[8] but in fact their plan had gone to pieces and they were jammed tightly against the irreducible needs of British policy, as government thinking construed them. Egypt must be defended by all the exertions of British diplomacy; but how was diplomacy to safeguard it, when French opposition was virulent, constant and effective?

[1] Marschall to German ambassador in London, 15 Jun. 1894, *Grosse Politik*, VIII, 2053.

[2] The German attitude emerges from *ibid.*, nos. 2031–71.

[3] The French attitude emerges from *D.D.F.*, XI, nos. 109, 113, 122, 123, 127, 134, 138, 139, 142, 151, 165, 178, 184, 193; for a copy of text of Agreement of 12 May 1894, *vide* C. 7358, P.P. (1894) XCVI, 23–9; a few protests from the Powers are printed in C. 7390, 33–40.

[4] C. 7549, *ibid.*, 43–5.

[5] Hornik, *loc. cit.*, 235; Taylor, 'Prelude to Fashoda', 67.

[6] Harcourt to Kimberley, 12 Jun. 1894, Gardiner, *op. cit.*, II, 318; same to same, 16 Jul. 1894, 319–20.

[7] Russian ambassador in London to Giers, 31 May/12 Jun. 1894, *Correspondance Diplomatique de M. de Staal*, (ed. A. Meyendorff), (Paris, 1929), II, 245.

[8] Rosebery to Queen Victoria, 14 Jun. 1894, *Q.V.L.*, 3rd ser., II, 404–5.

On 29 June Hanotaux had a violent interview with Lord Dufferin, and this made two things plain. The Foreign Minister emphasised that France would not countenance any lease of the Bahr-el-Ghazal by Britain, and the ambassador declared that his government would not countenance any activity in it by France.[1] This warning probably persuaded Hanotaux to hold out against his own colonial zealots and to insist that the projected expedition from the Congo should halt short of the Nile.[2] But the fact remained that the road lay open once more to a French advance; and the British could not close it, except by agreeing directly with Paris.

The Niger and the Nile

Rosebery now resigned himself to trying for such a settlement, and his terms show how closely he was sticking to the African priorities worked out by Salisbury. The Prime Minister hoped that the French would give way on the Nile in return for large-scale concessions on the west coast. Since 1889 Britain had already surrendered the hinterlands of her old west African colonies, and had allowed the French to push the boundaries of Senegal and the Ivory Coast into the western Sudan. Sacrifices of this sort were part of high policy, but they clashed with local British interests in the region. Once France had proclaimed her protectorate over Dahomey in 1893 and had started the move inland towards Borgu and the Lower Niger, both the Royal Niger Company and the Lagos Government were up in arms. An agreement would put an end to this bickering. In the same way there were the new French advances in Guinea to be regularised. By her treaty with Liberia France had cut off Sierra Leone from the Niger Valley; by her expansion on the Ivory Coast she was in process of encircling the Gold Coast.

So Rosebery had plenty to sell. When the negotiations started in August, he was ready to make concessions in all these regions, if only the French in return would recognize the British sphere on the Upper Nile.[3] In private his entourage were ready to go as far in west Africa as the most chauvinist of Frenchmen could have desired. 'Take all you want in Africa,' the London *chargé* reported them as saying, 'provided that you keep off the valley of the Nile.'[4]

[1] Memo. by Hanotaux, 29 Jun. 1894, *D.D.F.*, XI, no. 178.

[2] This is the interpretation in P. Renouvin, ' Les Origines de l'Expédition de Fachoda,' *Revue Historique*, 1948, 183–4. cf. C. Vergniol, 'Fachoda, les Origines de la Mission Marchand,' *Revue de France*, 1 Aug. 1936, pp. 431–2, 15 Aug. 1936, 639–42.

[3] British *chargé* in Paris to Hanotaux, 9 Oct. 1894, *D.D.F.*, XI, no. 243.

[4] French *chargé* in London to Hanotaux, no. 274, Confidential, 22 Sept. 1894, A.E. Angleterre, 897.

But Hanotaux stuck to his conditions before he would go down to the bargain basement. He knew that Colonel Colvile in Uganda was likely to move north to settle the Nile question behind the diplomats' backs, and all he was ready to offer was a standstill. If Colvile kept quiet in Buganda and Bunyoro, the French would keep out of the Nile Valley.[1] This was not enough for Rosebery, and on 7 November the negotiation vanished into thin air, taking with it the promised west African settlement.[2]

From now on the disputes over the Niger were sharpened. There was a factitious, an artificial quality about the British claims, since the Foreign Office prized them chiefly as a way of retaliating against French intransigence on the Upper Nile; in the eyes of London they could always be compounded, obliterated or comprehended in some larger settlement for the sake of the larger interest.[3] But from now on, this was not to be so easy. West Africa teemed with subjects for dispute, as was natural enough where Sir George Goldie was operating. Already he had launched Lugard on a filibuster into the Borgu country,[4] and Englishmen and Frenchmen were soon racing each other to be first at Nikki, its capital. Once the Royal Niger Company was explicitly committed to the struggle for Borgu, the Foreign Office had much less freedom of action to throw it away.

For the time being, there was still some room for manoeuvre, because 1894 was a bad year for the *enragés* of the French colonial party. After the striking victories of the previous year against the Muslim leaders of the western Sudan, the military were held back by the civilians in Paris who thought the advance had gone far enough. Yet if the French thrusts were braked in one place, they went on in others. From Dahomey the push towards the Niger continued, and the decision at the end of 1894 to subjugate Madagascar showed that the forward party were pressing once more.[5] The result was another fine crop of Niger disputes at the end of the year. Understandably Kimberley with his mid-

[1] Memo. by Hanotaux, 7 Oct. 1894, *D.D.F.*, XI, no. 240. For the whole negotiation *vide* A. J. P. Taylor, 'Prelude to Fashoda,' *English Historical Review*, 1950, 52–80.

[2] Memo. by Hanotaux, 7 Nov. 1894, *D.D.F.*, XI, no. 272. All that was salvaged from the west African wreckage was an agreement about the frontiers of Sierra Leone.

[3] For Rosebery's own estimation of these disputes, c.f. his remarks to the French ambassador about west African clashes earlier in the year: 'Do you find these African affairs interesting? They don't interest me at all, I tell you quite frankly. And I doubt very much whether we can win advantages from them,' (French ambassador in London to Casimir-Périer, no. 55, 27 Feb. 1894, A.E. Angleterre, 891.)

[4] Goldie's instructions to Lugard of 24 Jul. 1894 are summarised in Perham, *op. cit.* 493.

[5] A. Terrier and C. Mourey, *L'Oeuvre de la Troisième République en Afrique Occidentale* (Paris, 1910), 221–2, 242–8, 291–3; G. Hanotaux, *L'Affaire de Madagascar* (Paris, 1896), *passim.*

Victorian prejudices against tropical expansion felt gloomy about dealing with them. 'I often ask myself whether these African disputes are really worth taking seriously,' so he unburdened himself to the French ambassador. Northern and southern Africa apart, they were '. . . a matter of barren deserts or places where white men cannot live, dotted with thinly scattered tribes who cannot be made to work'.[1] Be this as it might, the deadlock on the Nile forced him to face up to the consequences on the Niger.

The Watch on the Nile

Once the British and French Governments had broken off negotiations, each suspected that the other's Nile project was more advanced than its own. In September 1894 the French embassy in London was seriously discussing whether Rosebery would chance an attack against the Dervishes.[2] In November the Council of Ministers were so afraid that Colvile might drive northwards from Uganda that they sent Liotard to the Upper Ubanghi, to begin the stroke planned the year before.[3] London too had its anxieties. Once the Anglo-Congolese agreement had broken down, Egyptian Intelligence forecast that '. . . ere long we may expect to hear of some interesting combinations in those districts which . . . form an easily accessible route to the Nile valley in the vicinity of Fashoda'.[4] By 1895 the threat was becoming open. The *Bulletin du Comité de l'Afrique française* was issuing glowing prophecies about the great *coup* impending on the Nile, and one of the colonial group had said as much in the Chamber.[5] This told the British Government nothing that they did not know already, but they went on steadily refusing another negotiation.[6] Indeed they translated their private warnings into public speech, when Grey, the Foreign Under-Secretary declared on 28 March that a French advance into the Bahr-el-Ghazal would be construed as 'an unfriendly act'.[7] This told the Quai d'Orsay in turn nothing which it did not know; but it was an interesting forerunner of the new diplomacy, with its addiction to public warnings.

[1] French ambassador in London to Hanotaux, 10 Jan. 1895, *D.D.F.*, XI, no. 333.
[2] French *chargé* in London to Hanotaux, no. 274, Confidential, 22 Sept. 1894, A.E. Angleterre, 897.
[3] Hanotaux to Delcassé, 5 Dec. 1894, *D.D.F.*, XI, no. 305; Hanotaux to French ambassador in London, no. 435, Confidential, 8 Dec. 1894, A.E. Angleterre, 899.
[4] Intelligence Report for Sept. 1894, encl. in W.O. to F.O., 29 Oct. 1894, F.O. 78/4986.
[5] cf. *D.D.F.*, XI, p. 618, fn. 2.
[6] French ambassador in London to Hanotaux, 23 Feb. 1895; same to same, 6 Mar. 1895, *ibid.*, nos. 377, 396.
[7] *Hansard*, 4th ser., XXXII, cols. 405–6.

This strident declaration that the ownership of a desert might be worth a war is the first note of the hysteria which was to overwhelm foreign policy toward the end of the century. It provoked the French at a time when Rosebery had good reasons for keeping them well disposed. His relations with Germany were bad, and he was acting for the moment with Russia and France in an effort to stop the massacre of Armenians in the Ottoman Empire. Moreover, Rosebery was conciliating the Russians by agreeing with them about the Pamirs on the northern frontiers of India, in an attempt to prop up the position in the Mediterranean and to halt the decline of British pre-eminence in China.[1]

Grey's Declaration was a confession of failure. Liotard and his men were still poised in Ubanghi, and the Nile was still open. That was one element of urgency in the situation. But the Foreign Office had a further reason for taking a belligerent stand on the Sudan. As Salisbury had said, the Dervishes would keep the bed warm until the Egyptian army came to stay. But from the early Eighteen nineties this comforting assumption grew less plausible, and the evidence grew that the Dervish power was breaking up. Intelligence officers in Egypt believed that the army of the Khalifate was past its best;[2] Father Ohrwalder, who escaped from the Sudan after ten years as a prisoner, reported that the country had been ravaged by famine;[3] and this testimony was confirmed by Slatin, who escaped in 1895 and brought new information to Cairo. Slatin asserted that 'a well-organised and well-led force of sufficient strength could undoubtedly re-occupy the Sudan within a reasonable period'.[4] This was encouraging up to a point, but it carried the cheerless corollary that Britain would not be the only Power which could mount such a force. The implications were not lost on Cromer. In November 1894 he was worried lest the Italians should beat the Khalifa too soundly, and 'fearful of having this abominable Sudan question forced on us prematurely'.[5] Egypt was still not strong enough to take the opportunity of reconquering the Sudan. In 1894 her treasury had a surplus of three-quarters of a million, but most of it was locked up in debt service or available only with the consent of the *Caisse*; and for

[1] *vide* Langer, *Diplomacy of Imperialism*; Israel, *op. cit.*, 64–7, who notes that on 11 Mar. 1895 Britain and Russia ratified their agreement over spheres of influence around the Pamirs. It provided for large British concessions. For the position in China *vide infra*, 340.

[2] F. R. Wingate, *Mahdiism and the Egyptian Sudan*, (1891).

[3] J. Ohrwalder, *Ten Years' Captivity in the Mahdi's Camp*, (1892).

[4] D.M.I. Egypt, General Report on the Egyptian Sudan, 18 Apr. 1895, encl. in Cromer to Kimberley, no. 44, Confidential, 20 Apr. 1895, F.O. 78/4668. The passage quoted was marked by an F.O. official.

[5] Cromer to Kimberley, 9 Nov. 1894, Zetland, *op. cit.*, 221.

1895 Cromer had framed a cautious Budget 'on the basis of maintaining the *status quo*'.[1] Evidently, not much was to be hoped for from Egypt. Neither could the British make sure of the Valley from the other end, for all Colvile's work to the north of Bunyoro. Without a railway from the east coast, Uganda could not serve as a forward base for any large operations on the Upper Nile. Consequently, the Foreign Office found itself without the means of exploiting what it took to be the crumbling of Dervish power,[2] when the French, or possibly the Italians or Belgians, seemed only too likely to do so. Grey himself put this dilemma two years later, when the British invasion had already begun:

> 'The pivot of the whole question of a movement into the Soudan has always seemed to me to be the condition of the . . . Khalifa's power. . . . When the Khalifa's power breaks up anarchy must ensue. This anarchy produces such disorder and weakness on the Egyptian frontier that you are almost bound to interfere: but it does more than this, it creates a standing temptation and provocation for other powers, be they Belgians or French, or some devilry working through Abyssinian intrigue, to interfere, to occupy, and to establish claims for themselves. . . . As long as the Khalifa was strong it did not so much matter. . . .'[3]

Hence Grey's blunt warning went out on 28 March, 1895.[4] Kimberley did something to tone it down,[5] but the fact remained that the British could not afford to wait much longer before reconquering the Sudan. As usual, it was Cromer who went straight to the point:

> 'The force of circumstances, much more than the faults of any Ministry or of any individuals, has driven us into a situation which renders war a not improbable solution of the whole mess. . . . I wish the works at Gibraltar were finished . . . I cannot . . . help thinking that it will not be possible or desirable to maintain a purely passive attitude much longer.'[6]

This was a bleak prospect, and the Rosebery government was in no case to accept it, if anything better could be obtained. Uneasily poised between the two alliances of Europe, edging towards Russia but yet

[1] Cromer to Kimberley, no. 23, 22 Feb. 1895, F.O. 78/4668.

[2] Of course theirs was a partial and external judgement. There is an assessment from Sudanese sources in J. A. Reid, 'Some Notes on the Khalifa Abdullahi . . . ,' *Sudan Notes and Records*, 1938, 207–11. c.f. also P. M. Holt, *The Mahdist State in the Sudan, 1881–1898*, (1958), 185–93.

[3] Grey to Munro Ferguson, Jan. 1897, G. M. Trevelyan, *Grey of Fallodon*, (1937), 62–3.

[4] No doubt Rosebery's petulance had something to do with it as well, as Mr. Taylor suggests, ('Prelude to Fashoda,' *loc. cit.*, 76–7).

[5] French ambassador to Hanotaux, 2 Apr. 1895, *D.D.F.*, XI, no. 423; same to same, Apr. 1895, *ibid.*, no. 429; same to same, 6 Apr. 1895, *ibid.*, no. 435.

[6] Cromer to Rosebery, 13 Apr. 1895, Zetland, *op. cit.*, 214–5.

afraid of German resentment, the ministry had much to gain from abating the clash with France. On 10 May Kimberley tried a last time. If the French would recognise the Egyptian (that is, the British) sphere on the Nile as far south as Fashoda, then he would agree to a stand-still arrangement in the remainder of the Valley. It was not much of a concession, and certainly not enought to attract Hanotaux. Nevertheless, this was as far as the Foreign Office dared to go. The French turned it down.[1] On 12 June the Nile negotiations were broken off.[2] Nine days later the government fell. Lord Rosebery had not solved the question of the Nile.

[1] Taylor, *loc. cit.*, 79; French ambassador in London to Hanotaux, 11 May 1895, *D.D.F.*, XII, no. 3.

[2] Memo. by Hanotaux, 12 Jun. 1895, *ibid.*, no. 62.

CHAPTER XII

The Way to Fashoda

The Invasion of the Sudan

On 25 June 1895, Salisbury returned to power after an election in which the coalition of Conservatives and Liberal Unionists had won an overwhelming victory.[1] Here was the first British Government during the partition which was not divided on large issues of foreign policy, and which was not distracted and jeopardised by the Irish question. The result was a steadiness in policy which had been absent since 1880. In addition, Salisbury now presided over one of the ablest Cabinets of the century.[2] But the presence of these active and powerful colleagues meant that the Prime Minister could not look forward to the same free hand in foreign affairs that he had enjoyed between 1887 and 1892. Out of nineteen Cabinet seats the Liberal Unionists had been given five — an indication of how much the Conservative leadership depended on their support; indeed, Salisbury went so far as to offer the Foreign Office to the Duke of Devonshire (the former Hartington). But if the Duke could be relied upon not to strive officiously for the spoils, it was not so with Chamberlain. He moved quickly into his stride, and soon aroused the irony and the disquiet of the Prime Minister. A relative of the Cecils noted that 'I never heard him talk of any colleague as he does of him, says Chamberlain wants to go to war with every Power in the World, and has no thought but Imperialism'.[3] If foreign policy was to be kept free from the

[1] After the election there were 340 Conservatives and 71 Liberal Unionists against 177 Liberals and 83 Irish Nationalists.

[2] *Lord Salisbury's third Cabinet*

Premier and Foreign Secretary:	Marquess of Salisbury.
First Lord of the Treasury:	A. J. Balfour.
Lord President:	Duke of Devonshire, Lib. U.
Chancellor of the Exchequer:	Sir Michael Hicks Beach.
Colonial Secretary:	Joseph Chamberlain, Lib. U.
Secretary for War:	Marquess of Lansdowne, Lib. U.
First Lord of the Admiralty:	G. J. Goschen, Lib. U.
Chancellor of the Duchy:	Lord James of Hereford, Lib. U.

The other eleven members of the Cabinet were all Conservatives.

[3] Journal of Lady Frances Balfour, 26 Nov. 1895, printed in her *Ne Obliviscaris*, (1930), II, 270.

interference of the Colonial Secretary, then it must justify itself by its successes.

But successes now were harder to win than in 1892. The whole international position was more complicated. Then, there had been a lull in the Egyptian question, but now things seemed to be moving swiftly towards a crisis. In 1892, again, the Near East had been quiet; and although the Franco-Russian combination might have made it doubtful whether the Straits could be defended, the Navy did not have to try. But in 1895 it looked as though that hour had come, for the Armenian massacres might well provoke drastic European intervention at Constantinople.[1] Lastly, the international position was now further complicated by a new issue which had arisen since Salisbury's second ministry. After April 1895 Germany, France and Russia had acted together to protect China against Japan, with the result that Britain lost her position as protector of Peking and arbiter in the Far East which she had held for half a century.[2]

These were all grave developments. Each of them was a continuation or a consequence of Anglo-Russian rivalry. Since the Eighteen twenties the two had struggled over the approaches to India and the balance of Europe, and now their interests clashed at one point after another between the Mediterranean and the Yellow Sea. The Franco-Russian alliance made these British positions increasingly hard to defend. Russian support helped the French to threaten Britain on the Nile; French support helped the Russians to threaten Britain at the Straits; joint action by the two was overturning British paramountcy in the Far East. Nor was it so easy as of old to counter this by the aid of the Triple Alliance. Here everything depended on Germany, and her action in destroying the Anglo-Congolese Agreement in 1894 and in joining with France and Russia in the Sino-Japanese crisis of 1895 showed that she could not be relied upon to help defend British interests.

Salisbury soon had fresh evidence of this. In July and August he held the celebrated interviews with Hatzfeldt and talked candidly about the possibility of breaking up Turkey and abandoning Constantinople to the Russians. The subsequent meeting between Salisbury and the Kaiser showed that the Germans would have nothing

[1] Langer, *Diplomacy*, 145–64; P. Cambon, *Correspondance*, 1870–1924, (Paris, 1940), I, 389–98.

[2] P. Renouvin, *La Question d'Extrême Orient, 1840–1940* (Paris, 1946) 139–76; H. Zuhlke, *Die Rolle des Fernen Ostens in den Politischen Beziehungen der Mächte, 1895–1905*, (Berlin, 1929), 46–64; P. Joseph, *Foreign Diplomacy in China, 1894–1900*, (1928), 124–72.

to do with such a plan, and it left both men thinking the worst about the other.[1]

Whether Salisbury was seriously intending to go ahead with the partition of Turkey is uncertain.[2] Certainly, he had no wish to see the Ottoman empire go down,[3] but things were as they were: Turkish power was rotten, the *Franco-Russe* would make naval protection ineffective. These were strong arguments for trying to settle with Russia, and so stabilise the position in China.[4] The very fact that Salisbury in 1895 was once more testing the notion of putting the Russians into Constantinople is itself a milestone along the road which finally led the British to write off the Turks in 1915.

His pessimism about holding Constantinople was soon to be confirmed. In fact, far from negotiating, the British and the Russians each suspected the other of designs on Constantinople.[5] On his side, Salisbury believed that the Tsar was preparing to rush the Straits and settle the whole matter out of hand without reference to British interests.[6] He now turned to the ultimate weapon of British diplomacy. He would send the Fleet to the Straits to enforce the will of England. But the old days were gone. The threat of the French fleet was too great, and without a

[1] Hatzfeldt to Hohenlohe, 10 Jul. 1895; Hatzfeldt to Holstein, 31 Jul. 1895; Hatzfeldt to German Foreign Office, 3 Aug. 1895; Kiderlen to German Foreign Office, 5 Aug. 1895; Hatzfeldt to German Foreign Office, 5 Aug. 1895; same to same, 7 Aug. 1895; *Grosse Politik*, X, nos. 2396, 2372, 2375, 2380, 2381, 2385.

[2] This controversy is not yet decided; *vide* F. Meinecke, *Geschichte des Deutsch-Englischen Bündnisproblems*, (Munich, 1927), 32–54; W. N. Medlicott, 'Lord Salisbury and Turkey,' *History*, (1927), 246–7; H. Preller, *Salisbury und die Türkische Frage im Jahre 1895*, (Stuttgart, 1930), *passim*; Langer, *Diplomacy*, 196–200; Israel, *op. cit.*, *passim*; Temperley and Penson, *op. cit.*, 494–5; L. M. Penson, 'The New Course in British Foreign Policy, 1892–1902,' *Transactions of the Royal Historical Society*, 1943, 132–3.

[3] Hatzfeldt to German Foreign Office, 3 Aug. 1895, *Grosse Politik* X, 2375.

[4] Two of his comments are of interest. '. . . We are engaged in slowly escaping from the dangerous errors of 1846–1856. . . . We have . . . the necessity of coping, practically alone, with the alliance of France and Russia. . . . It may not be possible for England and Russia to return to their old relations. But it is an object to be wished for and approached as opportunity offers,' (Salisbury to Iwan-Muller, 31 Aug. 1896, *B.D.*, VI, Appendix IV, 780.) cf. the interesting letter written five years later: 'I agree — and have long agreed — in the expediency of a closer friendship with Russia. By predilection I am an old Tory, and would have rejoiced if we had been able to maintain the friendship with Russia which existed in 1815.

But the possibility of improving our relations is constantly growing more questionable. . . .

I wish it were otherwise: but wishing is no good,' (Salisbury to Maccoll, 6 Sept. 1901, *Malcolm Maccoll, Memoirs and Correspondence* (ed. G. W. E. Russell,) (1914), 282–3.)

[5] French *chargé d'affaires* at St. Petersburg to Berthelot, 15 Nov. 1895; Russian embassy in Paris to *Directeur Politique*, 16 Nov. 1895; *D.D.F.* XII, 200, 202; German ambassador in St. Petersburg to Hohenlohe, 29 Oct. 1895, *Grosse Politik*, X, no. 2446.

[6] 'The Admiralty records show beyond a reasonable doubt that Salisbury's plan was actuated by the fear that Russia was preparing to execute a coup and seize Constantinople and the Straits,' (Marder, *op. cit.*, 245.)

guarantee of French neutrality, the Admiralty would have nothing to do with the plan.[1] Salisbury might sneer at the admirals with their porcelain ships, but the fact remained that it was the end of an epoch. The mailed fist could not strike. The enforced shift of interest in the Mediterranean from Constantinople to Cairo was practically complete.[2]

But it did not immediately lead Salisbury to take a more determined line over the Sudan. Ever since his return to the Foreign Office he had tried to reduce British dependence on the Triple Alliance, by tacking gently towards the Franco-Russian combination. There was nothing to be got out of Saint Petersburg, as the Straits crisis showed; but there were better prospects at Paris, where Hanotaux was not averse to winning some freedom of movement for French policy. The Egyptian question was too important and too difficult to be dealt with; but there were plenty of secondary issues where negotiation might be useful. On 13 August (a week after Salisbury's talks with the Germans over Turkey had ended so badly) he agreed to start negotiations with the French over Siam;[3] and on 23 October he promised that a commission should consider the claims of France and Britain in west Africa.[4]

Here the matter at issue was the troublesome question of Borgu. The French wanted it for the hinterland of Dahomey; but, resting on the agreement of 1890, the British claimed that since it lay to the west of the Niger bend south of the Say-Barruwa line, it was within their sphere. Acting for the Royal Niger Company, Lugard had made a treaty with Borgu. So had the French. Each side disputed the treaties of the other.[5] Moreover, Captain Toutée struck inland from Dahomey to the Niger, and in February 1895 he had set up a fort on the lower course of the river.[6] In this way the Foreign Office learned that Goldie's claims of effective occupation were grossly exaggerated.[7] But if all these quarrels seemed large to Sir George Goldie, they seemed small to Lord Salisbury. For reasons of world policy he wanted to settle with France as many local disputes as possible, in the hope that this would bring the

[1] *ibid.*, 244–5.

[2] German ambassador in Paris to Hohenlohe, 16 Jan. 1896, *Grosse Politik*, XI, no. 2650.

[3] J. D. Hargreaves, 'Entente Manquée: Anglo-French Relations 1895–1896,' *Cambridge Historical Journal*, 1953, 69–74.

[4] French ambassador in London to Hanotaux, 23 Oct. 1895, *D.D.F.*, XII, no. 181.

[5] Hanotaux to British ambassador in Paris, 18 Jul. 1895; British *chargé d'affaires* in Paris to Hanotaux, 15 Aug. 1895, *ibid.*, nos. 93, 129.

[6] Le Général Toutée, *Dahomé, Niger, Touareg*, (5th ed., Paris, 1917), 218–23, 348; *idem. Du Dahomé au Sahara*, (3rd ed., Paris, 1914), 197–216.

[7] Perham, *op. cit.* 539.

two countries into closer alignment. The quarrel on the Nile was too large to be mended in this way;[1] but the quarrel on the Niger was not. Once again British policy was turning to its favourite expedient of giving way in west Africa.

At the beginning of 1896 came a surprise which made French friendship more desirable than ever. On 3 January the Kaiser sent his celebrated telegram to Kruger, congratulating him on foiling the Jameson Raid.[2] To Salisbury the telegram seemed another German attempt '. . . to frighten England into joining the Triple Alliance';[3] its effect was to make him swing more closely to France. The Cabinet felt it '. . . to be important in the present state of things to settle as many questions with France as possible',[4] and on 15 January ministers decided to re-open the Niger negotiations. This gave the desired impression: '. . . we might yet live to see an *Entente Cordiale* of the Western Powers — new edition,'[5] prophesied Hatzfeldt. As a tactical move, the new course suited Salisbury's short-term interests well. It paid off the score of the telegram, and it cooled down the fire-eaters in west Africa.

The Niger commissioners met on 8 February. A week later they were at odds. The British claimed all the territory south of the line fixed by the Agreement of 1890, which would have secured their title to Sokoto and Bornu. The French retorted by claiming compensation west of the Niger bend, which raised once more the awkward question of Borgu and Nikki.[6] There was the usual parade of partisan theses, but not much was to be got out of the talks. It might help Salisbury's European situation to tack gently towards France, but for the highest reasons of Mediterranean policy, he could not go far. A general African settlement with France would have presupposed a settlement over Egypt and the Nile Valley, and here neither side trusted the other an inch. Here too Salisbury had nothing to sell. With the future of the Ottoman Empire so uncertain, it was obvious that he was not going to open the question of leaving Egypt;[7] and so when the French hinted at it, he replied with

[1] French ambassador to Hanotaux, 29 Sept. 1895, *D.D.F.*, XII, no. 161.

[2] Kaiser Wilhelm II to President Kruger, 3 Jan. 1896, *Grosse Politik*, XI, no. 2610. For its significance *vide infra*, 430–1.

[3] Salisbury to Queen Victoria, 12 Jan. 1896, *Q.V.L.*, 3rd ser., III, 21.

[4] Same to same, 11 Jan. 1896, quoted in Hargreaves, *loc. cit.* 75.

[5] German ambassador in London to Holstein, 21 Jan. 1896, *Grosse Politik*, XI, no. 2636.

[6] British Commissioners to Dufferin, 15 Feb. 1896, encl. in Dufferin to Salisbury, no. 22, Africa, 15 Feb. 1896, F.O. 27/3274. The proceedings of the commissioners are to be found in A.E. Angleterre, 913.

[7] French ambassador in London to Berthelot, no. 30, 11 Jan. 1896, A.E. Angleterre, 911.

the standard British references to the anarchy that would follow.[1] Deadlocked in the east, the negotiations in the west were bound to fall into the hands of the colonial zealots of both governments. Sir Percy Anderson wrote of 'the monstrous French pretension', and urged that the Royal Niger Company should be supported against it. Salisbury could see nothing for it but to concur,[2] although it was already suspected in the French embassy that government was tiring of Goldie's Company.[3] Nor was the Quai d'Orsay any more conciliatory. On west African matters Berthelot, the Foreign Minister, seems to have been screwed up to a high level of intransigence by the colonial party,[4] and he was giving little away. Not that it mattered very much. At last the great *coup* on the Nile was about to start — indeed Berthelot himself had signed the orders.

Liotard's mission in the Upper Ubanghi had been badly delayed by the pressure of the Congolese on French territory. Towards the end of 1895 the Colonial Ministry had called for action on the new proposals of Captain Marchand, who was confident of forcing a way to the Bahr-el-Ghazal and then to the Nile. Hanotaux had been too wary to give complete sanction to so explosive a scheme, but the colonial party had better luck with the unworldly chemist who succeeded him. On 30 November Berthelot agreed to the venture.[5] At the same time the French were clearing the way for a combined movement from the east. Menelek was willing to sign a treaty with them, and at the end of 1895 they managed to stop the Somali port of Zeyla from falling to the Italians. The supply line to Ethiopia was open. It might soon be needed.[6]

[1] Same to same, 19 Feb. 1896, *D.D.F.*, XII, no. 306. It might seem from this volume that a spirited Anglo-French negotiation on Egypt had begun in 1896. A.E. Angleterre 912 shows that this was not so.

[2] Minutes by Anderson, 17 Feb. 1896 and Salisbury, n.d. on Dufferin to Salisbury, no. 22, Africa, 15 Feb. 1896, F.O. 27/3274.

[3] French ambassador in London to Berthelot, no. 22, 20 Jan. 1896, A.E. Angleterre, 911.

[4] '. . . he is evidently disinclined to apply his own independent judgment to the consideration of a question to which he knows the Colonial group in the Chamber attach great importance, and he will undoubtedly continue to screen himself behind his Commissioners, who themselves probably take their orders from the French Colonial Office,' (Dufferin to Salisbury, no. 41, Confidential, 3 Mar. 1896, F.O. 27/3274.)

[5] This is not the place to analyse the timing of the Marchand Mission. Professor Renouvin has made the most instructive study of it in his article already cited. *vide* also C. Vergniol, 'Les Origines de la Mission Marchand,' *Revue de France*, 1 and 15 Aug., 1 Sept. 1936. The account in G. Lachapelle, *Le Ministère Méline* (Paris, 1928) adds little. For accounts by ministers *vide* G. Hanotaux, *Le Partage de l'Afrique: Fachoda*, (Paris, 1909), and A. Lebon, *La Politique de la France en Afrique, 1896–98*, (Paris, 1901); both untrustworthy.

[6] Memo by Hanotaux, 23 Jul. 1895; French ambassador in London to Berthelot, 18 Dec. 1895; Berthelot to French ambassador in London, 20 Dec. 1895, *D.D.F.*, XII, nos. 99, 240, 242, and c.f. *D.D.F.*, XIII, no. 76.

The British Foreign Office for their part realised only too well the danger of possible French thrusts to the Nile from west and east. In June 1895 British Intelligence at Cairo had again written a warning to this effect:

> 'Rumours have been current in Cairo of the arrival of a French expedition in the Bahr El Ghazal . . . there is no reason to assume that the arrival of French parties in that neighbourhood is impossible or unlikely . . . it is not unlikely that French agents may have come through the Galla country [*sc.* south-western Ethiopia] with a view to obtaining some influence along the line by which it is said they eventually hope to connect their Obok protectorate with their Haute Ubangi colony.'[1]

But in 1895 the danger was not thought to be pressing. In November Cromer was told that London was not contemplating an invasion of the Sudan in the near future.[2] Without any immediate threat to the Nile, Salisbury felt free to move closer to the French and further away from the Germans. He went on with the Niger negotiations. In January 1896, he hinted to the Germans that he might evacuate Egypt — a fable which partly succeeded in alarming Berlin.[3] At the beginning of February he refused an Austrian suggestion that the Mediterranean Agreements should be extended.[4] It is clear that the Triple Alliance was weakened considerably by the anxiety of both Austria and Italy at the worsening relations between London and Berlin.[5] Salisbury had no intention of breaking off the useful friendship with the Germans; but he had every intention of teaching them how valuable his friendship could be. He wished to improve relations with France, but he wanted to keep hold of Egypt and defend the Nile Valley still more.

Salisbury was the man in possession, and to him the Egyptian bird in the hand was worth much more than a flock of French promises in the bush. Egypt apart, he was ready to go on with the provisional policy of bettering relations with France, and trying to come to terms over the colonial disputes. Thus on 11 March there was a proposal that the west African problems should be thrashed out in London between Salisbury and the French ambassador[6]— much as the Anglo-German Agreement had been negotiated in 1890. On 12 March the Italian

[1] Intelligence Report, Egypt, no. 38, Confidential, 18 Jun. 1895; bound as Confidential Print in F.O. 78/4986.

[2] Cromer, *Modern Egypt*, (1908), II, 82; Zetland, *op. cit.* 223.

[3] German ambassador in London to Holstein, 21 Jan. 1896; Marschall to German ambassador in Vienna, 23 Feb. 1896; *Grosse Politik*, XI, nos. 2636, 2688.

[4] German ambassador in London to Hohenlohe, 8 Feb. 1896, *ibid.*, no. 2664.

[5] *ibid.*, cap. LXV, nos. 2659–69, cap. LXVI, nos. 2670–80.

[6] Hargreaves, *loc. cit.*, 82.

ambassador was reporting to Rome that relations between Britain and France seemed to be close.[1] Yet that same day Salisbury announced the invasion of the Sudan.

The Motives for the Invasion

The sudden decision to invade the Sudan was prompted by the Italian downfall in Ethiopia. In 1895 General Baratieri had advanced into the highlands and met such stiff resistance that on 7 December part of the army was beaten at Amba Alagi. Obviously the Italians were in trouble; obviously too, this did not worry Salisbury, who was no admirer of Crispi's. But the Foreign Office became suddenly alert when the Italians reported that Menelek and the Khalifa had agreed to launch a joint attack against Baratieri.[2] Salisbury at once mentioned the rumour to Cromer. He wrote that a Dervish attack on Kassala was 'not improbable' and enquired whether a demonstration in the neighbourhood of Wady Halfa would be useful 'to create a diversion'.[3] Cromer was against it. He was budgeting for a surplus of E £630,000 in 1896,[4] and he did not want it frittered away in the Sudan. The farthest he would go was to suggest a move inland from Suakin; but since there appeared to be no threat from the Dervishes, the plan was dropped for the time being.[5] The Italian position went from bad to worse, and Crispi tried desperately to drum up support from the Powers. But no one would help. He warned the British government that the Italians might be forced to withdraw from Kassala,[6] and Cromer himself underlined the warning by reporting that the Dervishes were massing around the town, and that it was 'on every ground most undesirable' that they should be allowed to re-occupy it. Once more he suggested a relief expedition from Suakin.[7] But Salisbury would have none of it. He telegraphed to Cairo:

> 'Military authorities here consider that occupation of posts you mention could not be effected without a conflict, and that if subsequently attacked and surrounded by Dervish forces operations for their relief on a considerable scale would be necessary.

[1] *D.D.I.*, 5–6. [2] Crispi, *La Prima Guerra d'Africa*, 369.
[3] Salisbury to Cromer, Telegram no. 1, 11 Jan. 1896; F.O. 78/4986.
[4] Cromer to Salisbury, no. 2, 11 Jan. 1896 (encl.); F.O. 78/4761.
[5] Cromer to Salisbury, Telegram no. 1, Confidential, 13 Jan. 1896; F.O. 78/4986. Salisbury to Cromer, Telegram, no. 2, 14 Jan. 1896; *ibid.*
[6] Memo. by Sanderson, 24 Feb. 1896; *ibid.*
[7] Cromer to Salisbury, 13 Mar. 1896; F.O. 78/4892; same to same, Telegram no. 17, Secret, 26 Feb. 1896; F.O. 78/4986.

I doubt if we are justified in risking these contingencies for a nominal advantage. We have no great interest in occupation of Kassala by Italy who went there without consulting us and rather against our wish. We have nothing to gain at present by occupying it ourselves. The power of the Khalifa tends steadily to diminish, and a waiting game is the obvious policy. *Whenever we are masters of the valley of the Nile Kassala will be easily dealt with. Till then it has little value.*'[1]

This is a revealing exchange. Plainly Cromer and Salisbury looked on the question of Kassala from different points of view. From the standpoint of Cairo it seemed important to take local action and keep the Dervishes off one of the affluents of the Nile. But in London the Foreign Secretary took a wider view. He had no wish to rush to the rescue of a member of the Triple Alliance, and was ready to see the Italians stew in their own juice. In any case, the Dervishes unaided would be unable to tamper with the flow of the river. Therefore he vetoed any sideshow from the east coast.

On 1 March came the great Italian disaster at Adua, where the Ethiopians routed the army of Baratieri. French rifles and Russian artillery advisers had worked well for Menelek.[2] Italian expansion in east Africa was brought to an end. It had never been popular in Italy. It was now detested.[3] Adua also threatened to complete Italy's detachment from the Triple Alliance; and in an effort to keep her in, the Kaiser now tried to patch up his quarrel with the British. On the evening of 3 March he called at the British Embassy and stayed until 1.30 in the morning, urging that France was making war against Italy in Ethiopia, that there was a deep Franco-Russian plot to despoil the British Empire, and that Salisbury would be well advised to go to the rescue of the Italians.[4] In other words, the Germans were now asking for support. Here was the vindication of Salisbury's policy of edging away from the Triple Alliance and teaching Berlin the value of his friendship. All the same, he refused to act. On 6 March he told the

[1] Salisbury to Cromer, Telegram no. 11, Secret, 29 Feb. 1896, F.O. 78/4986. The last two sentences (italics ours) were added in Salisbury's handwriting to the original draft.

[2] A. B. Wylde, *Modern Abyssinia*, (1901), 52.

[3] For the unpopularity in Italy of colonial adventures *vide* M. Hentze, *Pre-Fascist Italy*, (1939), 193–4, 199–201. cf. the remark of Crispi's successor: '*Non ci accingeremo mai a fare una politica di espansione. . . . Se anche il Negus ci offrisse il Tigre, noi lo rispingeremmo come un dono esiziale ai nostri interessi*', (quoted *ibid.*, 372). It is noteworthy that here is another country where expansion was unpopular during the so-called age of imperialism.

[4] Hohenlohe to German ambassador in London, 4 Mar. 1896. Memo. by Marschall, *c.* 4 Mar. 1896: *Grosse Politik*, XI, nos. 2770, 2771; Spring Rice to Villiers, 14 Mar. 1896, *The Letters and Friendships of Sir Cecil Spring Rice*, (ed. S. Gwynn), (1929), I, 200.

Germans he could do nothing to help in Ethiopia, and again on 8 March he turned down another appeal from the Italians.[1] Yet four days later the Cabinet decided upon an advance towards Dongola, nearly 200 miles south of the Egyptian frontier. What had made Salisbury change his mind?

Clearly, it was not the desire to save the Italian position at Kassala. He did not think that Kassala was worth saving, and in any case it lay across some 600 miles of desert from Dongola;[2] neither was he concerned to save the Italians, and indeed they saw that the move would not help them much.[3] Nor was it the case that he bent before the German importunity: he had paid little attention to the tirade of the Kaiser. Nor was the army sent forward because of some new French threat to the Nile: the British advance started on 12 March, whereas Marchand did not sail from France until 25 June, and in any case the Foreign Office had known about the French schemes for at least two years. It is unlikely that some shift of the European balance prompted Salisbury to invade the Sudan or that his moving purpose in doing so was to reconcile Germany at the cost of a renewed enmity with France.

Why Salisbury changed his mind may be deduced from the documents. On 10 March Ferrero, the Italian ambassador, again asked for British help. He reported that the position was critical. The Ethiopians and the Dervishes were both advancing on the Italian coastal strip at Eritrea, the former towards Asmara, the latter towards Keren. So the need for British help was greater than ever, and Ferrero asked for a diversion on the Nile ('*du côté du Nil*').[4] For the Italians in their desperation this was better than nothing; but for Salisbury it was better than he could have expected. It was in fact the opportunity he had been waiting for.

He explained his objectives privately to Cromer on the day after the Cabinet had agreed to the Dongola expedition.

> 'The decision . . . was inspired specially by a desire to help the Italians at Kassala, and to prevent the Dervishes from winning a conspicuous success which might have far-reaching results. In addition, we desired to kill two birds with one stone, and to use the same military effort to plant the foot of Egypt rather farther up the Nile. For this reason we preferred it

[1] German ambassador in London to Hohenlohe, 5 Mar. 1896; same to German Foreign Office, 6 Mar. 1896; same to same, 8 Mar. 1896; *Grosse Politik*, XI, nos. 2773, 2774, 2776.

[2] The lack of connexion between the offensive towards Dongola and the defensive needs of Kassala is lucidly set out in A. B. Theobald, *The Mahdiya* . . . , (1951), 194–5.

[3] *D.D.I.*, 16.

[4] Ferrero to Sanderson, 10 Mar. 1896; F.O. 78/4986.

to any movement from Suakim or in the direction of Kassala, because there would be no ulterior profit in these movements.'[1]

The Italian disaster provided the occasion; but it was not to help the Italians primarily that the British began the reconquest of the Sudan, as Lansdowne's explanation to the Cabinet shows:

> 'Our intervention was provoked by the imminent peril which at one moment appeared to threaten the Italian forces at Kassala and Adigrat. With the object of effecting a diversion in their favour, we have announced to the European Powers that we intend to advance up the Valley of the Nile, and that it seems to us expedient to occupy Dongola. Our explanations to Lord Cromer have, however, been more specific for we have told him that while the movement was intended to help the Italians, the ulterior object was to restore a portion of her lost territory to Egypt.
>
> It seems not unlikely that the original object of our interference may prove to be much less difficult of accomplishment than was anticipated. [The rains had saved Italian army from further disaster and it seemed that they might come to terms with Menelek.] But we shall not stop short of getting some permanent gain for Egypt.'

The War Minister went on to emphasise firmly that 'the ultimate aim' of the new policy was the reconquest of the Sudan, but echoing Salisbury's caution, he stressed that 'we must see how things go'.[2] The British attitude towards the Sudan hitherto had been based on the calculation that the Khalifate would decline far enough and fast enough for the Sudan to be occupied and the Nile to be protected before the French challenge materialised. It was Adua which upset this timetable. It had altered the balance within the entire region. The Dervishes would be immensely strengthened if they were joined by the victorious Menelek. The Ethiopians had proved much more formidable than had been expected. If they were in fact the tools of the French, then their defeat of Italy increased the threat to the Nile. The new menace from the east redoubled the old menace from the west. Thus Adua increased the long-term danger to Egypt. Salisbury reacted by ordering the long deferred invasion of the Sudan.

Thus the motives for opening the Dongola campaign lay in the strategy of the Nile Valley rather than in the play of the European balance. Since the end of 1889 the Foreign Office had striven to shut other Powers out of the Nile without ever quite succeeding. The British realised that surety could only be found in eventually occupying the whole of the Nile Valley, and Salisbury had long since laid his plans.

[1] Salisbury to Cromer, 13 Mar. 1896, Zetland, *op. cit.*, 223.

[2] Lansdowne, Cabinet Memo., 'Proposed Advance up the Nile Valley,' 24 Mar. 1896, S.P. (Private Cabinet Memo., 1895–1900, no. 10).

Sooner or later he would have to invade the Sudan from Egypt. But this would depend upon diplomatic opportunity, upon Egyptian finances and the strength of the Dervish power. The advance from the north might be too slow to beat the French, the Belgians and the Ethiopians to the Upper Nile. Therefore Salisbury had also envisaged the necessity for an advance from the south. Uganda was the base which he and Rosebery had taken for the purpose of reserving the southern Sudan; and by 1895, Salisbury was preparing to use the Protectorate as a base for regaining it.

It was for this reason that he urged on the building of the railway from Mombasa toward the Kikuyu country and Uganda. As Leader of the Opposition, Salisbury had castigated the Liberals for dallying over the line. He insisted that Britain could not afford to wait because 'there are four, if not five, Powers that are steadily advancing towards the upper waters of the Nile'.[1] No sooner was Salisbury back in office than he pressed forward the Uganda railway with all speed. In August the ministry announced its determination to push the line up to Lake Victoria — a distance of 650 miles.[2] At the end of the year, when Salisbury suspected Leopold II of new designs upon the Nile in collusion with the French, he candidly explained to the Queen the object of the railway. 'Our only chance', he wrote, 'is to keep the thing quiet until our railway to Uganda is sufficiently far advanced to enable us to send troops by it.'[3]

The government went to remarkable lengths for the sake of speed. It decided to build the line itself under the direction of a Committee sitting in the Foreign Office and immediately responsible to the Prime Minister.[4] By January 1896 the Committee was preparing estimates for the Treasury with but slight regard for financial prudence or technical practice. The plans were based on nothing better than the sketchy survey of the route made in 1892. Four years later, when Salisbury was explaining why the railway so far had cost two millions more than the estimate, he gave the real reason for the Committee's odd proceedings:

> 'Then it may be asked why we undertook a railway without a preliminary survey. My answer is that we did so with a perfect consciousness of what we were doing, and for the sake of speed. . . . There were considerations of a very cogent character which induced us to desire to finish, at the earliest period possible, what was practically our only access to those regions. At

[1] *Hansard*, 4th ser., XXX, col. 699 *et seq.* [2] *Hansard*, 4th ser., XXXVI, cols. 1290–7.

[3] Salisbury to Queen Victoria's Private Secretary, 5 Dec. 1895, *Q.V.L.* 3rd ser., II, 578. For Leopold's schemes, *vide* A. J. Wauters, *Histoire Politique du Congo Belge* (Brussels, 1911), 131–6.

[4] M. F. Hill, *Permanent Way, The Story of the Kenya and Uganda Railway*, (Nairobi, 1950), 132. This semi-official history of the line throws much light upon the strategic purpose of the railway.

> that time the battle of Omdurman had not been fought, the occupation of Fashoda had not taken place . . . and our position was one . . . of very considerable difficulty if any serious embarrassments with any European Power had arisen before we had done anything to make our military access to the place easier than it naturally was.'[1]

So, in April 1896 the military necessity for the Uganda line was enhanced by the same circumstances that dictated the advance on Dongola. In that month the Uganda Railway Committee decided that the line should be of heavy materials and of the same gauge as that chosen for the projected Egyptian line into the Sudan. It was hoped that the railway would reach the Lake in something less than four years and that the first hundred miles would be finished within one year.

At last in July 1896 the government went to the Commons for three million pounds to make the line.[2] No expense was to be spared and the second hundred miles was promised quickly. The debate on the Uganda Railway Bill,[3] as usual in things Egyptian, left the strategic point unsaid out of respect for French public opinion. Both front benches observed the customary conspiracy of silence.

In contrast with this sober planning to enter the Sudan from the south, the decision to invade from the north was abrupt. The Italian disaster provided the opportunity,[4] and opportunity was everything. The plight of the Italians at Kassala gave Salisbury a pretext for invasion which would be accepted by the House of Commons and also by the Triple Alliance.[5] Previously the move on Dongola would have

[1] *Hansard*, 4th ser., LXXXIV, cols. 584–5.

[2] The Chancellor of the Exchequer, Hicks Beach, like Goschen in 1891–2 dragged his feet over asking Parliament to vote the money for the Uganda Railway. Salisbury 'delivered his soul' to the Chancellor in protest and accused him of lack of courage. (Salisbury to Hicks Beach, 6 Apr. 1896, S.P. (Private, 1895–1900), Chancellor of Exchequer.)

[3] *Hansard*, 4th ser., XLIII, cols. 705–24, 1094–1109.

[4] To some diplomatic historians the opposite has seemed to be true. In his careful study of British policy in 1895–6, Mr. Hargreaves asserts that 'The decision to advance to Dongola . . . was really a moral gesture intended to reinsure England with the Triple Alliance'. (*Cambridge Historical Journal, loc. cit.*, 85.) Such a judgement assumes that British policy was governed entirely by the European considerations which guided other Powers. This was hardly the case. The Dongola decision was certainly a re-insurance, but it re-insured Britain in Egypt as much as it re-insured her with the Triple Alliance in Europe.

[5] This pretext was essential to Salisbury. He would not invade without it. The Italians themselves considered giving up Kassala. (J. L. Glanville, *Italy's Relations with England, 1896–1905*, Baltimore, 1934, 41.) For a moment Salisbury thought that they would let it go, and he telegraphed to Cromer that there would be no expedition. (Salisbury to Cromer, Telegram no. 20, 14 Mar. 1896, F.O. 78/4986.) The same day he learned that the Italians were going to hold on after all—and so the expedition was saved. As he commented to Cromer: 'If you think our proceedings abnormal, you will see that we have our difficulties to contend with. . . . Better not publish these oscillations of policy more than you can help.' (Salisbury to Cromer, Telegram no. 21, 14 Mar. 1896, F.O. 78/4986.)

been impossible, since Germany was estranged, and French opposition could be taken for granted. But now Germany was bound to support the advance for the sake of the Triple Alliance; and Germany controlled three votes on the *Caisse*. By helping the *Triplice* Salisbury helped himself. As in 1890, so in 1896, his moves in the Nile Valley were made when the diplomatic position was favourable. The state of Europe affected the timing of his advances in Africa; but what made those advances necessary were interests outside Europe.

There was also another consideration which ministers had to keep in mind. When Salisbury put the proposal to the Cabinet a most confused discussion took place.[1] Balfour and Chamberlain among others were fearful that the Sudan fiasco of 1884–5 might be repeated. If the Egyptian army should be beaten, they warned the Prime Minister, 'we should have to come to the rescue with a British army and I suppose that, besides other consequences, the Government would be deserted by its own followers.'[2] Salisbury agreed on the need for caution; but equally he insisted that if the advance was a mere demonstration, 'we shall miss a good opportunity.'[3]

Ministers, then, had their doubts; and not least about how the electors would respond to another adventure in the Sudan. The expedition was to be paid for by the Egyptian funds held by the *Caisse*. It would be no charge on the British taxpayer, and British soldiers would not be fighting. Moreover the House of Commons with its large Conservative majority was supposed to be imperialist in spirit. Nevertheless the government was so worried about the way in which members might react that they felt the expedition needed an elaborate justification.

The public reasons given for the move on Dongola were strange indeed. It was to prevent the invasion of Egypt. It was a sort of rescue party for the Italians. It was to check a serious set-back to 'the cause of civilisation in Africa'. It might ultimately go as far south as Dongola.

[1] 'I was asked a great number of questions connected with distances, and camels, and the rise of the Nile, and a variety of things on which Ministers could easily have got information from books and reports, the idea apparently in the minds of some of them being that the Dervishes might be squared by a commercial policy. . . . After answering various questions they finished the question of the Nile and began another without desiring me to withdraw. Lord Salisbury . . . discovered with horror that I was still in the room and gave me my *congé*. . . . Voluminous maps were on the table which very few of the Ministers were able to read. . . . It was an interesting experience to have had.' (*Memoirs of Field-Marshal Lord Grenfell*, (1925), 124–5.)

[2] Chamberlain to Salisbury, 11 Mar. 1896, Garvin, *op. cit.* III, 169–70.

[3] Salisbury to Chamberlain, 12 Mar. 1896; *ibid.*, 170–1. This serves to refute the unlikely story of de Staal that Salisbury was one of the last ministers to agree to the advance. (Russian ambassador in London to Lobanov, 1 Apr. 1896, de Staal, *op. cit.* II, 312.)

Kassala would be aided by the news of a forward movement 'even at many hundred miles distance . . . there is no better method'.[1] These singular propositions were repeated in a debate on Supply, when a number of stale telegrams were produced. But two points of great interest emerged from this second debate. The first was the powerful speech of Chamberlain in support of the expedition. The Colonial Secretary now said in public what Salisbury had for long been thinking in private. Speaking of Egypt, he said that in the past '. . . references were made to the periods at which the evacuation might possibly take place. That is a mistake which I do not think we are likely to repeat. All we say is . . . that the position in Egypt is such that the difficulties of evacuation are greater than we anticipated, and that it will take longer to make a self-supporting people of the Egyptian nation than we imagined to be possible. . . .' He went on to justify the advance by saying that '. . . the Nile is the life of Egypt, and that accordingly the control of the Nile is essential to the existence and security of Egypt'.[2] All these remarks might well have come out of the correspondence of Salisbury and Baring six years earlier; by 1896 they were becoming declared policy. But even Chamberlain was careful to point out that the aims of the advance were limited. The troops would move towards Dongola; but the scope of the advance would be determined by the amount of resistance they met.[3]

The other notable feature of the debate was the weakness of the Liberal opposition. Morley, and to a lesser extent Harcourt criticised the advance; but Grey's only objection to it was that the expedition was not going in by way of Suakin. As for the rest of the Liberal front bench, they did not speak. It was left to the Radicals and the Irish to come to Morley's support. Most of the Liberal leaders acquiesced in the invasion of the Sudan, as since 1891 they had come to accept the occupation of Egypt.[4]

Thus began the march on Dongola. With it there came what Chamberlain rightly called the 'new policy' towards the Sudan, which was in the

[1] *Hansard*, 4th ser., XXXVIII, cols. 1027–9 (Curzon), 1047–52 (Balfour).

[2] *Hansard*, 4th ser., XXXVIII, cols. 1500, 1506.

[3] Chamberlain's words indicate the goverment's uncertainty about the strength of the Dervishes: 'We have . . . been told by authorities from time to time . . . that the power of the Khalifa is waning. . . . But I think that it would be dangerous to place upon these statements anything like implicit reliance. I do not think it is possible to predict the effect of this advance. The advance itself will make clear whether . . . the Dervish power is hollow and a sham, or whether, on the contrary, it still stands so firmly as to make any assault upon it a dangerous and difficult operation.' (*ibid.*, cols. 1511–12.)

[4] *ibid.*, cols. 1478–96 (Morley), cols. 1512–18 (Labouchere), cols. 1520–2 (Grey), cols. 1537–45 (Dillon), cols. 1548–55 (Dilke), cols. 1564–71 (Harcourt).

end to take Kitchener on a journey of a thousand miles from the frontier of Egypt to the small fort at Fashoda. The decision to advance had been hurriedly taken amid doubts and confused opinions. The opportunism of Salisbury had snatched at the favourable moment and sharply altered the direction of British policy. He had been content to play a waiting game, but suddenly that was over and done with. The change in tactics was abrupt; but the purpose of strategy remained the same. It had been his set policy since 1889 to exclude European rivals from the Valley of the Nile. Now the time had come to do it once and for all. So too it was coming for the French. Three months later Marchand left for Africa.

The Consequences of the Invasion

'The expedition', wrote Baron de Staal from his vantage point in London, '. . . has completely modified everything. . . . It might be thought that the Triple Alliance is rising again from its ashes, that Britain is ready to turn towards it, and that Europe is once more divided into two hostile camps.'[1] Since the British government did not dare go to Parliament for the cost of the expedition, it had perforce to ask the *Caisse* for permission to use the appropriated revenues. The voting showed how the attack on the Dervishes had altered the relations between the Powers. Germany, Austria and Italy voted with the British; the French and Russian commissioners did not, and claimed that a split vote was invalid.[2] Paris might be reluctant to come to an outright break, but Saint Petersburg was not.[3] Indeed the Russians were at last really concerned about their ally's case in Egypt, for now that Lobanov had realised that the Suez Canal might have a bearing on the struggle fo. the Far East, he was out to break British control.[4] As usual, the rivalry in Cairo was faithfully reflected in Constantinople, where French and Russians pressed the Sultan to use what was left of his rights to stop the expedition, and Salisbury threatened him with sinister consequences if he did anything of the sort.[5]

Inevitably, the British détente with France came to an end. At the end of April Salisbury saw this so plainly that he announced that Britain would not evacuate Egypt until the whole of the Sudan was restored to

[1] Russian ambassador in London to Lobanov, 1 Apr. 1896, de Staal, *op. cit.* II, 313.

[2] Cromer to Salisbury, Telegram no. 64, 26 Mar. 1896, F.O. 78/4892.

[3] German ambassador in Paris to German Foreign Office, 18 Mar. 1896, *Grosse Politik*, XI, no. 2703; British ambassador in Paris to Salisbury, Telegram no. 9, 18 Mar. 1896, F.O. 78/4892.

[4] French ambassador in St. Petersburg to Bourgeois, 31 Mar. 1896, *D.D.F.*, XII, no. 361.

[5] Salisbury to British ambassador in Constantinople, Telegram no. 66, Very Confidential, 10 Apr. 1896, F.O. 78/4893.

her.[1] Six weeks later when Franco-Russian opposition had at last stopped the subsidy from the *Caisse*, he retorted that 'Dongola has many advantages, and one of its advantages is that it is on the road to Khartoum'.[2] So much for the protestations of March that Dongola would be the limit of the advance.

One of the first casualties of this rift was the west African negotiation. For a while the commissioners went on with their talks, but it was obvious that war on the Nile meant trouble on the Niger.[3] Several times that year Salisbury tried to mollify the French, and he hinted that the Royal Niger Company might be suppressed;[4] but faced with the larger conflict, Paris was not to be fobbed off with consolation prizes. So nothing could be done with France. But could something be done with Russia? Here Salisbury had everything to gain from a settlement. It would restore Britain's freedom to manoeuvre between the alliances. It would reduce the pressure in Egypt. Above all, it might put a brake on the attack against the old British pre-eminence in China, and might stop the open door closing against British trade.

There were equally cogent reasons for conciliating Russia in the Mediterranean. Salisbury therefore now tried to win Russia's friendship by writing off his losses at the Straits. Towards the end of 1896 he was offering the Russians an agreement over the future of Turkey and the opening of the Straits, which might well have sacrificed the traditional British interest at Constantinople. In a sybilline phrase, the Prime Minister hinted that 'the solution to the drama which is being played at Constantinople may help to give the solution to the drama in Egypt'.[5]

The questions which the Cabinet Defence Committee put to their strategical advisers in 1896 showed the way their minds were moving. They inquired: 'What would be the effect on British interests of opening the Straits (*a*) to all nations (*b*) to Russia' and also 'What is the strategical value to England of (*a*) Egypt (*b*) the Suez Canal?' Once again, the answer was that the Straits could not be defended.[6] The Director of Naval Intelligence wrote:

> 'The time . . . for jealously guarding the inviolability of the Dardanelles is passing away, and is not worth any important sacrifice now. [With

[1] This was the first public announcement; but the Prime Minister had already told the Queen that '. . . the ultimate object and intention was to go to Khartoum and restore it to Egypt. . . .' (Queen's Journal, 8 Apr. 1896, *Q.V.L.*, 3rd ser., III, 39.)

[2] *Hansard*, 4th ser., XLI, cols. 934–8.

[3] These futile negotiations can be followed in F.O. 27/3273, 3274, 3275.

[4] French ambassador in London to Hanotaux, 17 Dec. 1896, *D.D.F.*, XIII, no. 46.

[5] French ambassador in London to Hanotaux, 3 Oct. 1896, *D.D.F.*, XII, no. 468.

[6] D.M.I. Memo. on Naval Policy, 13 Oct. 1896, printed in Appendix III, Marder, *op. cit.*, 569–77; see also 268.

Russia in the eastern Mediterranean] . . .There would be only one way in which England could not only maintain herself in the Mediterranean at all, but continue to hold India, and that is by holding Egypt against all comers and making Alexandria a naval base.'[1]

By 1896 then the decision had finally been taken. The shift of British power from Constantinople to Cairo which had been going on since 1878 was complete.

But a settlement with Russia eluded Salisbury. This left the naval crisis in the Mediterranean still unsolved, and there was nothing for it except to go on expanding the fleet. The naval estimates rose sharply. Those presented by the Conservatives for 1896–7 were nearly twenty-two millions. By 1898–9 the figure had risen to twenty-four millions. Suspicion of the Russians and fear for the Mediterranean impelled this great building programme;[2] and the result was to give the British Mediterranean squadron a considerable superiority over the French. During the great crisis of 1898 this was to be decisive.

HESITATIONS IN THE SUDAN, 1896–7

Lord Cromer was intensely irritated by the decision to advance on Dongola. So hurriedly had it been taken, that he barely had time to run to the Khedive for his nominal consent before the newspapers published His Highness's orders to the Egyptian army.[3] But more than that, Cromer was an administrator rather than a statesman,[4] and he could see the invasion hampering the development programme in the Delta.[5] So his telegrams to London elaborated all the objections. The advance would cause a great deal of financial trouble.[6] It might lead to another diplomatic crisis.[7] It might give the agitators their chance. 'Native Anglophobe opposition was . . . very strong against the whole policy.'[8] Again,

'In the event of any sudden reverse . . . we might have trouble here for there can be no doubt that policy of advance is very unpopular among the

[1] D.N.I. Memo. on Naval Policy, 28 Oct. 1896, printed in Appendix IV, *ibid.* 578–80.

[2] Marder, *op. cit.* 260–82; A. D. Elliott, . . . *Life of* . . . *Goschen* (1911), II, 207, 213.

[3] Rodd, *op. cit.* II, 86–7. Salisbury apologised: 'We rather hurried on publicity by the advice of Lord Wolseley in order to assist the Italian garrison at Kassala.' (Salisbury to Cromer, Telegram, no. 18, 13 Mar. 1896, F.O. 78/4892.)

[4] As Salisbury put it: 'If the world was falling to pieces around his ears, but Egypt was left intact, Lord Cromer would not ask for more.' (French ambassador in London to Hanotaux, 3 Oct. 1896, *D.D.F.*, XIII, no. 468.)

[5] Cromer to Villiers Lister, Private, 30 Jan. 1896, F.O. 78/4761.

[6] Cromer to Salisbury, Telegrams nos. 28, 37, 40, 13, 16, 17 Mar. 1896, F.O. 78/4892.

[7] Same to same, Telegram, no. 28, 13 Mar. 1896, *ibid.*

[8] Same to same, Telegram, no. 39, 17 Mar. 1896, *ibid.*

most noisy part of the population, who declare that it is not dictated by regard for Egyptian interests.'[1]

The following day he telegraphed: 'I fear we are going to have considerable trouble with the Khedive.'[2] Here then was the result of thirteen years of occupation: a society inveterately anti-British, from the court to the market-place. Honest administration had not produced loyal collaboration. *La conquête des coeurs* was as far away as ever.

But the invasion was so important that Salisbury brushed aside the arguments of the Old India Hand. That did not mean that he was prepared to turn over the campaign either to the jingoes in the War Office or on the spot. Any amount of delay would be tolerated, rather than risk another disaster in the desert which might wreck the entire Nile Valley strategy. So the strength of the Mahdist state was to be slowly and cautiously probed;[3] Kitchener, the Sirdar of the Egyptian Army, was forbidden to rush beyond Akashah (one hundred miles south of the border) on his own initiative;[4] he was to drag the railway behind him; and control of the campaign was vested in Cromer himself, not in the War Office.[5]

All this deliberation and delay made it quite likely that the French would reach Fashoda before Kitchener had dealt with the Dervishes. But Salisbury could see no help for it. As he saw things, an all-out attack was politically impossible, since Parliament might jib at the expense this would involve.[6] The Cabinet was 'very strongly opposed' to sending Kitchener British reinforcements, and the furthest they dared go was to put Indian troops into Suakin.[7] Even when the Sirdar

[1] Same to same, Telegram, no. 41, Secret, 18 Mar. 1896, *ibid.*

[2] Same to same, Telegram, no. 44, Secret, 19 Mar. 1896, *ibid.*

[3] Salisbury to Cromer, Apr. 1896, Zetland, *op. cit.* 226.

[4] Sanderson (of F.O.) to Salisbury, Telegram, 1 Apr. 1896, F.O. 78/4775; Salisbury to Chamberlain, 12 Mar. 1896, Garvin, *op. cit.* III, 170.

[5] The transcript of a telegraphic conversation between Cromer and Kitchener brings out something of the mood at the time:

'Who is in the room with you?'

'Only Wingate,' [D.M.I., Egyptian Army.]

'I want you fully to understand the position . . . as regards the objects of the expedition . . . there can be no question of giving up the idea of going to Dongola, but you should fully understand that although in the more remote future a further advance may not impossibly be made, the objects of the present expedition are strictly limited to the capture of Dongola. There is at present no question of a general reconquest of the Soudan. . . . Even in the event of a further move forward in the more remote future the halt at Dongola will of necessity be in all probability of long duration.' (Transcript of 7 Apr. 1896, encl. in Cromer to Salisbury, no. 39, 7 Apr. 1896, F.O. 78/4893; c.f. Salisbury to Cromer, Telegram, no. 72, 1 May 1896, *ibid.*)

[6] Salisbury to Cromer, 1 Apr. 1896, Zetland, *op. cit.* 228.

[7] Same to same, Telegram, no. 64, 22 Apr. 1896, F.O. 78/4893. But it may also be that the Cabinet were reluctant to send troops to Egypt in the midst of their south African crisis; *vide* Salisbury to the Queen, 22 Apr. 1896, *Q.V.L.*, 3rd ser., III, 41.

captured Dongola in September, the Prime Minister was as despondent as ever about public opinion:

> 'The question of going forward to Khartoum is purely a question of money. There is no Egyptian money available. If it is done, it must be done with English money . . . my impression is that the House of Commons would *not* be disposed to authorise the expenditure.'[1]

But in the end the sophistications of the Nile Valley strategy had to be exposed to the whims of Demos. In November the British Treasury lent Egypt £800,000, to repay the money illegally borrowed from the *Caisse* and to pay for the railway and the gunboats. Hicks Beach, the Chancellor of the Exchequer, asked Parliament for approval of the loan, and added for good measure that by compelling Britain to make it, the decision of the Mixed Courts was 'rather likely' to prolong the occupation.[2] Yet only fifty-seven members voted against, and if they included Morley and Harcourt, they conspicuously did not include the rest of the Liberal leaders.[3] Clearly there was more jingoism in this House of Commons than Salisbury with his mid-Victorian notions had allowed for.

The decision to push the railway deeper into the Sudan was an irrevocable step to full-scale war. As the line crept on at the rate of a kilometre a day, Kitchener attacked once more, and by the end of August 1897 he had occupied Berber,[4] So the army now lay some two hundred miles from Khartoum. But the Khalifa and his emirs were still showing plenty of fight,[5] and it would need British troops to be sure of crushing them.[6] Cromer was against this for his usual administrative reasons; but Salisbury too was against any rapid overwhelming of the Sudan. He scouted:

> '. . . the diplomatic difficulties which might be interposed if any French explorer reaches the Nile before we have taken Khartoum. I am not greatly impressed by this danger, because we shall have to meet it anyhow. If we put into execution the claim of the Anglo-German agreement . . . I have no doubt we shall have a very lively protest from the French, and I doubt that it will be any the louder, or seriously louder, because upon some spot in the Nile Valley a French explorer may have succeeded in inducing some chief to accept a treaty. The diplomatic question will be interesting

[1] Same to same, 29 Sept. 1896, *ibid.*, III, 85.
[2] *Hansard*, 4th ser., XLV, col. 1444.
[3] Division List, Committee of Supply, *ibid.*, col. 1521.
[4] For the operations of 1897 *vide* H. S. L. Alford, and W. D. Sword, *The Egyptian Soudan, its Loss and Recovery*, (1898), 157–91.
[5] Holt, *op. cit.* 216–8.
[6] Cromer to Hicks Beach, 16 Dec. 1897, Zetland, *op. cit.* 231–2.

and difficult, but the increase of those qualities conferred by a French adventurer's "effective occupation" will not be serious.

It is to be remembered that by destroying the Dervish power we are killing the defender who is holding the valley for us now.'[1]

In the autumn of 1897 the Prime Minister could still play down the urgency of the Sudan campaign, for he had another weapon in the locker. Marchand might move faster than the Egyptian army, but he would not be the first at Fashoda. The British would win the race, not from Berber but from Uganda. The thrust from the south was put in to decide the swaying struggle in Ethiopia.

Frenchmen, Russians and Ethiopians

As the Sirdar built his railway deeper into the Sudan, French policy grew more enterprising in Ethiopia. It covered the eastern approaches of the Nile. It offered a river route to Fashoda.[2] Its emperor had good reason to be beholden to the French. By the end of 1896 they stood in great need of his help, for Marchand and his small party would not be a strong case for effective occupation, if they were confronted with Kitchener and his army. On the other hand, the French position would be vastly strengthened if Menelek and his hosts could be induced to move on to the river by agreement with the French. At the end of 1896 Lagarde was dispatched to reach such an agreement.

Ethiopia at this time was in transition. Menelek had the prestige of being the only African ruler who had got the better of the white man in war, and his independence had been starkly vindicated at Adua. None of the Powers was much inclined to rush in where the Italians had rushed out. At the end of the century Ethiopia became the haunt of a swarm of adventurers, freelances on the make, explorers and empire-builders. The country which had brought Rimbaud to his grave was enlivened by the activities of Greeks, Russians and Austrians, as well as citizens of those countries more usually connected with Africa. A Swiss engineer was Menelek's minister and councillor.[3] In 1897 and 1898 there were to be Cossacks, a French prince of the blood, and an English globetrotter. Most of this improbable set had their

[1] Salisbury to Lansdowne, 22 Oct. 1897, Lord Newton, *Lord Lansdowne*, (1929), 148.

[2] The River Sobat flows from western Ethiopia to join the Nile some hundred miles south of Fashoda.

[3] For a biography of him *vide* C. Keller, *Alfred Ilg*, (Leipzig, 1918). The Russian efforts are discussed in C. Jésman, *The Russians in Ethiopia, an Essay in Futility*, (1958). Other picturesque arrivals are mentioned in H. Le Roux, *Ménélik et Nous*, (Paris, 1905), and Count Gleichen, *With the Mission to Menelik, 1897*, (1898). In *Une Visite à l'Empereur Ménélik* the Prince Henri d'Orléans discusses his own arrival.

minds far away from the problems of the partition of Africa. But others were the rank and file in the great international struggle for the Nile.

Characteristically, the first statesman to see the possibilities in the country after Adua was Leopold of the Belgians, who made a bid the same year to take over the wreckage of the Italian sphere of influence.[1] It came to nothing, and Leopold went back to his schemes for reaching the Nile from the Congo Free State. The French mission was a much more serious affair. Lagarde was sent with one hundred thousand rifles and orders to make a treaty. On 14 March, 1897, he was told to encourage the Emperor to push a force up to the right bank of the Nile near Fashoda; this was 'indispensable'.[2] The reasons for haste are clear enough. It was already known that a British mission under Rennell Rodd, Cromer's chief assistant, was on its way to negotiate with Menelek; and moreover the French had heard a rumour that their Ubanghi expedition had reached the Nile. The British heard it as well.[3] The race was getting hotter.

In negotiating with the Emperor, Lagarde had several advantages over the emissaries of other Powers. There was the friendship which France had shown to Menelek in his adversity. There were the hundred thousand rifles. Above all there was the large addition of territory which France now offered to Ethiopia. On 20 March Lagarde got his treaty. The French Republic recognised Menelek's authority as far as a point about one hundred miles south of Khartoum, while he promised to 'give all the aid he can to the agents of the French government who will be on the left bank', from that point as far south as Lado.[4] This agreement neatly forestalled the Rodd mission, but it was important to get it into force before Rodd could try his blandishments on the Emperor. Two French parties were already reconnoitring the ground towards the Nile; Paris now spurred them on, and sent a further consignment of guns to keep Menelek in good heart.[5]

The British were well aware of these designs. In December 1896 Hicks Beach asked Salisbury '. . . whether it might not be well to send some kind of envoy to Abyssinia, to sooth away fears Menelek may have as to our Egyptian advance, and to find out whether he has any

[1] Langer, *Diplomacy*, 539–40, and references there cited.

[2] French minister of colonies to Lagarde, 14 Mar. 1897; *D.D.F.*, XIII, no. 149.

[3] French *chargé* in Cairo to Hanotaux, 17 Mar. 1897, *D.D.F.*, XIII, no. 154. He had already telegraphed the news to Paris. The Minister of Colonies knew it by 14 Mar.

[4] Convention for the White Nile, *ibid.*, no. 159. Menelek was to establish his authority on the right bank of the White Nile southwards from 14° N., and to help the French who would be on the left bank between 14° N. and 5·30° N.

[5] Minister of Colonies to Lagarde, 12 Apr. 1897; same to same, 19 Apr. 1897, *ibid.*, nos. 195, 203.

relations with the Mahdi'.[1] Should Ethiopia become a French base, and should its armies come to the rescue of the Khalifa, this would upset both Salisbury's strategy in the Nile Valley and Kitchener's tactics in the Sudan. The object of Rodd's mission was to keep Menelek neutral in the struggle.

Rodd had a poor hand to play. Salisbury empowered him to offer Menelek the same western frontier which the Prime Minister had offered to the Italians in 1891 and which had been carefully drawn up so as to keep them at a safe distance from the Nile.[2] If the Ethiopians would co-operate against the Dervishes, then the British government would agree to Menelek's frontier being pushed further along the Blue Nile as far as Karkuj and Famaka.[3] No doubt these seemed good terms in London, but in Addis Ababa they looked niggardly. Menelek was in the happy position of being able to auction his help, and he had already been made a better offer. The most that Rodd could get was a promise that the Emperor would not give guns to the Dervishes and a vague assurance of neutrality in the war against them.[4]

The failure of the British mission was inevitable. France could afford to be generous to Menelek with the land east of the Nile, but Salisbury could not. The campaign in the Sudan was meant to settle the Egyptian question once and for all. It was not meant to replace the Khalifa al-Mahdi by the Lion of Judah as the guardian of the Nile. The French could abet Menelek's ambitions in the west and turn them against the British; the British could not offer nearly so much, even to turn them against the Dervishes.[5] It was plain to Rodd and his advisers that the problem must be solved by the big battalions. Once Kitchener had fought his way to Khartoum and the British controlled the river down to Fashoda, Menelek was more likely to appreciate the justice of the British cause.[6]

When Salisbury learned of Rodd's failure, he was faced with an awkward decision. The bulk of the Egyptian army was still stuck at Dongola, and there was no hope of a rapid advance unless British regiments were put into the fighting. But in 1897 the Prime Minister did not want to use them, because he feared the diplomatic consequence

[1] Hicks Beach to Salisbury, 22 Dec. 1896, S.P. (Hicks Beach).

[2] *vide supra*, cap. X.

[3] F.O. to Rodd, Feb. 1897, F.O. 1/32. Karkuj is 12·58 N., 34·4 E., Famaka is 11·19 N., 34·46 E. The French had offered a frontier up to 14° N.

[4] Memo. by Wingate, encl. in Rodd to Salisbury, no. 18, Confidential, 9 May 1897, F.O. 1/32; Rodd, *op. cit.*, 171.

[5] J. R. Rodd, *Social and Diplomatic Memories, 1894–1901*, (1923), 171.

[6] Rodd to Salisbury, no. 21, Very Confidential, 14 May 1897, F.O. 1/32; Rodd, *op. cit.*, 168; Sir Ronald Wingate, *Wingate of the Sudan*, (1955), 112.

and he did not trust British opinion to support the commitment. As soon as Salisbury knew that Rodd had failed to detach Menelek from the French, he decided to deal with any possible Ethiopian advance on the Nile by putting in his long prepared push from Uganda.

In September 1896 the Prime Minister had felt that the Uganda railway was now an urgent matter,[1] and in that year government had obtained a vote[2] to extend the line from the Kikuyu country to Uganda. In March 1897 he observed: 'My impression is that there is more danger of French interference in the Nile Valley from the East than from the West.'[3] A month later he asked the Treasury for £35,000 to pay the cost of

> '. . . sending an expedition [from Uganda] to the east bank of the Nile to make friends with the tribes before the French get there from the west . . . the ostensible reason for despatch will be to explore the source of the Juba.'[4]

Macdonald, the commander in Uganda, hoped to capture Fashoda within a year.[5] Hicks Beach did not quite understand. 'Is it intended to take and keep Fashoda?' If so, the expedition seemed too small. If Macdonald's expedition was merely to make treaties with the tribes which the French, as in west Africa, would not respect, the force seemed too big.[6] Salisbury explained. In June 1897 Major Macdonald with five hundred men was ordered to march along the eastern side of the Nile toward Fashoda, making treaties as he went.[7]

The invasion from the south however was much less powerful than Salisbury had originally intended. For one thing, the builders of the railway inland from Mombasa had run into unforeseen obstacles and only eighty miles of line had been laid. Worse still, Macdonald's expedition was paralysed by the mutiny of the Sudanese garrison in Uganda

[1] Salisbury to Queen's Secretary, 2 Sept. 1896, *Q.V.L.*, 3rd ser., III, 72–3.

[2] The extension had inspired Labouchere's verse:

> 'What it will cost no words can express;
> What is its object no brains can suppose;
> Where it will start from no one can guess;
> Where it is going to nobody knows.'

[3] Salisbury, Minute on Macdonald to Barrington, 26 Mar. 1897, S.P. (Private Miscellaneous, Vol. 100).

[4] Barrington to Hicks Beach, 24 Apr. 1897, S.P. (Private, 1895–1900, Chancellor of the Exchequer).

[5] Macdonald to Barrington, 26 Mar. 1897, S.P. (Private Miscellaneous, Vol. 100). This volume contains the private correspondence about the expedition.

[6] Hicks Beach, Minute, 25 Apr. 1897, S.P. (Private, 1895–1900, Chancellor of the Exchequer).

[7] Salisbury to Macdonald, 9 June 1897, Low, *op. cit.*, 445–6; C. 8718 P.P. (1898) LX, 456.

in September, much to Menelek's satisfaction,[1] and then by Mwanga's rebellion in Buganda. As a result of these accidents, the expedition could not start out until the following year.[2] The Foreign Office knew by November 1897 that Macdonald could not get to Fashoda in time to affect the outcome. For all the long and careful preparation, the base in the Uganda protectorate supplied by the expensive Uganda railway proved useless in the event.

Thus by the beginning of 1898, the position in the Sudan seemed much more dangerous than Salisbury had foreseen. Rodd had failed to fend off the Ethiopians; Macdonald's mission had not yet started out; Kitchener had found the Dervishes so unexpectedly strong that he feared a counter-attack at Berber. Marchand, Menelek and the Khalifa all acting together might pose a problem that not even Kitchener's strong army could solve. The forces of Baker and Hicks had already been cut to pieces in that desert. To the Foreign Office these were gloomy memories to revive.

Salisbury's anxiety mounted after April 1897. He 'received unpleasant reports of the French having actually crossed the Nile, and if this is confirmed some other course may become necessary'.[3] If he was to confront Menelek and the French with a show of force then it would have to come from the north. Yet the Sirdar and his overlord in Cairo were at odds about how to push on. In November Kitchener was asking for British regiments for the storming of Khartoum. Cromer was against this, still hoping that an advance from Uganda would reach Fashoda in time. Hicks Beach and other ministers doubted whether Parliament and British opinion would approve of imperial money and troops being spent to take Khartum. The Chancellor wrote:

> 'As you know I have always sympathised with the advice Cromer now gives. There is, no doubt, a sentiment about Khartoum. But suppose it taken, after a stiff and costly fight, what then? Can we stop there? I think not: and if we did, our presence there would not prevent the French or Belgians taking Fashoda. If we want to anticipate them there, surely we could do it, at least risk and cost, by an expedition from the South, such as I thought Macdonald was now prospecting for. . . . And are we prepared to undertake the conquest and administration of all the country that used to be dependent on the Khedive in Ismail's time? Egypt certainly could not afford to do it now: possibly later she might.

[1] Lagarde to Hanotaux, 24 Dec. 1897, *D.D.F.* XIII, no. 386.

[2] For an account of the expedition *vide* H. H. Austin, *With Macdonald in Uganda*, (1903), espec., 7–8, 36–54. By Oct. 1898, Macdonald had got to Latuka, still more than five hundred miles from Fashoda. Here he had to turn back (*ibid.*, 157–9).

[3] Barrington to Macdonald, 8 Apr. 1897, S.P. (Private Miscellaneous, vol. 100).

This however is only part of the question. You and I can remember what happened in 1878–80. Our Afghan and Zulu misfortunes were the main cause of our defeat in 1880. We tried a forward policy in too many places at once. I am afraid of the same thing now. The Indian fighting is not yet done. When it is done, there will be a heavy bill . . . and it won't be popular. . . . I don't want to add a Khartoum expedition to our present engagements; to which, by the way, the soldiers would add the abnormal demands, at present in Crete and South Africa.'[1]

Yet when Kitchener telegraphed again for British troops on 1 January, 1898,[2] Salisbury was forced at last to take a direct part in the reconquest. As Cromer remarked:

'It looks as if the settlement of the Sudan business would be forced on us at once. Indeed, if we once begin to send English troops the sooner the whole thing can be settled and the troops brought back the better.'[3]

Now there was nothing for it but to send British troops.

Macdonald's was not the only project to break against the harsh facts of Africa. After Lagarde had reached his agreement with Menelek, the French had done their best to exploit this advantage. Two exploring parties, the one under Clochette, the other under Bonchamps, were moving towards the Nile. Prince Henri d'Orléans was in Addis Ababa, arranging for the opening up of the 'Equatorial Province' of Ethiopia, to which Menelek had just appointed as governer a rather shady Russian, Count Leontiev.[4] There was talk of forming an international syndicate to develop this territory, and as usual the resourceful Leopold II was one of its chief backers.[5] All this seemed promising enough, but in reality it was no more than a set of improvisations. Everything depended on Menelek's support and the success of Clochette and Bonchamps. The Emperor for his part meant to back the winner in this struggle between Europeans, and he would not commit himself deeply until he could see who that winner would be. Moreover the explorers came to

[1] Hicks Beach to Salisbury, 1 Nov. 1897, S.P. (Hicks Beach).

[2] Kitchener to Cromer, referred to in Cromer to Salisbury, no. 1, 1 Jan. 1898, F.O. 78/5049.

[3] Cromer to Salisbury, 1 Jan. 1898, Zetland, *op. cit.*, 232.

[4] Leontiev and d'Orléans told the French *chargé* in Cairo that the 'Equatorial Province' included the territory between the Juba, the whole of the Blue Nile, Galla-land, the Oromo and Lake Rudolph. (French *chargé* in Cairo to Hanotaux, 5 Aug. 1897, *D.D.F.*, XIII, no. 291.) This would have brought Ethiopian territory up to Khartoum and Uganda.

[5] Leopold also thought of sending a Congolese mission to Ethiopia. It was to have been headed by a Belgian priest, a former confessor of Menelek's. (Wauters, *op. cit.*, 147.)

grief as they toiled through the desolate country to the east of the Nile. In August Bonchamps caught up with the other party and found it in great distress; it was clear that Menelek was doing little to help,[1] and Bonchamps had to come back to Addis Ababa to remind the Emperor of his loyalty to France.

Meanwhile in Paris Hanotaux drove on the scheme as fast as he dared. In September he urged the Russians to combine more closely with the French agents in Ethiopia, since the independence of the country was 'of the very greatest importance'.[2] In October Paris sent peremptory orders that Bonchamps was to make another attempt to follow the River Sobat to the Nile.[3] So Bonchamps tried once more. By December he had struggled up to a point only one hundred miles from Fashoda. Hunger and exhaustion drove him back. Yet even this was not the end. On the way back the party met a large Ethiopian force sent by Menelek to establish his rule along the Sobat and up to the Nile.[4] Two of the Frenchmen went back westwards with this column, and so did a Russian from the legation at Addis Ababa. On 22 June, 1898, they finally reached the Nile, where it is joined by the Sobat. A short way upriver lay Fashoda, and they looked anxiously for the Marchand expedition. There was no sign of it. The heat, the fever, the swamps were too much, and they too had to turn back. Before leaving, they decided to plant a flag on an island in midstream, but only the Russian could still scrape the strength to do so. It was a Russian colonel who finally raised the flag of France on the Nile.[5] Then they withdrew. Three weeks later Marchand arrived at Fashoda.

He too had found it hard going. The mission had been delayed in the Congo by a native war and a quarrel with Brazza. Then he had come up the Congo in a steamer provided by Leopold II;[6] he had dragged a dismantled boat across Africa as far as Fort Desaix, and then put it together to sail down the streams of the Bahr-el-Ghazal. His timetables had gone all astray. He had hoped to reach the Nile before the end of 1897;[7] but at last in March 1898 he reported that the last stage of the

[1] Minister of Colonies to Lagarde, 27 Sept. 1897, *D.D.F.*, XIII, no. 334.

[2] Hanotaux to French *chargé* in Saint Petersburg, 10 Sept. 1897, *ibid.*, no. 321.

[3] Minister of Colonies to Lagarde, 30 Oct. 1897, *ibid.*, no. 347.

[4] This was one of four columns sent by Menelek in an effort to consolidate his frontiers. Of the others two went towards Lake Rudolf with French and Russian help; the other went along the Blue Nile.

[5] The efforts of the Bonchamps mission and the final scene by the Nile are described by the second in command. (C. Michel, *Vers Fachoda*, (Paris, 1901), *passim.*)

[6] This seems to argue an understanding between the Congo State and Paris. (M. P. Hornik, *Der Kampf der Grossmächte um der Oberlauf des Nil*, 158–63.)

[7] Marchand to Minister of Colonies, no. 5, 10 May 1897, M.F.O.M. Afrique, III, dossier 36b.

journey was close at hand.[1] This was good news in Paris, all the more so since their Intelligence had reported from London that the Macdonald mission was a failure, and that Britain had nothing but diplomacy with which to stop Marchand.[2] In fact nothing did bar his way, and on 10 July Captain Marchand pitched camp at Fashoda. Eight Frenchmen and one hundred and twenty Senegalese waited for the reinforcements from Ethiopia.[3]

The Meeting at Fashoda

After the failure of the thrust from Uganda the British government speeded up the reconquest of the Sudan. Once British troops were committed, Salisbury had to look ahead to the diplomatic consequences of victory. He well knew that there would probably be a clash with France at Fashoda;[4] the problem was so to phase it that his hands would be free of complications elsewhere. His best course was to isolate France at the moment of impact at Fashoda, and this was above all a problem of keeping on the right side of Russia. In the early months of 1898 the Russians were moving from strength to strength in China, and threatened to push the British out altogether. Salisbury had lost confidence that Britain could halt this advance, and in January 1898 he made a new approach to the Tsar. In both China and Turkey he offered 'a partition of preponderance': if Russia would recognise the British position along the Yangtse and in Egypt, Arabia and the southern reaches of the Euphrates, then Britain would respect Russian interests in northern China, the Straits and the Euphrates north of Baghdad.[5] This would have disposed of two anxieties with one bargain. It would have taken the pressure off British interests in the basin of the Yangtse; it would have left France in isolation during the coming struggle at Fashoda. As it happened, the Russians turned down the suggestion, but there is strong reason to believe that when Salisbury persevered with his policy of conciliating them, he did so with one eye

[1] Marchand to Minister of Colonies, Telegram, no. 5, 15 Mar. 1898, embodied in Liotard to Colonies, Telegram, no. 20, 21 Apr. 1898, M.F.O.M. Afrique, III, dossier 32a.

[2] Report from London, 2 Feb. 1898, encl. in Ministry of War to Ministry of Colonies, 10 Feb. 1898, M.F.O.M. Afrique, 14, dossier Oubangui/Marchand/Nil.

[3] Books on the Marchand Mission by those taking part: le Général Baratier, *A Travers l'Afrique*, (Paris, 1912); *idem*, *Vers le Nil*, (Paris, 1923); *idem*, *Fachoda*, (Paris, 1941); le Général Mangin, *Souvenirs d'Afrique*, (Paris, 1936); le Docteur Emily, *Mission Marchand*, (Paris, 1909); H. Bobichon, *Contribution à l'Histoire de la Mission Marchand*, (Paris, 1936); *idem*, *Le Vieux Congo*, (Paris, ?1938). There are some letters of Marchand's in J. Delebecque, *Le Général Marchand*, (Paris, 1936).

[4] e.g. Salisbury to Cromer, 29 Oct. 1897, Zetland, *op. cit.*, 259–60.

[5] Salisbury to British ambassador in Saint Petersburg, 25 Jan. 1898, I, no. 9.

cocked on the Sudan.[1] Indeed the disunity of France and Russia over the Fashoda crisis seems to show that his tactics met with some success.

The crisis was not long in coming. On 8 April, 1898, Kitchener routed a large Dervish force at Atbara to the south of Berber, and at last Khartoum was in sight. So too was the consequence of victory. The rumours of Marchand's coming were now strong,[2] and in June Cromer suggested that once Khartoum was taken, the British should press on along the White and the Blue Nile, so as to confront any raiders from either east or west.[3] Salisbury at his end was pondering on the future status of the Sudan. Once it was conquered, the Sultan might inconveniently claim his rights; in any case the French would no doubt remind him of them. The Prime Minister considered:

> 'In view of this move, we must be careful of acknowledging Egyptian title by itself any further south. Would it not be wise, if you take Khartum to fly the British and Egyptian flags *side by side*. We might treat Khartum as the capital of the Mahdi state: and the capture of Khartum would deliver by right of conquest the whole of the Mahdi state from Halfa to Wadelai into the power of the capturing army. That army would consist of two allied contingents. . . . If we can establish this position we shall shake free of a good deal of diplomatic hamper.'[4]

He would indeed. With a title based on conquest, Salisbury would be able to brazen it out with any casual force of French explorers who might be found in the Nile Valley.

These were not the only preparations for the last stages of the struggle. Now that Kitchener was closing in for the kill, the British government took another step to free Cromer's hands and to commit themselves more directly to the reconquest. On 27 June, 1898, Hicks Beach told the House of Commons that another £750,000 would be needed to complete the campaign; the borrowing powers of Egypt were limited to £1,000,000, and she already owed some £800,000 which Britain had advanced to her. He therefore proposed to remit the whole

[1] Mr. Kennedy, who has had access to the unpublished memoranda of Salisbury's biographer, says that they contain a reminiscence of the Prime Minister's attitude towards Russia in the Far Eastern crisis of Mar.–Apr. 1898. The Cabinet wanted to send a strong message to Saint Petersburg. Lady Gwendolen Cecil reports her father as saying: 'Of course the Russians have behaved abominably and if it would be any satisfaction to my colleagues I should have no objection to fighting them. But I don't think we carry guns enough to fight them and the French together. . . . In six month's [*sic*] time we shall be on the verge of war with France; I can't afford to quarrel with Russia now,' (A. L. Kennedy, *Salisbury* . . . , (1953), 276.)

[2] Cromer to Salisbury, no. 37, 23 Jan. 1898, F.O. 76/5049; same to same, Telegram no. 149, 16 May 1898, F.O. 76/5050.

[3] Memo. by Cromer to Salisbury, 15 Jun. 1898, F.O. 76/4956.

[4] Salisbury to Cromer, Telegram no. 47, Secret, 3 Jun. 1898, F.O. 76/5050 (from the handwriting, clearly drafted by Salisbury himself).

of this earlier loan, for the reconquest would be cheap at the price.[1] After a thin debate, the motion was passed by 155 to 81. Events were playing into the hands of the forward school. So split was the Liberal Front Bench that their only safe ground of objection was on the grounds of financial purism.[2] Yet even this was an outmoded cry by the later Eighteen nineties. These were prosperous years. In the financial year 1896–7 Hicks Beach found himself with a surplus of £3,500,000; the surplus in 1897–8 was to be even larger.[3] Important imperial enterprises could be financed without provoking the old cry that they meant new burdens for the taxpayer. The loan to Egypt in 1896 had come out of Exchequer balances. So had the grants for the Uganda railway. The Foreign Office floated its policies of expansion on the surpluses of the Exchequer. This had considerable political advantages.

The final preparation for the climax was to decide how to deal with the French after the Khalifa had been crushed. At the end of July the Foreign Office was drawing up these crucial instructions. The draft was twice before the Cabinet and then approved by the Queen. Care was indeed necessary: Kitchener's actions after he had entered Khartoum might well determine the issue of peace or war with France.

The despatch went to Cromer on 2 August. Salisbury wrote:

> 'In view of the substantial military and financial co-operation which has recently been afforded by Her Majesty's Government to the Government of the Khedive, Her Majesty's Government have decided that at Khartoum the British and Egyptian flags should be hoisted side by side. . . . You will . . . explain to the Khedive and to his Ministers that the procedure I have indicated is intended to emphasise the fact that Her Majesty's Government consider that they have a predominant voice in all matters connected with the Soudan, and that they expect that any advice which they may think fit to tender to the Egyptian Government, in respect to Soudan affairs, will be followed.
>
> [After the occupation of Khartoum Kitchener was to send a flotilla up the White Nile as far as Fashoda and another up the Blue Nile to Roseires. He was himself to go to Fashoda.]
>
> 'There are two points to which Sir Herbert Kitchener's attention should be specially directed.
>
> The first of these is that in dealing with any French or Abyssinian authorities who may be encountered, nothing should be said or done which would in any way imply a recognition on behalf of Her Majesty's Government of a title to possession on behalf of France or Abyssinia to any portion of the Nile Valley. . . .

[1] *Hansard*, 4th ser., LX, cols. 241–50.
[2] e.g. the speech of Harcourt, *ibid.*, cols. 250–6. The Division List follows col. 286.
[3] Hicks Beach, *op. cit.*, II, 49–50, 62.

The second point . . . is the necessity of avoiding, by all possible means, any collision with the forces of the Emperor Menelek.

It is possible that a French force may be found in occupation of some portion of the Nile Valley. Should this contingency arise, the course of action to be pursued must depend so much on local circumstances that it is neither necessary nor desirable to furnish Sir Herbert Kitchener with detailed instructions.'[1]

These orders to Kitchener were much on the lines that Cromer had already suggested, although he himself had advised against hoisting the two flags at Khartoum.[2] But the Prime Minister was looking further ahead. To him the all important question was the clash with France, and he wanted to base Britain's position in the Sudan on the right of conquest. Of this the Union Jack would be the symbol.

The conquest itself was not long delayed. As the railway advanced towards Atbara, Kitchener struck out once more. By the first day of September the gunboats were close enough to pound at the dome of the Mahdi's tomb. On 2 September the Dervishes came forward under the banners of their emirs. For five hours they advanced again and again towards Kitchener's machine guns. 'I never saw the Dervishes fight better', as Wingate wrote.[3] When eleven thousand of them were killed, the remnants fled away. Kitchener lost 386. That was the battle of Omdurman and the end of the Khalifate.

Already the Sirdar knew that almost certainly the French had reached Fashoda,[4] and it was reported that Menelek, allied with the Khalifa, was moving along the White Nile.[5] The time had come to implement Salisbury's plan. On 10 September the two flotillas sailed upstream. As they disappeared into the swamps they moved out of all contact with Europe, for the telegraph broke down and Kitchener had already muzzled the war correspondents. The anxious Foreign Ministries in London and Paris, unable to enquire or advise or command, waited for the inevitable clash.

In Paris alarm was growing. Things had changed since the days when Marchand had been launched. Khartoum had fallen, and the new Anglo-German Agreement over the colonies of Portugal[6] had removed any

[1] Salisbury to Cromer, no. 109, Secret, 2 Aug. 1898, F.O. 78/5050. The draft was printed for the Cabinet on 30 Jul. and again on 2 Aug. On that day it was approved by the Queen. The final text is printed in *B.D.*, I, no. 185. It included provisions for confronting the Belgians.

[2] Cromer to Salisbury, no. 163, Secret, 4 Jun. 1898, F.O. 78/5050.

[3] Wingate to his wife, 6 Sept. 1898, Wingate, *op. cit.*, 117.

[4] Rodd to Salisbury, Telegram no. 202, 27 Aug. 1898, F.O. 78/5050; note by Wingate, 27 Aug. 1898, Wingate, *op. cit.*, 117.

[5] Rodd to Salisbury, Telegram no. 222, 7 Sept. 1898, F.O. 78/5050.

[6] For this Agreement, *vide infra* 446–8.

chance that Berlin might side with Paris. At the Quai d'Orsay Delcassé was making unreal plans for halting Marchand before he reached the Nile.[1] The British found the new Foreign Minister most conciliatory; he '. . . showed none of the irritation which M. Hanotaux found it impossible to conceal when he had to allude to Egypt or to cognate subjects'.[2] But Salisbury took a firm line from the beginning. The former territories of the Khalifa had passed to Britain and Egypt 'by right of conquest'; this right was not 'open to discussion'. Still, even now he hinted at a settlement 'in regard to those regions which are not affected by this assertion'.[3] If Delcassé hoped to see an opening here about the main issue, he was quickly disabused; for the first time the British showed that the quarrel might go very far. Monson, the ambassador, reported from Paris:

> 'I said to His Excellency that I must tell him very frankly that the situation on the Upper Nile is a dangerous one. . . . Her Majesty's Government are determined to hold to the decision already announced. . . . It was right that I should state to him categorically that they would not consent to a compromise on this point.'[4]

Then on 25 September it became known that Kitchener and Marchand had met at Fashoda. The Sirdar had gone up the Nile determined to bring the French back with him.[5] He and Wingate had decided that once at Fashoda they would raise the Egyptian flag by itself, since this was less likely to jar upon their rivals.[6] In this, as in all else, Kitchener could go only on his own judgement. So it was with Marchand. Neither man knew what the diplomats were saying; both had to carry off the scene by their own sense of occasion.

The famous meeting took place on 19 September.[7] Marchand claimed

[1] Delcassé to Minister for Colonies, 7 Sept. 1898, *D.D.F.*, XIV, no. 329.

[2] British ambassador in Paris to Salisbury, no. 441, Confidential, 8 Sept. 1898, F.O. 78/5050; printed in part in *B.D.* I, no. 188.

[3] Salisbury to British ambassador in Paris, Telegram, Private, 9 Sept. 1898, *ibid.* Also *B.D.*, I, no. 189.

[4] British ambassador in Paris to Salisbury, Telegram, no. 137, 18 Sept. 1898, *ibid.* Also *B.D.*, I, no. 191. c.f. Memo. by Delcassé, 18 Sept. 1898, *D.D.F.*, XIV, no. 358.

[5] Rodd to Salisbury, Telegram no. 240, 22 Sept. 1898, F.O. 78/5050.

[6] Wingate, *op. cit.*, 118–9.

[7] Kitchener to Cromer, Confidential, 21 Sept. 1898, encl. in Rodd to Salisbury, no. 153, Secret, 29 Sept. 1898, F.O. 78/5051 (partly printed in C. 9054, *P.P.* (1899) CXII, 874–5); Wingate to his wife, 23 Sept. 1898, Wingate, *op. cit.*, 119–21; Wingate to Queen's Secretary, 23 Sept. 1898, *Q.V.L.* 3rd ser., III, 285–7. For later accounts by eye-witnesses *vide* Sir H. W. Jackson, 'Fashoda, 1898,' *Sudan Notes and Records*, III, (Khartoum, 1920), 1–11; Sir Horace Smith-Dorrien, *Memories of Forty-Eight Years' Service*, (1925) 121–29; Marchand to French Government, Telegram, no. 21, 22 Sept. 1898, *D.D.F.*, XIV, no. 445; letters between Kitchener and Marchand, 18–22 Sept. 1898, *ibid.* Appendix, A I–V. For other French accounts *vide* authorities cited above.

to have made a local treaty, and the news 'rather staggered' the Sirdar. He pointed out that this had produced '. . . a situation which might lead to hostilities'. The French commander said that he could not retire without orders, but he did not demur to the running-up of the Egyptian flag. Then the Sirdar left, after posting a detachment to keep an eye on Marchand, and making a formal protest against his presence.

Such was the Fashoda incident. For all the courtesy shown by the soldiers, their clash was to bring war in sight during the next fortnight, as Britain bluntly pressed for evacuation, and France desperately argued for delay.

Salisbury's position was both simple and strong. He held all the cards. The British had conquered the Sudan. Kitchener had an army, Marchand had seven Frenchmen marooned by the banks of the Nile; Salisbury had a united government, Delcassé had a tottering ministry; Britain had a navy ready for war, France had a pack of legal arguments. So the British demand was that Marchand should go, without quibbles or face-saving. Delcassé on the other hand, was playing from weakness, as he well knew. 'We have nothing but arguments and they have got troops', as he put it.[1] He could threaten to cancel the west African agreement which had been reached at last,[2] but there was no hope that the issue could be swayed by trivialities such as that. He could throw piquant hints that 'between ourselves he would much prefer an Anglo-French to a Franco-Russian Alliance';[3] but Salisbury was no more to be wheedled out of the Nile Valley than he was to be hustled. The prize was now in his grasp, and he did not mean to let go.

The last three days of September showed how far he was ready to go. On the twenty-seventh Delcassé, badgered by Britain and yet afraid of French opinion, begged that at least there should be a negotiation. '. . . if there was to be no discussion, a rupture could not be avoided,' and he appealed to the British '. . . not to drive him into a corner'.[4] But Salisbury paid no heed, and relentlessly turned the screw. If Paris would not recall Marchand, there were other ways of persuading him to leave. As Sanderson saw it from the Foreign Office: 'I do not think it will be a great calamity if Marchand is left a fortnight or so on short commons in order to demonstrate how helpless and derisory the supposed

[1] Letter of Delcassé, 26 Sept. 1898, printed in A. Maurois, *Edouard VII et son Temps*, (Paris, 1933), 88.

[2] Minute by Gosselin (British Commissioner for Niger Negotiations) 27 Sept. 1898 F.O. 27/3442.

[3] British ambassador in Paris to Salisbury, Telegram no. 154, Secret, 28 Sept. 1898, F.O. 78/5051; also printed in *B.D.*, I, no. 198.

[4] Monson to Salisbury, Telegram no. 151, 27 Sept. 1898, F.O. 78/5051; also printed in *B.D.*, I, no. 196.

occupation is'.[1] Salisbury himself went beyond this, and wrote: 'His position should be made as untenable as possible.'[2]

Both sides were raising their stakes and the crisis was coming. On 30 September Monson and Delcassé had a violent interview. The ambassador reported Delcassé as saying:

> 'All France would resent such an insult to the national honour as is involved in the proposal to recall M. Marchand and to treat the French occupation of Fashoda as an unjustifiable act. He could not think that it is wished in England to go to war over such a question, but France would, however unwilling, accept war rather than submit.
>
> I confined myself to saying that Her Majesty's Government had already through me signified their point of view, and that for my part I did not see how they could possibly retreat from it.'[3]

The following day Monson added his own view: '. . . as to the possibility that M. Delcassé was "bluffing" . . . I am bound to state that I believe that he . . . thoroughly meant what he said.'[4] In the face of all this Salisbury remained quite intransigent, and went on reiterating that the British claim rested on the right of conquest and that there was nothing to discuss so long as Marchand remained at Fashoda.[5]

Here then was the outcome of the long, intricate and determined struggle which Britain and France had waged for the control of the Nile Valley. Their rivalry for Egypt had been inveterate; nevertheless, Egypt had its minaretted cities and above all it had the Canal. But by October 1898, the struggle had spread far from the Delta to the desolate and intractable country of the Upper Nile. It was for the mastery of these deserts that Britain and France were now making ready for war.

At the same time, Salisbury had not quite lost his sense of proportion. In the second week of October there were signs that the French were weakening,[6] and the Prime Minister took a first step to meet them. He still would hear of no compromise about Marchand, but on 12 October

[1] Minute by Sanderson, n.d., on Rodd to Salisbury, Telegram no. 252, 29 Sept. 1898, F.O. 78/5051.

[2] Draft reply, Salisbury to Rodd, Telegram no. 92, Secret, 1 Oct. 1898, F.O. 78/5051. The despatch is printed in *B.D.*, I, no. 201, but the sentence quoted was omitted from the final version.

[3] Monson, British ambassador in Paris to Salisbury, Telegram no. 160, Secret, 30 Sept. 1898, F.O. 78/5051; also printed in *B.D.*, I, no. 200. Delcassé recorded his version in a memo. of 30 Sept., 1898, *D.D.F.*, XIV, no. 400.

[4] Same to same, no. 491, Secret, 1 Oct. 1898, F.O. 78/5051.

[5] Salisbury to British ambassador in Paris, no. 355 A, 6 Oct. 1898, F.O. 78/5051; also printed in *B.D.*, I, no. 203.

[6] British ambassador in Paris to Salisbury, no. 504, 9 Oct. 1898; same to same, no. 505, 10 Oct. 1898; same to same, Telegram no. 169, Secret and Most Confidential, 11 Oct. 1898 F.O. 78/5051; also printed in *B.D.*, I, nos. 206, 208, 209.

the French hinted that he might withdraw, and stated their demand for an outlet from the Ubanghi to the Nile. Salisbury said that he would take the suggestion to the Cabinet.[1] Nothing seems to have come of this first gesture, and on 24 October the government authorised naval preparations, and the reserve fleet was got ready.[2] At the same time the Foreign Office kept up a facade of uncompromising resolution.[3] But behind the scenes the Cabinet was not so unanimous. On 26 October Curzon expressed to Chamberlain his anxiety lest the government should consent to a French enclave on the Nile.[4] Curzon was a fire-eater, but he had just left the Foreign Office, where he had been Salisbury's Under-Secretary. His fears were justified, for on the following day the Prime Minister said that there could be discussion of the frontier in those regions if the French would remove Marchand.[5] But the days were past when Salisbury could conduct a foreign policy of his own without let or hindrance. He had masterful colleagues, who took a much more extreme line than he favoured himself: Chamberlain, Hicks Beach and Devonshire in particular, were strongly opposed to concession.[6] Indeed, Salisbury's whole conception of the diplomacy of limited liability was rapidly losing ground. Chamberlain and Goschen at this time were reported to be in favour of war over Fashoda,[7] and there is a story that the Colonial Secretary was hoping to trounce the French and dispose of their rivalry for once and for all.[8] But in holding

[1] Salisbury to British ambassador in Paris, Telegram no. 223, 12 Oct. 1898, F.O. 78/5051. c.f. French ambassador in London to Delcassé, Telegram no. 196, 13 Oct. 1898, *D.D.F.*, XIV, no. 433.

[2] Marder, *op. cit.*, 321–2.

[3] German *chargé* in London to Hohenlohe, 22 Oct. 1898, *Grosse Politik*, XIV (2), no. 3895.

[4] Curzon to Chamberlain, 26 Oct. 1898, Garvin, *op. cit.*, III, 229.

[5] Salisbury to British ambassador in Paris, Telegram no. 255, Confidential, 30 Oct. 1898, F.O. 78/5052. *B.D.*, I, no. 223. c.f. French ambassador in London to Delcassé, 28 Oct. 1898, *D.D.F.*, XIV, no. 459; also the subtle and understanding analysis of Salisbury's difficulties in same to same, 29 Oct. 1898, *ibid.*, no. 465.

[6] Garvin, op. cit., III, 230.

[7] Report of German naval *attaché* in London, 25 Oct. 1898, *Grosse Politik*, XIV (2), no. 3898.

[8] Prussian minister in Hamburg to German Foreign Office, 6 Nov. 1898, *ibid.*, no. 3908. Chamberlain is reported to have said: 'I am afraid Lord Salisbury himself has not got the strength of mind to bring about the necessary crisis and choose the right moment to strike. . . . You may be certain however that *all* my colleagues, *even* Mr. Arthur Balfour are of the same opinion as I am, namely that Lord Salisbury's policy "peace at any price" cannot go on any longer, and that England has to show to the whole world that she *can act.* I consider that the present moment is very favourable for us and you will see what is going to happen as soon as our *war preparations* are finished. . . . As soon as we are ready, we shall present our bill to France *not only in Egypt*, but all over the globe and should she refuse to pay, *then war.*' This is an anonymous account of a conversation with Chamberlain, and there are grounds for supposing that it may have been touched up in the re-telling. Garvin, however, (*op. cit.*, III, 231–3) accepts it as substantially true.

back, this swashbuckling Salisbury had the support of another great architect of British expansion. Queen Victoria was strongly opposed to '. . . a war for so miserable and small an object',[1] and her views were put before the divided Cabinet.[2] Even so, it was still common knowledge among the foreign ambassadors at the end of the year that Salisbury was having trouble in holding back the hotheads in the ministry.[3]

But in the end his caution prevailed. At the end of October Marchand had left Fashoda without permission from Paris, and thereafter the French case crumbled quickly. On 3 November the French government instructed him to evacuate Fashoda.[4] Thereafter the tension and the bad temper might drag on, but the French challenge to the Nile was removed. Now it was only a matter of recognising the facts, and on 21 March, 1899, this was at last done. The Anglo-French Declaration of that date delimited the spheres of the two Powers. France kept the Central Sudan from Darfur in the east to Lake Tchad in the west, but she was totally excluded from the Nile Basin.[5] On 26 March the Queen met Lord Salisbury in France. 'We talked of many things,' she noted, 'and rejoiced at the success of the arrangement with the French, which gives us entire possession of the valley of the Nile.'[6] They had good reason to rejoice.

The Way back from Fashoda

The Fashoda incident became the Fashoda crisis because of the condition of French politics. Just as Paris heard that Marchand and Kitchener had met, the Dreyfus Affair was reaching its crescendo. On 3 September Cavaignac, the minister for war, had resigned, and from now until the end of 1898 France was in deep crisis, as the anti-Dreyfusards closed their ranks and threatened the Republic for insulting the army.[7] Hence the Brisson ministry had only the narrowest of ground on which to negotiate about Fashoda. A climb

[1] Queen Victoria to Salisbury, 30 Oct. 1898, *Q.V.L.*, 3rd ser., III, 305.

[2] Queen's Journal, 25 Oct. 1898; Salisbury to Queen Victoria, 27 Oct. 1898; *ibid.*, 298–9.

[3] German ambassador in London to Hohenlohe, 20 Dec. 1898; same to same, 22 Dec. 1898, *Grosse Politik*, XIV (2), nos. 3923, 3925; cf. de Staal, *op. cit.*, II, 396, reporting a similar opinion by de Courcel. Also French ambassador in London to Delcassé, 5 Nov. 1898, *D.D.F.*, XIV, no. 491.

[4] British ambassador in Paris to Salisbury, Telegram no. 200, 3 Nov. 1898, *B.D.*, I, no. 226.

[5] Text of Declaration in *P.P.* 1899, CXII, 958–9. The British finally came to terms with Menelek on 15 May 1902, and with Leopold II on 9 May 1906.

[6] Queen Victoria's Journal, 26 Mar. 1899, *Q.V.L.*, 3rd ser., III, 355.

[7] For the progress of the *Affaire* in 1898 *vide* G. Chapman, *The Dreyfus Case* (1955).

down in the Sudan might precipitate the catastrophe in France; while across the Channel the British Government insisted that nothing but a climb down would satisfy them. This is why the crisis dragged on through October. By the twenty-fifth Monson was thoroughly alarmed. Chanoine, the new minister for war, had just resigned, and this seemed to the ambassador the prelude to:

> '. . . a military domination which threatens to become a despotism. The step taken by General Chanoine may well imply . . . the suspension of constitutional Government . . . the advent of a military Government or of a nominally civilian Government in the hands of the Military party, would, as far as I can see, render the settlement of our existing dispute with France far more difficult than it is at this moment; and that, I need not say, is quite difficult enough.'[1]

A military *coup d'état* seemed likely; and the distraught civilian government might try to save the Republic from war at home by launching a war abroad. Without a doubt, it was fears of this sort which led the British to send war orders to the Mediterranean fleet on 26 October.[2]

But once they had done so, the outcome of the crisis was inevitable. France could not hope to match the British sea power. In the Mediterranean she could put only fifteen battleships against eighteen; her reserve fleet was much weaker.[3] These naval facts governed the outcome of the crisis. Domestic strife made it dangerous for the French to yield; but they had no choice. Delcassé himself saw no hope: 'How are we to combine the needs of honour with the necessity of avoiding a naval war which we are in no state to undertake, even with Russian help: that is the problem.'[4]

So long as the British stayed firm, there could be only one result; and for a stake such as the Nile Valley even Lord Salisbury was ready to be firm. The French surrendered over Marchand on 3 November. Two days later Brett wrote in his journal: 'The war has blown over for the present, although the risk still remains. It seems that the French cannot fight at sea in *winter*.'[5]

In any case there was no help from Russia. Salisbury throughout

[1] British ambassador in Paris to Salisbury, no. 546, 25 Oct. 1898, F.O. 27/3397.
[2] Marder, *op. cit.*, 326. [3] *ibid.*, 321.
[4] Letter of Delcassé, 22 Oct. 1898, Maurois, *op. cit.*, 90. There seems to be little ground for the elaborate speculations of M. B. Giffen, *Fashoda, the Incident and its Diplomatic Setting*, (Chicago, 1930), that the French surrender was caused by diplomatic weakness, 110, 156–8, 182–4.
[5] Esher, *op. cit.*, I, 223.

went on the assumption that the Russians would not support the French when it came to war for the Sudan, and they never looked as though they would.[1] Monson reported that the Foreign Minister was convinced '. . . that it would be too dangerous to continue to buoy up the courage of France by allowing her to trust to her ally for material aid'.[2] Nevertheless Delcassé well knew that with Russian help or without it, a naval war was impossible for France.

The Meaning of Fashoda

At first sight there is a certain absurdity about the struggle for Fashoda. The massive advance of Kitchener's army took two and a half years, and it ended by browbeating a few men marooned by the side of the Nile. There was a strange disproportion between ends and means, as there was in building two railways from points two thousand miles apart to run into the deserts of the Upper Nile. A still deeper absurdity seems to lie in the French speculation about damming the river and in the labours of the British to stop them. Even Marchand himself came to see that the scheme was hare-brained, for it turned out that there was no stone within miles of Fashoda.[3] To this extent, the great rivalry for the Upper Nile was based on a myth. The greatest absurdity of all might seem to be that for two months two great Powers stood at the brink of war for the ownership of the *sudd* and desert of the Upper Nile.

It is true that after 1895 there was an irrational fringe to the British attitude towards the Nile. It is no less true that this attitude commanded the assent of British opinion during the dramatic climax of the struggle. Nearly all the English newspapers stood firm behind the government during the crisis,[4] and their tone was considerably more strident than that of the French press.[5] The abstract analysis of editorials is not worth much as an evaluation of public opinion, but there is no doubt that there was plenty of warlike spirit in the country.[6] Even the British

[1] Langer, *Diplomacy*, 562–4. This remains an obscure matter, but the editors of the *Documents Diplomatiques Français* state that they are unable to find in the archives any assurances of Russian co-operation. (*D.D.F.*, XIV, pp. 657–8 fn.)

[2] British ambassador in Paris to Salisbury, no. 580, Most Confidential, 7 Nov. 1898, F.O. 27/3397.

[3] Langer, *Diplomacy*, 558.

[4] T. W. Riker, 'A Survey of British Policy in the Fashoda Crisis,' *Political Science Quarterly*, XLIV, (New York, 1929), 54–78. Seven daily papers are here listed as 'trying to outdo one another in virulence', while two others talked openly of force, 65–6.

[5] Carroll, *op. cit.*, 173–5.

[6] Even so violent an anti-imperialist as Wilfrid Blunt admitted this. (W. S. Blunt, *My Diaries* (new edition, 1932), 303.) c.f. French ambassador in London to Delcassé 26 Oct. 1898 *D.D.F.*, XIV, no. 455.

and Foreign Arbitration Association let it be known that while they remained devoted to their doctrine they did not think that it should be applied to Fashoda.[1]

The aggressive mood of 1898 has often been regarded as an example of the hysterical passion for aggrandisement which is supposed to have swept through Britain at the end of the century. This 'new imperialism' is said to have been produced by the spread of literacy, the coming of the mass vote and the rise of the yellow press.[2] This may be so, or it may not. At the end of the century there may have been a new imperial spirit rising in some sections of English society. Perhaps the new voters and the new readers may have applauded a policy of swagger and bluster towards the foreigner. The newly fashionable theories of Social Darwinism may have introduced a racial arrogance towards lesser breeds without the law.[3] More people by this time may have come to believe that Africa could be made into another India.

All this may have been true; but it is not to say that new public pressures drove the government down the road to Fashoda, or that popular demand in September 1898 compelled government to do what it would otherwise not have done. During the Fashoda crisis the leaders of both parties came out openly in favour of the Nile Valley strategy. In a speech on 12 October, Rosebery warned the French not to make a mistake '. . . which can only lead to a disastrous conflagration'; the next day Asquith spoke in the same sense; on 28 October Harcourt spoke of the need for national unity; while Campbell-Bannerman said on 24 November that '. . . we ranged ourselves as one man in determining to resist the aggression'.[4] This chorus of patriotic union was joined by the Liberal and Radical press.[5] Among the politicians only Morley, among the newspapers only the *Manchester Guardian* stood out against this general line of approval and support for the British government. At the time of Fashoda opinion in the country was being exhorted by two political parties both saying the same thing and both casting it in stereotypes of the national honour and the civilising mission. It may well be true, as Chamberlain asserted, that British policy was strengthened

[1] Raphael, *Cape to Cairo Dream*, 467, n.

[2] E. Halévy, *A History of the English People in the Nineteenth Century*, V, (English translation, 2nd ed., 1951), 8–9.

[3] For criticisms of this *vide* L. T. Hobhouse, *Democracy and Reaction*, (1904), 83–118; J. A. Hobson, *Imperialism*, (1902), Book II, cap. 2; for a vindication, J. A. Cramb, *The Origins and Destiny of Greater Britain*, (1915), 190–7, 218–26.

[4] Crewe, *op. cit.*, II, 555–6; Gardiner, *op. cit.*, II, 470–1; J. A. Spender, *Life of . . . Campbell-Bannerman*, (1923), I, 209–12; J. A. Spender and C. Asquith, *Life of . . . Asquith*, (1932), I, 118–9.

[5] Riker, *loc. cit.*, 69.

by '. . . the spectacle of a united nation',[1] but it does not follow that the policy was determined by that spectacle. To assert that it was, is to study the situation of 1898 from the standpoint of other centuries and, it may be, from the standpoint of other countries.

The Fashoda crisis was not the outcome of a ferocious popular will then, although it evoked signs of one. It was the logical conclusion of a strategy followed by the Foreign Office for a decade. Of the calculations and interests involved in this, the public knew very little. The leaders of both parties understood the strategy, and most of them approved of it; but time after time they refrained from any public explanation of the vital issues it involved, lest this should hinder British diplomacy abroad and provoke the intervention of the ignorant at home. Foreign policy was a matter for an *élite*, and they conducted it according to their own view of national interest and world policy. The British electorate found that their country now enjoyed a condominium over the Sudan, whether they liked it or not.[2] However it may have appeared to the man in the street, to the initiated few Fashoda was simply the climax to an old policy of imperial defence.

In the eyes of the real makers of policy, there was obviously a scramble in Africa; but it was hardly for Africa or for empire for empire's sake. Throughout the partition their over-riding concern was to claim those regions of the continent which seemed vital for security in the Mediterranean and therefore in the world.

[1] Speech of 15 Nov. 1898, quoted in Riker, *loc. cit.*, 77. It is worth remark that at the time of the crisis the Foreign Office went to the trouble of briefing the British press. (Kennedy Jones, *Fleet Street and Downing Street*, (1920), 96–7.)

[2] cf. the remarks of W. T. Stead in *The Review of Reviews*, Apr. 1899, 311; 'We are supposed to be a self-governed people. But when and where did the British electors have any opportunity of saying ay or no to the question whether they should be saddled for all time with the immense responsibility of policing and civilising the Soudan. . . . If the Unionists who carried last General Election had been charged by their opponents with the intention of adding 1,500,000 square miles of African territory to the burden of the British Empire, they would have repudiated the charge as a calumny. . . . Yet they have done it, without a mandate and almost without a protest.'

CHAPTER XIII

'Imperialist' Beginnings in West Africa

THE LONG STANDSTILL 1890–1895

In west Africa between 1890 and 1895 British governments had held back. Compared with the resolution shown elsewhere, here their purpose and power remained diffident. There were no wealthy financiers or eager settlers, no Egyptian army and treasury to forward spacious claims. On the west, there was only the small trader; and official aid to him was stinted. Ministries were content if they could save the existing field of British commerce from French and German advances. Little was done to stake off large colonial estates for future exploitation, since private enterprise, except in Goldie's Niger Company, showed little energy for carrying British claims inland. In the official settlements as well, trade and revenue were far too slender to empower the administrators to enlarge their territory. Imperial aid for the purpose was usually refused. So fettered, government in west Africa carried out no grand strategy as on the Nile or in southern Africa; and ministers protected the commercial network only where the merchant could bear the charge. They deliberately skimped the coat of empire to the poor cloth of trade. The depression of west African commerce between 1885 and 1895 sapped the strength of commercial expansion; and the Foreign Office went on yielding to European rivals on the west, the better to defend the strategic interest on the Nile.

Salisbury merely attempted to hold what he had in west Africa. Since the Berlin Conference, the French had driven their power from Senegal and Guinea deep into the western Sudan. By the end of the Eighteen eighties, they were engulfing the British settlements of the Gambia and Sierra Leone.[1] But Salisbury did little to save them their hinterlands. The Colonial Office for many years had been able to think of no better use for the Gambia than to hawk it to France[2] for a consideration elsewhere. But the bargain had never been clinched; and the colony had

[1] Holland to Salisbury, 3 Jun. 1887, S.P. (Holland). c.f. J. Méniaud: *Les Pionniers du Soudan* (Paris, 1931), I, 301–21, 391–527.

[2] A. W. L. Hemming, 'Memorandum: Proposals which have been made involving the cession of the Gambia to France, and Proceedings in Parliament relating thereto,' Nov. 1888, C.O. African No. 357.

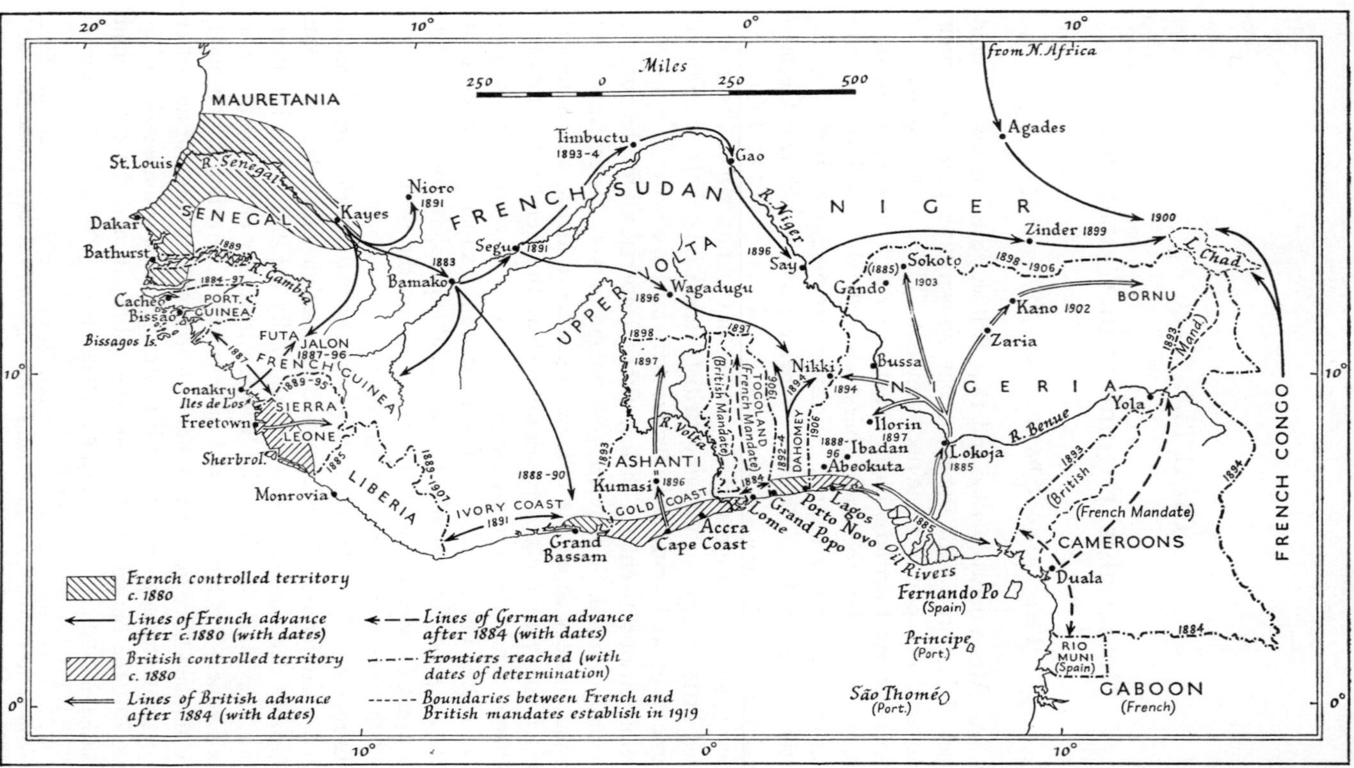

From J. D. Fage: An Atlas of African History: Edward Arnold

European Advance into West Africa, *c.* 1880–1900

been kept because the French refused to pay a price for it.[1] What little trade it gave had long since fallen into the hands of the merchants of Marseilles.[2] British revenue from French enterprise was but a few thousand pounds;[3] and the Administrator of the Gambia, G. T. Carter, did not know how to make his tiny domain meet the costs of administration. As a commercial prospect, the Gambia seemed a dead loss. Like his predecessors, Carter blamed African shiftlessness and political disorder. Unless the 'industrious Oriental' was brought in to set the example,[4] and order was imposed inland so that the peasant could be sure of reaping where he had sown, Carter feared that the African would never grow crops for export. But in the Gambia as elsewhere in the west African spheres, development and order still awaited more trade and revenue. And trade and revenue, as they had for decades, awaited administration and capital.

Further to the south, the colony of Sierra Leone was in no better shape to challenge the French for the hinterland. It was as much as its short-lived officials could do to manage the existing fever-ridden settlement. Slave-raiding upcountry[5] pinned down the commerce of Freetown. With the heavy falls in oil prices after 1885, the colony's revenue shrank smaller than twenty years before.[6] As far as the Governor could see in 1894, the colony had no future, unless other staples could be developed to replace the decaying palm oil trade.[7]

[1] Salisbury and Holland again considered ceding the Gambia to France as part of a general west African settlement in 1888. Holland reported that the Liverpool merchants had dropped their opposition. (Holland to Salisbury, 31 Oct. 1888, S.P. (Holland).)

[2] Administrator to Knutsford, 2 May 1890, Gambia Report on the Blue Book for 1889, C. 5897, P.P. [1890] XLVIII, 255.

[3] (in £s sterling, round figures)

Gambia	*Imports*	*Exports*	*Revenue*
1881	143,000	140,000	24,000
1890	149,000	164,000	30,000
1895	97,000	94,000	21,000
1900	278,000	282,000	49,000

Sources: P.P. (1890–1, XC 660–1, 682–3, 688–9; P.P. (1901) LXXXVI, 660–1, 668–9, 682–3, 688–9).

[4] Administrator to Knutsford, 2 May 1890, C. 5897, P.P. [1890], XLVIII, 22.

[5] Sierra Leone, Report on the Blue Book for 1889, C. 6221, P.P. [1890–1] LV, 161.

[6] Sierra Leone: (in £s sterling round figures)

Years	*Imports*	*Exports*	*Revenue*	*Debt*
1871	306,000	440,000	80,000	27,000
1881	374,000	366,000	70,000	73,000
1890	390,000	349,000	74,000	58,000
1895	427,000	453,000	98,000	50,000
1900	558,000	362,000	169,000	none

Sources: (P.P. (1884–5) LXXXIII, 6–7, 22–3, 28–9; P.P. (1890–1) XC, 660–1, 682–3, 688–9, 668–9; P.P. (1901) LXXXVI, 660–1, 668–9, 682–3, 688–9).

[7] Cardew, quoted in 'Report on the Administration of the Niger Coast Protectorate, 1894–95', (C. 7916), P.P. (1895) LXXI, 66.

So Salisbury at the end of the Eighteen eighties could draw his own conclusions. The merchants of Liverpool and London trading to Bathurst and Freetown pressed the government to save their hinterlands from French encirclement.[1] But the west African traders had none of the compelling influence in British politics enjoyed by the great Eastern and Indian interests. The Prime Minister had a bad case for resisting French claims in this region, and he was not sorry to encourage French aspirations in west Africa which might help to divert their efforts from Egypt and the Nile.[2] So while he was bringing Germany to accept the Nile Valley as a British sphere, he had given generous compensation to France in west Africa. By the Agreements of 10 August, 1889, and 9 June, 1891,[3] the frontiers of French Senegambia and Guinea were drawn tight round the Gambia and Sierra Leone. The treaties in effect strangled the extension of the colonies inland once and for all. In Liverpool and London the Chambers of Commerce might complain:

> 'In west Africa the British Governments of the last decade have been outstripped by Germany and France; the Gambia has dwindled; the Cameroons has been lost; two foreign powers have intervened between Lagos and Gold Coast Colonies — which Colonies should have been coterminous — the French have spread themselves over Senegambia, and the British Governments have yielded the districts of the Northern Rivers of Sierra Leone . . . the Chamber is of opinion that wherever in the unappropriated territories of Africa a preponderance of British trade existed, there British interests should have been secured, by proclaiming such territories spheres of British influence.'[4]

But Salisbury refused to peg out claims to tropical estates on the speculation that the British merchant might one day make use of them. France, he admitted, was building up a large empire in west Africa. 'Great Britain, on the other hand,' he declared, 'has adopted the policy of advance by commercial enterprise. She has not attempted to compete with the military operations of her neighbour.'[5] British activities in west Africa were based on merchants, the French, on soldiers whose professional interest in attack and victory sometimes outran the wishes

[1] Holland to Salisbury, 27 Jan. 1888, S.P. (Holland).
[2] Cecil, *op. cit.*, IV, 252–3.
[3] Hertslet, *op. cit.*, II, 729–43.
[4] Liverpool Chamber of Commerce, Report on Affairs of the West African Colonies, (1892), encl. in Liverpool Chamber of Commerce to Foreign Office, 22 Aug. 1893, F.O. 83/1242; London Chamber of Commerce to C.O., 4 Apr. 1892, and 8 Mar. 1892, C.O. Africa (West), 448, pp. 7–8, 1–2.
[5] Salisbury to Dufferin, 30 Mar. 1892, C. 6701, P.P. [1892] LVI, 778.

of the politicians in Paris. Nothing more, the Prime Minister contended could have been done to enlarge the Gambia and Sierra Leone. The French had been ready to pay and they had won. As he put it:

> 'The Colonies of the Gambia and Sierra Leone, with limited revenues barely sufficing for their administrative expenditure would have been unable to bear any strain in the direction of military expenditure, and the sanction of Parliament was not to be expected for the employment of Imperial resources adequate for the purpose.'[1]

In other words, the value of the trade was not worth the taking of more territory. It was good Gladstonian and Treasury doctrine. Mid-Victorian principles of private enterprise and informal influence still governed policy toward west Africa. Except on the Niger, the traders, who were lamed by depression and disorders,[2] could not carry far inland a government which refused to go anywhere, except upon their backs.

When the last decade of the century opened, the interior of the Gold Coast looked like going the same way as the hinterlands of Sierra Leone and the Gambia. From the Upper Niger, from the Ivory Coast and later from Dahomey, the French were pressing forward into the Upper Volta regions to the north of Ashanti; while the Germans were reaching inland from Togoland. British merchants trading with the Gold Coast urged the government to reserve the regions behind the colony as far north as the River Niger.[3] But here also, Salisbury measured out British claims according to priorities elsewhere. What could be done without straining French or German relations or local finances, would be done. But shackled in this way, the British stride was to fall far short of the Upper Niger. Little more was done in the event than to claim formally the region which had long been under British informal influence.

Here again it was the same story of an administration too weak to

[1] *ibid.*

[2] *Trade and Revenues of British West Africa*

Quinquennial Averages: in thousands of pounds sterling

	Exports and Imports	*Revenues*
1871–75	2,322	187
1876–80	3,020	246
1881–85	3,028	263
1886–90	2,707	264
1891–95	4,166	433
1896–1900	6,266	795

Source: A. McPhee, *The Economic Revolution in British West Africa*, (1926), App. 'A'.

[3] London Chamber of Commerce to C.O., 8 Mar. 1892, C.O. African (West), 448,

push inland or repel foreign rivals. The slump in oil prices[1] crippled the local government. So too did the turmoil in the oil-bearing forest belt, for disorders in and about Ashanti frequently stopped exports from reaching the ports.[2] At the end of the Eighteen eighties, the Settlement's commercial foundation seemed to be slipping.[3] The Governor, Sir Brandford Griffith revived schemes of 'economic agriculture' which had always failed in the past. New staples — cotton, coffee, indigo — would have to be developed to replace the declining palm export.[4] Roads and railways would have to be built and the administration should provide them. Direct taxation would have to be imposed to pay for them and Ashanti would have to be pacified. Otherwise the Colony would have no future. But like some of his predecessors, Griffith found that 'direct taxation is impossible in this Colony' except at the risk of African revolt.[5] The lack of revenue and imperial help prevented the ordering and development of the territory already acquired; and until that had been done, the administration had little strength to push northward and repel the French.

Salisbury was left with little but diplomacy to defend British claims to the regions north of Ashanti; and he chose to concentrate this resource upon more important interests in Egypt, east Africa and the Mediterranean. Commercial interests in the Gold Coast hinterland came low in his list of African priorities. In 1888 and 1890 his arrangements with Germany[6] made this clear. Needing German support elsewhere, he bought immunity from the *bâton égyptien* at the expense of

[1] Average Quinquennial Prices in Pounds Sterling of Palm Oil per ton in United Kingdom:

1871–75	£34·2	1886–90	£20·4
1876–80	33·0	1891–95	23·6
1881–85	31·0	1896–1900	21·4

Source: McPhee, *op. cit.*, 33, fn. 1.

[2] Griffith to Knutsford, 19 May 1891, C. 7917, P.P. [1896] LVIII 503 *et seq.*

[3] Trade and Revenue of Gold Coast.

(in £s sterling round figures)

	Imports	*Exports*	*Revenue*	*Debts*
1871	251,000	295,000	29,000	none
1881	398,000	373,000	116,000	none
1890	562,000	601,000	156,000	none
1895	924,000	878,000	230,000	none
1900	1,289,000	885,000	333,000	none

Sources: (P.P. (1884–5) LXXXIII, 6–7, 22–3, 28–9; P.P. (1890–1) XC, 660–1, 682–3, 688–9, 668–9; P.P. (1901) LXXXVI, 660–1, 668–9, 682–3, 688–9).

[4] *vide*, Report of Gold Coast Committee on Economic Agriculture, (C. 5897) P.P. (1890) XLVIII, 355 *et seq.*; Griffith to Knutsford, 10 Nov. 1890, (C. 6270), P.P. (1891), LV, 558–9.

[5] Griffith to Ripon, 8 Jul. 1893, Gold Coast Annual Report, (C. 6857), P.P. (1893–4) LIX, 344.

[6] Hertslet, *op. cit.*, I, 73; III, 903.

west Africa.[1] Hence Salisbury admitted the possibility of German claims in the Gold Coast hinterlands north of the ninth latitude. The Anglo-German agreement set aside these countries as a neutral zone in which both Powers abjured political extension. It was a tactic of weakness, such as was never used in east Africa or on the Nile.

At the same time, Salisbury's arrangements with the French were equally unambitious. The agreements of 10 August, 1889, and 26 June, 1891, defined the boundary between the British field of influence on the Gold Coast and the French Ivory Coast as far north, as the ninth parallel of latitude.[2] Ashanti was thus reserved. But further north, the hinterland was left open to the French advance. If the Gold Coast Colony had not been completely sealed off like the Gambia and Sierra Leone, neither had Salisbury claimed the hinterland beyond the ninth parallel. The issue remained to be settled by 'effective occupation'.

The Gold Coast government could hardly compete with the French military expeditions in this region without pacifying Ashanti first. Still unsubdued, the Confederacy lay between the colony and the disputed hinterland. Wolseley's expedition of 1874,[3] designed to make the Ashanti kingdom a respectful if still independent client of Britain, had only shattered its unity and turned it into a menacing disorder.[4] In May 1891 the Governor reported: '. . . Ashanti as a whole, besides being gradually broken up, is steadily retrograding, both in its entirety . . . and in the portions which have separated themselves from the nominal Government at Kumasi, which is powerless to check the downward tendency. . . .'[5] Griffith insisted that Ashanti must be pacified and tried to persuade the Ashantis to accept a British protectorate.[6] But the Colonial Office which Griffith had not consulted, wanted no such commitment.[7] Knutsford held that the colony had no resources to spare for what might prove a large military task. His Liberal successor, Ripon, upheld the veto against moving across the Prah,[8] although the merchants and officials of the Gold Coast still pressed for action. The colony could not foot the bill, and London would not underwrite it. Ashanti was left to enjoy the consolations of anarchy.

[1] Marschall to Hatzfeldt, 17 May 1890, *Grosse Politik*, VIII, no. 1677.
[2] Hertslet, *op. cit.*, II, 730, 743–4.
[3] *vide supra*, 30–1.
[4] On the strife in Ashanti, *vide* Memo. by G. E. Ferguson; 'Ashanti and the Brong Tribes or the Attabubus in their Relations with the Kingdom of Ashanti . . .' C. 7917, P.P. [1896] LVIII, 600 *et seq.* Hodgson to Knutsford, 9 Dec. 1889, *ibid.*, 476; and 11 Jan. 1890, *ibid.*, 480–3.
[5] Griffith to Knutsford, 19 May 1891, *ibid.*, 505.
[6] Griffith to Knutsford, 19 May 1891, *ibid.*, 503–23.
[7] C.O. to Griffith, 3 Sept. 1891, *ibid.*, 540.
[8] Ripon to Hodgson, 30 Jan. 1894, *ibid.*, 613–4.

But north of Ashanti the empire made one half-hearted effort. In March 1892 Salisbury decided that '. . . it would . . . be advisable to anticipate French agents by the conclusion of treaties'[1] with the chiefdoms of Dagomba, Gondja, Mossi and Gourounsi. The project was ambitious enough. It was intended to cover all the country from the backlands of the Gold Coast to the Niger Company's territories on the east, thus cutting off the French in Dahomey and the Germans in Togoland from access to the interior.[2] Ferguson's missions of 1892 and 1894 attempted to rig up this ring of treaties. But the British were pitting a single African agent against the French army. Ferguson's paper fences proved too flimsy. His treaties merely bound the chiefs to have no dealings with other Powers and promised nothing in return.[3] Hence they were unlikely to be observed. By an oversight, the treaties which were to give a claim to the region connecting the Gold Coast with Borgu were never made,[4] and others were either amended or withdrawn altogether when the Germans objected toward the end of 1894.[5] These paper claims, so negative in content, so easily yielded, show the feeble imperial interest in the Gold Coast hinterland before 1895. The inertia was the more marked since the Foreign Office and the merchant had for decades offset the disappointments of the coast trade with bright visions of commerce with the richer and more civilised peoples of the western Sudan. Once again in 1894, Gold Coast officials invoked this ancient spell in appealing to London for action. 'Mohammedans by religion,' F. M. Hodgson, the Gold Coast colonial secretary wrote, 'more intelligent and industrious by nature than the negro of the coast lands, they have advanced considerably further in civilization. Their wants are more numerous, and they present in every way a prospective source of profit to the English merchant.'[6]

But the Palmerstonian dream of tapping the supposed wealth of the Sudan from the coastal stations had few charms left in the early Eighteen nineties. They did not entice ministers to exchange the traditional policy of protecting existing commerce for one of staking off large territories for empire. 'Our object', as Salisbury put it later was, '. . . not territory, but facility for trade.'[7] As the British negotiators found when they came to settle with the French four years later, practically nothing had been

[1] F.O. to C.O., 24 Mar. 1892, C.O. African (West), 448, 5.

[2] Sir E. Monson, Memo., encl. Monson to Salisbury, 12 Jan. 1898, *B.D.*, I, 138.

[3] F.O. to C.O., 31 Mar. 1892, C.O. African (West), 448, 6–7; Knutsford to Griffith, 5 Apr. 1892, *ibid.*, 8–9.

[4] Monson, Memo., *B.D.*, I, 138.

[5] J. A. Tilley, Memo., 5 Jan. 1905, *ibid.*, 322–3.

[6] Annual Report of the Gold Coast, 1894, C. 7944, P.P. [1896] LVII, 358.

[7] Salisbury to Monson, 28 Jan. 1898, *B.D.*, I, 139.

done to reserve the Gold Coast hinterlands, '. . . either by occupation or by indisputably valid Treaty rights.' Britain, they concluded, had not apparently '. . . consider[ed] such acquisition to be consistent with her interests'.[1] This was an accurate description. There were officials who wished to do something; yet there was no minister who desired the country enough to go to Parliament for money.

At Lagos as at Cape Coast, the British administration during the decade after 1885 lacked the means of empire-building inland.[2] 'Lagos.' the Colonial Secretary wrote, 'in common with all the other West African Colonies, exists only as a trading station for the native producers and depends, unfortunately upon the produce of the palm trees of the surrounding tribes.'[3] But the depression[4] and the continual strife of the people of Oyo and Ibadan against the Ijebus and Egbas[5] across the inland trade paths fettered the expansion of Lagos, as much as the disruption of Ashanti crippled the Gold Coast. 'Were a permanent peace established [in Yorubaland], the acting-Governor declared in 1889, '. . . the imports and exports of Lagos would soon be nearly doubled, but this can never be effected until what is known as the Ibadan-Ilorin war is brought to a termination.'[6]

The deadlock remained unbroken throughout the Eighties and early Nineties. Emissaries from Lagos tried and failed to bring about peace inland. Mere influence was not enough, yet until 1893 the Colonial Office refused all the traders' and officials' requests for troops. When French agents from Dahomey went up to Abeokuta, heralding an attempt to lop off the main source of Lagos trade, Salisbury's government, after a flurry of treaty-making with the chiefs in the region, again

[1] Monson to Salisbury, 20 Jan. 1898, *ibid.*, 138.

[2] Trade and Revenue of Lagos.

(in £s sterling, round figures)

	Imports	*Exports*	*Revenue*	*Debt*
1871	392,000	590,000	45,000	14,000
1881	334,000	460,000	116,000	716
1890	501,000	595,000	56,000	none
1895	816,000	986,000	142,000	none
1900	830,000	885,000	211,000	1,000,000

Source: (P.P. (1884–5) LXXXIII, 6–7, 22–3, 28–9; P.P. (1890–1) XC, 660–1, 682–3, 688–9, 668–9; P.P. (1901) LXXXVI, 660–1, 668–9, 682–3, 688–9).

[3] (C. 6857), P.P. (1893–4) LIX, 698.

[4] *Palm Oil Prices per Ton realised in England, 1880–92:*

1860 — 52	1884 — 29–40	1888 — 19	1892 — 22–24
1881 — 30	1885 — 25–29	1889 — 23	
1882 — 30–35	1886 — 21–22	1890 — 22–24	
1883 — 26–40	1887 — 22–25	1891 — 22–24	

Source: Lagos Annual Report, 1892, (C. 6857), P.P. (1893–4), LIX, 699.

[5] *vide* S. Johnson, *The History of the Yorubas*, (1921), caps. XXIII–XXXIV.

[6] Denton to Knutsford, 26 Nov. 1889, C. 5897, p. 9.

relied on diplomacy in Paris to make up for lack of effective occupation. If Salisbury would not extend the empire, he would keep France from annexing Britain's customers if he could. By his general west African Agreement with France in August 1889[1] he achieved this, but no more. A boundary between the Lagos and Dahomey spheres of influence was drawn from the coast northwards up to the ninth latitude, and this kept the palm forests of Yorubaland within the British sphere. On the other hand, the hinterland beyond the ninth parallel, like that of the Gold Coast, remained open to foreign invasion.[2] The Lagos authority remained too weak to contend for it. Increased liquor duties had to be imposed in 1892 before the ordinary administrative expenses could be met.[3]

At last in 1893, the Colonial Office allowed the Governor, Sir Gilbert Carter, to impose free trade upon the Egbas of Abeokuta and peace upon Ibadan and Ilorin.[4] It was not an extension of administration or territory. New treaties were made with the chiefs in place of the old. Yet the chiefdoms retained their formal independence. British interference was kept deliberately to a minimum. Carter's 'active interior policy' merely re-asserted the informal sway of Lagos which had broken down.

But pacification alone did little to improve the colony's trade or income.[5] British officials in Lagos as in the other colonies hoped against hope to introduce the African to peasant agriculture. Without cash crops, the settlement's economy seemed unlikely to survive the decay of the palm oil staple. In Lagos too there was much talk of the need for roads and railways — and the same absence of capital with which to build them. The old Coast system — based on *laisser faire* and informal influence — was dying. But the vitality of British interests in west Africa was as yet too weak to put anything in its place.

The Royal Niger Company

Salisbury made his biggest claims, not on behalf of the colonies, but of the Niger Company. For Goldie in the Niger basin he tried to stake out a far handsomer estate, stretching northward to the seventeenth parallel and the edge of the Sahara. 'In this matter', Salisbury declared, 'the interests of this country are the interests of the Royal Niger Company.'[6]

[1] Hertslet, *op. cit.*, II, 732, 736.
[2] Salisbury to Aberdare, 23 Jul. 1889, S.P. (Secretary's note book).
[3] Lagos, Annual Report for 1892, C. 6857, P.P. [1893–4], LIX, 684.
[4] Carter to Ripon, 11 Oct. 1893, C. 7227, P.P. [1893–4], LXII, 600, 632, 597–654.
[5] *vide* McCullum to Chamberlain, 15 Jan. 1898, C.O. 147/129.
[6] Salisbury to Egerton, Private, 10 Aug. 1890, S.P. 59.

Reserving these territories was part of his purpose in the Anglo-French Agreement of August 1890.[1] France gained title to a huge region from the confines of Algeria southward to '. . . a line from Say on the Niger, to Barruwa on Lake Tchad, drawn in such a manner as to comprise in the sphere of action of the Niger Company all that fairly belongs to the Kingdom of Sokoto. . . .'[2] By this line Salisbury defined the northern limit of his territorial ambition on the Niger. Its eastern and western limits remained unsettled; but British and French commissioners were to negotiate a western boundary in the country south and west of the Middle and Upper Niger.

Such extensive territorial prospects pleased even the Niger Company.[3] In yielding so much elsewhere, Salisbury meant to pluck the prize of the Niger. The choice was deliberate. In putting his biggest claim here, the Prime Minister was obeying the same necessity that was holding him back everywhere else in west Africa. The nation as a whole had no more aspirations to empire on the Niger than in Sierra Leone or the Gold Coast. Parliament and Treasury would have subscribed to it even less cheerfully on behalf of the Company than of the colonies. But on the Niger as nowhere else, private enterprise mustered strength enough to stake out claims far inland.

Elsewhere the traders had not pierced far inland from the coasts. African resistance still barred their way. Depression and cut-throat competition sapped their resources. But in the eyes of the Foreign Office, Goldie's Company had the virtue of success.[4] On the Niger he had great advantages over the merchants of the coast. The river gave easier

[1] Salisbury to Aberdare, 23 Jul. 1890, S.P. (Secretary's note book); Salisbury to Mackenzie, 26 Jul. 1890, *ibid.*

[2] C. 6130, P.P. [1890] LXXXI, 512–3; Hertslet, *op. cit.*, II, 738–9.

[3] Aberdare to Salisbury, 31 Jul. 1890, S.P. (Aberdare).

[4] *Territory Administered by the Royal Niger Company: Statistics, 1887–98*
(in £s sterling)

	Finance		*Trade*	
Years	*Revenue*	*Expenditure*	*Imports*	*Exports*
1887	42,396	71,324	73,819	223,450
1888	55,771	73,830	120,878	230,073
1889	57,652	82,870	139,465	260,846
1890	62,430	92,258	180,692	286,200
1891	89,667	107,975	224,729	335,000
1892	103,155	107,115	181,012	341,800
1893	110,756	99,255	159,989	405,935
1894	74,160	104,001	'cannot be stated'	
1895	87,806	108,963		
1896	102,330	117,905		
1897	94,045	135,637		
1898	113,305	135,093		

Source: P.P. (1901) LXXXVI, 988.

access to populous regions and a promising trade. The British government had concentrated its efforts on this entry for decades. Here African resistance to European advances inland had been broken earliest. The Palmerstonian vision of the Niger as the inlet to rich markets in the Moslem north had not quite faded in the Foreign Office when Goldie came, promising to make it come true at no public expense. His private enterprise, once chartered with power to conquer and to rule, and endowed with a virtual monopoly of trade, could overcome the competition, depression and disorder which held up lesser merchants and colonial governments. Able to make a profit as much by ruling as by peaceful commerce, the Niger Company alone had broken through the rain-forests and was pushing northward into the Sudan beyond.

Salisbury's policy was to help the merchants who helped themselves. Hence it was only on the Niger that he, like Granville before him, claimed a large west African hinterland. As Salisbury explained:

> '. . . The spirit and energy of the Royal Niger Company have, without the expenditure of Imperial funds, or the sacrifice of the life of a single British soldier, placed under the protection of the Crown, the whole of the Lower, a great portion of the Central, Niger, and its affluent, the Benue, up to Yola. The Company has concluded treaties with the powerful Sultan of Sokoto, and with the Sultan of Gandu, whose power extends over vast territories on both sides of the Niger. On the rivers an effective administration has been established, and security is maintained by patrolling steamers and police.'[1]

But the Anglo-French Agreement of 1890 was only a paper protection for the Company's sphere. French agents soon invaded it from the south and west. In 1890 Captain Monteil struck inland from Senegal, passed eastward through Say to Sokoto, Bornu and Lake

Protectorate of Southern Nigeria: Total Value of Imports and Exports
(in £s sterling)

Years	*Revenue*	*Expenditure*	*Imports*	*Exports*
1892–93	97,749	98,611	726,889	843,501
1893–94	173,606	138,539	929,333	1,014,088
1894–95	127,352	176,331	739,864	825,099
1895–96	155,513	145,044	750,975	844,333
1896–97	112,441	128,411*	655,978	785,605
1897–98	153,181	121,901	639,699	750,223
1898–99	169,568	146,752	732,640	774,648
1899–1900	164,108	176,140	725,798	888,955

*inclusive of £20,000 paid to the Royal Niger Company as compensation for the Akassa Raid.

Source: P.P. (1901), LXXXVI, 987–8.

[1] Salisbury to Dufferin, 30 Mar. 1892, C. 6701, P.P. [1892] LVI, 778.

Tchad and then wheeled northward to Tripoli.[1] Immediately the Niger Company sent an expedition under MacIntosh to Bornu to make treaties in Monteil's wake. As long as the western bounds of the Company's hinterland lay open, the Say-Barruwa line in the north gave little security against the French.

It seemed for a time in 1892 that the boundary between the British and French spheres west and south of the Middle and Upper Niger, might soon be settled. The Anglo-French Commission proposed a compromise. The disputed area was to be divided along a line running from Say on the Niger south-westward to Bonduku on the Volta River, the western frontier of the Gold Coast. All the country to the north and west of the line would have fallen to France; that to the south and east to Britain.[2] The British design in all this was plain; and once more they gave the Niger Company's claims priority over all else in west Africa. The Foreign Office intended to secure the Borgu region immediately south and west of the Middle Niger, and so keep the French away from the navigable reaches of the river. A French establishment on the Middle Niger would have damaged Goldie's monopoly of trade and transport and the Company's vitality as a British instrument. To fend off this danger, the Foreign Office was offering France most of the Gold Coast hinterland — the chiefdoms of Gurma, Mossi, Mamprussi, Gurunsi and Dagarti.

This proposal would have settled the question once and for all. But France rejected it. The renewed Anglo-French struggle over the Nile prevented agreement on the Niger. After 1892 the French pressed energetically into the disputed territories. General Dodds broke the kingdom of Dahomey, and opened the way for a northward drive into Nikki and Borgu. General Archinard drove south-eastwards from the Sudan towards Mossi and the Niger bend, to link up with the northern push from Dahomey. The entire territory from Mossi and Dagarti on the west to Borgu on the east quickly became the arena for gladiators of empire; those of the crowned company against those of the army of the republic.

Between 1892 and 1895 the Liberal government followed Salisbury's lead in backing up Goldie; and they did so for the same reasons. While one skirmish was beginning in the Niger bend, another flared up in the north-east of the Company's sphere about Lake Tchad. Monteil between 1891 and 1893 carried French influence to Bornu, while

[1] P. L. Monteil, *De Saint-Louis à Tripoli par le lac Tchad*, (Paris, 1895).

[2] *vide* Prof. Westlake, 'England and France on the Niger,' *Contemporary Review*, (Mar. 1898), LXXXIII, 591–2.

Mizon appeared in Muri. Rosebery's reaction to the French intrusion was vehement. He insisted upon the recall of Mizon.[1] In November 1893 he went so far as to call in the Germans to stop further French efforts at extending their claims east of Tchad. By the Anglo-German treaty of that date, Rosebery agreed that the German Cameroons' hinterland should extend northward up to the Lake. The German sphere of influence was also to include the entire Shari River basin stretching from Tchad eastward to the western borders of the former Egyptian Sudan.[2] Here something more was at stake for Rosebery than mere commercial claims. Sliding the Germans into these vast regions of west central Africa was meant to block the French from reaching the Upper Nile from the Upper Niger and the Congo. As a French diplomat protested, the agreement would interpose vast British and German spheres between the French bases in Algeria, Senegal, and Upper Niger and those on the Congo. It would destroy all chance of the French joining their west African protectorates with those on the Red Sea coast.[3] Skirmishing over the northern boundaries of the British Niger sphere had become part of the greater struggle for the Upper Nile. Hence the Niger Company's commercial claims indirectly served the supreme British interest in the security of Egypt.[4] The French however quickly turned the tables on Rosebery. In March 1894 the Germans conceded their Cameroons sphere in turn to France and opened the way once more to the Upper Nile.[5] It was another sign of the comparative weakness of British interest in western Africa that the Foreign Office in 1893 had to rely on pushing Germany forward, as it had pushed Portugal in the Congo ten years earlier.

After the failure of the Cameroons and Congolese treaties, Rosebery and Kimberley showed once more that they would give up much on the west to obtain French recognition of the Nile Valley as a British sphere. In October 1894 such an agreement was within sight. But in the end Paris refused the strict guarantees which London demanded on the Nile, and the negotiations broke down. Henceforward the French let loose expedition after expedition to invade the British claims in the Gold Coast hinterland and the Niger bend. Their efforts to establish themselves on the banks of the navigable reaches of the river grew more

[1] Rosebery to Queen Victoria, 30 Jun. 1893, *Q.V.L.*, *op. cit.*, 3rd ser., II, 268–9. For the 'Affaire Mizon', *vide* Dufferin to Develle, 30 Oct. 1893, *D.D.F.*, X, no. 410; French Chargé d'Affaires in London to Develle, 30 Nov. 1893, *ibid.*, no. 451.

[2] Hertslet, *op. cit.*, III, 914.

[3] French Chargé d'Affaires in London to Develle, 1 Dec. 1893, *D.D.F.*, X, no. 455.

[4] *vide* Marschall to Wilhelm II, 16 Nov. 1893, *Grosse Politik*, VIII, no. 2021.

[5] Hatzfeldt to Caprivi, 14 Apr. 1894, *ibid.*, no. 2022.

forthright. More French money and soldiers were poured out.[1] The rivals' treaty-making and claim jumping spread over Mossi, Gurma and Borgu. At the end of 1894 Kimberley was still hopefully dangling west African concessions before France, in hopes of softening her militancy over Egypt and the Nile.[2] But no agreement could be found on the Nile; and so rivalry on the Niger raged on, each treaty and claim being contested as a pawn in the general settlement that must come in the end. So the struggle for the Nile, as it moved to a climax, gave momentum to the lesser skirmishing on the Niger.

Nothing is more striking about the selection of British claims in tropical Africa between 1882 and 1895 than the emphasis on the east and the comparative indifference to the west. The British chose to concentrate on the Nile and its approaches. Their over-riding concern was not with tropical Africa as such but with security in the Mediterranean and the Orient. To this supreme purpose, the reserving of so much of tropical Africa had been largely incidental. The concentration on east Africa shows the preoccupation with supreme strategic interests. The neglect of west African claims on the other hand, shows a relative indifference to tropical African commercial gains.

Trade prospects had always seemed better in western than in the eastern regions. The west if anywhere, was the place to extend the empire's tropical plantations. More thickly settled and more sophisticated, the western peoples offered larger markets, better labourers and more raw materials. The trading connection with the west coast was much older, the possibilities better known. Yet it was not these commercial options that the late-Victorians were most anxious to claim. They preferred to make the empire safer in poorer east Africa than to make it wealthier in the richer west.

Until 1895 the aim of pegging out tropical estates for the future had played little part in British policy toward the partition. Few responsible ministers saw any serious need for them. It is true that they talked much in public of new African markets; but then it was of temperate rather than tropical Africa that they spoke. There were few shortages of tropical raw materials while the 'Great Depression' lasted. If prices were any indication, palm oil was in plentiful supply; and Lancashire did not lack for raw cotton until the century closed.[3] There was little need to bring tropical Africa into production, as long as America and

[1] *vide* Perham, *op. cit.*, cap. XXII; F. A. Edwards, 'The French on the Niger,' *Fortnightly Review*, (1898), LXIII, 576–91.

[2] Courcel to Hanotaux, 19 Dec. 1894, *D.D.F.*, XI, no. 319.

[3] Redford, *op. cit.*, II, 19–20.

India were saturating Europe's demand for raw materials. Contrary to the classical doctrine of economic imperialism, no strong pressure for the acquisition and development of tropical African estates existed among British manufacturers and investors or the British public at large, until the partition was almost over. The call until 1895 appears to have been restricted to west coast merchants and officials — an energetic but not a compulsive lobby in British politics. It arose out of the difficulties of declining profits in Africa, and not from the demands of economic growth in Europe.

After 1880 the West Coast merchants had pressed government to extend and develop the west African empire because their traditional system seemed to be breaking down. Politically that system had been based on mercantile influence rather than rule. It's arrangements for peace and free trade depended largely on the authority and good will of the African chiefdoms. Its international security upon the self-denial of the Powers. But the authority of the chiefs seemed to be declining. There was anarchy inland; and with the imperial advance of France and Germany, commercial influence was not enough. The British merchant needed British rule to protect and extend his trade.

Commercially also, the traditional coast system seemed more and more unsatisfactory to British traders and officials. Just as the existing native polities no longer met the needs of order, so the native economies were failing to supply commodities for a profitable trade with Europe. The entire system stood or fell with palm oil. A wild forest product only requiring collection and transport, it was a staple which the native economies yielded up easily, without European intervention. But throughout the Eighties and early Nineties, profits and oil revenues were falling. Merchant and administrator looked to the introduction of commercial agriculture for recovery. Yet without drastic intervention from European agencies, African tribal society seemed unlikely to meet so revolutionary a demand. A century of fruitless effort showed that only railways, taxation, and close administration would induce west Africans to take up farming for export. Hence the 'Coasters' urged government to provide these requisites of development, and to make west Africa an imperial estate.

But the ministers in London nearly always refused. If they were willing to negotiate spheres of influence for the protection of existing trade, they did not think it their duty as yet to administer or develop them at public expense. Though the old coast system was breaking down, the imperial government would accept no larger role than that of auxiliary to the merchant. Nor did it liberalise its strict financial rules. Proposals for pacifying expeditions and extended administration were almost always rejected, unless the local revenue could bear the charge. Native wars and collisions with the large northern Muslim states were to be avoided.[1] At the same time, the Treasury would not embark the state's capital in developing west Africa. Ministers refused to guarantee loans for railway-building, doubting whether west Africa would ever produce enough for the lines to carry or to make them pay. What private enterprise could not, the government would not do. Public works and pacification awaited surpluses which never came.

To judge by their actions before 1895, British ministers felt no urgent need to develop west Africa. They did not act like men desperately putting imperial power and capital to work in west Africa for the purpose of raising new markets and sources of supply. They were slow to bring the existing field of commerce under imperial rule. They were even slower to use administration in west Africa directly to graft new forms of production into the native economy. To imagine that the needs of British industry drove the late-Victorians to acquire enlarged tropical estates in west Africa, is to exaggerate their activity and misread their minds.

It is often supposed that tropical Africa was brought under imperial rule to create more business for Britain. But in west Africa, before 1895, it would be truer to say that the merchant was expected to create empire, that government, as in mid-Victorian times, expected him to do without imperial rule, to make do with the protection of a sphere of influence, and to pioneer his own way inland.

Chamberlain's Doctrine of Tropical African Estates

The coming of Joseph Chamberlain to the Colonial Office in 1895 opened a new era in west African policy. It was he who first tried to release expansion from the shackles of the old informal system. He was the first British statesman to prize west African territory highly enough to risk fighting France to get it. It was he who first called a halt to the long British retreat in the west. Chamberlain brought a new incentive to the British movement into tropical Africa. Its largest territorial claims hitherto had been collaterals of the supreme interests in the Mediterranean, in south Africa and in the Orient. Not until the eleventh hour did another, less sophisticated motive intervene: the aim of taking territory for its own sake as an estate for posterity. This was Chamberlain's special if belated contribution. It made little difference

[1] Salisbury to Mackenzie, 26 Jul. 1890, S.P. (Secretary's note book).

to the map of Africa by treaty, for most of that had been drawn already. Yet his radical approach to empire left a more lasting monument. Because he was the first Colonial Secretary to believe in the need for developing tropical Africa as a state enterprise, he set a new value on the possession of territory. He was too late to add much of it to the empire; but he inspired the beginnings of its modern administration and development.

For all his enforced fellowship with Cecils and Cavendishes, Chamberlain in 1895 remained the uncomfortable Radical. His radicalism was not philosophic like Morley's and not dilettante like Labouchere's. Neither was he of those who criticised the 'Establishment' only to enter into it. The Unitarian screw-maker, the social reformer of Birmingham, represented a genuine radicalism of nonconformity and conscience, nourished in the great towns among the small business men and craftsmen from whom he sprang. Angularly dissatisfied with his own times, he combined a good deal of Pym-like 'root and branch' with much Wentworthian 'thorough'. He was in earnest to 'improve' society. Unlike his backward-looking colleagues salvaging a golden age of aristocracy from a naughtier world, Chamberlain was hurrying toward a better future. From his discontent with the social ills of the *laisser-faire* state, he turned to state action. Legislation and administration seemed to him the only hope of progress. 'It is our business', he had said, 'to extend [government's] functions, and to see in what ways its operations can be usefully enlarged.'[1] His was the 'progressive' radicalism of moderate, collectivist social reform.

Chamberlain's imperialism was in one sense his radicalism writ large.[2] His alliance with the Conservatives in defence of Irish union frustrated his programme of reform at Home.[3] But it was understood between him and his colleagues that he might find less dangerous scope for his ideas in the colonial field. Hence Chamberlain began by demanding state action to remedy the diseases of *laisser-faire* in the British Isles; and ended by trying to apply his remedy to the *laisser-faire* empire. The necessities of domestic politics helped to divert overseas his Benthamite passion for constructive administration. Chamberlain fused radical collectivist and traditional notions of empire in a single doctrine.

[1] Perhaps the best statement of Chamberlain's views on government, politics and society is contained in his speech to the Eighty Club, 28 Apr. 1885: *Mr. Chamberlain's Speeches* (ed. C. W. Boyd), (1914), I, 163.

[2] This interpretation is well put in E. Gulley, *Joseph Chamberlain and English Social Politics*, (New York, 1926), 322.

[3] Selborne to Salisbury, 7 Apr. 1895, S.P. (Selborne); Balfour to Salisbury, 31 Jul. 1892, S.P. (Balfour).

The enlarged idea of the national importance of empire which he attained thereby went far beyond his conservative colleagues' beliefs.

The Colonial Secretary declared his doctrine as soon as he took office. Progress and prosperity in Britain, he preached, depended upon developing the empire.[1] But private enterprise had neglected its colonial opportunities in the tropics, particularly in the West Indies, Cyprus[2] and east and west Africa. The imperial government had also failed in its duty to improve the condition of its subjects. As Chamberlain put it to his colleagues:

> 'Up to the present time the Imperial Government has done hardly anything to aid our Colonies and Dependencies in opening up the Countries which are under the British Flag. We have trusted entirely to individual enterprise and capital . . . yet it is certain that in many cases progress has been delayed, and in some cases absolutely stayed, because the only methods by which improvement could be carried out were beyond the scope of private resources.'[3]

Therefore, the Colonial Secretary argued, the state must take the lead in empire-building from the merchant and investor. If the vast 'undeveloped estates' claimed by Britain in tropical Africa and elsewhere were not to be liabilities on the Treasury, a new policy was needed. Imperial activity in tropical Africa had been restricted hitherto to the aim of excluding foreign rivals. Now it should urgently promote development 'by opening up new fields for private enterprise and new markets for British industry'.[4]

It was no longer enough for this purpose to rely on local revenues, on diplomacy and spheres of influence. The Imperial Treasury should provide loans to make the roads, railways and harbours, the lack of which had turned away the private merchant and investor.[5] The imperial government should bring its spheres of influence under effective rule, it should impose peace, encourage the African to contribute his labour and taxes, and hold even the balance of justice between European and African interests. 'Scientific' administration, Chamberlain hoped, would create wealth and engineer progress for the African, as for the British urban and agricultural poor. Like other nonconformist business-

[1] Chamberlain to West African Railways Deputation, 24 Aug. 1895, Garvin, *op. cit.*, III, 20.
[2] Chamberlain to Salisbury, 1 Aug. 1895, S.P. (Chamberlain).
[3] Cabinet Memo., enclosed in Chamberlain to Salisbury, 26 Nov. 1895, S.P. (Colonial Office, Private, 1895–1900).
[4] *ibid.*
[5] Cabinet Memo., 25 Nov. 1895, Garvin, *op. cit.*, III, 177.

men of conscience, he held that profit and social justice must go together. It was his special aim in tropical Africa to curb the liquor traffic, and to abolish slavery and forced labour. Otherwise he explained, '. . . We should kill the goose that lays the golden eggs — the people we want to be our best customers.'[1] Chamberlain brought colonial 'development' and 'welfare' into the vocabulary of policy toward the African tropics.

In some ways such an outlook was not new. Something like it had been applied to the Indian empire since the Eighteen forties; but there the British investor, not the taxpayer, had willingly supplied the capital, because the Indian government's revenue offered good security. Other ministers from 1889 onward had occasionally talked in Chamberlain's tones. Salisbury himself had spoken publicly of the government's duty to make smooth the path for the merchant, just as he had complained of foreign tariffs excluding British trade from Africa. In 1893 Rosebery had turned a gilded phrase for it when he spoke of 'pegging out claims for the future.'[2] But hitherto the Victorians had paid only lip-service to the doctrine of tropical estates. It had sometimes helped in public to justify their advances in tropical Africa. It had rarely inspired them. To most ministers, talk of the prospects there was little more than sugar to help a trading nation swallow a sophisticated strategy. With Chamberlain it was not so. He meant to open the bolted Treasury and the closed minds of Parliament and the electorate to the need for state enterprise. He intended to make a business of the tropical African fields which others had staked out mainly with an eye to security.

In August 1895 the Colonial Secretary appealed to British opinion for support:

> 'I regard many of our Colonies as being in the condition of undeveloped estates, and estates which can never be developed without Imperial assistance.'[3]
>
> 'I may submit to you . . . what is in a certain sense a new policy. . . . If the people of this country are not willing to invest some of their superfluous wealth in the development of their great estate, then I see no future for these countries, and it would have been better never to have gone there. I shall appeal to the opinion of the country, which is gradually ripening, and I think I shall meet with a satisfactory response.'[4]

[1] *Hansard*, 4th ser., XXXVI, col. 642.

[2] Speech at the Royal Colonial Institute, 1 Mar. 1893, *The Foreign Policy of Lord Rosebery*, (1901).

[3] *Hansard*, 4th ser., XXXVI, col. 642.

[4] Speech to Deputation on West African Railways, 23 Aug. 1895. Garvin, *op. cit.*, III, 20.

Chamberlain admitted that the policy represented a radical departure. It is also notable that he spoke not as one representing a strong national demand for developing tropical Africa, but as one trying to evoke it. His tone and tenour confirm that hitherto no such demand had arisen in British opinion. In his opinion at least, the British investor, manufacturer and merchant generally had been hugely indifferent to the possibilities of the African tropics. Their need of markets and raw materials had played little part in instigating British claims.

But now, Chamberlain thought, the trend was more favourable. Imperial sentiment perhaps was rising. Sections of British business, beginning to feel the force of foreign tariffs and industrial competition, were turning toward protectionism, perhaps to imperial preference. Capital was cheap, and investors would welcome new outlets. Depression was lifting, and industrial growth meant a rising demand for tropical materials. Chamberlain hoped for support, not from the few east and west African merchants alone, but from the many businessmen whom he envisaged as coming to see the importance of developing a specifically imperial economy. Perhaps the Colonial Secretary's impressions were to some extent true. Yet when he came to carry out his schemes, he found the nation's interest in turning tropical Africa into another India still dwarfed beside its objections to more taxation and state enterprise, its respect for *laisser-faire* tradition, and its scepticism about the region's resources in lands, minerals and labour. What was more, the stiffest opponents of a radical departure were among his own Cabinet colleagues.

In August 1895 the Colonial Secretary asked the Cabinet to turn the large profits of the government-owned Suez Canal shares into a colonial development fund. The money would be used for loans to build colonial railways and other public works.[1] His private argument for tropical estates however, suggests that he was more immediately concerned to avoid asking Parliament for grants-in-aid of the derelict colonies and unprofitable railway projects already on his hands, than with the long-term promotion of imperial trade. His plea to Salisbury was simply: '. . . If I can get just a little money I believe something may be done to make Cyprus a paying proposition.'[2] There was a similar problem in the West Indies. In Chamberlain's proposal to the Cabinet, the whole cost of the Uganda railway which was vital to Salisbury's Nile Valley strategy, was to be the first charge on the proposed fund.[3]

[1] Chamberlain to Salisbury, 1 Aug. 1895, S.P. (Chamberlain). [2] *ibid.*
[3] Chamberlain, Cabinet Memo., enclosed in Chamberlain to Salisbury, 26 Nov. 1895, S.P. (C.O., Private, 1895–1900).

But Hicks Beach at the Exchequer and Sir Edward Hamilton strongly objected. As the British taxpayer had bought the shares, so the profits should be spent in the United Kingdom. Chamberlain's proposal was financial heresy. Parliament would reject it as a 'crooked expedient' to evade its control over expenditure. There was nothing in the plan which would justify such high political risks.[1] The Cabinet put Chamberlain's development fund into cold storage.

But the Colonial Secretary was freer in his own department. West African colonial trade and revenue were improving, especially in the Gold Coast which was enjoying a minor gold boom. Towards the end of 1895 he authorised the west African administrations to make a start with the inland railways which merchants and officials alike had been demanding since 1883.[2] At the same time Chamberlain, without consulting the Cabinet,[3] was able to clear the path towards the gold of Ashanti. For a decade Knutsford and Ripon had refused the merchants' petitions for this undertaking, waiting until the local Treasury could pay for it.[4] Chamberlain would wait no longer. He unleashed an expedition to bring Ashanti under control[5], and advanced the Gold Coast administration the money to pay the cost.[6] In Sierra Leone, Cardew was allowed to bring the protectorate under closer administration, and in the Gold Coast, Chamberlain endorsed Maxwell's attempts to introduce land reform, to gain control of the chiefs and to levy a house tax on Africans.

These were the small beginnings of Chamberlain's large plan of 'scientific' development. Imperial control was to be extended; and the interior pacified; the chiefs were to be brought under official supervision. Railways were to open the interior, attract European capital and stimulate African production, before French and German railways could divert the inland trade to foreign ports. But the greatest difficulty was to make the railways pay. Each administration was to be equipped with a strong agricultural department which would at last persuade the

[1] Hicks Beach, Cabinet Memo., 29 Dec. 1895; Sir E. Hamilton, Cabinet Memo., 14 Dec. 1895, S.P. (C.O., Private, 1895–1900).

[2] *vide Construction of Railways in Sierra Leone, Lagos and the Gold Coast*, Cd. 2325, P.P. [1905], LVI, 361–410. *vide Correspondence on Proposed Concessions of Railways in the West African Colonies*, C.O. African (West), 448.

[3] Chamberlain to Salisbury, 8 Nov. 1895, S.P. (Chamberlain).

[4] Ripon to Hodgson, 30 Jan. 1894, C. 7917, P.P. [1896] LVIII, 613–4; Ripon to Maxwell, 15 Mar. 1895, C. 7918, P.P. [1896], LVIII, 761–2; *vide* C. 7917, C. 7918 *passim*.

[5] Chamberlain to Maxwell, 22 Nov. 1895, *ibid.*, 847–9.

[6] The charges of the expedition were regarded as a loan to the Gold Coast, which was expected to recover the expenses eventually from the Ashanti themselves. The expedition cost about £99,000. (Gold Coast Annual Report, 1902, Cd. 1768, P.P. (1904), LVI, 379.)

African through the chiefs to grow cotton, kola nuts, fibres, cocoa and rubber.[1] Where necessary, tribal land tenures were to be reformed and the progressive peasants given a secure, individual title. Waste and unoccupied lands were to be brought under government's control. But the administrations could do none of these things without money. Chamberlain and his officials hoped to tax the African population directly, both as a spur to production and for revenue. European enterprise must also contribute a higher share of royalties on its concessions and trade. The remainder would have to be made up from imperial loans and grants-in-aid. Where the British merchant and investor, the African chief and the native economies had failed, the administrator was to organise African society for production and progress.

Chamberlain henceforward ran a financial steeple-chase with the rising cost of colonial development. African resistance — rebellion in Sierra Leone and the threats of another in the Gold Coast — frustrated the attempts at direct taxation. The projects for land reform had to be withdrawn as too explosive. The west African merchants of Liverpool, Manchester and London accused Chamberlain of ruining their trade and resisted his attempts to raise more revenue. They wanted railways; but they did not want an expensive, 'high-class' bureaucracy battening on their profits. Hicks Beach at the Treasury was tired of Chamberlain's demands for grants, and Parliament looked suspiciously at the rising Colonial Office votes. The Colonial Secretary once more proposed imperial guarantees for loans to develop the Crown Colonies. Hicks Beach, who was anxious to find an outlet for surplus capital, brought a Colonial Loans Fund Bill before Parliament in the middle of 1898. But strong opposition compelled him to withdraw it.[2] A year later, the extent to which Chamberlain's developments had exceeded Parliamentary authority and colonial financial resources became plain. The ministry reluctantly forced through an emergency measure guaranteeing loans of three and a half million pounds for west African and West Indian railways and harbours. As Chamberlain admitted, the works were already being carried out. The loans had been largely anticipated and spent.[3] A slightly chastened and more experienced Colonial Secretary came through these African and Parliamentary troubles. '*Festina lente*', he wrote, when refusing to bring Yorubaland under

[1] For a characteristic statement of west African development plans at this time, *vide* C.O. Memo. on the British Possessions in West Africa (H.J.R.), 12 May 1897, C.O. African (West) 534.

[2] *Hansard*, 4th ser., LXII, col. 173 *et seq.*

[3] *Hansard*, 4th ser., LXXVI, col. 518 *et seq.*

closer administration, 'is a just motto in the development of colonies in the possession of barbarous tribes.'

CHAMBERLAIN AND THE NIGER, 1897–1898

Chamberlain's influence upon the last phase of the Anglo-French struggle on the Niger was as distinctive as his contribution to tropical African administration. His colleagues looked upon the disputed Niger claims as little more than pawns in the strategy of the Nile. How far they were to be made good, they were willing to leave to diplomatic convenience and the activity of Goldie's Niger Company to decide. Chamberlain, on the other hand, regarded them as an urgent national trading interest. He would uphold them for their intrinsic value. For expansion, as for development, he insisted that the imperial government must take the lead from the faltering merchants. Granted his belief in tropical African estates, so vehement an approach to the Niger question could be expected. Yet during his first two years in office, he accepted Salisbury's leadership without protest.

The Prime Minister was intent, not upon pegging out estates in west Africa, but upon buttressing world security on the Upper Nile. It seemed essential in 1895 to conciliate France, and through her, Russia, to relieve their pressure in the Mediterranean, India and China. The Cabinet 'felt [it] to be important in the present state of things to settle as many questions with France as possible'.[1] Salisbury hoped to clear the way for a *rapprochement* by settling minor Anglo-French quarrels first. Graver negotiations over the Nile and China might follow. Disputes in Tunis, Morocco and Siam were already being settled in a spirit of give and take. The petty west African disputes were to be similarly composed. In December 1895 Chamberlain proposed a comprehensive settlement of colonial difficulties with France and Germany. He was prepared to cede the Gambia and Dominica to France in exchange for Dahomey, and then to pass that territory to Germany in return for a free hand in the neutral zone behind the Gold Coast.[2] The Niger question, which would have been settled in 1894 but for the disagreement over the Nile, also seemed ripe for solution. In August 1895 Salisbury and Hanotaux were rejecting each other's treaties in Nikki and Borgu;[3] but both sides looked upon

[1] Salisbury to Queen Victoria, 11 Jan. 1896, J. D. Hargreaves, 'Entente Manquée; Anglo-French Relations, 1895–96,' *C.H.J.*, XI, no. 1, (1953), 75.

[2] Chamberlain to Salisbury, 16 Dec. 1895, S.P. (Chamberlain).

[3] Hanotaux to Dufferin, 18 Jul. 1895, *D.D.F.*, XII, no. 93; British Chargé d'Affaires to Hanotaux. 15 Aug. 1895, *ibid.*, no. 129.

this as a matter for petty bargaining. They agreed in January 1896 that the Anglo-French commission, which had sat intermittently since 1892, should begin again.[1]

Once more however, the struggle on the Nile brought the Niger Commission to deadlock. On 12 March, 1896, Salisbury told the French of the advance on Dongola. The fat was in the fire and the west African negotiations were swallowed up in the blaze.[2] Salisbury, adamant about Egypt and the Nile, his German relations strained by the Jameson Raid, became the more anxious to be reasonable about the Niger. On 27 April, 1896, the British Foreign Office offered generous concessions to French claims, only for Paris to ask for more.[3] In October Salisbury spoke benevolently of giving the French access to the lower reaches of the Niger[4], and in December, of getting rid of the Niger Company whose trading monopoly angered both Paris and Berlin.[5] Far from pressing British claims on the Niger, the Foreign Office was ready to yield part of the sphere which it had claimed in 1890 and 1892. Salisbury was friendliness itself in the '*petits litiges africains*' in the west. But with the British advancing to their objectives on the Nile, the French government could not afford to be bought off with west African compensations. 'It is the whole Egyptian situation', Courcel said, 'which forces us too often to treat questions of business as questions of politics.'[6] The more Britain worsted France in Egypt, the more France raised her claims in west Africa to strengthen her bargaining position and to provide her politicians with successes. While Kitchener pressed forward from Dongola toward Khartoum, and the Niger Commission disputed in Paris, more French expeditions fanned outward from Dahomey on to the Middle Niger. Bretonnet occupied Ilo and Bussa for the French. Other challenges appeared to the north in Gandu and Sokoto. French pressure in the Niger bend mounted. In October, Baud reached Camirama; Vermeersch occupied Nikki, where Lugard had made a treaty. The French also took Gomba and were plainly making for control of the west bank of the big river from Say as far south as Bussa or even Jebba. The Niger Company could not cope with these many-headed advances into its sphere. Early in 1897 Goldie managed to occupy

[1] This decision may be followed in Courcel to Hanotaux, 14 Aug. 1895, *D.D.F.*, XII, no. 128, and 29 Sept. 1895, no. 161; Hanotaux to Courcel, 21 Oct. 1895, no. 179; Salisbury to Hanotaux, 29 Nov. 1895, no. 217; Courcel to Berthelot, 20 Dec. 1895, no. 243, and 15 Jan. 1896, (annexe).

[2] *vide supra*, cap. XII.

[3] Salisbury to Dufferin, 12 May 1896, Hargreaves, *op. cit.*, 92.

[4] Courcel to Hanotaux, 3 Oct. 1896, *D.D.F.*, XII, no. 468.

[5] Courcel to Hanotaux, 11 Dec. 1896, *D.D.F.* XIII, no. 40.

[6] Courcel to Hanotaux, 27 Jan. 1897, *D.D.F.*, XIII, no. 77.

Nupe and Ilorin. Yet Salisbury forbade him to move north of Jebba. These French advances did not perturb him. Things were going well on the Nile. The security of Egypt which had been the crux of his African policy since 1889 was within sight of consummation. It seemed foolish to provoke the French unnecessarily in west Africa at such a time; and the Niger territory, which private business had proved incapable of holding, was not worth a war with France or a national effort. The Prime Minister was still concerned with protecting facilities for British trade rather than with empire-building.[1] He remained the exponent of that classical imperialism which painted red only as much of the map as was occupied by colonists or seemed vital to world power.

But Chamberlain early in 1897 began jogging Salisbury's elbow toward a more imperial foreign policy. The Colonial Secretary's newfound experience of foreign affairs was bringing him to heretical conclusions. A friend noted:

> 'He talked of China and West Africa, and of France and Russia, with an amplitude of view and phrase that would have astonished Birmingham ten years ago. He has lately had a strong difference of opinion with Lord S. He believes we are at the parting of the ways and that we must stand fast for Imperial expansion now or never, whatever the result.'[2]

It was characteristic of Chamberlain's 'scientific' approach to politics. More than any of his contemporaries, he reached his opinions by analysing 'the trend of the times' and forecasting the future in terms made popular by Seeley, the Cambridge historian. How the Colonial Secretary foresaw the world in the twentieth century, he revealed in a famous passage:

> 'It seems to me that the tendency of the time is to throw all power into the hands of the greater empires, and the minor kingdoms — those which are non-progressive — seem to be destined to fall into a secondary and subordinate place. But if Greater Britain remains united, no empire in the world can ever surpass it in area, population, in wealth, or in the diversity of its resources.'[3]

Already Chamberlain was hurrying to prepare a British empire to survive in a world of continental super-states. A sense of crisis — of now or never — henceforward inflamed his already vehement temper toward desperate action. Altogether, he was coming to identify the

[1] Salisbury to Monson, 28 Jan. 1898, *B.D.*, I, 139.

[2] *Journals and Letters of Viscount Esher*, (ed. Brett), 29 Jan. 1898, I, 210–11.

[3] Chamberlain's speech to the Royal Colonial Institute, 31 Mar. 1897, Boyd, *op. cit.*, II, 5.

future of the British Isles with the future of its empire. No more than Disraeli and Palmerston, had Salisbury ever regarded empire as the most important element in national power and prosperity. Therefore he had never made the pursuit of empire the first aim of policy. But Chamberlain from 1897 onwards came near to doing so. Upon his world picture, it seemed reasonable for the first time to extend British rule wherever possible, even at the risk of a European war.

The Colonial Secretary concluded at the beginning of 1897 that, since France had shown herself irreconcilable, she must yield to strength. He protested frequently against the Prime Minister's weakness in the Near Eastern crisis, with some support from other ministers. Salisbury did not want to go too much against him '. . . for fear of breaking up the Cabinet'.[1] The Colonial Secretary extended his campaign for a pugnacious foreign policy to Egypt and the Far East. 'Mr. Chamberlain', Salisbury told the Queen, 'is a little too warlike, and hardly sees the other side of the question.'[2] From April 1897, the Colonial Secretary's indignation with France and his zeal for imperial expansion began to press on the Niger negotiations. Goschen at the Admiralty gathered that Chamberlain wanted to break them off and asked for a Cabinet to cool his belligerence. The treating with the French went on; but Salisbury wearily admitted that in the Niger question he was 'yoked to Chamberlain' and felt bound to compromise for the sake of keeping him in the Cabinet.[3] During the following months, the Colonial Secretary obtained a free hand to prepare a thorough-going counter-offensive against the French invasion in the Gold Coast hinterland and the Niger bend.[4] By the autumn he was determined to resist the French push toward the Lower Niger from the west, 'even at the cost of war'.[5]

The Niger Company had outlived its usefulness for this purpose, as well as for others. It was not a suitable instrument of Chamberlain's plans for investing imperial capital in west African colonial estates. That its monopoly must go had already been agreed in principle with the French. In any case, the chartered company was too weak and unco-operative to resist their military incursions. Chamberlain thought it was time to 'expropriate [Goldie] lock, stock and barrel'.[6] He had to

[1] Salisbury to Queen Victoria, 17 Feb. 1897, *Q.V.L.*, 3rd ser., III, 133; Queen's Journal, 1 Apr. 1897, *ibid.*, 147.
[2] Queen's Journal, 14 Nov. 1897, *ibid.*, 209.
[3] Goschen to Salisbury, 19 Apr. 1897, S.P. (Goschen).
[4] *vide* Perham, *op. cit.*, 632 *et seq.*
[5] Chamberlain to Selborne, 28 Sept. 1897, Garvin, *op. cit.*, III, 208.
[6] Chamberlain to Selborne, 19 Sept. 1897, *ibid.*, III, 210.

wait until December 1899 to get his way about this; but in the meantime he had created an official instrument to do what Goldie could not. Chamberlain cajoled his colleagues into allowing him to organise the West African Frontier Force and confront the French army in the hinterlands. The Colonial Secretary wanted to play the west African game with new rules. He was introducing the 'imperial' factor to extend British territorial claims and the day of chartered companies was over, except in Rhodesia. He was calling a halt to Salisbury's policy of trading the strategically worthless west for the economically worthless east.

To the Prime Minister and some of his colleagues it seemed that Chamberlain was wilfully confusing priorities and raising the Niger stakes at the worst possible time. Marchand was making for Fashoda. The Cabinet knew that Kitchener's Egyptian army would have to be reinforced with British troops to speed the advance to Khartoum. With the Sudan crisis impending, it seemed wiser to conciliate France by conceding the lesser issues on the Niger. Goschen and Hicks Beach pressed this view on Salisbury throughout 1897. If it was our policy seriously to settle the trivial Anglo-French disputes in west Africa, they asked, what was the point of mustering the West African Frontier Force? Aggressive action would only anger the French and embitter negotiation; and all for absurdly unimportant interests.[1] The Chancellor thought the ministry was going forward in too many places at once. A price would be paid in unpopularity at the next elections. 'What is going to happen in Nigeria and the Gold Coast Hinterland,' he protested, 'I really don't know; but Chamberlain will try to do a good deal if you don't stop him.'[2] Goschen urged that 'the moment . . . did not seem very suitable for a quarrel with the French who had lost their heads'.[3] It is almost certain that the Cabinet toward the end of 1897 told Chamberlain that there could be no question of fighting France for Bussa or Mossi.[4] For all that, the Cecils compromised with the Colonial Secretary to keep him from leaving the government. The ministry henceforward pursued a double-headed policy. Chamberlain was allowed to go ahead with his military policy in west Africa; while Salisbury went his conciliatory way in Paris.

At the end of October 1897 the Anglo-French commissioners resumed their negotiations about the Niger. The Prime Minister was

[1] Hicks Beach to Salisbury, 1 Oct. 1897, S.P. (Hicks Beach).

[2] Hicks Beach to Salisbury, 1 Nov. 1897, S.P. (Hicks Beach).

[3] Goschen to Salisbury, 19 Sept. 1897, Elliott, *op. cit.*, II, 211.

[4] *vide* Perham, *op. cit.*, 633, 641. Brett's Journal notes that Chamberlain had had a row with Salisbury in September. (Esher, *Journals*, I, 210–11.)

willing to concede a French demand for access to the river between Leaba and Bajobo and a connecting corridor through Gurma to French territory.[1] Chamberlain on the other hand strongly opposed the suggested enclave.[2] In February 1898 he launched his West Africa Frontier Force into the Lagos hinterland, to occupy as much territory as its commanders dared without provoking war with France.[3] By May and June Willcocks stood face to face with the French army in Borgu; and Chamberlain was fuming and blustering against Salisbury's weakness in Paris. Nevertheless, once Hanotaux had been shown that the Niger negotiation was not to be linked to the Nile question, a settlement slowly emerged.[4] By the beginning of June the haggling had narrowed down to the ownership of Ilo and Bona. Hanotaux insisted that the entire bargain stood or fell on French possession of Ilo. Salisbury 'confidently' counselled that France should have it.[5] But Chamberlain again protested:

> 'I think that we shall not be the greatest losers even if the present negotiations fall through. In that case I hope we may take steps to put ourselves in a better position before they are resumed. There is no reason why we should not follow the example of the French and occupy places in *their* hinterland which would give us something to exchange. . . .'[6]

Now, as throughout the Niger negotiations Chamberlain did not want a diplomatic settlement of west African disputes. He wanted time to develop his counter-offensive and extend his occupation of the Gold Coast and Niger hinterlands.

But this time Salisbury and the Cabinet had their way. The Prime Minister wrote:

> 'It will be a pity if we break off the negotiations, for it will add to our difficulties in the Nile Valley. . . . If we are to send British or Indian troops in the hope of fighting another Plassey with Lugard as our Clive and Sokoto as our Bengal, the prospect becomes very much more serious. Our Clive will be in no danger of being astonished at his own moderation. There is no loot to get except in Goldie's dreams. If you wish to come to terms it would be prudent to do so before we take Khartum. We shall get nothing out of the French Assembly after that event.'[7]

[1] Salisbury to Gosselin, 30 Dec. 1897, *B.D.*, I, no. 157.
[2] Chamberlain, Cabinet Memo., 25 Jan. 1898, Garvin, *op. cit.*, III, 212–14; Salisbury Minute, 11 Jan. 1898, *B.D.*, I, no. 159.
[3] *vide* Perham, *op. cit.*, cap. XXX.
[4] Monson to Salisbury, 1 May 1898, *B.D.*, I, no. 177. For the British view of the negotiations *vide ibid.*, nos. 174, 176, 178.
[5] Salisbury to Chamberlain, 2 Jun. 1898, Garvin, *op. cit.*, III, 218–19.
[6] Chamberlain to Salisbury, 2 Jun. 1898, Garvin, *op. cit.*, III, 220.
[7] Salisbury to Chamberlain, 3 Jun. 1898, *ibid.*

The Niger Convention was signed on 14 June 1898, three months before Fashoda. By its terms the French obtained access to the navigable Niger and they retained the disputed regions of Mossi and Nikki. Borgu was divided between the contestants. British claims had receded considerably since Salisbury hopefully drew the Say-Barruwa line in the Anglo-French Agreement of 1890. But the French accepted the British claim to Sokoto and Ilo while retaining Bona. In effect, the partition of west Africa was over. As it had begun so it ended — a disturbance stirred largely by the struggle for Egypt and the Nile.

The disagreement between Chamberlain and Salisbury underlines once again the contrast between the new radical and the traditional outlooks on imperial expansion. The Prime Minister and several members of the Cabinet regarded the west African issues as trivial brawls over expendable places; the Colonial Secretary, as serious exertions in a field important to the commercial future. Salisbury played for limited stakes and was ready to forego tropical estates in the west African interior. Chamberlain, on the other hand, demanded territory on the Niger and in the Gold Coast hinterland, as well as in the Sudan. He wanted everywhere to raise the betting and sweep the board in a game of winner take all. He had succeeded in pegging out a few additional claims on the Niger. But his imperialism of tropical estates for posterity came too late, it was too constricted by free trade tradition to contribute significantly to the motivation of empire in tropical Africa or to alter greatly its ultimate boundaries.

An empire's motives for claiming territory are often very different from the motives which inspire its subsequent administration and development. The modern administration of British west Africa originated in administrative rather than commercial needs. Chamberlain was the first minister to face the problem of making the territories already claimed repay the cost of governance. Revenue was his constant anxiety; and administrations had to take the lead in commercial development if they were ever to become solvent. Perhaps a new imperialism helped to inspire Chamberlain's programme. Yet the strongest incentive seems to have been the inability of the old Coast system to stand the financial strain of foreign rivalry and the enlarged territorial burdens imposed by the partition.

Henceforward public enterprise pioneered the development of east and west Africa. Although after 1900 European demand for tropical materials rose sharply, it was government which provided the bulk of the capital, and administrative agencies which did most to organise the African native economies for production. What prompted colonial governments to develop their territories was Parliamentary pressure to cut down grants-in-aid, to repay loans and to swell the revenue. The partition of Africa had left them unexpected but compulsive legacies. In Kenya and Uganda they were compelled to stimulate the economy to repay the cost of the Uganda Railway. The unforeseen outcome of Salisbury's pursuit of security in Egypt was to be the white settler in Kenya and the African cotton farmer in Uganda and the Sudan. In the same way, colonial governments in west Africa were spurred into development to pay for pacification, administration and Chamberlain's railways.

The British colonies and protectorates in tropical Africa had not been claimed originally because they were needed as colonial estates. Rather, they had been claimed for strategic reasons, and they had to be developed as colonial estates to pay the costs of their administration. Their economic development was more a consequence than a motive of the 'Scramble'. As an explanation of European rule in tropical Africa, the theory of economic imperialism puts the trade before the flag, the capital before the conquest, the cart before the horse.

CHAPTER XIV

South Africa: another Canada or another United States?

Fashoda closed the twenty-year-old crisis of British security on the Nile. Meanwhile, the Jameson Raid of 1895 had re-opened that crisis of imperial supremacy in south Africa which British statesmen had feared since the Transvaal rebellion of 1881. The second Boer War followed hard upon Fashoda. At first sight these spectacular African aggressions at the end of the century might suggest a full-blooded drive for empire — a climactic 'new imperialism'. But this was not how ministers saw their onslaughts upon the Sudan and the Transvaal. What moved them to reconquer the Sudan was the ancient pursuit of security in the Mediterranean. What brought them in the end to absorb the Transvaal was the belief that otherwise their influence over south Africa would be lost.

In a sense the logic behind the intervention in the Transvaal was like that behind the occupation of Egypt in 1882. As in Egypt so in south Africa, an inpouring of trade and capital combined with a nationalist reaction against foreign interference to crack British paramountcy. In both cases the routes to the East were threatened. In Egypt, Anglo-French commercial expansion by 1882 had undermined the Khedivate — the basis of the dual political influence. Interference to restore it had provoked the Arabist revolution and completed the collapse; and the failure to come to terms with the Egyptian nationalists and with France had rooted the British on the Nile. The connection between the growth of trade in south Africa and the eventual engulfing of the Transvaal was somewhat similar. By 1896 economic growth had released the South African Republic from the stranglehold of the British colonies and reversed the supremacy of the Cape and the dependence of the Transvaal. Statesmen had assumed that the colony would absorb the republics into a British dominion, but now it seemed more likely that the republic would draw the colonies into a 'United States' of south Africa. As in Egypt, aggression began where investment left off and external hegemony became uncertain. The attempt at repair damaged it further. The

Jameson Raid, like the bombardment of Alexandria, provoked nationalist resistance and made supremacy by influence unattainable. What inspired the assault on the Transvaal was the fear that the political ties binding south Africa to the empire were snapping.

Rhodes Against the Trend, 1890–1895

This cataclysmic view, from which the imperial government was never to escape, came from Rhodes after the ruin of his schemes for redressing the local balance in favour of the empire. In 1890 they seemed to have every chance of success. His British South Africa Company was colonising Matabeleland, he was Prime Minister of the Cape Colony, in alliance with Hofmeyr and the Bondsmen; and Knutsford and later, Ripon in London were doing everything to support the touchy champion of an imperial south Africa.

After hemming in the Transvaal on the north, Rhodes' next move was in Swaziland. Since 1887 Natalians and trekboers had disputed for the possession of this country; but London had no desire to annex it, since all its potential sources of public revenue had passed into private hands. Neither did it interest the Cape colonists. Swaziland was the bait which Rhodes and Hofmeyr would use to draw Kruger into a commercial union with the Cape, and to persuade him to leave Matabeleland to the South Africa Company.[1]

In 1890 after most of the Swazi settlers had declared in favour of republican rule, Robinson and de Winton, the British agent, recommended that Swaziland should be yielded to the Transvaal at this price. At the same time Hofmeyr exerted all his influence upon Kruger to agree;[2] and Knutsford offered to let Kruger build a railway through Swaziland to Kosi Bay and absorb the 'Little Free State'— the part of Swaziland which the Transvaalers had occupied. What was left was to be policed jointly by republican and imperial officials until that too could be handed over to the Transvaal.[3] There were two conditions:

[1] Knutsford explained to Salisbury: 'We should be much abused in this country if we let the Boers annex Matabeleland and Mashonaland . . . but we shall have to face considerable danger of conflict with the Boers; if we bar them from extension to the North, I should be inclined to compromise with them by letting it be known that if they come to terms with Umbandine [King of Swaziland] we shall not prevent them from protecting and annexing that country. This will bring them to the sea, which is their chief desire,' (Knutsford to Salisbury, 28 Jan. 1889 and 9 Jun. 1889, S.P. (Holland).) Goschen objected to giving the Transvaalers access to the sea. (Goschen to Salisbury, Dec. 1889, S.P. (Goschen).)

[2] For Hofmeyr's part in the negotiations *vide* Hofmeyr and Reitz, *op. cit.*, cap. XXIII.

[3] *vide* Knutsford to Loch, 17 Sept. 1891, (drafts), S.P. (Holland).

the republic must join the Cape customs union and admit the Cape railway. But this attempt to bribe the Transvaal into the colonial commercial system failed when Kruger's Volksraad rejected the Swaziland Convention of 1890, preferring their separatist aspirations. All that was left of the agreement was a Transvaal undertaking to keep out of Zambesia[1] and to share the policing of Swaziland for the time being.

Kruger did hold back his trekkers from invading the South Africa Company's field in Mashonaland; and at last in December 1891, he gave the colony its rail link with Johannesburg in the Sivewright agreement. Rhodes' ministry lent the republic's Netherlands Railway Company the capital to extend the Cape line to the Rand. In return, the republic gave the Cape government control of the freight rates on the northern section of the line for the next three years. But the republic could not be kept commercially dependent on colonial ports. In June 1892, the wealth of the Rand enabled the republic to borrow in London the money for the rest of the Delagoa Bay line. It was Rhodes' friend, Rothschild who raised the loan. The financial and mining interests of Johannesburg demanded the shortest route to the sea, to cut their working costs. Economic growth was bursting south Africa's political frontiers. But her rigidities of loyalty and sentiment remained. In the struggle to shape development into the republican or the colonial patterns of politics, the Transvaal now seemed to hold every advantage. Cape Town and London hastened to settle with Kruger before he opened the Delagoa line and took control of the Cape extension.

Hopes of improving the colonial bargaining position were pinned upon Delagoa Bay, the *Uitlander* franchise in the Transvaal and the Rhodesian counterpoise in Matabeleland. But the acquisition of Delagoa Bay was hedged with diplomatic thorns. It seemed not at all unlikely that Kruger's government might confidently defy the imperial power and take over Swaziland. Apart from this, there was the danger that he might let his trekkers loose into Matabeleland and upset all Rhodes' northern schemes. Yet a full-blooded quarrel with Kruger in either Swaziland or Matabeleland might break Rhodes' alliance with Hofmeyr and the Bond in Cape Town and shake the loyalty of the Cape government. Aware of these risks, the Cape ministry again pressed Ripon to accept the republic's claims in Swaziland, if it would veto an invasion of Matabeleland.[2]

How anxious the Colonial Office was about the weakening position in south Africa, how dependent upon Rhodes and his company to

[1] Hertslet, *op. cit.*, I, 243.

[2] Ripon to Loch, 1 Dec. 1892, C. 7212, P.P. (1893–4) LXII, 289–92.

buttress it, is shown by a departmental memorandum of October 1892. This pointed out the 'great danger' of the Transvaalers invading Zambesia. Boer sympathies in the Orange Free State and even in the Cape Colony would be with the trekkers. 'Unless we are prepared to resist this by force, we shall have to abandon Mr. Rhodes and the British South Africa Company and the whole idea of British supremacy in the interior to a "New Republic", which will be hostile to British capital and enterprise.'[1] But, the official continued, another Transvaal war, particularly in defence of the chartered company, would be exceedingly unpopular at Westminster. It would be disastrous for imperial relations with the Afrikaners everywhere and above all, to Rhodes' influence in the Cape Colony. It was essential to avoid a rupture between Rhodes and the Bond. Only this combination, the Colonial Office believed, could lay the ghost of Afrikaner disloyalty arising from the first Boer war. 'The racial animosity excited by the Transvaal war of 1880–1', the Colonial Office noted, 'has by a policy of conciliation, greatly died out,— due to Mr. Rhodes.'[2] But conflict with the South Africa Republic would envenom it. An explosion in Swaziland would be as dangerous to Rhodes as a crisis in Matabeleland. If war broke out between the settlers and the Swazi, Ripon could see no way of preventing the republic from occupying the country to restore order.[3] Harcourt at the Treasury was urging him to withdraw from the temporary police arrangement set up by the Swaziland Convention of 1890.[4] The same fears that had prompted Knutsford to take Matebeleland, brought Ripon to give away Swaziland.

In December 1892 Ripon offered to leave the republic in sole possession of Swaziland[5] under certain conditions. He asked for franchise concessions for the *Uitlanders* of the Transvaal, hoping to undermine republican separatism from within. But this Kruger rejected. Ripon also insisted that no railway eastward from Swaziland to the coast should be built without British permission. To this Kruger agreed, for his Delagoa railway was in sight. Ripon had renewed his safeguard against the republic obtaining independent access to Kosi Bay. But as a sop to British humanitarians he insisted that the Swazis should formally assent before coming under the republic. Upon this

[1] C.O. Memo., 'The Swazi Question,' 19 Oct. 1892, C.O. African (South) 438, 16.
[2] *ibid.*, 15.
[3] Ripon to Loch, 1 Dec. 1892, C. 7212, P.P. (1893–4), LXII, 289–92.
[4] The Treasury wished to relieve '. . . Imperial funds of a charge for which it seems . . . difficult to find any adequate defence,' (Treasury to C.O., 19 Jan. 1893, *ibid.*, 251–2.)
[5] For a resumé of these negotiations *vide ibid.* See also *Hansard*, 4th ser., XXX, cols. 153 *et seq.*

point the second Swaziland Convention of November 1893 broke down. Instead of consenting, the Swazi queen regent sent a deputation to claim British protection, much to Ripon's embarrassment. The dangerous question remained unsettled.

Three possible solutions of the Swazi crisis were put to the Cabinet in May 1894. Ripon's arguments showed the same sense of imperial weakness, the same fears of republican expansion and Afrikaner solidarity as had run through the memorandum of the previous year. 'To do nothing' was the first possibility; but this was too risky. The Transvaalers might stir up trouble as a pretext for annexing Swaziland. If the Swazi resisted, Ripon argued, 'we might find ourselves in the position of having to sit back while the South African Republic carried on a Swazi war.' To go to war with the Boer over Swaziland seemed out of the question.[1] All south Africa would side with the Transvaal. A second possibility was that the Colonial Office should take sole responsibility for order. But Afrikaner opinion would hotly resent it. An imperial protectorate in Swaziland would damage Anglo-Boer relations badly; and at Home, Party and Parliament would object to the expense. The third solution, the Colonial Secretary argued, would be the best — to hand the territory over to the Transvaal. South African opinion demanded it. But it would be difficult to reconcile a surrender with the government's pledge that Swazi rights would be guaranteed.[2] Ripon observed wryly: 'It must be remembered that a feeling exists in this country against what is called "handing over the Swazis to the Boers" not only among philanthropists, but among chambers of commerce and bodies of that kind.' Upon the protests of the London Chamber of Commerce and the Aborigines' Protection Society against transfering Swaziland to the republic,[3] Ripon remarked: 'I do not attach much importance to their opinion . . . knowing how they are manufactured.'[4]

Swaziland's fate, like Zambesia's was settled more by south African nationalists than by British imperialists. Apparently Ripon was authorised to transfer the Swazis to the Transvaal after obtaining special securities for their land rights and legal customs; and the Colonial Secretary set out to persuade the queen regent and her council to agree.[5] In December 1894, the territory passed under republican rule.[6]

[1] Ripon to Rosebery, 4 Sept. 1894, Wolf, *op. cit.*, II, 225–6.
[2] *Hansard*, 4th ser., XII, 139.
[3] London Chamber of Commerce to C.O., 21 Dec. 1892, C. 7212, P.P. (1893–4), LXII, 237–8; Swaziland Committee to C.O., 16 Nov. 1892, *ibid.*, 213–4.
[4] Ripon, Cabinet Memo., The Swazi Crisis, 21 May 1894, C.O. African (South) 466, 3–4; Ripon to Rosebery, 4 Sept. 1894, Wolf, *op. cit.*, II, 224–8.
[5] Ripon to Loch, 19 Oct. 1894, C.O. African (South) 476, 1.
[6] Hertslet, *op. cit.*, I, 255–60.

Gladstonian though he was, Ripon made sure that this concession should not give the Transvaalers independent access to Kosi Bay. Therefore he annexed Trans-Pongoland in April 1895, and in May re-annexed Amatongaland.[1] *The Economist* correctly explained the Colonial Secretary's reasoning: 'We should be the last to prevent the access of the Boers to the sea on grounds of trade. We merely wish to prevent the Boers from acquiring a political right to a sea-frontier . . . which . . . may be embarrassing to us in our dealings with Foreign Powers.'[2] This principle had prompted Stanley to annex Natal in 1844. In 1895 the Colonial Office was still following the same rule.

In Zambesia the British government promoted colonial enterprise so as to turn south Africa toward the empire; in Swaziland it held up republican enterprise in an effort to lever the Transvaal into a commercial union. But the force and expansion of republican separatism in Swaziland had proved too strong. Neither in Zambesia nor in Swaziland did the new imperialists in Britain decide the issue.[3] Both questions were determined by the struggle for supremacy in south African politics.

The Fall of Cape Supremacy 1894–1895

In addition to the colonisation of southern Zambesia and the cession of Swaziland, Rhodes saw a third chance of off-setting the rise of the Transvaal: to get control of Delagoa Bay. There, the colony might regain the stranglehold on the republic's commerce. If Rhodes could buy the Portuguese terminus of the republic's railway, he would be able to counter the control of the Transvaal section of the Cape–Johannesburg line which would fall to Kruger when the Sivewright agreement expired at the end of 1894. Its effort to construct a separatist system thwarted, the republic would be readier to enter a commercial union on Cape terms. Lourenço Marques was for Rhodes the key to the south African deadlock.

No sooner had the Sivewright agreement been signed than Rhodes tried again to buy the province and its railway from the bankrupt Portuguese government.[4] Success seemed the more likely since Salisbury by the Anglo-Portuguese Convention of 1891 had renewed the British right of pre-emption over all Portuguese possessions south of the

[1] Wolf, *op. cit.*, II, 229–34. [2] *The Economist*, 11 May 1895, 611.
[3] For the Transvaal-Swaziland Debate of 6 Feb. 1895 *vide Hansard*, 4th ser., XXX, cols. 133–64.
[4] Raphael, *op. cit.*, 158–60.

Zambesi. Yet the bid failed.[1] So did all Rhodes' subsequent offers. 'I have for several years done my best to obtain for the Colony, by purchase, or otherwise, the Portuguese Province of Lourenço Marquez . . .', he complained; 'The whole circumstance was known to Her Majesty's Government. They are aware that the Cape is prepared to purchase the Province.' But 'as a Government, they could do nothing to help him'.[2] The difficulty was diplomatic rather than financial. Concentrating on Egypt and the Nile Valley, Rosebery, like Salisbury before him, did not have enough diplomatic resources left to extract the 'key to South Africa' from Lisbon.

Fear of German reaction held up and in the end stopped Rhodes' designs on Delagoa Bay. When the Portuguese government in agreement with Kruger had confiscated the Lourenço Marques railway in 1889, Salisbury's protest had been almost conciliatory.[3] He did nothing to forward Rhodes' bid. The ultimatum to Portugal in January 1890, which might have been used to seize Lourenço Marques, was used instead to secure the Shiré and Mashonaland. Berlin had agreed to the one[4] but might have objected strongly to the other. Desiring German aid in Egypt and the Mediterranean, needing German agreement to a British sphere in Uganda and the Upper Nile Valley, Salisbury would risk no attempt upon Delagoa Bay.

Rosebery was similarly inhibited between 1893 and 1894, not only by difficulties over colonial questions with Germany, but also by his Cabinet colleagues. They objected to being embroiled with Berlin over more colonial trifles. His ill-judged attempt in the Anglo-Congolese treaty of May 1894 to settle two questions at once, put an end to Rhodes' chances of buying Delagoa Bay. Germany and France together overthrew the agreement. They seemed about to make common cause against Britain on all colonial questions, and above all, on the question of Egypt. The Gladstonians in the Cabinet, Harcourt, Morley and Asquith, censured Rosebery for provoking the Powers in order to satisfy the unreasonable territorial ambitions of the self-governing colonies. Over Samoa for example, Harcourt protested:

> 'These colonial gentlemen expect us to quarrel on their behalf with the great military Powers of Europe, and to add millions to our expenditure,

[1] Merriman blamed the lack of support from the British government. Van der Poel, *Railway and Customs Policies in South Africa*, 61.

[2] Rhodes Minute of March 1894, quoted in L. Michell, *Life of C. J. Rhodes*, II, 94.

[3] Salisbury to Petre, 10 Sept. 1889, Petre to Salisbury, 15 Aug. 1889, in C. 5903, P.P. [1890] LI, 349, 357.

[4] Marschall to Hatzfeldt, 31 Aug. 1890, *Grosse Politik*, VIII, no. 1686.

to which they refuse to contribute a single farthing and leave the whole burden to fall on the English taxpayer.'[1]

Several ministers insisted upon the Foreign Office walking 'very warily' in Africa. 'We have never been so destitute of friends or so "*mal vus*" by the Powers,' fumed Harcourt. 'We have to count on the negative if not positive hostility of Germany on African questions as well as of France. The less we attempt any move which requires their friendly co-operation the better — for we assuredly shall not get it.'[2] Rosebery would have had difficulty in carrying his colleagues into another *imbroglio* with Germany to get Delagoa Bay for the Cape Colony.

By 1894 Rosebery's ministry knew that Delagoa Bay would be very costly indeed. For the first time the German government specified its opposition to any change in the *status quo* of the Transvaal and Delagoa Bay, on pain of retaliation in Egypt. In June the Germans protested against British attempts to persuade Kruger to extend the franchise to the *Uitlanders*.[3] Six months later Marschall objected, '. . . to encroachments by Mr. Cecil Rhodes on the sovereignty of Portugal [at Lourenço Marques] and the commercial independence of the port or of the railway.'[4] The ambassador, Hatzfeldt, warned the Foreign Secretary that 'Germany would not "permit" us [Britain] to annex the Portuguese East African colonies.' Kimberley replied: 'England [was] a great Sea Power and could in such a matter "speak the strongest" word,' But Hatzfeldt pointed out that Germany 'could make her power felt elsewhere',[5] particularly in Egypt.[6]

In June 1894 Rosebery told Rhodes that he must give up all hope of acquiring Lourenço Marques or its railway.[7] The Germans had vetoed the project. Lesser and more wayward causes had helped frustrate Rhodes at Lourenço Marques — New Zealand's aspirations in Samoa, the Gladstonians' exasperation with the great colonies' demands upon the mother country, their insistence upon peace and economy, and Harcourt's rivalry with Rosebery. Yet from Rhodes' point of view, the British government had sacrificed supremacy in south Africa for security in Egypt. With the completion of the Delagoa Bay Railway, the Transvaal freed itself at last from dependence on colonial ports. Commercial hegemony seemed to be passing from Cape Town to

[1] Harcourt to Kimberley, 8 Dec. 1894, Gardiner, *op. cit.*, II, 326.
[2] Harcourt to Kimberley, 16 Nov. 1894, *ibid.*, II, 324.
[3] *Grosse Politik*, IX, 2103.
[4] F.O. Memo. by J. A. C. Tilley, 5 Jan. 1905, *B.D.*, I, 325.
[5] Kimberley to Harcourt, 7 Dec. 1894, Gardiner, *op. cit.*, II, 325.
[6] *B.D.*, I, 325. [7] Walker, *op. cit.*, 447.

Pretoria. Natal in February 1894 joined the Transvaal in a commercial alliance against the Cape–Orange Free State customs union. In return Kruger admitted the Natal railway to the Rand, promising a third share of the gross traffic to Durban and another third to Delagoa Bay. When the Sivewright Agreement expired in December 1894, he regained control of freight rates on the Transvaal section of the Cape line and began to divert the flow of the Rand's wealth away from the Cape into his own system. From carrying 80 per cent of the Rand traffic, the Cape Railway became suitor to the republic for one-third. Politically as well as commercially, the Transvaal was replacing the colony as the dominant state in the sub-continent.

By the beginning of 1895, republican expansion had evaded all the holds which Rhodes, followed lamely by the Colonial Office, had tried to keep upon it. The circle had been broken at Delagoa Bay. Inadvertently Rothschild had helped to break it in the interests of the Rand mining industry. The cession of Swaziland had gained neither commercial union nor a vote for the *Uitlanders*. Although English and Dutch at the Cape had been drawn closer together by Rhodes and Hofmeyr, the separatism of the Transvaal remained unshaken. Worse still, the expected counterpoise in the north had turned out to be a feather. Six years earlier it had been commonly supposed that the gold fields of southern Zambesia would be as rich if not richer than those of the Transvaal.[1] Rhodes had gambled the strategy of his mineral kingdom on this assumption, as had the British government its policy in the South Africa Company charter. There remained little doubt by 1894 that Rhodes' mining advisers had guessed wrongly. The beginnings of deep level work at Johannesburg, which touched off the gold boom of 1894 to 1895, showed the whereabouts of the true Rand. But reports held little promise of any such strikes in the chartered company's fields. Many of Rhodes' heroic dispositions of capital and territory on behalf of British influence were being overturned by the incidence of gold. Without a gold rush, Matabeleland and Mashonaland could not be turned into a powerful colony quickly. Indeed, the settlers who might have filled it were joining the immigrants in Johannesburg. Henceforward hopes of strengthening British influence turned away from the company's colonists to Kruger's *Uitlanders*. With Kruger in possession of the Rand, it seemed likely that the Pretoria-Delagoa Bay connection must soon entirely eclipse the Cape-Bechuanaland-Zambesia railway

[1] E. d'Erlanger, 'History and Finance of the Rhodesian Railways,' Weinthal, *op. cit.*, I, 641; C. Tainton, 'Early Days on the Rand,' *ibid.*, 709; W. Ingram-Lyon, 'Rhodesia: the Industrial Link,' *ibid.*, 714–7.

and commercial system. The balance of wealth and power in south Africa was swinging heavily against the Cape Colony. For all Rhodes' hammering, the massive movement of neutral capital and business had become unmalleable to the design of an imperial dominion.

As if the moment had come to decide the shape of south Africa's future once and for all, a sense of ultimate crisis gripped colonial and imperial leaders from the end of 1894. Rhodes and Jameson talked openly of capturing the republican citadel to free the *Uitlanders*. There were rumours of risings and fears of civil war on the Rand. The High Commissioner, Loch, looked to a re-occupation of the Transvaal as the quickest way to re-assert supremacy. If an *Uitlander* rebellion took place, he proposed to take the opportunity of occupying the republic.[1] But at first, Rosebery's government took a more detached and a less desperate view. To Ripon's mind, removing the obstructive republic by force seemed unnecessary and self-defeating. In winning the Transvaal by such methods, all south Africa might well be lost to the empire. The Colonial Office felt that 'every nerve should be strained to prevent such a disgrace as another African war.'[2] 'Under the influence of . . . gold and the consequent immigration'[3] the republic would be bound sooner or later to give the *Uitlanders* the vote and they would make it join a federation with the colonies. The danger to British supremacy from an Anglo-Boer explosion seemed far greater than the threat from Pretoria. In September 1894 Ripon rejected Loch's proposals. The *Uitlander* agitation was to be left to run a constitutional course.

But although their standpoint was not that of Rhodes and Loch, British ministers believed imperial supremacy in south Africa was now at stake. Their fear of German interference heightened their anxiety to avert an internal catastrophe. The Colonial Secretary wrote nervously: 'The German inclination to take the Transvaal under their protection is a very serious thing. To have them meddling at Pretoria and Johannesburg would be fatal to our position and our influence in South Africa. . . .'[4] Kimberley also feared German designs upon Delagoa Bay. He warned the Austrian ambassador for Berlin's information that supremacy south of the Zambesi was so essential to England that to keep it, she would be unable 'to recoil from the spectre of war'.

'If England were ever to permit Delagoa Bay to pass to other hands,

[1] J. Van der Poel, *The Jameson Raid*, (1951), 16–20.

[2] E. M. Drus, 'The Question of Imperial Complicity in the Jameson Raid,' *English Historical Review*, Oct. 1953, 592–3.

[3] Ripon to Rosebery, 4 Sept. 1894, Wolf, *op. cit.*, II, 222: Salisbury, *Hansard*, 4th ser. XXX, 701, 14 Feb. 1895; *The Economist*, 21 Jun. 1890, 782.

[4] Ripon to Kimberley, 25 Nov. 1894, Wolf, *op. cit.*, II, 232–3.

Cape Colony, whose interests would thereby be most seriously damaged, would immediately secede from the Mother Country and separate from England.

The maintenance of the Cape Colony was perhaps the most vital interest of Great Britain because by the possession of it communication with India was assured, which otherwise might be cut off any day. Cape Colony was of even greater importance to England than Malta or Gibraltar, and it was this that the German cabinet would not understand — that the English government are compelled to support the interests of Cape Colony because they do not want to lose it.'[1]

After granting self-government to their white colonists in an effort to lighten Britain's load, it was ironic that the imperial authorities should now have to dance to their subjects' tune, to keep them in the empire. British security in the world seemed to be at stake in the Colony's struggle for the leadership of south Africa. Hence Kimberley told Berlin to 'keep their hands off' and to stop 'coquetting with the Republic'.[2] 'For England, the Transvaal was a "*point noir*" of no less importance than Egypt.'[3] In reply the Germans repeated their resistance to any change in the republic's status. They would regard any attempt to force it into a commercial union as the first step toward its political extinction.[4]

Not since 1885 had a European rival seriously threatened the British position in south Africa. But now the possibility of German aid to the Transvaal aggravated the internal tension. Disturbances in Johannesburg or in Swaziland might bring the Germans to Kruger's side, and even the weak and conciliatory Rosebery ministry fore-armed itself against this possibility. It is likely enough that Ripon authorised the High Commissioner early in 1895 to intervene at Johannesburg with imperial troops, if there was any danger of German meddling.[5] By March even the anti-imperialist Harcourt admitted that 'the relations of the Cape Colony and the English Government towards the Transvaal and Kruger are of a most critical character.'[6] The crisis of imperial supremacy which British statesmen had foreseen and feared since the first Transvaal war seemed to be coming to a head.

[1] Deym to Kálnoky, 1 Nov. 1894, (rpt. of conversation with Kimberley), quoted in L. M. Penson, 'The New Course in British Foreign Policy, 1892–1902,' *T.R.H.S.*, 1943, p. 128.

[2] Kimberley to Ripon, 25 Nov. 1894, Wolf, *op. cit.*, 233; Marschall, *Memo.* 1 Feb. 1895, *Grosse Politik*, VIII, no. 2017.

[3] *ibid.*, no. 2018. [4] *ibid.*, no. 2029.

[5] *vide* van der Poel, *Jameson Raid*, 22–3; cf. E. Drus, *E.H.R.*, Oct. 1953, 592–3.

[6] Harcourt to Ripon, 5 Mar. 1895, Gardiner, *op. cit.*, II, 338.

THE RHODES–JAMESON PLAN, 1894–1896

By 1895 Rhodes was convinced that the Transvaal republic was becoming the dominant state in south Africa. At the railway conference in April, Kruger had offered the Cape line one quarter of the Rand traffic, whereas Rhodes had tried to insist upon forty per cent. What he had foreseen and worked to stave off for ten years had come about. The republic, in control of the pivot of the economy, could now dictate terms to the rest of the sub-continent. It seemed to Rhodes that the state which held economic power and appealed to Afrikaner sentiment would soon draw its neighbours into a republican federation. As he explained later, 'I [became] so anxious . . . that we should get a change [in the Transvaal] and obtain the union of Africa' under colonial auspices before it was too late.[1] Kruger's *régime* in Pretoria had to be toppled over at once.

By June, Rhodes saw 'a certain . . . conjunction of matters that would bring about this change'.[2] His opportunism indeed had a certain virtuosity. The climax of the commercial duel between the Cape and the Transvaal seemed to offer a rare tactical opening for a *coup* at Johannesburg. Hitherto Rhodes' indispensable supporters, the Cape Bondsmen, might have sided with Kruger in case of an *Uitlander* uprising against him. The Bond probably would have avenged Kruger's downfall by turning Rhodes out of office in Cape Town. For this reason the Cape premier had publicly regretted the *Uitlanders*' demonstrations of June 1894.[3] But a year later his chance seemed to have come. The Cape Dutch by that time seemed inflamed sufficiently by the republic's attacks on their agrarian and commercial interests for the Bond to acquiesce in Kruger's overthrow.[4]

Opportunity beckoned Rhodes at the same time from Johannesburg, with a warning that if he did not take it, others would. The *Uitlanders* appeared to have reached the point of revolt. But from Rhodes' point of view it promised to be a revolution of the wrong kind. The immi-

[1] Second Report of Select Committee on South Africa, P.P. (1897), IX, Q. 686–7, 115; *vide* van der Poel, *Jameson Raid.*

[2] Second Report of Select Committee on South Africa, P.P. (1897) IX, Q. 687, 115.

[3] van der Poel, *Jameson Raid*, 14 *et seq.*

[4] Rhodes explained: 'Then there had been trouble continually with Cape Colony, we desiring to have free trade for the interchange of products, and the Transvaal shutting out our products, and doing their best to interfere with our railway systems, which had cost us a huge sum of money. So that there was isolation from Cape Colony, and there was the feeling of the people there, and I felt . . . that the time had come to bring about that change which must come. . . . It must come, as certain as we are sitting here,' (Second Report of Select Committee on South Africa, P.P. (1897) IX, Q. 687, 115.)

grants by this time were thought to outnumber the Boer burghers heavily. Their Transvaal National Union had hoped to beat Kruger at the elections of 1894 with the aid of Joubert and Esselen, the leaders of the liberal faction of the enfranchised burghers.[1] They had failed; but they were now agitating hard for the franchise. Moreover, they had gained august patrons, in the heads of Wernher-Beit and of Consolidated Goldfields, two of the largest mining interests. According to Rhodes, they were prompted by the economics of deep-level mining.[2] They wanted to get rid of Kruger 'because the indirect taxation levied upon the gold mines by [his] regime rendered the poorer reefs "non-payable".'[3] 'Payability' depended upon cutting mining costs; and Kruger's dynamite monopoly, his high import duties and railway rates, his failure to organise the supply of African labour, stood in the way.[4]

But the movement in Johannesburg in 1894 was by no means as favourable to Rhodes' political interests as it might have appeared. The leaders of the gold mining industry were divided. If the 'Anglo-Saxons' were backing reform, the 'Cosmopolitans' were supporting Kruger.[5] There was no good reason why the Johannesburg capitalists as a class should have entered politics at this time. During the fantastic 'Kaffir' boom of 1894 and 1895, all alike were making enormous profits from company flotation rather than the actual mining of gold.[6] Upon one thing the Johannesburg capitalists agreed — Kruger's *régime* might be a heavy encumbrance upon their industry's future, but a British colonial government would be heavier still. Neither the *Uitlanders* nor the mine-owners wished to take the Transvaal into the empire. 'They dislike[d] the native policy of England — they dislike[d] the meddling of the House of commons and of the philanthropic societies. . . .'[7] Taxation of the industry would be no lighter,[8] the recruitment of labour no easier, under colonial government. The mine-owners were loath to turn their industry from the milch cow of the Transvaal into one for an entire south African confederation. They were aiming at an anglicised and

[1] J. P. Fitzpatrick, *The Transvaal from Within*, (1899), 118.

[2] *vide* F. H. Hatch and J. Chalmers, *The Gold Mines of the Rand*, (1895), VIII, 272.

[3] Second Report of Select Committee on South Africa, P.P. (1897) IX, 45.

[4] Hatch and Chalmers, *op. cit.*, 246–7, 249, 252, 271.

[5] Of the ten large mining houses, the cosmopolitans so-called were J. B. Robinson, Barnato, Neumann, Albu, Goerz, and Lewis and Marks. The 'Anglo-Saxons' were Wernher-Beit, Consolidated Goldfields, Farrar's Anglo-French group and Abe Bailey's syndicate.

[6] *The Economist*, 2 Nov. and 3 Aug. 1895, 1429–30, 1011.

[7] Robinson to Chamberlain, 4 Nov. 1895, Garvin, *op. cit.*, III, 60.

[8] J. Curle, *Gold Mines of the World*, (1899), 28.

independent republic. Having failed to achieve it by constitutional means at the elections of October 1894, some of them had decided, according to Rhodes, upon revolution. But a new republic devoted mainly to the business interests of international capital would hardly join a south African union on the Cape Colony's terms.[1] Rhodes therefore decided that he must capture and divert the Johannesburg movement. When the uprising came, the full weight of imperial influence would be needed to swing the issue toward union with the Cape and the empire.

When the reform leaders brought Rhodes into their scheme in April 1895, it was with deep misgivings about his political enthusiasms, his militancy and his chartered company.[2] On the other hand, they needed his help to arm their revolt, and to make sure that the British government would hold the ring against German intervention. By June, Rhodes and Beit with the reformers were organising what promised to be an easy and 'bloodless revolution' for the end of December. As soon as the *Uitlanders* rose in Johannesburg, Dr. Jameson was to cross the border with a force of British South Africa Company police to consolidate success.

Rhodes had laid his Johannesburg mine before Chamberlain took office in June 1895. But the new Colonial Secretary helped to explode it.[3] He probably heard in August that 'the long-expected . . . rising of the Uitlanders . . . would shortly take place, and that being so it was desirable that an armed force should be stationed on the Transvaal border available for use'.[4] Two months later he handed over to the chartered company the territory which was to provide Jameson with his base in Bechuanaland.

Meanwhile the Colonial Secretary took the High Commissioner's advice on certain questions. 'Is a change likely to come soon [in the Transvaal]?' 'The chances . . . are that a change will be brought about by violence.' 'What would be the effect of a change?' 'Nine out of every ten Englishmen in the Transvaal would prefer an Anglicised and liberalised Republic to a British Colony in any shape'; but the best

[1] Second Report of Select Committee on South Africa, P.P. [1897/ IX, Q. 686–7, 115.

[2] P.P., [1897], IX, Qs. 811–15, 122; *vide* V. Harlow, 'Sir Frederick Hamilton's Narrative of Events relative to the Jameson Raid,' *English Historical Review*, Apr. 1957, p. 290; Beit to Phillips, 15 Jul. 1894, P.P., [1897], IX, Q. 754, 119.

[3] E. Drus, 'The Question of Complicity in the Jameson Raid,' *English Historical Review*, LXVIII, 582–93; *eadem*, 'A Report on the Papers of Joseph Chamberlain relating to the Jameson Raid and the Inquiry,' *Bulletin of the Institute of Historical Research*, XXV, 33–62; J. van der Poel, *The Jameson Raid*, (1951), *passim*.

[4] Grey to Chamberlain, 10 Dec. 1896, E. Drus, *Bulletin of Institute of Historical Research*, XXV, 56.

hope of federation would be to hoist the British flag. 'What action should be taken in case of the outbreak of Civil War' on the Rand? Robinson proposed to go up to Pretoria and call an assembly elected by all adult males in the Transvaal, to settle the future form of government. 'Whether such a Convention would decide upon independence, or a self-governing British colony, is a matter of conjecture . . . but our weight should be thrown into the scale of the latter.' A large British force meanwhile should be held ready to go to south Africa if necessary, to forestall German intervention. Lastly, Chamberlain asked the Commissioner: 'What would be the attitude of the Cape?'[1] The reply underlined Rhodes' opportunism:

> 'The Cape Dutch sympathised with their Transvaal kinsmen in the war of 1881, but the ungrateful and hostile attitude of President Kruger since, and the conciliatory policy of H.M. Government, have greatly changed that feeling.
>
> Nevertheless, if a race war broke out, the ill-deeds of Kruger might be forgotten in a burst of national sentiment. On the other hand, if the High Commissioner's intervention were directed to the prevention of race war, he would probably receive the support of both races; and it must be remembered that the material interests of the Cape farmers would be on the side of some closer union with the Transvaal in the matters of customs and railways than can be looked for under the present regime.'[2]

The High Commissioner's diagnosis was that of Rhodes. Kruger had struck hard at Cape commercial interests and the ensuing Drifts crisis of October and early November offered the best chance since 1877 of absorbing the republic without losing the Cape Colony and antagonising the Orange Free State. On 6 December Chamberlain telegraphed to the High Commissioner: 'Agree generally with your idea. . . . I take for granted that no movement will take place unless success is certain, a fiasco would be most disastrous.'[3] He advised later that the rising should either come at once or be put off for a year or two, in view of the crisis over Venezuela with the United States.[4] On 26 December he told Salisbury that the outbreak in Johannesburg was imminent. Two regiments were on their way to the Cape, in addition to the usual garrison. Rhodes had the Bechuanaland police. 'If the rising is successful,' Chamberlain believed, 'it ought to turn to our advantage.'[5] The Prime Minister acquiesced in the Colonial Secretary's

[1] Robinson to Chamberlain, 4 Nov. 1895, Garvin, *op. cit.*, III, 59–62.
[2] *idem*, 61–2.
[3] Chamberlain to Robinson, 6 Dec. 1895, *ibid.*, 63.
[4] Chamberlain to Meade, 18 Dec. 1895, *ibid.*, 72.
[5] Chamberlain to Salisbury, 26 Dec. 1895, S.P. (Chamberlain).

course, but he had qualms about Rhodes, about the Germans and about provoking a Boer War:

> 'I am very much obliged to you for your letters about the Transvaal. It is evident that sooner or later that State must be mainly governed by Englishmen: though we cannot yet precisely discern what their relations to the British Crown or the Cape Colony will be, I am not sorry that at this stage the movement is only partially successful. If we get to actual fighting, it will be very difficult to keep the Cape forces — or our own — out of the fray. In such a case we should have an angry controversy with Germany. Of course Germany has no rights in the affair, and must be resisted if the necessity arises: but still it would be better if the revolution which transfers the Transvaal to British rulers were entirely the result of the action of internal forces, and not of Cecil Rhodes' intervention, or of ours.'[1]

Salisbury and his ministers left little evidence of their own analysis of the south African situation during their first months in office or of why they acquiesced in Robinson's plan. No record of fundamental discussion between members of the Cabinet, such as sometimes goes before a critical decision, has yet come to light. Chamberlain, it seems, had something like a free hand. Throughout the life of this ministry indeed, his Conservative colleagues disliked to interfere with him in the colonial field. Their restraint did not imply that his plans were always right, but that his position was always strong. Balfour, who was closest to Salisbury, feared that to lose Chamberlain would do great damage to the Conservative cause, for he could best give it the colour of progressive social reform which seemed to attract the electorate. This was also the view of Selborne, the Prime Minister's son-in-law and Chamberlain's Under-Secretary at the Colonial Office.

But the respect of Balfour and Selborne for Chamberlain was personal as well as tactical. In a half-patronising way, they felt obliged to him for his part in defending the Union, and they knew him for an ambitious, hyper-sensitive man. They knew also how much it had hurt him to desert the Liberals and give up his chance of becoming premier. Chamberlain craved the Conservative leaders' sympathy and trust. They tried to sooth him. It was understood that three times out of four, they would have to say 'no' to his schemes of domestic reform. That in part was why Chamberlain had to turn his ambition from the Home to the colonial scene, if he was to co-operate with the Conservatives. They in their turn felt bound to compensate him for his sacrifice and to retain his loyalty. The Tories feared to cross him

[1] Salisbury to Chamberlain, 30 Dec. 1895, Drus, Report on Chamberlain Papers, *op. cit.*, 36–7.

too often in his new work lest he feel 'stabbed in the back' by his new friends and retire from public life. His colleagues therefore bent over backwards to say 'yes' three times out of four to his colonial proposals.[1]

By force of circumstance as well as personality, Chamberlain was the most powerful Colonial Secretary of the century. Policy is fragile to the touch of temperament. His vehement temper and imperial conviction in place of Ripon's experienced inertia worked in favour of Rhodes' plan. The self-made 'Man from Birmingham' was a more complete imperialist than either his colleagues or his predecessors. They regarded empire as a natural, inevitable growth; he tended to believe that it should be urgently manufactured. Where they usually preferred to wait and see, he strained after constructive triumph. It was partly because the Radical conceived of power as the means to progressive change; the Whigs and Tories, as the means to letting well alone. Commercially as well as politically, Chamberlain attached more importance to the national interests in the empire than to those outside it. For him, more than for any other statesman of the century, the future of the British Isles lay in uniting and developing the empire. In the traditionalists' judgement, considerations of peace and relation with Europe habitually outweighed mere 'colonial', as distinct from 'imperial' interests. Chamberlain, on the other hand put imperial expansion before everything else. If this full-blooded approach to empire was rare among responsible leaders, Chamberlain's confidence that the mass electorate, if properly informed, would support it, was rarer still. The rest of Salisbury's ministry had no such confidence. With Chamberlain all-out imperialism won a powerful place in a strong government for the first time.

His imperial conviction brought a new element into policy. Yet it seems likely that his decision to accept Robinson's plan for exploiting an *Uitlander* rising was swayed more by the crisis in south Africa than by new ambition in London. The contrast with Ripon's rejection of Loch's proposals for action in 1894 can be carried too far. At that time there was good hope of a constitutional settlement between Kruger and the *Uitlanders*; and the Cape Colony and the republic had not reached the verge of war over the railway and tariff question. Ripon had room and time for non-intervention, as long as these two interacting crises did not become fused. Moreover, Rhodes' ministry and Cape Dutch opinion frowned upon Loch's proposals. But by 1895

[1] These insights into Chamberlain's relations with the Conservatives come largely from two personal letters: Balfour to Salisbury, 31 Jul. 1892, S.P. (Balfour), and Selborne to Salisbury, 7 Apr. 1895, S.P. (Selborne).

the two crises seemed to have reached the point of mutual detonation. An *Uitlander* revolution seemed inevitable; the Drifts crisis showed the danger of war between the colony and republic; and Rhodes and Cape opinion had changed. Chamberlain agreed to Robinson's plan in 1895, not so much because he was more of an imperialist than Ripon but because a conflict seemed inevitable. Furthermore, he felt bound to take those precautions against disturbance and German interference which Ripon could afford to put off. This was how the Colonial Secretary explained his decision privately to Salisbury in June 1896.[1] The Prime Minister himself accepted the explanation as a fair statement of Chamberlain's policy.[2] In their own eyes at least, they were not beginning a new drive for empire. Nor were they accomplices in an underhanded plot to overthrow an independent state. They calculated like men forced to prepare against an internal conflict in south Africa which they had not provoked, could not avert, and hoped against hope to turn to advantage.

Substantially all this was true. By 1895 south Africa had passed beyond the British government's direct control. For six years the empire had ridden gratefully upon Rhodes' coat-tails. Power and initiative lay with Rhodes on the one hand and with Kruger on the other, not with the Colonial Office. Once the two south African rivals and their systems became irreconcilable, Chamberlain, like Ripon, had little choice but to follow and support Rhodes, with whose financial and political empire British influence had become largely identified. Imperial supremacy had no other leg to stand on. Chamberlain on this occasion was partly the victim of an inherited situation.

Yet the deepest reasons why Chamberlain and Salisbury adopted Robinson's plan were probably unwritten. They were too well known and agreed to need explanation between colleagues. Traditional ideas of supremacy in south Africa probably had the largest share in this decision. Inherited notions of policy in mature bureaucracies sometimes carry ministers along with a logic and momentum of their own. Salisbury and Chamberlain were prisoners of their own conceptions of what had been, what was, and what should be in south Africa. They tended to see the *Uitlander* crisis not as it was in Johannesburg, but as British ministers had long expected it would be.

Like most statesmen since the Eighteen sixties, Salisbury and Chamberlain looked upon Transvaal independence as a temporary expedient. They assumed that sooner or later the republic would be

[1] Chamberlain, Memo., 12 Jun. 1896, Garvin, *op. cit.*, III, 48.
[2] Salisbury to Chamberlain, 12 Jun. 1896, Drus, Report on Chamberlain Papers, *op. cit.*, 51.

absorbed into a British confederation. They saw, as Colonial Secretaries had seen since 1887, that their external hold upon the Transvaal was loosening and they regretted the Conventions of 1881 and 1884 as blunders. But for a decade they had expected all to come right. Immigration in the end would make the Transvaal British, without the risk of another Boer war. Salisbury and Chamberlain thought that the inevitable moment had come. The immigrants' disabilities seemed intolerable to British pride. That the majority should take over the government from the Boer minority seemed right. As Chamberlain put it, 'it was no business of mine either to promote or hinder the political designs of any party in the Transvaal.'

But it was his duty to guard against German interference, if the uprising came to a head.[1] German pretentions disturbed Salisbury and Chamberlain,[2] as they had Kimberley and Ripon. For the two Unionists in 1895, as for Carnarvon twenty years earlier, Delagoa Bay was the key to south Africa. Thence Germany might step into south African affairs as the Transvaal's ally. It was there that the republic had escaped from Cape colonial control. As early as September, Chamberlain pointed out to the Prime Minister the possibility of a German threat:

> 'Portugal cannot pay [the Berne Award] and must seek assistance. It is possible that Germany may offer this assistance if we do not — and may be offended if we do. The possession of the [Delagoa] line by a foreign power would be disastrous and ought to be prevented if possible. Selborne has a suggestion for buying up the Mozambique territory from Portugal and dividing with Germany which he will explain later.'[3]

In the last resort the Royal Navy could thwart German interference. But an *Uitlander* rising in Johannesburg would certainly evoke German reactions for Berlin had entered a *caveat* against any change in the *status quo*. Yet Anglo-German rivalry does not seem to have been the root cause of the south African crisis of 1895. Rather, that rivalry was called forth by the internal conflict within the Transvaal.

If an *Uitlander* uprising broke out and Chamberlain had to safeguard against German meddling, he meant to try for the British flag and avoid a 'capitalist republic'. He claimed:

> '. . . whatever defects may exist in the present form of Government of the

[1] Chamberlain, Memo., 12 Jun. 1896, *ibid.*, 51.

[2] The two Unionists were perturbed to find that the London Convention of 1884 contained nothing to prevent Kruger from negotiating with foreign powers and left them only a power to veto his formal treaties. Chamberlain apologised for this to Salisbury: 'Alas! it all happened when Gladstone was consul and when I was in office,' (Chamberlain to Salisbury, 13 Nov. 1895, S.P. (Chamberlain).)

[3] Chamberlain to Salisbury, 4 Sept. 1895, S.P. (Chamberlain).

Transvaal, the substitution of an entirely independent Republic governed by or for the capitalists of the Rand would be very much worse for British interests in the Transvaal itself and for British influence in South Africa.'[1]

Neither Salisbury nor Chamberlain trusted the gold mining financiers to co-operate with imperial interests. It would appear that they prepared to intervene, not to promote the gold industry, but to prevent its declaration of independence. Once more the south African problem for British ministers was not so much one of promoting trade and investment as one of composing them to their political design.

Chamberlain's aims in all this were nothing new. Confederation and the upkeep of a supreme influence had been settled policy since the Eighteen sixties. Carnarvon, Kimberley, Knutsford and Ripon, each in his different way, had worked to absorb the Transvaal into an imperial dominion. For eight years the *Uitlanders* had been expected to do the trick; and for six years Colonial Secretaries had feared that with the rise of the Transvaal and the completion of the Delagoa railway, the imperial supremacy of influence would decline. Chamberlain, faced with a more acute south African crisis than any of his predecessors, sought to carry out the logic of tradition. That he followed Robinson's advice less warily than Ripon had Loch's, was perhaps due to his inexperience and to his anxiety to get things done. When Chamberlain at last discovered that the revolt, far from being irresistible, was a fiasco, it was too late for him to turn back.

On 29 December the Colonial Secretary told the Prime Minister: 'I think that the Transvaal business is going to fizzle out. Rhodes has miscalculated the feeling of the Johannesburg capitalists.'[2] Lack of zeal and dislike of the Union Jack had made them back out of the rising. Perhaps most of them had never intended to go beyond a threat of rebellion that would scare Kruger into making concessions. In any case, the gold houses of London did not want a rising.[3] On that same day Jameson invaded the Transvaal with his small force, hoping to put heart into the Johannesburg revolution. All he did was to reveal Rhodes' plan to the world. Chamberlain wrote to Salisbury:

'I am sorry to say that the Transvaal risings have entered on a more acute stage. Having failed to get up a revolution in Johannesburg Rhodes . . . has apparently sent in Dr. Jameson. . . . This is a flagrant piece of filibustering for which there is no justification that I can see in the present state of things in the Transvaal. If it were supported by us it would justify

[1] Drus, Report on Chamberlain Papers, *op. cit.*, 49.
[2] Chamberlain to Salisbury, 29 Dec. 1895, S.P. (Chamberlain).
[3] van der Poel, *Jameson Raid*, 83.

the accusation by Germany and other powers that having first attempted to get up a rebellion in a friendly state and having failed, we had then assented to an act of aggression and, without any grievance of our own, had poured in British troops. It is worth noting that I have no confidence that the force now sent, with its allies in Johannesburg, is strong enough to beat the Boers — and if not we should expect that a conflict would be the beginning of a Boer war in S. Africa.'[1]

Chamberlain immediately disavowed Jameson's action, and Robinson ordered him to withdraw. But the quixotic doctor went on to defeat and surrender at Krugersdorp. On the High Commissioner's advice, *Uitlander* rebels, who for a time controlled Johannesburg, likewise surrendered unconditionally to their republican masters. But the Colonial Secretary still hoped to force Kruger to enfranchise the immigrants and to ease their taxes. Robinson went up to Pretoria for the purpose, but disgusted Chamberlain by leaving without accomplishing anything. The High Commissioner, finding that the Raid had strengthened Kruger and damaged the imperial position throughout south Africa, decided that he was impotent to extract concessions.[2]

Effects of the Raid

Tension between the British and German press,[3] if not between their two governments, reached flash point when the German Emperor sent his congratulations to Kruger. Continental opinion was indignant against Britain for the Raid. The German Foreign Office hoped to show Salisbury the weakness of Britain's isolation, and to force him closer to the Triple Alliance.[4] And so during the first months of 1896 the Germans were thinking of getting France and Russia to join in guaranteeing the *status quo* in the Transvaal and Mozambique against Britain.[5] The Raid and the Kaiser's telegram focused popular attention sharply upon the Transvaal question for the first time since Majuba. Chamberlain called for an ' "Act of Vigour" . . . to soothe the wounded vanity of the nation'[6], and a naval squadron was sent to nullify the meagre German force in the Delagoa Bay region. Responding to the heat of British opinion, the Colonial Secretary went far towards staking his

[1] Chamberlain to Salisbury, 31 Dec. 1895, S.P. (Chamberlain); part of this letter is quoted in Garvin, *op. cit.*, III, 90.

[2] The best account of his reasons and Chamberlain's reception of them is in R. H. Wilde, *Joseph Chamberlain and the South African Republic 1895–1899*, in *Argriefjaarboek vir Suid Afrikaanse Geskiedenis*, *1956*, 22–4.

[3] *vide*, O. J. Hale, *Publicity and Diplomacy*, (Charlottesville, Virginia, 1940) cap. V.

[4] *vide*, *Grosse Politik*, XI, nos. 2577–639. [5] *idem.*

[6] Chamberlain to Salisbury, 4 Jan. 1896, Garvin, *op. cit.*, III, 95.

reputation upon getting justice for the *Uitlanders* and forcing Kruger to a settlement. Chamberlain wanted the republican government to 'frankly recognize the superior interests of the Paramount Power in the welfare of South Africa'. Something had to be done to restore British influence after the Raid[1] and he hoped that Kruger could be brought to London for personal negotiations. Chamberlain told the Prime Minister: 'I think it wise in the present "crisis" to get the old man here and we have much to gain from him while he has very little to ask from us.'[2]

Kruger however was unmoved by the Colonial Secretary's diplomacy of threat and bluff. Far from making concessions to the *Uitlanders*, the Boer President rejected the British claim to meddle in the republic's internal affairs and demanded the ending of imperial controls over its foreign relations. The Transvaal was aiming at full independence.[3] How its Executive hoped to achieve this aim British ministers now learned from a secret agent's reports of its meetings. Dr. Leyds was going to Europe to get German, and if possible French and Russian, support for the abrogation of the London Convention. He was to ask the German government to help the republic buy the Delagoa Railway from Portugal; and Portugal was to turn Lourenço Marques into an open neutralised port guaranteed by the two south African republics and the European Powers against English designs. The German and Dutch foreign ministers had already promised to press this proposal in Lisbon.[4] Kruger was bent upon checkmating the Empire at Delagoa Bay. He refused to come to London. The Transvaal was arming heavily. Burghers in the Free State were showing a militant temper and talking loudly of the part they would play in the coming struggle. The High Commissioner left no doubt that the republic had decided upon armed defiance.[5]

Chamberlain and Selborne were alarmed at this news. It seemed to them that but two hopes of saving imperial supremacy remained. The Colonial Secretary again urged Salisbury to buy the Delagoa Railway from Portugal;[6] but this was for the time being a diplomatic impossibility. There appeared to be nothing for it but to force Kruger to give the *Uitlanders* their rights under the threat of war. Selborne in sending Robinson's telegrams on to the Prime Minister wrote:

[1] Chamberlain to Robinson, 17 Mar. 1896, Wilde, *op. cit.*, 33.
[2] Chamberlain to Salisbury, 24 Jan. 1896, S.P. (Chamberlain).
[3] Robinson to Chamberlain, (telegram), 21 Mar. 1896, enclosed in Selborne to Salisbury, 26 Mar. 1896, S.P. (Selborne).
[4] Greeve to Rosmead, 26 Mar. 1896, S.P. (C.O. Private 1895–1900).
[5] Robinson to Chamberlain (telegram), 21 and 22 Mar. 1896, enclosed in Selborne to Salisbury, 26 Mar. 1896, S.P. (Selborne).
[6] Chamberlain to Salisbury, 18 Mar. 1896, S.P. (Chamberlain).

'Leyds is the inevitable villain of the South African piece. Strained, straineder, broken, relations seem to me the future foreshadowed in these telegrams. I don't break my heart over that, but there is no denying that it will be a biggish business.

The present advantage is in the knowing where we are.'[1]

This probably was Chamberlain's reaction too, for he often left Selborne to make the Colonial Office's case privately to the Prime Minister. At the end of March the two Colonial ministers inclined towards an ultimatum.[2] But Salisbury calmed them down.[3] Only a few days before, the Cabinet had ordered the advance on Dongola, with the blessing of the Triple Alliance.[4] It was no time either militarily or diplomatically to risk another Boer war. Salisbury once again gave priority to the position in the Mediterranean and on the Nile.

Chamberlain and Selborne were no more anxious than Salisbury for war with the Transvaal; but the threat of war seemed the only weapon left after the Raid. The Colonial Secretary wrote on 5 April:

'I shall never go into such a war with a light heart, and at the present time we have no reason — either of right or interest — which would justify the enterprise.

If we ever were forced into it against our will I should try to seize and defend the gold bearing districts. This is the key of S. Africa and if we could hold this we need not follow the Boers into the wilderness.

I do not believe that there will be war — but Kruger will not be wise if he dismisses that possibility altogether from his calculations. . . .

I cannot feel the least sympathy with either Kruger or his antagonists [the Johannesburg capitalists].

The former is an ignorant, dirty, cunning and obstinate man who has known how to feather his own nest and to enrich all his family and dependents.

The latter are a lot of cowardly selfish blatant speculators who would sell their souls to have the power of rigging the market.

In spite of all this our business is to bring about a fair settlement.

We shall not do it, I admit, by a policy of empty menace or arbitrary impatience — neither I think, shall we succeed if we underestimate our own reserve force and allow Kruger to have it all his own way.'[5]

[1] Selborne to Salisbury, 26 Mar. 1896, S.P. (Selborne).

[2] *vide*, Wilde, *op. cit.*, 34.

[3] On 30 Mar. Selborne wrote to Salisbury: 'I have heard you give expression lately to opinions about S. African politics with which I cannot as yet see my way to agree. I have therefore, put my views into the form of a memorandum, which I send to you herewith, and solicit your destructive criticism when next we meet,' (S.P. (Selborne). The memorandum is not with this letter in the Salisbury Papers.)

[4] Lansdowne, Cabinet Memo., 'Proposed Advance up the Nile Valley,' 24 Mar. 1896, S.P. (Private Cabinet Memoranda, 1895–1900).

[5] Chamberlain, Minute, 5 Apr. 1896, Wilde, *op. cit.*, 35.

Chamberlain was frustrated and exasperated. But he was held back from going too far toward the edge of war not only by Salisbury's view of the diplomatic position but also by south African opinion. The Cape and Natal ministries protested that this was no time for an ultimatum or troops;[1] and the High Commissioner explained why:

> '. . . In the event of hostilities on any issue growing out of the Jameson raid, the . . . Republic will be openly assisted by the Orange Free State, and . . . a large number of the Dutch, both in Cape Colony and Natal . . . [will sympathise with Kruger and secretly, if not openly assist him.] The feeling of the Dutch and Afrikander population . . . has undergone a complete change since the Jameson raid and they would now neither sympathize with nor support any forcible measures undertaken by the Imperial Government to secure the redress of the Uitlanders' grievances. . . . [Even if we won in the end we would have to govern a population] . . . torn asunder by race hatred and internal dissensions, which would for generations require the maintenance of a large standing garrison.'[2]

Chamberlain was learning that the Raid had played havoc with imperial influence and had united all south African governments against further imperial intervention. Kruger's own hold on the Transvaal burghers had been strengthened. At the Orange Free State elections, held two months after the Raid, Steyn's pro-Kruger party had come to power. Worst of all, Hofmeyr and the Cape Bondsmen had broken with Rhodes and turned him out of office. The colossus, upon whose shoulders the weight of British influence had rested for five years, had fallen. Henceforward the colonial government was in the grip of neutralist Dutch. South African suspicion that Rhodes and Jameson had acted as tools of the Colonial Office was not allayed by the inquiries into the Raid held at Pretoria and Cape Town. The Afrikaner nationalists of the interior and the Cape Dutch were coming together again, as they had in the first Transvaal war of 1881, in defence of republicanism. The Raid had made Kruger almost invulnerable. In the end Chamberlain had to accept Robinson's conclusion that 'all we can do is wait'.[3] As the Rand and the Delagoa Bay railway had turned the economics, so the nationalist reaction to the Raid set the politics of south Africa against imperial federation in favour of a republican future.

[1] *ibid.*, 37. [2] Robinson to Chamberlain, 28 Apr. 1896, *ibid.*, 38.
[3] Robinson to Chamberlain, 22 Mar. 1896, S.P. (Selborne); Wilde, *op. cit.*, 38–40.

Another Canada or Another United States?

The crisis of March and April 1896 persuaded Chamberlain and Selborne that the imperial supremacy of influence had collapsed. Unless it could be restored quickly, and the south African states soon formed into a British dominion, the superior wealth and power of the Transvaal seemed likely to draw the colonies out of the empire into a 'United States of South Africa'. The Prime Minister was sceptical of this cataclysmic view. On 30 March, 1896, he read a Colonial Office memorandum about imperial prospects in south Africa. Drafted by Selborne,[1] so important a document must have been discussed with Chamberlain before it was sent. It is perhaps the best evidence of the fundamental considerations which inspired Chamberlain and Selborne henceforward and which in the end dragged the ministry into the Boer War.

'British African Dominion, question of creating.

Are the British Possessions in South Africa more likely to become separated from the British Empire,

1. If they become confederated with the two Republics under the British flag as a British African Dominion, or
2. If they remain as now separate units under various forms of Government and continue to have as their neighbours two independent Republics?

In endeavouring to answer this question I take as my postulate the fact, as I believe it to be, that the key to the future of South Africa is in the Transvaal. It is the richest spot on earth. The only properly speaking populous spots in South Africa are already within it; and while the population of Cape Colony, of Natal, of Rhodesia etc. will increase but slowly and gradually, the population of the Transvaal has increased, and will continue to increase, by leaps and bounds, and in fifty years time will probably be reckoned in millions.

My postulate therefore is that the Transvaal is going to be by far the richest, by far the most populous part of South Africa, that it is going to be the natural capital state and centre of South African commercial, social and political life.

1. Now given that the Cape Colony, Natal, the Chartered Company's territories, and the various Imperial administrations, such as Basutoland, Zululand etc., have with the present Transvaal and Orange Free State Republics, been somehow welded into one British South African Dominion on the analogy of Canada, what will be the probable eventual result?

[1] Although the Memo. is unsigned, it is clearly Selborne's work. It mentions 'the editor of the *Daily News*, who was at school with me'. In 1896 the editor was Edward Cook (born 1857) who had been educated at Winchester. So had Selborne (born 1859).

I admit to the full that such political combinations have by nature a centrifugal tendency — yet there are other forces which so far have in some very important instances counter-acted that tendency — Canada and Australia are both examples. . . .

Now I think that in the case of the supposed British South African Dominion there are three forces which would combine to counteract the centrifugal tendency.

A. External pressure

Germany is firmly planted on the West in Damaraland and Namaqualand, and France on the East in Madagascar.

As regards Germany it is notorious how much she covets Walfisch Bay which belongs to the Cape Colony. The next day after the United States of South Africa had declared their independence Germany would walk into Walfisch Bay.

Moreover Germany is anxious to connect her possessions on the West Coast of Africa with those on the East Coast by a strip running parallel to the Zambesi and then across to Lake Nyassa. This ambition she could probably realise, if she chose, against a United States of South Africa but not against the British Empire.

. . . Therefore the external pressure on a British South African Dominion would be very great. With Germany on the West and France on the North and East — would not that Dominion feel the need of the protection of the Mother Country?

B. Internal rivalries

Dutch and English; English and Dutch. Most curiously though sprung from the same stock, the two races do not amalgamate. It shows what a lot of Celtic and Norman blood must be infused in us.

. . . The present Government of the Transvaal teaches the English what they would have to expect if the dominating influence in a United States of South Africa were Dutch. The Dutch on the other hand are strongly imbued with the idea that if the English element got the upper hand of them, and there was no moderating Imperial influence, they would receive but scanty consideration.

C. There are material advantages and sentimental advantages in being part of the British Empire. There are corresponding material and sentimental disadvantages. I believe the former to outweigh the latter, and that the evidence of this fact (as I assume it to be) is in a continuous degree impressing itself on men's minds who find themselves within the Empire.

2. But if the Cape Colony and Natal remain separate self-governing Colonies; if Rhodesia develops into a third self-governing Colony, and if the Transvaal and the Orange Free State remain independent Republics, what then? I think nothing can prevent the establishment of a United States of South Africa.

A. There being no centralised government of South Africa the external pressure will not be so clearly perceived; it will lose its cohesive effect in being diffused over a congeries of separate provincial Governments.

B. The racial rivalry will exist in a less generalised form. The preponderance of advantages over disadvantages in belonging to the British Empire will also exist, but again in a less concentrated form. But both these factors of attraction to the Empire will be outweighed and rendered nugatory by the immediate commercial interests of the British South African States. The Transvaal will be the market for South Africa: the market for the manufactures of Cape Colony and Natal: the market for the agricultural products of those Colonies and of Rhodesia. The commercial interest of the closest connexion with the Transvaal will outweigh all other considerations. These British Colonies will sue for closer commercial union. The Transvaal will reply that so long as these Colonies remain British they will not grant it; that they have no intention of becoming British, but that if these Colonies will unite with them in forming a United Republic of South Africa they will welcome them with open arms.

If the Transvaal were always going to remain a Dutch Republic, I admit that this danger would not be so imminent. Racial jealousies might temporarily postpone the effects of commercial interests. But . . . the Transvaal cannot permanently remain a Dutch Republic. There has never been a census; but the best information obtainable gives a maximum of 25,000 male Boers and a minimum of 50,000 Uitlanders, of whom ¾ are British. Before Jameson's criminal blunder the Uitlanders were said to be pouring into Transvaal at the rate of 500 males a week. Just think what would be the result of 10 or 20 years of an immigration maintained at one-fifth or even one-tenth of this rate! Therefore according to all the experience of history, this country so powerful in its future wealth and population . . . situated at the geographical centre of political South Africa would assuredly attract to itself all British Colonies in South Africa.

A great part in the working out of this problem will be played by the Delagoa Bay Railway. If we could secure the control over it we should effect two great results. We should, by holding the balance even between the South African railway systems give an immense assistance to the Cape Colony, to Natal, and to the Orange Free State to maintain their commercial and financial position against the Transvaal. We should also bring conviction at last to the Transvaal Government that their best interests lay in coming to a complete understanding with us. They would feel themselves irrevocably hemmed in. They would renounce their foreign intrigues as of no further practical utility, and they would come to terms with us. If on the other hand the control of the railway passed to the Transvaal, or to a Foreign Power working with the Transvaal against British interests, the results would be very serious. They could then secure a monopoly of all Transvaal trade for the Delagoa Bay Railway with the effect not only of supplanting British imports by (say) German imports, and not only of inflicting grievous commercial injury on the trading classes of the Cape Colony and Natal, but they could also reduce the Governments of those two Colonies and that of the Orange Free State to the verge of financial bankruptcy, so dependent are they upon their railway revenue. It needs no words to prove what a powerful use could be made of this instrument in squeezing the British South African Colonies into joining in a United South African Republic.

I maintain, therefore, that it is a matter of vital importance to us to prevent the Delagoa Bay Railway passing into the control of any power whatever except the Portuguese or British Governments, nor would I like to see it under the control of the Cape Colony or Natal Governments. No one seems to believe that Portugal will be able to afford to retain the railway long after the Berne Award is given and doubtless the Portuguese Government would be afraid to sell direct to us. We ought, however, to have a private buyer ready, who will afterwards transfer it to us. I was greatly surprised the other day to hear a doubt expressed whether the House of Commons would be willing to find the money, say 2½ millions, for the purchase. I feel simply positive myself that the majority of the House of Commons would hail the vote with acclamation. . . .

My opinion, therefore, is that

1. If we can succeed in uniting all South Africa into a Confederacy on the model of the Dominion of Canada and under the British Flag, the probability is that that confederacy will not become a United States of South Africa.
2. If South Africa remains as now a congeries of separate States, partly British Colonies and partly Republics, it will inevitably amalgamate itself into a United States of South Africa.
3. That we must secure the control of the Delagoa Bay Railway for the British Imperial Government if Portugal is not able to retain the control herself.'[1]

The Prime Minister unfortunately did not record his comments on the colonial ministers' argument. They doubtless exaggerated to make a case. But according to the canons of supremacy which had held good since mid-Victorian times, their logic had force. That the south African reaction to the Raid, together with the economic revolution, had done immense damage to the old imperial paramountcy of influence could not be denied. Paramountcy since the Eighteen sixties had meant two things: the exclusion of rival European states; and power enough to guide south African development toward a loyal imperial confederation. For nearly forty years British ministers thought they had been building their dominion upon the rock of Cape Colony, and more recently, upon

[1] C.O. Memo., 26 Mar. 1896, S.P. (C.O. Private, 1895–1900, no. 12).

the Cape Colony and Rhodesia. By 1896 they knew that they had built on sand. The real stone of south African union lay out of reach in the Transvaal.

Indirect supremacy had been based upon the loyalty of the Cape government, its preponderance in south Africa and the existence of external checks upon the Transvaal republic. With the cleavage between Dutch and English after the Raid, the colonial ministry could no longer be relied upon as the architect of a British dominion; and Afrikaner sentiment in the colonies and Orange Free State was rallying to Kruger. The opening of the Delagoa railway and the growth of the Rand had overthrown Cape hegemony[1] and released the South African Republic from one form of external control. At Lourenço Marquez the republican had defeated the colonial axis in the struggle to direct the development of south Africa as a whole. As long as Delagoa Bay remained open and Kruger controlled the Rand, it seemed that the gold mines would work ever more in favour of a republican south Africa. The port and railway had also opened a large inlet for the spread of German influence there. Germany might be a weak naval Power. If she challenged Britain openly in south Africa, naval force could thwart her locally, if it came to war. But German diplomacy in 1894–6 as in 1884–5 was exploiting Britain's south African difficulties to gain advantages in other parts of the world; and the bigger those difficulties became, the more inconvenient German meddling seemed. Altogether, the warning in the Colonial Office memorandum of 1896 that south Africa was drifting out of the empire was well grounded in traditional notions of the requisites for south African supremacy.

In appraising the fall of paramountcy, Chamberlain and Selborne were contending that the imperial government itself must now intervene directly, if south Africa was to be welded into a British dominion. Since the end of the Eighteen eighties, Chamberlain's ambition had been to re-assert the 'Imperial factor'. Many of his colleagues apparently wondered if it was not too late already. The memorandum of 1896 seems to have been addressed to Salisbury and other ministers who, like Ripon in 1894, doubted whether the Transvaal should be forced into an imperial dominion, or indeed whether a south African

[1] The colony's rail traffic and revenues dropped heavily after 1895, as those of the Transvaal rose. By 1898 the Cape railways profit, which in 1896 amounted to £349,000, had dwindled to almost nothing, and the colonial treasury had a deficit of more than half a million. In 1897 the Cape lines carried 30% less traffic to the Transvaal than in the previous year while the Delagoa line carried 60% more. Thenceforward the Delagoa line drew more and more traffic from both the colonial lines. But part of this colonial decline at least was due to a slump in Johannesburg. (*vide* van der Poel, *Railway and Customs Policies*, 97–104.)

confederation would best secure British influence or stay for long within the empire. To most Liberals and some Conservatives 'supremacy' over white dominions seemed by now a word to call fools into a circle. Hence the Prime Minister is likely to have argued[1] against Chamberlain and Selborne in the crisis of 1896 that it might be better for British interests to be content with a divided south Africa than to try and force the incorporation of the Transvaal. It hardly seemed worth while to risk a Boer war in pursuit of a south African dominion, when imperial authority over dominions was becoming a fiction. The Colonial ministers' memorandum of March was meant to rebutt that objection. They asserted that unless the Transvaal could be controlled once more from Delagoa Bay, or be swiftly incorporated into a dominion, south Africa would be united as a republic. They hinted that British trade and investment would be damaged by this outcome. Perhaps they argued in the Cabinet Defence Committee that a United States of South Africa would deprive Britain of the Cape Town naval base.

It seemed in 1896 to be still vital to imperial security. Goschen at the Admiralty gave warning that the Navy could not keep the Mediterranean route to the East open for merchant ships in case of war.[2] Much shipping would be diverted round the Cape and to cope with it, the Admiralty was already extending coaling facilities and docks at the Cape and Mauritius.[3]

Strategy was one element in the Colonial Office pressure for an active south African policy. But there were wider considerations as well. In proclaiming the bankruptcy of the traditional system of influence, the memorandum implied the necessity of a new departure. Chamberlain and Selborne insisted that it was worth the effort and the risk. Their older Tory colleagues doubted it. At bottom, the difference in outlook on the south African crisis reflected two different predictions about the future of the empire as a whole. Chamberlain hoped to reconstruct it as a unit of defence, and perhaps also of trade, under a central federal authority in London. Without imperial federation, he doubted whether the United Kingdom would survive as a great power in the twentieth century alongside the continental giants, the United States and Russia. If south Africa was to be included in a federation of the whole empire, it was urgent to absorb the Transvaal and make a

[1] Unfortunately there are few of Salisbury's own letters on South Africa for this period in the Salisbury Papers so that his precise views are for the time being a matter of deduction and perhaps of speculation.

[2] Elliott, *op. cit.*, II, 210; 'It was the consensus of naval opinion that the Suez route would have to be abandoned by merchant shipping in war time in favour of the Canadian-Pacific or preferably the Cape route,' (Marder, *op. cit.*, 226.)

[3] *ibid.*, 227.

British south African union before it became too late. Salisbury and the Conservative leaders on the other hand were more impressed with the hazards than the needs for haste. They had had more experience of the immense obstacles in the way of imperial federation. They doubted whether the growth of Canada and Australia towards independent nationhood could be compressed into a federated empire. More sceptical about the possibility of strengthening central authority over dominions in matters of defence, foreign affairs and trade, they were in no hurry to turn south Africa into another dominion. In this sense perhaps, the memorandum of March 1896 was the new imperial federationists' manifesto in the south African case.

But upon the need to restore supremacy over south Africa the Colonial ministers and their critical colleagues all agreed. If they were divided about the degree of risk to be taken, the Cabinet accepted the breakdown of indirect influence and colonial agency as a fact. Ministers resigned themselves to intervention. At the same time they did not want another Anglo-Boer war. The Prime Minister and the rest of the Cabinet thought Chamberlain 'impulsive'.[1] But it seemed that only two ways of strengthening imperial influence remained; to press Kruger with the full weight of British diplomacy into enfranchising the *Uitlanders*; and to get control of Delagoa Bay. Of the two, Chamberlain and Selborne regarded Delagoa Bay as much the more effective issue. It was there that German interference might be blocked, the British grip on the Transvaal regained and the south African balance redressed in favour of the colonies. *Uitlander* representation and a British confederation would surely follow. On the other hand, to enfranchise the immigrants would not in itself solve the question. Chamberlain and Selborne knew that it would only lead to a British republic. Their task was as much to bring the unwilling *Uitlanders* as the intransigent Boers into the empire.

During the remainder of 1896, Salisbury, urged on by Chamberlain, pursued the main chance in Lisbon. The Prime Minister's pessimism about extracting Delagoa Bay or the railway from Portugal was confirmed. German and French opposition strengthened Portugal's natural reluctance to part with her possession. In December the Colonial Secretary complained: 'Delagoa Bay is the key of the situation in S[outh] Africa — it is to us of supreme importance; yet we can get no kind of satisfaction [from Lisbon].' He pressed Salisbury 'to take a

[1] Selborne in reporting a private talk with Chamberlain to Salisbury wrote: 'I thought you would be interested to learn this singular confirmation of your view of the impulsiveness of his nature,' (7 Apr. 1895, S.P. (Selborne).)

more decided line'. 'Could we make [the Portuguese Government] choose between us and Germany?'[1] The Prime Minister with all his diplomatic troubles over China and the Sudan, decided that nothing could be done to compel Portugal; and Chamberlain bowed to his authority. In Lisbon as at Pretoria the Colonial Secretary concluded: '. . . we have nothing to do but to stand upon our rights and wait events.'[2]

But in fact Chamberlain felt that he could not afford to stand still. Germany and France might forestall Britain at Delagoa Bay. With the successive inquiries into Jameson's raid in Pretoria, Cape Town and now in London, south African sentiment was still swinging in Kruger's favour. The Transvaal was still arming. The Orange Free State in 1897 joined the sister republic in an offensive and defensive alliance. In November 1896 Chamberlain asked the Cabinet to reinforce the colonial garrisons, in order to '. . . prevent the Boers from putting forward impossible claims and from taking aggressive action'.[3] But Lansdowne, the Secretary for War, had refused. Kruger meantime passed a new Aliens Immigration Law to strengthen the burghers' *régime* against the *Uitlanders*. Early in 1897 Chamberlain was advised that the law was contrary to the Convention and he decided to constrain the republican executive to repeal it. If necessary he would go almost as far as an ultimatum for the purpose. A battlefleet was to be sent to Delagoa Bay to impress Kruger and to ward off German interference; and Chamberlain again asked for military reinforcement to defend the colonies against a possible republican attack. In April 1897 Chamberlain felt bound to give the *Uitlanders*' cause the full support of the imperial authority just as he had done the year before. The Parliamentary inquiry into the raid was about to open in London. Perhaps it was as well to bring their grievances before the British public. Chamberlain had pledged himself to obtain redress from Kruger, and as yet he had achieved nothing. A diplomatic success was needed. But his arguments for putting pressure on the republic were mainly defensive:

> 'None of us believe it likely that the Boers will take the aggressive, but none deny the possibility and effects [of reinforcements] would be great on the attitude and allegiance of the Orange Free State and Cape Dutch toward one side and another. . . . The Transvaal are daily giving proof of trying to wear out our patience and whittle away the Convention.'[4]

Apparently Chamberlain felt compelled to act forcibly in order to

[1] Chamberlain to Salisbury, 16 Dec. 1896, S.P. (Chamberlain).
[2] Chamberlain to Salisbury, 19 Dec. 1896, *ibid.*
[3] Chamberlain, Cabinet Memo., 10 Nov. 1896, Garvin, *op. cit.*, III, 139.
[4] Chamberlain to Salisbury, 8 Apr. 1897, S.P. (Chamberlain).

strengthen the morale of the 'loyalist' pro-British parties and impress the Afrikaner moderates throughout south Africa.

Faced with Chamberlain's proposals, the Cabinet hesitated between the risk of war and the danger of losing all influence in south Africa by default. Hicks Beach had no wish to reconquer supremacy until 'a policy of patience' had been tried and had failed. Otherwise '. . . we should not get on our side such an amount of public opinion, both in the Cape Colony and here, as is essential to a successful issue'.[1] But the Chancellor agreed to reinforcements in April 'for political reasons'.[2] Lansdowne summed up the dilemma: 'I do not see how we are to intimidate Kruger without provoking him;'[3] but he protested that he could not find more troops for south Africa. Balfour quizzically agreed to reinforcement. He criticised Chamberlain's '. . . favourite method of dealing with the S[outh] African sore . . . by the free application of irritants'; but he added:

> '. . . I cannot think it wise to allow him to goad on the Boers by his speeches, and to refuse him the means of repelling Boer attack, when, as responsible minister, he earnestly and persistently presses for them. My own view is that a Boer attack is exceedingly improbable: and that it will only take place if the Boers come to the conclusion that we are fixed in a determination to attack *them*, and that what *must* come, had better come *soon*. The production of the Harris telegrams before the S. African committee (which seems to be now inevitable) may foster this frame of mind, and it is a nice point whether the sending out of 3000 or 4000 men will prove to be a sedative or a stimulant.'[4]

Goschen reluctantly agreed to Chamberlain's demand for a demonstration of force;[5] but at the same time the First Lord poured scorn on the scale of the naval demonstration at Delagoa Bay, and privately urged Salisbury to bring his battleships back to the Mediterranean where they were most needed. Goschen also complained to the Prime Minister against Chamberlain's wanting to break off the Niger negotiations with France. 'I fancy', Goschen wrote, 'Chamberlain is not so averse to a war [with France] as many others may be.'[6] Distrusting Chamberlain's impetuosity, Goschen and Hicks Beach begged Salisbury to restrain him.

[1] Hicks Beach to Milner, 22 Mar. 1897, Lady V. Hicks Beach, *Life of Sir Michael Hicks Beach*, (1932), II, 102.
[2] Chamberlain to Salisbury, 8 Apr. 1897, S.P. (Chamberlain).
[3] Lansdowne to Salisbury, Apr. 1897, Newton, *Lord Lansdowne*, 144–5.
[4] Balfour to Salisbury, 10 Apr. 1897, S.P. (Balfour); quoted in part in Dugdale, *op. cit.*, I, 248.
[5] Chamberlain to Salisbury, 8 Apr. 1897, S.P. (Chamberlain).
[6] Goschen to Salisbury, 19 Apr. 1897, S.P. (Goschen).

Nevertheless the Prime Minister, anxious not to thwart the Colonial Secretary too often, accepted Chamberlain's opinion of imperial weakness in south Africa 'which has been maturing for some time'. But Salisbury warned him that 'For reasons . . . unconnected with Africa I should look with something like dismay to a Transvaal war. It might mean the necessity of protecting the North-East of England as well as the South.'[1] Already embroiled with France and Russia, he did not want to provoke Germany as well.[2] The Colonial Secretary replied:

> 'The [south African] situation is most difficult and is made much more so by the political and international considerations indicated in your letter.
>
> There are two possibilities to guard against. The first is a war with the Transvaal which might be (though I am not certain that it would be) unpopular in England and which might easily strain our relations with Germany.
>
> The other is the loss of the confidence of the British in South Africa which would certainly lead to a republic — the elimination of the Imperial factor. Of the two this is the greatest evil, yet there is undoubtedly a strong party anxious to bring it about.
>
> I have come to the conclusion that there is only one way of avoiding these two possible contingencies, and that is by convincing Kruger that we are in earnest and mean to defend the [London] Convention. . . . My hope is that he will then give way.'

Chamberlain asked Salisbury to do what he could to isolate the Transvaal diplomatically from Germany.[3]

Evidently the Colonial Secretary was sticking to his catastrophic view of the imperial position. Already Chamberlain had made up his mind that his problem was to prevent the Transvaal from absorbing the colonies into a 'United States of South Africa'. He was prepared in the last resort to risk a Boer war to do it. Better a war than a policy of inaction which would demoralise the British party — the only strong force left working for an imperial south Africa. It was Chamberlain's tragedy that the Jameson Raid and the economic revolution seemed to have deprived the empire of all south African allies except the Rhodesian and *Uitlander* interests. Henceforward Chamberlain was tied to them. He had to follow and support them, however much he disliked and distrusted them. The economics of their situation made their eventual capitulation to Kruger only too likely. To disappoint their expectation

[1] Salisbury to Chamberlain, 16 Apr. 1897, Garvin, *op. cit.*, III, 141.

[2] *vide supra*, 345–6, 363–4.

[3] Chamberlain to Salisbury, 19 Apr. 1897, S.P. (Chamberlain); Garvin quoted part of this letter but omitted the third paragraph. (Garvin, *op. cit.*, III, 141–2.)

of imperial aid might drive them to surrender politically. For this reason Chamberlain from 1896 onwards did all that his colleagues would allow to promote and defend the *Uitlander* cause.

They accepted the Colonial Secretary's case with misgivings. Ministers were '. . . governed by two prominent considerations — (1) to protect the British flag in South Africa so as to secure its predominance, and (2) to avoid war'.[1] They agreed to send half the number of troops that Chamberlain had requested. The ultimatum and the show of force brought Kruger to repeal the Aliens Immigration Law, and in May the crisis passed. Chamberlain was pleased to have 'scored a point'.[2] But in fact the imperial position in south Africa had hardly been improved. Strong measures only confirmed Afrikaner and Dutch suspicion that the British had determined to provoke and reconquer the Transvaal.

For the next eighteen months Chamberlain and his colleagues watched and waited. They reverted to the policy of patience. There were good reasons. Ministers believed that the public's enthusiasm for empire was by no means ripe for war with the Transvaal — evidence enough that they were not driven on by imperialist hysteria in the Country. As Chamberlain told the new High Commissioner, Sir Alfred Milner, unless the Boers were the aggressor, a war would be 'extremely unpopular' in Britain. And it would 'certainly rouse antagonism in the Cape Colony, and leave behind it the most serious difficulties in the way of South African union'.[3] Hicks Beach was protesting against the bills he would have to meet for expeditions in the Sudan and in west Africa, fighting in India and the troubles in Crete and China. 'You and I', he complained to the Prime Minister, 'can remember what happened in 1878–80. Our Afghan and Zulu misfortunes were the main cause of our defeat [at the election] in 1880. We tried a forward policy in too many places at once. I am afraid of the same thing now. . . . Chamberlain will try to do a good deal if you don't stop him.'[4] The older ministers were still frightened of the shadow of Midlothian. They still remembered vividly the disasters which Carnarvon's annexation of the Transvaal had brought down both upon the government at Home and upon the empire in south Africa. And the expected collision with France over Fashoda

[1] Lord James, a member of the Cabinet: Askwith, *Lord James of Hereford*, (1930), 256–7.

[2] Wilde, *op. cit.*, 59.

[3] Chamberlain to Milner, 16 Mar. 1898, *The Milner Papers*, (ed. C. Headlam), (1931–3), I, 227.

[4] Hicks Beach to Salisbury, 1 Nov. 1897, S.P. (Hicks Beach). Hicks Beach here was complaining particularly against Chamberlain's active measures in west Africa; but he had similar objections to letting the Colonial Secretary loose in south Africa.

dictated caution in dealing with Germany, with Portugal and with Kruger. Chamberlain, himself, now accepted that:

> '. . . Our policy for the present was to let the Boers "stew in their own juice", fight out their internal quarrels and not be able to raise prejudice and confuse the issues by pointing to external interference as the danger to be feared.
>
> The decision may be right or wrong, but I intend that it shall have a fair trial.'[1]

As Salisbury put it in November 1898, the government's policy was 'to keep the peace with Kruger unless he did something outrageous'.[2] There was still hope of bringing Kruger to reform by constitutional agitation from within. There remained a chance of getting practical control of Delagoa Bay from a bankrupt Portugal.[3] In June 1898, Salisbury and Balfour in consultation with Chamberlain began working to detach Germany from the Transvaal, and remove her opposition in Lisbon to British designs upon Delagoa Bay.

During the lull of 1897 to 1898, Milner entirely confirmed the analysis of imperial decline in south Africa set down in the Colonial Office memorandum of March 1896. Like Chamberlain and Selborne, the High Commissioner was an imperial federationist of the new school. He had gone out to Cape Town believing that south Africa would unite as a republic if the British government did not intervene to make a dominion soon. The task as he saw it was to prevent 'the weakest link in the Imperial chain' from snapping.[4] Milner's standard of what British influence in south Africa should be was correspondingly high; his judgements of its actual weakness, alarming. The High Commissioner reported the collapse of paramountcy precisely and dogmatically.

'It is idle to suppose,' he wrote, 'that for years and years to come, if ever, we shall have any hold on the place beyond that which a strong garrison, a considerable squadron . . . will give us. A united and loyal S[outh] Africa — on the Canadian pattern . . . is a thing of the very distant future.'[5] The fall of Rhodes and the revival of the Bond's co-operation with Kruger appeared to have broken the Cape Colony as the chief instrument of imperial influence. Milner reported: 'Half the white people in this Colony, indeed I fear more than half . . . are

[1] Chamberlain, C.O. Minute, Nov. 1897, quoted in Wilde, *op. cit.*, 73.
[2] Chamberlain to Salisbury, 30 Nov. 1898, S.P. (Chamberlain).
[3] Chamberlain to Salisbury, 29 May 1897, S.P. (Chamberlain).
[4] Milner to Parkin, 28 Apr. 1897, *Milner Papers*, I, 42.
[5] Milner to Dawkins, 25 Aug. 1897, *ibid.*, 87.

at heart fellow-citizens with the Free Staters and Transvaalers.' At best the colonists might be neutral. 'But the moment Great Britain and either of the Republics are at loggerheads, they side openly and vehemently with the latter.'[1] He feared the 'overwhelming preponderance in wealth and opportunity on the side of the Transvaal [which] may turn the scale against us, unless we have some means to bring very effective pressure to bear upon that country.'[2] Once Britain had her hands full elsewhere, the republics might easily denounce the Conventions and assume complete independence.[3] It seemed to Milner as to Chamberlain that south Africa was in danger of developing towards a republican union.

'The remedy may be found in time', wrote Milner, 'in an English party in the Transvaal getting the franchise.'[4] But short of intimidation and ultimatum, the chances of forcing Kruger's hand seemed slim indeed. Or 'Rhodesia must develop *very* rapidly' if it was to off-set 'the overwhelming preponderance . . . of the Transvaal'.[5] But 'now the *very rapid* development of Rhodesia', Milner reported in July 1898, 'is more than doubtful . . . I do not believe it is going to be a rival to the Transvaal for many years to come.'[6] The Eldorado which would attract an inrush of British immigrants to the Zambesi had not been found. But Milner, as one might have guessed, saw one last chance of winning back all that had been lost since 1895: to obtain practical control of Delagoa Bay — 'the best chance we have of winning the great game between ourselves and the Transvaal for the mastery in South Africa without a war'.[7] If it could be done, the empire would have the 'trump card in the game of uniting S[outh] Africa as a British state'.[8] That alone would restore imperial external control over the Transvaal, and then Kruger could be forced into enfranchising the *Uitlanders*. Delagoa Bay could decide the struggle between the Afrikaner republican and the British imperial parties, and bind south Africa to the empire.

Delagoa Bay: The Last Chance, 1898

Negotiations had opened and closed in Lisbon, but Salisbury refused to go to extremes for the purpose. He had a certain regard for international legality, a sharp sense of the borderline where diplomacy lurched over the brink of war. The Prime Minister had done no more

[1] *idem.* [2] Milner to Chamberlain, 6 Jul. 1898, *ibid.*, 267–8.
[3] Milner to Chamberlain, 16 Mar. 1898, *ibid.*, 229.
[4] Milner to Dawkins, 25 Aug. 1897, *ibid.*, 87.
[5] Milner to Chamberlain, 6 Jul. 1898, *ibid.*, 267–8. [6] *idem.*
[7] *idem.* [8] Milner to Hutchinson, 18 Sept. 1898, *ibid.*, 268.

than offer bankrupt Portugal a loan to be secured upon the revenues of Mozambique and her other African colonies.

In June 1898 the Germans threatened to work against Britain everywhere, unless Salisbury admitted them to a share in the loan — and in the Portuguese colonies in case of default.[1] The clash with France in the Sudan was near, and Salisbury felt it wiser to settle with Berlin. The basis of his proposal was that if Portugal accepted loans from Britain and Germany, the customs revenue of Mozambique south of the Zambesi, and Angola north of Egibo, would be pledged to the British. The remainder of the two Portuguese colonies would stand security for the Germans.[2] But Bulow, trying to raise the price of German abstention in the Transvaal and at Delagoa Bay,[3] asked in addition for Blantyre, Timor, Walfisch Bay.

Chamberlain in August was dissatisfied not only with German demands but with Salisbury's weakness. The Colonial Secretary wanted Delagoa Bay immediately. It was not enough to hope that Lisbon would accept a loan and then to wait for her default. Salisbury's proposals left the supreme objective dependent on too many contingencies. But the Prime Minister, on holiday in France, replied that it was impracticable to do more:

> 'I do not see how any different arrangement, giving us control of Lorenzo [sic] Marques before default, is possible. It is only after default that Portugal would have any motive whatever for conceding to us control over Lorenzo [sic] Marques or any other portions of her Colonies. Default is the essence of the whole matter. Occupant Portugal would have no reason to surrender any right or any territory.
>
> If you think this was not what the Cabinet understood by the proposals, further negotiation had better be deferred till they meet again. There is in reality no hurry as Portugal is resolved at present to borrow from nobody.'[4]

Salisbury apparently had some respect for the rights of the occupant in a territorial question. Nor had he much hope that Portugal would accept a loan on the Anglo-German terms. It seemed to him now as for ten years past, that there was but a hollow chance of getting effective control over Delagoa Bay and its railway. At this Chamberlain seems to have lost faith in the Anglo-German arrangement. On 19 August he wrote to Balfour: '. . . the only advantage to us is the promise of Germany's abstention from further interference in Delagoa Bay and

[1] Bulow to Hatzfeldt, 20 Jun. 1898, *Grosse Politik*, XIV, no. 3816.
[2] Hatzfeldt to German Foreign Office, 13 Jul. 1898, *ibid.*, no. 3831.
[3] Hatzfeldt to German Foreign Office, 21 Jun. 1898, *ibid.*, no. 3817.
[4] Salisbury to Balfour, (telegram), 13 Aug. 1898, S.P. (Balfour).

the Transvaal — in other words, we pay blackmail to Germany to induce her not to interfere. . . .'[1] But to stave off German meddling in south Africa would not restore imperial supremacy over the Transvaal republic. Four days later Chamberlain wrote: '. . . I am much less eager than I was for any arrangement, and I should not break my heart if the negotiations [with Germany] came to an end. I never anticipated that the Germans would be so greedy.'[2]

Salisbury and Balfour however went on to sign the Anglo-German agreement. It was too late to break off negotiations without giving offence in Berlin. The treaty it was true, was no guarantee that Portugal would accept Anglo-German loans or that she would default on repayment; and until she did, the clauses assigning practical control of Delagoa Bay to Britain would not come into force. But the agreement had its advantages. As Balfour put it:

> '. . . it secures for us the absolute exclusion of every other Power, including Germany, from what, for shortness, I may call our sphere of influence — in other word, Germany resigns . . . a claim to regard Delagoa Bay as a port of international interest, whose fate Portugal and England could not be permitted to settle at their own sweet will. Resigning this, she also resigns all concern in Transvaal matters. That she would ever have actively supported the Transvaal is, indeed, more than doubtful; but unquestionably her supposed friendliness to the Boers encouraged them to adopt a policy towards this country, which, now that they are shut out from all hope of European assistance, may perhaps be modified to our advantage.
>
> We obtain further a complete defensive alliance with Germany against any third Power desiring to intervene in Mozambique or Angola.'[3]

The Anglo-German treaty isolated the Transvaal from European aid. It ended the efforts which Germany had made since 1894 to claim compensation for any change in the international status of Mozambique and the Transvaal. But as German interference had never been a serious menace to imperial supremacy in south Africa, so the removing of it did little to restore that supremacy. The rise of the Transvaal and the internal conflicts within south Africa, not the rivalry within the European balance, had done most to slacken the British hold upon south Africa. By 23 October the Portuguese government had rejected Anglo-German financial aid and raised a loan in Paris instead.[4] Salisbury's

[1] Chamberlain to Balfour, 19 Aug. 1898, S.P. (C.O. Private, 1895–1900).

[2] Chamberlain to Balfour, 23 Aug. 1898, S.P. (C.O. Private, 1895–1900).

[3] Balfour, Memo., 5 Sept. 1898, S.P. (Private Secretary and Memoranda, 1895–1900).

[4] Tattenbach to German Foreign Office, 23 Oct. 1898, *Grosse Politik*, XIV, no. 3881; and 30 Sept. 1898, no. 3879.

gloomy forecast had been fulfilled. Delagoa Bay, the 'trump card in the game of uniting S[outh] Africa as a British state' had once again eluded Chamberlain and Milner.

By the end of 1898, all the British moves to restore paramountcy and to counteract the political and commercial preponderance of the Transvaal had failed. The Portuguese would not part with Delagoa Bay. Hope of a northern Rand in Rhodesia had faded. Every attempt to breach the burghers' monopoly of power in the Transvaal on behalf of the *Uitlanders* had boomeranged; and the nationalist reaction had turned towards Kruger the sympathies of the Orange Free State and many of the Cape Dutch. In spite of Rhodes' re-entry into politics and his organisation of the South Africa League, the Bondsmen won the Cape election in the autumn of 1898 and took office under Schreiner. The best that Milner expected of such a ministry was neutrality;[1] whereas at the Transvaal election of February, Kruger had won an overwhelming majority. The *Uitlanders'* hope of victory for the liberal burghers had again been disappointed.

THE RESTORATION OF SUPREMACY

It seemed to Milner that only one way to restore supremacy was left — the British government must compel Kruger to admit the *Uitlanders* to power. As early as February 1898 his mind was turning toward this desperate solution. 'Looking at the question from a purely South African point of view,' he had written, 'I should be inclined to work up to a crisis. . . .'[2] Chamberlain however had damped his heat. After an interview with the Colonial Secretary, one of Milner's officials reported in July:

> '. . . Chamberlain will *not* do anything, owing to the fear that the party would suffer by proposing a line of policy which would not command the support of the Opposition, or even of a certain number of the supporters of the Govt. . . . [Chamberlain] insisted on the fact that public opinion would not support him in taking action unless a distinct and serious breach of the Convention could be brought home [against the Transvaal]. . . .'[3]

A war to free the Johannesburg mine-owners from the dynamite monopoly would have been extremely unpopular with the British public. Milner himself found that home opinion was still 'dormant' on the subject of south Africa at the beginning of 1899.[4] In the estimation of

[1] Milner to Chamberlain, 20 Jul. 1898, *Milner Papers*, I, 265.
[2] Milner to Chamberlain, 23 Feb. 1898, *ibid.*, 220–4.
[3] Conynham Greene to Milner, 22 Jul. 1898, *ibid.*, 236–7.
[4] Milner to Selborne, 31 Jan. 1899, *ibid.*, 301–2.

those whose job it was to know, there was no irresistible urge in British politics or business to conquer the Transvaal. When Milner came home in November 1898 to press for decisive action, he found that 'the "no-war" policy is still in favour in the highest quarters'.[1] But he returned to Cape Town in February 1899 thinking that 'If I can advance matters by my own actions . . . I shall have support when the time comes'.[2] If British opinion still slept, at least the international position had brightened. The crises with France at Fashoda and on the Niger had come and gone. The Chinese crisis was passing. Germany had withdrawn from south African affairs.

But once again it seems to have been the British party in south Africa that forced Chamberlain to turn the screw on Kruger again. Since November 1898, he had suspected that Kruger was coming to a settlement with the Johannesburg mine-owners, in return for a loan. Such a bargain would have reconciled the capitalists without breaching Kruger's *régime* and would have taken the heart out of the reform movement. The Colonial Secretary warned the gold mining houses against 'selling [themselves] and the Uitlander position rather cheap'.[3] At the same time, the Cape and Free State governments were proposing a conference between the four south African states to smooth their disputes. Chamberlain and Milner did their best to discourage Schreiner's proposal, fearing that it was meant to take the settlement out of imperial hands.[4] In April 1899, Kruger offered the *Uitlanders* comprehensive concessions in the 'Great Deal', if they would cease their agitation against the republic in Johannesburg and in London. Chamberlain commented:

> 'Whether this offer is genuine or not I regard it as the most important move made since the Raid. . . .
>
> My own opinion is that the govt. of the S.A.R. *are* anxious to settle. Their financial difficulties, the strength of the S[outh] A[frican] L[eague], their position with regard to the dynamite monopoly, the loss of support from Germany, the altered position of England since Fashoda — all works in favour of a settlement — of course on their own terms.
>
> The terms will not do.
>
> It is no use for the financiers to undertake what they cannot perform and if the majority of the Uitlanders get no satisfaction the agitation must go on — even though the millionaires are satisfied.'[5]

[1] Milner to Fiddes, 25 Nov. 1898, *ibid.*, 299.
[2] Milner to Selborne, 31 Jan. 1899, *ibid.*, 302.
[3] Chamberlain to Salisbury, 30 Nov. 1898, S.P. (Chamberlain), Wilde, *op. cit.*, 92–4; E. Drus, 'Select Documents from the Chamberlain Papers Concerning Anglo-Transvaal Relations, 1896–99,' *Bulletin of the Institute of Historical Research*, 170–2.
[4] Wilde, *op. cit.*, 91–2. [5] *ibid.*, 92–3.

Chamberlain wished the *Uitlanders* to insist upon full municipal status for Johannesburg. The 'Great Deal' failed because of the Reformers' increased demands, and they were joined by the mine-owners in a renewed campaign for the franchise. In the middle of April Chamberlain received their mass petition for imperial aid. Milner implied that an imperial refusal to intervene this time might drive the pro-British parties in south Africa to make their own bargains with the republic. The Colonial Secretary's dilemma of April 1896 and April 1897 had recurred. He was forced to choose between an ultimatum to the republic and antagonising the south African 'loyalists'. The Cabinet was informed:

> 'Our relations with the Transvaal have again reached a critical stage.
>
> We have to reply to an Uitlander petition of 21,000.
>
> If we ignore altogether the prayer of the petitioners, it is certain that British influence in South Africa will be severely shaken.
>
> If we send an ultimatum to Kruger, it is possible, and in my opinion probable, that we shall get an offensive reply. . . .
>
> We cannot expect any support from the present Cape Government which is a Bond Government with strong leanings towards the Transvaal.
>
> . . . The present state of things is a source of constant danger, and cannot continue indefinitely.'[1]

Chamberlain proposed a threatening despatch to Kruger which would stop short of an ultimatum, yet keep the 'loyalists' ' hopes high.

Neither the Colonial Secretary nor the Cabinet in May 1899 were deliberately manoeuvring the republic into war. They feared the outcome of Milner's belligerence. Balfour objected to Chamberlain's draft remonstrance:

> '. . . If the Transvaal were to be dealt with on ordinary principles, [of international law] there does not seem to me anything like a *casus belli* established.
>
> . . . Now your despatch as at present drafted does not go beyond a friendly remonstrance, but I think that such a remonstrance if it leads to no ulterior consequences, and if it remains unattended to by Kruger, will do us no good in South Africa, but will rather make our position in the eyes of our friends worse than it is at present.
>
> . . . If we are to insist at the point of the bayonet upon anything, I still feel that the most plausible demand would be for a measure of municipal reform sufficiently comprehensive to give our countrymen . . . reasonable security for liberty and property. . . . The main objection to such a scheme

[1] Cabinet Paper, 28 Apr. 1899, S.P. (S. African Cabinet Papers, Box III); partly quoted in Wilde, *op. cit.*, 99; and Drus, *Select Documents*, 173.

is that (as you tell me) it will not satisfy the Uitlanders. I must say that if this is so, they are rather unreasonable.'[1]

Salisbury's Cabinet felt that Milner and the *Uitlanders* were hurrying them toward an ultimatum which British opinion might think unjustified. The government reluctantly agreed to a diplomatic offensive in support of the reformers' claims, but was still anxious to steer clear of war. It eagerly accepted proposals from the Free State and colonial ministers for negotiations between Kruger and Milner at Bloemfontein.

The High Commissioner demanded the vote for all *Uitlanders* who had resided in the republic for five years, as well as more seats in the Volkraad. Kruger offered a limited seven year franchise. On 5 June, Milner broke up the conference. As he put it, 'they want to squeeze the new-comers into the existing mould. I want them to burst it.'[2] Chamberlain and his colleagues thought that Milner had been much too abrupt. In mid-July however, Kruger, pressed by the Free State and the colonial governments, at last proposed a law giving substantial concessions to the immigrants. The High Commissioner thought that Kruger was merely playing for time. 'No franchise measure should be accepted as satisfactory,' he wrote, 'unless its provisions are agreed between the two governments and guaranteed by compact between them. This is only chance of obtaining decent measure. . . . To assert our power and retain confidence of loyalists are after all the main objects to keep in view.'[3]

Chamberlain on the other hand mistook the new franchise law at first as a sign that Kruger's government was on the run. The Colonial Secretary wrote to Salisbury:

'. . . I really am sanguine that the crisis is over. . . . If my expectations are justified by official confirmation tomorrow the result will be a triumph of moral pressure — accompanied by special service officers and 3 Batteries of artillery.'[4]

Thus encouraged, Chamberlain seized the opportunity to stretch his advantage further, and assert the imperial authority's right to examine and approve the franchise bill jointly with the republican government. He wrote to Milner:

'If . . . S.A.R. has really given seven years retrospective franchise and five seats, I congratulate you on a great victory. No one would dream of

[1] Balfour to Chamberlain, 6 May 1899, quoted in Wilde, *op. cit.*, 101; Drus, Select Documents, 175.

[2] Milner to Sir Edward Grey, 7 Aug. 1899, *Milner Papers*, I, 478.

[3] Milner to Chamberlain, 18 Jul. 1899, Wilde, *op. cit.*, 119.

[4] Chamberlain to Salisbury, 18 Jul. 1899, S.P. (Chamberlain).

fighting over two years in qualification period . . . S.A.R. will have been driven by successive steps to almost exact position taken by you. We ought to make the most of this and accept it as basis of settlement. . . .

If report of the new concession is confirmed I propose to send you despatch . . . concluding with the suggestion for another conference in Capetown to arrange details so as to secure bona fide representation . . . and to discuss all remaining points of difference between the two governments.

Periodical Conferences are better security than new Convention which would stereotype terms obtained, whereas we consider them as part of gradual advance towards equality promised in 1881.

Any attempt hereafter to nullify present concessions would place us in very strong position to protest.'[1]

Under the illusion of victory, the Colonial Secretary had changed from defence to attack. Hitherto he had been moved mainly by the need to retain the *Uitlander* and Rhodesian parties' loyalty to the empire. Now Milner felt confident enough to contemplate turning the Transvaal into an English republic. 'In forcing S[outh] A[frican] R[epublic] in direction of equal rights and genuine self-government', Chamberlain, as much as Milner, now intended 'the practical assertion of British supremacy'[2] in its internal affairs.[3] Exulting over the apparent triumph of moral pressure in the franchise question, he impulsively committed himself and his colleagues to winning back supremacy over the Transvaal by diplomatic force.

By the end of August it was plain that moral pressure was not sufficient to impose the increased imperial demands. But they could not now be withdrawn. There was nothing for it but an ultimatum. Ministers unhappily discussed their mistaken opportunism. Hicks Beach wrote: '. . . I hope Milner and the Uitlanders will not be allowed to drag us into war.'[4] The Prime Minister also blamed the High Commissioner and the extreme British party in south Africa.

'The Boers will hate you for a generation, even if they submit,' he complained to Lansdowne:

'If they resist and are beaten, they will hate you still more. . . . [Milner's] view is too heated, if you consider the intrinsic significance and importance of the things which are in controversy. But it recks little to think of that now. What he has done cannot be effaced. We have to act upon a moral field prepared for us by him and his jingo supporters. And therefore I see

[1] Chamberlain to Milner, 18 Jul. 1899, Wilde, *op. cit.*, 120.
[2] Milner to Chamberlain, 26 Jul. 1899, *Milner Papers*, I, 471.
[3] Here we follow Dr. Wilde's interpretation of this turning point in Chamberlain's policy.
[4] Hicks Beach to Salisbury, Aug. 1899, S.P. (Hicks Beach).

before us the necessity for considerable military effort — and all for people whom we despise, and for territory which will bring no profit and no power to England.'[1]

The rest of the Cabinet heartily disliked Chamberlain's and Milner's methods. Yet in the end they approved them. They preferred not to drive Chamberlain to resign. It seemed too late to draw back. Above all they agreed that supremacy in south Africa must be regained.

On 28 August Chamberlain replied to the Transvaal's latest offer of a five years retrospective franchise and a quarter of the Volkraad seats for the *Uitlanders*. In return Kruger's executive expected the imperial government to give up its claim to suzerainty, to refer disputes in future to the arbitration of the south African governments, and to stop further intervention in the republic's internal affairs. The British government accepted the franchise and arbitration proposals, but insisted upon its own suzerainty and right of intervention. Required to agree to these imperial terms under threat of an ultimatum, the republic refused to yield; and Chamberlain asked for troops to go to Natal. Since war seemed inevitable, he suggested raising the British terms. Milner and the south African loyalists wanted '. . . to take some security that all the conditions of a settlement [of the Transvaal] shall be observed'. On 2 September Chamberlain told the Prime Minister: 'I can only think of three ways in which this might be effected, viz., Occupation, Disarmament or Federation, and neither [*sic*] could be secured except as the result of a successful war.'[2]

Chamberlain's case for an ultimatum in September 1899 was remarkably like that in March 1896:

'What is now at stake is the position of Great Britain in South Africa — and with it the estimate formed of our power and influence in our Colonies and throughout the world. . . .

The population at the present time of British and Dutch South Africa is (very roughly) estimated at 4,000,000, of which 430,000 are of British origin, 410,000 are Dutch, and the remaining 3,160,000 natives. The contest for supremacy is between the Dutch and the English.

. . . We have no dispute of any kind with the Orange Free State for nearly a generation. To the Dutch in our own Colonies we have given equal rights and privileges with those of our own nationality — we have allowed political agitations to continue to the point of treason — we have seen, without objection, a Dutch minority returning a majority of Members to the Cape Legislature and thus securing a Ministry wedded to Dutch interests.

[1] Salisbury to Lansdowne, 30 Aug. 1899, Newton, *Lansdowne*, 157.
[2] Chamberlain to Salisbury, 2 Sept. 1899, Drus, *Select Documents*, 179.

Yet in spite of all this we are today in doubt whether the Orange Free State and a considerable proportion of our Dutch fellow-subjects will not make common cause with our enemies, and we know as a fact that their sympathies will be with them, even if their fears and self-interest prevent them from giving material aid.

The reason for this lies wholly in the existence of the Transvaal Republic and in the policy which has been purused by the Oligarchy at Pretoria.

The Dutch in South Africa desire, if it be possible to get rid altogether of the connection with Great Britain, which to them is not a mother-land, and to substitute a United States of South Africa which, they hope, would be mainly under Dutch influence. This idea has always been present in their minds. . . . Indeed, I am not certain that Mr. Rhodes did not play up to this ideal when he talked of "the elimination of the Imperial factor" some years before the Raid. But it would probably have died out as a hopeless impossibility but for the evidence of successful resistance to British supremacy by the South African Republic. The existence of a purely Dutch Republic . . . flouting successfully British control and interference, is answerable for all the racial animosities which have become so formidable a factor in the South African situation.

. . . It depends upon the action of the British Govt. now whether the supremacy which we have claimed so long and so seldom exerted, is to be finally established and recognised or for ever abandoned. . . . I think that the object of the Government should now be to formulate its demands in a form to which a categorical yes or no may fairly be demanded.'[1]

Chamberlain vehemently argued the necessity of reconquering the Transvaal to save south Africa for the empire. Since a military solution seemed inevitable, he wished to raise Britain's demands on the republic. But Salisbury and Hicks Beach saw no advantage in asking for more, so long as hope of peace remained.[2] On 17 September Kruger's executive rejected the British demands. War seemed unavoidable. The Cabinet agreed to formulate final terms for a settlement to be imposed by ultimatum.

Ministers had not aimed deliberately at provoking war. They had arrived at it with regret and foreboding, while trying to assert a disappearing supremacy. Hicks Beach probably best expressed their mood on the eve of war:

'I am sure . . . that none of us (except possibly J[oseph] C[hamberlain] though I am by no means sure about him) likes the business. But we all feel that it has got to be done — and though I feel grave doubts as to the

[1] Chamberlain, Cabinet Memo., 'The South African Situation', 6 Sept. 1899, S.P. (S. African Cabinet Papers, Box III).

[2] Salisbury, Cabinet Memo., 5 Sept. 1899, S.P. (South African Cabinet Papers, Box III); quoted in full in Drus, *Select Documents*, 179–80.

effects of a war, both in South Africa and on the fortunes of our party here, the Dutch in South Africa can hardly like us less than they do now, and I hope at the end will have learned to respect us.'[1]

Salisbury had written in the same vein, and even more pungently. But by now Salisbury was not the ruthless and poised statesman who had presided over the partition. He was growing old. He was failing. Above all his wife was dying, and the Prime Minister was a man of sorrows. He doubted with Hicks Beach whether war would be popular with the British electorate. 'Public opinion here', he wrote, 'is not very irritable [with the Boers]. . . . Public opinion in South Africa is no doubt rabid. . . .'[2] The government had not been driven into war by imperialist hysteria at Home but by British south African opinion. Ministers all along had believed that Home opinion had to be educated and manufactured to give them support in case of conflict with the Transvaal. Lord James had preferred peace to a war to restore imperial paramountcy. 'But at last I was convinced', he admitted, 'that the Boer Government meant war.'[3]

The ultimatum drafted on 9 October shows what the imperial aims had become, once war was inevitable. A new convention was to provide for the repeal of all legislation since 1881 imposing disabilities upon alien residents of the republic. They were to be re-instated in all the privileges open to them at the time of the retrocession. Full municipal rights were to be granted to the mining districts, and the independence of the courts of justice was to be guaranteed. The republic was to be restricted in its armaments. Upon these conditions the British government offered to guarantee the independence of the republic against external aggression.[4] The essential demand was for equality between the white races in the Transvaal. As Hicks Beach put it:

'I see no reason for proposing anything now which would be taken as a revocation of independence. We can never govern from Downing Street any part of South Africa in which the whites are strong enough to defend themselves against the natives: so that equality of white races in the Transvaal would really secure all we can desire, viz. British predominance.'[5]

The Colonial Secretary agreed: '. . . we do not want in any case to make ourselves responsible for the Government of the Transvaal.' But he

[1] Hicks Beach to Lady Londonderry, 30 Sept. 1899, Hicks Beach, *op. cit.*, II, 108.
[2] Salisbury to Chamberlain, 19 Sept. 1899, Drus, *Select Documents*, 181.
[3] Askwith, *op. cit.*, 256–7.
[4] 'Proposed Ultimatum to the South African Republic,' Cabinet Paper, 9 Oct. 1899, Drus, *Select Documents*, 182–6.
[5] Hicks Beach to Chamberlain, 29 Sept. 1899, *ibid.*, 187.

added, 'It must be a Republic or a self-governing Colony — under the British flag in either case.'[1]

But the British ultimatum was never sent. On 9 October, the Transvaal presented its own ultimatum, demanding the withdrawal of British troops from the republic's borders. The Boer war began. In January 1900 Chamberlain outlined his plan for the eventual settlement. Both republics were to be annexed. The Transvaal would become a self-governing colony with a British majority in control. The Crown was to keep command of the armed forces of both colonies for some time after the peace. Immediate provision was to be made for a full railway and customs union of all the south African colonies. 'There remains', Chamberlain ended, 'the question of federation. It seems to me that this subject will not be ripe until there is a clear British majority with a British Government in four at least of the five States of British South Africa.'[2] As Milner had advised: 'It is our duty to provide for the influx of a selected British population, who will do much to consolidate South African sentiment in the general interests of the Empire.'[3]

Not until the Boer war had begun, did the Cabinet decide to annex the Transvaal, as extremists had been urging them to do since 1895. But once hope of peaceful compromise had gone, ministers determined to take the key of south Africa away from the anti-imperial Boers and to place it in the hands of loyal Britons. They would use it to turn south African development firmly away from republican union into imperial federation, and to settle the internal commercial and political conflicts between its races and sections once and for all.

Motives

Salisbury's Cabinet had not set out intending to reconquer south Africa for the empire. Such proposals indeed would have seemed wild and anachronistic. Half a century of experience seemed to show that the party which adopted them would get short shrift from the British electorate. Conservative leaders recalled only too well how Carnarvon's annexation of the Transvaal had set south African opinion against Britain. All south Africa could be lost in reconquering the republic. Aware of the penalties at Home and in south Africa, Salisbury and his ministers did not deliberately provoke a Boer war. Their purposes were more immediate and defensive. What prompted them to try

[1] Chamberlain to Hicks Beach, 27 [29?] Sept. 1899, *ibid.*, 188.

[2] Chamberlain, Cabinet Memo., 10 Jan. 1900, S.P. (S. African Cabinet Papers, Box III).

[3] *Milner Papers*, II, 283.

and force the republic into a settlement at the risk of war was their fear of losing British south African loyalty, their hope of impressing Afrikanerdom with a sense of imperial strength, and their determination to halt the decline of their paramount influence. In the Transvaal in 1899 as in Egypt in 1882, a British government fell over the brink of war in trying to make a mid-Victorian system of supreme influence work after it had broken down.

The risks of using threat and ultimatum to force the republic into a compromise settlement were foreseen and calculated. Yet the ministry accepted the chances of a war which promised to unite Dutch and Afrikaner implacably against the empire. Such grave risks made little sense, except on certain assumptions. No other means of pressure upon the Transvaal remained. The Afrikaner elements were already unreliable or alienated. The republic would dominate the colonies and decide south Africa's future. A republican union was inevitable, so long as Kruger's *régime* lasted in Pretoria. But if the President was convinced that the imperial authority was in earnest, he would give way. The balance of these few hopes and many fears prompted Salisbury's government to press Kruger so hard for an agreed settlement that it committed itself at last to dictate terms at all costs.

The ministry's own arguments reflect the deeper motives for the renewal of direct imperial intervention in south African politics after 1895. They do not fit easily into any of the conventional theories of imperialism. It does not appear that public demand in Britain actively compelled the government to enforce its will on the republic. Instead, ministers felt obliged to educate and lead British opinion, if they were to obtain the necessary support. The subsequent enthusiasm for the imperial cause owed more to war hysteria than to thirst for empire.

Nor did purely commercial reasons or business pressure weigh heavily with ministers, although war propaganda was later to make much of Kruger's hostility to British trade interests. The existence of the republic did not prevent British exporters from enjoying most of its trade; and British goods already had most favoured nation treatment under the London Convention. It mattered little to the British manufacturer and merchant whether the Rand trade passed through colonial ports or through Delagoa Bay. Neither did the investor demand to see pro-British politicians governing the Rand, before he would put his money in it. Intervention in the Transvaal was hardly needed to turn it either into a market or into a field of investment.

No more than business pressure or imperialist sentiment did diplomatic rivalries compel ministers to force the issue with Kruger. It is true that German collaboration with the republic between 1894 and 1898 did excite alarm. Interference from Berlin sharpened the inconveniences of Transvaal independence. But Germany was neutralised and France over-awed before intimidation proceeded. German designs and European alignments did not give the spur to the onslaught on Pretoria. The crisis stemmed from Africa rather than Europe. It arose from swift economic and political growth in south Africa, more than from change in the aims of British imperialism, from the collision of rival waves of internal colonisation, rather than from conflicts within the European balance.

After a quarter of a century of retirement, the imperial power to compose south African factions and their competing railway and tariff systems had dwindled. Commercially, the Cape Colony seemed to have lost the struggle against the republican system based on the Rand and Delagoa Bay. Politically, the raid left south Africa cleft on racial lines. The British factions stood over against the triumphant Afrikaner neutrals or republicans in every state. Moderates of both races were either discredited or absorbed into the extremes. It seemed as if the British colonial agencies of imperial supremacy would either yield to the republican attraction or fall into decline.

Whether this was or was not the actual situation in south Africa, it was the impression in London. For a decade imperial influence had become largely identified with the success of Rhodes' political and mineral kingdom and of his allies among the Johannesburg *Uitlanders*. After their blunders and failures in 1895, the British government's commitment to them became almost inescapable. The Transvaalers emerged intransigent and triumphant. The moderate Boers and British were for the time being eclipsed. With the south African balance swinging commercially and politically toward republicanism, the empire never had more need of powerful collaborators in south Africa. None remained but the Rhodesian and *Uitlander* interests. According to the view in London, they offered the last hope for imperial influence in south Africa. The wreck of external holds over the Transvaal and the loss of Boer sympathies in the Cape Colony and Orange Free State left the imperial government captives of Rhodes' South Africa League and the Johannesburg reform movement.

Salisbury and his ministers found their situation humiliating and inexpedient. Dependence on Rhodes and the south African mining interest was not to their taste. The Cabinet mistrusted the men of Johannesburg, and doubted whether their British loyalties were proof against the economic attractions which Kruger's *régime* might offer.

Rhodes had been the declared enemy of the imperial factor in south Africa's internal affairs. The *Uitlanders* had not wanted the British flag in 1895; and the Great Deal seemed to have tempted the Johannesburg capitalists. It was the fear of British south Africans defecting from the imperial cause which drove the Cabinet to give way to their clamour for direct action against Kruger's *régime*. On the three occasions when Chamberlain pressed for an ultimatum to be sent, the compelling consideration was to retain the British party's loyalty. Ministers in the end consented. Their own belief that imperial influence in south Africa was set into decline prevented any escape. They could find no way of keeping south Africa permanently within the empire but to follow where the Rhodesians and *Uitlanders* led them.

It would seem likely that the pressures which impelled the ministry against the republic were exerted not by Home, but by British south African opinion. There were economic interests which demanded action; but they were not those of the British economy. They were sections of the south African mining industry and the Cape and Rhodesian trading and railway interests. The British government was too closely tied to these factions not to protect and promote them locally and commercially. But its purpose in doing so was primarily imperial and political. It had no other means of saving supremacy in south Africa.

Evidently, most ministers were sceptical of this forecast of imperial cataclysm. But Chamberlain and Selborne, Milner and Rhodes believed it. Their outlook on south Africa was coloured by new and extremist notions of the empire's importance for Britain's future greatness. Chamberlain emerged from his introduction to world politics with an oppressive sense of the relative decline of British power.[1] He was in a hurry to offset it by re-uniting 'Greater Britain' overseas with the British Isles under a strong central authority. The Colonial Secretary's urgency for imperial federation spurred him to tighten the imperial grip on south Africa. To this extent a new and more urgent pursuit of imperial unity lay behind the onslaught against the Transvaal.

But the Cabinet reached substantially similar conclusions on essentially mid-Victorian ideas. Salisbury and Hicks Beach, Goschen and Balfour were cautious realists in their outlook on imperial affairs. They were not hurrying to turn south Africa into a British dominion as a

[1] Esher noted, 29 Jan. 1898: '[Chamberlain] talked of China and West Africa, and of France and Russia, with an amplitude of view and phrase that would have astonished Birmingham ten years ago. . . . He believes we are at the parting of the ways, and that we must stand fast for Imperial expansion now or never, whatever the result.' (Esher, *Journals*, *op. cit.*, I, 210–11.)

first step toward the federated empire of the twentieth century. But they believed in the traditional conception of supremacy in south Africa and in the vital importance of the Cape Town naval base to imperial defence.[1] It seemed indisputable, even by their more modest standard of imperial needs, that the paramountcy over the republics was bankrupt. His colleagues were no less determined than Chamberlain to restore British predominance; and although they distrusted his methods they approved his aims.

Their course seems paradoxical on any of the orthodox theories of imperialism. Drastic imperial action took place at a time when British enterprise had at last achieved high profit and great success in developing south African resources. The motive behind intervention was therefore not the contriving of commercial success. Rather it was commercial success which raised up republicanism and undermined British influence. And the late-Victorians' imperial instincts, their determination to secure the long route to the East and fear of losing their British allies in south Africa, brought them to restore their supremacy and shape a loyal dominion. The restoration of supremacy in Canada or Australasia would have been as pointless as it was unthinkable. It was the melancholy distinction of south Africa to have been regarded as strategically vital and politically unreliable.

But the paradox goes deeper than that. Restoring imperial supremacy in this white man's country might seem imperative; but in the long run it was to prove impossible. Statesmen in London were taking a course that cut against the grain of all their historical experience. The empire went to war in 1899 for a concept that was finished, for a cause that was lost, for a grand illusion.

[1] Hicks Beach declared that Britain could not risk losing south African supremacy because '. . . That would mean the loss of the Cape of Good Hope, perhaps the most important strategical position in the world and one of the main links of our great Empire'. (Hicks Beach, *op. cit.*, II, 113.) Chamberlain also stressed '. . . the immense importance for England of the position of the Cape. It forms the cornerstone of the whole British colonial system. In the event of a European war, the Suez route will become impassable and the Cape route is the only one which can guarantee the security of the Indian Empire. Fortifying and consolidating Cape Colony is therefore . . . a vital interest for Great Britain. . . .' (de Staal, *op. cit.*, II, 420.)

CHAPTER XV

Nationalism and Imperialism

Did new, sustained or compelling impulses towards African empire arise in British politics or business during the Eighteen eighties? The evidence seems unconvincing. The late-Victorians seem to have been no keener to rule and develop Africa than their fathers. The business man saw no greater future there, except in the south; the politician was as reluctant to expand and administer a tropical African empire as the mid-Victorians had been; and plainly Parliament was no more eager to pay for it. British opinion restrained rather than prompted ministers to act in Africa. Hence they had to rely on private companies or colonial governments to act for them. It is true that African lobbies and a minority of imperialists did what they could to persuade government to advance. Yet they were usually too weak to be decisive. Measured by the yardstick of official thinking, there was no strong political or commercial movement in Britain in favour of African acquisitions.

The priorities of policy in tropical Africa confirm this impression. West Africa seemed to offer better prospects of markets and raw materials than east Africa and the Upper Nile; yet it was upon these poorer countries that the British government concentrated its efforts. These regions of Africa which interested the British investor and merchant least, concerned ministers the most. No expansion of commerce prompted the territorial claims to Uganda, the east coast and the Nile Valley. As Mackinnon's failure showed, private enterprise was not moving in to develop them; and they were no more useful or necessary to the British industrial economy between 1880 and 1900 than they had been earlier in the century. Territorial claims here reached out far in advance of the expanding economy. Notions of pegging out colonial estates for posterity hardly entered into British calculations until the late Eighteen nineties, when it was almost too late to affect the outcome. Nor were ministers gulled by the romantic glories of ruling desert and bush. Imperialism in the wide sense of empire for empire's sake was not their motive. Their territorial claims were not made for the sake of African empire or commerce as such.

They were little more than by-products of an enforced search for better security in the Mediterranean and the East. It was not the pomps or profits of governing Africa which moved the ruling *élite*, but the cold rules for national safety handed on from Pitt, Palmerston and Disraeli.

According to the grammar of the policy-makers, their advances in Africa were prompted by different interests and circumstances in different regions. Egypt was occupied because of the collapse of the Khedivial *régime*. The occupation went on because the internal crisis remained unsolved and because of French hostility which the occupation itself provoked. Britain's insistent claims in east Africa and the Nile Valley and her yielding of so much in west Africa were largely contingent upon the Egyptian occupation and the way it affected European relations. In southern Africa, imperial intervention against the Transvaal was designed above all to uphold and restore the imperial influence which economic growth, Afrikaner nationalism and the Jameson fiasco had overthrown. Imperial claims in the Rhodesias, and to a lesser extent in Nyasaland, were contingent in turn upon Cape colonial expansion and imperial attempts to offset the rise of the Transvaal. The times and circumstances in which almost all these claims and occupations were made suggest strongly that they were called forth by crises in Egypt and south Africa, rather than by positive impulses to African empire arising in Europe.

To be sure, a variety of different interests in London — some religious and humanitarian, others strictly commercial or financial, and yet others imperialist — pressed for territorial advances and were sometimes used as their agents. In west Africa, the traders called for government protection; in Uganda and Nyasaland, the missionaries and the anti-slavery groups called for annexation; in Egypt, the bondholders asked government to rescue their investments; in south Africa, philanthropists and imperialists called for more government from Whitehall, while British traders and investors were divided about the best way of looking after their interests. Ministers usually listened to their pleas only when it suited their purpose; but commercial and philanthropic agitation seldom decided which territories should be claimed or occupied or when this should be done, although their slogans were frequently used by government in its public justifications.

It is the private calculations and actions of ministers far more than their speeches which reveal the primary motives behind their advances. For all the different situations in which territory was claimed, and all the different reasons which were given to justify it, one consideration, and one alone entered into all the major decisions. In all regions north of Rhodesia, the broad imperative which decided which territory to reserve and which to renounce, was the safety of the routes to the East. It did not, of course, prompt the claiming of Nyasaland or the lower Niger. Here a reluctant government acted to protect existing fields of trading and missionary enterprise from foreign annexations. In southern Africa the extension of empire seems to have been dictated by a somewhat different imperative. Here the London government felt bound as a rule to satisfy the demands for more territory which their self-governing colonials pressed on them. Ministers did this in the hope of conserving imperial influence. Nevertheless, the safety of the routes to India also figured prominently in the decision to uphold British supremacy in south Africa. It was the same imperative which after impelling the occupation of Egypt, prolonged it, and forced Britain to go into east Africa and the Upper Nile, while yielding in most of west Africa. As soon as territory anywhere in Africa became involved, however indirectly, in this cardinal interest, ministries passed swiftly from inaction to intervention. If the papers left by the policy-makers are to be believed, they moved into Africa, not to build a new African empire, but to protect the old empire in India. What decided when and where they would go forward was their traditional conception of world strategy.

Its principles had been distilled from a century and more of accumulated experience, from far-reaching and varied experiments in the uses of power to promote trade and in the uses of trade to promote power. Much of this experience confirmed one precept: that Britain's strength depended upon the possession of India and preponderance in the East, almost as much as it did upon the British Isles. Therefore, her position in the world hung above all upon safe communications between the two. This was a supreme interest of Victorian policy; it set the order of priorities in the Middle East and Asia, no less than in Africa, and when African situations interlocked with it, they engaged the serious and urgent attention of the British government. At the first level of analysis, the decisive motive behind late-Victorian strategy in Africa was to protect the all-important stakes in India and the East.

An essentially negative objective, it had been attained hitherto without large African possessions. Mere influence and co-operation with other Powers had been enough to safeguard strategic points in north Africa; while in south Africa control of coastal regions had sufficed. The ambition of late-Victorian ministers reached no higher than to uphold these mid-Victorian systems of security in Egypt and south Africa. They were distinguished from their predecessors only in this: that their security by influence was breaking down. In attempting to restore it by intervention and diplomacy, they incidentally marked out the ground on which a vastly extended African empire was later to arise. Nearly all the interventions appear to have been consequences, direct or indirect, of internal Egyptian or south African crises which endangered British influence and security in the world. Such an interpretation alone seems to fit the actual calculations of policy. Ministers felt frankly that they were making the best of a bad job. They were doing no more than protecting old interests in worsening circumstances. To many, the flare-up of European rivalry in Africa seemed unreasonable and even absurd; yet most of them felt driven to take part because of tantalising circumstances beyond their control. They went forward as a measure of precaution, or as a way back to the saner mid-Victorian systems of informal influence. Gloomily, they were fumbling to adjust their old strategy to a changing Africa. And the necessity arose much more from altered circumstances in Africa than from any revolution in the nature, strength or direction of British expansion.

Hence the question of motive should be formulated afresh. It is no longer the winning of a new empire in Africa which has to be explained. The question is simpler: Why could the late-Victorians after 1880 no longer rely upon influence to protect traditional interests? What forced them in the end into imperial solutions? The answer is to be found first in the nationalist crises in Africa itself, which were the work of intensifying European influences during previous decades; and only secondarily in the interlocking of these crises in Africa with rivalries in Europe. Together the two drove Britain step by step to regain by territorial claims and occupation that security which could no longer be had by influence alone. The compelling conditions for British advances in tropical Africa were first called into being, not by the German victory of 1871, nor by Leopold's interest in the Congo, nor by the petty rivalry of missionaries and merchants, nor by a rising imperialist spirit, nor even by the French occupation of Tunis in 1881 — but by the collapse of the Khedivial *régime* in Egypt.

From start to finish the partition of tropical Africa was driven by the persistent crisis in Egypt. When the British entered Egypt on their own, the Scramble began; and as long as they stayed in Cairo, it continued until there was no more of Africa left to divide. Since chance and miscalculation had much to do with the way that Britain went into Egypt, it was to some extent an accident that the partition took place when it did. But once it had begun, Britain's over-riding purpose in

Africa was security in Egypt, the Mediterranean and the Orient. The achievement of this security became at the same time vital and more difficult, once the occupation of Egypt had increased the tension between the Powers and had dragged Africa into their rivalry. In this way the crisis in Egypt set off the Scramble, and sustained it until the end of the century.

British advances in tropical Africa have all the appearances of involuntary responses to emergencies arising from the decline of Turkish authority from the Straits to the Nile. These advances were decided by a relatively close official circle. They were largely the work of men striving in more desperate times to keep to the grand conceptions of world policy and the high standards of imperial security inherited from the mid-Victorian preponderance. Their purposes in Africa were usually esoteric; and their actions were usually inspired by notions of the world situation and calculations of its dangers, which were peculiar to the official mind.

So much for the subjective views which swayed the British partitioners. Plainly their preconceptions and purposes were one of the many objective causes of the partition itself. There remain the ultimate questions: how important a cause were these considerations of government? What were the other causes?

The answers are necessarily complicated, because they can be found only in the interplay between government's subjective appreciations and the objective emergencies. The moving causes appear to arise from chains of diverse circumstances in Britain, Europe, the Mediterranean, Asia and Africa itself, which interlocked in a set of unique relationships. These disparate situations, appraised by the official mind as a connected whole, were the products of different historical evolutions, some arising from national growth or decay, others from European expansion stretching as far back as the Mercantilist era. All of them were changing at different levels at different speeds. But although their paths were separate, they were destined to cross. There were structural changes taking place in European industry cutting down Britain's lead in commerce. The European balance of power was altering. Not only the emergence of Germany, but the alignment of France with Russia, the century-old opponent of British expansion, lessened the margins of imperial safety. National and racial feelings in Europe, in Egypt and south Africa were becoming more heated, and liberalism everywhere was on the decline. All these movements played some part in the African drama. But it seems that they were only brought to the point of imperialist action by the idiosyncratic reactions of British statesmen to internal crises in Africa. Along the Mediterranean shores, Muslim states were breaking down under European penetration. In the south, economic growth and colonial expansion were escaping from imperial control. These processes of growth or decay were moving on time scales different from that of the European expansion which was bringing them about.

By 1882 the Egyptian Khedivate had corroded and cracked after decades of European paramountcy. But economic expansion was certainly not the sufficient cause of the occupation. Hitherto, commerce and investment had gone on without the help of outright political control. The thrusts of the industrial economy into Egypt had come to a stop with Ismail's bankruptcy, and little new enterprise was to accompany British control. Although the expanding economy had helped to make a revolutionary situation in Egypt, it was not the moving interest behind the British invasion. Nor does it seem that Anglo-French rivalry or the state of the European balance precipitated the invasion. It was rather the internal nationalist reaction against a decaying government which split Britain from France and switched European rivalries into Africa.

But the cast of official thinking profoundly influenced the outcome of the emergency. Moving instinctively to protect the Canal, the Liberals intended a Palmerstonian blow to liberate the progressives and chasten the disruptive elements in Egyptian politics. But instead of restoring their influence and then getting out, the need to bottle up anarchy and stave off the French forced them to stay on. This failure to work the mid-Victorian techniques, by coming to terms with the nationalists and finding Egyptian collaborators, meant that Indian solutions had to be applied to Egypt as well. The disenchantment of the 'Guardians' was replacing the liberal faith in voluntary co-operation; and Gladstone's sympathy with oppressed mationalities was hardening into Cromer's distrust of subject races. For similar reasons, official pessimism deepened about the reliability of the Turkish bastion in the Mediterranean; and as the balance tilted against Britain in the inland sea, her rulers realised that they were in Egypt to stay. Weighing the risks of Ottoman decay and the shifts in the European balance, remembering Indian experience and distrusting Egyptian 'fanatics', England's rulers pessimistically extended the search for security up the Nile to Fashoda, and from the Indian Ocean to Uganda and the Bahr-el-Ghazal.

The causes of imperial expansion in southern Africa were altogether different. It was essentially unconnected with the contemporary crisis in Egypt and its consequences in tropical Africa; it moved on a different time-scale, and the impulses behind it were separate. Unlike Egypt and tropical Africa, south Africa was to a great extent insulated from the rivalries of European Powers. Unlike them also, it was being rapidly developed by British commercial interests. The crisis which faced British governments was produced by colonial growth, and not by the decay of a native government. It arose from internal conflicts among the colonists, rather than from rivalries among the Powers. But the south African and Egyptian crises were alike in this: neither was precipitated by drastic changes in the local purposes of British expansion; but in both, the late-Victorians strained to keep up their supreme influence against a nationalist threat, and they were drawn at last into reconquering paramountcy by occupation.

South Africa was a case of colonial society receding beyond imperial control. It was also a case of economic development raising the enemies of the imperial connection to political preponderance over the colonial collaborators. By 1895 the new found commercial supremacy of the Transvaal was sustaining republicanism and threatening to draw the colonies into a United States of South Africa.

Here also the subjective appraisals of the policy-makers combined with objective situations to produce imperial advances. British aims in the south were specifically imperial, as they were not in tropical Africa. For years it had been assumed without question that south Africa must eventually turn into another Canada. But it was not only in London that official thinking was crucial. Their special historiography had taught ministers that with self-governing colonials it was prudent to follow their friends and rash to push or thwart them. As a result throughout the south African crisis, policy had to be warped to the theorems of the British colonial party.

In 1881 Gladstone had hoped to stultify Afrikaner nationalism by conciliation, as he was to try to do in Ireland. He switched policy back to the mid-Victorian technique of resting imperial supremacy upon a responsible ministry at the Cape and indirect influence over the Boer republics. It was assumed until 1895 that British immigrants and business would engulf the republicans and strengthen the natural imperial ties of self-interest and kinship. Nationalism would be killed by kindness. So long as London kept in line with colonial opinion and Britain's collaborators were upheld, south Africa would eventually turn itself into a loyal dominion. In this belief, Colonial Secretaries from Kimberley to Ripon kept intervention to a minimum, so as to avert another war between Boer and Briton and the risk of another Ireland. Hence they went on dismantling the 'Imperial Factor'. But by 1896 this system of imperial influence at second hand seemed to have broken under the strain of internal conflicts. South Africa had outgrown imperial supremacy in any form; it had passed beyond the power of British influence to compose the rivalry of its separate states. As Chamberlain saw it, economic development and political catastrophe had wrecked the imperial position in south Africa. It was the Rhodesians' thesis that the Transvaal must be brought under the control of an English-speaking majority. Fearing to lose their last allies, Chamberlain and Milner became their prisoners and followed them over the edge of war. Drawn on by hopes of re-integrating the empire, hardened by the recalcitrance of Afrikaner, as of Irish nationalists, and haunted by the fear of declining national greatness, the Unionists feared that free association would no longer keep south Africa in the empire. The nostrums of the Durham Report had not worked with the nationalists of the Transvaal, as they had done with those of Quebec. South African pressure drove ministers into action as anomalous as that taken at Fashoda. Admitting that imperial supremacy over white colonies was fast becoming a fiction, they were drawn into trying to restore it in south Africa by compulsion.

There are many evidences that towards the end of the century the wearing out of well-tried devices and the emergence of so many intractable problems shocked ministers out of their self-confidence and turned them to desperate expedients. The beliefs which had inspired earlier expansion were failing. Palmerston's axioms were giving way to Salisbury's re-appraisals. Liberal values could not be exported to all with cases of Birmingham hardware. Self-government would not always travel. Some nationalisms could not be killed by kindness. The growth of communities into harmonious commercial and political partnership with Britain was not after all a law of nature. The technique of collaborating classes had not worked everywhere. And as difficulties and doubts mounted, the men presiding over the destinies of the British Empire found themselves surrounded by the Eumenides.

Why were these catastrophes overtaking them? All the processes of British expansion were reaching their peak. The metropolitan society was putting forth its strongest energies. It was at this climactic point that the social changes in its satellites were quickest and most violent. Hence it was at this time that their relations with the metropolis tended to move into crisis. The colonial communities were breaking off toward full independence; while anti-western nationalism and social upheaval were estranging the non-European partners of British interests. The effects of growth were also coming back to roost at Home. England's rulers were alarmed by the symptoms of disintegration the demand for collectivism, the decay of the landed interest and the running sore of Ireland. The late-Victorians were confronted with nationalist upsurges in Ireland, Egypt and south Africa, and with their beginnings in India. They were losing the faith of their fathers in the power of trade and anglicisation to turn nationalists into friends and partners. They were no longer so sure as they had been that revolutionary change worked naturally and inevitably to advance British interests. And so they ceased to foster and encourage change and tended to be content to preserve the *status quo*. They became less concerned to liberate social energies abroad and concentrated on preserving authority instead.

Canning and Palmerston had known that the liberals of the world were on their side. But the late-Victorians had to find their allies more and more among Indian princes, Egyptian pashas or African paramount chiefs. Finding themselves less successful in assimilating nationalists to British purposes, their distrust of them grew. And becoming uncertain of the reliability of mere influence, they turned more often from the technique of informal control to the orthodoxies of the Indian *raj* for dealing with political anomalies and for securing their interests. They were ceasing to be a dynamic force and becoming a static power. They were more and more preoccupied throughout the world to guard what they had won; and they became less able to promote progress, as they lapsed into the cares of consolidation.

Fundamentally, the official calculations of policy behind imperial expansion in Africa were inspired by a hardening of arteries and a hardening of hearts. Over and over again, they show an obsession with security, a fixation on safeguarding the routes to the East. What stands out in that policy is its pessimism. It reflects a traumatic reaction from the hopes of mid-century; a resignation to a bleaker present; a defeatist gloss on the old texts of expansion. Perhaps at the deepest level the causes of the British share in the African partition are not found in strategic imperatives, but in the change from Canning's hopes for liberalism to Salisbury's distrust of nationalism, from Gladstone's old-fashioned concern not to turn south Africa into another Ireland, to Chamberlain's new-fangled resolve to re-forge it into another Canada.

The notion that world strategy alone was the sole determinant of British advances is superficial. For strategy is not merely a reflection of the interests which it purports to defend, it is even more the register of the hopes, the memories and neuroses which inform the strategists' picture of the world. This it is which largely decides a government's view about who may be trusted and who must be feared; whether an empire assumes an optimistic or pessimistic posture; and whether the forces of change abroad are to be fostered or opposed. Indeed any theory of imperialism grounded on the notion of a single decisive cause is too simple for the complicated historical reality of the African partition. No purely economic interpretation is wide enough, because it does not allow for the independent importance of subjective factors. Explanations based entirely on the swings of the European balance are bound to remain incomplete without reference to changes outside Europe.

Both the crises of expansion and the official mind which attempted to control them had their origins in an historical process which had begun to unfold long before the partition of Africa began. That movement was not the manifestation of some revolutionary urge to empire. Its deeper causes do not lie in the last two decades of the century. The British advance at least, was not an isolated African episode. It was the climax of a longer process of growth and decay in Africa. The new African empire was improvised by the official mind, as events made nonsense of its old historiography and hustled government into strange deviations from old lines of policy. In the widest sense, it was an offshoot of the total processes of British expansion throughout the world and throughout the century.

How large then does the new African empire bulk in this setting? There are good reasons for regarding the mid-Victorian period as the golden age of British expansion, and the late-Victorian as an age which saw the beginnings of contraction and decline. The Palmerstonians were no more 'anti-imperialist' than their successors, though they were more often able to achieve their purposes informally; and the late-Victorians were no more 'imperialist' than their precedessors, though they were driven to extend imperial claims more often. To label them thus is to ignore the fact that whatever their method, they were both of set purpose engineering the expansion of Britain. Both preferred to promote trade and security without the expense of empire; but neither shrank from forward policies wherever they seemed necessary.

But their circumstances were very different. During the first three-quarters of the century, Britain enjoyed an almost effortless supremacy in the world outside Europe, thanks to her sea power and her industrial strength, and because she had little foreign rivalry to face. Thus Canning and Palmerston had a very wide freedom of action. On the one hand, they had little need to bring economically valueless regions such as tropical Africa into their formal empire for the sake of strategic security; and on the other, they were free to extend their influence and power to develop those regions best suited to contribute to Britain's strength. Until the Eighteen eighties, British political expansion had been positive, in the sense that it went on bringing valuable areas into her orbit. That of the late-Victorians in the so-called 'Age of Imperialism' was by comparison negative, both in purpose and achievement. It was largely concerned with defending the maturing inheritance of the mid-Victorian imperialism of free trade, not with opening fresh fields of substantial importance to the economy. Whereas the earlier Victorians could afford to concentrate on the extension of free trade, their successors were compelled to look above all to the preservation of what they held, since they were coming to suspect that Britain's power was not what it once had been. The early Victorians had been playing from strength. The supremacy they had built in the world had been the work of confidence and faith in the future. The African empire of their successors was the product of fear lest this great heritage should be lost in the time of troubles ahead.

Because it went far ahead of commercial expansion and imperial ambition, because its aims were essentially defensive and strategic, the movement into Africa remained superficial. The partition of tropical Africa might seem impressive on the wall maps of the Foreign Office. Yet it was at the time an empty and theoretical expansion. That British governments before 1900 did very little to pacify, administer and develop their spheres of influence and protectorates, shows once again the weakness of any commercial and imperial motives for claiming them. The partition did not accompany, it preceded the invasion of tropical Africa by the trader, the planter and the official. It was the prelude to European occupation; it was not that occupation itself. The sequence illuminates the true nature of the British movement into tropical Africa. So far from commercial expansion requiring the extension of territorial claims, it was the extension of territorial claims which in time required commercial expansion. The arguments of the so-called new imperialism were *ex post facto* justifications of advances, they were not the original reasons for making them. Ministers had publicly justified their improvisations in tropical Africa with appeals to imperial sentiment and promises of African progress. After 1900, something had to be done to fulfil these aspirations, when the spheres allotted on the map had to be made good on the ground. The same fabulous artificers who had galvanised America, Australia and Asia, had come to the last continent.

TABLE SHOWING THE PROGRESS MADE IN THE DELIMINATION OF BRITISH FRONTIERS IN AFRICA

Red Nos. on Map.	Name of Boundary	Length, Miles	Date of Treaty	Number of Document	Page	Delimitation Survey	Marked on Ground	Protocol signed	No.	Page	Finally approved	No.	Page	Map	
														Facing Page	No. in Atlas
1	Gambia (Anglo-French) . .	425	Aug. 10, 1889	226	729	Nov., 1890, to May, 1891.	May, 1891.	June 9, 1891.	231	742	—	—	—	730	—
1	,, ,, ...	—	,, ,, ...	,,	,,	1895–6.	—	—	—	—	—	—	—	—	—
1	,, ,, ...	—	,, ,, ...	,,	,,	1898–9.	—	—	—	—	—	—	—	—	—
1	,, ,, ...	—	April 8, 1904	251	816	1905–6.	—	—	—	—	—	—	—	—	—
2	Sierra Leone—French Guinea . . [From the Coast to Tembi-Kunda.]	260	Aug. 10, 1889 . . . . Jan. 21, 1895	226 237	729 757	Dec., 1891, to April, 1892	—	—	—	—	—	—	—	—	6
2	Sierra Leone—French Guinea . . [From the Coast to Tembi-Kunda.]	—	,, ,, ...	,,	,,	Dec., 1895, to May, 1896.	1895, 1896.	April 9 and 30, 1896.	239	765	June 14 and 16, 1898.	243	794	—	7, 8
2	Sierra Leone—French Guinea . . [Tembi-Kunda Eastwards.]	8	Aug. 10, 1889 . . . . Jan. 21, 1895	226 237	729 757	1900 and Jan. 15, 1903.	1903.	Mar. 12, 1903.	247	809	Exchange of notes, Mar. 22 and April 5, 1904.	250	815	—	11
3	Sierra Leone—Liberia	195	Nov. 11, 1885	351	1132	Jan., 1903, to July, 1903.	1903.	June 25, 1903.	352	1136	—	—	—	—	39, 40
4	Gold Coast—Ivory Coast (Anglo-French).	450	July 12, 1893	236	754	May, 1902, to Feb. 1903.	1902 to 1903.	Feb. 1, 1903.	246	803	May 11 and 15th, 1905.	255	832	756	12 to 17
5	Gold Coast, Northern Territories —French Sudan, Senegambia-Niger (Anglo-French Boundary North of Gold Coast).	195	June 14, 1898	241	785	1900.	—	Aug. 16, 1901.	—	—	—	—	—	—	9, 10
5	,, ,, ,,	,,	Mar. 18/April 25, 1904 . .	253	822	—	1904.	Oct. 19, 1904.	254	827	May 24/ July 19, 1906.	257	847	—	20 to 23

TABLE SHOWING THE PROGRESS MADE IN THE DELIMITATION OF BRITISH FRONTIERS IN AFRICA—*continued*

Red Nos. on Map.	Name of Boundary	Length, Miles	Date of Treaty	Number of Document	Page	Delimitation Survey	Marked on Ground	Protocol signed	No.	Page	Finally approved	No.	Page	Map: Facing Page	Map: No. in Atlas
6	Gold Coast, Northern Territories—Togo (Anglo-German).	165	Nov., 14, 1899	277	919	Dec., 1901, to Sept., 1902.	—	July 21, 1902.	Note	935	—	—	—	—	—
6	,, ,, ,, [North of 9th parallel only.]	,,	June 25, 1904	283	935	—	Sept., 1904, to Dec. 15, 1905.	—	—	—	—	—	—	—	29
7	Gold Coast—Togoland (Anglo-German).	125	July 1, 1890, Art. IV . .	270	899	May, 1904, to Oct., 1904.	1904.	Oct. 11, 1904.	—	—	—	—	—	904	—
8	S. Nigeria (Lagos)—Dahomey (Anglo-French). [From 9° N. Lat. to Niger.]	235	June 14, 1898	241	785	1900.	—	Dec. 22, 1900, and Jan., 1905.	245	797	Oct. 19, 1906.	258	849	—	9, 10
9	S. Nigeria (Lagos)—Dahomey (Anglo-French). [From the Coast to 9° N. Lat.]	200	Aug. 10, 1889	226	729	1895–6.	—	Oct. 12, 1896.	240	780				—	24, 25
			June 14, 1898	241	785	1900.	—	—	—	—					
10	Niger—Chad (Anglo-French . .	860	June 14, 1898 . . . . April 8, 1904	241 251	785 816	Nov., 1902. Jan., 1904.	—	April 9, 1906.	256	843	—	—	—	—	9, 10, 18, 19
10	,, ,, ,,	,,	May 29, 1906	256	843	1906, 1907.	1907. 1908.	Feb. 25, 1908.	Note	846	—	—	—	—	18, 19
11	Yola—Chad (Anglo-German) . .	350	Nov. 15, 1893 . . . . Dec. 12, 1902	275 281	913 930	Aug. 10, 1903, Feb. 1903, to Feb., 1904 and 1905.	—	Feb. 24, 1904, and Mar. 19, 1906.	282 284	933 937	July 16, 1906.	284	941	914	30 to 33
11	,, [From ,, Gorege to ,, Lake Chad.] . .	40	(Local Commission)	—	—	—	1906 to 1907.	Feb. 12, and Mar. 11, 1907.	Note	86	—	—	—	—	—

11	Yola-Chad (Anglo-German) .. [From Uba, on Yedseram River, to River Benue.]	81	,, ,, ..	—	—	—	1907.	Mar. 11, 1907.	Note	86	—	—	—	—	—
12	Cross River (Southern Nigeria—Kameruns). [Cross River to the Sea.]	140	April 29 and May 7, 1885 July 27 and Aug. 2, 1886 July 1, 1890 April 14, 1893 .. .. Nov. 15, 1893	260 263 270 273 275	868 880 899 910 913	1895.	—	—	—	—	—	—	—	910	—
12	,, ,, ,,	,,	,, ,, ...	—	—	Dec., 1905, May, 1906.	1906.	1906.	—	—	—	—	—	—	—
13	Cross River Rapids—Yola Arc ..	285	Nov. 15, 1893	275	913	1907.	—	—	—	—	—	—	—	—	—
14	Barotseland—Angola	710	June 11, 1891 .. .. Arbitration award, May 30, 1905.	310 326	1016 1074	—	—	—	—	—	—	—	—	1076	—
15	Walfish Bay	75	July 1, 1890 .. .. Proclamation of annexation, Mar. 12, 1878.	270 19	899 175	—	—	—	—	—	—	—	—	—	—
16	Bechuanaland—German South-West Africa.	1,113	July 1, 1890, Art. III (A.G.) Dec. 30, 1886, Art. I (G.P.) June 11, 1891, Art. IV (A.P.)	270 216 310	901 703 1019	Nov., 1898, to Oct., 1903.	1898 to 1903.	—	—	—	—	—	—	902	—
16(*a*)	Cape Colony—German South-West Africa (Orange River).	—	July 1, 1890, Art. III ..	270	901	—	—	—	—	—	—	—	—	—	—
17	Amatongaland—Portuguese East Africa.	30	June 11, 1891, Art. III ..	310	1018	Aug., 1896, to Dec., 1896.	—	—	—	—	—	—	—	—	—
17	,, ,, ,,	,,	,, ,, ,, ,,	,,	,,	—	Aug. and Oct., 1897.	Oct. 2, 1897.	316	1066	Dec. 29, 1898/Jan. 25, 1899.	319	1070	—	35
18	Swaziland—Portuguese East Africa.	65	Conference, April to June, 1907.	—	—	1888, 1894, and 1897.	April, 1907.	—	—	—	—	—	—	—	—
19	Transvaal — Portuguese East Africa.	255	July 29, 1869 .. .. Feb. 27, 1884	29 28	245 227	1887, 1890, and 1894.	1887, 1890, 1894.	—	—	—	—	—	—	232	—

TABLE SHOWING THE PROGRESS MADE IN THE DELIMITATION OF BRITISH FRONTIERS IN AFRICA—*continued*

Red Nos. on Map.	Name of Boundary	Length, Miles	Date of Treaty	Number of Document	Page	Delimitation Survey	Marked on Ground	Protocol signed	No.	Page	Finally approved	No.	Page	Map: Facing Page	Map: No. in Atlas
20	Limpopo River to Sabi River (Anglo-Portuguese).	115	June 11, 1891, Art. II ..	310	1018	Dec., 1902, to July, 1903.	—	Dec. 21, 1903/July 19, 1904.	325	1073	June 3, 1907. (20 and 21)	329	1078	—	34
21	Mazoe or Manica Boundary (Anglo-Portuguese, 18° 30′ S. to Sabi River).	235	June 11, 1891, Art. II .. Arbitral award, Jan. 30, 1897.	310 315	1018 1036	1892.	1898. 1899.	June 5 and 28, 1898, and Dec. 14 and 15, 1898.	318	1069					
22	Barué Boundary (Anglo-Portuguese, River Mazoe to 18° 30′ South).	145	June 11, 1891, Art. II ..	310	1018	1898.	1905.	June 28 and Dec. 6, 1898.	317	1069	Mar. and April, 1902, Jan. and April, 1904.	322 324	1071 1073	—	—
23	Anglo - Portuguese Boundary South of River Zambesi.	215	June 11, 1891, Art. II ..	310	1018	1903–4. April, 1905, to Oct., 1905.	1905.	Oct. 24, 1905.	327	1077	—	—	—	—	—
24	Anglo - Portuguese Boundary North of Zambesi.	260	June 11, 1891, Art. I ..	310	1017	June, 1904 to Nov., 1904	1904.	Nov. 21, 1904.	327	1077	—	—	—	—	—
25	Nyasaland Protectorate—Portuguese East Africa (Anglo-Portuguese).	660	June 11, 1891, Art. I ..	310	1017	July to Nov., 1899, Oct. to Dec., 1900.	1899–1900.	Dec. 8, 1900.	320	1071	*Sept. 15, 1906.	328	1077	—	—

* Provisional confirmation of recommendations of Boundary Commissioners, 1899 and 1900 (Procés-Verbal, December 8, 1900).

25	Nyasaland Protectorate—Portuguese East Africa (Anglo-Portuguese). [To make some alterations to previous line. Beaconed from B. P. 38 to Mt Kapiriuta.]	91	(Local Commission) . .	—	—	—	1907.	—	—	—	—	—	—	—	—
26	Nyasa-Tanganyika (Anglo-German).	225	July 1, 1890, Art. I, § 2 . .	270	900	1898.	1898.	Nov. 11, 1898.	276	916	Feb. 23, 1901.	279	925	900	28
27	North-West Rhodesia—Belgian Congo.	1,200	May 12, 1894	163	578	—	—	—	—	—	—	—	—	580	—
28	Uganda and Sudan—Belgian Congo.	800	May 12, 1894 . . . . May 9, 1906	163 165	578 584	Jan., 1907, to present.	—	—	—	—	—	—	—		
29	British—German East Africa (Indian Ocean to Lake Jipe).	118	July 1, 1890, Art. I . .	270	899	1892.	—	July 25, 1893.	274	911	—	—	—	—	—
29	,, ,, ,,	,,	July 25, 1893	274	911	1897.	1900.	Jan, 28, Feb. 14, and April 25, 1900	278	921	July 27, 1900.	Note	921	912	{ 26 { 27
30	British—German East Africa (South end of Jipe to Lake Victoria).	350	July 1, 1890 . . . . July 25, 1893	270 274	899 911	April, 1904, to Jan., 1906.	1904 to 1906.	July 18, 1906.	285	942					
30	Uganda—German East Africa . .	150	July 1, 1890	270	889	July, 1902, to April, 1904.	1904.				—	—	—	—	—
31	British East Africa — Italian Somaliland.	375	March 24, 1891	288	948	—	—	—	—	—	—	—	—	—	—
31(*a*)	British Somaliland — Italian Somaliland.	710	March 24, 1891 . . . . May 5, 1894	288 290	948 951	— —	— —	— —	— —	— —	— —	— —	— —	— 952	— —
32	British Somaliland—Abyssinia . .	—	May 14, 1897 . . . . June 4, 1897	99 99	423 428	— —	— —	— —	— —	— —	— —	— —	— —	— —	— —
33	British Somalilans — French Somali Coast.	50	Fenruaty $\frac{2}{9}$, 1888 . .	225	726	—	—	—	—	—	—	—	—	—	—
34	Uganda and East Africa—Abyssinia.	760	December 6, 1907 . .	103	445	1900–01. Oct., 1902, to July, 1903.	—	—	—	—	—	—	—	—	{ 3 { 4

TABLE SHOWING THE PROGRESS MADE IN THE DELIMITATION OF BRITISH FRONTIERS IN AFRICA—*continued*

Red Nos. on Map.	Name of Boundary	Length, Miles	Date of Treaty	Number of Document	Page	Delimitation Survey	Marked on Ground	Protocol signed	No.	Page	Finally approved	No.	Page	Map: Facing Page	Map: No. in Atlas
35	Sudan—Abyssinia	760	May 15, 1902	100	431	1903.	1903.	—	—	—	—	—	—	950	—
36	Sudan—Eritrea .. .. .. [R. Stetit to Abe Gamal.]	530	April 15, 1891	289	949	1903.	—	—	—	—	—	—	—	1116	—
			June 25 / July, 7, 1895	338	1108										
			December, 7, 1898 ..	340	1110										
			June 1, 1899	342	1113										
			April 16, 1901	343	1115										
			November 23, 1901 ..	291	952										
			May 15, 1902	100	433										
	Sudan—Eritrea .. .. .. [From Sabderat North-Eastwards.]	,,	,, ,, ,,	—	—	1899. 1901.	—	—	—	—	—	—	—	—	36
37	Anglo-French —From Congo Nile Watershed to Tripoli.	1,950	March 21, 1899	244	796	—	—	—	—	—	—	—	—	—	—
38	Egypt—Tripoli		—	—	—	—	—	—	—	—	—	—	—	—	—
39	Egypt—Turkey, Sinai Peninsula	140	Firman, 1841	178	614	1906.	1906.	—	—	—	Oct. 1, 1906.	373	1201	—	{ 43 44

INDEX